JUSTICE AND DEMOCRACY

JUSTICE AND DEMOCRACY
Cross-Cultural Perspectives

Edited by

Ron Bontekoe
Marietta Stepaniants

University of Hawai‘i Press
Honolulu

Library of Congress Cataloging-in-Publication Data

Justice and democracy : cross-cultural perspectives / edited by Ron
    Bontekoe and Marietta Stepaniants.
        p.   cm.
    Selected papers delivered at the Seventh East-West Philosophers'
Conference in Honolulu.
    Includes bibliographical references and index.
    ISBN 0–8248–1926–8
    1. Democracy—Congresses.   2. Social justice—Congresses.
3. Liberty—Congresses.   I. Bontekoe, Ronald, 1954– .
II. Stepaniants, M. T. (Marietta Tigranovna)   III. East-West
Philosophers' Conference (7th : 1996? : Honolulu, Hawaii)
JC423.J87   1997
321.8—dc21   97–5096
                                                          CIP

This volume is dedicated to Eliot Deutsch and to the memory of Charles A. Moore—the latter for having conceived of and initiated the series of East-West Philosophers' Conferences, and the former for his wisdom and hard work in continuing this tradition over the past three decades.

CONTENTS

5. Postmodern Perspectives

6. Principles of Cultural Dialogue

PREFACE

The papers included in this anthology represent a selection of the best that were delivered at the Seventh East-West Philosophers' Conference in Honolulu, the most recently held in a series of international conferences on comparative philosophy initiated by Charles Moore in 1939. The choice of theme for this seventh conference, "Justice and Democracy," was inspired in large part by two important recent developments on the world scene: first, the collapse of the Soviet Union and of the communist system it had maintained in Eastern Europe, followed by the introduction of a market economy and democratic institutions into those regions; and second, a pronounced worldwide resurgence of violence grounded in ethnic, religious, and cultural differences—a resurgence of violence that reminds us once again of how difficult it seems to be for human beings to resolve their disagreements through discussion.

The conference in Honolulu attracted well over a hundred philosophers and political theorists from every continent and region in the world, and they agreed perhaps on only one thing—that today democracy (understood in a number of quite different ways, however) is the only form of government that enjoys moral legitimacy. But the practical problems involved in establishing and preserving truly democratic institutions vary dramatically from culture to culture. Thus the papers presented at the conference explored the nature of democracy from an almost bewildering range of perspectives. In order to highlight certain recurrent themes and issues, the papers in this volume have been arranged under six headings.

The essays in Part 1, "Theoretical Approaches," are all concerned, in one way or another, with the problem of protecting the individual's sense of self against the possibility of its submergence in, and domination by, the collective identity. How do we guarantee the individual the freedom to determine

1

his or her own identity? And more specifically, to what extent does this require an appeal to formalized rights, justified in terms of some universal norm? Is it possible, perhaps, as Richard Rorty suggests, to accomplish this by means of the individual's own identification with various subgroups? Indeed, might identification with, or loyalty to, a group be all that we really mean by "justice"? Erikh Solovyov, for one, contemplating the prevalence of populist invective in contemporary Russian politics, suggests not.

In Part 2, "Contemporary Problems of Application," the essays are all concerned with what happens to democracy in concrete circumstances—with its tendency to either flourish or degenerate. There are, of course, a number of factors that can undermine the health of democratic institutions or prevent their taking hold. Thus Cass Sunstein and Frank Cunningham, for example, focus on the threat posed to political unity and the possibility of concerted action by fundamental disagreements regarding moral, religious, and philosophical issues. While Cunningham sees the cultivation of "elementary tolerance" as the best response to this danger, Sunstein stresses the value of "incompletely theorized agreements." J. E. Tiles draws attention to the fact that real progress in the pursuit of democracy is impossible unless the culture in question lends support to the project. (Where this support is lacking, two questions arise: first, can anything be done to move the culture in question closer to the ideal of democracy? and second, *should* anything be done?) Finally, Ted Honderich and Svetozar Stojanović address the essential injustice of the gross disparities in wealth that tend to arise in capitalist economies, and the distortion in democratic decision-making that this occasions.

The papers collected in Part 3, "Asian Perspectives," focus on issues relating to the reconciliation of democratic values with the indigenous religious and social values of the major Asian cultures—with Confucianism in China, with Hinduism in India, and with Islam in the countries of the Middle East. Ambrose King, for example, observes that while a "democratic Confucian" political system, like liberal democracy, cherishes and respects individuals and their rights, it defines these primarily in communal and social terms. For this very reason, Confucianism offers us, according to Chung-Ying Cheng, an indication of how to go about integrating two separate—and often, it seems, conflicting—facets of justice: justice as virtue on the personal level and justice as fairness on the state level. Yü Ying-shih contends that if there is in Western democracies a crisis arising from the comparative scarcity of qualified leaders, Confucianism might help us to address that problem by showing us how to produce "men of character." Daya Krishna, too, focuses on the leadership issue and, writing from an Indian perspective, argues that the common Western assumption that equality between human beings can only be achieved by reducing or minimizing inequalities of all sorts is fundamentally mistaken. Finally, Javid Iqbal and Majid Fakhry stress the parallels that exist between Islamic and Western conceptions of justice, parallels suggesting that democracy can be expected to grow in the Muslim world.

The lessons that Asia may have to offer the West is also the general focus of Part 4, "Comparative Perspectives." Here Roger Ames and David Hall, reflecting on the importance of *li* (ritual action) in the promotion and maintenance of a community of shared experience in China, propose that the West too might profit by tying its recognition of rights and duties more immediately to extralegal institutions and practices, enforceable by social pressures rather than punishments. David Loy and Michael Barnhart draw similar conclusions from their considerations of Buddhist ethics. They observe that whereas Western culture emphasizes the individuality of the self, so that individual freedom has always been strongly associated in Western thought with subject-object dualism, Buddhism takes as one of its central principles the denial of the self's autonomy. For the Buddhist, freedom or *mukti* means freedom from ignorance about the self, freedom from the passions, and freedom from suffering. This freedom, however, is grounded in an appreciation of the essential codependence of things—a codependence that implies that compassion, rather than a categorical derivation of standards and principles, must serve as the basis upon which we achieve social justice.

A number of our contributors represent that trend of contemporary thought known as radical postmodernism. Rosi Braidotti, for example, claims that we need to radicalize our vision of universal values, and proposes that we accomplish this by embracing the concept of "nomadism"—by which she means an ethical consciousness that resists settling into socially determined modes of thought and behavior, without, however, embracing relativism. Ernesto Laclau also focuses on the tension between the universal and the particular. While the universal, he contends, is "empty" and can only be filled, in different contexts, by concrete particulars, it is nonetheless absolutely essential for any kind of political interaction. Difference and particularity may be the necessary starting points for truly democratic politics, but starting from them, it is still possible to find a way to a "relative universalization of values." Through pragmatic negotiations, hybridization results, which is understood by Laclau as the empowerment of existing identities, since the particular can only fully realize itself if it keeps constantly open and constantly redefines its relation to the universal. Chantal Mouffe takes a similar line, defending and even celebrating the universality of antagonism, which she views as constitutive of the particular and irreducible. The aim of James Buchanan's paper is to "rethink democracy in the light of technology," the impact of which on the structure and development of democratic society, he contends, has been inadequately appreciated.

Part 6, or "Principles of Cultural Dialogue," focuses on the danger of mistaking a universalist attitude for the actual inclusion of others in social dialogue. A number of our contributors point out, for example, that insofar as the West is permitted to define the terms and values that govern our investigations into the nature of justice and the problems of democracy, the resulting discussion is liable to be seen by non-Westerners as merely another instance of cultural imperialism. In this respect, Fred Dallmayr, in particular, brings into view the basic tension intrinsic to justice: its tendency to oscillate between the poles of neutral indifference and solicitous attention to difference. His paper explores the implications for ethical theory of the "blindness" of justice—the fact that justice is meant to apply equally to everyone, irrespective of color, creed, race, or gender. Dallmayr concludes that "in seeking to promote 'universal' standards, including the principle of universal rights, Western culture paradoxically tends to foster monolingual conformity."

Given the diversity of perspectives represented, one thing of which we can assure the reader is that monolingual conformity is not a problem in this collection.

Ron Bontekoe and Marietta Stepaniants

ACKNOWLEDGMENTS

The editors are sincerely grateful to all those who made this volume possible. Our acknowledgments go first to the University of Hawai'i which, in cooperation with the East-West Center, sponsored the Seventh East-West Philosophers' Conference. The presidents of the two institutions supported the idea of the project, while a number of people associated with either the university or the center, such as Judith Hughes, Dean of the College of Arts and Humanities, contributed to its practical realization through their personal efforts. We would also like to thank the University of Hawai'i Press and, in particular, Sharon Yamamoto for her help in all phases of the editing and production of this volume.

For six decades now the Department of Philosophy at the University of Hawai'i has maintained the tradition of the conferences. Special thanks should be addressed to the members of the Steering Committee: Roger T. Ames, Chung-Ying Cheng, Eliot Deutsch, Kenneth Kipnis, Mary Tiles, and K. N. Upadhyaya. A particularly important role was played by Professor Eliot Deutsch, who replaced Charles A. Moore as the "keeper of the flame." Professor Roger Ames, the editor of the journal *Philosophy East & West*, itself an "offspring" of the conferences, provided the Director of the Seventh Conference with valuable advice and support. Much hard and time-consuming work was performed efficiently, with affection and enthusiasm, by the Assistant to the Director—Virginia Suddath.

The constellation of distinguished academics and promising new scholars was assembled with the help of counseling from the members of the International Advisory Committee: Zygmunt Bauman, Jürgen Habermas, Daya Krishna, Zehou Li, and Richard Rorty.

In recent years, the continuation of the conference series has been due in large measure to contributions from the Hawai'i business community, rallied by the enlightened businessman, Dr. Hung-Wo Ching. On this occasion, he graciously agreed to be the honorary chairman. However, as honorary chairmen go, he proved to be a very unusual one: he worked almost every day for the success of the conference and was involved in all of the details of the project. It would be more precise, then, simply to call Dr. Ching the Chairman of the Seventh East-West Philosophers' Conference. The difficult responsibilities of the fundraising chairman were taken on and fulfilled by one of the youngest and most distinguished businessmen of the local community—Mr. Warren K. K. Luke. Financial aid for the publication of the conference volume comes from a permanent supporter of the conferences—Alexander & Baldwin, Inc.

Marietta Stepaniants, Director
Seventh East-West Philosophers' Conference

Part 1. Theoretical Approaches

Richard Rorty

JUSTICE AS A LARGER LOYALTY

All of us would expect help if, pursued by the police, we asked our family to hide us. Most of us would extend such help even when we know our child or our parent to be guilty of a sordid crime. Many of us would be willing to perjure ourselves in order to supply such a child or parent with a false alibi. But if an innocent person is wrongly convicted as a result of our perjury, most of us will be torn by a conflict between loyalty and justice.

Such a conflict will be felt, however, only to the extent to which we can identify with the innocent person whom we have harmed. If the person is a neighbor, the conflict will probably be intense. If a stranger, especially one of a different race, class, or nation, it may be considerably weaker. There has to be *some* sense in which he or she is "one of us," before we start to be tormented by the question of whether or not we did the right thing when we committed perjury. So it may be equally appropriate to describe us as torn between conflicting loyalties—loyalty to our family and to a group large enough to include the victim of our perjury—rather than between loyalty and justice.

Our loyalty to such larger groups will, however, weaken, or even vanish altogether, when things get really tough. Then people whom we once thought of as like ourselves will be excluded. Sharing food with impoverished people down the street is natural and right in normal times, but perhaps not in a famine, when doing so amounts to disloyalty to one's family. The tougher things get, the more ties of loyalty to those near at hand tighten, and the more those to everyone else slacken.

Consider another example of expanding and contracting loyalties: our attitude toward other species. Most of us today are at least half-convinced that the vegetarians have a point, and that animals do have some sort of rights. But suppose that the cows, or the kangaroos, turn out to be carriers of a newly mutated virus, which, though harmless to them, is invariably fatal to humans. I suspect that we would then shrug off accusations of "speciesism" and participate in the necessary massacre. The idea of justice between species will suddenly become irrelevant, because things have gotten very tough indeed, and our loyalty to our own species must come first. Loyalty to a larger community—that of all living creatures on our home planet—would, under such circumstances, quickly fade away.

As a final example, consider the tough situation created by the accelerating export of jobs from the First World to the Third. There is likely to be a continuing decline in the average real income of most American families. Much of this decline can plausibly be attributed to the fact that you can hire a factory worker in Thailand for a tenth of what you would have to pay a worker in Ohio. It has become the conventional wisdom of the rich that American and European labor is overpriced on the world market. When American business people are told that they are being disloyal to the United States by leaving whole cities in our Rust Belt without work or hope, they sometimes reply that they place justice over loyalty.[1] They argue that the needs of humanity as a whole take moral precedence over those of their fellow-citizens and override national loyalties. Justice requires that they act as citizens of the world.

Consider now the plausible hypothesis that democratic institutions and freedoms are viable only when supported by an economic affluence that is achievable regionally but impossible globally. If this hypothesis is correct, democracy and freedom in the First World will not be able to survive a thoroughgoing globalization of the labor market. So the rich democracies face a choice between perpetuating their own democratic institutions and traditions and dealing justly with the Third World. Doing justice to the Third World would require exporting capital and jobs until everything is leveled out— until an honest day's work, in a ditch or at a computer, earns no higher a wage in Cincinnati or Paris than in a small town in Botswana. But then, it can plausibly be argued, there will be no money to support free public libraries, competing newspapers and networks, widely available liberal arts education, and all the other institutions that are necessary to produce enlightened public opinion, and thus to keep governments more or less democratic.

What, on this hypothesis, is the right thing for the rich democracies to do? Be loyal to themselves and each other? Keep free societies going for a third of mankind at expense of the remaining two-thirds? Or sacrifice the blessings of political liberty for the sake of egalitarian economic justice?

These questions parallel those confronted by the parents of a large family after a nuclear holocaust. Do they share the food supply they have stored in the basement with their neighbors, even though the stores will then only last a day or two? Or do they fend those neighbors off with guns? Both moral dilemmas bring up the same question: Should we contract the circle for the sake of loyalty, or expand it for the sake of justice?

❋   ❋   ❋

I have no idea of the right answer to these questions, neither about the right thing for these parents to do, nor about the right thing for the First World to do. I have posed them simply to bring a more abstract, and merely philosophical, question into focus. That question is: Should we describe such moral dilemmas as conflicts between loyalty and justice, or rather, as I have suggested, between loyalties to smaller groups and loyalties to larger groups?

This amounts to asking: Would it be a good idea to treat "justice" as the name for loyalty to a certain very large group, the name for our largest current loyalty, rather than the name of something distinct from loyalty? Could we replace the notion of "justice" with that of loyalty to that group—for example, one's fellow-citizens, or the human species, or all living things? Would anything be lost by this replacement?

Moral philosophers who remain loyal to Kant are likely to think that a *lot* would be lost. Kantians typically insist that justice springs from reason, and loyalty from sentiment. Only reason, they say, can impose universal and unconditional moral obligations, and our obligation to be just is of this sort. It is on another level from the sort of affectional relations that create loyalty. Jürgen Habermas is the most prominent contemporary philosopher to insist on this Kantian way of looking at things: the thinker least willing to blur either the line between reason and sentiment, or the line between universal validity and historical consensus. But contemporary philosophers who depart from Kant, either in the direction of Hume (like Annette Baier) or in the direction of Hegel (like Charles Taylor) or in that of Aristotle (like Alasdair MacIntyre), are not so sure.

Michael Walzer is at the other extreme from Habermas. He is wary of terms like "reason" and "universal moral obligation." The heart of his new book, *Thick and Thin,* is the claim that we should reject the intuition that Kant took as central: the intuition that "men and women everywhere begin with some common idea or principle or set of ideas and principles, which they then work up in many different ways." Walzer thinks that this picture of morality "starting thin" and "thickening with age" should be inverted. He says that, "Morality is thick from the beginning, culturally integrated, fully resonant, and it reveals itself thinly only on special occasions, when moral language is turned to special purposes."[2] Walzer's inversion suggests, though it does not entail, the neo-Humean picture of morality sketched by Annette Baier in her book *Moral Prejudices.* On Baier's account, morality starts out not as an obligation but as a relation of reciprocal trust among a closely knit group, such as a family or clan. To behave morally is to do what comes naturally in your dealings with your parents and children or your fellow clan-members. It amounts to respecting the trust they place in you. Obligation, as opposed to trust, enters the picture only when your loyalty to a smaller group conflicts with your loyalty to a larger group.[3]

When, for example, the families confederate into tribes, or the tribes into nations, you may feel obliged to do what does not come naturally: to leave your parents in the lurch by going off to fight in the wars, or to rule against your own village in your capacity as a federal administrator or judge. What Kant would describe as the resulting conflict between moral obligation and sentiment, or between reason and sentiment, is, on a non-Kantian account of the matter, a conflict between one set of loyalties and another set of loyalties. The idea of a *universal* moral obligation to respect human dignity gets re-placed by the idea of loyalty to a very large group—the human species. The idea that moral obligation extends beyond that species to an even larger group becomes the idea of loyalty to all those who, like yourself, can experience pain—even the cows and the kangaroos—or perhaps even to all living things, even the trees.

This non-Kantian view of morality can be rephrased as the claim that one's moral identity is determined by the group or groups with which one identifies—the group or groups to which one cannot be disloyal and still like oneself. Moral dilemmas are not, in this view, the result of a conflict between reason and sentiment but between alternative selves, alternative self-descriptions, alternative ways of giving a meaning to one's life. Non-Kantians do not think that we have a central, true self by virtue of our membership in the human species—a self that responds to the call of reason. They can, in-stead, agree with Daniel Dennett that a self is a center of narrative gravity. In nontraditional societies, most people have several such narratives at their dis-posal, and thus several different moral identities. It is this plurality of identi-ties that accounts for the number and variety of moral dilemmas, moral philosophers, and psychological novels in such societies.

Walzer's contrast between thick and thin morality is, among other things, a contrast between the detailed and concrete stories you can tell about your-self as a member of a smaller group and the relatively abstract and sketchy story you can tell about yourself as a citizen of the world. You know more about your family than about your village, more about your village than about your nation, more about your nation than about humanity as a whole, more about being human than about simply being a living creature. You are in a better position to decide what differences between individuals are morally relevant when dealing with those whom you can describe thickly, and in a worse position when dealing with those whom you can only describe thinly. This is why, as groups get larger, law has to replace custom, and abstract prin-ciples have to replace *phronēsis*. So Kantians are wrong to see *phronēsis* as a thickening up of thin abstract principles. Plato and Kant were misled by the fact that abstract principles are designed to trump parochial loyalties into thinking that the principles are somehow prior to the loyalties—that the thin is somehow prior to the thick.

Walzer's thick-thin distinction can be aligned with Rawls' contrast between a shared *concept* of justice and various conflicting *conceptions* of justice. Rawls sets out that contrast as follows:

> the concept of justice, applied to an institution, means, say, that the institution makes no arbitrary distinctions between persons in assigning basic rights and duties, and that its rules establish a proper balance between competing claims. . . . [A] conception includes, besides this, principles and criteria for deciding which distinctions are arbitrary and when a balance between competing claims is proper. People can agree on the meaning of justice and still be at odds, since they affirm different principles and standards for deciding these matters.[4]

Phrased in Rawls' terms, Walzer's point is that thick "fully resonant" *conceptions* of justice, complete with distinctions between the people who matter most and the people who matter less, come first. The thin concept, and its maxim "do not make arbitrary distinctions between moral subjects," is articulated only on special occasions. On those occasions, the thin concept can often be turned against any of the thick conceptions from which it emerged, in the form of critical questions about whether it may not be merely arbitrary to think that certain people matter more than others.

Neither Rawls nor Walzer think, however, that unpacking the thin concept of justice will, by itself, resolve such critical questions by supplying a criterion of arbitrariness. They do not think that we can do what Kant hoped to do—derive solutions to moral dilemmas from the analysis of moral concepts. To put the point in the terminology I am suggesting: we cannot resolve conflicting loyalties by turning away from them all toward something categorically distinct from loyalty—the universal moral obligation to act justly. So we have to drop the Kantian idea that the moral law starts off pure but is always in danger of being contaminated by irrational feelings that introduce arbitrary discriminations among persons. We have to substitute the Hegelian-Marxist idea that the so-called moral law is, at best, a handy abbreviation for a concrete web of social practices. This means dropping Habermas' claim that his "discourse ethics" articulates a transcendental presupposition of the use of language, and accepting his critics' claim that it articulates only the customs of contemporary liberal societies.[5]

❀   ❀   ❀

Now I want to raise the question of whether to describe the various moral dilemmas with which I began as conflicts between loyalty and justice, or rather as conflicting loyalties to particular groups, in a more concrete form. Consider the question of whether the demands for reform made on the rest of the world by Western liberal societies are made in the name of something not merely Western—something like morality, or humanity, or rationality—or are simply expressions of loyalty to local, Western, conceptions of justice. Habermas would say that they are the former. I would say that they are the latter, but are none the worse for that. I think it is better not to say that the liberal West is better informed about rationality and justice, and instead to say that, in making demands on nonliberal societies, it is simply being true to itself.

In a recent paper called "The Law of Peoples," Rawls discusses the question of whether the conception of justice he has developed in his books is something peculiarly Western and liberal or rather something universal. He would like to be able to claim universality. He says that it is important to avoid "historicism," and believes that he can do this if he can show that the conception of justice suited to a liberal society can be extended beyond such societies through formulating what he calls "the law of peoples."[6] He outlines, in that paper, an extension of the constructivist procedure proposed in his *A Theory of Justice*—an extension which, by continuing to separate the right from the good, lets us encompass liberal and non-liberal societies under the same law.

As Rawls develops this constructivist proposal, however, it emerges that this law applies only to *reasonable* peoples, in a quite specific sense of the term "reasonable." The conditions that nonliberal societies must honor in order to be "accepted by liberal societies as members in good standing of a society of peoples" include the following: "its system of law must be guided by a common good conception of justice . . . that takes impartially into account what it sees not unreasonably as the fundamental interests of all members of society."[7]

Rawls takes the fulfillment of that condition to rule out violation of basic human rights. These rights include "at least certain minimum rights to means of subsistence and security (the right to life), to liberty (freedom from slavery, serfdom, and forced occupations) and (personal) property, as well as to formal equality as expressed by the rules of natural justice (for example, that similar cases be treated similarly)."[8] When Rawls spells out what he means by saying that the admissible nonliberal societies must not have unreasonable philosophical or religious doctrines, he glosses "unreasonable" by saying that these societies must "admit a measure of liberty of conscience and freedom of thought, even if these freedoms are not in general equal for all members of society." Rawls' notion of what is reasonable, in short, confines membership of the society of peoples to societies whose institutions encompass most of the hard-won achievements of the West in the two centuries since the Enlightenment.

It seems to me that Rawls cannot both reject historicism and invoke this notion of reasonableness. For the effect of that invocation is to build most of the West's recent decisions about which distinctions between persons are arbitrary into the conception of justice that is implicit in the law of peoples. The differences between different *conceptions* of justice, remember, are differences between what features of people are seen as relevant to the adjudication of their competing claims. There is obviously enough wriggle room in phrases like "similar cases should be treated similarly" to allow for arguments that believers and infidels, men and women, blacks and whites, gays and straights should be treated as relevantly *dis*similar. So there is room to argue that discrimination on the basis of such differences is *not* arbitrary. If we are going to exclude from the society of peoples societies in which infidel homosexuals are not permitted to engage in certain occupations, those societies can quite reasonably say that we are, in excluding them, appealing not to something universal, but to very recent developments in Europe and America.

I agree with Habermas when he says, "What Rawls in fact prejudges with the concept of an 'overlapping consensus' is the distinction between modern and premodern forms of consciousness, between 'reasonable' and 'dogmatic' world interpretations." But I disagree with Habermas, as I think Walzer also would, when he goes on to say that Rawls

> can defend the primacy of the right over the good with the concept of an overlapping consensus only if it is true that postmetaphysical worldviews that have become reflexive under modern conditions are epistemically superior to dogmatically fixed, fundamentalistic worldviews—indeed, only if such a distinction can be made with absolute clarity.

Habermas' point is that Rawls needs an argument from transculturally valid premises for the superiority of the liberal West. Without such an argument, he says, "the disqualification of 'unreasonable' doctrines that cannot be brought into harmony with the proposed 'political' concept of justice is inadmissible."[9]

Such passages make clear why Habermas and Walzer are at opposite poles. Walzer is taking for granted that there can be no such thing as a non-question-begging demonstration of the epistemic superiority of the Western idea of reasonableness. There is, for Walzer, no tribunal of transcultural reason before which to try the question of superiority. Walzer is presupposing what Habermas calls "a strong contextualism for which there is no single 'rationality'." On this conception, Habermas continues, "individual 'rationalities' are correlated with different cultures, worldviews, traditions, or forms of life. Each of them is viewed as internally interwoven with a particular understanding of the world."[10]

I think that Rawls' constructivist approach to the law of peoples can work if he adopts what Habermas calls a "strong contextualism." Doing so would mean giving up the attempt to escape historicism, as well as the attempt to supply a universalistic argument for the West's most recent views about which differences between persons are arbitrary. The strength of Walzer's *Thick and Thin* seems to me to be its explicitness about the need to do this. The weakness of Rawls' account of what he is doing lies in an ambiguity between two senses of universalism. When Rawls says that "a constructivist

liberal doctrine is universal in its reach, once it is extended to . . . a law of peoples,"[11] he is not saying that it is universal in its validity. Universal reach is a
notion that sits well with constructivism, but universal validity is not. It is the
latter that Habermas requires. That is why Habermas thinks that we need really heavy philosophical weaponry, modeled on Kant's—why he insists that
only transcendental presuppositions of any possible communicative practice
will do the job.[12] To be faithful to his own constructivism, I think, Rawls has
to agree with Walzer that this job does not need to be done.

Rawls and Habermas often invoke, and Walzer almost never invokes, the
notion of "reason." In Habermas, this notion is always bound up with that of
context-free validity. In Rawls, things are more complicated. Rawls distinguishes the reasonable from the rational, using the latter to mean simply the
sort of means-end rationality that is employed in engineering, or in working
out a Hobbesian *modus vivendi*. But he often invokes a third notion, that of
"practical reason," as when he says that the authority of a constructivist liberal doctrine "rests on the principles and conceptions of practical reason."[13]
Rawls' use of this Kantian term may make it sound as if he agreed with Kant
and Habermas that there is a universally distributed human faculty called
practical reason (existing prior to, and working quite independently of, the
recent history of the West), a faculty that tells us what counts as an arbitrary
distinction between persons and what does not. Such a faculty would do the
job Habermas thinks needs doing: detecting transcultural moral validity.

But this cannot, I think, be what Rawls intends. For he also says that his
own constructivism differs from all philosophical views that appeal to a source
of authority, and in which "the universality of the doctrine is the direct consequence of its source of authority." As examples of sources of authority, he
cites "(human) reason, or an independent realm of moral values, or some
other proposed basis of universal validity."[14] So I think we have to construe
his phrase "the principles and conceptions of practical reason" as referring to
whatever principles and conceptions are in fact arrived at in the course of creating a community.

Rawls emphasizes that creating a community is not the same thing as
working out a *modus vivendi*—a task which requires only means-end rationality, not practical reason. A principle or conception belongs to practical reason, in Rawls' sense, if it emerged in the course of people starting thick and
getting thin, thereby developing an overlapping consensus and setting up a
more inclusive moral community. It would not so belong if it had emerged
under the threat of force. Practical reason for Rawls is, so to speak, a matter
of procedure rather than of substance—of how we agree on what to do rather
than of what we agree on.

This definition of practical reason suggests that there may be only a verbal difference between Rawls' and Habermas' positions. For Habermas' own

attempt to substitute "communicative reason" for "subject-centered reason" is itself a move toward substituting "how" for "what." The first sort of reason is a source of truth, truth somehow coeval with the human mind. The second sort of reason is not a source of anything, but simply the activity of justifying claims by offering arguments rather than threats. Like Rawls, Habermas focuses on the difference between persuasion and force, rather than, as Plato and Kant did, on the difference between two parts of the human person— the good rational part and the dubious passionate or sensual part. Both would like to de-emphasize the notion of the *authority* of reason—the idea of reason as a faculty which issues decrees—and substitute the notion of rationality as what is present whenever people communicate, whenever they try to justify their claims to one another, rather than threatening each other.

The similarities between Rawls and Habermas seem even greater in the light of Rawls' endorsement of Thomas Scanlon's answer to the "fundamental question why anyone should care about morality at all," namely that "we have a basic desire to be able to justify our actions to others on grounds that they could not reasonably reject—reasonably, that is, given the desire to find principles that others similarly motivated could not reasonably reject."[15] This suggests that the two philosophers might agree on the following claim: The only notion of rationality we need, at least in moral and social philosophy, is that of a situation in which people do not say "your own current interests dictate that you agree to our proposal," but rather "your own central beliefs, the ones which are central to your own moral identity, suggest that you should agree to our proposal."

This notion of rationality can be delimited using Walzer's terminology by saying that rationality is found wherever people envisage the possibility of getting from different thicks to the same thin. To appeal to interests rather than beliefs is to urge a *modus vivendi*. Such an appeal is exemplified by the speech of the Athenian ambassadors to the unfortunate Melians, as reported by Thucydides. To appeal to your enduring beliefs as well as to your current interests is to suggest that what gives you your *present* moral identity—your thick and resonant complex of beliefs—may make it possible for you to develop a new, supplementary, moral identity.[16] It is to suggest that what makes you loyal to a smaller group may give you reason to cooperate in constructing a larger group, a group to which you may in time become equally loyal or perhaps even more loyal. The difference between the absence and the presence of rationality, on this account, is the difference between a threat and an offer—the offer of a new moral identity and thus a new and larger loyalty, a loyalty to a group formed by an unforced agreement between smaller groups.

In the hope of minimizing the contrast between Habermas and Rawls still further, and of rapprochement between both and Walzer, I want to suggest a way of thinking of rationality that might help to resolve the problem I posed earlier: the problem of whether justice and loyalty are different sorts of things, or whether the demands of justice are simply the demands of a larger loyalty. I said that question seemed to boil down to the question of whether justice and loyalty had different sources—reason and sentiment, respectively. If the latter distinction disappears, the former one will not seem particularly useful. But if by rationality we mean simply the sort of activity that Walzer thinks of as a thinning out process—the sort that, with luck, achieves the formulation and utilization of an overlapping consensus—then the idea that justice has a different source than loyalty no longer seems plausible.[17]

For, on this account of rationality, being rational and acquiring a larger loyalty are two descriptions of the same activity. This is because *any* unforced agreement between individuals and groups about what to do creates a form of community, and will, with luck, be the initial stage in expanding the circles of those whom each party to the agreement had previously taken to be "people like ourselves." The opposition between rational argument and fellow-feeling thus begins to dissolve. For fellow-feeling may, and often does, arise from the realization that the people whom one thought one might have to go to war with, use force on, are, in Rawls' sense, "reasonable." They are, it turns out, enough like us to see the point of compromising differences in order to live in peace, and of abiding by the agreement that has been hammered out. They are, to some degree at least, trustworthy.

From this point of view, Habermas' distinction between a strategic use of language and a genuinely communicative use of language begins to look like a difference between positions on a spectrum—a spectrum of degrees of trust. Baier's suggestion that we take trust rather than obligation to be our fundamental moral concept would thus produce a blurring of the line between rhetorical manipulation and genuine validity-seeking argument—a line that I think Habermas draws too sharply. If we cease to think of reason as a source of authority, and think of it simply as the process of reaching agreement by persuasion, then the standard Platonic and Kantian dichotomy of reason and feeling begins to fade away. That dichotomy can be replaced by a continuum of degrees of overlap of beliefs and desires.[18] When people whose beliefs and desires do not overlap very much disagree, they tend to think of each other as crazy or, more politely, as irrational. When there is considerable overlap, on the other hand, they may agree to differ and regard each other as the sort of people one can live with—and eventually, perhaps, the sort one can be friends with, intermarry with, and so on.[19]

To advise people to be rational is, on the view I am offering, simply to suggest that somewhere among their shared beliefs and desires there may be enough resources to permit agreement on how to coexist without violence. To conclude that someone is irredeemably *irrational* is not to realize that she is not making proper use of her God-given faculties. It is rather to realize that she does not seem to share enough relevant beliefs and desires with us to make possible fruitful conversation about the issue in dispute. So, we reluctantly conclude, we have to give up on the attempt to get her to enlarge her moral identity, and settle for working out a *modus vivendi*—one which may involve the threat, or even the use, of force.

A stronger, more Kantian, notion of rationality would be invoked if one said that being rational guarantees a peaceful resolution of conflicts—that if people are willing to reason together long enough, what Habermas calls "the force of the better argument" will lead them to concur.[20] This stronger notion strikes me as pretty useless. I see no point in saying that it is more rational to prefer one's neighbors to one's family in the event of a nuclear holocaust, or more rational to prefer leveling off incomes around the world to preserving the institutions of liberal Western societies. To use the word "rational" to commend one's chosen solution to such dilemmas, or to use the term "yielding to the force of the better argument" to characterize one's way of making up one's mind, is to pay oneself an empty compliment.

More generally, the idea of "the better argument" makes sense only if one can identify a natural, transcultural relation of relevance, which connects propositions with one another so as to form something like Descartes' "natural order of reasons." Without such a natural order, one can only evaluate arguments by their efficacy in producing agreement among particular persons or groups. But the required notion of natural, intrinsic relevance— relevance dictated not by the needs of any given community but by human reason as such—seems no more plausible or useful than that of a God whose Will can be appealed to in order to resolve conflicts between communities. It is, I think, merely a secularized version of that earlier notion.

Non-Western societies in the past were rightly skeptical of Western conquerors who explained that they were invading in obedience to divine commands. More recently, they have been skeptical of Westerners who suggest that they should adopt Western ways in order to become more rational. (This suggestion has been abbreviated by Ian Hacking as "Me rational, you Jane.") On the account of rationality I am recommending, both forms of skepticism are equally justified. But this is not to deny that these societies *should* adopt recent Western ways by, for example, abandoning slavery, practicing religious toleration, educating women, permitting mixed marriages, tolerating homosexuality and conscientious objection to war, and so on. As a loyal Westerner, I think they should indeed do all these things. I agree with Rawls about what it takes to count as reasonable, and about what kind of societies we Westerners should accept as members of a global moral community.

But I think that the rhetoric we Westerners use in trying to get everyone to be more like us would be improved if we were more frankly ethnocentric, and less professedly universalist. It would be better to say: Here is what we in the West look like as a result of ceasing to hold slaves, beginning to educate women, separating church and state, and so on. Here is what happened after we started treating certain distinctions between people as arbitrary rather than fraught with moral significance. If you would try treating them that way, you might like the results. Saying that sort of thing seems preferable to saying: Look at how much better we are at knowing what differences between persons are arbitrary and which not—how much more *rational* we are.

If we Westerners could get rid of the notion of universal moral obligations created by membership in the species, and substitute the idea of building a community of trust between ourselves and others, we might be in a better position to persuade non-Westerners of the advantages of joining in that community. We might be better able to construct the sort of global moral community that Rawls describes in "The Law of Peoples." In making this suggestion, I am urging, as I have on earlier occasions, that we need to peel apart Enlightenment liberalism from Enlightenment rationalism.

I think that discarding the residual rationalism that we inherit from the Enlightenment is advisable for many reasons. Some of these are theoretical and of interest only to philosophy professors, such as the apparent incompatibility of the correspondence theory of truth with a naturalistic account of the origin of human minds.[21] Others are more practical. One practical reason is that getting rid of rationalistic rhetoric would permit the West to approach the non-West in the role of someone with an instructive story to tell, rather than in the role of someone purporting to be making better use of a universal human capacity.

NOTES

1. Donald Fites, the CEO of the Caterpillar tractor company, explained his company's policy of relocation abroad by saying that "as a human being, I think what is going on is positive. I don't think it is realistic for 250 million Americans to control so much of the world's GNP." Quoted in Edward Luttwak, *The Endangered American Dream* (New York: Simon & Schuster, 1993), p. 184.

2. Michael Walzer, *Thick and Thin: Moral Argument at Home and Abroad* (Notre Dame: Notre Dame University Press, 1994), p. 4.

3. Baier's picture is quite close to that sketched by Wilfrid Sellars and Robert Brandom in their quasi-Hegelian accounts of moral progress as the expansion of the circle of beings who count as "us."

4. John Rawls, *Political Liberalism* (New York: Columbia University Press, 1993), p. 14n.

5. This sort of debate runs through a lot of contemporary philosophy. Compare, for example, Walzer's contrast between starting thin and starting thick with that between the Platonic-Chomskian notion that we start with meanings and descend to use, and the Wittgensteinian-Davidsonian notion that we start with use and then skim off meaning as needed for lexicographical or philosophical purposes.

6. Rawls, "The Law of Peoples" in *On Human Rights: The Oxford Amnesty Lectures, 1993,* Stephen Shute and Susan Hurley, eds. (New York: Basic Books, 1993), p.

44. I am not sure why Rawls thinks historicism is undesirable, and there are passages, both early and recent, in which he seems to throw in his lot with the historicists. (See the passage quoted in note 11 below from his recent "Reply to Habermas.") Some years ago I argued for the plausibility of an historicist interpretation of the metaphilosophy of Rawls' *A Theory of Justice* in my "The Priority of Democracy to Philosophy," reprinted in my *Objectivity, Relativism and Truth* (Cambridge: Cambridge University Press, 1991).

7. "The Law of Peoples," pp. 81, 61.

8. Ibid., p. 62.

9. All quotations in this paragraph are from Jürgen Habermas, *Justification and Application: Remarks on Discourse Ethics* (Cambridge: MIT Press, 1993), p. 95. Habermas is here commenting on Rawls' use of "reasonable" in writings earlier than "The Law of Peoples," since the latter appeared subsequent to Habermas' book.

When I wrote the present paper, the exchange between Rawls and Habermas published in *The Journal of Philosophy* (vol. 92, no. 3, March 1995) had not yet appeared. This exchange rarely touches on the question of historicism versus universalism. But one passage in which this question emerges explicitly is to be found on p. 179 of Rawls' "Reply to Habermas": "Justice as fairness is substantive . . . in the sense that it springs from and belongs to the tradition of liberal thought and the larger community of political culture of democratic societies. It fails then to be properly formal and truly universal, and thus to be part of the quasi-transcendental presuppositions (as Habermas sometimes says) established by the theory of communicative action."

10. Loc. cit.

11. "The Law of Peoples," p. 46.

12. My own view is that we do not need, either in epistemology or in moral philosophy, the notion of universal validity. I argue for this in "Sind Aussagen Universelle Geltungsansprüche?" *Deutsche Zeitschrift für Philosophie, (Band* 42, 6/1994), pp. 975–88. Habermas and Apel find my view paradoxical and likely to produce performative self-contradiction.

13. "The Law of Peoples," p. 46.

14. Both quotations are from "The Law of Peoples," p. 45.

15. I quote here from Rawls' summary of Scanlon's view at *Political Liberalism,* p. 49n.

16. Walzer thinks it is a good idea for people to have lots of different moral identities. "[T]hick, divided selves are the characteristic products of, and in turn require, a thick, differentiated, and pluralistic society" (*Thick and Thin,* p. 101).

17. Note that in Rawls' semitechnical sense an overlapping consensus is not the result of discovering that various comprehensive views already share common doctrines, but rather something that might never have emerged had the proponents of these views not started trying to cooperate.

18. Davidson has, I think, demonstrated that any two beings that use language to communicate with one another necessarily share an enormous number of beliefs and desires. He has thereby shown the incoherence of the idea that people can live in separate worlds created by differences in culture or status or fortune. There is always an immense overlap—an immense reserve army of common beliefs and desires to be drawn on at need. But this immense overlap does not, of course, prevent accusations of craziness or diabolical wickedness. For only a tiny amount of nonoverlap about cer-

tain particularly touchy subjects (the border between two territories, the name of the One True God) may lead to such accusations, and eventually to violence.

19. I owe this line of thought about how to reconcile Habermas and Baier to Mary Rorty.

20. This notion of "the better argument" is central to Habermas' and Apel's understanding of rationality. I criticize it in the article cited above in note 14.

21. For a claim that such a theory of truth is essential to "the Western Rationalist Tradition," see John Searle, "Rationality and Realism: What Difference does it Make?" *Daedalus* (vol. 122, no. 4, Fall 1992), pp. 55–84. See also my reply to Searle in "Does Academic Freedom Have Philosophical Presuppositions?" *Academe* (vol. 80, no. 6, November/December 1994), pp. 52–63. I argue there that we should be better off without the notion of "getting something right," and that writers such as Dewey and Davidson have shown us how to keep the benefits of Western rationalism without the philosophical hangups caused by the attempt to explicate this notion.

Erikh Solovyov

LAW AS POLITICIANS' MORALITY

Everywhere the process of formation of democratic institutions is accompanied by a severe and demanding moral criticism of political practice.[1] Such was the case in Western Europe in the eighteenth century, such is the case today in those countries that develop a model of a *democratic constitutional state*. The historic experience of modern Russia is of great (and maybe, exclusive) interest in this respect.

The rapid changes that have occurred in our country after 1985 have awakened a mass interest in the subject of morality and politics. The conditions of *glasnost* allowed the veil over the mechanisms of political domination to lift slightly. The charges of political cynicism, escobarism,[2] and criminal corruption of the political leadership have taken a prominent place in the verdicts that have been passed by the forming democracy against the exhausted totalitarian communist regime. These charges stand firm in the arsenal of today's publicists. However, since the beginning of 1992, they have been more and more frequently turned *against the democratic power itself*.

The moral criticism of the *perestroika* period had a mainly liberal and politico-juridical character; the moral criticism of the past few years has become mainly populist and moralistic. The primary form of today's discourse of invective is the rally. Its style subordinates to itself everything—parliamentary speeches, publicism, and scientific discussions. As a result, moral and political discourse suffers probably more than any other. It gravitates to invocations ("by the name of the people!"), to maximalism, and to the terseness of a street slogan. As if illegitimately confined by the rules of public meetings, it bypasses any—and first of all its own—ethical reasoning.

Hardly anyone will dare to assert that the present moral condemnation of the Russian ruling democracy is groundless and unsubstantiated. Yes, there are many precise verdicts advanced. As a rule, though, these appear in those

23

cases where the charge is based on some legal criterion—violation of the constitution, the rigging of elections, corruption in government, administrative abuses, the nonobservance of agreements and promises, etc. By contrast, whenever the question of a moral evaluation is raised, indistinctness and eclecticism predominate. A politician acting in the environment of a democratic constitutional state (although a very, very imperfect one) is judged on the basis of standards and ideals borrowed from completely different political worlds. A member of parliament is exposed according to the moral standards, not of a representative democracy, but of a direct-plebiscite democracy, represented by the soviets at their best: he is seen as a worthless "servant of the people" and a bad executor of the voters' mandate. A public figure of a constitutional state is evaluated according to the stereotypes of a moral-police state. Ministers of a federated republic are reproached for the absence of virtues characteristic of the public figures of the Russian monarchy.

But especially gladly (and with particular success among the public) they judge the politician who has long been dealing with a market economy, still in the process of forming, by the standards appropriate to the politician who commands a planned economy.

But this is not all. The populist opposition is generally inclined to interpret democracy as a bankrupt executor of a social project that was adopted and published by the communist reformers in their time. In 1985–1988 the great mottos of *glasnost* and democratization ranked on a par with the adventurist slogan of "acceleration"—i.e., of immediate renovation and perfection of the economy. *Perestroika* solemnly and complacently declared that it is canceling communist asceticism in the name of the future and thinks that it must satisfy the daily needs of the present generation. Populism imputes this public promise of "a quick success" to democracy and then, pointing a finger at today's calamities, denounces not only the actions of democracy but also its institutions and its constitutional and legal standards as a *worthless means* by which to reach this "quick success."

If we combine all these accusations, we shall see that the modern politician is judged according to absolutely fantastic, far-fetched, and ethically dubious criteria. He must possess every imaginable perfection as well as the unimaginable practical efficiency that he once allegedly claimed for himself. No wonder that the progovernment publicism is inclined today generally to exempt politics from the moral judgment. Politics, it asserts, is a "national park" of pragmatism, and the agent of political actions must be judged exclusively by the results he achieves within the space of real possibilities. This is an unacceptable position. First, it is wrong in principle; second, it is deadly for democracy, which itself has risen on the bayonets of merciless exposures of Communism.

Democracy must answer populist moral invective with its own version of political ethics which is organized around the following question: What does the concept of a *democratic constitutional state* itself demand from a moral politician? There is a sea of literature dedicated to the political ethics of democracy. But it is too time-consuming to apply it to the ideological conflicts experienced by modern Russia. The present paper does not pretend to achieve this goal. I am interested rather in the main postulate distinguishing the political ethics of democracy. Being a historian of moral and political philosophy, I try to substantiate this postulate as it is addressed to the genesis of a democratic constitutional state or, more exactly, to the original civilized effort establishing it as a concept and a practice. At the same time, I never forget that my actual opponent is modern Russian populism.

I

A democratic constitutional state—both as an ideal and as a reality—is based on two equally important principles: on the idea of *the sovereignty of the people*, and on the idea of *human rights* ("rights to freedom," "basic rights," "inalienable subjective rights of a person"). The first presumes that the will of the people is the highest law and that all power comes from the people (i.e., it becomes legitimate only through the people's will). The second demands that power—wherever it comes from—recognize the basic rights of every single person (the rights to freedom, to life, to property, to participation in the formation of the public will).

Both the sovereignty of the people and the notion of human rights are concepts with a long tradition. We already meet the idea that the will of the people is the highest law in the old communal "public meetings" known to many cultures. (The democracy of the ancient *polis* is only their classic example.) The idea of inalienable freedom is perceived—or at least felt—everywhere people fight against the oppression of faith. (The radical formulae of freedom of conscience that emerged at the end of the Reformation in Western Europe, and which paved the way to declarations of human rights, are only the most consistent expressions of this tendency.) Therefore, we may say that neither the idea of the sovereignty of the people nor the idea of basic rights are in principle alien to any of the traditional cultures. (National liberation movements in all regions of the world have usually taken them as long foreseen truths.)

Combining these ideas in the composition of a democratic constitutional state, however, is entirely another thing. This was not suggested by any tradition and appeared as an invention of the people.

Paradoxical as it may seem, the standards and institutions of legally normalized democracy are "foreign," "borrowed," "Western" *for every* ethnos and local culture. They were born in the New World on the other side of the Atlantic, in a country which did not have its own stable traditions yet, and moved eastward, conquering first France and then—in a long struggle—the minds of politically active classes in Germany and in the states of Eastern Europe, in Russia, and in the Asian countries. There was not a single country in the Old World which did not resist the experience of this new democracy and which did not advance rather serious objections on behalf of its cultural and political identity. What is astonishing is not that these arguments have been (and continue to be) persistently put forward,[3] but that, in spite of these arguments, the concept and practice of a democratic constitutional state have established themselves in such culturally diverse countries as France and Germany, Holland and Italy, Israel and Japan, Costa Rica and New Zealand. In every country where the people had enough patience to wait for "matured democracy," it has rather successfully assimilated their unique cultural and political experience.

As an out-of-tradition popular invention, a democratic constitutional state reveals a certain similarity to technical inventions. At the same time (and this must be stressed), it is absolutely nontechnical by virtue of its semantic construction. You cannot consider legally normalized democracy as a kind of institutional mechanism, which, after it is once adjusted and wound up, works automatically, using the energy of habit. Not only its improvement but also its stable functioning demands a constant and successive effort. The contents of this effort determine the manner of amalgamation of the two similarly important principles included in the concept of a democratic constitutional state. I mean *the autonomous will of the people* as the recognition of human rights.

A democratic constitutional state exists from the moment the people, which already possesses the whole of power, voluntarily restricts its power and its will through the recognition of human rights. The people itself puts these rights higher than any of its wishes, interests and considerations of advantage; it itself, as a sovereign, establishes *the primacy of the idea of human rights over the idea of the people's sovereignty*. Such is the first effort of self-discipline and self-obligation which through renewal becomes permanent, subordinating step by step the positive law of the people's state, its political institutions and procedures, its corporations and associations, and its economic practice to its recognition of basic rights.

Let us listen attentively to the striking political vocabulary of the "Age of Enlightenment" that was born in America, coined in France, and clearly—for all future times—interpreted in Germany, in the works of Wilhelm von Humboldt and Immanuel Kant.

Human rights, when they were born, were called *inherent, sacred,* and *inalienable.* In the nineteenth, and even twentieth centuries, many thinkers regarded these expressions with haughty irony, seeing in them rhetorical clichés of the naturalistic, theological, and dogmatic legal language that has lived out its life. But they missed the main point: the perception of self-value and the unconditional significance of human rights that was rather well-conveyed in each of these expressions.

a) The naturalistic term "inherent" fixed the understanding of human rights as such individual competences that exist before and regardless of any human regulations, of the whole of legal practice and of policy itself. Kant said about it: People "have absolutely similar *inherent right* (i.e., the one that belongs to them before any legal action is taken)."[4]

b) The expression "sacred," reminding us of the conceptual relation of human rights with the "divine law" of the late Middle Ages, had, at the same time, an exact analogue in secular, nontheological language. "Sacred rights" were called here "unconditional" and "undisputed." Kant explained that to recognize the sanctity of inherent rights meant to see in them the "supreme principle from which all the maxims concerning society must stem and which cannot be restricted by any other principle."[5]

c) But probably most significant is the authentic meaning that was originally given to the concept of "inalienable rights." First, it meant that the basic rights are "imprescriptible"—i.e., are given to a person forever. Second, an obliterated and lost meaning of the expression "inalienable" was that a person had no power to give away his rights or to abandon them due to some attendant considerations. None of the citizens of a constitutional state has the right to sell himself into slavery, having exchanged his freedom for a modest guaranteed income. You can sacrifice your life, but not the freedom of dealing with your life; you can alienate property, but not the right of property. Or, as Kant said, "everybody has inalienable rights which he has no power to relinquish, even if he wanted to."[6] But if no single citizen has the right to relinquish freedom, then the people as a whole also cannot do this.[7] Recognizing the basic rights of a person as "inalienable," the people takes an eternal pledge to a free political existence.

The very solemnity of the expressions "inherent," "sacred," and "inalienable" brings to mind the language of a vow. Yes, the declarations of the late eighteenth century were, in their essence, vows to treat from then on the right to freedom as a prepolitical, unconditionally significant, and unabolishable basis of statehood. And every people that includes human rights in its constitution reiterates this vow. Such is the hidden, repeatedly reproduced deontology of democratic conscience. Its politico-juridical expression is the understanding of human rights as an unchangeable part of the constitution. The relevant articles may only be supplemented; they may not be interpreted with the aim of restricting them.

❧   ❧   ❧

Now, let us see what all this means for political ethics. In a democratic society, the politician is one who receives power from the hands of his or her people and who takes an oath before the people. In this oath, he or she joins the sacred vow that was given by the people itself at the moment of the constitutional establishment of statehood. But in this way the politician as a personality interiorizes, reproduces in him- or herself the very autonomy of the people's will. Subordination to the constitutional and legal principles of democracy becomes his or her own basic principle. That is the meaning of the formula that I have adopted for my paper's title: Law as Politicians' Morality. It is time to explain its full meaning.

I understand "law" as (a) human rights as they are declared in the constitution, (b) formulae of positive law (civil, procedural, and criminal) explicating human rights in the sense of subjective personal rights, and (c) political institutions, rules and procedures explicating human rights in the sense of the right of active citizenship (i.e., the constitutional and legal framework of democracy). I understand "morality" (in accordance with all post-Kantian ethical tradition) as unconditional moral demands that cannot be reduced to any calculation of advantages. I understand by "politician" a democratic politician defending the good of the people as this lends itself to an expression in the formulae of a lawful common interest. Thus when I speak about the law as politicians' morality I mean the following: that the demand to preserve and to observe the law (in the sense I have just explained) has the same unconditional priority for a democratic politician defending the good of the people as morality has for a human being in pursuing his own good.

This means that any demands addressed to a politician on behalf of the common good, expediency, urgent people's needs, etc. he recognizes as significant, binding, but still *conditional* imperatives. Before he decides to begin to fulfil these demands, the politician must find out whether this is expedient, whether such (and, first of all, such) is the need of the people, and so on. Everything that is connected with the good of the people should be considered rationally and empirically. This reasoning is tested in the course of a free political discussion and allows for a palliative and compromise recognition. But the demand of the preservation and observance of a right is a *categorical imperative* of political practice. Moreover, it is an "absolute condition," a condition *sine qua non,* in the process of discussing any rationally founded demands and propositions. If the condition and the price of a meliorative (or even urgently rescuing) measure turns out to be the relinquishing of at least some basic rights, the measure should be rejected out of hand. If a democratic politician, recognizing another way of thinking, allowed a performative contradiction in determining his own role (the role of a spokesman for, and a defendant of, the *legitimate* interests of the people) he would, simply speaking, relinquish this role, by using his powers to deny his powers.

The formula "law as a morality of politics" presupposes a certain mandatory hierarchy of normative preferences which structures the moral personality of a politician. I would like to give some examples of this hierarchy, deploying them in the form of peculiar "triads":

a) The imperative of constitutional procedures has primacy over the imperative of the general good, which, in turn, has priority over any demand formalizing special interests.
b) The respect for the other's right as a maxim of practical reason is higher than political expediency as a maxim of common sense, though the latter itself prevails over a selective sense of compassion.
c) The virtue of justice must be given preference over the virtue of social prudence, though the latter has dominance over the virtue of mercy.

In my opinion, rigorously consistent observance of this hierarchy of the normative preferences is the main precept with which a democratic politician must reply to the eclectic and heterogeneous criticism of modern populism. Of course, he should reply with his deeds and with self-criticism, and not merely by public self-justification.

However, there is another—and probably the most important—question that is put by today's moral and political invective. Must a democratic politician subordinate himself to the direct demand of the people's will (which expresses itself through, for example, mass manifestations or a referendum) if this demand contradicts the constitutional expression of the people's will?

The politician has no right to treat the will of the people expressed in a plebiscite as a conditional imperative. (Otherwise, he would simply reject the principle of the people's sovereignty.) And yet, a democratic politician cannot, categorically, subordinate himself to this will if it is unconstitutional and is directed against the law. Politically and ethically, he could express his will in the following way. A person possessing legitimate power is authorized not by a spontaneous but by an autonomous people's will. All of his responsibilities stem from the solemn constitutional promise that the people has given before God, the world community, and its own conscience. The people is violating this oath by the will expressed in a plebiscite. But the will of a violator of such an oath has no obligatory force.

I have deliberately used in this "ultimatum of disobedience" an obsolete language echoing the moral and legal vocabulary of the eighteenth century. But the ultimatum could be expressed also in modern politological terms. Robert A. Dahl writes,

> Basic rights (including political) are in a certain sense preceding democracy. They stem from moral guidelines and the basis of human existence. They are not only preceding democracy [as the power of the people] but they are also higher. Therefore, they may be interpreted as the rights which a citizen [in our

context, a politician] may use if necessary to defend himself from the vicissitudes of the democratic process.[8]

This question is not at all scholastic for today's Russia. It is in the background of many discussions and corrodes political thought like an acid. It is not by chance that in the last documents that are specifically codified appear the things that are practically evident: "A referendum may not be considered valid if its results contradict the Constitution."[9]

II

One of the methods widely used by populism in the moral criticism of democracy is an *historical evaluation of its effectiveness.* In essence, this approach is based on a social and utilitarian criterion: recognition of the political regime as a means of attaining the general good. But the trick here is that the criticism is presented on behalf of a history which seems to be sacred. Political philosophy has long known this kind of evaluation and, replying to it, has stressed as a rule that the proof of democracy's value may be recognized as historical only if history is considered in the long-term. We can get to know the virtue of democracy only when it reaches a venerable age. Nothing is more harmful to its formative process than the craving "for easy success and present enjoyment."[10] These wise maxims are quite sufficient to parry the commonplace invectives which sound in today's Russia approximately like this: "We have lived under democracy already for three years, but we still don't see that it promotes the progress of our society." This discussion, however, has not yet reached the core of the matter. We shall continue to dwell on the surface of the issue until such time as we ask whether history can be taken as an absolute, infallible judge of a democratic constitutional state at all.

First, we should consider the phenomenon indicated by Tocqueville, and ask why, strictly speaking, the beneficial influence of democracy on society turns out to have a remote—one might even say, delayed—effect. Judging it on the basis of an historical test of effectiveness implies that democracy, together with its constitutional and legal construction, is a political *means* of social progress. I believe that such an interpretation is correct only with respect to a given democratic government. It is hard to deny that any such government is responsible for whether or not "it contributed to progress," whether it demonstrated will and persistence, competence and skill in pragmatic adjustment, all of which it required to meet social and historical needs.

But democracy itself, as a constitutional and legal structure, is another matter entirely. It is not a means of progress in any immediate sense of this word. Rather it is more "a means for a means"—i.e., an aggregate of rules in accordance with which a government "working for progress" can be elected and controlled. However, as was long ago noticed by operationalist philosophy, "a means for a means" can be effective only if in some respect it is rec-ognized as an end in itself. Politicians who studied the history of democracy also noticed this long ago. In various contexts, and in different expressions, they drew attention to the following paradox: The law turns out to be a good means to attain the end (of progress) exactly when it is not interpreted as a means and is valued regardless of the end to which it contributes. Thus the main goal is attained as if it were a secondary one—independently of any pro-gram, with delays, "by the will of Providence."

This is remarkably similar to the interpretation of morality in ethically qualified theology: the execution of the commandments is a means of salva-tion, but only if it is not treated as a means—i.e., if the commandment is ex-ecuted "from one's heart" or rigoristically, without the expectation of any advantages to be gained in heaven. The imperativeness of the moral com-mandment does not depend on soteriology. Rather soteriology subsumes the moral action, which is imperative in itself, into the structure of its per-ceptions concerning means and ends. I think that the same situation is to be found with respect to the law. By itself, in its primary meaning, the law has nothing to do with the problems of government "working for progress." At the same time, it can make an important contribution to this work, if it is observed scrupulously, strictly, and without any instrumental adaptation to the goal.

But if the law is external to the whole practice of pursuing progress, then where has its meaning come from? What spiritual effort has given birth to it in this world rushing toward future benefits—private, special, public, and global? It seems to me that a brief answer may be given as follows: the law (as I have defined it earlier) is born from the spirit of rejection of the previous absence of rights, or from an act of *political and juridical remorse.* Political freedom is based on the determination that "this will not be repeated."

To see that this is really the case, it is enough to get acquainted with three most important declarations of human rights. As is well known, the first of them, the Declaration of Independence (1776), marked the secession of the American colonies from the insolently despotic parent state. But simultane-ously, this was also an act of alienation from the whole of the Old World with its religious persecutions, land expropriations, and monarchical tyrannies. The French Declaration of Human and Citizen's Rights (1789) directly pro-claimed in its preamble the renunciation by the nation of its own despotic past. The declaration was prepared for by a half-century of criticism of absolutism—criticism in which the absolutist state was portrayed almost as a criminal state. Finally, the Declaration of Human Rights adopted by the United Nations in 1948 is in its essence an antitotalitarian legal document. Its basis is the Nuremberg tribunal. It codifies the condemnation by the world community of Hitler's "new order." And every new state that signs this dec-laration joins the global antitotalitarian oath.

When I use the word "remorse" to characterize the general civilizational meaning of the recognition of basic rights, I do not mean any outward expression of spiritual sorrow. The remorse does not necessarily involve gestures of repentance; it may even reject them. In its original (Greek) significance, repentance means simply *metanoia*—i.e., the full and irreversible alteration of thought. It corresponds to the solemn language of a sworn renunciation. But this is the language of the declarations of human rights. Of course, the language of hope permeates their texts as well—the hope for a perfect future for mankind. In the list of basic rights we find promotional promises or "ideal rights" that society cannot provide in practice. But the conceptual unity of the document is not determined by this.

> André Glucksman, a French philosopher, was absolutely right when he said, The idea of human rights acquires its definite outline not because we know what an ideal human being should be, what he should be by his nature or as a perfect human being, a new human being, a human being of the future and so on. No, the idea of human rights becomes definite because we imagine very clearly what a human being should not be.[11]

The meaning of basic rights is perceived in the negative experience of humiliation and the endurance of violence in its many forms (enslavement, despotism, dictatorship, manipulation, authoritarian guardianship, compulsory happiness, and so on). Basic rights are declared when the people come to understand that they will never again endure certain forms of violence— that there are no circumstances or goals that could make them endure it. The latter is especially important in the context of our discussion. The absence of rights (and especially the total absence of rights) cannot be the means for the achievement of any purpose. This postulate is present in the whole law of democracy.

Human rights (especially in the twentieth century) are the product of a terrible knowledge of history—a knowledge which does not allow us to consider history to be some sort of sinless judge of political practice. We have no naïve faith in objective historical tasks and challenges any more. They themselves are subject to our scrutiny. There is also no longer any latent moral notion of progress. The time is past when social utilitarianism (the pursuit of the social or the general good) could dress itself up in a toga of sacred historical demands.

A ban on what should not be has priority over what is possible and even necessary. This is one more rule of normative preference supposed by the law and obligatory for political ethics. The resistance of illegal methods of resolving social problems (the consistency, duration, and strength of this resistance) is the main thing to be taken into account in the historic evaluation of the effectiveness of democracy. It is more important than any progressive reforms made by democratic governments, more important than any measures aimed at bringing the kingdom of the people's prosperity nearer.

The preventive and defensive functions of the law were well understood by the best minds of the past, who did not yet know the social nightmares of our century. At the end of the nineteenth century, the Russian philosopher Vladimir Solovyov coined the following wonderful formula: "The task of the law is not at all to turn the world lying in evil into God's Kingdom, but only not to let it turn into Hell ahead of time."[12]

We may say that the law and legal conscience involve a guarded, reconnoitering way of thinking. They look ahead from the perspective of the negative experience of the absence of rights and try to prevent its recurrence. This allows us to properly understand the remarkable injunction with which Alexis de Tocqueville finishes his book, *Democracy in America:* "Let us, then, look forward to the future with that salutary fear which makes men keep watch and work for freedom, not with that faint and idle terror which depresses and enervates the heart."[13] This "salutary fear" obviously contradicts the pathos that, for a very long time, was instilled by the doctrines of guaranteed and implacable progress. Tocqueville, a rigoristic defender of the unconditional value of basic rights, was, at the same time, one of the first critics of these doctrines. Was it accidental? I think it was far from accidental.

The concept of inherent, sacred, and inalienable rights (or the new "natural law") appeared along with the religion of progress and soon it formed a close ideological union with the latter. At the beginning of the nineteenth century, it was taken for granted that to defend the "natural law" was the same thing as to defend the main premises of the progressive development of society. However, the union of the "natural law" and the religion of progress was shaken as soon as the latter took historicist forms, declaring its "natural stages," its "dialectical denials," and, above all, its "implacable historical necessity"—which necessitated huge expenses and demanded the legalization of these expenses. Succumbing to new forms of progressivist thinking, jurisprudence went down the drain of juridical positivism and then of juridical nihilism. The inherent spiritual discord between the "natural law" and the religion of progress was exposed. It became obvious that it was impossible to recognize an unconditional significance of basic rights and at the same time to profess historicism, the main juridical credo of which was "If this is necessary—for progress—then it is legitimate."

Does this mean, then, that a developed legal conscience cannot look for support in any theory of historical process? No. Perfectly compatible with it is the version of open history that was advanced for the first time by A. de Tocqueville, A. Cavour, and A. Herzen, and which was given a serious grounding in the modern epistemology of history.[14] The future, this epistemology asserts, is irrevocably uncertain, too uncertain and multivarious for us to follow any single, theoretically comprehended "command" of history. But it is precisely because of this that the future depends upon our ethically grounded principles and positions—upon our irrevocable freedom to choose and, therefore, to reject at least such actual challenges of history as may have as a condition of their fulfillment the return to already condemned forms of historical practice. Open history demands the law as a significant criterion of an acceptable future: the progressive is that which is legitimate. We can say that this is the rule in accordance with which history unfolds inside democratic societies. At the same time, this is a final, integral maxim of political ethics adequate to the notion of a democratic constitutional state.

The question of the relation between the concept of human rights and the religion of progress has one more aspect important to the subject of our conference. The doctrine of the guaranteed and implacable improvement of society is a product of West European, which is to say, *one special regional, culture*. It is a secular synopsis of the Judaeo-Christian perception of the universe. The doctrine of guaranteed progress is infected with "Eurocentrism" from the beginning. However, when it is absorbed by people of other cultures as an evolutionary or dialectical scheme, it immediately shifts its center. The vision of the ultimate condition to which history aspires is different; history's natural stages and formations are interpreted in a different way. And of course, every culture tries, in one way or another, to join the historic vanguard—that which is most progressive and selected for the victory that is inevitably supposed by the doctrine of guaranteed progress in its historically developed forms (see Comte, Fichte, Hegel, and Marx). In my opinion, there is no other philosophy in today's world that is so conducive to the estrangement of people and to the cultivation of their social and group as well as ethnic and confessional ambitions. The logical construction of a predetermined general history that yields to arbitrary interpretations and transformations is the best speculative instrument available for the support of special historical missions and for isolationist or aggressive fixation on cultural peculiarities.

The human rights concept has quite a different semantic orientation. I remind the reader once more of a deep thought of André Glucksman: "The idea of human rights becomes definite exactly because we understand quite well what a human being should not be. The experience of inhumanity is much more tangible and understandable to us than the experience of perfect humanity."[15] I would add, "more tangible, understandable, and yielding to generalization." There is no people that would not find the absence of rights a negative experience and, therefore, the main premise of human rights theory may be given general expression. From this point of view, it is similar to negative moral commandments like "do not lie," "do not kill," "do not sell," "do not steal," which are recognized by all mankind.

Of course, there is cultural peculiarity in the absence of rights. But who would brag about it?! I have yet to meet a thinker who would applaud the uniqueness of his or her culture with reference to the special refinement of torture or to an unusually long preservation of serfdom. The experience of the absence of rights unites people through the rejection of that absence of rights.

It is naïve to expect that some day people will be united by a single dream about a perfect future world. But it seems to me that it may nonetheless be possible for them to come to an agreement in their judgments of the conditions on which a perfect world can *never* be built. There are reasons to believe, therefore, that the recognition of human rights opens not only a new stage in the political unification of mankind. It may open as well an era of cultural and civilizational rallying around a supratraditional, universal ideal of the democratic constitutional state, in contrast to the traditionally European and forcibly general, spontaneously estranging religion of progress. It is also possible that in both of these processes (the political and the cultural-civilizational) politicians, accepting the law as a supreme moral code, will play a significant role.

NOTES

1. Here and further, political practice is understood as the acquisition, preservation, and use of legitimate power.

2. That is, "The end justifies the means."

3. We can demonstrate that the main types of these arguments were exhausted by the end of the nineteenth century. All later arguments in favor of identity turn out to be "borrowed" and "Western."

4. Immanuel Kant, *Werke*, vol. 8 (Leipzig: Academieausgabe, 1923), p. 292. (My translation.)

5. Ibid., p. 298.

6. Ibid., p. 304.

7. Kant explains this in relation to the problem of social treaty, Wilhelm von Humboldt in relation to the problem of "limited government."

8. Robert A. Dahl, *A Preface to Economic Democracy* (Los Angeles: University of California Press, 1981), p. 28.

9. Draft Constitution of the Ukraine. Kharkov, 1994.

10. Alexis de Tocqueville, *Democracy in America*, vol. II (New York: Alfred A. Knopf, 1945), p. 17.

11. "The New Ethics: Solidarity of the 'Shaken'," an interview with A. Glucksman, *Voprosy Filosofii* (vol. 3, 1991), p. 86.

12. V. S. Solovyov, *V. S. Solovyov: A Two Volume Edition*, vol. 1 (Moscow: 1988), p. 454.

13. Alexis de Tocqueville, *Democracy in America*, vol. II, p. 330.

14. Convincing proofs of this thesis are given in the works of my colleague, A. S. Panarin, a member of The Institute of Philosophy of the Russian Academy of Sciences.

15. Op. cit., p. 86.

María Pía Lara

JUSTICE AND SOLIDARITY: THE CASE OF RECOGNITION

Today democracy is almost universally acclaimed as the criterion of legitimacy for political systems. The consensus regarding its worth is the result of painful historical experiences in this century. The revival of political philosophy in academic circles reflects a need to rethink some basic issues concerning what democracy is and how it should be conceived. Political philosophers are discussing whether democracy is merely a form of government, or a political way of life, and how proceduralism relates to questions concerning the good, or if it is even capable of dealing with such substantial issues. Communitarianism and feminism have raised many questions regarding this subject, making it one of the most discussed issues of our time.[1] The problem is not a simple one. We are now facing not only the challenge of pluralist and non-homogenous societies, but also the question of how we should deal with difference and recognition, the possible relationship between formalism and substantial notions of the good, and, above all, the revision of what, for us, has been the legacy of modernity. What is at issue here is which key notions of political liberalism should survive the present criticisms of democracy as these are conceived in postconventional societies.

Much of the literature written in recent years, especially among political philosophers, is related in one way or another to the interpretation of these legacies of modernity. Rousseau and Kant are frequently invoked to defend or attack certain approaches toward the ideal of the homogeneity of will, the tradition of republicanism as a core notion of collective forms of government and the tradition of liberalism as linked to the idea of the individual. Many authors have based their theses on reinterpretations of Kant's ideas of respect and autonomy.

Democracy is still the best political means for people to convert their agreements and disagreements into new interpretations of the law, the political order and its institutions. However, modern societies face serious problems stemming from immigration and their attempts to assimilate different groups, giving rise to questions regarding our notions of plurality and political solutions based on these notions.

In this paper, I want to deal not so much with the problems that have already been on the agenda of political philosophy for the last ten years, such as the aprioristic separation between the public and the private, ideas of community and the individual, of citizenship and the state, or the respective merits of the republican model versus the liberal one. All of these have attracted a great deal of attention and generated a variety of interpretations. Rather, I want to focus on the "anonymous public conversations"[2] that use the public sphere as a space for the deliberation, disagreement, and argument that help to form the public opinion of civil society. Some social scientists have already offered interesting interpretations of the ways in which public debates have strengthened democracy and become important political tools. Those empirical and social studies have focused on the interrelationship of justice and the good, which are already intertwined in the public sphere due to the free and spontaneous processes of communication.

My aim is to situate the public sphere as part of the culture of civil society. I understand this according to the proposal of Jeffrey C. Alexander: that is, as the "arena in which social solidarity is defined in universalistic terms,"[3] an independent civic sphere, differentiated from the state and the market, but also linked to solidarity through a special kind of recognition of the individual. In my opinion, it is here that we can relate the political to the moral dimension. I want to argue that the public sphere is where we work out a shared vision of how justice can be interpreted and applied. Then I would like to focus on the relevance of solidarity as an example of how the ethical and the political influence our conceptions of justice and the good.

Because justice and solidarity are related to our cognitive and emotional selves and we can only demand recognition of our identities through an appeal to justice, these demands have to be displayed in the public sphere. Here the subjects of recognition can become the authors of a new definition of justice as recognition. It is in the public sphere that we struggle for recognition, not only as social groups but also as individuals. And if modern societies have developed simultaneous processes of individuation and socialization, our biographies have become principles of individuation that, with the mediation of public dialogues, have acquired a moral status. Through the public discussion of our need for recognition, the moral status of our identities interconnects with the political base, and this interrelatedness produces what I will call here the "new illocutionary form" developed through our modern ways of conceiving our identities. By "new illocutionary form" I understand self-presentations with which one justifies a complex validity claim before a second person or a public: "a claim to recognition of the irreplaceable identity of an ego manifesting itself in a conscious way of life."[4]

THE PUBLIC DOMAIN AS A SPHERE OF SOLIDARITY

Hannah Arendt is now seen as one of the major political thinkers to have revived the idea of the public sphere as a key to the development of a democratic society.[5] Since *Situating the Self*, Seyla Benhabib has been among those who argued most persistently that the public sphere, despite the criticisms leveled by feminists that it is a male political gathering,[6] is an element of the utmost importance for developing a deliberative model of democracy. It is here that matters of collective deliberation are conducted and decided among free and equal individuals, and solely in terms of arguments and counterarguments.

Ever since Habermas published *The Structural Transformation of the Public Sphere*, many theorists have correctly insisted that deliberative processes can become, and in fact are, very important for collective decision-making. More recently, however, interest has focused on some features of deliberation that seem particularly important for any coherent model of participatory democracy. Social arenas have provided the opportunities for individuals to express their concerns about violations of their normative standards of justice. And in our contemporary societies, these claims seem always to be related to demands for respect and recognition of individuals and groups. That is why the real shift in interest to the public sphere as an arena for discussion and communication is due to the fact that our societies have assumed that social recognition is related to the expectations of subjects entering into communicative interaction, as Axel Honneth aptly pointed out.[7] Also, as Seyla Benhabib claimed in her essay, "Deliberative Rationality and Models of Democratic Legitimacy," the process of gathering new information and the variety of experiences being described can enlarge[8] us and make us aware of problems not previously known or fully understood. Active participation in dialogue helps us develop a reflective attitude and gain conceptual clarity in order to argue and understand the other's point of view, to see such views and experiences as seeking recognition and as possible bases for new interpretations that can reconcile our normative standards of justice and our divergent conceptions regarding values and their order. It provides us, in fact, with the necessary contrast we need if our visions are to be clarified by a reflexive effort; active participation in dialogue enables each of us to be regarded and identified as a special human being, a particular person in need of attention. Furthermore, this exercise of dealing publicly with matters that we care about is now seen as an important element of a learning process whereby we come to acknowledge and respect other peoples' unique, different, and multiple ways of being.[9] Public discussions are thus an important factor in constructing a democratic culture of "civil society," because they provide an arena of communication for the intersubjective presuppositions of human identity development and their claims for recognition.

Because it provides us with the chance to reflect on our conceptions of the good life and the lives we want to lead, the public arena immediately situates us in a place in which we and others have the possibility of finding a voice, of making our point, of being understood, of being able to defend or attack what we consider important to our lives in common and as individuals. But it is also the arena in which we can better situate what we can now call interpretations of needs and rights, the new contextualizations of our struggles to achieve or find legitimate recognition and dignity.

According to the proceduralists, these dialogues take the form of new interpretations or revisions of law, thus assuring their institutional acceptance. But the only way to legitimize legal norms is through their acceptance by all participants. Therefore, the legitimacy of a democracy depends upon people being able to construct new interpretations of their needs in their search for recognition. Depending on how these new views of the good are absorbed by institutional processes and reflected on a normative level, we can say that the community has achieved a decentralized and pluralist structure or has failed to do so.[10]

Our visions of the good play a very important role in the new reordering of values in which the institutional basis of justice is grounded. And this is where solidarity comes in as a basis for connecting this horizon of different views of the good to the various life projects of individuals and their expectations that those claims will meet with recognition and, therefore, can be discussed in the public sphere. Solidarity demands channels for these voices to be heard and to become part of the culture, of the shared values, of the strong evaluations with which Charles Taylor has been so concerned.

In what follows, I want to draw attention to these interconnections of solidarity and where they can come from, because it is my thesis that it is only through solidary ties, by means of "illocutionary claims" of recognition in the public sphere, that individuals and collectives can succeed in making their demands part of our vision of justice.

SOLIDARITY AND RECOGNITION AS AN "ILLOCUTIONARY FORM"

Habermas has dealt extensively with the relationship between justice and solidarity; in fact, he sees them as two sides of the same coin. Nevertheless, his interpretation of solidarity is also linked to a very Kantian conception of autonomy and a strict separation of justice and the good. This has been one of the elements of his thought most criticized by communitarians and feminists. I cannot discuss in detail here the many works dealing with this subject. Rather, I would like to focus on a proposal made by Maeve Cooke, and a very important suggestion advanced by Paul Ricoeur, which makes it possible to link solidarity to processes of recognition.

In "Selfhood and Solidarity,"[11] Maeve Cooke distinguishes two conceptions of solidarity: what she refers to as "esteem-based" solidarity, on the one hand, and "respect-based" solidarity, for which Habermas' solidarity is paradigmatic, on the other. Cooke is concerned both with distinguishing between "esteem-based" and "respect-based" solidarity, and with developing possible interconnections between the two. Of particular importance is her integration of Charles Taylor's and George Herbert Mead's claim that originality is a central element in the conception of the individual as it has developed in modernity. Connected with this is a new vision of the individual as irreplaceable.

It is no accident that in recent thinking on ethics there has been a significant recovery of Aristotle's main insights, for he stressed the relations of love and friendship and their significance in moral and political life. One important interpretation of Aristotle's conception of love and friendship has been put forward by Paul Ricoeur, who tries to reconcile our present need for recognition as autonomous individuals with the arenas provided by public debate in which "friendly discussions" can take place. In *Oneself as Another*, Ricoeur shows the possible connection between justice and solidarity as a dialectic of self-esteem and friendship that becomes action and affection. Here the asymmetrical relation between doing and undergoing highlights two important issues that are always present when we claim recognition. First, the action of the thing done, and the reception of the impact of the action, involve two different protagonists. Second, we can appeal to Kant's "moral point of view" in considering that roles are reversible; we can place ourselves in the position of the other and thus enlarge our mentality. Within this dynamic, Ricoeur sees a relationship between the need for esteem and solidarity coming from the Aristotelian view and the place of responsibility where justice comes into play.

Maeve Cooke's "esteem-based solidarity" allows us to work out a notion of solidarity that is not only based on the abstract concept of autonomy, derived mainly from Kant and providing the basis for Habermas' view of solidarity, but which is also connected with strong evaluations and an expressive view relating to our ideas of authenticity.

First, I understand the processes of socialization and individuation as developing simultaneously, as suggested by George Herbert Mead and, later, by Habermas (in his own interpretation of Mead's theory). In Habermas' conception of this process of individuation, he adopts Mead's view of the need for recognition from the other, thus connecting with the works of Humboldt and Kierkegaard. Habermas writes,

> individuation is pictured not as the self-realization of an independent subject carried out in isolation and freedom, but as a linguistically mediated process of socialization and the simultaneous constitution of a life history that is conscious of itself. The identity of socialized individuals forms itself simultaneously in the medium of coming to an understanding with others in language and in the medium of coming to a life-historical and intersubjective understanding with oneself. Individuality forms itself in relations of intersubjective acknowledge-ment and of intersubjectively mediated self-understanding.[12]

This passage seems of particular interest because here Habermas acknowl-edges the possibility of linking two types of recognition: one connected with the abstract conception of the moral subject, with the idea of autonomy, but also, and as a simultaneous process, another connected with the individual's account of her own biography, with the individual as a contextualized being, and with direct reference to the category of authenticity, in which the irre-placeable individual human being seeks the recognition of others.

Although Habermas has not developed this insight further, it is an impor-tant idea which allows a connection to be established between Ricoeur's con-ception of solidarity and responsibility and Maeve Cooke's notion of "self-esteem" solidarity. Cooke criticizes Habermas' view of solidarity be-cause she believes there is an *alternative* notion of solidarity in which the recognition implied is understood as "mutual," as a "reciprocal recognition that has a strong affective dimension" and that is closely bound to interpre-tations of the good life. It is important to note here that both types of recog-nition are important and neither excludes the possibility of the other. Furthermore, they need to be conceived as two distinct forms of solidarity once we acknowledge Ricoeur's dialectic between responsibility and solidar-ity, intertwined in the categories of action and affection.

Habermas is primarily interested in Humboldt's idea of linguistic under-standing. However, he also points to a possible basis for the other type of sol-idarity (the one Maeve Cooke refers to as "esteem-based solidarity") in discussing Kierkegaard: "the idea that each individual must first make itself into that which it is would be honed by Kierkegaard into the act of taking re-sponsibility for one's own life history."[13] For Habermas, biographies function as a principle of individualization, because "only if it is transposed by such an act of self-choice into an existential form for which the self is responsible"[14] can the subject claim recognition of her identity, the authenticity that lies at the basis of this sphere of validity. And this entails a need to address those needs to others and to be open to other life-histories that also claim authen-ticity. With the possibility that Paul Ricoeur envisioned of shifting from "doer" to "sufferer" and with this vision of one's own demand for validity being submitted to others while one may also judge the authenticity of the other's life, the abstract notion of solidarity is replaced by a more concrete approach to others. Kierkegaard rather than Kant takes precedence here in stressing the interconnectedness of a responsibly assumed way of life. But we must bear in mind Kant's notion of respect, of the responsibility we have to consider others as ends in themselves, never as means. That each person has the right to submit her project for the recognition of validity claims in terms of normative and expressive standards can be understood if we consider her as a human being capable of acquiring life-projects as a simultaneous act of self-determination and self-realization.[15]

In this interpretation by Habermas, one can find the indication of a close connection between these two types of recognition, as can be seen in his historical reconstruction of the interconnection of individuality and linguistic intersubjectivity and individuality and biographical identity. When we are compelled to claim recognition by addressing others, the validity claims— normative and expressive—tend to become open to new moral judgments. What I have called the "illocutionary force" is our need to be understood and valued as persons, and the claims that we submit to the public arena force us to address others as necessary for the completion of our demand for recognition. As Ricoeur observes, "It is through public debate, friendly discussion, and shared convictions that moral judgement in situation is formed."[16]

And while Kierkegaard made his demand of being true to oneself and assuming the responsibility and risks of one's own biography into a religious confession, it was Rousseau who transformed this confession before God into a public self-confession, "which the private man circulated before the reading audience of the *bourgeois public*. The prayer was deflated to a *public conversation*" (my emphasis).[17]

According to this perspective, it is possible to assert that the concept of the individual is linked to this claim for recognition. In Habermas' historical reconstruction, this has become the secularized vision of the performative use of the concept of individuality. In this view, biographies of individuals are not descriptions or self-descriptions, nor are they self-observations, but rather self-presentations that are in need of recognition through a new validity claim—one related to the recognition "of the irreplaceable identity of an ego manifesting itself in a conscious way of life."[18]

In my view it is this interpretation of recognition that allows us to link solidarity in a concrete sense, based on the specificity of life projects and the identities of individuals and collectives, with the public sphere, as necessary for the redemption of its validity claims, because only others can validate them in terms of a new normative standard relating to an expressivist sphere.[19] Making my identity part of a public confession in need of recognition, on a performative level, is what makes this new way of addressing the other an illocutionary form. We need others to help us understand ourselves, to define our identities through our acquisition of rich human languages of expression. No one is able to acquire those languages on her own. We are introduced to them by our exchanges with others, the others *who matter to us,* "those significant others," as Mead would say. Our ability to find richness in our modes of expression and our ability to articulate ourselves in language is directly linked to claims of authenticity and to the dialogical character of this concept, its expressive domain.[20] Our modern identities have acquired this expressive facet not only because we struggle with demands for recognition, but also because we have found ways to express these demands as clear examples of how justice can be redefined by our interpretations of needs and our own ways of relating those needs to our self-definitions. This is the double nature of recognition when it has been developed through arenas of the public sphere.[21]

(Today we are able to think of examples of this kind thanks, mainly, to the problems brought to the public sphere by feminism and the various feminist demands for recognition. Not only have these gained the acknowledgment and solidarity of others, they have also contributed toward the creation of a new order of values, toward new interpretations of needs, and toward new definitions that have helped to extend the domain of justice.)

ORIGINALITY AND PLURALITY IN THE PUBLIC DOMAIN

Charles Taylor's explorations of the concept of authenticity linked to a new moral insight have been widely discussed, and there is no doubt that his interpretation of authenticity has allowed us to visualize and analyze many of the problems of recognition and the challenge our societies face with regard to phenomena like multiculturalism. Particularly relevant is Taylor's account of how the notion of authenticity displaced the moral accent through the idea that we, as individuals, have an obligation to ourselves to be "true and human beings," and that the source of this can be found only in our inner selves. Habermas drew attention to Rousseau as the originator of the idea that there is no other source for this knowledge except our inner selves. And, just as Habermas pointed to Rousseau as the first to secularize the religious confession into a public moral confession in need of recognition, Taylor develops his idea of recognition with reference to this same thinker, emphasizing that it was he who first conceived morality as "the voice of nature within us."[22] Then in a careful reconstruction, Taylor draws on Herder to support the idea that each human being also develops the capacity to be "original," within her own measure.[23]

This "expressivistic turn" has links to rich new interpretations of authenticity and processes of recognition.[24] A key element in this new moral conception of individuals as original selves is the idea of irreplaceability—that is, the idea that the uniqueness of individuals is central to the individuation of the self. In the political domain this can be understood as the irreplaceability of subjects, for "I alone can speak on behalf of myself." Therefore, uniqueness is what makes the individual ethically significant. This is because the original projects we submit to the public sphere can enlarge our minds, make us more open to new ideas or values, or enable us to learn from them. This is morally good, for it entails the learning process of first becoming tolerant, and then broadening our horizons to redescribe ourselves through the possibilities that others have shown us.

However, the openness of the self has been equated in the culture of modernity with its reflexive distance from all particular identities, forms of life, and traditions. This mechanism of reflexive distance is itself a tradition, as Habermas has argued, or a "second order tradition" as Wellmer would formulate it, and it presupposes a historical break with regard to the dogmatism of traditional ways of life. This historical break forces all of the participants in public discourse to submit their projects for criticism and recognition. Tolerance here has played a major role in the acceptance of different and plural visions of the good. But we have also learned that tolerance is not enough when what we claim is the recognition of our identities, for tolerance is "perceived as non-egalitarian . . . not satisfactory for long, and the imperatives of democratic equality seem to press further towards the *recognition of equal worth*."[25]

The feminist demand for equal recognition for women springs from our understanding of justice and the way the struggle for recognition has led us to reinterpret justice from a different perspective, from the woman's point of view. Differences here require a kind of solidarity that can deal with the value of plurality. Society would become better, more democratic, if a way could be found whereby plurality were conceived as profoundly enriched by the diversity of life projects and their claims, through public discussions on the reordering of our values and choices.

The abstractly conceived notion of respect leads only to the possibility of tolerance, or to the first phase of the dynamic where subjects can be seen as ends in themselves. Tolerance and distant respect are not enough when we have to deal with difference and the experiences of subjects who need to be considered as equal to ourselves.[26] The idea of interrelating processes of recognition and solidarity in the public domain also implies that postconventional identities are formed through differences. Where those differences make us aware of the possibilities of different worldviews, we learn to contrast them and exercise our capacity for judgment and reinterpretation of values and needs. In this sense, our postconventional identities are seen not as finished projects or dogmatic choices, but as open and contingent unfinished ones.[27] Democracy, in this sense, seems to have the capacity for developing a "special engagement" with difference, as Anne Phillips would say. But in addition to this, as various different groups and individuals submitting our life projects to discussion in the public domain, we exercise our capacity to learn and to be transformed through these differences.

As we can see from Habermas' and Taylor's interpretations of individuals as unique and irreplaceable beings (promoting with their demands a revision of our normative standards and broadening our views of the good life), *recognition is now seen as a need,* closely linked to the acceptance that our pluralist societies value. The interrelation between responsibility and solidarity arises when, as Paul Ricoeur observes, there is a mediation of "the opening of the Same onto the Other and the internalization of the voice of the Other in the Same," brought about as "language contribute[s] its resources of communication, hence of reciprocity, . . . [in] an exchange that reflects a more radical one, that of the question and answer in which the roles are continually reversed."[28]

In this vision, two processes are bound together: our claims for recognition in the public sphere, and the way we develop our identities through dialogue. Conceiving of recognition and authenticity as moral values has compelled us to think of solidarity not only as "respect-based," but also as "esteem-based." The importance of individuation and socialization as processes that develop the proposed ideal of authenticity can only be defined in dialogical terms.[29]

Thus recognition has become a social and individual need. But as we have seen, we are no longer dealing only with problems relating to the notion of autonomy and its domain (the normative sphere), from which we can draw the two key concepts of this view, respect and tolerance. In contemporary democracies, we are now confronted with the threat of pluralism and multiculturalism, with the reflexive and critical insights of feminism, which have raised the problem of difference to the normative level. That is why the connection between a solidarity rooted in "self-esteem" that acknowledges individuals as equals and develops its bonds through affective ties and shared horizons of a reflexive distance, combines autonomy and authenticity. The place where this dynamic tests its "illocutionary force" is the public sphere, for it is there that our concepts of culture and values develop and unfold new meaning, there that new interpretations of justice and the good are to be discovered and, finally, there that we are enabled to explore deeper and potentially richer notions of what human beings are and how we might stimulate their projects within our institutional framework, so that it will protect and nourish pluralities as dimensions of the modern world we inhabit. As Habermas so aptly stated,

> Cultures survive only if they draw the power for *self-transformation from criticism and secession.* Legal guarantees invariably refer only to everyone retaining the capacity to regenerate this power in his or her own cultural milieu. And this power, in turn, is not generated only by marking one's cultural identity off

from others, but at least as much from the interaction with those others who are foreign to it and with stimuli that are alien to it.[30]

Translated by Laura Gorham

NOTES

1. Concerning the good and justice, the subject and citizenship, as understood by communitarianism, see for example, Michael Walzer, *The Spheres of Justice* (New York: Basic Books, 1983); Michael Sandel, *Liberalism and the Limits of Justice* (Cambridge: Cambridge University Press, 1982); and Alasdair MacIntyre, *After Virtue* (Notre Dame: University of Notre Dame Press, 1982). For feminist perspectives, see Seyla Benhabib, *Situating the Self: Gender, Community and Postmodernism* (New York: Routledge, 1992); Nancy Fraser, *Unruly Practices: Power, Discourse and Gender in Contemporary Social Theory* (Cambridge: Polity Press, 1989); Seyla Benhabib and Drucilla Cornell, eds., *Feminism as Critique* (Cambridge: Polity Press, 1987); and Iris Young, *Justice and the Politics of Difference* (Princeton: Princeton University Press, 1990).

2. To use Seyla Benhabib's phrase. See her "Deliberative Rationality and Models of Democratic Legitimacy," *Constellations* (vol. 1, no. 1), p. 35.

3. Jeffrey C. Alexander, "The Paradoxes of Civil Society," *Social Sciences Research Center,* Occasional Paper 16 (Hong Kong: The University of Hong Kong in association with the Department of Sociology of Hong Kong), p. 21.

4. Jürgen Habermas, "Individuation through Socialization: On Mead's Theory of Subjectivity" in *Postmetaphysical Thinking* (Cambridge: MIT Press, 1992), p. 167.

5. See her *The Human Condition* (New York: Penguin Books, 1977).

6. See Joan B. Landes, *Women and the Public Sphere in the Age of the French Revolution* (Ithaca: Cornell University Press, 1988) and Iris Young, *Justice and the Politics of Difference* (Princeton: Princeton University Press, 1990).

7. Honneth claims that "Generalizing these results beyond their particular research context, we arrive at the conclusion that the normative presupposition of all communication action is to be seen in the *acquisition of social recognition* [my emphasis]: Subjects encounter each other within the parameters of their reciprocal expectation that they receive recognition as moral persons and for their life achievements." Axel Honneth, "The Social Dynamics of Disrespect: On the Location of Critical Theory," *Constellations* (vol. 1, no. 1), p. 262.

8. Benhabib uses this term, borrowing it from Hannah Arendt, who in turn focused on the Kantian idea of learning from other people's point of view as an exercise in—what Arendt called—enlarged mentality." See Hannah Arendt, *Between Past and Future* (New York: Penguin Books, 1977); Hannah Arendt, *The Life of the Mind* (New York: Harcourt Brace Jovanovich, 1978); and Hannah Arendt, *Lectures on Kant's Political Philosophy* (Chicago: University of Chicago Press, 1982).

9. Habermas, for example, observes that "the process of implementing the law is embedded in contexts which precisely also require ethical discourses as an important strand of political discussions about a shared conception of the good and a desired life form that is jointly recognized as the authentic one. These are deliberations in which

those who are involved clarify how they want to see themselves as citizens of a specific republic, as inhabitants of a specific region, as heirs to a specific culture, which traditions they want to perpetuate or discontinue, and how they want to deal with their historical destiny, with another and with nature, etc." Jürgen Habermas, "Struggles for Recognition in Constitutional States," *The European Journal of Philosophy* (vol. 1, no. 2), pp. 128–55.

10. As Albrecht Wellmer points out, what is needed is "a network of autonomous associations, institutions and public spaces *below* the level of the state. And only where it happens, i.e., where a democratic form of ethical life penetrates the many-voiced prose of everyday life, can liberal rights and [the] democratic form of legitimacy coalesce into the social union of liberal and democratic society." Albrecht Wellmer, "Conditions of a Democratic Culture: Remarks on the Liberal-Communitarian Debate," lecture delivered in Spain in 1994.

11. "Selfhood and Solidarity," *Constellations* (vol. 1, no. 3).

12. Jürgen Habermas, "Individuation through Socialization: On Mead's Theory of Subjectivity" in *Postmetaphysical Thinking* (Cambridge: MIT Press, 1992), pp. 152–53.

13. Ibid., p. 162.

14. Ibid., pp. 164–5.

15. Paul Ricoeur claims that, "[t]he force of the morality of communication lies fundamentaly in the fact that it has merged the three Kantian imperatives into a single problematic: the principle of autonomy following the category of unity, the principle of respect following the category of multiplicity, and the principle of the kingdom of ends following the category of totality. In other words, the self is founded in a single stroke in its dimension of universality and in its dialogic dimension, interpersonal as well as institutional." *Oneself as Another* (Chicago: University of Chicago Press, 1992), p. 281.

16. Ibid., pp. 290–1.

17. Jürgen Habermas, *Postmetaphysical Thinking*, p. 165.

18. Ibid., p. 167.

19. See Charles Taylor, *Sources of the Self: The Making of Modern Identity* (Cambridge: Harvard University Press, 1989), especially "The Expressivist Turn," pp. 368–92.

20. See Charles Taylor, *The Ethics of Authenticity* (Cambridge: Harvard University Press, 1991), p. 34.

21. I would like to thank Ron Bontekoe for raising the question of whether we could acquire this recognition when others have no interest in hearing of our life projects. Proceeding from Paul Ricoeur's work on the "doer" and the "sufferer," I think we can argue that solidarity in the public sphere can be stressed if we are open to listening and changing ourselves. All we need is to implement our struggle so as to make those arenas spontaneous places, part of the democratic culture and differentiated from the state, the market and the family.

22. *The Ethics of Authenticity*, p. 27.

23. As Taylor observes, "This idea has entered very deep into modern consciousness. . . . But this gives a new importance to being true to myself. If I am not, I miss the point of my life, I miss what being human is for *me.*" *The Ethics of Authenticity*, p. 29.

24. See, for example, Alessandro Ferrara, *Intendersi a Babele. Autenticità, phronesis e progetto della modernità* (Roma: Rubbetino, 1994); and Axel Honneth, "The Social Dynamics of Disrespect," *Constellations* (vol. 1, no. 2), pp. 255–69.

25. Anne Phillips, "Dealing with Difference: A Politics of Ideas or a Politics of Presence?" *Constellations* (vol. 1, no. 1), p. 75.

26. According to Anne Phillips, "Tolerance is perceived as non-egalitarian, resting in some way on a distinction between the majority and minority deviance and incorporating some implied preference for a particular way of life. . . . [T]he democratic solution of difference expects us to engage more directly with each other. We bring our differences to the public stage; we revise them through public debate." Ibid., pp. 79–80.

27. "In modernity, rigid lifeforms succumb to entropy." Jürgen Habermas, "Struggles for Recognition in Constitutional States," *The European Journal of Philosophy* (vol. 1, no. 2), p. 143.

28. *Oneself as Another,* p. 339.

29. I have also worked on the idea of women's autobiographies in "The Construction of Women's Identity," a chapter of my forthcoming book, tentatively titled *Moral Textures.*

30. Jürgen Habermas, "Struggles for Recognition in Constitutional States," *The European Journal of Philosophy* (vol. 1, no. 2), p. 143.

Kenneth Baynes

EQUALITY AND DIFFERENCE IN DEMOCRATIC THEORY

Critics of liberal equality have traditionally argued (somewhat paradoxically) either that the idea of equality is empty and has no independent value apart from its relation to other ideals or that its unchecked pursuit conflicts with other political values, such as liberty.[1] Recently, these (generally "conservative") critics of equality have been joined by more "progressive" feminists and "multiculturalists." Liberal equality, for these critics, is a wholly formal and abstract idea that in practice perpetuates inequalities by privileging those who conform to the underlying (and for the most part unspoken) norms in light of which judgments of equality and difference are made.[2] According to both sets of criticisms, liberal equality presents a vision of society in which differences are illegitimately excluded and in which everyone is forced to be the same.

I do not want to claim that these criticisms cannot find any foothold within liberal theory; liberalism is, after all, a large and diverse tradition. I do want to claim, however, that they do not apply to the better arguments for liberal equality. In particular, I shall argue that recent discussions of "liberal egalitarianism" go a long way toward showing a strong internal connection between equality and other liberal values (such as freedom and responsibility).[3] Liberal equality is thus neither an empty ideal nor inevitably in deep conflict with other values. On the other hand, the reservations voiced by some feminist and multicultural critics suggest that the attempts to specify an adequate conception of equality have not yet been successful. In particular, they suggest that its connections with notions of autonomy, choice and power must be explored further.

My own survey of the literature has uncovered two somewhat distinct fields of discussion. On the one hand, guided by the question "equality of what," there is a body of literature that has sought to identify a general measure or metric of equality that could be used to compare the life prospects of otherwise diverse individuals and groups. This literature is primarily concerned with what can be called "equality of condition" or "equality of life prospects."[4] On the other hand, there is a literature centered around questions of equal citizenship.[5] Here focus is on the attempt to give substantive content to the formal principle of equality—treat equals equally—within a variety of different social contexts: with respect to, for example, what is required for legal, political, economic, sexual, or racial and ethnic equality, and the best arrangement of these equalities among themselves and with other values. In each of these contexts, the formal imperative to treat equals equally requires interpretation about who is to be considered an equal and what it means to treat them equally. Iris Young captures this second set of concerns nicely when she writes: "Equality refers not primarily to the distribution of social goods, though distributions are certainly entailed by social equality. It refers primarily to the full participation and inclusion of everyone in a society's major institutions, and the socially supported substantive opportunity for all to develop and exercise their capacities and realize their choices."[6] In the context of discussions on multiculturalism and sex equality, this principle of equal citizenship has sometimes led to the call for special group rights.[7]

What I shall claim is that these two areas of discussion are not as widely separate as is sometimes suggested. Rather, attempts to address the question of equality of condition cannot avoid the difficult questions raised in the so-called "difference" debate. On the other hand, attempts to go "beyond equality and difference" or to "reconstruct" the idea of equal citizenship must address considerations raised in the discussions concerning equality of condition. On its best interpretation, I shall argue, liberal equality refers to the equal access of all individuals to the conditions required for self-realization and self-determination or, to borrow Habermas' recent formulation, to the conditions required for an effective exercise of citizens' private and public autonomy.[8] The presence in a society of any disadvantage in access to such conditions that is not attributable to the genuine choices of the individual makes the society to that extent less egalitarian.

I. "EQUALITY OF WHAT?": FROM RAWLS TO COHEN

Recent discussions of equality of condition or equality of life prospects are greatly indebted to Rawls' critique of utilitarian and, more generally, welfarist conceptions of equality. Equality of welfare is committed to promoting the most equitable distribution of utility or preference compatible with other values. However, this position is subject to what has been called the "expensive tastes" objection.[9] If Bill has preferences that are much more costly to satisfy than the preferences of Sam, then it seems equality of welfare requires distributing more resources to bring Bill up to the same level of welfare as Sam. As Rawls points out, however, this approach ignores the extent to which individuals may be responsible for the preferences they have. What a truly egalitarian metric ought to measure is not all preferences and desires, but those that are not due to genuine choices of the individual. To borrow Ronald Dworkin's terminology, we need a distinction between "brute luck" and "option luck" and it is only (or at least primarily inequalities resulting from the former that should command the attention of egalitarians.[10] Society, it would seem, has little—if any—obligation to redistribute in the direction of greater equality if the inequalities are the result of genuine choices individuals have made.

However, as critics have noted, Rawls' introduction of an account of primary goods and other resourcist accounts of metric of equality—such as Dworkin's—do not necessarily follow from this critique of welfarism, and they run into difficulties of their own.[11] One of the better-known criticisms has been offered by Amartya Sen. Although he agrees with the critique of welfare metrics, Sen argues that the resource or goods approach is "fetishistic."[12] Resourcists like Rawls and Dworkin focus on what it is that individuals have, rather than on what they are able to do or be with what they have. This has led Sen to propose what he calls a capabilities or functionings account of the egalitarian metric. The aim then is to identify a range of human functionings or capabilities relative to a (now culturally defined) notion of wellbeing. Such functionings range from "elementary" ones such as escaping morbidity and mortality, being adequately nourished, and having mobility to "higher" or more complex ones such as being happy, achieving self-respect, taking part in the life of the community, and appearing in public without shame.[13] A society is more egalitarian to the extent that it provides equally a real opportunity for each citizen to develop and exercise the relevant range of human capabilities.[14]

Finally, in what can be called a third round in the discussion, critics such as Richard Arneson and Gerald Cohen have pointed to difficulties in this capabilities approach. In particular, there is a problem of indexing, since individuals have a diversity of capabilities and since any two individuals may have very different sets. Thus if one attends to capabilities rather than utility or primary goods, there seems to be no common measure in terms of which judgments of equality can be made. According to Arneson, this implies that Sen's capabilities approach must either adopt an objective or perfectionist account (which he finds unacceptable in liberal democratic society) or it collapses into a modified form of welfarism—what Arneson calls equality of opportunity for welfare.[15] Cohen, by contrast, claims that Arneson's retreat to welfarism is overly hasty, and introduces a notion of "midfare" as an alternative to Sen's notion of capabilities.[16] Midfare refers to a heterogeneous set of goods, something between utility and goods, that comprise the conditions for well-being:

not utility, since it is not simply a matter of an individual's mental state or desires, but not goods, since the concern is with what goods do for the individual. Further, he claims that, while it may be difficult to develop a complete or full metric, it is nonetheless possible and worthwhile to develop a list of basic midfare, corresponding to a "normal human existence." These would include such fundamental goods as health, nutrition, and housing. Only when it is a matter of the "higher" or more complex capabilities do issues of pluralism complicate his own model.[17] Nonetheless, according to Cohen, his focus on midfare remains true to the egalitarian concern that no one should be lacking in an "urgent desideratum" through no fault of her own.

While clearly preferable to some of the available alternatives, Cohen's proposal, which he calls "equality of access to advantage," is still inadequate. Despite its attention to fundamental capabilities, it remains captive to what Iris Young has called the "distributive paradigm" in theories of justice and equality.[18] His notion of midfare focuses on basic capabilities—health, nutrition, and housing—to the neglect of "higher" capabilities that, at least in many current social movements, are the focus of attention. In this respect, it even falls behind Rawls' concern to secure an equal and effective exercise of the two moral powers—namely, the capacity to form and pursue a conception of the good and the capacity to have a sense of justice. If, following Iris Young, the capabilities whose equal and effective opportunity for development society ought to insure is broadened to include self-expression and self-determination, the resources required would have to be modified. In particular, they would have to include greater access to decision-making structures and processes, a more extensive reconfiguration of the social division of labor, and greater participation in the production and interpretation of cultural meanings. In short, as it presently stands, Cohen's model would seem to have the least to offer on just those questions that many recent social movements regard as most important.

II. EQUAL CITIZENSHIP AND THE DILEMMA OF DIFFERENCE

Once this predominantly theoretical question of finding an equality metric is posed in terms of the question of determining what counts as a "normal human existence," it seems clear that no sharp distinction between this question and the question of equality of citizenship can be maintained. The question of what counts as "normal human existence" or what are the fundamental capabilities and capacities that should be socially supported on the basis of considerations of equality are themselves contestable matters—especially if one does not restrict oneself to a minimal set of basic needs.

It is at this point, I think, that some of the recent literature on equality and difference, particularly what has emerged from the context of feminist legal theory, is relevant. A central criticism made by many of these theorists is that the formal principle of equality—and especially notions of legal equality— always operates against a prior and more substantive norm with reference to which judgments of equality and difference are made. This norm, however, quite frequently reflects features of a particular dominant group—generally, white, heterosexual men—and treats these as "normal." Examples of this abound—in legal decisions concerning sexual harassment and rape, in laws regulating working hours and other conditions of employment, in policies related to pregnancy and maternity leaves, and in many other areas of legal decision. Legal equality is formal equality and, since it operates against inegalitarian background norms, it frequently serves an ideological function.

Moreover, attempts to secure sex equality in law have thus far generally pursued either an "assimilationist model" (which emphasizes the extent to which we are all alike) or an "accommodation model" (which seeks to create "special rights" on the basis of "real" differences). As some feminists point out, however, both models founder upon the same problem. In attempting to determine which differences deserve legal remedies and which should be ignored, the background norms that establish terms of relevance and in light of which judgments of similarity and difference are made frequently go unchallenged.[19] Martha Minow points to a difficulty in both strategies in illustrating what she calls "the dilemma of difference":

> By taking another person's difference into account in awarding goods or distributing burdens, you risk reiterating the significance of that difference and, potentially, its stigma and stereotyping consequences. But if you do not take another person's difference into account—in a world that has made that difference matter—you may also recreate and reestablish both the difference and its negative implications. If you draft or enforce laws you may worry that the effects of the laws will not be neutral whether you take difference into account or ignore it.[20]

One alternative model of equality, proposed by Christine Littleton, seeks to avoid this dilemma.[21] In rejecting both assimilationist and accommodationist models, it neither denies difference nor accepts recognized differences as deviations from a norm requiring "special treatment." Rather, on this model of "equality as acceptance" the aim of legislation and judicial interpretation should be to "make difference costless" by removing the various types of "cost" that attach to sex and gender differences. For example, Littleton calls for establishing "gendered complements" so that different forms of traditionally "women's work," such as caregiving, can be compensated in ways comparable to the equivalent work of men. More importantly, however, the model of "equality as acceptance" also requires critically questioning and examining the "cultural meanings" that inform the way such valuations are made. The underlying norms and valuations that inform judgments of "gendered complements" must, it would seem, be seen as "social constructs" that are open to revision in light of contested need interpretations.

Despite the advantages of this approach—especially as a legal remedy for dealing with difficult instances of sexual inequality—objections have been raised against it as well. In particular, some feminists worry that the legal recognition of culturally defined differences will only contribute to their perpetuation—to the view that women, as socially and culturally constructed, really are better at some kinds of activities than others. For example, the notion of "gendered complements" in the workforce might tend to perpetuate a kind of "mommy track" in which caregivers or dependency workers, despite receiving higher salaries, would nonetheless continue to be mostly women.[22] On this model, there seems to be little incentive to redefine or even abolish gender identities and little incentive to alter the sexual division of labor. In a similar vein, Catharine MacKinnon warns that over-attention to questions of difference can obscure questions of unequal power which should be the real concern in sex equality law.[23]

What seems clear from these reservations about the model of "equality as acceptance" is that, at a minimum, any measures taken to make difference costless must also critically scrutinize the origin of those differences and, more importantly, the multiple functions they may be serving in the prevailing social arrangement of power and opportunities. Furthermore, such a critical scrutinizing would itself seem to presuppose a genuinely pluralist or heterogeneous public sphere in which background norms and need interpretations can be contested.

In *Justice and the Politics of Difference,* Iris Young develops Littleton's conception of equality as acceptance in connection with her own idea of a "heterogeneous public." Rather than an ideal of the universal citizen that transcends difference and requires that each citizen be treated the same, she argues for a positive affirmation and proliferation of group differences as the best means for achieving equality. "In this vision the good society does not eliminate or transcend group difference. Rather, there is equality among socially and culturally differentiated groups, who mutually respect one another and affirm one another in their differences." On this view, "social justice . . . requires not the melting away of differences, but institutions that promote reproduction of and respect for group differences without oppression."

According to Young, this "politics of difference" will require specific measures to guarantee the representation of oppressed or disadvantaged groups within the political process. She proposes, among other things, public funding to enable group organization and policy-formation, mechanisms to insure that the appropriate decision-makers have considered proposals offered by disadvantaged groups, and even group veto power regarding specific policies that affect a group directly.[24] As examples of this last proposal, she suggests veto rights for women in relation to reproductive rights policy and veto rights for Native Americans over the use of reservation lands.

I will forgo here any assessment of her specific policy recommendations, which, as she acknowledges, must be designed with a view toward a variety of considerations, including general equal opportunity rights. Rather, what I wish to draw attention to is Young's general proposal that equality requires not "difference-blind" policies, but policies that self-consciously recognize group differences. In this respect, her proposal is similar to that offered by Charles Taylor in the context of debates about multicultural rights. In both cases, equality requires attending not to the respect in which individuals are the same, but to the ways in which individuals are different or unique.[25]

Does this call for a heterogeneous public and special rights to group representation require a radical break with the idea of liberal equality as some have suggested, or is it, as Will Kymlicka suggests, simply "an old idea with a new twist"?[26] It would, I think, be a significant break if it were a call for the representation of disadvantaged groups in order to secure their parity and ongoing survival. This, in fact, seems to be Taylor's position in his remark that cultures can validly claim a right to survive "through indefinite future generations."[27] Young, however, is more ambiguous. At times she does speak of the need to achieve "equality between groups," but in other formulations she states that justice is concerned with "the institutional conditions necessary for the development and exercise of individual capacities and collective communication and cooperation."[28] This would locate her position more squarely within a liberal egalitarian conception that need not be hostile to limited forms of group representation—not to insure the indefinite continuation of distinct groups, but to provide individuals with the conditions for meaningful and genuine choice in their lives.

This reference to "genuine choice" brings us back to our earlier discussion of "equality of condition." The concern there, as we saw, was that individuals not be disadvantaged, through no fault of their own, in the realization of a relevantly defined set of capabilities. What the literature of "difference" brings to this discussion, I believe, is a radical questioning of—indeed, deep suspicion about—the way in which the relevant set of capabilities is defined. Genuine choice is undermined not only when individuals are denied access to specific cultural and material resources, but also when choices are constrained by cultural norms and standards that the individuals in question could not reasonably play a role in defining. On this view, the genuine choices of some can undermine the choices of others if values arising from the former become the basis for defining the norms or standards that are used to judge the equal condition of others. Equal access to advantage, then, requires that all the individuals in question have an equal opportunity to define the norms or standards in light of which judgments of equality are to be made, and it means that the norms or standards informing the genuine choices of some should not become the basis for defining what counts as the genuine choice of others. To give one example, as has often been observed, it is difficult not to believe that legal cases concerning pregnancy leave would have been treated differently if more Supreme Court justices could have become pregnant.

The questions that this account of equality opens up are admittedly immense. Most obviously, it requires an account of genuine choice—an idea that many would consider to be a chimera. However, what I think this account also shows is that if no plausible sense can be given to the idea of genuine choice, then all differential advantage is unjust.[29] It is thus unlikely that locating a notion of freedom or choice at the center of liberal equality in the way I have proposed will bring any comfort to its libertarian critics. I hope, however, that it will strengthen the case for liberal equality.

NOTES

1. Peter Westen, "The Empty Ideal of Equality," *Harvard Law Review* (vol. 95, 1982); W. Letwin, ed., *Against Equality* (London: Macmillan, 1983); and J. Lucas, "Against Equality," *Philosophy* (vol. 40, 1965).

2. For some examples of this literature, see Iris Young, *Justice and the Politics of Difference* (Princeton: Princeton University Press, 1990); Zillah Eisenstein, *The Female Body and the Law* (Berkeley: University of California, 1988); and Charles Taylor, *Multiculturalism and the 'Politics of Recognition'* (Princeton: Princeton University Press, 1992).

3. For a good discussion of the "internal connection" between equality and liberty, see S. Lukes, "Equality and Liberty: Must They Conflict?" in *Moral Conflict and Politics* (New York: Clarendon Press, 1991), pp. 50–70.

4. I borrow this term from the helpful survey of equality offered by Richard Arneson, "Equality," in *A Companion to Contemporary Political Philosophy*, R. Goodin and P. Pettit, eds. (Oxford: Blackwell, 1993), pp. 489–507.

5. For a useful discussion of this "principle of equal citizenship" within the context of U.S. Constitutional theory, see Kenneth Karst, "Why Equality Matters," *Georgia Law Review* (vol. 17), pp. 245–89.

6. *Justice and the Politics of Difference*, p. 173.

7. In addition to the works cited by Iris Young and Charles Taylor, see Will Kymlicka, *Liberalism, Community and Culture* (Oxford: Clarendon Press, 1989).

8. See Jürgen Habermas, *Faktizität und Geltung* (Frankfurt: Suhrkamp, 1992) chap. 3, and my discussion of public and private autonomy in "Democracy and the *Rechtsstaat*" in *The Cambridge Companion to Habermas,* S. White, ed. (New York: Cambridge University Press, 1995). Interestingly, in his "Reply to Habermas," Rawls also describes his model of "justice as fairness" as an attempt to secure citizens' public and private autonomy (forthcoming in *The Journal of Philosophy*).

9. John Rawls, "Social Unity and Primary Goods" in *Utilitarianism and Beyond*, A. Sen and B. Williams, eds. (New York: Cambridge University Press, 1982), pp. 168–69; and G. Cohen, "On the Currency of Egalitarian Justice," *Ethics* (vol. 99), pp. 913f.

10. Ronald Dworkin, "What is Equality?", *Philosophy and Public Affairs* (vol. 10, 1981); and Cohen, "On The Currency of Egalitarian Justice," p. 931.

11. Gerald Cohen, "Equality of What? On Welfare, Goods, and Capabilities" in *The Quality of Life*, M. Nussbaum and A. Sen, eds. (New York: Oxford University Press, 1993), p. 13.

12. "Equality of What?" in *Liberty, Equality, and Law: Selected Tanner Lectures on Moral Philosophy*, S. McMurrin, ed. (Salt Lake City: University of Utah Press, 1987), p. 158.

13. "Capability and Well-Being" in *The Quality of Life*, p. 37.

14. Sen, "Equality of What?" and *Inequality Reexamined* (New York: Clarendon, 1992).

15. Arneson, "Equality," p. 25.

16. Cohen, "Equality of What?" p. 27.

17. Cohen, p. 27.

18. *Justice and the Politics of Difference*, chapter 1.

19. See Christine Littleton, "Reconstructing Sexual Equality" reprinted in *Feminist Jurisprudence*, P. Smith, ed. (New York: Oxford University Press, 1993), pp. 110–35; Deborah Rhode, *Justice and Gender* (Cambridge: Harvard University Press, 1989); Catharine MacKinnon, "Difference and Dominance: On Sex Discrimination" in *Feminism Unmodified* (Cambridge: Harvard University Press, 1987), pp. 32–45.

20. Martha Minow, "Justice Engendered" in *Feminist Jurisprudence*, p. 232.

21. "Reconstructing Sexual Equality" in *Feminist Jurisprudence*. The same approach has also been defended by Deborah Rhode in "The Politics of Paradigms: Gender Difference and Gender Disadvantage" in *Beyond Equality and Difference*, G. Bock and S. James, eds. (New York: Routledge, 1992), pp. 149–63.

22. Nancy Fraser, "After the Family Wage: What Do Women Want in Social Welfare?" *Political Theory* (1994).

23. Catharine MacKinnon, "Difference and Dominance" in *Feminism Unmodified*.

24. *Justice and the Politics of Difference*, pp. 163, 47, 184.

25. *Multiculturalism and the 'Politics of Recognition'*, p. 38.

26. Will Kymlicka, "Three Forms of Group-Differentiated Citizenship Rights in Canada," *Ethics* (1994).

27. *Multiculturalism and the Politics of Recognition*, p. 41 n.16.

28. Compare her remarks on p. 163 and p. 39.

29. In this I agree with Cohen's conclusion in "Equality of What?" p. 28, though I am perhaps more optimistic about the possibility of developing a workable (compatibilist) notion of genuine choice or autonomy.

Ron Bontekoe

GROUNDING A THEORY OF RIGHTS IN FALLIBILIST EPISTEMOLOGY

In listening to Richard Rorty's paper (see "Justice as a Larger Loyalty" in this volume), it struck me yet again that what Rorty fails to appreciate sufficiently is that workable social arrangements are *discoveries*. As someone who identifies himself as a pragmatist, but one who hews to the Peirce-Dewey line rather than to Rortian neopragmatism, I think we need to take our discoveries rather seriously. While I agree that we should eschew paying ourselves and our ways of doing things empty compliments by designating them as "rational" in some transcendental sense, I feel as well that we should avoid needlessly denigrating the significance of our discoveries by insisting that they are "merely how *we* do things." *If* we have in fact discovered an especially satisfying social arrangement, this is no doubt because the social arrangement on which we have stumbled relates in important respects to human nature—that human nature in the existence of which Rorty has no faith. And if our discovery relates in important respects to human nature, it will in all likelihood have significance not only for those of us who have already benefitted from its discovery but for others as well.[1] I would suggest, for example, that the liberal values of tolerance espoused by John Stuart Mill have universal applicability. In any event, the paper that follows is predicated on that assumption.

※　※　※

In their efforts to defend the integrity of the individual, advocates of the deontological view in ethics tend to privilege the claims of justice over the pursuit of the good. Now establishing the primacy of justice in this respect requires, of course, that its principles be derivable independently of any particular vision of the good. For if our derivation of the principles of justice *were* to depend upon some given conception of the good, this could only be because the good, so defined, takes precedence, and justice would then be

61

merely a means to its attainment. Thus the deontologist needs to find some "Archimedean point" from which to assess what it is that human beings owe to one another. The most celebrated recent offering of such an "Archimedean point," however, that advanced by John Rawls in his thought experiment of the original position, proved less than entirely convincing. (And so we have seen Rawls, in the years since the first appearance of *A Theory of Justice*, backing away from the notion that what the original-position argument offers is a strict derivation of the universal principles of justice.) In this paper I would like to propose an alternative "Archimedean point." The foundation upon which our speculations concerning the nature of justice should be based, it seems to me, is the fact of human finitude and the limitations of human understanding.

Let us consider for a moment the significance of the fact that every individual human being finds herself in a particular situation. To be in a situation is to see things, as Gadamer puts it, from "a standpoint that limits the possibility of vision." Hence an essential component of our conception of a situation is our conception of an *horizon,* which might be defined as "the range of vision that includes everything that can be seen from a particular vantage point."[2] According to Gadamer, moreover, to be in a situation means that "we are not standing outside of it and hence [that we] are unable to have any objective knowledge of it." Our own situation, and especially the way in which it distorts our understanding by predisposing us to see things in a particular way, is thus something of a mystery to us. We could know for certain how it affects our understanding only if we could somehow leave our situation behind and observe the world as it is in itself. But this, of course, is impossible. While we can, to an extent, leave behind our current situation, we can only do so by entering a new one. There is thus no sweeping aside of all that is pregiven and contingent in experience for beings, like ourselves, that exist historically.

This is not to say, however, that there is no way of improving upon our current understanding or expanding the bounds of our horizon. On the contrary, there are two such ways available to us. The first involves allowing the things that we encounter in the world to assert themselves against our expectations. The second, which is a variation on this, involves receptively listening to the interpretations of things that are advanced by other human beings. These individuals, because they are situated differently from ourselves, will necessarily have horizons of understanding that are different from our own. It follows, then, that if we take seriously the possibility that there are truths as yet unknown to us to be found in these unfamiliar interpretations, and genuinely try to see things in the light of these interpretations, what Gadamer calls a "fusion of horizons" may take place—a fusion in which the best that is contained in our own understanding and in that of the person to whom we are listening will tend to be preserved, and from which the most distorted elements in each of the two interpretations will tend to fall away. Thus although we can never escape altogether the distortive influences in our understanding, given that we are essentially situated (i.e., historical) beings, we can nonetheless both expand the range of things that we understand and gradually eliminate many of the particular errors that at any given time mislead us.

These consequences of human finitude, I would argue, are of the utmost importance for a reexamination of the nature of justice. For given the centrality of the individual's understanding (and more especially of her viewpoint) to her identity, the individual's status as a "knower," as a fellow-inquirer and potentially unique source of insight, seems in some respects to be a more natural place to ground her rights—which are integrally related to her dignity as a human being—than on her status as an independent "chooser" of her own ends. For one thing, there is the priority of understanding over choice to be considered. After all, a choice that is in no way determined by the quality of one's understanding or misunderstanding (one made by flipping a coin, say) is insignificant; in no way does it reflect upon the individual's nature. A significant choice, on the other hand, insofar as it is based on the individual's understanding of what is at stake in the act of choosing, invariably goes some distance toward identifying the chooser.

And here, I would suggest, we can begin to see just how far off the mark deontologists like Kant and the early Rawls have drifted. For the Kantian transcendental subject and the Rawlsian party to the original position, insofar as they are pure rational choosers stripped of contingent interests and desires, are nobody in particular. According to Kant and Rawls, everything that makes the individual human being the unique person that she is is irrelevant to her possession of human dignity. But offering dignity as a matter of principle, without regard for who the recipient might be *as a real person* is cold comfort—better than nothing perhaps, but far from satisfying. No wonder, then, that Rawls and Kant find themselves advocating forms of justice that readily conflict with the *warmer* virtues of love, benevolence, and fraternity. By way of contrast, if we ground the individual's rights on her ownership of a perspective, the individual acquires dignity precisely because of who she actually is. The contingencies of her experience that account for her specific interests, desires, and opinions are what render her insights unique and thus significant as a potential spur to growth on the part of others. Seen in this light, of course, justice is continuous with fraternity rather than opposed to it, for underlying each is a concern for the possibilities of enrichment that flow from mutual association and the sharing of insight.

A consideration that is seldom dwelt upon by traditional deontologists is the comparative unimportance for person A of person B's being a "chooser," except perhaps in the negative sense that if B's choices are frustrated, he may become a threat to A. If this possibility is ruled out, however, as it is whenever B is seriously weaker than A, there would seem to be no need for A to respect B at all. At this point, of course, the Kantian deontologist would be inclined to reply, "True, A *may not* respect B if he has nothing to fear from him, but that is simply to say that A's attitude towards B is *immoral*." This misses the point, I think. The question "Why should I be moral?" may be vacuous if it means "Why should I act in accordance with those precepts that I recognize define right conduct?" but if it means "Why should I act in accordance with *your* conception of right conduct?" it is a perfectly reasonable question. The Kantian deontologist, in other words, does have to make his grounding of justice in a recognition of the individual's status as a rational chooser *convincing*. And this means that A must be shown that he has good reason to care that B too is a possessor of free will.

Now in the context of Rawls' thought experiment, A, as a self-interested party to the original position, will no doubt wish to see that all social roles that he might possibly find himself occupying once the veil of ignorance is lifted are as comfortable as possible. But this is not at all the same thing as caring what happens to B. A could, quite consistently with wanting to maximize equality across the social roles that the parties to the original position have met to define, wish that particular fellow party to the original position, B, would go straight to hell! (This is, of course, merely an illustration that caring about the description of *roles* is not the same thing as caring about the individuals who might occupy those roles. As Michael Sandel has pointed out, in *Liberalism and the Limits of Justice*, it would be quite impossible for the parties to the Rawlsian original position to disagree about anything, since they are ciphers with no discernible characteristics that might differentiate them, and thus A could not "really" wish to harm B.) In fact, however, the Rawls of *A Theory of Justice* only defines justice as what would be agreed to in the original position because he takes it as a given that being a chooser carries with it very significant entitlements. As a result, his thought experiment is meant not so much as a *proof* that justice is what would be agreed to in the original position as it is an attempt to persuade the rest of us that we too *already* share his assumption that justice has to do with our entitlement to equal consideration by virtue of our being choosers. In *Political Liberalism*, of course, all of this is made explicit, for there Rawls gives this assumption the name "reasonableness" and makes a virtue of necessity by declaring that the *reasonable* attitude is not to be derived from the *rational*—or self-interested—standpoint, but is rather to be thought of as equally fundamental to the human situation.

Kant, on the other hand, at least attempts to demonstrate that B's status as a transcendental subject *should* matter to A in a personal sense. A will be guilty of rational inconsistency, Kant claims, if, in determining the principles according to which he would wish to see the world governed, he makes an exception of his own case—if he desires others to be honest while granting himself the option of lying, for example. There are, however, at least two serious problems with this line of reasoning. First, there is nothing irrational about recognizing one's own case as exceptional since, in point of fact, one's own case *is* exceptional. After all, in choosing to lie, or tell the truth, or commit murder, or sacrifice one's life, one chooses always and only *for oneself.* One's own case is, in a significant sense, the *only* case over which one has any say. Kant would remark, of course, that each individual is entitled to see his case as exceptional in *this* sense, and therefore that this constitutes no grounds for any given individual making an exception of himself with respect to the rules of conduct that he would approve for others.

But at this point the second difficulty comes into play. For as Nelson Goodman has demonstrated in *Fact, Fiction and Forecast,* we have no *a priori* sense of what lawlike statements look like. One might object, of course, that while Kant had *prescriptive* laws in mind here, Goodman's observations relate exclusively to *descriptive* laws. But in that the formulation of a prescriptive law depends upon our ability to identify the particular class of individuals to whom the law properly applies—all human beings, say—and this, in turn, depends upon our ability to say what it is that those individuals *share* that makes the law appropriate, every prescriptive law which is not merely arbitary and which applies to a nondenumerable class—like the class of human beings—must be grounded on some sort of *descriptive* law. And this, in turn, cannot be formulated without the identification of *projectible predicates*—which, according to Goodman, we cannot recognize *a priori*. It follows, in other words, that A can easily manage to have it both ways when he is pressed not to make an exception of his own case, but to act on the basis of a precept that he can consistently will as a law governing the behavior of all individuals. If he wishes to lie in order to gain some personal benefit, he simply thinks of himself as acting on the basis of some such law as the following: Never lie unless you happen to be . . . , and here he fills in a fairly specific description of himself. In the absence of strict criteria determining lawlikeness, we cannot convict A of any inconsistency here. (Indeed, making an exception of himself in *this* way no more undercuts the lawlikeness of A's principle than making an exception of foreign diplomats undercuts the lawlikeness of our traffic regulations.) And thus the question becomes at this point a purely practical one: What are the grounds that should convince the individual who is searching for a definition of morality that rational consistency of the kind that Kant identifies (which rules out making even a "lawful" exception of oneself) is to be preferred to the privileging of one's own case? Once the idea that we have an *a priori* sense of lawlikeness has been undermined, Kant has no satisfactory reply to give to this question. Especially since the pursuit of self-interest—for finite, "situated" beings such as ourselves—is in one sense entirely rational.

But this is not to suggest, of course, that *all ways* of pursuing one's self-interest or, for that matter, all *conceptions* of one's self-interest, are equally rational. On the contrary, it is quite possible to misunderstand one's own nature, or to misunderstand how the world might be made to accommodate that nature. Indeed, the young and the inexperienced often make mistakes of this kind (and each of us, it is worth bearing in mind, is, in a great many respects, inexperienced). The question of what one's true self-interest actually *is,* then, and how it might best be pursued, is not only perhaps the most important question that the individual has to ask herself, it is also a question concerning which *other* human beings are in position to offer considerable insight. Thus even if *B*'s being a "chooser" is, ordinarily, a matter of comparative practical indifference to *A*, the fact that *B* is also a "knower," the owner of a unique perspective, and consequently someone from whom he can potentially learn is, by contrast, a matter of positive significance for *A*. And if it is not, of course, then one of the first things that *A* stands in need of learning—for his own sake—is that it *should be.*

Another way of putting this, perhaps, is to say that there is something fundamentally right about Rorty's contention that, if our moral sentiments are grounded in anything, they are grounded in our recognition of someone as a potential partner in conversation. What is right about this claim is that it places due emphasis on the importance for each of us of *our* interests, more specifically in this case, of our interest in sharing insights, and dispenses with the notion that our appreciation of the other person's integrity is something compelled from us by our recognition of her independent status as a chooser. At the same time, however, it should be remarked that there is also something fundamentally wrong about the contention that we have moral obligations only with respect to those whom we *recognize* as potential partners in conversation—if this means, as Rorty apparently intends it to mean, that our lack of interest in what someone may have to say is justification enough to place her outside the realm of our moral concerns.[3] For one thing, a person does not have to be speaking to us directly in order to be contributing to the improvement of our understanding. Even if *we* do not hear her—whether because of her distance from us or our indifference to what we take her to be saying—she may well be improving the quality of "the conversation of mankind" in such a way as to benefit us indirectly.

In other words, our recognition of another person's rights should not be made to depend upon our assessment of the likelihood of her making a valuable contribution to one or another of those conversations with which we happen to identify most closely. This practical consideration comes into play, of course, in certain situations—when we are selecting, for example, teachers for our children or lawyers to represent us in court. Because not just anyone can be expected to do an effective job in these cases, we extend the *provisional right* to represent us only to individuals whom we consider to be qualified. But if the point of extending certain *basic rights* to those whom we recognize as the owners of perspectives is to foster in society as a whole the improvement of understanding that attends upon open discussion and the sharing of insights, we should bear in mind that one of the implications of human finitude is that we are never in a position to declare with certainty *who* will make a valuable contribution to a discussion, or *when* such a valuable contribution might be forthcoming. Among the owners of perspectives, no one is so intelligent and well-informed as to know everything, and no one is so deficient in these respects that we can say in advance that she will have nothing of value to offer. Our categorical recognition of another person's rights, then, should be understood as both *positively* grounded in our recognition of her as the owner of a perspective and in a sense *negatively* grounded in our awareness of our own incapacity to know in advance what contributions she might have to offer to the conversation of mankind.

It may seem ironic that we should be establishing the rights of the individual, even in part, on the basis of a consideration of the individual's *incapacities*. At the very least, this constitutes something of a contrast with the standard deontological emphasis on the individual's powers as a rational chooser. But talk of rights is essentially just talk of how we should agree to treat each other, since rights are the correlates of obligations, and obligations are simply those recommended lines of action to which we have agreed to commit ourselves. And, of course, considerations of our weaknesses or incapacities are often as germane as considerations of our strengths to the proposing and justifying of various lines of action.

The time has come, then, to ask specifically which rights are called for by this resiting of the "Archimedean point." In addressing this question, we need first of all to elaborate upon the distinction just made between *basic* and *provisional* rights. The former are those rights which, in that they represent the minimum conditions necessary to guarantee genuinely open discussion, should be granted as categorically as possible to all potential contributors to the conversation of mankind (subject, of course, to their being willing to recognize that other individuals possess them as well). Because these rights define the preconditions of our being able to *recognize* the good, it is *these* rights that should be thought of as constraining our pursuit of the good. Provisional rights, by contrast, will be understood as those entitlements that a given society grants to some (and sometimes to all) of its members in order to bring about a specific good the pursuit of which has been generally agreed upon *within* the political dialogue of the society in question. These rights, obviously, will be subject to change from generation to generation and to variation from place to place. Insofar as our resiting of the "Archimedean point" implies the existence of certain rights, then, it is *basic* rights that we are speaking about.

The first and most obvious of the rights implied by our focusing on the significance of the individual's ownership of a perspective is the right to life—which is to say, the right not to be killed by another person—since without life there *is* no perspective. Almost as obvious is the right to freedom from violence and coercion, since actual and threatened violence damage not only the body, but also the psyche, and thus warp the understanding. These rights are implied by our interest in *protecting* the individual's perspective. There are also, however, certain rights that are implied by our desire to secure the *interaction* of perspectives. Three come readily to mind: the rights to freedom of speech, freedom of association, and—what amounts to the converse of freedom from coercion—the freedom to cultivate one's own (spiritual and intellectual) potential. These, then, are the basic rights to be extended to the mature human being. With respect to children, clearly the important point to bear in mind is that nothing should be done that would in any way damage their potential before it is realized. To some extent, this will require the curtailment of their freedom and the forcible cultivation, through education, of some of their potential until such time as they are ready to take over responsibility for themselves.

Now insofar as the point of conferring upon individual human beings certain basic rights is to foster the improvement of understanding that attends upon the sharing of insights, it is important that these rights should not be inflated beyond what is necessary to sustain genuinely open exchanges, for adhering to this restriction promises significantly to improve the quality and texture of our discussions about the relative merits of various goals. There are, obviously, any number of different goals that we could pursue in our lives, but given that our energies and resources are limited, we must choose from among them. The point of ethical discussion, and ultimately also of our inquiries into human nature and the nature of the world in which we find ourselves, is to enable us to choose wisely from among the various claimants to the title of "a good worthy of pursuit." There is no reason to presume, however, with the utilitarians (and there seem to be excellent reasons to doubt), that a single hedonic calculus can be found or devised that will do justice to the needs and interests of all human beings. No doubt certain important goods can only be achieved if they are pursued collectively. Everyone in a society, perhaps, should be interested in the quality of its schools and in the improvement of economic prospects for the poor. On the other hand, a great many goods can be successfully pursued by the individual acting more or less alone—as we see, for example, in the creation of an artwork or the cultivation of a skill. Between these two extremes lie those goods that can be achieved only through the cooperative efforts of a number of individuals, but which do not require the commitment of society as a whole. Each member of society, it goes without saying, will voluntarily commit herself to the pursuit of a number of these ends—some public, some local, some private—and the exact combination will reflect her uniqueness as an individual. Now if the point of ethical discussion is to provide us with the insights necessary to make wise selections from among the many (sometimes conflicting) ends on offer, the point of the extension of the basic rights that we listed a moment ago is, first, to provide a climate within which serious discussion is possible and, second, to guarantee the individual a measure of freedom from coercion by others who wish to insist on *their* vision of the good.

Both of these benefits of the extension of basic rights, however, can be gained only if we avoid defining those rights in such a manner as to make one person's enjoyment of his rights conflict with another person's enjoyment of hers. When basic rights begin to proliferate beyond the range of what is *essential* for the continuation of life and the individual's cultivation of her (spiritual and intellectual) potential, conflicts among rights and between rights and the more important natural goods become inevitable. Precisely because rights represent a kind of ethical bedrock, however, because they are meant to constrain our pursuit of the good and thus are supposed to be inviolable, spurious rights constitute a tempting trump card to deal oneself before launching into ethical debate. In discussions about the underrepresentation of minority groups in positions of influence, for example, (I am thinking here of academic and judicial positions) it is all too tempting to appeal to the "rights" of minorities to equal representation—a move that is meant to settle the issue and close down further discussion, so that we can get on to the important business of making changes in the way we do things. Such an appeal *may* have significance, of course, *if* the society in question has in fact defined equal representation for all groups as a right—which is to say, as a provisional right, one that has been generally agreed to in the process of political dialogue, and subsequently been protected with some form of legislation. Ordinarily, however, the fact that such an appeal is made is evidence that the issue has *not* been settled. The appeal to such "rights"—which, in the absence of any supporting legislation, must be characterized as "natural" (or what I have been calling "basic")—is made rhetorically, in the hope that it will clinch the public debate. Because this rhetorical move constitutes an appeal to a spurious right, however, all that it actually brings about is an equally spurious response. One's opponent appeals in turn to his "right" to have the best qualified people possible in positions of influence, and productive discussion is at an end. The rival parties continue to grimace at each other and play their trump cards—to use Ronald Dworkin's metaphor—but no one gets to claim the pot. Clearly both things that have been misrepresented here as rights *are* goods: we want minority groups and their views to be adequately represented, and we want positions of influence to be filled by the best qualified people available. Insofar as these two goods can conflict, however, it is necessary that we be ready and willing to discuss how they should be made to accommodate each other. In other words, by keeping clearly in mind the actual status of the rival claimants to our loyalties—their status as goods to be achieved if possible—we keep the door open for productive compromise and reduce the confrontational character of ethical discussion.

As Sidney Hook suggests in *The Paradoxes of Freedom,* because "moral rights develop out of the marriage of interests and intelligence," it follows that "the extent of our rights and obligations is . . . a continuing discovery."[4] I would amend this ever so slightly by specifying that it is primarily the extent of what I have been calling "provisional rights" which is a continuing discovery. The basic rights that were specified earlier, insofar as they represent the minimum conditions necessary to guarantee open discussion concerning the nature of the good and the means that should be employed in its pursuit, must be thought of as possessing a more permanent status. Because they rest, not upon any of our specific and possibly shifting interests, but upon our need to be able to adjudicate between the claims of our various specific interests, these rights are *never* spurious. According to Hook,

> in the inescapable conflict of rights and duties, obligations and responsibilities, there can be no absolute obligation except . . . the moral obligation to be intelligent. Intelligence alone is an absolute value because . . . it mediates the conflicts of all other values, and sets limits of scope, timing, and appropriateness to their expression.[5]

True intelligence, however, is a function of one's recognition that one's own perspective is limited and stands in need of augmentation through a consideration of the insights that others are in a position to offer. Thus if we agree with Hook that "the moral obligation to be intelligent" *is* in some sense absolute, it follows that the extension of what I have been calling basic rights—or those rights that safeguard our access to the insights of others, and that thus make *possible* the intelligent mediation of conflicts of values—must also be, in a comparable sense, absolute.

The connection between the conception of justice adumbrated here and democracy should not be difficult to anticipate. Given our assumption that the sharing of insights improves our ability to identify the good, political institutions should be favored on the basis of their demonstrated practical value in fostering open discussion (or at least on the grounds that they appear *likely* to improve the degree of openness to be found in current political discussion). Thus democracy's preferability to the various forms of authoritarianism is a function of its providing better safeguards against the coercion of viewpoints. It is important, moreover, that individuals possess real power to effect changes not only in their private lives, but also in the development of their society. This is implied by their possession of a basic right to cultivate their own potential. The individual's identity, after all, is a matter not only of her personal tastes, talents, and interests, but is also defined in significant respects by the society of which she is a member (in that she speaks its language, observes its customs, enjoys the privileges it affords her, and bears responsibility for her attitude towards its practices). It follows, then, that if her society shapes her identity in a manner that she finds disagreeable, her right to cultivate her own potential entitles her at least to attempt to effect changes in that society—in the same way that it entitles her to attempt to make changes in her tastes, talents, and interests. But having the right to pursue meaningful political action—such as voting and campaigning—without fear of imprisonment or death does not imply, of course, that society is obliged to accept the individual's recommendations. Here again we must distinguish between the individual's *right* to speak and the *likelihood* of her being taken seriously.

An issue that is closely bound up with the political dimension of the individual's right to cultivate her own potential is the question of education. Earlier I remarked that the individual should be thought of as possessing a basic right to education. But to what *kind* of education should the individual be thought to possess a basic right? Obviously, we have to avoid getting too specific here, for while the value of education in a general sense is unquestioned, there is also tremendous disagreement about the relative merits of specific educational programs. It must be borne in mind, moreover, that while education opens up some avenues for the student, it simultaneously closes off—or at least diverts attention from—other avenues. A worthwhile education, we might stipulate, then, is any that has the virtue of opening up more opportunities than it appears to seal off. There can be no question, of course, of the individual's having a right to an "ideal" education. For given that we have not finished exploring the world in which we find ourselves, and thus given that there are improvements in the quality of our understanding still waiting to be made, we are not in a position to say with any confidence what an ideal education would look like. But the reason for extending a universal basic right to an education in the first place is simply to guarantee that the individual's horizon of understanding is not constricted through the intellectual equivalent of starvation. And just as any number of different diets will stave off starvation, so any number of different types of education will foster the development of the child's horizon of understanding. The crucial thing, then, is that the individual be provided with the intellectual means to engage productively with the "conversation of mankind." This requires, at a minimum, that the child be taught a language, and such other basic tools of interaction as reading, writing, and arithmetic. But if this is the minimal education to which each individual should have a right, it is not yet the kind of education that we might wish to see universally extended. There remains one more important feature of such education that needs to be specified.

I have been arguing in this paper that ultimately what should lie at the foundation of our sense of justice is our recognition of the person standing opposite us as the owner of a unique perspective, and consequently, as a potential contributor to our understanding. But if the conception of justice that is grounded in this recognition is to become widespread, we will need to foster among ourselves a fuller appreciation of our interdependence as finite beings. Limited and incomplete as we are, we need each other—for love, for friendship, for the benefits of cooperative labor, but preeminently for the sharing of insights. The sharing of insights, I want to insist, is preeminent in that it underlies and makes possible cooperation, love, friendship. We need, then, to cultivate our sense of belonging to a community—a community that nurtures us and to which we consequently owe our allegiance. This community, however, is not restricted to those with whom we actually happen to have dealings. As was mentioned earlier, a person does not have to be speaking to us directly in order to be contributing to the improvement of our understanding. Even if *we* do not hear her—because of her distance from us in time or space or frame of mind—her insights may benefit us indirectly. The community to which we need to cultivate our sense of belonging, then, is the community of mankind, a community that encompasses not only all of those presently alive but past and future generations as well. The conversation that binds together this community, after all, began long before we arrived on the scene and should, if good fortune and good management are with us, continue long after we have left it. We are the beneficiaries of the accumulated understanding of earlier generations, and if we are to repay our debt to them, we can do so only with respect to posterity, in relation to which we will come to stand as both teachers and object lessons.

But this raises the practical question of how we are to foster in the individual human being this sense of belonging to the community of mankind. The means are ready-to-hand; they have only to be properly employed by individuals who, in that they already identify with this extended community, can lead by example as well as instruction. As Dewey, Mill, and countless others have observed, our best hope for improving the condition of mankind "lies in utilizing the opportunities of educating the young to modify prevailing types of thought and desire."[6] What is needed, specifically, in order to cultivate our sense of belonging to the community of mankind is liberal education that portrays history as an adventure in the growth of understanding. This is not to suggest, of course, that history should be misrepresented. Obviously, the growth of understanding has been anything but smooth. The wars, the tyrannies, the tragedies brought about by superstition and half-baked ideology, however, all need to be remembered as examples of what makes the adventure *significant*. Pain and death, fulfillment and life are at stake in the decisions we make, which are subsequently recalled as history. History, then, must not be approached as entertainment. But if its study is to foster our sense of belonging to the extended community of mankind—which is to say, if we are to break out of the self-perpetuating cycles of sectarian strife— neither can it be approached as a way of nurturing grievances. Thus we must teach the young to identify, not with that conqueror or this sectarian cause, but with those moments when ignorance and prejudice in one form or another have given way to insight. What is needed, in other words, is a view not unlike that which Hegel tried to provide us, in which history is seen as the unfolding drama of Spirit and Reason, and each of us is important by virtue of the part we play in the furthering of that drama.

NOTES

1. For a fuller discussion of my objections to Rorty's position, see "Rorty's Pragmatism and the Pursuit of Truth," *International Philosophical Quarterly* (vol. XXX, no. 2, June 1990), pp. 221–44.

2. Hans-Georg Gadamer, *Truth and Method* (New York: Crossroad, 1982), p. 269.

3. In "Postmodernist Bourgeois Liberalism," Rorty explains that "it is part of the tradition of *our* community that the human stranger from whom all dignity has been stripped is to be taken in, to be reclothed with dignity," and that "this Jewish and Christian element in our tradition is gratefully invoked by free-loading atheists like [him]self" (*Journal of Philosophy*, 1983, p. 588). But he also makes it clear that there are, in his estimation, no grounds *other* than tradition—which, of course, is always subject to change—to which one might appeal in justifying the adoption of this attitude toward the outsider. The implication, then, is that, depending on how we feel about openness and tolerance, we might well decide to *constrict* the range of those with whom we identify and to whom we consequently accord dignity.

4. Sidney Hook, *The Paradoxes of Freedom* (Berkeley: University of California Press, 1962), p. 5.

5. Ibid., pp. 61–2.

6. John Dewey, *Human Nature and Conduct* (New York: Modern Library, 1922), p. 127.

Part 2. Contemporary Problems of Application

Frank Cunningham

ON RELATING JUSTICE AND DEMOCRACY: A STRATEGY AND A HYPOTHESIS

A standard socialist argument has been that democratic political rights are shallow unless economic equality affords everyone a realistic opportunity to make use of them. Collapse of most of the world's socialist governments in the name of democracy evidently challenges those, like myself, who continue to regard this claim sound. Nor is it enough simply to assert that socialism is necessary though not sufficient for a robust democracy. The project of this contribution, then, is to explicate and modify a strategy behind the earlier argument and to offer a hypothesis about how that strategy might be employed. The prescribed strategy should be defensible independently of specifically socialist commitments; though at the end of the article I shall return to socialism.[1]

THE STRATEGY

The element of a socialist approach to the relation between justice and democracy I think worth retaining in a modified form is its effort to "displace" purely theoretical disputes onto practical terrain. According to the earlier view, tensions between abstract conceptions of democracy and justice are superseded when the latter is interpreted as egalitarian economic policy and implemented in circumstances appropriate to democratic politics. On the socialist perspective associated with Marxism, democracy and justice were conceived of in class-relativized terms, so "bourgeois democracy" was to be replaced by a different, "proletarian" kind of democracy. Justice was valued, if at all, for its potential to autodestruct in a communist future "beyond justice."

77

Among the several contestable features of this viewpoint (embraced by not all socialists or even all Marxists) was a propensity shared with many nonsocialists to regard democracy and justice as states of affair either present or absent rather than as matters of more or less. Instead of arguing that socialism could be more democratic or more just than capitalism, it was supposed to embody superior forms of these things. A contrasting viewpoint is that each of democracy and justice admits of degree. It is thus an open question what economic and political arrangements are conducive to progress in democracy and justice, which latter, having univocal senses, can serve as common standards by which to evaluate such arrangements.

The election of parliamentary representatives in countries like my own (i.e., Canada) constituted a democratic advance from the time when legislation was imposed by an imperial power. The later enfranchising of women rectified a serious democratic deficiency, but continuing exclusion of resident noncitizens, insufficient accountability of elected representatives, and disproportionate political power of a variety of nonelected potentates constitute persisting limitations. Similarly, in the United States one can identify progressions in justice regarding available education, job categories, and pay scales for blacks, while informal but systemic obstacles make it all too easy to envisage a more just society. Many other examples contrary to all-or-nothing conceptions come readily to mind.

Examples also come to mind of regress in justice and in democracy. Furthermore, to come to the crucial component of this strategy, there are situations where justice and democracy work against one another or where they are mutually reinforcing. One illustration of opposition is when affirmative action programs generate widespread backlashes. By contrast, to the extent that gains in justice achieved by the civil rights and women's movements expanded public participation and the franchise, justice and democracy were mutually reinforcing. The relationship might be pictured as a spiral that can move in an upward or a downward direction. The sad history of late socialism exhibited a downward spiral, where initial gains in economic justice were offset by antidemocratic politics, which in turn facilitated unjustified privileges. Perhaps we are witnessing the birth of an upward justice/democracy spiral in South Africa.

Of course, the spiral claim does not tell us what justice and democracy are, beyond pretheoretical intuitions. A radically pragmatic socialist displacement strategy could make do without precision on this score, since it was thought that success in radical politics would make theoretical debates unnecessary. Although I think the spiral thesis should apply to a range of interpretations of justice and democracy, I do not wish to endorse such a leap-before-you-look approach, which sustained an antidemocratic power politics. The conceptions of democracy and justice employed are, therefore, to be considered placeholders awaiting further elaboration and defense.

Democracy, as I shall conceive it for this purpose, is measured by success in the efforts of any ongoing collection of people whose actions have effects on one another jointly to make their shared situations conform to their individual wishes. On this broad interpretation of popular sovereignty, the more people there are in a country, a city, a neighborhood, a region of the world, a family, a school, a religious organization, a voluntary association, or any other such situation, who are able by any of a variety of means for taking joint action (informal negotiation, reaching consensus, voting, delegating discretion, and so on) to make the situation conform to their wishes, the more democratic that situation is.[2] Justice, as I shall regard it, is interpreted in terms of equality such that a society (again broadly interpreted) is more or less just to the extent that nobody is, in a coercive way, denied the opportunities and the capacities to enjoy the society's advantages or to be exempted from its burdens.[3]

How much of democracy or justice is possible or desirable and how justice and democracy relate to other valued things are matters of ongoing debate among political theorists which will not be addressed in this paper. Also, any political philosopher will recognize the several problematic terms and contested decisions involved in these conceptions, to which there are well-established alternatives. For example, one might agree with a popular sovereigntist definition of "democracy," but narrow it to the availability of *opportunities* for full participation. Or a popular sovereignty approach might be rejected in favor of one that focuses just on methods for making collective decisions. Similarly, accepting equality as the genus of justice, alternative interpretations of what is to be equalized are possible, or one could limit justice to matters of retribution or acquisition.

Fully recognizing the importance of these differences, the strategy of this paper attends rather to the mutually reinforcing or mutually antagonistic natures of justice and democracy, which I believe clearly apply to versions of the popular sovereigntist and egalitarian conceptions sketched above. Perhaps they also apply to other pairs of alternative conceptions, but even if they do not, the core of the strategy would have force provided that popular sovereignty and equality of capacities and opportunities have a *bearing* on the degrees of democracy and of justice otherwise conceived.

Practical displacement on the recommended strategy is achieved by promoting conditions conducive to an upward justice/democracy spiral or that at least inhibit a downward one. Socialist displacement looked to economic conditions for this purpose—either policies favoring economic equality or changes in class structure. The approach is not unique to socialists, as a pro-capitalist analogue is defended by some advocates of thoroughgoing free markets. Also, economic conditions are not the only potentially displacing ones. In Canada, as in other multinational and multicultural countries much imagination has been devoted to seeking constitutional political arrangements as frameworks for the promotion of democracy and justice.

Notwithstanding the enthusiasm of champions of economic or political displacement, caution about how much can be achieved is in order. It is for this reason that I prefer to talk of displacing conditions as promoting or inhibiting, where this means that they are regarded as facilitators or privileged background conditions rather than as strict causes. Moreover, it is unlikely that large scale and persisting progress in democracy and justice could be promoted by economic or political conditions alone. Nor are they likely to be strong enough facilitators of upward justice/democracy spirals in combination. Required in addition are popular values of political culture. The point is not new and, despite charges of an exclusively economic orientation against classic socialists, was recognized by them. Hence the effort of late socialism was to combine economic transformations with constitutional reform while trying to enforce a culture of what was called "socialist man." This suggests another modification of the earlier displacement strategies best introduced in explicating a hypothesis about political values.

A HYPOTHESIS

In the remainder of this paper I shall seek to identify a value (or those values) the general harboring of which in popular political culture facilitates or would facilitate an upward justice/democracy spiral. Let me emphasize that this quest is independent of the prescribed strategy, which one could accept while rejecting my candidate for a facilitating value. Indeed, one could accept the strategy and try to defend some version of economic or political displacement dispensing with considerations of popular values.

Another negative lesson to be learned from earlier socialist efforts concerns the level of ambition aimed at in identifying displacing values. Quite apart from shortcomings of the content of the "socialist man" value, and apart too from the heavy-handed and, as in the case of Stalinism or the Maoist Cultural Revolution, brutal measures employed to try forcing it onto a population, this value was too far removed from preexisting political culture to be realistically nurtured for the purpose in question. As a purely hypothetical endeavor the task would be too easy: in a society where people generally and strongly favored both justice and democracy the desired spiral would be facilitated.

At the other end of a spectrum one might, in the manner of current Hobbesist thinking, select the "value" of self-interest and try to show that properly enlightened self-interested people will comport themselves in ways that facilitate a justice/democracy spiral. Though he does not frame his project in these terms, something like this approach motivates David Gauthier's attempt to ground morality. Self-interest is best served when people are mutually trusting of commitments made to one another. Rationality thus dictates that a culture of promise-keeping and other values that go with it be inculcated in oneself and every other member of a society.[4] This is not the place to present a general critique of the neo-Hobbesist approach. Instead, I shall content myself with expressing scepticism about its adequacy for the matter at hand. It seems to me that final appeal to self-interest fails to explain or to motivate moral behavior or else it does so by smuggling crypto normative elements into accounts of enlightened interest. Even if this dilemma can be avoided for some purposes, I do not think self-interest is an adequate base from which to start in pursuing the present strategy.

Justice and democracy, as conceived here, constitute a potential spiral, the upward direction of which is facilitated by some still unidentified value or values. This means that the facilitating values will themselves be part of such a spiral and, like democracy and justice, could figure in a downward direction. The difference between such a value and either democracy or justice is that the value(s) should not admit of degree in the same way. While democracy and justice can and, alas, often do descend to very low levels—or, what comes to the same thing, yield to high degrees of undemocracy and injustice—one is seeking a facilitating value that, as well as providing for upward motivation, also constitutes a floor, a sort of safety net or bungee cord as protection against a justice/democracy plummet. In such a circumstance, however, bare self-interest would function more as a gravitational pull.

Less metaphorically expressed, the reason that self-interest is an inadequate starting place is that each of justice and democracy involves irreducible normative components. Institutions required for democratic practices and policies promoting justice sometimes, and perhaps typically, are of such magnitude in time and space that sustaining them will often require sacrifices of self-interest on the part of individuals who cannot reasonably gamble on personal gain in the long run. The point might obtain even if democracy is thinly conceived along Schumpeterian lines as majority vote for candidates of competing elites or if justice is limited to justice in acquisition. Abiding by majority opinion will not always be regarded as being in one's long-term self-interest. Sincere advocates of acquisitive justice must be prepared to make sacrifices to redress unjustified past acquisitions.

Similar considerations pertain to promise-keeping, which I accordingly doubt can be motivated exclusively by reference to self-interest. Nor does this value, viewed as a norm of popular culture, seem sufficient to facilitate a justice/democracy spiral. However, since I think that promise-keeping comes close, indicating strengths and weaknesses will illustrate the interrogation of politically relevant values required by the strategy prescribed here. Promise-keeping has the advantage of being a minimal norm—one it is not unrealistic to suppose prevalent as a sincerely held popular value. A minimal value need not directly sustain the desired spiral, but one must at least be able to see how its nurturing might progressively lead in the direction of enforcing attitudes with this effect. These attitudes are not hard to identify in the case of justice and democracy. They are, respectively, *concern* for the well-being of others and *respect* for their autonomy.

Justice is clearly best served in a populace whose members are concerned about one another. Democracy is the more secure when people are prepared to share decision-making with others, many of them anonymous and with diverse interests, and a society in which people are mutually respectful is conducive to this situation. Promise-keeping implicates elements of both attitudes, as is evidenced by the contrary stances of promise breakers, who show both lack of concern and disrespect toward those to whom the broken promises had been made.

To a certain extent, the value of promise-keeping also admits of nurturing. As the term is used here, two sorts of activity are involved in "nurturing" a value of popular political culture—one at which philosophers are quite good and one at which they are rather poor. Activities at the core of the philosopher's stock-in-trade are tracing conceptual connections, drawing out implications, giving arguments, and identifying commitments. Whether by linguistic, conceptual, or phenomenological examination of popular values such as promise-keeping, philosophers should be able to show what activities or other attitudes a sincere promise-keeper is committed to or against, what social or moral worldview (or views) cohere(s) with promise-keeping, how actual comportment exhibits or fails to exhibit sincerity, and, in general, to trace connections between it and other aspects of a normative landscape.

An activity at which philosophers are less adept is persuasive communication of such findings among a populace. But this does not mean the task is impossible. I think of four personas in which philosophers might be able to affect political culture which I digress to list, since it is crucial to my overall argument that there be means to nurture facilitating values.

Intervenors. By this I do not mean putting aside one's philosophical tools and taking to the streets (though this is not always a bad idea either), but using philosophical talents and theories in public forums around major political issues and in ways that communicate with more than just other philosophers. An example in Canada has been provided by the interventions of Charles Taylor and Will Kymlicka in our constitutional debates.[5]

Teachers. Presumably the students taught by political theorists who are professors are also citizens, current or future parents, employers and employees, politicians, writers, and otherwise beings in the world. While propagandizing in the classroom is both pedagogically unsound and usually futile, the effect of training in critical thinking about political values can have lasting effects, especially if pursued in a way that addresses current issues and engages student participation.

Organic Intellectuals. I hope it is now generally acknowledged that some of the most vibrant recent political theorizing has been by feminist philosophers. In nearly every case, this has been due in part to their active engagement in social movements for the liberation of women. Just as feminist theory has drawn strength from these movements, so has it had an influence on their members and thus indirectly on society as a whole, not to mention the effect on students of bringing engaged theory to the classroom. Analogous comments can be made about active intellectuals in earlier and later social movements: labor, for national liberation, antiracist, ecological, and others.[6]

Experts. Shortly after military suspension of elections in Algeria to prevent fundamentalist success, I was phoned as a resident democratic theorist by a columnist for a local paper, asking for an analysis. Reflecting later on my mumbled and hedged response, I realized that this was an excellent opportunity to put political-philosophical training to use where it would reach a broad public. That, at least in North America, the occasion seldom arrives regarding the media and other forums is only partly due to anti-intellectualism. Had I been better prepared to address a hard and real situation and better at articulating my views, the interview might have been used, and I could have been phoned again.

Returning now to promise-keeping, perhaps enough has been said to show that this value has a purchase on norms promoting democracy and justice capable of being nurtured. Still, I do not think it will serve, at least not exclusively, as the facilitating value now sought. It is not enough that a value admit of nurturing; it must be nurturable in *contexts* appropriate to a given end. Chief among the contexts in which an upward justice/democracy spiral is both most needed and most precarious are those involving, on the one hand, persisting and large scale differences of life aims in a population—differences which make democratic politics difficult—and, on the other hand, wide disparities in people's abilities successfully to pursue their chosen ends—disparities which, in particular, make the achievement of justice difficult.

Promise-keeping typically involves face-to-face interactions among individuals similarly situated economically and socially. An exception is to be found in the case of long standing historical promises, such as the (broken) promises made by Europeans to the aboriginal peoples in North America. The first (interpersonal) context is too narrow, the second too historically broad for the purpose of exhibiting connections between promise-keeping and such values as respect and concern in the contexts of democracy and justice.

This does not mean that somebody agreeing with the prescribed strategy could not employ it to nurture values of promise-keeping. The same may be said regarding other values: civic virtue, public mindedness, some popularly exhibited forms of respect or concern themselves, and perhaps other candidates. Maybe there is no privileged facilitating value and a diversified approach is the best one. Though not at all hostile to this conclusion, I should nonetheless like to advance a candidate for what I take to be an especially well-situated value of popular political culture—if for no other reason than to encourage analogous interrogation of other candidates by example. I have in mind toleration taken in a weak or thin sense, which I shall label "elementary."

"Toleration," as used here, refers to the pluralist value that, other things being equal, people ought to be able to pursue their own goods in their own ways. Toleration is elementary to the extent that the *ceteris paribus* clause in this formulation is generously interpreted. One standard vitiating condition is when the pursuit of some good or some manner of pursuit of a good would undermine toleration itself. A yet more stringent constraint would override toleration when it is thought that a good pursued is in fact a bad. Toleration is the most elementary when somebody is unsympathetic to anyone else's pursuit of a good whenever this would interfere with his or her own pursuits. I intend to defend elementary toleration even in its weakest sense as a justice/democracy spiral facilitator. Since this is a very weak sense indeed, deliberately chosen partly in virtue of its weakness, I should first point out that it nonetheless defines a line between bare toleration and flat out intolerance. Somebody otherwise sympathetic to the paper's strategy and hypothesis, but who thinks elementary toleration too weak could, of course, identify a stronger version of toleration; however, it would have to be recognized that there is a trade-off between the strength of facilitating values and the breadth of a nurturable popular base.

Prescriptions with *ceteris paribus* riders are weakened, but at the same time they retain presumptive force. Sincerely to adhere to elementary toleration means that one actually does favor others being able to pursue their own goods and assumes a burden on oneself to justify exceptions. This rules out that version of nationalism which is premised on fear or hatred of other nationalities, where some people's nationality is partly constituted by denigration of other national cultures. It also rules out the approach of colonialism and neocolonialism where religious or ethnic features of a colonized nation are cynically manipulated in home country interests. A recognized shortcoming of elementary toleration is that it permits passivity in the face of others' frustrations, but when the attitude that others should lead their lives as they wish as long as I am not interfered with passes over into active or passive complicity in Apartheid-type oppression (a life nobody could reasonably be expected to wish to lead), expressions of elementary toleration become hypocritical. Elementary toleration rules out religious bigotry, while clearly being consistent with ecumenicism. Evangelism is a grey area, shading in some cases into hypocrisy and bigotry, in other cases into overridable presumptive toleration.

Toleration, even in its elementary form, is more closely conceptually linked to respect and concern than to promise-keeping. Not only does intolerance involve disrespect and lack of concern but, more positively, somebody who sincerely harbors the value of toleration recognizes that people with other goods are nonetheless people and can empathize with the form if not the content of their satisfaction in achieving goods other than one's own and their frustration in failing to achieve them. Intolerance, on the other hand, seems to me always to involve denial of personhood or denigration of life goals different from one's own.

The first attitude is especially prominent in the case of sexism or racism, the second in that of ethnic or religious chauvinism. In general, toleration and intolerance will have somewhat different characters depending on their "targets," though I suspect that a blend of denial of personhood and lack of empathy functions in all of them. Unlike promise-keeping, the context of toleration is one where there are ongoing, cohabiting social differences, and these differences cut across class and other lines typically dividing advantages and disadvantages. That is, it shares the contexts where democracy and justice are especially important.

By contrast with some of the other candidates mentioned above—public mindedness, civic virtue, and so on—elementary toleration has the advantage of being minimal and hence realistic, thus making it more readily assessable to somebody wishing to nourish it. Of course, minimalism also means that such a person will have a longer way to go in using elementary toleration as a point of entry to encourage more securely justice and democracy promoting popular consciousness. But this is exactly the point of a strategy of practical displacement: to substitute for an exclusively theoretical burden (abstractly relating justice and democracy) a practical burden (participating in public forums to make constructive changes in popular thinking).

Techniques for nurturing elementary tolerance no doubt depend on specific circumstances. Aboriginal people in Canada are increasingly demanding self-government, and in classroom and other forums it is not uncommon to hear expressions of sympathy for this demand in principle, but without any willingness to support its actual implementation. One way to nurture respect here is to wed abstract arguments about self-determination with accounts of what aboriginal self-government might concretely mean. For example, students who learn how community-centered and nonconfrontational trials are conducted and who can see the advantages for native communities and for the nonnative communities increasingly experimenting with this "circle sentencing" strengthen their tolerance with comprehending respect. Care-promoting empathy is best nurtured by supplementing ethical theory and statistics about the quality of native life with first-hand accounts—for instance, in autobiographies or novels. Advocates of affirmative action are often frustrated to find agreement with its goals but resistance to its policies. The attitude can, however, be turned to advantage by directly confronting the question of what consistency in practical reasoning involves, while explicating the nature of systemic disadvantage, again concretely and in personally assessable ways.

The general advantages I see in elementary toleration can be explained and defended by contrasting this approach with an orientation toward toleration on the part of contemporary liberal philosophy illustrated in the recent work of John Rawls. A central concern of liberal political philosophy for him is to understand how "a just and free society" is possible under conditions of "deep doctrinal conflict with no prospect of resolution."[7] Toleration plays two, related, roles in his endeavor. Insisting on the priority of civil rights over the ability of groups to impose their conceptions of the good on individual citizens, the state enforces tolerant behavior. At the same time, the state itself is not to promote or to become captive of any individual's or group's conception of the good, thus protecting pluralistic toleration among them. Much of Rawls' analysis is devoted to showing that toleration is an inescapable "burden of judgment" and to defending the priority of the right over the good.

The effort of this paper is of a different sort than that of Rawls, though success should be welcomed by Rawlsian as by non-Rawlsian liberal democrats. Rawls' primary concern is to justify giving toleration-promoting rights legal priority over goods-pursuing behavior. The displacement project is to facilitate popular values favorable to democracy and to justice (in a sense compatible with that at least of the left Rawlsian)[8] while remaining agnostic about how toleration should be ranked relative to other values in ethical theory or whether it should be legislatively prioritized. Where Rawls is concerned to justify acceptance of toleration in a sufficiently strong sense to sanction state imposition of it, this paper assumes toleration in a weak sense as a widely shared value and seeks ways to nurture it.

That arguments are needed to justify toleration might be taken by a champion of the Rawlsian approach to indicate that this is not a widespread value and hence that there is not enough to nurture. Alternatively, recognizing that Rawlsian argumentation is aimed at something more than elementary toleration, it might be admitted that the latter is a generally held value, but urged that unless a commitment to toleration is strong enough to accept its state enforcement, elementary toleration is insincere or little more than window-dressing for otherwise intolerant behavior.

As the first of two steps in responding to such an objection, it must be urged that elementary toleration, assumed in this step to be a widespread value, is more than insignificant window-dressing. One might consider what a society where it was not at all held would be like: people with different visions of a good life would regard one another not just as misguided but as nonpersons; the unhappiness of people who failed to realize goals other than one's own would not be thought in the least unfortunate. Lamentably, there are individuals who exhibit such attitudes, and there may even be times and places where they constitute large numbers of a society. But surely the difference between social worlds where this was the norm and where it was an aberration is significant from a moral and a political point of view.

Among other differences, the world of elementary toleration would offer a base, lacking in the other world, from which to build advanced toleration. Here is another nurturing task appropriate to the talents of philosophers. An attitude of elementary toleration is advanced to the extent that the presumption in favor of it is strengthened by challenging the toleration-overriding conditions referred to earlier. Here the plausibility of standard arguments given by, among others, Rawls himself suggests its feasibility. Recognition of conflict among intelligent people over fundamental questions of morality and ethics suggests that intolerance based on ascriptions of evil should be tempered with intellectual modesty. A good way of minimizing, if not ever completely overcoming, the liberal paradox generated by intolerance of the intolerant is by as much as possible replacing force with education—that is, by nurturing toleration itself. The inescapability, in a shrinking world and in increasingly multicultural societies, of people with different values counsels toleration on grounds of self-interest, appeal to which need not be altogether shunned, even while recognizing the insufficiency of such arguments noted above.

The second step in responding to the constructed liberal argument is to give reasons to believe that elementary toleration is in fact sufficiently widespread to be a good facilitator. One general argument for this conclusion, which I find expressed in different ways by Michael Walzer, Ernesto Laclau and Chantal Mouffe among others, links attitudes of toleration with conceptions of the self. Extreme intolerance, on this view, involves attitudes of dogmatism and fanaticism emanating from unidimensional and completely self-assured subjects. However, the nonfixity of people's natures and the confusions of the "divided self"—both arguably typical of the human condition—require exceptional and transient circumstances for such intolerance to be sustained.[9] An even more philosophically general argument is the quasi-transcendental one of Habermas that toleration is engraved in the presuppositions of ordinary discourse.[10] One need not accept the conclusions for high ethical theory that he draws from this observation to agree that ongoing human interaction at least requires mutual recognition of personhood.

Whatever the strengths of such general theories, I suspect that the burden of the present argument must finally be borne empirically. I do not intend to try marshaling an empirical argument, which those sympathetic to this paper's strategy and at least intrigued by the toleration hypothesis may undertake by drawing on whatever resources are at their disposal. In such an undertaking it must be kept in mind that the claim only regards *elementary* toleration, and that exceptions are admitted provided there is still assurance that tolerant attitudes are sufficiently widespread to be nurtured. Of course, a defender of the hypothesis should also be able to give plausible explanations for the exceptional cases, as, for example, Walzer does in referring to the effects of insecurity in explaining violent ethnic conflicts in such places as the former Yugoslavia.[11]

It is also pertinent to distinguish debate about toleration from two other debates often confused with it. While skepticism about knowledge of the good may be conducive to toleration, it is also possible to defend toleration from within antiskeptical perspectives, as each of contemporary Utilitarianism and Kantian deontology illustrates. Similarly, toleration does not entail antitraditionalism. A common individualist complaint against communitarians is that they sanction the suppression of individuals by intolerant traditions of their own communities. However, as some individualists recognize,[12] to the extent that people give meaning to their lives by embracing traditional values, it can also be intolerant to suppress a tradition. Also, as several communitarians argue, major traditions have within themselves resources for the critique of intolerant propensities.[13]

This last point bears more attention, since it challenges the opinion sometimes voiced in secular, liberal-democratic societies that toleration is a value unique to these societies and not found in more traditional ones. (Though it does not advance defense of my hypothesis, the chauvinism in such claims should be noted, as the Western democracies are not without their intolerant fundamentalists, whether religious or nationalist.) I am inclined to think that this opinion confuses toleration with the specific political-institutional structures designed to protect it in liberal-democratic societies, and that there are other ways of expressing and enforcing toleration in other traditions.

An example of this claim is the ecumenicism to be found in every one of the world's major religions. This does not mean that all religious believers are tolerantly ecumenical or that ecumenical attitudes toward those of other faiths automatically yields comparable toleration toward those of one's own. However, what is required is confidence that there is some ground for a culture of toleration, if not within the theologies of any or all religions—a matter of continuing theological debate—then in their institutional comportments and in the ordinary beliefs of their members. Regarding what are sometimes called "traditional" societies (as if developed liberal-democratic societies lack traditions), codes of behavior governing the treatment of strangers or visitors often exhibit a more tolerant attitude toward these categories of people than is found in societies priding themselves on their modernity. If, despite these putative examples to the contrary, it is thought that toleration is only sufficiently widespread to serve as a justice/democracy facilitating value in liberal-democratic countries of the developed world, somebody would need to seek alternative values in other societies.

I now conclude by returning to the question of economic equality and responding to an anticipated socialist criticism. It might be agreed that cultural changes are necessary for making progress in democracy and justice, and it might even be agreed that in some kind of world elementary toleration would be conducive to justice and democracy. But, the argument goes, the world as it actually exits is marked both country by country and, most dramatically, among the world's regions by extreme material inequalities. Elementary toleration or even more advanced toleration is at best ineffective faced with these inequalities. Those in relatively comfortable circumstances will not be prepared to make sacrifices in their lifestyles even if they are tolerant of those in whose interests such sacrifices would be made. Moreover, inequalities of wealth are not accidently correlated with inequalities of power, which those who possess it are both loathe to give up and can use to protect their privileged positions.

By themselves, I do not think that these apt and quite accurate observations challenge the hypothesis of this essay. The strategy of the essay recognizes that cultural transformations in the absence of economic and political ones are insufficient and aims to contribute not to an automatic upward spiral, but to one that requires persistent activity on all three of the economic, political, and cultural fronts. Nor is elementary toleration seen as a sufficient value of the cultural component of such campaigns, but as a realistic and nurturable point of entry. The envisaged objection gains more force against the hypothesis if it employs a standard socialist critique of liberalism to argue that a culture of pluralistic toleration, far from being nurturable, is antithetical to the required value transformations. On this view, toleration encourages anti-communal social atomization and neoliberal attitudes in favor of tending one's own garden. This is a weighty objection, full reply to which would require an extensive excursion into major intersocialist debates.[14]

My thinking on this score is influenced by that of my late colleague, C.B. Macpherson. He was a strong critic of those aspects of liberal democracy that serve to perpetuate power imbalances and promote a pernicious culture of "possessive individualism," but he also saw positive potentials in liberal-democratic values and accordingly regarded their "retrieval" as the best place for transformatory politics in Western democracies to start. On this perspective, the world of political culture contains not just good values (communal feeling, concern, respect) and bad values (selfishness, greed) but also *contested* values which lend themselves to alternative interpretations and prompt conflicting modes of behavior. It is precisely because they are sufficiently popularly engaging to be contested that these sorts of value are good places to start.[15]

Elementary toleration is such a value. That this toleration is so easily overridable makes it susceptible to a neoliberal interpretation; that it includes favorable recognition of other people's goods works against classic neoliberalism and looks in a more communal direction. If anyone who is in broad sympathy with the hypothesis of this paper has a better realistic candidate, I would very much welcome knowing what it is.

NOTES

1. In preparing this article, I profited from interventions at the 1995 East-West Philosophers' Conference, where its draft was read. Thanks are also due to Nancy Fraser, Dow Marmur, Ludwig Nagl, Herta Nagl-Docekal, George Sher, and Wayne Sumner for helpful suggestions and criticisms.

2. This informal conception is filled out and key terms are defined in my *Democratic Theory and Socialism* (Cambridge: Cambridge University Press, 1987), chap. 3. Those who conceive of democracy as outcomes, rather than as processes, can still regard democracy as a matter of degree by estimating how closely less than perfectly democratic situations approximate these outcomes.

3. This conception of justice combines the claim, well argued by Christopher Ake, that justice may be considered a matter of equality with a characterization of equality recently defended by G. A. Cohen. Christopher Ake, "Justice as Equality," *Philosophy and Public Affairs* (vol. 5, no. 1, Fall 1975), pp. 68–89; G. A. Cohen, "On the Currency of Egalitarian Justice," *Ethics* (vol. 99, no. 4, July 1989), pp. 906–44. Following Cohen, the stipulation about coercion is included to indicate that justice does not (typically) require rectifying burdens that result from one's own, uncoerced choices.

4. David Gauthier, *Morals by Agreement* (Oxford: Oxford University Press, 1985). I take promise-keeping to be the vital link in Gauthier's attempted derivation of morality from rational self-interest. It might be thought that the link is Locke's famous proviso, a version of which Gauthier accepts, that individual appropriation be constrained to leave enough and as good of the world's resources for others to try to appropriate, and that this is a good facilitator. I do not pursue such an hypothesis, since I think that the context within which it is most appropriately believed (one of appropriation for private use) is also the context where belief in it is the most tenuous.

5. Taylor's interventions were in a variety of forums—special publications, public speeches, presentations to commissions of inquiry—and are collected in his *Reconciling the Solitudes* (Montreal: Queen's-McGill Universities Press, 1993), chaps. 7, 8, and 9. Kymlicka has also spoken in public forums and has been a regular contributor to a discussion bulletin addressing questions of pressing Constitutional concern, *Network Analyses,* an Ottawa-based publication of a nongovernmental organization, "Network on the Constitution." An example of an intervention by Kymlicka is an article coauthored with Wayne Norman, "The Social Charter Debate" (no. 2, January 1992).

6. I discuss the relation of democratic theory to social movements in my *The Real World of Democracy Revisited* (Atlantic Highlands: Humanities Press, 1994), essay 7.

7. John Rawls, *Political Liberalism* (New York: Columbia University Press, 1993), p. xxviii. Lecture IV of this book is the most relevant to the topic of the current paper.

8. Rodney Peffer derives a concept of justice compatible with the one employed here from a critical reading of Rawls in *Marxism, Morality, and Social Justice* (Princeton: Princeton University Press, 1990), chaps. 9 and 10.

9. Ernesto Laclau and Chantal Mouffe, *Hegemony and Socialist Strategy* (London: Verso, 1985), chap. 3; Michael Walzer, *Thick and Thin* (South Bend: University of Notre Dame Press, 1994), chap. 5. In defending "moral minimalism," Walzer wishes to extend the general ("thin") values of philosophers across cultures, while preserving the cultural specificity of popular ("thick") morality. The present paper asks

how some (elementary) popular values might be nurtured so as to encourage the harboring of more robust popular values as well. Further, it is assumed that each of the elementary and more advanced values have both culturally specific and cross-cultural dimensions.

10. Habermas applies his views on discourse to democracy in *Legitimation Crisis* (Boston: Beacon Press, 1973) and more recently in *Faktizität und Geltung* (Frankfurt am Main: Suhrkamp, 1992), chap. 7. An interesting treatment of specifically multicultural issues by Habermas bearing on the current paper is his comment on some views of Charles Taylor, "Struggles for Democratic Recognition in the Constitutional State" in *Multiculturalism*, Amy Gutman, ed. (Princeton: Princeton University Press, 1994), pp. 107–48.

11. Walzer, op. cit., pp. 79ff.

12. For example, Will Kymlicka, *Liberalism, Community, and Culture* (Oxford: Clarendon Press, 1989), chap. 8.

13. Central communitarian sources are Alasdair MacIntyre, *Whose Justice? Which Rationality?* (Notre Dame: University of Notre Dame Press, 1988); and Michael Walzer, *The Company of Critics: Social Criticism and Political Commitment in the 20th Century* (New York: Basic Books, 1988). See too Charles Taylor's essay, "Shared and Divergent Values," *Reconciling the Solitudes*, chap. 8, for an application.

14. I survey these arguments and defend a version of liberal-democratic socialism in *Democratic Theory and Socialism*, Part Two.

15. C. B. Macpherson, *Democratic Theory: Essays in Retrieval* (Oxford: Oxford University Press, 1973). I take stock of the relevance of Macpherson's views in the post-1989 world in *The Real World of Democracy Revisited*.

Cass R. Sunstein

DELIBERATION, DEMOCRACY, DISAGREEMENT

INTRODUCTION

What is the relationship between democracy and justice? No simple answer could make sense. There are many different conceptions of both democracy and justice. Some conceptions produce conflicts, others do not.[1]

If we understand democracy as simple majority rule, and if we understand justice as entailing the protection of certain rights, democracy and justice may well conflict, at least if majorities are not respectful of rights. Majorities may well violate rights. Thus on plausible assumptions, majoritarian conceptions of democracy are incompatible with justice. Those who find justice to be an overriding goal will therefore seek to limit the scope of democracy, and no one should doubt that many conceptions of justice and democracy require us to make choices between the two. On the other hand, we could define justice and democracy as mutually reinforcing. Perhaps political equality is a requirement of justice, and if this is how we understand things, we may well be led to see democracy and justice as compatible.

My principal interest here is democracy rather than justice, and it may be helpful to point out that observers might find three different conceptions of justice, or three families of conceptions, in Western political traditions. On one view, democracy is closely associated with the protection of certain basic rights. Democracy is seen principally as a way of securing those rights. Democracy is part of the set of rights that justice requires people to have, and democracy should be constituted so as to ensure that all rights are protected. This conception of democracy may well entail institutional arrangements designed to limit what government may do, as in the ideas of checks and balances or judicial review—antimajoritarian measures designed to ensure that justice is done. Undoubtedly aspects of this conception of democracy will

93

play a role in any sound understanding, but that role is partial and not the complete picture. The principal point is that the "rights" view of democracy does not offer a developed understanding of a democracy at all. If people are concerned with the protection of antecedently given rights, it may not be easy to explain why democracy is desirable and, in any case, the appeal of democracy is not likely to be adequately explained.

On a second view, democracy is understood not as a system for protecting rights but instead as a mechanism for aggregating private preferences. On this view, a democratic process has the signal advantage of ensuring that the number and intensity of preferences are reflected in governmental outcomes. What the system tries to achieve is a form of "political equilibrium." Democracy is thus a kind of market, one that is specially suited to the pervasive problem of aggregating preferences.

There is truth in this view too. In the real world, and in theory too, democracies must attempt some form of preference-aggregation when unanimity cannot be achieved, but I think that the aggregative view does not offer a good understanding of what democracy is all about. That view takes preferences as given, and in this sense it fails to do what democracy should—that is, to offer a system in which reasons are exchanged and evaluated. A well-functioning system of democracy rests not on preferences but on reasons. The democratic interest in reason-giving is associated with familiar understandings of liberty and justice. We might think that freedom entails not simply an opportunity to satisfy your preferences, but an opportunity too to scrutinize them and to see whether they can be defended. It also seems reasonable to say that under the right circumstances, a system of reason-giving is likely to prevent injustice. At any rate it is plausible to think that if someone is going to be deprived of benefits, or faced with burdens, government ought to generate a public-regarding reason for that result. Aggregative conceptions of democracy do not require reason-giving, and this seems a key defect.

Ideas of this sort lead naturally to a third conception of democracy, one that might be labeled deliberative. Deliberative democrats attempt to combine a measure of popular sovereignty and commitment to justifications for the distribution of benefits and burdens. They want representatives to be accountable to the public at large, but they are not simple majoritarians, since they also seek to ensure that all government action is accompanied by reasons. Their preferred system of politics is representative, on the theory that direct democracy is less likely to be pervaded by reasons. But they want reason-giving to be characteristic of citizens generally as well. In fact, they prize active citizenship as indispensable to democracy, and they do not see the desire to participate in politics as simply another "taste." Deliberative democrats believe too in a norm of political (not economic) equality, and they see political equality as a precondition for a well-functioning republic of reasons. Finally, deliberative democrats are likely to be constitutional democrats.

They do not see constitutionalism and democracy as antonyms. They think that constitutionalism, properly conceived, is a precondition for a good system of democracy, insofar as constitutionalism protects rights of freedom of speech, religious liberty, and the rule of law, all of which are necessary for deliberative democracy.

I cannot attempt in this space to set out a full account of deliberative democracy or to respond to the many possible challenges to this ideal.[2] It is clear that there is a pervasive problem of social pluralism and disagreement, and that this problem can make democratic deliberation quite difficult. Deliberative democracy appears to prize unanimity as a result of reasoned argument, but unanimity is highly unlikely in a heterogeneous world. People disagree about what counts as good or right. They disagree about the best way to accommodate different goods and different rights. They disagree about whether the good is prior to the right or vice versa. They disagree about what is even admissible as good or as right. Some of these disagreements are explicitly religious in character. Some of them involve disagreements among religion, agnosticism, and atheism. Other disagreements might be described as quasi-religious, in the sense that they involve people's deepest and most defining commitments.

There is much dispute about whether well-functioning democracies try to resolve such disagreements, and about how they should do so if they do try. One important strategy, discussed below, is to attempt to obtain social agreement on a range of abstractions—free speech, private property, due process—and thus to ensure that disagreements will occur at a "subconstitutional" stage when hard particular questions arise. Another strategy is to urge government to seek an "overlapping consensus"[3] among reasonable people, thus allowing agreements to be made among Kantians, utilitarians, Aristotelians, and others. Perhaps participants in a liberal democracy can agree on the right even if they disagree on the good. On the Rawlsian account, "comprehensive views" should be put to one side as incompatible with the best understandings of political legitimacy. Thus a sympathetic observer, summarizing a widespread view, refers to the liberal "hope that we can achieve social unity in a democracy through shared commitment to abstract principles."[4]

In many ways this is a promising approach to the problem of disagreement, and the Rawlsian project is certainly compatible with that of deliberative democracy.[5] But an investigation of actual democracy, and of law in actual democracies, draws this view into doubt. Democracies, and law in democracies, must deal with people who very much disagree on the right as well as the good. Democracies, and law in democracies, must deal with people who tend to distrust abstractions altogether. Public officials are certainly not ordinary citizens. But neither are they philosophers. Indeed, officials—like citizens generally—may lack a high-level theory of any kind, and they will likely disagree with one another if they have one. Many decisions must be made rapidly in the face of apparently intractable social disagreements on a wide range of first principles. In addition to facing the pressures of time, these diverse people must find a way to continue to live with one another. They should also show each other a high degree of mutual respect or reciprocity. Mutual respect may well entail a reluctance to attack one another's most basic or defining commitments, at least if it is not necessary to do so in order to decide particular controversies.

My principal suggestion in this essay is that well-functioning democratic systems sometimes adopt a special strategy for producing agreement amidst pluralism. Participants in controversies try to produce *incompletely theorized agreements on particular outcomes*.[6] They agree on the result and a narrow or low-level explanation for it; they need not agree on fundamental principle. The distinctive feature of the account is that it emphasizes agreement on (relative) particulars rather than on (relative) abstractions. This is an important source of social stability and an important way for diverse people to demonstrate mutual respect. For those who emphasize incompletely theorized agreements, the goal is to try to stay with the lowest level of abstraction necessary to decide what to do on a disputed issue, and to raise the level of theoretical ambition only if required.

Consider some examples. People may believe that it is important to protect endangered species, while having quite diverse theories of why this is so. Some may stress obligations to species or nature as such; others may point to the role of endangered species in producing ecological stability; still others may point to the possibility that obscure species will provide medicines for human beings. Similarly, people may invoke many different foundations for their belief that the law should protect labor unions against certain kinds of employer coercion. Some may emphasize the democratic character of unions; others may think that unions are necessary for industrial peace; others may believe that unions protect basic rights. So too, people may favor a rule of strict liability for certain torts from multiple diverse starting-points, with some people rooting their judgments in economic efficiency, others in distributive goals, still others in conceptions of basic rights. Of course people disagree about these matters; what I am suggesting is that such convergence as we have may well emerge from low-level principles.

When the convergence on particular outcomes is incompletely theorized, it is because the relevant actors are clear on the result without reaching agreement or being clear on the most general theory that accounts for it.[7] Often they can agree on an opinion, or a rationale, usually offering low-level or mid-level principles and taking a relatively narrow line. They may agree that a rule—forbidding discrimination on the basis of sex, protecting endangered species, allowing workers to unionize—makes sense without agreeing on the foundations of their belief. They may accept an outcome—reaffirming the abortion decision, *Roe v. Wade,* or protecting sexually explicit art—without understanding or converging on an ultimate ground for that acceptance. Reasons are almost always offered, but what ultimately accounts for the opinion, in terms of a full-scale theory of the right or the good, is left unexplained. Higher levels of abstraction are avoided. The model I have in mind is one in which people from divergent starting-points, or with uncertainty about their starting-points, can converge on a rule of a low-level judgment.

Incompletely theorized agreements have obvious disadvantages, but I believe that they have crucial virtues as well. Their virtues extend as well to social life, even workplace and familial life, and also to democratic politics. In many ways, incompletely theorized agreements offer an approach to social pluralism that complements or competes with the existing alternatives, including political liberalism, which offers large-scale abstractions on which social agreement may or may not be likely under reasonably favorable conditions. I will note these possibilities without discussing them in detail here.

My emphasis on incompletely theorized agreements is intended partly as descriptive. These agreements play an important function in any well-functioning democracy consisting of a heterogeneous population. But I want to make some normative claims as well. There are distinctive advantages to incompletely theorized agreements in law and elsewhere. Such agreements are especially well-suited to the institutional limits of many democratic institutions, which are composed of multimember bodies, consisting of highly diverse people who must render many decisions, live together, avoid error to the extent possible, and show each other mutual respect.

I. AGREEMENTS WITHOUT THEORY

A. In General

Incompletely theorized agreements play a pervasive if infrequently noticed role in law and society. It is rare for a person or group completely to theorize any subject—that is, to accept both a general theory and a series of steps that connect the theory to a concrete conclusion. In fact, people often reach *incompletely theorized agreements on a general principle.* Such agreements are incompletely theorized in the sense that people who accept the principle need not agree on what it entails in particular cases. People know that murder is wrong, but they disagree about abortion. They favor racial equality, but they are divided on affirmative action. Hence there is a familiar phenomenon of a comfortable and even emphatic agreement on a general principle, accompanied by sharp disagreement about particular cases. This sort of agreement is incompletely theorized in the sense that it is *incompletely specified.*

When content is given to the agreement, much of the key work must be done by people who have not agreed to the general principle, often at the point of application.

Sometimes constitution-making and democratic stability become possible through this form of incompletely theorized agreement. Consider the case of Eastern Europe, where constitutional provisions have been adopted with many abstract provisions on the specification of which there will be (indeed, has been) sharp dispute. A similar phenomenon lies at the heart of contemporary law, for the creation of large regulatory agencies has often been possible only because of incompletely specified agreements, in which legislators converge on general requirements that regulation be "feasible" or "reasonable," or that it provide "a margin of safety." The task of specification is left to people who were not parties to the agreement.

There is a second and quite different kind of incompletely theorized agreement. People may agree on a mid-level principle but disagree about both general theory and particular cases. They may believe that government cannot discriminate on the basis of race, without having a large-scale theory of equality, and without agreeing whether government may enact affirmative action programs or segregate prisons when racial tensions are severe. The connection is left unclear between the mid-level principle and general theory; it is equally unclear between the mid-level principle and concrete cases. So too, people may think that government may not regulate speech unless it can show a clear and present danger, but disagree about whether this principle is founded in utilitarian or Kantian considerations, and disagree too about whether the principle allows government to regulate a particular speech by members of the Ku Klux Klan.

My special interest here is in a third kind of phenomenon—incompletely theorized agreements on particular outcomes, accompanied by agreements on the low-level rules or standards that account for them. Judges and other public officials have to decide particular issues, and so it is especially important that those who disagree on high-level theories agree on particular results.[8]

Perhaps the participants endorse no high-level theory, or perhaps they believe that they have none. Perhaps they find theoretical disputes irrelevant, confusing, or annoying. Perhaps they disagree on the right or the good. What is critical is that they agree on how a case must come out. The argument applies to legal rules, which are typically incompletely theorized in the sense that they can be accepted by people who disagree on many more general issues. People may agree that to receive social security benefits, people must show "disability," defined in a rule-bound way, without having a theory of which disabled people deserve what. Thus a key social function of rules is to allow people to agree on the meaning, authority, and even the soundness of a governing legal provision in the face of disagreements about much else.[9]

B. How People Converge

It seems clear that people may converge on a correct outcome even though they do not have a high-level theory to account for their judgments. Jones may know that dropped objects fall, that bees sting, that hot air rises, and that snow melts, without knowing exactly why these facts are true. The same is true for law and morality. Johnson may know that slavery is wrong, that government may not stop political protests, that every person should have just one vote, and that it is bad for government to take property unless it pays for it, without knowing exactly why these things are so. We may thus offer an epistemological point: People can know that X is true without entirely knowing why X is true.

There is a political point as well. People can agree on individual judgments even if they disagree on high-level abstractions. Diverse judges may believe that the great American abortion decision, *Roe v. Wade*,[10] should not be overruled, though the reasons that lead each of them to that conclusion sharply diverge. Some people emphasize that the Court should respect its own precedents; others think that *Roe* was rightly decided as a way of protecting women's equality; others think that restrictions on abortion are unlikely to protect fetuses in the world, and so the case rightly reflects the fact that any regulation of abortion would be ineffective in promoting its own purposes. We can find incompletely theorized political agreements on particular outcomes in many areas of law and politics—on both sides of the affirmative action controversy, on both sides of disputes over the death penalty, and on both sides of the dispute over health care.

C. Rules and Analogies

There are two especially important methods by which a society might resolve disputes without obtaining agreement on first principles: rules and analogies. Both of these methods attempt to promote a major goal of a heterogeneous society: *to make it possible to obtain agreement where agreement is necessary, and to make it unnecessary to obtain agreement where agreement is impossible.*

The fact that we can obtain an agreement of this sort—about the meaning of a rule or the existence of a sound analogy—is no guarantee of a good outcome, whatever may be our criteria for deciding whether an outcome is good. A rule may provide that no one under the age of twenty is permitted to work, and we may all agree on what it means, but such a rule would be neither just nor efficient. The fact that there is agreement about the meaning of a rule does not mean that the rule is desirable. Perhaps the rule is bad, or perhaps the judgments that go into its interpretation are bad.

Some of the same things can be said about analogies. People in positions of authority may agree that a ban on same-sex marriages is analogous to a ban on marriages between uncles and nieces, but the analogy may be misconceived, because there are relevant differences and because the similarities are far from decisive. The fact that people agree that case A is analogous to case B does not mean that case A *or* case B is rightly decided. Problems with analogies and low-level thinking might lead us to be more ambitious. Participants in law may well be pushed in the direction of general theory—and toward broader and more ambitious claims—precisely because low-level reasoners offer an inadequate and incompletely theorized account of relevant similarities or relevant differences.

All of this should be sufficient to show that the virtues of incompletely theorized outcomes—and the virtues of decisions by rule and by analogy—are partial. Those virtues should not be exaggerated. But no system is likely to be either just or efficient if it dispenses with incompletely theorized agreements; in fact, it is not likely even to be feasible.

II. THE CASE FOR INCOMPLETE THEORIZATION

What might be said on behalf of incompletely theorized agreements, or incompletely theorized judgments, about particular cases? As I have said, incompletely theorized agreements may be unjust or otherwise wrong. Indeed, we are accustomed to thinking of incomplete theorization as reflective of some important problem or defect. Perhaps people have not yet thought deeply enough. We are accustomed to thinking of incompletely theorized judgments as potentially wrong. When people raise the level of abstraction, they do so to reveal bias, or confusion, or inconsistency. Surely participants in a democratic system should not abandon this effort. There is a good deal of truth in these usual thoughts, but they are not the whole story. On the contrary, incompletely theorized judgments are an important and valuable part of both private and public life.

First, and most obviously, incompletely theorized agreements are well-suited to a world containing social dissensus. By definition, such agreements have the large advantage of allowing a convergence on particular outcomes by people unable to reach anything like an accord on general principles. This advantage is associated not only with the simple need to decide cases, but also with social stability, which could not exist if fundamental disagreements broke out over every incident of public or private dispute.

Second, incompletely theorized agreements can promote two goals of a liberal democracy and a liberal democratic system: to enable people to live together,[11] and to permit them to show each other a measure of reciprocity and mutual respect. The use of rules or low-level principles allows judges to find commonality and to decide cases without producing unnecessary antagonism. Both rules and low-level principles make it unnecessary to reach areas in which disagreement is fundamental.

Perhaps more important, incompletely theorized agreements allow people to show each other a high degree of mutual respect or reciprocity. Frequently ordinary people disagree in some deep way on an issue—the Middle East, pornography, gay marriages—and sometimes they agree not to discuss that issue much, as a way of deferring to each other's strong convictions and showing a measure of reciprocity and respect (even if they do not at all respect the particular conviction that is at stake). If reciprocity and mutual respect are desirable, it follows that officials, even more than ordinary people, should not challenge one another's deepest and most defining commitments if there is no need for them to do so.

To be sure, some fundamental commitments might appropriately be challenged in the legal system or within other multimember bodies. Some such commitments are ruled off-limits by the authoritative official materials. Many provisions involving basic rights have this function. Of course it is not always disrespectful to disagree with someone in a fundamental way; on the contrary, such disagreements may sometimes reflect profound respect. When defining commitments are based on demonstrable errors of fact or logic, it is appropriate to contest them. So too when those commitments are rooted in a rejection of the basic dignity of all human beings, or when it is necessary to undertake the contest to resolve a genuine problem. But these cases, though far from self-defining, are relatively rare. Most cases can be resolved in an incompletely theorized way, and more complete theorization is not justified on grounds of necessity, demonstrable error, or basic dignity.

This point suggests a third consideration. Any general theory of a large area of the law or democratic life—free speech, contracts, property—is likely to be too crude to fit with our best understandings of the multiple values that are at stake in that area. Monistic theories of free speech or property rights, for example, will be ill-suited to the range of values that speech and property implicate. Human goods are plural and diverse, and they cannot be ranked along any unitary scale without doing violence to those very goods.[12] People value things not just in terms of weight but also in qualitatively different ways. We are unlikely to be able to appreciate the diverse values at stake unless we investigate the details of particular disputes. In the area of free speech, a top-down theory—stressing, for example, autonomy or democracy—is likely to run afoul of powerful judgments about particular cases. For this reason such theories are usually inadequate precisely because of their generality and simplicity.

Analogical thinking—a form of casuistry—is especially desirable here. This way of proceeding allows participants in law to build doctrine with close reference to particular cases and thus with close attention to the plurality of values that may well arise. This plurality will confound "top-down" theories that attempt, for example, to understand speech only in terms of democracy, or property only in terms of economic efficiency. General theories are too likely to contain errors.

Of course a "top-down" approach might reject monism and point to a wide range of plural values.[13] But any such approach is likely to owe its genesis and its proof—its point or points—to a range of particular cases to which it can refer. In this way, incompletely theorized judgments are well-suited to a moral universe that is diverse and pluralistic, not only in the sense that people disagree, but also in the sense that each of us is attuned to pluralism when we are thinking well about any area of social life.

Fourth, incompletely theorized agreements have the crucial function of reducing the political cost of enduring disagreements. If officials disavow large-scale theories, then losers in particular cases lose much less. They lose a decision, but not the world. They may win on another occasion. Their own theory has not been rejected or ruled inadmissible. They have not been disenfranchised or ruled out of court. When the authoritative rationale for the result is disconnected from abstract theories of the good or the right, the losers can submit to legal obligations, even if reluctantly, without being forced to renounce their largest ideals. To be sure, some theories should be rejected or ruled inadmissible; this is sometimes the point of authoritative official materials. But it is an advantage, from the standpoint of freedom and stability, for a democratic system to be able to tell most losers—many of whom are operating from foundations that have something to offer, or that cannot be ruled out of bounds *a priori*—that their own deepest convictions may play a role elsewhere.

Fifth, incompletely theorized agreements may be especially desirable in contexts in which we seek moral evolution over time. Consider the area of constitutional equality, where considerable change has occurred in the past and is likely to occur in the future. If the legal or political culture really did attain a theoretical end-state, it might become too rigid and calcified; we would know what we thought about everything, whether particular or general. The idea of equality would be frozen at a particular point in time. By contrast, incompletely theorized agreements—a key to debates over constitutional equality, with issues being raised about whether gender, sexual orientation, age, disability, and others are analogous to race—have the important advantage of allowing a large degree of openness to new facts and perspectives. Such agreements enable disagreement and uncertainty to turn into consensus. They promote a good deal of flexibility. At one point, we might think that homosexual relations are akin to incest; at another point, we might find the analogy bizarre. Of course, a high-level theory of equality might be right and perhaps it should be adopted if right, but judges deciding cases are unlikely to arrive at it through high-level theorizing and, if they do, they may well fail to implement it in light of their institutional limitations.[14]

Sixth, incompletely theorized agreements may be the best approach that is available for people of limited time and capacities. The search for full theorization may be simply too difficult for participants attempting to reason through difficult problems. And when compared with the search for theory, incompletely theorized agreements have the advantage of humility and modesty. To enter into such agreements, one need not take a stand on large, contested issues of social life, some of which can be resolved only on what will seem to many a sectarian basis.

III. FEATURES OF ANALOGY

I now turn to analogical thinking as an illustration of incompletely theorized agreements on particular outcomes. This way of proceeding is pervasive in law and in everyday life. In ordinary discussions of social questions, the ordinary mode involves not high-level principles but analogies. This is how people ordinarily talk and deliberate. You think that racial hate speech is not protected by the first amendment; does this mean that the government can silence George Wallace or Louis Farrakhan? A familiar argumentative technique is to show inconsistency between someone's claim about case *X* in light of his views on case *Y*. Analogical thinking is a form of casuistry; it is based on close attention to individual instances.

In analogical thinking, as I understand it here, such theories are not deployed. They seem too sectarian, too large, too divisive, too obscure, too high-flown, too ambitious, too confusing, too contentious, too abstract. On the other hand, analogizers cannot reason from one particular to another particular without saying something at least a little abstract. They must invoke a reason of principle or policy to the effect that case *A* was decided rightly *for a reason,* and they must say that that reason applies, or does not apply, in case *B*. I will try to show that this method of proceeding is ideally suited to a legal system consisting of numerous judges who disagree on first principles, who lack scales, and who must take most decided cases as fixed points from which to proceed.

1. Analogies outside of law and public life.   Outside of law and public life, analogical reasoning often helps to inform our judgments. I have a German shepherd dog, and I know that he is gentle with children. When I see another German shepherd, I assume that he too will be gentle with children. I have a Toyota Camry, and I know that it starts even on cold days in winter. I assume that my friend's Toyota Camry will start on cold winter days as well. This is a usual form of reasoning in daily life, but it will readily appear that it does not guarantee truth. The existence of one or many shared characteristics does not mean that all characteristics are shared. Some German shepherd dogs are not gentle with children. Some Toyota Camrys do not start on cold days in winter. For analogical reasoning to work well, we have to say that the relevant, known similarities give us good reason to believe that there are further similarities as well and thus help to answer an open question. Of course, this is not always so. At most, analogical thinking can give rise to a judgment about probabilities, and these are of uncertain magnitude.

2. *Analogical thinking in law and public life: its characteristic form.* Analogical reasoning has a simple structure in law and public life. Consider some examples. We know that an employer may not fire an employee for agreeing to perform jury duty;[15] it is said to follow that an employer is banned from firing an employee for refusing to commit perjury. We know that a speech by a member of the Ku Klux Klan, advocating racial hatred, cannot be regulated unless it is likely to incite and is directed to inciting imminent lawless action;[16] it is said to follow that the government cannot forbid the Nazis to march to Skokie, Illinois.[17] We know that there is no constitutional right to welfare, medical care, or housing; it is said to follow that there is no constitutional right to government protection against domestic violence.[18]

From a brief glance at these cases, we can get a sense of the characteristic form of analogical thought in law and public life. The process appears to work in five simple steps. (1) Some fact pattern A—the "source" case—has characteristics W, X, and Y. (2) Fact pattern B—the "target" case—has characteristics X, Y, *and* Z, or characteristics W, X, Y, and Z. (3) A is treated a certain way in law. (4) Some low-level principle, discovered in the process of thinking through A, B, and their interrelations, explains why A is treated in the way that it is. (5) Because of what it shares in common with A, it is concluded that B should be treated in the same way. It is covered by the same low-level principle.

It should readily appear that analogical reasoning does not guarantee good outcomes or what we might describe as truth. For analogical reasoning to operate properly, we have to know that A and B are "relevantly" similar, and that there are not "relevant" differences between them. Two cases are always different from each other along at least some dimensions. When lawyers say that there are no relevant differences, they mean that any differences between the two cases (a) do not make a difference in light of the precedents, which foreclose certain possible grounds for distinction, or (b) cannot be fashioned into the basis for a distinction that makes sense or is genuinely principled. A claim that one case is genuinely analogous to another—that it is "apposite" or cannot be "distinguished"—is parasitic on conclusion (a) or (b), and either of these must of course be justified.

The key task for analogical reasoners is to decide when there are relevant similarities and differences. Categories must be constructed rather than found, and both precedents and statutes force interpreters to make complex evaluations. To see whether a precedent or a statute "applies" to a particular context, we must develop some principles separating the cases that are covered from those that are not—step (4) in the assessment described above. The judgment that a distinction is not genuinely principled of course requires a substantive argument of some kind. What, then, are the characteristics of a competent inquiry into analogies?

3. *The features of analogy.*   In law, analogical reasoning has four different but overlapping features: *principled consistency; a focus on particulars; incompletely theorized judgments; and principles operating at a low or intermediate level of abstraction.* Taken in concert, these features produce both the virtues and the vices of analogical reasoning in law. I offer some brief remarks on each of these features.

First, and most obviously, judgments about specific cases must be made consistent with one another. A requirement of coherence, or principled consistency, is a hallmark of analogical reasoning (as it is of reasoning of almost all sorts). It follows that in producing the necessary consistency, some principle, harmonizing seemingly disparate outcomes, will be invoked to explain the cases. The principle must of course be more general than the outcome for which it is designed.

Second, analogical reasoning is focused on particulars, and it develops from concrete controversies. The great American jurist, Oliver Wendell Holmes, Jr., put it in this suggestive if somewhat misleading way: A common law court "decides the case first and determines the principle afterwards."[19] The suggestion is misleading since, in order to decide the case at all, one has to have the principle in some sense in mind; there can be no sequential operation of quite the kind that Holmes describes. But Holmes is right to say that ideas are developed from the details, rather than imposed on them from above. In this sense, analogical reasoning is a form of "bottom-up" thinking.

Despite the analogizer's focus on particulars, we have seen that any description of a particular holding inevitably has some theoretical components. One cannot even characterize one's convictions about a case without using abstractions of some sort and without taking a position on competing abstractions. We cannot know anything about case X if we do not know something about the reasons that count in its favor. We cannot say whether case X has anything to do with case Y unless we are able to abstract, to at least some extent, from the facts and holding of case X. The key point is that analogical reasoning involves a process in which principles are developed from, and with constant reference to, particular cases.

Third, analogical reasoning operates without anything like a deep or comprehensive theory that would account for the particular outcomes it yields. On this count analogy-making shares an important characteristic with rule-interpretation. The judgments that underlie convictions about, or holdings in, the relevant case are incompletely theorized, in the sense that they are unaccompanied by anything like a full apparatus to explain the basis for those judgments. Of course, there is a continuum from the most particularistic and low-level principles to the deepest and most general. We might compare the idea that government may not discriminate on the basis of point of view with the notion that the First Amendment is based on a certain well-developed notion of autonomy. There is no qualitative distinction between the low-level and the deeply theorized. I suggest only that analogizers avoid those approaches that come close to the deeply theorized or the foundational and that, to this extent, lawyers are generally analogizers.

Fourth, and finally, analogical reasoning produces principles that operate at a low or intermediate level of abstraction. If we say that an employer may not fire an employee for accepting jury duty, we might mean, for example, that an employer cannot require an employee to commit a crime. This is a principle, and it does involve a degree of abstraction from the particular case, but it does not entail any high-level theory about labor markets, or about the appropriate relationship between employers and employees. If we say that a Nazi march cannot be banned, we might mean that political speech cannot be stopped without a showing of clear and immediate harm, but in so saying we do not invoke any large theory about the purposes of the free speech guarantee, or about the relation between the citizen and the state. People can converge on the low-level principle from various foundations, or without foundations at all. In analogical reasoning, as I understand it here, we usually operate without express reliance on any quite general principles about the right or the good.

4. *Why analogy?*   There is an underlying issue. Why might we think analogically? Would it not be better to proceed directly to the merits, rather than to compare cases with one another? I think that the ultimate answer is highly eclectic. The case for analogies is pragmatic; it involves an array of diverse social interests. I offer a brief outline here.

First, the analogizer is committed to a certain kind of consistency or equal treatment. A litigant in case *A* may not be treated differently from a litigant in case *B*, unless there is a relevant difference between them. This idea operates as a barrier to certain forms of prejudice and irrationality. Second, analogies can be a source of both principles and policies. A judge who looks at a stock of precedents will be able to learn a great deal. Investigation of analogies may not be the best way to do policy science or to investigate issues of principle. But it may contribute a little bit to that process. Third, the resort to decided cases, as analogies, helps judges to avoid hubris. A judge who respects what others have done is less likely to overstep, by invoking theories that are idiosyncratic, highly divisive, or sectarian. Fourth, analogical reasoning, if based on precedent, promotes the interest in fostering and protecting expectations. Cases may encourage people to believe that the law is a certain way, and they may act on that belief. Fifth, analogical thinking saves time by establishing a wide range of conventions. If judges had to start from scratch in each case, the legal system would be overwhelmed. For judges and lawyers, following precedent is thus enabling rather than constraining. It ensures that people of limited time and capacities can take much for granted. Finally—to return to our main theme—analogies facilitate the emergence of agreement among people who diverge on most or many matters. Judges A, B, and C may disagree on a great deal. But to say the least, it is helpful if judge A can invoke certain fixed points for analysis, so that judges B and C can join the discussion from shared premises. Perhaps judge B can invoke some fixed points that argue in a surprising direction. We cannot exclude the possibility that ultimately the judges really do disagree. But with analogies, at least they have begun to talk.

As a description of common law case in Anglo-American legal systems, this account should be unsurprising. Judges typically decide particular controversies by exploring how previous cases have been resolved. They rely on precedents, and reason from them. They look for relevant similarities and relevant differences. In the end, they will produce a rule or a standard, or more likely a series of rules and standards. But rules are not given in advance of encounters with particulars; they are generated through close encounter with the details of cases. Moreover, the rules that emerge from the cases are not simple rules, for they can be changed at the moment of application, especially when the court encounters a case that seems to have new or unanticipated characteristics.

The fact that the common law operates by analogy does not mean that the common law is without rules. Far from it. The common law is pervaded by rules, many of which are followed even in cases in which a return to first principles, or to the justifications for the rules, would call for some refashioning of the rules during the confrontation with particular cases. In the abstract, a common law system may be even more rule-like than a civil law system. Many of the laws of a civil law system are really standards, filled with ideas like "reasonable" and "good faith"—ideas that have not been given fixed content. Many areas of the common law have eschewed standards or factors and yielded a large number of rules, settling issues in advance. Nonetheless, it remains true that many common law courts do perceive themselves as authorized to change the rule, or to reconceive the rule, when the particulars of the case so require. Often courts feel free to examine a wide range of policies and principles in deciding whether the application of a previous "rule" makes sense in novel cases.

IV. ANALOGIES IN CONSTITUTIONAL LAW

In American constitutional law, it is often suggested that the actual and appropriate foundations of decision are text, structure, and history. The suggestion is right, but it is often a conceit.[20] Sometimes judges do ask about the relation between the case at hand and constitutional text, structure, and history. But this approach often produces insoluble difficulties. The difficulties may stem from the fact that there are large ambiguities in the three sources of law. They may result because high-level ideas like "equal protection" must be specified in order to be usable. Or the problem may be that of applying a general document to particular problems, many of which were unanticipated.

Those who believe that constitutional cases often turn on something other than text, structure, and history tend to suggest that large-scale moral or political claims play a role in resolving constitutional gaps. But this view poses problems of its own, especially on a multimember court consisting of people who are uncertain about, or who disagree on, first principles. Judges do invoke moral principles, to be sure, but usually those principles operate at a low level of abstraction, and judges try to avoid the largest and most disputable claims. This is a key part of the ethos of constitutional adjudication, exemplified not least in the idea that unnecessary constitutional rulings should be avoided, an idea that is meant to limit disagreement over fundamental principles.

Consider, for example, the question whether a ban on flag-burning violates the constitutional protection against laws abridging the freedom of speech. The constitutional text does not say whether flag-burning falls within "the freedom of speech," nor whether laws preventing that act "abridge" any such freedom. The history behind the provision is not very helpful. To come to terms with that history, we need to make complex judgments about the transplantation of the framers' general commitments and particular conclusions to a new era. There is no simple "fact" with which judges can work. Moral and political argument can certainly help here; but if it is abstract, it may produce confusion or stalemate, and may not be productive among heterogeneous judges who disagree on a great deal. Many judges will find the moral argument on the free speech principle—about liberty, democracy, utility—too confusing to be helpful. Others will disagree too sharply on the governing values.

Judgments become far more tractable if constitutional interpreters try to proceed, as they do in fact, through analogies. There is general agreement—indeed there is a holding—that draftcard burning is not protected by the constitution, at least if the government is trying to make sure that people do not lose their draftcards. Is a ban on flag-burning relevantly similar or relevantly different? This is the start of an inquiry into a large number of analogies, some involving decided cases, others involving hypotheticals. This is also how judges proceed. The conclusion is that our constitutional tradition is largely a common law tradition.[21] It has more in common with English constitutionalism, and with our own common law, than is generally recognized.

This understanding of American constitutionalism raises a question of democratic legitimacy. Often the legitimacy of a constitution, or of constitutional law, is traced to the fact that the document reflects considered judgments of the people as a whole. In this view, judicial review—the extraordinary process of judicial invalidation of measures having democratic pedigree—is justified by the fact that judicial decisions are a product of the people's will.[22] Of course, this understanding is in some ways a charade. But most recognizable theories of judicial review attempt to connect constitutional judgments to constitutional text and history, and the absence of some plausible connection would be extremely disturbing to nearly all people concerned with constitutional legitimacy. Without a conception of democratic judgments, on what authority do courts invalidate statutes?

There is much to say on this difficult topic. Part of the answer lies in the rule of law values associated with following precedent. The process of precedent-following disciplines judicial discretion and also makes it plausible to say that there has been public acceptance of, acquiescence in, or at least nonrejection of, constitutional decisions. Some of the answer lies in the fact that, in constitutional cases, judges rely on defining moments or defining precedents—the Civil War, the New Deal, the civil rights movement, and *Brown v. Board of Education*—that have a high degree of popular approval and that operate as fixed points for inquiry, whatever the judges think of them as a matter of political theory. A large part of what disciplines judicial judgments, and at least some part of what legitimates them, is not constitutional text or history, but the need, perceived by judges as well as by everyone else, to square current judicial decisions with previous judicial decisions. When a court concludes that a ban on flag-burning violates the constitutional protection of free speech, it may of course seek to connect its conclusion with constitutional text and history and also with a good conception of the free speech principle. But much of the apparatus behind the conclusion is not text or history, and not general principle, but previous judicial decisions—ruling some approaches off-limits, placing others on the table and, in any case, establishing tracks along which reasoning must go. This apparatus is not sufficient for judicial legitimacy. But it certainly contributes to such legitimacy, because it limits judicial hubris, produces a kind of consistency among people who are similarly situated, and builds (under good conditions) on the wisdom of the past.

Let us turn now to the role of moral judgments in constitutional law. Some people think that constitutional law is or should be deeply philosophical, and it is easy to understand the basis of this belief. How can we decide the meaning of the word "equal," or "liberty," or "reasonable" without making philosophical claims? But there is a problem with this view, and the problem is connected to the fact that legal solutions must operate in a world with distinctive limitations. Some philosophers think, for example, that a free speech principle that places a special premium on political discussion is extremely attractive.[23] But judges may not be able to agree on this idea, and agreement is indispensable in light of the fact that cases have to be decided. Perhaps too, this approach would be too readily subject to abuse in the real world. Perhaps any institutional judgments about the category of what counts as "the political" would be too biased and unreliable to be acceptable. For good institutional reasons, we might adopt a free speech principle of a low-level or philosophically inadequate sort, simply because that inadequate approach is the only one that we can safely administer.

All of this suggests that legal conclusions need not be justified from the philosophical point of view, and that deep philosophical justifications may not yield good law, because of the institutional constraints faced by participants in any legal system. The point is connected with the role of analogies. Analogical thinking is unlikely to provide an adequate understanding of any area of law. But perhaps analogical reasoning, whatever its limits, is well-adapted to some of the institutional disabilities of courts. This is hardly a basis for celebrating analogical thinking in the abstract. But it might be enough to explain why this way of proceeding has such appeal for participants in law (and for people confronting moral questions in everyday life).

V. ANALOGY AND INCOMPLETELY THEORIZED AGREEMENTS

In this section, I discuss some challenges to incompletely theorized agreements as a key part of democratic deliberation in the face of social pluralism and disagreement. I have the legal system in mind as a key example, but the points extend to democratic deliberation more generally.

A. Analogy and Burke

An initial challenge, traceable to Jeremy Bentham, is that incompletely theorized agreements, and especially the method of analogy, are unduly tied to existing intuitions and, partly for this reason, are static or celebratory of existing social practice. The objection is that analogical reasoning works too modestly from existing holdings and convictions, to which it is unduly attached. It needs to be replaced by something like a general theory—in short, by something like science. Analogizers are Burkeans, and their approach suffers from all the flaws associated with Burke's celebration of the English common law. It is too insistently backward-looking, too skeptical of theory, too lacking in criteria by which to assess legal practices.

At first glance, the claim seems mysterious. Whether analogical reasoning or incompletely theorized judgment calls for the continuation of existing practice turns on the convictions or holdings from which analogical reasoning or the relevant judgment takes place. Without identifying those convictions or holdings, we cannot say whether existing practices will be celebrated. It is surely conceivable that the process of testing initial judgments by reference to analogies will produce sharp criticism of many social practices and, eventually, will yield radical reform. Legal holdings that are critical of some social practices may well turn out, through analogy, to be critical of other practices as well.

In fact, analogical thinking has often produced dramatic reform. In the United States, the great case of *Brown v. Board of Education* invalidated racial segregation in education. By analogy to *Brown,* courts invalidated racial segregation elsewhere as well. More than that, they have reformed prisons and mental institutions, struck down many racial classifications, including affirmative action programs, invalidated sex discrimination, and prevented states from discriminating on the basis of alienage and legitimacy. Whether incompletely theorized judgment is conservative or not depends not on the fact that it is incompletely theorized, but on the nature of the principles brought to bear on disputed cases.

B. Analogy and Realism

A separate objection is not to incompletely theorized agreements in general but to analogical thinking in particular; it questions whether this way of proceeding actually has the virtue claimed for it. Does it really allow for agreement on particulars by people who disagree on general principles? On one view, reasoning by analogy is utterly indeterminate in the absence of social consensus or a degree of homogeneity that will exist in no properly inclusive legal system. According to those skeptical of analogical thinking, we can reason in this way only if we already agree on certain fundamental questions. Otherwise people will simply differ, and there will be no way to reason through their differences.

To some degree the objection is valid. If someone thinks that the government can punish political speech whenever that speech poses any risk of any degree to the government, it will be hard to reason with them, through analogies, to a sensible system of free expression. (Note, however, that it may be possible to undermine this very position with analogies.) In this sense, it is right to think that reasoning by analogy depends on a degree of commonality among participants in the discussion. If people have little or nothing in common, they may be unable to talk. We might ask, however, whether this really amounts to an objection at all. The need for a degree of consensus is hardly a problem distinctive to analogy. It applies to all forms of reasoning.

In coming to terms with this objection, we need to distinguish between analogical reasoning in law and analogical reasoning elsewhere. In law, there are greater constraints on the process. Existing legal holdings sometimes provide the necessary commonality and the necessary consensus. People who disagree with those holdings usually agree that they must be respected; the principle of *stare decisis* so requires. Within the legal culture, analogical reasoning imposes a certain discipline, and a widespread moral or political consensus is therefore unnecessary. Hence people who would not use analogies to reach closure in politics or morality can often do so in law.

Analogies may well be less helpful in politics or morality, simply because of the possible absence of precedents that can help generate an incompletely theorized agreement on particular outcomes. The differences lead to two important conclusions. First, the method of analogy may indeed be less determinate outside of law. Second, there can be a real difference between the legally correct outcome and the morally correct outcome. The difference lies in the fact that analogies will operate as entirely "fixed points" in legal reasoning, whereas many of these are revisable in morality. Consider, for example, the fact that lawyers must take *Roe v. Wade* as authoritative so long as it stands, even if they think the decision abhorrent from the moral point of view. If *Roe* is authoritative, it disciplines discussion of certain topics—the right to withdraw medical equipment, the right to use contraceptives, the right to euthanasia—and the discipline would be removed if the abortion issue were itself up for moral judgment.

Even outside of law, however, the objection from indeterminacy is not entirely persuasive. Very diverse people may have sufficient commonality on fundamental matters to permit considerable progress. When there appears not to be such commonality, a good deal of movement can occur through simultaneous engagement with what various participants in the discussion say and think—engagement that includes narratives about diverse experiences or history, personal and otherwise, as well as more conventional "reasons." (Note that the case method operates in part through narratives.) Much of moral discussion involves this form of casuistry, in which people test their provisional judgment by reference to a range of actual or hypothetical cases. We have no reason to disparage this process in advance. Sometimes people really do disagree. But analogical reasoning can at least help to discover exactly where they do, and exactly why.

C. Analogy and Conceptual Ascent

The third objection comes from Henry Sidgwick. On this view, there is often good reason for officials to resort to large-scale theory, and it stems from the transparent limits of incompletely theorized agreements, analogical thinking, and attention to particulars. When our modest judge uses analogical reasoning to say that case *A* is like case *B,* he has to rely on a principle. Perhaps the principle is wrong because it fails to fit with other cases, or because it is not defensible as a matter of political morality. If the judge is reasoning well, he should have before him a range of other cases, *C* through *Z,* in which the principle is tested against others and refined. At least if he is a distinguished judge, he will experience a kind of "conceptual ascent," in which the more or less isolated and small low-level principle is finally made part of a more general theory. Perhaps this would be a paralyzing task, and perhaps our judge need not often attempt it. But it is an appropriate model for understanding law and democratic deliberation.

The conceptual ascent is especially desirable in light of the fact that incompletely theorized agreements and analogical thinking will allow large pockets of inconsistency. Some areas of the law may make internal sense, but because the categories with sense are small, they may run into each other if they are compared. We may have a coherent category of law involving sex equality (though this would be fortunate indeed) and a coherent category involving racial equality (same qualification), but these categories may have a strange relation to the categories involving sexual orientation and the handicapped. More ambitious forms of reasoning, going well beyond analogical thinking, seem necessary in order to test the low-level principles.

There is some truth in this response; to say how much would take me far beyond the present discussion.[24] Perhaps moral reasoners should try to achieve vertical and horizontal consistency, not just the local pockets of coherence offered by analogy. And sometimes judges and other officials must raise the level of abstraction in order to decide justly, or in order to decide at all. But the response does not offer a complete picture; it ignores some of the distinctive characteristics of the arena in which real-world officials must do their work. Some of these limits involve what should happen in a world in which people face various constraints, but some of them involve political morality and appropriate mutual interaction in a world in which people disagree on first principles. In light of these limits, analogical thinking has several major advantages. Those advantages have everything to do with the virtues of incompletely theorized agreements. Recall here that such agreements involve low-level principles on which people can converge from diverse foundations, that people of limited time and capacities are unlikely to be able to reach full integrity, and that incompletely theorized agreements reduce the costs of enduring agreements and are well-suited to the need for moral evolution.

VI. INCOMPLETELY THEORIZED AGREEMENTS OVER TIME

Incompletely theorized agreements have virtues, but their virtues are partial. Stability, for example, is brought about by such agreements, and stability is usually desirable, but a system that is stable and unjust should probably be made less stable. In this final section, I offer some qualifications to what has been said thus far. In brief, they are as follows. Some cases cannot be decided without introducing a fair amount in the way of theory. If an outcome cannot be achieved at all without a good deal in the way of theorizing, courts must theorize a good deal. Moreover, some cases cannot be decided well without introducing theory. If a good theory is available, and if judges can be persuaded that the theory is good, there should be no taboo on its judicial acceptance.

Thus far the discussion has offered a static description—a description in which judges or other officials are deciding what to do at a certain time. Of course low-level principles are developed over long periods, and a dynamic picture shows something different and more complex. First, the understanding may shift and perhaps deepen. Second, a characteristic role of observers of the democratic process is to try to systematize cases and practices in order to see how best to make sense of them, or in order to show that no sense can be made of them at all. In any process of systematization, a rather high-level theory might well be introduced. Often observers will try to invoke some higher-level idea of the good or the right in order to show the deep structure of the system, or to move it in particular directions, or to reveal important, even fatal inconsistencies. A demonstration that the law makes deep sense might be a source of comfort and occasional reform. A demonstration that the system makes no sense, or reflects an *ad hoc* compromise among competing principles, might produce discomfort and large-scale change. Third, sometimes the law or political practice reflects more ambitious thinking or reacts to these more ambitious efforts by outsiders.

In a society respectful of social heterogeneity, and apart from those abstractions that can command general agreement, it is relatively rare for any area of law or social practice to be highly theorized. Much of the time, people from divergent starting-points[25] can accept relevant outcomes. But I do not mean to say that it would necessarily be bad for theories to be introduced; nor do I deny that small-scale, low-level principles can become part of something more ambitious. A descriptive point first: It is important to note that after a period of time, the use of low-level principles may well result in a more completely theorized system. To engage in analogy, a reason is always required and, after a period, the low-level reasons may start to run into each other, perhaps producing debates at a higher level of abstraction. During those debates, the concrete rulings may be synthesized and a more general principle may emerge. Sometimes the process of low-level thinking will yield greater abstraction or a highly refined and coherent set of principles. An especially interesting phenomenon occurs when a once-contestable analogy becomes part of the uncontested background for ordinary work, or when the uncontested background is drawn into sharp question via analogies.

Now let us turn to the question of what judges and other officials should do. At least if people can agree on the high-level theory, and at least if the theory can be shown to be a good one, acceptance of a high-level theory may hardly be troubling, but, on the contrary, an occasion for celebration. Who could object to public adoption of what is by hypothesis a good theory? Some areas may therefore become more fully theorized than incompletely theorized agreements allow in the short run. But any such theory will likely have been developed through generalizing and clarifying incompletely theorized outcomes, and doing so by constant reference to concrete cases, against which the theory is measured. The theory will not be free-standing. In many contexts, moreover, officials will not be able to know whether an apparently good theory really is right. The acceptance of a theory will create an excessive risk of future error. These possibilities are sufficient for the claims defended here. Officials should adopt a more complete theory for an area of law only if they are very sure that it is correct.

Of course, it would be foolish to say that no general theory can produce agreement, even more foolish to deny that some general theories deserve general support, and most foolish of all to say that incompletely theorized agreements warrant respect whatever their content. What seems plausible is something more modest: except in unusual situations, and for multiple reasons, general theories are an unlikely foundation for law and democratic judgment, and caution and humility about general theory are appropriate for judges and other public officials, at least when multiple theories can lead in the same direction. This more modest set of claims helps us to characterize incompletely theorized agreements as important phenomena with their own special virtues. They represent a distinctive solution to social pluralism and, in any case, a crucial aspect of the exercise of reason in a deliberative democracy.

NOTES

1. This essay overlaps with the first of my two Tanner Lectures on Human Values, presented at Harvard University in 1994, and appearing as "Political Conflict and Legal Agreement," *The Tanner Lectures on Human Values: 1996*. A book based on

these lectures, *Legal Reasoning and Political Conflict*, was brought out by Oxford University Press in 1996.

2. For relevant discussion, see Cass R. Sunstein, *The Partial Constitution* (Cambridge: Harvard University Press, 1993); Cass R. Sunstein, "Beyond the Republic Revival," *Yale Law Journal* (vol. 97, 1988), p. 1536.

3. See John Rawls, *Political Liberalism* (New York: Columbia University Press, 1993), pp. 133–72.

4. Joshua Cohen, "A More Democratic Liberalism," *Michigan Law Review* (vol. 92, 1994), pp. 1503, 1546.

5. See Cass R. Sunstein, *Democracy and the Problem of Free Speech* (New York: Free Press, 1993), chap. 8.

6. Compare the notion of overlapping consensus as set out in Rawls, supra, at 133–172. The idea of an incompletely theorized convergence on particulars is related. Both ideas attempt to bring about stability and social agreement in the face of diverse "comprehensive views." But the two ideas are far from the same. I am most interested in the problem of producing agreement on particulars, with the thought that often people who disagree on general principles can agree on individual cases. Rawls is more interested in the opposite possibility—that people who disagree on particulars can agree on abstractions, and use that agreement for political purposes, see idem at 43–45. Of course this is also true. I do not attempt here to sort out all the relations between the idea of an overlapping consensus and the notions that I have in mind.

7. Interesting issues of collective choice lurk in the background here. Important problems of cycling, strategic behavior, and path dependence may arise in multi-member bodies containing people with divergent rationales, each of whom wants to make their rationale part of law. See Kenneth Arrow, *Social Choice and Individual Values*, 2nd edition (New York: Wiley, 1962). There may also be complex bargaining issues as some officials or judges seek to implement a broad theory as part of the outcome, while others seek a narrow theory, and still others are undecided between the two. Cf. Douglas Baird et al., *Game Theory and the Law* (Cambridge: Harvard University Press, 1994), chap. 1.

8. There is no algorithm by which to distinguish between a high-level theory and one that operates at an intermediate level. We might consider, as examples of high-level theories, Kantianism and utilitarianism, and see legal illustrations in the many (academic) efforts to understand such areas as tort law, contract law, free speech, and the law of equality as undergirded by highly abstract theories of the right or the good. By low-level principles, I mean to refer to the general class of justifications that are not said to derive from any particular large theories of the right or the good, that have ambiguous relations to large theories, and that are compatible with one or more such theories.

9. See Joseph Raz, *The Morality of Freedom* (Oxford: Oxford University Press, 1985), p. 58.

10. 410 U.S. 113 (1973). On the refusal to overrule *Roe,* see *Planned Parenthood v. Casey,* 112 S. Ct. 2791 (1992).

11. This aspect of liberalism is emphasized in Charles Larmore, *Patterns of Moral Complexity* (Cambridge: Cambridge University Press, 1987).

12. See Elizabeth Anderson, *Value in Ethics and Economics* (Cambridge: Harvard University Press, 1993); Charles Taylor, *Philosophy and the Human Sciences* (Cambridge: Cambridge University Press, 1985), pp. 230, 243; Sen, "Plural Utility,"

Proceedings of the Aristotelian Society (vol. 81, 1981), p. 193; Cass R. Sunstein, "Incommensurability and Valuation in Law," *Michigan Law Review* (vol. 92, 1994), p. 779.

13. See Sen, supra note, and Amartya Sen, *Commodities and Capabilities* (New York: Elsevier Science Publishers, 1985) for examples.

14. See Gerald Rosenberg, *The Hollow Hope* (Chicago: University of Chicago Press, 1992).

15. See *Petermann v. International Brotherhood*, 344 P. 2d. 25 (Cal. 1959).

16. See *Brandenburg v. Ohio*, 395 U.S. 444 (1969).

17. See *Collin v. Smith*, 578 F. 2d. 1197 (7th Cir. 1978).

18. See *DeShaney v. Winnegago County*, 109 S. Ct. 998 (1989). In the legal examples, we are dealing with noninductive analogical reasoning. We are not making a prediction about likely facts in an unknown case, but instead making claims about how an as-yet-undecided case should be resolved in light of its similiarity to a decided or clear case.

19. Holmes, "Codes and the Arrangements of Law," *Harvard Law Review* (vol. 44, 1931), p. 725; reprinted from *American Law Review* (vol. 5, 1870), p. 11.

20. See Strauss, *Common Law Constitutionalism* (forthcoming).

21. The best discussion is Strauss (forthcoming); see also Wellington, "Common Law Rules and Constitutional Double Standards," *Yale Law Journal* (vol. 83, 1973), p. 221.

22. This is a widely shared view. For all of their differences, both Robert Bork, *The Tempting of America* (New York: Free Press, 1989), and Bruce Ackerman, *We the People* (Cambridge: Harvard University Press, 1991), accept it.

23. Alexander Meiklejohn, *Free Speech and its Relation to Self-Government* (New York: Harper, 1948).

24. See Raz, supra note. Arrow's Impossibility Theorem—see Kenneth Arrow, *Social Choice and Individual Values*—raises important problems for coherence theories in law, notably including Dworkin's account. I cannot discuss those problems here, but on a multimember judicial body, there may be serious cycling problems, in which, paradoxically, result *A* is favored over result *B*, which is favored over result *C*, which is (and here is the paradox) favored over result *A*; or decisions may turn, arbitrarily, on the order in which issues happen to arise ("path dependence"). See Frank Easterbrook, "Ways of Judging the Court," *Harvard Law Review* (vol. 95, 1982), pp. 802, 811–31. A strong theory of *stare decisis*, combined with a commitment to analogical thinking, may alleviate some of the cycling problems of path dependence. Idem at 817–21. The point suggests that it will be difficult to achieve real coherence through decentralized, multimember courts, and that the Hercules metaphor will run into real difficulty. A system built on analogical reasoning aspires to less and can diminish cycling, but the problem of path dependence will result in a high degree of arbitrariness.

25. Not all of them. Some starting-points are palpably confused or invidious, as in those that deny the basic equality, for political purposes, of all human beings.

DEMOCRACY AS CULTURE

> *Democracy is a word of many meanings. . . . [O]ne of the meanings . . . denotes a mode of government, a specified practice in selecting officials and regulating their conduct as officials. This is not the most inspiring of the different meanings of democracy; it is comparatively special in character. But it contains about all that is relevant to* political *democracy.*[1]
>
> John Dewey, LW 2, p. 286

Political democracy may not be the only meaning of "democracy," but has it not been profoundly inspiring? Have not wars and revolutions been fought so that the people might have a voice in saying who is to govern them? Is that not what all who labor under the yoke of tyranny yearn for?

Of course, desires of all kinds, including the yearnings of the oppressed, are directed at objects which may not be adequately understood. To succeed in business is not necessarily to put financial worries behind one. To marry is not necessarily to live happily ever after. A government of the people, *chosen by* the people is not necessarily a government *by* the people or *for* the people. Plato—no friend of Athenian democracy—could with equal degrees of irony and plausibility praise Athens for its aristocracy,

> a form of government which receives various names, according to the fancies of men, and is sometimes called democracy, but is really an aristocracy or government by the best which has the approval of the many (*Menexenus* 238cd).[2]

A government of the people, which is by the few, however great and good those few are and however enthusiastically they are approved by the people, will not necessarily be a government for the people.

119

If the best could be relied upon to govern for the people instead of in their own interests, then obviously it would be best for the best (at governing) to govern. But experience supports Lord Acton's grim maxim about the corrupting influence of power, and the lesson commonly drawn is that it is best, although not ideal in practice, for the people to choose those whom they regard as best able to govern on their behalf—which is not ideal in practice because the choice is commonly between representatives of special interests on whose behalf the elected will in fact govern. Political democracy, as this market in influence is known, is not after all such an inspiring reality. The hope for a government of the people, by the people, and for the people turns out in reality to be a government *by* a few, approved by a large number (not always a majority), *for* one or another coalition of special interests. And if, as often happens, the special interests check one another so that pressing problems go unresolved, ordinary citizens begin to hanker for a more authoritarian style of government.

The alternative of taking the etymology of "democracy" seriously and placing the responsibility for decision-making directly on the electorate[3] seems unworkable for multiple reasons. As interests fragment down to the individual voter, the chances of reaching a decision appear to decrease to a vanishing point. Society, moveover, is too complex; the details of the legal instruments needed to regulate it are too intricate; the effort needed to keep abreast in order to judge any of the many issues facing those who would vote is too time-consuming. Best to delegate responsibility, and appoint a limited number of representatives to decide on behalf of the people.

But the problem, as we have seen, is to ensure that the decisions of the delegated representatives are made in the interests of the people as a whole. Ideally, the people would approve only those officeholders best able to decide what will be best for the people as a whole. So the ideal democracy turns out to be precisely what Plato, engaging in ironic flattery, called Athens, "a true aristocracy . . . government by the best which has the approval of the many." Political democracy—ostensibly "by the people and for the people"—turns out not to work very democratically in practice, and the best form of it that can be imagined remains hard to distinguish from its supposed antithesis. Perhaps it takes suffering under the toils of tyranny to derive much inspiration from such a *faut de mieux.*

So what would be a more inspiring sense of "democracy"? What Dewey had in mind was not primarily a form of government—although it certainly could apply to the administrative structures of cities, districts, and nations—but rather a form of "associated living" (*LC*, p. 90)[4] or "the idea of community life itself" (*LW* 2, p. 328). Dewey here explicitly uses "idea" in a Platonic sense as a synonym of "ideal": what associated life would be if a recognizable tendency within it were carried out in full, completed, perfected (ibid.). The idea/ideal was that individuals should have a responsible share according to capacity in forming and directing the activities of the groups to which [they belong] and in participating according to need in the values which the groups sustain . . . in harmony with the interests and goods which are common (*LW* 2, pp. 327–8).[5]

The idea/ideal yields a criterion by which to judge "a habit, a custom, or an institution." It is

> to be judged good when it contributes positively to free intercourse, to un-hampered exchange of ideas, to mutual respect and friendship and love—in short, to those modes of behaving which make life richer and more worth living for everybody concerned; and conversely, any custom or institution which impedes progress towards these goals is to be judged bad (*LC*, p. 90).

It would not be inappropriate to say that this is a conception of democracy as a moral ideal. But lest current (individualistic) connotations of "moral" distort the point,[6] it is best to summarize by saying that what Dewey took to be a more inspiring sense of "democracy" was a form of culture—a set of practices, attitudes, and expectations, which, in an ideal society, would pervade every aspect of human interaction.

To see in greater detail what this idea(l) involves, we must consider three important components: community, publicity, and experimental rationality. All three terms, like "democracy," are easily misunderstood. "Community," for example, can nowadays be applied to any group of people who have something in common (e.g., "the handicapped community" or "the business community") regardless of whether they act together to further some common interest. For Dewey, a community is not merely a group of people with some common distinguishing feature; it is not even a group of people who work together because their joint activity satisfies their diverse individual desires. Dewey's community is a group of people who derive a significant portion of their satisfactions from the prosperity of the common enterprise in which they participate, and from the way in which it sustains not only those who contribute to it directly, but also more inclusive groups (the wider community).

People who work in a business only to satisfy their individual needs and desires will compete for the prestige and material rewards of advanced positions regardless of whether the enterprise would better prosper under another's direction. They will work to maximize what they can derive as benefits for themselves, indifferent to what it may cost their fellow workers. They will consider the impact of their business on the wider community only to the extent that it might affect what they derive from the enterprise. On the other hand, people who want to see some common enterprise succeed—and succeed by making a contribution to the well-being of those who do not contribute directly to that enterprise—will think carefully about what role they can best fill, and will neither reach for responsibility that they cannot handle nor decline to contribute when they are able. Since the satisfaction they take from participating is based in part on the benefits other people derive, their ambitions are not fulfilled by tactics that beggar their co-workers or their fellow citizens. Such people are able to constitute what Dewey would be prepared to call a "community," and if they are engaged in a manufacturing or service industry, their business would qualify as a community.[7] A society whose people took this attitude wherever and whenever they worked or acted together would constitute "The Great Community" (*LW* 2, p. 325ff.).

For this attitude to pervade any common undertaking, there has to be a certain level of communication between those involved. It is not possible to specify in advance the precise form that this communication should take; what goes on in a parliament, a town meeting or a board room is not uniquely appropriate in all circumstances. What can be said is that there must be, on the part of all participants, an awareness of the problems (requiring decisions) their joint undertaking faces, of the relevant circumstances and resources to meet those problems, of the apparently available courses of action, and of the consequences of each available course of action. In addition, there must be opportunities for each participant to contribute to the understanding of the problems, suggest resources, propose courses of action, and clarify the values in terms of which courses of action will be assessed. The guidance of the enterprise, in other words, must take place in a public space to which all have an appropriate degree of access. Community can only thrive on publicity. "Publicity" here clearly does not mean mind-numbing exposure to attention-grabbing tricks; it means what Dewey called "co-operative publicity" (*LC*, p. 170)[8]—the creation of an open space where common concerns are on display for, and contributions welcome from, all who share the concerns.

What takes place in this public space should, Dewey urged, be structured by the principles of "experimental rationality." His actual phrase was "experimental logic," but "logic" has since become closely associated with a project of reducing thought processes to mechanical steps represented by formal mathematical structures, which is quite the opposite of what Dewey was talking about. "Experimental rationality" is itself easily enough misunderstood. It invites confusion with "instrumental rationality," a harnessing of imagination and critical judgment in a single-minded pursuit of means to realize some antecedently determined goal. Indeed, experimental method has been diligently employed not only to settle theoretical questions, but to discover the means to material comforts and economic advantage. Dewey did not, however, regard either of these uses as essential to the method.

To be sure, experimental method (as Dewey sees it—see *LC*, pp. 248–49) does involve a search, not a search that is haphazard (trial and error), but one based on established experience, guided by a plan that is built around a hypothesis. The consequences of following the plan serve to test the hypothesis and suggest how it and subsequent plans based on it should be modified.

Hypotheses, for Dewey, are not confined to theoretical generalizations about the facts of nature; they also serve to articulate the values to be realized by an enterprise, and any expression of a value should be treated as a hypothesis. Using the method, the members of a community may not only apply their collective intelligence to gain mastery over their material circumstances, but may also consider how developing circumstances are affecting the values they hoped to realize through carrying out the plan and whether those developments call for a better articulation of their shared values. Experimental method has, in other words, an applicability in practical reasoning which extends well beyond the discovery of instrumental means.

The conscientious application of experimental method in a community would have two important consequences. On the one hand, it would reinforce the publicity on which community thrives.[9] A description of the results of an experiment (its bearing on any part of the plan that had the status of a hypothesis) has authority only to the extent that its appropriateness is evident to everyone with an interest in it. Experiments, the conduct and interpretation of which is not open to the community, are like ceremonies of divination (auguries and haruspicies) open instead to abuses of power.

On the other hand, the application of the experimental method keeps the ways by which decisions are made on behalf of the community from ossifying. When one group of people and one form of organization works well, and the community realizes some of the values it has been seeking, it is both natural and wise to try to preserve this pattern of success by making a tradition of it. But the value of tradition can easily be treated as intrinsic and come to conflict with the value of community itself, particularly where one segment seizes and holds onto an opportunity to pursue a particular interest and preserve privileges that do not contribute to the community as a whole. As Dewey told a Chinese audience in 1920, the experimental method

> is real conservatism in that it promotes the conservation of those aspects of the culture which have been verified by experiment, and it is real radicalism in that it does not hesitate to reject those aspects of traditional culture which do not stand up under experiment (*LC*, p. 249).

A genuine spirit of experiment is easy to smother by limiting the oxygen of publicity. Persuade enough people that it is not their responsibility, their role, their place to contribute to the determination of policy by interpreting events and prevailing values and the result will be a structure of power which is the antithesis of community—one which realizes the values of a privileged few and limits the possibilities of the rest.

To say that community, publicity, and experimental rationality articulate a conception of democracy as a form of culture is to acknowledge that one can look for the presence or absence of this pattern at all levels of society from union local to state legislature, from country club to congress, from the Women's Institute to the National Academy of Sciences. It is to recognize that whatever habits of initiative and deference people have acquired in one arena, they will carry into another. It is to expect that where the democratic pattern is absent, people whose reflex is always to ask "Who is in charge here?" will not be able to understand a collective decision. It is to realize that people who do not expect to participate in determining the direction of the groups to which they belong or share equitably in the benefits joint action brings about will view their roles with apathy and think no further than their private likes and dislikes.

Judging by the standards of this more thorough conception of democracy, no one can apply the term "democratic society" without deep misgivings. Few who live under systems of government that can boast of being political democracies, can also boast that these are more than empty forms. Voter turnout is commonly low—symptomatic of an apathy born of the experience of powerlessness. The choice, after all, is more often than not between competing interests and values in which ordinary citizens will share hardly at all. "Political democracy" works in practice as a safety device to preserve what with any degree of honesty can only be described as oligarchies: when the policies of one set of oligarchs become oppressive, the people have the opportunity to elect a different set. What pressure may have built up on the part of the people for a real say in how things are run bleeds off into hopes vested in a new regime—and this for the very good reason that experience of the alternative pattern is simply not salient. In school, at work, in church, at play, without thinking, without intending, people impose and accept patterns of dominance and deference. They "elect" officers far more frequently as a ritual confirmation of those patterns, than as an opportunity to examine the options that face them and the values that they as a group are pursuing.

Can anything be done to move a culture closer to the ideal of democracy? Should anything be done? The second question may appear to claim priority, but nevertheless consider first, briefly, a unique body of historical experience that bears on the first question. At the beginning of this century as the vigor of the Ch'ing (Manchu) dynasty waned, China found itself threatened by commercial and military imperialism from Japan and from several Western nations. The Chinese confronted the possibility that their traditional culture would not sustain their survival as a nation without an extensive overhaul. Events during the first two decades of the century ensured that relatively more of the Chinese who studied abroad would do so in the United States and that more of them would find their way to Columbia University, where John Dewey taught, than to any other American university.[10]

By 1919, there were already in China a number of these students who had returned from studying under or near John Dewey and had begun to propagate the message of *How We Think* (*MW* 6, pp. 177–356) and *Democracy and*

Education (*MW* 9). Hearing that Dewey was to visit Japan, some of his former students invited him to China for a visit that came to last for well over two years. Dewey arrived in time to catch a wave of popular discontent, which crested on the fourth of May, 1919,[11] and popular receptivity augmented by these events together with assiduous efforts on the part of his Chinese sponsors combined to give Dewey and his views maximum public exposure.

Dewey was almost certainly the foreign thinker who was most widely heard and read in China during the early 1920s, although that may not have meant a great deal. Only those who attended his lectures heard his words translated into Chinese; only the literate, estimated at 2 percent of the population,[12] could read reports of what he had said. It is less instructive to ask whether Dewey's message came near to reaching a critical mass of the Chinese people than to inquire how Dewey's sponsors operated and what happened to them. They were, after all, the sole channel through which Dewey's thought went out and the primary testament that what he was saying was relevant to China's situation.

It cannot be said that, in translating and publishing records of Dewey's lectures, his sponsors distorted the message. We have no record of what Dewey said in English, but translations from Chinese into English of what he was reported to have said (*LC* and *ALC*) sound very like him and constitute a reliable primer of his philosophy. Nor do Dewey's disciples appear to have been predisposed to distort the message. Already in 1911, while still a student at Berkeley (before going on to Columbia), Chiang Meng-lin had specified the problem very precisely. "Our motto [has been] this: A government of the people by the educated class, and for the people. To change 'by the educated class' into 'by the people' is our new political philosophy."[13]

It is, of course, much easier to articulate a new political philosophy such as this than to put it into practice. At what point is the *demos* mature enough to take up the burden of *kratos*? The educated classes believe that they have seen the goal, but also believe that they have seen the obstacles that obscure it for others. It would appear that the new philosophy cannot be implemented immediately. As Hu Shih put it in 1915,

> The best form of government for a somewhat benighted country like China, it seems to the present writer, is one which will enable the enlightened class of people to utilize their knowledge and talents for the education and betterment of the ignorant and the indifferent.[14]

This might be a symptom of an incurable elitism which in the long run prevented the *praxis* of Dewey's followers from ever measuring up to the message of Dewey's philosophy.[15] It might equally be an indication that Hu grasped Dewey's message that democracy is a form of culture and was not fool enough to think its practice could arise spontaneously from a society bound by thousands of years of undemocratic tradition.

Hu, as "the spearhead and amazingly vital leader of the *pai hua* move-ment,"[16] made his goal a literate and well-informed populace. Literacy in China, he realized, could not advance until there was a widely accepted writ-ten version of the spoken language (*pai hua*); the ordinary citizen could not be expected to learn what was in effect the dead language of the classical tra-dition (*kuo wen*) in order to read. The movement was successful in promot-ing written *pai hua,* even if this did not lead immediately to widespread literacy. But did the tireless Hu set his sights too low? He saw, on the one hand, the need for cultural reform (literacy) as well as the first step that needed to be taken and, on the other hand, the thorough corruption of the warlord governments that had replaced imperial authority. He urged his fel-low reformers to abstain from even discussing politics for twenty years.[17] Was this to enshrine the very sort of dualism (politics and culture) that Dewey con-tinually fought, or merely a pragmatic decision to invest energies where there was some hope of progress?

Chiang, who as writer and editor "assumed the role of a chief ideologist"[18] of the education reform movement in China, twice served for extended pe-riods as acting chancellor of Beijing National University (*Peita*). Caught as he was between recalcitrant students and obdurate government, his experiences injected increasing tones of pessimism and despair into his writing. Kuo Ping-wen, the first Chinese scholar to earn a doctorate from Teacher's College at Columbia, became president of Nanjing Higher Normal School and suc-ceeded in having it raised to the status of the National Southeastern Univer-sity. But Kuo could not keep his institution independent of political affiliation, and when (in 1925) the showdown came between the Kuomintang and the local warlord, his opponents within his own university found the leverage to have him dismissed and thereby terminated his influence on ed-ucation. Politics is only one aspect of general culture, but political power can effectively frustrate general cultural reform. (See note 22 below.)

Nor does one escape the constraints of political power by descending from the office of the president of a university to the grass roots. T'ao Hsing-chih, arguably the man who came to have the deepest appreciation of how Dewey's message should apply to China,[19] concluded, after years of writing, editing, and organizing teacher's associations, that the campaign had to be taken di-rectly to the people. He pointed out to Chiang how embarrassing it was that the acting chancellor of China's leading university should have illiterates in his household and proceeded to teach Chiang's butler and other staff to read.[20] To overcome the barriers created by his privileged education, he adopted peasant clothes (cotton tunic and leggings, and watermelon skull-cap). Distressed by events (particularly the sacking of Kuo), T'ao worked ex-clusively at the village level after 1925. In 1927, he founded an experimental school outside Nanjing, where potential teachers had to join peasants in their daily work and where, as an illustration of the "union of teaching, learning and doing," village meetings were held which included the teachers and were presided over by students from the school.[21] T'ao's school was closed by Kuomintang troops in 1930—yet another illustration of how political power constrains the possibilities of cultural reform.

Early conflict with the authorities (arrest, prison, and exile to the International Settlement in Shanghai) may well have pushed Ch'en Tu-hsiu to a conclusion that others of the group, which had enthusiastically translated and endorsed Dewey's words in 1919, could fully appreciate only after years of fruitless effort: that a culture is inseparable from the system of power and privilege it embodies. It is not possible to leave that system intact and change the culture either from a privileged position within that system or from beneath it.[22] Ch'en embraced Marxism and became a founding member of the Chinese Communist Party. After four decades of revolutionary struggle and consolidation, the Communist Party was in a position to conduct one of the most extensive experiments in social engineering ever attempted. Regrettably, the Cultural Revolution focused on breaking China's age-old patterns of dominance and deference, rather than on fostering cooperative publicity and experimental rationality. But one cannot look at what appear to be the lasting effects of the Cultural Revolution without a profound sense of the limitations on what can be done to change a culture by "politics in command."[23]

Most nations in the northern hemisphere today do not have a mass of illiterate peasants and do not need to reform their written language before they can even begin to tackle the problem of social reform. There are problems of functional illiteracy which are insufficiently appreciated, but the most serious obstacles that confront those who would spread the idea(l) of a democratic culture are rather the very well-functioning channels of communication that daily reinforce a complacency about existing political institutions, a set of assumptions about the most that can be expected of the motives of those who accept the responsibility of wielding power within those institutions, and anxieties about demands being made by other segments of society—channels of communication which reinforce all of that and which, incidentally, provide a great deal of distraction as well. Freedom of expression is now an accepted norm, but only a few are heard above the cacophony. Many nations of the North are relatively free of political repression, but everywhere there is a widespread feeling of powerlessness.

The experience of Dewey's Chinese disciples is relevant to those who wish to promote a genuinely democratic culture not because they face the same problems, but because the available avenues of action remain very similar. One can work from a position of privilege within existing institutions and discover how few degrees of freedom are afforded even by a tolerant institution and how intense will be the pressure to live the values that sustain that institution. One can go to the grass roots and discover in time how hard it is to propagate what a system of power and privilege must regard as weeds. One can reach for sufficient political power—difficult in a system that survives by repeatedly dissipating potential concentrations of power in the hands of a few identifiable people—and if fortunate enough to succeed, discover that changing the direction of a culture is at least as difficult as changing that of a supertanker.

"The Dewey Experiment in China" must be encouraging to those who were inclined to answer "no" to the question postponed above: Should anything be done to move our culture closer to the democratic ideal? Whether they are content with what power and privileges they have managed to amass for themselves or simply have no faith that any but the most exceptional of human beings (saints) can constitute a genuine community at any level of society, the Chinese experience should reassure them that little can be done. Cynics will point to recent events and claim that they turn on its head the rhetoric Dewey used before a Chinese audience in 1920:

> Why do men work for democratic governments? Is it just because under a democratic government they pay less in taxes, or enjoy a higher standard of living? Quite the contrary. . . . Men struggle to achieve democratic government because they want to have a voice in the determination of their own destiny . . . (*LC*, p. 165).[24]

There is little doubt that not everyone who has recently called for "more democracy" has been demanding participation in Dewey's Great Community, and little to suggest that what real grass roots democracy that there is[25] will soon make the prairie bloom in any but the most sporadic fashion. Indeed, those of us who would answer "yes" to the "Should we?" question must avoid either illusions about the hearts of our fellow men or faith in the destiny of true democracy, but we must nevertheless at least try to stay clear in our minds about what our ideal entails.

NOTES

1. References to the writings of John Dewey will be given in the text as follows:

MW   The Middle Works, 1899–1924 in fifteen volumes (Carbondale: Southern Illinois University Press, 1978).

LW   The Later Works, 1924–1952 in seventeen volumes (Carbondale: Southern Illinois University Press, 1984).

LC   Lectures in China, Robert W. Clopton and Tsuin-Chen Ou, trans. & eds. (Honolulu: University of Hawai'i Press, 1973).

ALC   Additional Lectures in China, translated by Robert W. Clopton and Tsuin-Chen Ou, typescript archive [B945 D41 C55] and microfilm [SO1453], Honolulu, HI, Hamilton Library, University of Hawai'i at Manoa.

2. The basis of the plausibility was the function of the Areopagite Council, chosen for life by the assembly from among "knights," which acted as a constitutional court, and which frequently thwarted the assembly. See A. R. Burn, *The Pelican History of Greece* (Harmondsworth: Penguin Books, 1966), p. 157. The irony is to be found in Plato's belief that Athens had never discovered how to identify the men best qualified to govern it. If Plato does not have the Areopagite Council specifically in mind, but is thinking rather of the function of the demagogues (the few whose policies were approved by the many), there may be a further, much heavier irony in this funeral oration that Socrates claims to have heard from Aspasia, the mistress of Pericles.

3. It appears impractical, given the size of our cities and the career and employment expectations of individuals, to involve anything like the proportion of ordinary citizens (i.e., not continuously on a government payroll) in the day-to-day running of civic affairs that the Athenians achieved under the reforms of Kleisthenes (Burn, p. 156). Nevertheless, the idea that even momentous decisions with far-ranging implications should be referred to the electorate as a whole appears to have hardly any place in the constitutions of countries that claim to be democratic.

4. Given the use that I propose to make later of the reception of Dewey's philosophy in China, I will, where possible, cite from *LC* and *ALC*. In China, Dewey was inclined to treat political democracy as a less qualified source of inspiration. For example, his recommendation of democratic politics and its three fundamental rights (of person, property, and free thought) to the Private Fukien College of Law and Administration (Spring 1921, *ALC*, pp. 87–90) is fulsome. But the contrast with what democracy might yet be is already clearly present in his thought. He closes by saying, "democratic politics in any full sense of the term is still in its beginning stages, and has not been adequately developed anywhere, even in the West."

5. This 1927 formulation is an echo of that Dewey used in *Democracy and Education* (1916), *MW* 9, p. 89. Some of the illustrative material in the surrounding context ("robber band") is the same.

Those who are prone to confuse Dewey's communitarianism with welfare statism or his "social democracy" with "democratic socialism" would find a useful corrective in, for example, the lecture he gave to the Fukien Shang-iou Club (July 1921, *ALC*, pp. 83–88), where he urges not only cooperative self-help, but in effect cautions against what conservatives now stigmatize as "the culture of dependency" on central government.

6. Bear in mind that Dewey and his colleague James Tufts had defined morality as a reflective response to the customs and usages that constitute the *mores* of a society (the backbone of its culture) and for them "complete morality" included a commitment to "a progressive social development in which every member of society shall share" (*MW* 5, pp. 7, 74).

7. This is what is supposed to distinguish a "cooperative" from a privately owned company. Cooperatives may or may not conduct their affairs in a way that is mindful of the wider community, but only the former would satisfy Dewey's criterion. State-owned enterprises are ostensibly operated only with a view to serving the wider community and are thus not commonly structured to foster community among their employees.

8. Dewey's discussion on this and the following page of the reported lecture indicates clearly that when he called for improvements in the arts of communication—as

he did frequently throughout his career—he did not have material technology primarily in mind, but rather cultural forms by means of which individuals might convey to one another both the facts as they perceived them and their thoughts about how to proceed in the light of those facts.

9. The relationship between experiments and the public which is to certify the authority of their results has not received the attention it deserves by philosophers of science. A notable exception is to be found in the account that Steven Shapin and Simon Schaffer give, in *Leviathan and the Air Pump* (Cambridge: Cambridge University Press, 1985), of the debates between Hobbes and the Royal Society (in particular, Robert Boyle) over the status of experiments designed to prove the possibility of a vacuum.

10. See Barry Keenan, *The Dewey Experiment in China: Educational Reform and Political Power in the Early Republic* (Cambridge: Council on East Asian Studies Harvard University, 1977), pp. 14–21.

11. See Chow Tse-tsung, *The May Fourth Movement* (Cambridge: Harvard University Press, 1960), for a history of the movement to which that date gave its name. Dewey in fact had arrived in China three days before and was lecturing in Shanghai when the unrest erupted in Beijing. Within a year, the circle of Chinese scholars that had sponsored him came to regard the continuing unrest as serving only to interfere with their goal of deeper cultural reform and were urging students to return to their studies.

12. Chiang Meng-lin, one of Dewey's followers (see below), estimated that only 25 percent of those who could read were reading the May Fourth periodicals in which Dewey's lectures were published, which meant that one-half of one percent of China's population received Dewey's message (Keenan, op. cit., pp. 70–1). Chiang used this calculation to call into question Hu Shih's policy (see below) of staying aloof from political involvement.

13. Keenan, op. cit., p. 123.

14. Ibid.

15. It is alleged that the practice of the circle of Dewey's Chinese sponsors was often very elitist. Nancy F. Sizer, in "The Failure of Chinese Educational Leadership 1919–1930," *History of Education Quarterly* (vol. 19, 1979), pp. 381–92, relates (on p. 386) how Hu Shih, after a lecture at the Beijing National University, refused to answer a question from Mao Tse-tung, who worked in the university library, because Mao was not enrolled as a student.

Dewey may not himself have been sufficiently careful to match his *praxis* and that of his progressive associates in the United States to either his rhetoric or his ideals. This at least is the burden of several historical studies done over recent decades. See, for example, items 14, 31, 34, 47, and 61 in J. E. Tiles, ed., *John Dewey: Critical Assessments* in four volumes (London: Routledge, 1992).

16. Sizer, op. cit., p. 385.

17. Keenan, op. cit., p. 26. Keenan raises the question whether this was a move that implicitly followed the Confucian advice to the gentleman to stay out of politics when the way does not prevail in the state. The circle associated with Dewey, however, hardly allowed themselves "to be folded up and safely put away" (*Analects* XV 7). To be sure, the emphasis on culture as the foundation of good government is Confucian, but Confucius nowhere suggests that cultural reform can be brought about

through any means other than the example of a virtuous ruler. The reform movement did appeal to Confucius where convenient for rhetorical effect, but by no means should be thought of as a new neo-Confucianism. "In particular [Chiang] singled out the Confucian precept *jen* (benevolence), which, as a principle of governing, embraced the ideal of peace but treated the people as flocks of animals to be shepherded. As Chiang saw it, the fundamental system of values required change" (ibid., p. 63; cf., pp. 68–69).

18. Ibid., p. 63.

19. Keenan considers the extent of T'ao's departures from Dewey's doctrines. But there is little in the account of T'ao's thinking after 1923 that is not already explicit in lectures Dewey gave during his two years in China. Compare the accounts given in Keenan's chapter IV with, for example, *ALC*, pp. 185–97 (Lecture before the students of the Normal School at the Headquarters of the 10th Regiment of the Infantry of the Shan-si Army, October 12, 1919). T'ao's innovation was to couple the "bottom-up" theory of Deweyan democracy with a "bottom-up" praxis of reform, instead of trying to change things by reaching down from the office of the chancellor of a university.

20. Keenan, op. cit., p. 92.

21. Ibid., pp. 100–1.

22. Keenan (ibid., p. 154) summarizes as follows the argument of an article that Ch'en published on May Day 1921, and in which he disputes Hu Shih's policy of political abstinence: "the idea of falling back on the separation of culture from politics as a strategic ploy, while expecting the real connection between the two to begin political reform, was unrealistic."

23. "Unlike the cultural revolution in the People's Republic of China in the 1960s, the ingredient missing in Chiang [Meng-lin]'s plan was 'politics in command'. Political power was totally out of the reformers' control, in fact, and acted relentlessly to frustrate cultural reform efforts" (Keenan, ibid., p. 72).

24. It is plausibly suggested that what brought about the reunification of Germany was not a desire on the part of East Germans for a voice in their own destiny, but their constant exposure to images of the standard of living enjoyed by West Germans.

25. For current grassroots examples of what the authors believe is " 'living democracy' where citizens participate in public life, defining a culture of shared responsibility, and values," consult Frances Moore Lappé and Martin DuBois, *The Quickening of America: Rebuilding Our Nation, Remaking Our Lives* (San Francisco: Jossey-Bass, 1994).

Ted Honderich

HIERARCHIC DEMOCRACY AND THE NECESSITY OF MASS CIVIL DISOBEDIENCE

If we make an uncontroversial list of the liberal democracies, certainly including the United States and Great Britain, and if we then try to conceive of or understand them in a general way, we may arrive at what can be called the Ordinary Conception of them. It boils down to three propositions.[1]

1. The people, legitimately influenced during an election, choose representatives who promise certain policies, and afterwards the people legitimately influence the elected representatives.
2. There is universal suffrage in the election—one person, one vote—and approximate equality in both the influencing of the people during the election and their subsequent influencing of the elected representatives.
3. The society's actual policies are chosen by the representatives in accordance with their promises, and the policies do take effect.

The Ordinary Conception is no good.[2] For starters there is the embarrassing electoral fact that in liberal democracies it is typically not the people who vote and thereby choose the representatives, but only about half of the people. There is also the fact—partly having to do with governmental structure and perhaps the rulings of a Supreme Court—that the society's actual policies can rarely be regarded as just the policies promised by the elected representatives. A third fact is that the choosing of representatives in the election is far better seen as made not by individuals, as the Ordinary Conception supposes, but by groups of individuals with a common interest—by interest groups. This third fact is fundamental. Indeed, the first two facts, about who actually votes and about actual policies being different from promised policies, are also better described in terms of interest groups and a history of them.

133

Such a criticism of the Ordinary Conception is not unusual. If you remain inclined to go on thinking about individuals rather than groups of them, several simple reminders may give you pause. One is that understanding and explaining anything whatever is typically served by generalization, the use of general categories. No one dreams of explaining brain function only in terms of single neurons, or of characterizing a Dickens novel sentence by sentence, or of writing a history of a war in terms of individual soldiers as against platoons, regiments, and armies. The second reminder has to do with organization. Interest groups need not be organized, but some are. A collection of individuals with a common interest or purpose achieves more when somehow organized. Fully to explain some outcome, you may really have to attend to facts of organization and hence groups.

What can be called the Pluralist Conception of the liberal democracies also boils down to three propositions.[3]

1. Interest groups legitimately influence the choosing and do the choosing of representatives who promise policies, and after the election legitimately influence them.
2. There is universal suffrage, and there is approximate equality among the groups.
3. Actual social policies are chosen by the representatives, to some degree mindful of their promises, and the policies take effect to a considerable degree.

This conception is like the Ordinary Conception in sharing a feature with pretty well all conceptions of liberal democracy. Almost all conceivers or definers of liberal democracy introduce into it an idea of equality. One reason is etymology, usage, and political tradition, all of which associate democracy with equality. Another reason is that democracies involve *more* political equality than do dictatorships and oligarchies. A third is that the definers of democracy want the kind of government that they are conceiving to be true to, or defendable by, certain general principles about equality.

Those who favor something like the Pluralist Conception of the liberal democracies, however, are also under a certain pressure: the real world. For starters, mass communicators like Mr. Rupert Murdoch have more influence on elections and on what happens subsequently than, say, London bus drivers, let alone London beggars. That is to say, of course, that the mass communicators have more legitimate influence, influence owed to activities in accord with the rule of law. So those who favor something like the Pluralist Conception cannot take the liberal democracies to involve any plain or downright equality. What they say instead, in a variety of ways, is what is said in the second and vague proposition of the Pluralist Conception: There is *approximate* equality among the interest groups.

Is the Pluralist Conception better than the Ordinary Conception? Above all, is it better at explaining how a society comes to have its actual policies? Not much. The conception is vague, and hence far from really explanatory. It is vague about more than equality. It is vague about what we are to count as the interest groups. All that we have so far is the idea that the voters and influencers divide into such groups, each with a common interest. We do not know what they are, let alone what degrees of power or influence they have. Are we to think of men as constituting such a group? Property owners? Farmers? People in a geographical region? Mass communicators? Leftists? Churchgoers who are gun owners? All is uncertainty here.

Let us try again.

In the liberal democracies, there are great differences between tenths of population ranked in terms of wealth. The tenth of the population that is richest has between 52 percent (in Sweden) and 70 or 72 percent (in Great Britain and the United States) of the society's total personal wealth. The poorest tenth has barely any wealth worth speaking of, far less than 1 percent.[4] So the richest tenth has some large multiple of roughly 60 times as much wealth as the poorest tenth. As for income, the best paid tenth has between about five (in Scandinavia) and twelve times (in the United States) as much as the worst paid tenth.[5] It would be partly a technical job for economists, and one that they seem not to have undertaken, but obviously someone's wealth and income could be combined into a single summative measure. Thus we can consider a new ranking in terms of what might be called *economic power.* Without further ado, let me offer a proposition which is certainly an underestimate, maybe a grotesque underestimate. It is that the top tenth of the population has at least 30 times the economic power of the bottom tenth.

Economic power correlates with fundamental things. That is why it is important. The thing relevant now is *political power,* understood as power legitimately to influence and to enter into the process which issues in a society's actual policies. How strong is this correlation in ordinary circumstances? That will depend on which determinants of political power cluster together with economic power. At least most do, partly because at least most of these determinants of political power can be bought. Let me mention just two different ones: knowledge, as against confusion and ignorance, and constraints on the range of promised policies really on offer in an election, whatever wider range the law or the constitution may allow.

Without further ado, let me offer another proposition about the top and bottom tenths of the population in terms of economic power. It is that in ordinary circumstances the top tenth has at least 15 times the political power of the bottom tenth. There is this hierarchy in political power, determined or pretty well determined by a hierarchy in economic power. This is fast political science, following on fast economics. For several reasons, it seems to me no apology is needed. It is the economists and political scientists who have to catch up, not we who have to slow down. Real life, and real death, have to be thought about, as best we can.

The Pluralist Conception of the liberal democracies, as we saw, is vague about both equality and interest groups. This can now be remedied—by making a reasoned judgment as to the identity of the *dominant* interest groups in ordinary circumstances, the interest groups that dominate the process that issues in actual social policies. I happen to be no Marxist, or ex-Marxist, or market-Marxist either. You need not be any of these to conclude that the dominant interest groups are best thought of as exactly all the ten tenths of the population in terms of their economic power. We thus come to a third conception of the liberal democracies, one that is also a lot clearer about equality.

1. Interest groups identified in terms of economic power are dominant both in legitimately influencing the choosing of representatives who promise policies, and in doing the choosing, and in the legitimate influencing after the election of the representatives.
2. There is universal suffrage, but gross inequality among the interest groups in the influencing and choosing, with the best-off interest group or tenth of the population having at least 15 times the political power of the worst-off.
3. Actual social policies are chosen by the representatives, to some degree mindful of their promises, and the policies are somewhat effective.

That is the Hierarchic Conception of the liberal democracies.[6] Or, as we can say, referring not to the tokens or particular systems but to the type, that is Hierarchic Democracy. It assigns an explanatory dominance to the hierarchy of interest groups identified by economic power or, of course, the lack of it. The idea is not that the upper tenths have more political power, which is, of course, true. It is that all *these* groups, including the ones at the bottom with small or insignificant amounts of power, dominate the process that issues in a society's actual policies. It is all these groups, not other groups that we can think about—men or Leftists or whatever—that are important. You can almost always explain actual policies on the basis of these groups alone. I will not try to be precise about or make a quantifying guess about the dominance of the chosen interest groups. As you will gather, I propose not to be put off saying what seems to me to be true by the difficulty of being precise and, more generally, by the difficulty of satisfying political scientists.

Let me just glance at one question in this connection. I have taken voters and influencers only as members of the ten economic interest groups. Could it be that voters and influencers in the top tenth have in the end somewhat less than 15 times the political power of the voters and influencers in the bottom tenth because the members of each tenth are also members of other interest groups? The truth is almost certainly just the opposite. Members of the top tenth are more likely to be members of other groups that are more rather than less influential. They are more likely to be members of more influential rather than less influential racial groups, for example. So with geographical groups and employer-employee groups.

Consider now Hierarchic Democracy's actual policies and, more important, the contribution of those policies to the satisfaction and frustration of fundamental human desires, desires not only of its own citizens but also of people elsewhere. To my mind, there are six of these connected desires.

We all want to live, to have lives of decent length. We want them for ourselves and for those close to us. In the hierarchic democracies, and mainly because of those systems of government, the lives of the poor are shortened, by something like six years.[7] This fact comes together with another one more awful—that the hierarchic democracies in the economically developed world continue to have a large role in securing cut-off lives for people elsewhere, say parts of Africa. The life expectancy for males in a number of African countries is not about 72, as in Great Britain and the United States, but not much over forty. In Sierra Leone it was recently 39.4. It is as if these men were of a different species.[8]

We all want not only the means that make for lives of decent length, but the further means that make for a certain quality of material life. The hierarchic democracies in the developed world deliver, for some of their citizens, only food and drink for something like subsistence. They deliver wretched rooms, if rooms at all, and grim environments, chronic bad health, no means of travel, nothing much to sweeten life. Our hierarchic democracies, too, continue to be more than implicated in the grisly deprivations of this kind suffered by other societies, say river blindness and child labor.

We all want freedom and power, of various kinds. To speak of political freedom, what the hierarchic democracies give to their own citizens is gross inequality. That is the nature of these political systems. If we need to remember that this inequality is better than dictatorship or oligarchy, we also need to remember that it is appallingly inferior to other possible systems of democracy. As for the contribution of our own hierarchic democracies, say the United States and Great Britain, to freedom and power in many other societies, two policies are followed. Our governments seek to advance Hierarchic Democracy where that suits the interests they serve, and they support dictatorship and oligarchy where that does so. Latin America has been invaded by the United States about 100 times in this century.[9]

We all want respect and self-respect. In a number of our hierarchic democracies over the past decade, to mention but one relevant fact, millions of men and women have been denied the minimal dignity of a job. Most of the governments in question have not taken perfectly possible direct action, historically proven, to alleviate this destruction of morale. It is as if the New Deal had never happened. Their international economic policies have entrenched poor countries and peoples in the debt and poverty that perpetuates something near to denigration and self-denigration.

We all want to be together with other people. That is, we want satisfactory personal or familial and also wider human relationships. These are in important ways dependent on the satisfaction and frustration of the fundamental desires already noted. In the hierarchic democracies, to speak only of the desire for a sense of membership in a society, it is frustrated for many by poverty and powerlessness.

We all want, finally, the goods of culture. No one would prefer ignorance or incompetence or shallowness, whatever disdain they may pretend to have for what has been denied to them. For some in the hierarchic democracies, education is made difficult, entertainment trivial, and group traditions unsustaining. With respect to this desire for culture, and the desire for human relationships just mentioned, there is little need to speak of the grim contribution our hierarchic democracies have made to the problems of other societies.

So much for a brief account of the contribution of the actual policies of our hierarchic democracies to the satisfaction and frustration of fundamental desires. The account should not come as a surprise. It is something that might have been expected of systems of government and societies that are instances of Hierarchic Democracy, systems dominated by the general fact of grossly unequal economic and political power. It is worth remarking, too, that these actual policies constitute an argument for the correctness of the Hierarchic as against any other conception of our systems of government. These are not the sorts of policies that would suggest that our systems are correctly described by either the Ordinary Conception or the Pluralist Conception of liberal democracies.

Something needs to be added. The contributions of our hierarchic democracies to the cutting-off and deadening of lives would remain criminal if, as so many have hoped, those contributions were slowly decreasing. That is, the situation would remain criminal if it were slowly improving. The truth is that since about 1979 the conditions of life about which we are thinking have been worsened. England has been dragged down by vicious politicians. The United States has used still less of its wealth to help even unlucky Americans, let alone anyone else.[10] We pass by a certain dismal truth too quickly now, like the Oxfam photographs. The truth is that since about 1979 the poor have been made poorer while the rich have been made richer. No amount of callous dissembling touches the fact. It is made plain even by the research departments of the governments of selfishness in question.[11] As a result, the poor are dying younger than before.[12] Samuel Johnson was right to say that a decent provision for the poor is the true test of civilization.[13] We might add that reducing an indecent provision for the poor is the true test of barbarism.

The account given of Hierarchic Democracy's contributions to satisfaction and frustration, as you will have noted, has not been a merely factual one. It has implied a moral judgement. Let me make that judgement or feeling more explicit by setting out a principle from which it derives. That is the Principle of Equality.[14] In one bare formulation, it is as follows:

> We should have effective policies which make well-off those who are badly-off—policies which will remove individuals from the class of the badly-off—and we should seek to act on these policies partly by having certain practices of equality.

The principle depends on definitions of being badly-off and well-off, which can be stipulated in terms of satisfaction and frustration of the fundamental human desires at which we have glanced. The principle applies to human beings generally, and the policies it mentions are not necessarily policies of democratic governments however conceived. The policies are these: (i) increasing the total of means to satisfaction, (ii) transferring means from the well-off without significantly affecting their position, which is certainly possible, (iii) transferring means that *do* affect their position, and, no less important, (iv) reducing demands by social contributors, including entrepreneurs and the like, for favorable economic incentives or inequalities.

The Principle of Equality seems to me the foundation of a decent morality. It may bring to mind what is perhaps the best-known political philosophy of the late twentieth century, that of John Rawls, and in particular his principles of justice.[15] Let me distinguish the Principle of Equality and say a word or two for it.

It is not subordinate to or constrained by any other principle. The principle that is most like it in Rawls' philosophy *is* subordinate to a principle of traditional individual liberties, including a liberty having to do with private property. Rather, the Principle of Equality incorporates a limited respect for such liberties. This is primarily a matter of its attention to the fundamental desire for freedom and power.

Further, the Principle of Equality differs from the particular principle in Rawls' philosophy that is most like it, the Difference Principle. This specifies allowable and obligatory socio-economic differences or inequalities between people. The Difference Principle states, in sum, that we may and must have any socio-economic differences or inequalities that make a worst-off group better-off than it would be without those differences. The idea behind this is that some people may demand favorable socio-economic inequalities in return for their contributions to society, but other people benefit from the contributions. The most familiar variant of the principle in ordinary political thinking is that we are to have any inequalities in wealth that make the poorest less poor than they would be without the inequalities. That is a thought closely related to the "trickle-down theory."

The Difference Principle seems to me wonderfully indeterminate. It is a striking instance of the hesitancy and uncertainty of liberalism. What I have in mind is that, despite some of Rawls' remarks to the contrary,[16] it appears to justify, indeed oblige us to have, wholly different possible societies. This depends on what silent assumptions are made about the demands of social contributors. Hence it makes no determinate recommendation about societies. Let me show this.

Imagine a society where social contributors simply do not demand favorable socio-economic inequalities for their contributions, which is to say extrinsic incentives, and where socio-economic goods are distributed absolutely equally. This society would have the full support of the Principle of Difference. So, on the given assumption about certain demands, the principle justifies a society of utopian egalitarianism. Now imagine a society in which social contributors are more rapacious than social contributors in our societies. They demand rewards that are in excess, whatever degree of excess, of the rewards demanded in our own societies. It is a society of whatever degree of socio-economic inegalitarianism. This, it seems, is also justified by the Difference Principle.

The Principle of Equality, if it has not been so impressively elaborated as Rawls' principle, is in this crucial respect different. It is fundamental to it, as remarked, that we reduce demands by social contributors for economic rewards. It recommends the formation of and reliance on intrinsic rather than extrinsic incentives. It is therefore greatly less indeterminate. As you will have gathered, I take it to be more morally defensible than Rawls' Difference Principle and his liberal political philosophy generally.

Let us take stock. We have an understanding of the liberal democracies, the Hierarchic Conception. We have an idea of the contributions of our hierarchic democracies to fundamental satisfactions and frustrations, and of the worsening situation. We also have a principle by which to judge these political systems and their contributions, the Principle of Equality. That brings us to the question of whether those of us whose moral convictions are in some accord with the Principle of Equality should support Hierarchic Democracy. Should we be Hierarchic Democrats?[17]

One alternative that may come to mind is support for what there is reason to call Egalitarian Democracy—which is to say, for people's democracies or the Communist system. Another idea, certainly a better one, is support for Third Ways in politics and economics—Third Ways being compromises between Hierarchic and Egalitarian Democracy.[18] These are not the alternatives I wish to consider. My main reason is not that Egalitarian Democracy has been disproved by the battle between West and East and the fall of Communism, as some absurdly say, or that both these alternatives may seem to be utopian dreams. In fact, I am attracted to Third Ways. Rather, one of my reasons has to do with a certain concern for means rather than ends, with the means to getting one or another of certain governmental and economic systems rather than a specific system chosen in advance as the end.

There is nothing unusual about this concern. It is in fact often the case that we can and should make up our minds about a means before we have made up or can possibly make up our minds about a specific end. There may be a strong or even overwhelming case for trying to move in some general direction, toward a set of possible outcomes, between which we have not made a final choice, and may never have the chance of making a final choice. These outcomes, as in the present case, may have as their most important characterization just that any of them would be more morally tolerable than the situation in which we find ourselves.

Should we then adopt some means, other than or in addition to just the means of Hierarchic Democracy, of moving toward better systems of government and societies of moral decency? More particularly, should we adopt means *other than legitimate ones*? That is, should we adopt means other than those in accordance with the rule of law? Still more particularly, should we, in our hierarchic democracies, not limit ourselves to influencing voters and governments by activities in accordance with the rule of law?

These questions may lead you to think of a worn answer—violent revolution, or the replacement of a hierarchic democracy with an egalitarian democracy by means of force. But, as already implied in what was said about means and ends, I do put aside the worn answer. Another reason for doing so is my belief that, whatever may have been true in the past, a kind of compromise with our hierarchic democracies is now, and will continue to be, essential to progress toward moral decency. The supposed means of violent revolution is, in fact, now no means at all, since it is bound to be defeated by violence and repression. It would be wrong on this ground alone, without reference to anything about means and ends or to any evils or shortcomings of Egalitarian Democracy itself.

Hence there remain two possible additional means to moral progress. One means is another kind of political violence. In at least its defiance of legitimacy, it is in conflict with Hierarchic Democracy, but it does not aim at replacing it with Egalitarian Democracy.[19] The second means, of which I shall have more to say, is *mass civil disobedience and noncooperation*. It, too, since civil disobedience departs from the rule of law, is in conflict with Hierarchic Democracy. But it too does not aim at replacing Hierarchic with Egalitarian Democracy.

Mass civil disobedience, for present purposes, is to be understood as consisting in actions by very many people in a hierarchic democracy—actions aimed at effecting change in the society's policies, but not at the establishing of Egalitarian Democracy. The actions are illegal but nonviolent. Also, those who commit the offences in question do not seek to conceal the fact, and they do not seek to avoid the penalties involved.[20] Mass noncooperation, for present purposes, is to be understood as consisting in actions having the same aim, but actions that are legal. The particular civil disobedience and noncooperation that is relevant, of course, is the kind directed at the change intimated earlier—the satisfaction of fundamental human desires, satisfaction that is morally imperative and called for by the Principle of Equality.

What will come to mind as historical examples of civil disobedience are the Civil Rights campaign against racial discrimination and the campaign against the Vietnam War, both in the United States, and the campaigns against that war and against nuclear arms in Great Britain. As for noncooperation in the past, it has mainly consisted of strikes, including general strikes, and boycotts, notably boycotts of products and services, including national products.

What also need to be kept in mind are certain historical struggles that do not fall within our narrow definitions, since they did not take place in hierarchic democracies. They are entirely relevant, and in a way, are of even greater importance. They include the successful struggle for independence in India led by Gandhi, seminal for the tradition of civil disobedience. Above all, they include the recent Eastern European demonstrations, occupations, and marches. Since 1989 these have precipitated nothing less than political and economic transformations, nonviolent revolutions. The occupation of Tiananmen Square in Beijing may also come to have a large significance.

What is the general strategy in mass civil disobedience and noncooperation? An idea owed to Rawls is too restricted and elevated. It is the idea of civil disobedience as *a mode of address,* an appeal within a nearly-just society to that society's shared sense of justice.[21] Clearly there is no need to restrict civil disobedience to nearly-just societies in certain senses of that term. It might even be out of place in such societies. Perhaps, however, Rawls does not actually intend much restriction, since it may be that the nearly-just societies in his sense do actually include the United States and Great Britain. Such, I am tempted to say, is the moral world of liberalism. It is also clearly not necessary for civil disobedience that there exists in a society something that actually deserves the name of a shared sense of justice. I doubt that anything ever does. The idea is too elevated.[22]

Still, the general strategy in mass civil disobedience and noncooperation does include a moral appeal. It is an appeal to act on what many already feel to be wrong, or an appeal to come to feel that something is wrong. But to say no more would be to underdescribe the strategy, and make less likely a proper judgment of civil disobedience and noncooperation. Mass civil disobedience and noncooperation is not just supplication.

It is a kind of coercion, although what might be called coercion by persuasion rather than coercion by force. It is a refusal to continue in helpful compliance with injustice, often a refusal to continue in self-injuring behavior. It brings pressure on a society and, more particularly, on its government. It expresses moral hatred, hostility, disgust or exasperation, a determination to condemn or shame a government and a society, to press them into decent human sympathy and into action based on it. It is also part of this coercion, of course, that mass civil disobedience makes life harder for governments, their servants, and others. It may cost police time, reduce profits, disrupt order, and at least threaten incidental violence and damage. Officially peaceful demonstrations are very likely to include broken windows and broken arms.

So we can contemplate, at least for a moment, two possible means to moral progress—mass civil disobedience and noncooperation, of which we now have an idea, and the political violence of which I have had less to say, the kind that has the same aim of moral decency in our societies, rather than the old aim of creating an egalitarian democracy.

What is always said against political violence is that it *is* violence, the illegal use of force, and violence that kills and maims. No one in his senses could try to minimize the fact. Still, if it looked like it might work, it would not be so easy to think about as is commonly supposed. We are all constrained by a customary morality that owes much to those who benefit from it. Hence we are mesmerized by violence and distracted from any real contemplation of other things. We concentrate on violent death to the exclusion of lives cut off or ruined legitimately. Unspeakably more decent living time has been subtracted from the twentieth century by the institutionalized and legal frustration of fundamental human desires than by all of the political violence, even if war is included in it.

But we need not think for much more than a moment about the kind of political violence in question. At any rate, we need not try to think about it except in the special case of violence on behalf of the political freedom and independence of a people, which liberation struggles can call on singular resources of determination and sacrifice, and are often enough effective. We need not think of the rest of the kind of political violence in question, because it does not look like it might work. The situation is, in this important respect, the same as with violent revolution, the attempt to replace Hierarchic by Egalitarian Democracy. The political violence that we now have in mind would kill and maim, and would then almost certainly be defeated by the state and its supporters.

What would make it wrong would mainly be the effects of the state violence and repression used in opposition to it, and the absence of any compensating gain. That the opposition to this political violence arguably would be wrong would not diminish the wrongfulness of the political violence itself. An act of mine does not become right—although there are philosophers who try to think so—if it leads to disaster only through someone else's (anticipated) wrongful opposition.

Why would the governments of the hierarchic democracies and their natural supporters almost certainly win? One part of the reason is that they are better at violence, through practice. Another more important part of the reason is that the fighting would drive out truth. Fighting would disarm one side, the side against the indecencies owed to or contributed to by Hierarchic Democracy. Fighting would disarm this side of its best weapon. That weapon *is* truth, including what can be called moral truth. No one attends to grim life expectancies elsewhere or river blindness or racial self-denigration when there are tanks in the street and children are being killed.

To turn to mass civil disobedience, you will anticipate that part of what can be said in favor of it is that it is unlikely, or not greatly likely, to be met by state violence. In speaking of state violence, I mean more than the use of riot police and the intelligence services. State violence, in this sense, although I shall not pause to define it, is likely to involve the army and to carry a significant possibility of civil war. To say mass civil disobedience is unlikely to be met by state violence is to assume something about a sense of proportion on the part of the governments of hierarchic democracies. It is also to assume that they have a sense of the possible penalty that may be paid for using state violence against civil disobedience. State violence against it, as the Left has rightly calculated before now, may win some support to the cause of those who are civilly disobedient.

Should we be hierarchic democrats or should we instead supplement voting and legitimate influencing with the influence of mass civil disobedience? Before answering, I should like to look quickly at one matter. It concerns a proposition of mine that will have been anticipated—that mass civil disobedience, unlike the related political violence, *does* allow truth and moral truth to be heard and to have their rightful effect. Some will disagree. They will disagree because this disobedience, as already noted, is in fact not just supplication. It is a kind of coercion, a confrontation, which, despite its commitment to nonviolence, carries the threat of incidental violence. Historically, mass civil disobedience *has* issued in incidental violence by demonstrators.

It is possible to insist in reply that mass civil disobedience *does* allow truth to be heard, indeed *makes* truth heard. It itself, the main fact of it, is not violence. It is not such an abandoning of our conventions for dealing with disagreement as to madden both sides and leave no thought but defence and retaliation. What is often stressed in this connection by lawyers and the like who are sympathetic to civil disobedience is one of its defining features—that it is open and public and that those who engage in it do not attempt to escape the penalties for their offences. This, the lawyers say, shows the restraint of respect for law. This misses the point a little, as lawyers are likely to do in political philosophy.

It is not *law* that is being in a way respected by the civilly disobedient who break it, not law in general, not something that includes the law of a tyrant-state or an oligarchy. What is respected in a way by the civilly disobedient is the law of, exactly, a hierarchic democracy, and, really, a hierarchic democracy itself. *It* is accorded a respect for the reason, among others, that

Hierarchic Democracy too, as implied earlier, must be regarded as a possible means to a society of moral decency and a less imperfect democracy. This respect cannot be missed by the adversaries of the civilly disobedient. It is what leaves room for truth, and makes perception and reflection possible.

But saying this, I suppose, misses another point—perhaps as philosophers are likely to do. We need not seek just to *argue* our way toward the conclusion that civil disobedience leaves room for truth and hence for moral progress, to *argue* that there is something that makes for such a fact. The historical record by itself establishes the fact. Alabama and Leipzig come to mind. They not only left room for truth to be heard, but got it a hearing it had not had before.

I therefore do advocate, without reserve, mass civil disobedience and also noncooperation. This seems to me a moral necessity.

We ought to engage in and support such mass civil disobedience in order to resist further advances in social criminality by our governments: vicious taxation, yet more repressive pieces of legislation about assembly or ways of living, more turning of hospitals and universities into profit-centers, more vandal roads, more profiteering by privatization, more venality of elected representatives, more hypocrisy about wars and refugees, more indifference to famine.

We ought to engage in and support disobedience not only on new issues of this kind as they come up, but we ought also to engage in and support disobedience against the standing conditions of the societies of Hierarchic Democracy: shortened and cut-off lives both in them and outside of them, stunted lives including some that might almost be better if they were shorter, constraint and weakness in place of freedom and power, denigration and self-denigration, the impeding and wrecking of human relationships, ignorance and vulgarity in place of culture.

We ought not to pay tax. We ought to strike and march illegally. There ought to be demonstrations against our elections in hierarchic democracies, before, during, and after them. It is possible both to vote and to advocate voting, and also to damn a way of voting, and the cheat built into it. We ought to find new forms of civil disobedience.

So too with mass noncooperation, in connection both with new evils and standing evils. We ought not to buy from the corporations and companies that do so much to frustrate the will of our representatives when those representatives remember some of their promises. Those of us who are attracted to an inner core of religion should withdraw from churches, which in their meekness accomodate the true immorality of our societies. We ought to find new forms of noncooperation.

This, you may say, is utopian. Well, that is a right of philosophy, a right which has served us all very well. And I am not sure it is utopian. It was easier to be sure about that before the fall of Communism, before the civil disobedience that precipitated a once-impossible thing. There is an old saying, perhaps a saying of the Left. It is that only power can defeat power. Sometimes those who have said it have had in mind the idea that state power can only be defeated by the power of violence. That proposition has been refuted by the fall of Communism.

Hope of decency in our societies, hope with reason, depends on the thought of many people coming to share a moral feeling. You will know that I speak of disgust and condemnation, and also guilt. It is possible that many will come to share that feeling, and that it will issue in civil disobedience and in noncooperation. The globalization of information may do us a service here, despite the controls on it. So may education, and argument, and the realization that economism is not an answer to the right questions about societies, and the greater economic success of such more egalitarian economies as Japan, and the actual experience of misery coming to the aid of insufficient moral imagination, and the fact that those who drag down societies also lose.

It is possible to hope, with reason, and I do.

NOTES

1. I am grateful to A. B. Atkinson, Robin Blackburn, Kiaran Honderich, and David Zimmerman for help with this paper. They will be relieved to hear that they bear no responsibility for what is said in it.

2. Perhaps the Ordinary Conception is now asserted only by politicians. (Even most of them, by the way, have given up the conception of liberal democracy as *rule* by the people, which was not true even of ancient Athens.) The Ordinary Conception is not far from one of the polyarchies contemplated in R. A. Dahl, *A Preface to Democratic Theory* (Chicago: University of Chicago Press, 1956), chap. 3 and appendix; and not far from from models II and IIIb in David Held, *Models of Democracy* (Cambridge: Polity Press, 1987), pp. 70, 102. See also H. B. Mayo, *An Introduction to Democratic Theory* (New York: Oxford University Press, 1960), chap. 4.

3. The Pluralist Conception, partly because of its contained claim about equality, is not to be identified with several accounts of democracy with similar names. See, for example, R. A. Dahl, *Dilemmas of Pluralist Democracy* (New Haven: Yale University Press, 1982). On pluralism generally, see Held, op. cit., chap. 6.

4. It is possible, as A. B. Atkinson has remarked to me, that the poorest tenth has less than zero percent. That is, its debts are greater than its assets.

5. E. N. Wolff, *International Comparisons of the Distribution of Household Wealth* (Oxford: Clarendon Press, 1987), esp. pp. 153, 127, 137; A. B. Atkinson, "What Is Happening to the Distribution of Income in the UK?" in *Proceedings of the British Academy* (1992); A. B. Atkinson, L. Rainwater, and T. Smeeding, "Income Distribution in European Countries," Discussion Series of the Microsimulation Unit at the University of Cambridge (forthcoming); D. Kessler and E. N. Wolff, "A Comparative Analysis of Household Wealth Patterns in France and the United States," *Review of Income and Wealth* (vol. 37, no. 3, September 1991).

6. The Hierarchic Conception, and also the Ordinary and the Pluralist Conceptions, are set out more fully in "Hierarchic Democracy," *New Left Review* (no. 207, 1994). There are some differences between what is said here and in that article.

7. The life expectancy of American black males was recently 7.4 years shorter than for American white males. For black as against white females, it was 5.5 years shorter. Source: United States Bureau of the Census, *Statistical Abstract of the United States: 1991* (Washington, D.C., 1991). I am not able to produce recent British statistics in support of the uncontroversial claim that the lives of the poor are shortened, because life expectancies by social class are no longer available from the relevant government research department, no doubt for political reasons. For older statistics, see my *Violence for Equality: Inquiries in Political Philosophy* (London: Routledge, 1989), p. 2 ff., p. 204. According to these statistics, men in the fifth social class had life expectancies about six years shorter than men in the first social class. It is very unlikely indeed that the situation has improved.

8. United Nations *Demographic Year Book, 1991* (New York, 1992), Table 22, p. 460ff.

9. Eduardo Galeano, "A Child Lost in the Storm" in *After the Fall: the Failure of Communism and the Future of Socialism,* Robin Blackburn, ed. (London: Verso, 1991), p. 252.

10. My account of the governments in question is given in *Conservatism* (Boulder: Westview Press, 1990).

11. For an excellent summary of increasing income inequality in Great Britain, see A. B. Atkinson, "What Is Happening to the Distribution of Income in the UK?" cited above, and also A. B. Atkinson, L. Rainwater, and T. Smeeding, "Income Distribution in European Countries," cited above. See also F. Levy and R. J. Murnane, "U.S. Earnings Levels and Earnings Inequality: A Review of Recent Trends and Proposed Explanations," *Journal of Economic Literature* (September 1992); and *Income and Wealth,* a report for the Joseph Rowntree Foundation (February 1995).

12. *British Medical Journal* (30 April 1994).

13. *Boswell's Life of Johnson,* G. B. Hill, ed. (Oxford: Clarendon Press, 1934), vol. 2, p. 130.

14. The Principle of Equality is stated more fully in "The Problem of Well-Being and the Principle of Equality," *Mind* (1981), reprinted as chap. 2 of my *Violence for Equality: Inquiries in Political Philosophy* (London: Routledge, 1989). The article also considers more fully the six fundamental human desires mentioned above.

15. *A Theory of Justice* (Cambridge: Belknap Press, 1971). For other objections to the theory, see "The Use of the Basic Proposition of a Theory of Justice," *Mind* (1975). It has been remarked to me, by the way, that the present paper leaves out consideration of the thinking of the New Right. Indeed it does. One reason is that I am no longer inclined to dignify by discussion such a view as that a perfectly just society may be one in which people are starving and have no moral right to food, the perfect justice being owed to the fact that the distribution of goods in the society has a certain history. That, I take it, is propounded in Robert Nozick, *Anarchy, State and Utopia* (New York: Basic Books, 1974).

16. Op. cit., sections 13, 26, 48.

17. It is only weaker general principles and considerations having to do with equality that issue more or less automatically in support for Hierarchic Democracy.

Sometimes there is not enough difference between the supposed premises and the conclusion to make a real argument.

18. See, for example, Blackburn, op. cit.

19. Cf. the discussion of Democratic Violence in *Violence for Equality: Inquiries in Political Philosophy.*

20. See the excellent collections edited by H. A. Bedau, *Civil Disobedience: Theory and Practice* (New York: Pegasus, 1969) and *Civil Disobedience in Focus* (London: Routledge, 1991).

21. Rawls, op. cit., sections 55, 57, 59. They are reprinted and discussed in Bedau, ed., *Civil Disobedience in Focus.*

22. I take it, a little uncertainly, that what is said of a shared sense of justice in *A Theory of Justice* is heavily qualified in Rawls's *Political Liberalism* (New York: Columbia University Press, 1993). See, for example, pp. xvi, xviii, 8.

Svetozar Stojanović

POSTCOMMUNISM, DEMOCRACY, NATIONALITY, AND CAPITALIST ECONOMY

Postcommunist development followed the demise of monopoly structural control on the part of the communist-statist class over the state and, through it, over the economy and all other sectors. Until the nature of the new social orders crystallizes sufficiently, we have to designate as "postcommunism" a "transition period" in which, along with the supposed break, considerable continuity with the previous situation will persist, particularly as regards cadres and the economy.

Postcommunism constitutes *a mix of communism, precommunism and capitalism* that differs significantly from country to country and the final form of which depends on what prevails from among these three tendencies. For this reason, I argue for comparative research on postcommunism.

With regard to the extent of the break with communism, we can arrange postcommunist countries along a continuum. In East Germany we encounter the greatest break with communism as it rapidly integrated into West German capitalism. At the opposite pole we find several examples. In Serbia, for instance, communism did not implode; rather, it (self-)transformed into postcommunism. However, Serbia is not unique either in that respect or with respect to the violent collapse to which multinational Yugoslavia has succumbed. Serbia represents a completely separate case due to the international blockade imposed against it for the past couple of years.

One can, as well, classify postcommunist countries according to the continuity exhibited with the precommunist juncture of authoritarianism, nationalism, an immensely powerful state, and a weak "civil society." Of all the postcommunist countries, in the Czech Republic, prior to the establishment of communism, those characteristics were least pronounced. At the opposite end of the postcommunist spectrum stands Croatia as one of the leading states in perpetuating precommunist traditions (particularly those

149

nationalistic in nature). In it prevails an anticommunist and antiYugoslav revanchism, based in part on the darkest past in World War II.

The theory of the disintegration of communist statism is still in its infancy, while the theory of postcommunist development is still in the embryonic stage. I now turn to the structural dimensions of postcommunist development, beginning with *the tension—even contradiction—between postcommunist democracy and postcommunist capitalism,* especially since the ideological illusion prevails that democracy and capitalism always go hand in hand.

In truth, until recently (prior to the breakup of communist statism) *all* democratic states functioned as market economies. Conversely, a number of market economies still function within undemocratic states. Indeed, there is no strict parallelism between a privately based market economy and democracy, much less a cause and effect relationship between the two. Not only does democracy not necessarily always lead to a market economy, but at times it can even constitute an impediment to it. Such an economy and such a political arrangement represent forms of social organization as well as aspects of culture and mentality that only *in the long run* are mutually supportive and reinforcing.

In capitalism, it was only *partial democracy* that had existed until relatively recently: the right to vote had been limited to taxpayers and literate citizens (exclusively men)—i.e., to those who were interested in seeing capitalism succeed. As capitalism spread and increased in strength, the electorate also grew. Only much later and under great social pressure did *the symbiosis between capitalism and general democracy* (in a formal sense) come into being. Marx envisioned that in some highly developed countries the capitalist system would be eliminated by the universal right to vote, while it is precisely in those countries that a capitalism imbued with democracy blossoms.

In postcommunism as a rule there are no electoral limitations, and consequently *general democracy* (in a formal sense) already exists within it. However, between postcommunist democracy and postcommunist aspirations concerning the development of market-based production, entrepreneurship, and distribution, there is a tension and even a contradiction. More specifically, the greater part of the electorate does not support the procapitalist parties, particularly those that threaten it with the social-Darwinistic measures of "instant capitalism." Procapitalistic elitism is encountering enormous resistance on the part of anticapitalistic populism.

History knows of no mass popular movements in the name of private, profit-oriented market business practices. Instead, such movements have been in the name of justice, equality, freedom, and civil, national and human rights, and against hunger, unemployment, and exploitation. In postcommunism as well one should not expect any mass movements in support of capitalism.

Some anticommunist dissidents fantasized about a *sui generis* "original position" in which they almost at will build a new society. But communist nihilists already attempted "a complete break of the new with the old," and it is well known how their radical social engineering wound up. Both the former and the latter are characterized by the belief in a magic effect of systemic changes in history.

It seems as if the pendulum of social illusions has been moving from one extreme to the other: while for the communists private ownership, the market and profit exemplified a negative utopia, for many anticommunists these institutions have come to represent a kind of positive utopia. The anticommunists hope that the "visible hand" of the government will suddenly ("the great leap forward"!) make possible the functioning of the "invisible hand" of the market. But that u-topia also suffers from u-chronia: it turns out that capitalism cannot burst forth and abruptly spring into being.

Since there is no capitalist class, the procapitalist political elite has to play the role of "class substitute"! In a certain sense, one could say that in postcommunism there is still not even a working class. Stated more clearly, the labor force inherited is in keeping with the system of communist statism, and, with regard to interests, mentality, and expectations, it bears little resemblance to the for-hire market workforce that is indispensable for the development of capitalism. The "old working class" still needs to be transformed into the "new working class." That assertion doubtlessly sounds ironic if we recall the leftist discussions in the West of thirty years ago regarding the "new working class" as the principal socialist hope in capitalism.

It is through politics, as the dominant factor in postcommunism, that many are expecting to bring about (by intervention from above) the sudden transformation of statism in its entirety as a socio-*political* formation into capitalism as a socio-*economic* formation. The postcommunist political elite is principally made up of elements from the noneconomic spheres which, for that reason, attempt to maintain the dominance of politics over the economy, despite their noisy declarations in favor of capitalism (in which the relationship between politics and the economy is precisely the reverse). The economic *dilettantism* of many of the postcommunist governments resembles the economic incompetence of the leading communists at the time of their assuming power.

It is estimated that due to enlarged reproduction of the communist-statist "original sin" at least one fourth of the communist super-enterprises are not economically viable. Indeed, the ruling class's industrial grandomania was not in the least accidental: it was easier to run large enterprises by "plan" and, in so doing, garner prestige at home and abroad. Which of today's postcommunist governments possesses the power and mandate required to eliminate that *enterprise-leveling* (*uravnilovka*) overnight?

Such statist egalitarianism constitutes only one aspect of the "monopolistic-paternalistic syndrome": in order for it to accept or at least to tolerate its lack of any control over the ruling class, the citizenry was "corrupted" by, among other things, guaranteed jobs in secure nonmarket enterprises. The masses gladly approved the elimination of the dictatorial aspect of communism but, in return, they have not been prepared to renounce the social security obtained under its auspices. After all, economic reforms in statism had failed owing to resistance both on the part of conservative communists and on the part of citizens reluctant to trade·those guarantees for the uncertainties of economic liberalization.

Postcommunism will have major difficulties with inherited *proletproduction* in which the manual labor of the "immediate producers" was proclaimed as the main source of newly created economic value. In communism extensive development based on cheap labor was acclaimed, but communism lapsed into a "comparative crisis" as soon as knowledge, information and innovation became the main "productive forces" in capitalism.

By means of deconstruction it is not difficult to show that "equality," as the supposedly central value of statist communism, concealed class privileges and other types of privileges as well. The ruling "vanguard" eliminated the labor market ostensibly to prevent exploitation, but in the process it came to have at its disposal a labor force considerably below its potential market value. Since the power structure was of a class nature, the distribution of housing under "social ownership" also favored the ruling class and other well-positioned groups, while an *anti-private-property ideology* masked this structure. As a rule, those in power by no means wanted main income discrepancies to be expressed in monetary terms (and consequently the haves would build apartments at their own expense, while the have-nots would live in socially provided living quarters) since the extent of social differentiation would then be totally transparent. The absence of private medical practice played a similar role, because in any event the more wealthy and powerful already had privileged access to the best physicians in public practice.

Such an atmosphere strongly provoked the resentment of the masses, but it also redirected it away from the statist class toward the private sector— getting rich, entrepreneurial activity, competition, innovation, etc. In good measure this continues to be the case under postcommunism as well. The masses continue to attack "enrichment without work," subsuming under that heading (also) enrichment on the basis of private ownership, as if the market economy could exist without it. People speak out in favor of private ownership, market incentives, and competition, but only as long as it adversely affects someone else. Thus strikes continue to be of an exceedingly political nature: they demand of the government that redistribution satisfy the needs of those employed in the public sector, even at the expense of someone else's income.

One of the most ironic consequences of the fall of communism is the sudden acquisition of wealth on the part of a number of members of the former ruling class and their descendants, who in their private business dealings make use of previously acquired connections, experience, information, knowledge, and material resources. At one time Trotskyists warned that by usurping the nationalized means of production Stalinists could easily become a class of private owners. Somewhat similarly, a part of the former statist class is currently becoming just that.

However, the working people do not want to see the fruit of many decades of their labor, manifest as social and state ownership, expropriated for a song through privatization. The Proudhonian ideological formulation of "Property is theft" takes on a convincing ring as the masses get the clear impression that private ownership originates with the *sui generis* theft of state-social ownership. Some countries attempt to avoid such forms of *primitive postcommunist accumulation* through the allotment of enterprise shares to employees or even to the entire populace. However, that idyll of shareholding egalitarianism quickly gives way to a new class differentiation between those who, for a trifle, purchase shares and those who have to sell them.

With regard to the ideological rationalization of this newly created situation, a very interesting reversal has occurred. In order to discredit capitalism, communist ideologues used Marx's opposition of *formal equality and material inequality*, while the new capitalists from the ranks of the former communists do not even wish to hear of this distinction. For them it is totally unimportant that a material handicap exists for those who have to sell their shares; all that matters is that these transactions take place under formal conditions of equality.

The same type of reversal has occurred with respect to democracy. The communist-statist class had the habit of discounting bourgeois democracy as merely *formal*, while simultaneously prolaiming its own dictatorship as being a *substantially* democratic form of government. With the fall of communism, the monopoly structural control over the state on the part of that class disappeared, but that, of course, does not mean that no differences exist between social groups with respect to their real possibilities of influencing the state in postcommunism. On the contrary, the new power holders—often former communists and now usually nationalists or liberals—make use of the mass of inherited advantages (of cadres, organization, finances, information, etc.), while they define democracy as a mere formal procedure (involving the existence of the universal right to vote and multiparty elections). On the other hand, opposition parties that are in that respect handicapped, even when they declare themselves antiMarxist, still (unconsciously) appeal to the Marxist-substantive view of democracy in attacking the new situation as undemocratic.

In analyzing the relationship between democracy and capitalism in postcommunism, one must take into account international factors. International "capitalist encirclement" significantly contributed to the collapse of communism, and its effect on the postcommunist development and denouement will surely not abate. Nevertheless, the West had better guard well against triumphalistic postcommunist social engineering from outside. It is extremely important to know, for example, that the Russian people have experienced the external pressure in favor of "capitalistic shock therapy" as an attack not only upon their material interests, but also upon their national independence and dignity.

It is essential not to lose sight of the tension and even the contradiction between postcommunist democracy and international "capitalist encirclement": the preferences of the domestic electorate do not coincide with the radically capitalist demands on the part of western governments, business circles, and financial institutions. True, foreign capital can help a great deal, but it is not in a position to substitute a (yet nonexistent) capitalist class in the postcommunist countries.

President Clinton's strategy of a "proliferation of market democracies" fails to take sufficiently into account the aforementioned contradiction. To say nothing of the vicious circle into which that strategy falls, in that the United States is not prepared to extend more abundant material assistance to the postcommunist countries (above all, to Russia) prior to their exhibiting clear evidence of having successfully undertaken a capitalist path, even though the United States knows that these countries are not in a position to do that without generous foreign aid.

How do we find a way out of this postcommunist situation in which the majority of the electorate does not support capitalism? Increasing numbers of its protagonists (for example, Henry Kissinger and Zbigniew Brzezinski) are reaching the conclusion that, in order for the capitalist transformation to be speedy and more successful, what will be needed are authoritarian, rather than democratic, postcommunist governments. That is why, in the final analysis, the West supported Yeltsin's violent crushing of the opposition parliament in the fall of 1993.

In that context, however, an analogy with the Bolsheviks immediately comes to mind. They relied on dictatorship, unpreoccupied with any expectation that the masses would give an advantage via free elections to their own "long-term and objective interests" (as understood by the Bolsheviks) over their own "short-term and subjective" preferences. Nevertheless, we all know to what extent that dictatorship was "temporary." Moreover, where is the guarantee that the authoritarian forces under postcommunism would use the "temporary" suspension of democracy to effect just capitalist changes?

✤   ✤   ✤

Three multinational communist federations disintegrated into twenty-two states (as a rule, national) and, most likely, this process of dissolution is still not complete. But if the breakup of communism was an enormous surprise, it is not clear why the explosion of nationalism accompanying it should also have been a surprise, since nationalism is a significantly older and more thoroughly studied historical phenomenon than communism. Many former communists in nationalist-separatist confrontations employ violence, which they had otherwise not used to defend their communist governments and system.

Soviet power-holders imagined that they could adequately deal with their nationalities' problems by reducing them to national *cultures* and these in turn to "national *forms*" whose differences were allegedly overcome by a common "socialist *content*." Czeslav Milosz correctly pointed out ("Swing Shift in the Baltics," in *The New York Review of Books*, November 4, 1993) that "Soviet" nations took the official formula, "*National* culture as to form, *socialist* culture as to content," and turned it around in practice to read: "Socialist culture as to form, national culture as to content."

Naturally, the former ideological formula would not have been of any use to the Soviet government—save as a self-delusion—had it not by means of dictatorship imposed a single "socialist content" (more often than not, as *kitsch*), i.e., had it not hindered "national forms" from creating and manifesting differences of content. When that dictatorship weakened, and especially when, under Gorbachev, radical liberalization was introduced, then the differentiating, nationalistic and even separatist potential of "national forms" put an end to the obligatory "Soviet content," not only in culture but also in politics. Were the new slogan formulated explicitly, it would be expressed as: Politics and culture—national both in form and in content.

One should not be too amazed that in the new politics many former communists again play an important and, at times, crucial role. Above all, since communists already utilized nationalism and separatism for the destruction of the previous regimes and to gain power, it was entirely logical that many of them were prepared to use nationalism and separatism in postcommunism as well to remain in the political game. Moreover, the transition from one (communist) type of Manichaeism to another (nationalist) one was not so difficult. In discovering a (new) enemy in other nations of the former common state, such communists quickly found a common language with the original nationalists whom they had formerly severely persecuted. They even compete with such nationalists in radicalism, to some extent owing to a feeling of guilt and somewhat due to an attempt to divert attention by means of political noise away from their own repressive antinationalist past. That political-psychological mechanism strongly recalls the effort of the communists of bourgeois origin to demonstrate the most extreme anticapitalist position possible in the eyes of their party comrades of proletarian origin.

I have no intention here of going more exhaustively into the doctrinaire-historical background of the Soviet government's underestimation of "form." Suffice it to remind the reader that it began with the Bolsheviks' belittling of the *liberal and democratic* "form" of capitalism and their reducing it to an "illusion" behind which was supposedly hidden, from the point of view of "content," merely the *class rule of the bourgeoisie*. For that communist nihilism *vis-à-vis* social "form" Lenin bears full responsibility. In truth, he elaborated that position with a series of simplifications drawn from Marx's analysis of the ontology (architectonics) and ideology of capitalism. Nonetheless, it should be said that Marx himself in some of his formulations significantly opened up the possibility for such vulgarizations.

During their first twenty years in power, the declared position of the Yugoslav communists toward the nationality question was quite reminiscent of that of the Soviets. However, in the second half of the 1960s the CPY rejected "Yugoslav-ness" and initiated a nationalization (ethnization) of the constituent states, and somewhat later, of its own (party) makeup.

In the independent national states separated from the communist federations there is a strong tendency to create *ethnic societies*, rather than *civil societies*. Indeed, the nationalist-separatist forces—for instance, in the former Yugoslav republic of Slovenia—abundantly employed the ideology of "civil society," but only until such time as they broke away from the federation, and then, in practice, they have shown that they had their own ethnic (Slovenian) society in mind. There existed at least two reasons for this ideological cover-up: in this way it was incomparably easier, first, to mobilize domestic liberal-democratic circles to fight against the central Yugoslav government and, second, to obtain legitimacy and support from the West.

We have already established that democracy represents a certain impediment to the capitalist transformation in postcommunism. However, that transformation is incomparably more frustrated by the aspiration to a closed ethnic society. I say incomparably more, because in the long run capitalism and democracy share a universalistic homology, since the institutions of "buyer-seller" and "citizen-voter" disregard diverse characteristics of people, while nationalism (ethnic society) adopts the discriminatory particularity that contradicts capitalist logic both in the short and in the long time frame. After all, in postcommunism capitalism has yet to be established, while nations have been in existence for a long time. Superficial critics of nationalistic tendencies usually point out that a nationality is an "abstract collective," overlooking that it is more concrete and closer to the masses than the totality composed of "buyers and sellers" and "citizens and voters."

In nationalist circles the communist system of the past and its remnants are less and less being blamed for the difficult economic situation. Instead, accusations are increasingly being leveled at other nations, particularly the former "ruling nation." The new ruling parties attempt to establish "national sovereignty" over economies in which state-social ownership still predominates. Owing to the symbiosis of nation and state, political interventionism in the economy does not abate. In an ethnic economy and an ethnic society it is difficult to develop profit-market business dealings because the basic agents would have to be owners, entrepreneurs, capitalists, workers, and not a political-demographic totality like a nation.

Radical nationalist governments are concerned that, through privatization, state-social ownership (especially of the "national soil") will fall into the hands of those who belong to other nations. Therefore, *postcommunist ethnic society* is in conflict with the international "capitalist encirclement." The West should not be amazed that the masses offer resistance to the capitalist domination of outsiders. How can one convince them to accept the competition of overbearing international capital if it is known that the far more powerful capitalist economies enjoy state protectionism? If the transfer of "national wealth" into foreign hands cannot be avoided, nationalist power-holders would rather relinquish it to foreigners from faraway nations (and not to their former countrymen), and even more to their own compatriots and their descendants abroad ("ethno-business").

War and other conflicts with the breakaway states, and also with the separatism that, from within, threatens the new independent states, constitute one of the basic reasons for establishing an *ethnic-command economy*. What is at issue is a *war-ethnic postcommunism*. While, in the name of a communist utopia, earlier power-holders called upon the populace to sacrifice during the "transition period," the new power-holders now demand sacrifices from it for the sake of national interests, the national state and the national future.

How can we reconcile all of these observations regarding ethnic society with my assertion that general formal democracy is established in postcommunism? Obviously, I have to introduce one qualification into that assertion: in postcommunist countries with dominant nationalist orientations the right to vote is tacitly limited in the sense that citizenship is automatically granted to the members of the ethnic group whose name the state bears, while other inhabitants face numerous obstacles. Thus the former Stalinist "political correctness" is replaced by ethnic correctness.

Great conceptual and emotional confusion has been generated among internationalist leaning intellectuals in postcommunist countries, particularly where inter-nationality and inter-faith wars have broken out. Those who have not degenerated into nationalists and chauvinists, but who have also failed to attain a realistic attitude to the nation and the nation state, compensate for their lack of comprehension by a surplus of condemnation.

Indeed, it is difficult to orient oneself in the collective "limit situations" that came about with the breakup of the states, civil wars of ethnic and religious origin, crimes that yesterday's countrymen carry out against each other, mass flight. That return to a "natural state" tragically validates the thesis of "foundational violence" in the history of nations and their states. The newest evidence for this is represented by the case of the Muslims of Bosnia-Herzegovina. Up until the disintegration of Yugoslavia and especially until the outbreak of the war there with the Serbs, and somewhat later with the Croats as well, many Muslims vacillated between a Muslim, a Yugoslav, an "undefined," a Serb, and a Croat *national* identity (although there was no such hesitation regarding their religious identification). Afterward it took "only" two years of war to feel and nationally define themselves definitively as Muslims. The analysis of this sudden shift in identification could stimulate us to an elaboration of the notion of "late-comer nations," but we will not go into that at this time.

What practical effect can one's opposing of the nationalist metaphysics via the characterization of a nation as an "historical construct" exert, when a people in practically no time moves from being a national *construct* to being a national *given*? After all, the thesis about an historical construct is valid only in a collective-diachronic perspective, while, for the individual, the nation is, as a rule, a given (involving ethnicity, language, religion, culture, tradition, and custom) in which one is born.

Therefore, in the newly formed postcommunist states the national democrats have an incomparably better chance than do the non-national democrats in their political competition with the nationalist *anti*democrats. The non-national democrats are unable, for instance, to explain why even the democratic Germans wanted to reunify with other Germans, but not to unify with other East European democrats, or why democratic Germany should automatically adopt into its citizenry only those foreigners who have German, and not some other, ancestry. They also cannot convincingly explain why the combined force of Czech and Slovak democrats was so ineffectual that it could not impede the breakup of the Czecho-Slovak federation into two national states. It is unclear why the West was so surprised by the success of national and nationalistic parties and by the relative failure of the non-national-democratic parties in the latest elections in Russia. How is it that they expected the Russians to lend electoral support to those parties in which they did not see the best guarantee for their *national* interests?

Postcommunist nationalism cannot be successfully countered simply by counterposing a civil state to the national state, and even less by reactions declaring that "It's not borders that matter, but rather democracy," because it is widely known that many states in the West are predominantly national and that democracy functions there as well in a state framework in which only its citizens have the right to vote. Therefore, the real dilemma for the twenty-two states originating with the collapse of three communist federations is to become either a *democratic national* state or an *antidemocratic nationalistic* state. The first nurtures equality of all citizens without regard to whether or not they belong to the *majority* ethnic group for whom the state is named, while the second is disgraced by ethnic discrimination and the implementation of campaigns for ever-increasing "ethnic purity."

Confused internationalistic intellectuals have led themselves into an absurd position: they are trying to persuade the nations drawing borders between themselves in blood that in "the European world"—particularly since it has taken on a postmodern character—time is a far more important factor than is space. Moreover, behind "European-ness" is often concealed an attempt to impose the identity and power of one half of the continent upon the other half. I have nothing against "European identity" being further defined, say, by humanism and democracy (which in any case is a "Balkan" invention and creation!) but solely on condition that fascism and colonialism are also included in it. Why the effort to define the national, regional, or continental identity as homogeneous, instead of as a structure full of internal tensions and contradictions?

Part 3. Asian Perspectives

Ambrose Y. C. King

CONFUCIANISM, MODERNITY, AND ASIAN DEMOCRACY

NEW WAVE OF DEMOCRATIZATION

The political revolution in 1989 in Eastern Europe and the dramatic events of August 1991 in Moscow did not only mark the end of the Cold War era, but also the beginning of a worldwide wave of democratization. Marc F. Platter hailed the arrival of democracy on the ruins of Leninist Socialism as "the democratic moment" and stated that "we may at last be entering a sustained period of peaceful democratic hegemony—a kind of 'Pax Democratica'."[1] Samuel P. Huntington saw that, between 1974 and 1990, at least thirty countries made transitions to democracy, doubling the number of democratic governments in the world. He called it democracy's "third wave." Although Huntington, as a political realist, cautioned that the third wave of democratization might be followed by a third reverse wave, nonetheless he pondered the question: "were these democratizations part of a continuing and ever-expanding 'global democratic revolution' that will reach virtually every country in the world?"[2] Francis Fukuyama, in his now famous article entitled "The End of History," advanced a strong claim that we may be witnessing "the end point of man's ideological evolution and the universalization of Western liberal democracy as the final form of human government." He has taken the view that "the triumph of the West . . . is evident first of all in the total exhaustion of viable systematic alternatives to Western liberalism."[3] He further writes,

> What is emerging victorious, in other words, is not so much liberal practice, as the liberal idea. That is to say, for a very large part of the world, there is now no ideology with pretensions to universality that is in a position to challenge liberal democracy.[4]

163

Fukuyama's optimism for liberal democracy, though extraordinary, is not unprecedented in history. In fact, several times before in the past century it seemed that democracy had won universal acceptance, but the acceptance was much less trustworthy than had been imagined. In 1900–1901, leading newspapers announced the good news that the twentieth century was to be the century of democracy.[5] History, with "the cunning of reason" perhaps, proved that wrong, and future events will probably do the same to Fukuyama and other like-minded prophets. There is no shortage of scholars who see the uncertainties in the "democratic age."[6] Charles S. Maier recently talked about the "moral crisis" of democracy and wrote, "on the aftermath of 1989's collapse of communism, a . . . feeling of anticlimax has succeeded initial euphoria."[7] It is not difficult to be carried away by the sudden triumph of democracy. However, the triumph of democracy probably has less to do with the "success" of democracy than with the widespread disenchantment with communism. More than forty years ago, Louis Hartz wrote, "the competition between democracy and communism . . . is . . . a curious one, a kind of reverse competition in the process of disillusionment."[8] The central problem seems to stem from a discrepancy between ideal and practice. Democracy, as an ideal, has promised much, but the ideal of communism has promised even more. The "realities" of both liberal democracy and communism have betrayed these promises, but communism's betrayal is considerably greater, and thus it brought about its own defeat in the "competition of disillusionment." No one could fail to notice that the end of communism does not signal the end of the problems facing liberal democracy. Ken Jowitt has rightly reminded us:

> Liberal capitalist democracy has aroused a heterogeneous set of opponents. . . . For all the real and massive differences that separate these diverse oppositions, one can detect a shared critique. Liberal capitalist democracy is scorned for an inordinate emphasis on individualism, materialism, technical achievement, and rationality. . . . Liberal capitalism is indicted for undervaluing the essential collective dimension of human existence.[9]

MODERNITY AND THE QUESTION OF THE UNIVERSALIZABILITY OF LIBERAL DEMOCRACY

John Dun said some time ago, "we are all democrats today because we so transparently ought to be. Democratic theory is the public cant of the modern world. . . . All states today prefer to be democracies because a democracy is what [it] is virtuous for a state to be."[10] Ernest Gellner made a perceptive observation concerning democracy:

> Looking at the contemporary world, two things are obvious: democracy is doing rather badly, and democracy is doing very well. . . . Democracy is doing very

badly in that democratic institutions have fallen by the wayside in very many of the newly independent "transitional" societies, and they are precarious elsewhere. Democracy, on the other hand, is doing extremely well in so far as it is almost (though not quite) universally accepted as a valid form.[11]

Indeed, it is no exaggeration to say that democracy—the meaning of which is simply "the rule of the people"—is now so transparently a virtuous form of government that no state can afford not to be democratic. But it is one thing to say that there is no viable ideological rival to democracy in the contemporary world; it is quite another thing to say that there is no alternative to *liberal democracy*, which is a very special form of democracy. For the moment, the disintegration of communism has left the idea of liberal democracy standing alone, with no viable ideological competitor in sight. But this does not render valid the idealist, ahistorical assertion that liberal democratic civilization is the absolute end of history, the definitely final civilization. It seems to me that to ask whether there is an alternative to liberal democracy is not as pertinent as is the question: "Is liberal democracy universalizable?" As David Held rightly points out,

the celebratory view of liberal democracy neglects to explore whether there are any tensions, or even perhaps contradictions, between the "liberal" and "democratic" components of liberal democracy. . . . Furthermore, there is not simply one institutional form of liberal democracy. . . . An uncritical affirmation of liberal democracy essentially leaves unanalyzed the whole meaning of democracy and its possible variants.[12]

It should be noted that liberal democracy is a blend of liberalism and democracy and its two components have different historical-cultural roots. It has been well argued that

the conjunction "liberal democracy" is paradoxical, because the relationship between liberalism and democracy has been a deeply ambiguous one. Liberalism has provided not only the necessary foundation for, but also a significant constraint upon democracy in the modern world.[13]

Both democracy and liberalism are creations of the West, and the question of the universalizability of liberal democracy inevitably touches upon the issue of culture and modernity.

Since the eighteenth century, modernity, which originated in Europe, has spread progressively across the globe.[14] Today the whole world is willy-nilly involved in modernization. The so-called Third World, voluntarily or not, is "condemned to modernization,"[15] to use the phrase of Octavio Paz, the Mexican poet and Nobel Prize Winner. Clearly, the category of modernity "remains incorrigibly Western in most of its terms of reference."[16] However, the assertion that Western modernity will eventually be the universal form of modernity is, to say the least, questionable, if not downright wrong. Surprisingly or not, most modernization theories are hardly sensitive to cultural factors. Charles Taylor renders a great service to the debate by distinguishing two kinds of theories of modernity—i.e., "cultural" and "accultural." As he sees it, the dominant theories of modernity over the past two centuries have been of the accultural sort. Accultural theory of modernity is "defined by a rational or social operation which is culture-neutral." According to this kind of theory, "modernity is conceived as a set of transformations that any and every culture can go through and that all will probably be forced to undergo." Indeed, "just relying on a cultural theory," warned Taylor, "would make us neglect certain important facets of the transformation." On the other hand, according to Taylor, it would be equally wrong to rely on a purely accultural theory, which tends to make the mistake of "seeing everything modern as belonging to one Enlightenment Package." Fully convinced of the existence of alternatives to Western modernity, Taylor writes,

> In short, exclusive reliance on an accultural theory unfits us for what is perhaps the most important task of social science in our day: understanding the full gamut of alternative modernities that are in the making in different parts of the world. It locks us into an ethnocentric prison, condemned to project our own forms onto everyone else, and blissfully unaware of what we are doing.[17]

Bearing in mind this sage advice, let us look at the cultural particularities of liberal democracy that are part and parcel of Western modernity.

THE CULTURE OF LIBERAL DEMOCRACY

Democracy made its first appearance in the Athenian city-state. Liberal democracy, by contrast, did not emerge in Europe until the seventeenth century.[18] Athenian democracy, which manifested itself in the universal device of having the people manage their own affairs, was grounded in a sense of community. The claims of the state were given a unique priority over those of the individual citizen. It was a form of collective existence—a case of a community ruling itself. This is probably why Gastil would like to call classical Athenian democracy "tribal" or "community" democracy.[19] Athenian democracy's legacy to posterity is the concept of "rule by the people," which has indeed become the ground of legitimacy for any kind of government called a democracy.[20] In contrast, liberal democracy, though it shared the concept of "rule by the people" with classical democracy, was grounded on the individual. The root is liberalism, "defined as that set of social and political beliefs, attitudes and values which assumes the universal and equal application of the law and the existence of basic human rights superior to those of state or community."[21] Liberalism affirms the basic worth of individuals. The heart of liberalism is that it takes the individual as the ultimate and irreducible unit of society. In other words, "the individual is conceptually and ontologically prior to society and can in principle be conceptualized and defined independently of society."[22] The true mark of liberal democracy, then, is not that individual rights are cherished and respected, but that rights are not defined in "social" or "communal" terms. It is thus not accidental that liberalism is seen to be a form of "individualism." The liberal idea—derived from a variety of religious and secular tenets of the West—is culturally and historically specific. And a democracy based upon such a culturally-specific principle can hardly claim to be intrinsically universal in nature.

At this juncture, it is worth noting that whether the individualism/collectivism antithesis is the central shared orientation of modernity is very much in doubt.[23] Only the extreme version of the accultural theory of modernity—to use Taylor's concept—would tend to presume that the individualistic principle of liberal democracy defines the only truly modern polity. Eisenstadt, while recognizing that the spread of modernity from the West to the rest of world has produced a "very strong convergence" in different modern societies, asserts,

> But while modernity has spread to most of the world, it has not given rise to a single civilization, and one pattern of ideological and institutional response but to several, or at least to many basic variants, which are constantly developing their own closely related but not identical dynamics. A great variety of modern or modernizing societies, sharing many common characteristics but also evincing great differences among themselves, developed out of these responses.[24]

True enough, democracy is now the "Moral Esperanto" of present nation-states. But the appeal of "liberal democracy" is far from universal. Bhikhu Parakh demonstrates convincingly the cultural particularity of liberal democracy, and provides a useful decoupling of liberalism and democracy. He points out that "the democratic part of liberal democracy, consisting of such things as free elections, free speech and the right to equality have proved far more attractive outside the West and is more universalizable than the liberal components." He makes it unmistakably clear that while non-Western societies have no difficulty in accepting democratic values, they are very uneasy with, if not downright hostile to, liberal values. He writes,

> millions in non-Western societies demand democracy, albeit in suitably indigenized form, whereas they shy away from liberalism as if they instinctively felt it to be subversive of what they most valued and cherished. This is not because it leads to capitalism, for many of them welcome the latter, but because the Third World countries feel that the liberal view of the world and way of life is

at odds with their deepest aspirations and self-conceptions. As they understand it, liberalism breaks up the community, undermines the shared body of ideas and values, places the isolated individual above the community, encourages the ethos and ethic of aggressive self-assertions . . . weakens the spirit of mutual accommodation and adjustment.[25]

The problem of liberal individualism is not that it places too much weight on the rights of the individual, but that the rights of the individual are defined in "asocial" or "nonsocial" terms. In liberalism, to be an individual is almost synonymous with being an individualist. John Dun perceptively noted,

> To be individual is to be distinctive, and to be an individual is simply the common fate. But to be an individualist is to embrace this fate with a suspicious alacrity, to make a vice out of necessity. Being individual—in aspiration at least—is simply doing one's own thing, a private concern or a consensual pleasure. But being an individualist is well on the way towards disregarding the interests of others or denying the presence of any basic affective commitment of one human being towards another.[26]

In short, to be an individualist is to be an egocentric individual without regarding the larger society of which one is a part. America as a land of individualism was first described with acuity by Tocqueville. He saw that the Americans, though individualistic in many private pursuits, were remarkably capable of combining in voluntary associations to pursue collective interests. In a word, the independence and assertiveness of individuals were coupled with a significant level of responsibility. However, according to Riesman, a truly dramatic change has taken place in the United States in the growth of public approval of egocentric behavior.[27] It is interesting to note that in recent years certain American academics, including sociologists like Robert Bellah and Amita Etzioni, have been advocates of the social-political philosophy of communitarianism, which, loosely speaking, is intended to temper the excesses of American individualism in the light of a strong assertion of the rights of the larger society. The communitarian theorists have openly challenged the primacy of the "unfettered" individual. Amita Etzioni and his coeditors of *Quarterly Journal, The Responsive Community*, declared in their statement of purpose: "we say that the rights of individuals must be balanced with the responsibilities to the community." And, interestingly, the February 1991 issue of *Harper's* featured a symposium on whether the United States Constitution needs a Bill of Duties to offset the Bill of Rights.[28]

America, in both contemporary and historical terms, is a liberal democracy *par excellence*. However, the coupling of liberalism and democracy in the United States was circumstantial rather than deliberate in nature. In the last two hundred years, liberalism and democracy in American politics have coexisted in a "creative tension" and have had a "deeply troubled relationship."[29] From an historical and developmental perspective, the communitarian "movement" represents but the latest phase of the troubled relationship between liberalism and democracy in American political culture.

MODERNITY, CONFUCIANISM, AND ASIAN DEMOCRACY

The rapid ascendancy of the East Asian economy in the last two to three decades has made this region the focal point for students of development of different persuasions. Peter Berger calls it the "second case" of capitalist modernity.[30] The great German sociologist, Max Weber, in his classic entitled *The Religion of China,* asserted that Confucianism as a rationalism of adjustment was responsible for the "non-development" of capitalism in Imperial China.[31] In light of the phenomenal success in economic development of East Asia, which is, culturally speaking, a Confucian region, the Weberian thesis has been subjected to various criticisms. In my view, Weber's work on Confucianism is not without problems,[32] but these do not refute his thesis because today's Confucianism is not the Confucianism that Weber wrote about—which should be thought of as Imperial Confucianism or what I call "Institutional Confucianism."[33] What is pertinent to our discussion here is that the success of East Asian economic development has made it imperative to rethink the role of Confucianism as a cultural system in relation to modernization. Admittedly, the economic success of East Asia has a great deal to do with institutional factors.[34] Nevertheless, students of East Asian modernization believe that the economic features of East Asia are linked to its distinctive social and cultural features, which include "a very strong achievement-oriented work ethic, a highly developed sense of collective solidarity, and the enormous prestige of education." There should be little doubt that these social and cultural features are also part of the "East-Asian model."[35]

Whether the authoritarian system is the "cause" of economic development in East Asia is far from being agreed upon among scholars. I tend to agree with Huntington that "economic reform requires a strong authoritative government, although not necessarily authoritarian government".[36] But there is no denying the fact that Taiwan, South Korea, Singapore, and to some extent, Hong Kong all achieved their miraculous economic success under a development-oriented authoritarian system of one kind or another. What is more remarkable is that these East Asian societies, following the success of economic development and industrialization, have made a fundamental shift in their political orientation. The authoritarian systems have undergone a basic transformation toward democracy. The East Asian experience, which demonstrates unmistakably that there is a strong empirical correlation between economic factors and political democracy, confirms what Seymour Lipset asserted years ago.[37] The present study does not attempt to disentangle the causes of democracy in East Asia.[38] Suffice it to say that industrial capitalism is a necessary, though not a sufficient, condition for political democracy.[39] A fact that must be recognized is that in East Asia, after Japan, the so-called dragons, like Taiwan and South Korea, have clearly embarked on the road toward democracy. What this paper argues is that, although East Asia's democratization is not only desirable but also feasible, East Asian democracy does not necessarily follow the Western model of liberal democracy. In short, East Asian countries are consciously or unconsciously searching for an alternative to Western liberal democracy.

Fukuyama's unbounded faith in liberal democracy does not make him entirely oblivious to the challenges liberal democracy might face. He admits that

> The most significant challenge being posed to the liberal universalism of the American and French revolutions today is not coming from the communist world, whose economic failures are evident for everyone to see, but from those societies in Asia which combine liberal economics with a kind of paternalistic authoritarianism.[40]

Elsewhere he writes,

> For us in the West, we have to wonder whether rather than being at a stage of evolution toward being more like us, Confucian democracies have found a route toward 21st century modernity that we really don't know about.[41]

Gilbert Rozman reminds us that the distinction between capitalist and socialist provides a useful way of perceiving our century. "Yet we see an advantage in redrawing this dichotomy somewhat so that more distinctions can be made. Above all, we propose to add a 'third dimension' to the analysis in order to capture the East Asian qualities labeled here as 'Confucian.'"[42] But what will be the nature of democracy informed by the Confucian heritage in East Asia? Huntington, speaking of the Asian democracies that are still being developed, asserts that they may meet the "formal requisite of democracy," but differ significantly from the Western democratic systems. He writes, "This type of political system offers democracy without turnover. It represents an adoption of western democratic practices to serve not Western values of competition and change, but Asian values of consensus and stability."[43] Although Huntington believes that "In practice, Confucian or Confucian-influenced societies have been inhospitable to democracy," he deems that Confucianism, like any major cultural tradition, "has some elements that are compatible with democracy, just as both Protestantism and Catholicism have elements that are clearly undemocratic." He observes that "Confucian democracy may be a contradiction in terms, but democracy in a Confucian society need not be."[44]

The phrase "Confucian democracy," as it is used by Fukuyama and Huntington, is loose but interesting. It is worth mentioning in passing that "capitalist democracy," not unlike "Confucian democracy," is also a contradiction in terms. According to Ralph Milband, who sees capitalist democracy as another name for liberal democracy,

> capitalist democracy is a contradiction in terms, for it encapsulates two opposed systems. On the one hand there is capitalism, a system of economic organization that demands the existence of a relatively small class of people who own and control the main means of industrial, commercial, and financial activity, as well as a major part of the means of communication.... On the other hand there is democracy, which is based on the *denial* of such preponderance, and which requires a rough *equality of condition* that capitalism, as Fukuyama acknowledges, repudiates by its very nature. Domination and exploitation are ugly words that do not figure in Fukuyama's vocabulary but they are at the very core of capitalist democracy, and are inextricably linked to it.[45]

I am not prepared here to settle the scores between Confucian democracy and capitalist (or liberal) democracy. What is worth noting is that both Fukuyama and Huntington have shown a concern for the relationship between culture and democracy, though neither of them has provided a systematic exposition of the cultural particularities of Asian democracy.

The East Asian democratic experience shows that most countries in this region have adopted democratic institutions, but they have not followed truly liberal principles. Lipset, in a paper entitled "The Centrality of Political Culture," states that "cultural factors deriving from varying histories are extraordinarily difficult to manipulate, political institutions—including electoral systems and constitutional arrangements—are more easily changed."[46] To call East Asian democracy "Confucian democracy," as Fukuyama does, is not unreasonable, since East Asia's culture evolved through centuries within the orbit of China and the once hegemonic cultural system that was Confucianism. According to Rozman, "Justification for a regional focus is not hard to find. This focus is evident in the common heritage of the region, which is customarily, although somewhat imprecisely, called the Confucian heritage."[47] Today, though Institutional Confucianism is long dead, Confucian ethics and values are still a living cultural force. For East Asia, if democracy is going to be fully developed, it has to come to terms with Confucianism.

Confucianism never advocated the democratic form of government; in fact, it was not concerned with "forms" of government as such. To the great Confucians of the past, the paramount issue was how a government was to be justly administered. In a fundamental sense, Confucianism deals with the Tao (way) of administration but not with the Tao of politics.[48] While saying that Confucianism was no advocate of democracy, we cannot characterize Confucianism as simply antidemocratic. Confucianism is a complex system which cannot be interpreted unidimensionally as "for" or "against" democracy. Richard Solomon lists three tensions inherent in the Confucian tradition: (1) dependence on hierarchical authority versus self-assertion; (2) social harmony and peace versus hostility and aggression; (3) self versus group.[49] Confucianism not only contains elements or seeds of democracy, but arguably also offers a sinicized version of the "liberal tradition."[50] The most salient political component in Confucianism is the *minben*. The Confucian dictum, "The people are the basis of the state" is consistently and unequivocally articulated by great Confucians throughout Chinese history. Mencius said, "It is the people who are primary, the gods second, and the ruler last." In the words of the great Ming Confucian, Huang Tsung-hsi, people should be the "masters," the ruler the "guest." True, *minben* (people-as-the-basis) is not democracy. It contains the essence, perhaps, of what Lincoln meant by "of the people" and "for the people," but it does not extend to "by the people."[51] On balance, *minben*, which can be seen perhaps as containing the seed of democracy, has serious limitations if taken as material out of which modern democracy can be built. De Bary, who forcefully expounded that there is a liberalism in the Confucian tradition, particularly in Huang Tsung-hsi's work, finds that there is "trouble" with Confucianism. He writes,

> even though Huang (Tsung-hsi) went further than any other Confucian in asserting the primacy of the people—that they should be masters of the land, and the ruler the guest—he still was unable to articulate the means whereby the people as commoners (*min*) could actually assume this magisterial function.

Furthermore, he adds,

> In the end, however, what failed the Confucians repeatedly . . . was not the lack of a prophetic voice but the lack of an articulate popular audience—the absence of a political and social infrastructure that would have given the people themselves a voice.[52]

The "trouble" with Confucianism was first revealed in China's encounter with Western civilization in the nineteenth century. The civilization state of the Middle Kingdom was assaulted and defeated by the Western powers, which had already been baptized by industrialization and modernization. China was faced with a challenge unprecedented in her long history. Reluctant at first, China had no choice but to learn from the West. In a real sense, China was "condemned to modernization." The old moral-political order collapsed. China was challenged with twin crises: a crisis of the political order and an intellectual crisis or an "orientational crisis."[53] And a search for a new moral-political order by the Chinese intellectuals ensued, driven by the impulse to gain "wealth" and "power" for the "new" nation of China.[54] The readiness of Chinese intellectuals to be attracted to the idea of democracy as a new "form" of government can only be understood within this historical context. However, for Yen Fu and other like-minded intellectuals, democracy or liberal ideas were treated—as Benjamin Schwartz makes clear—as a means to an end.

> Liberty, equality (above, all, equality of opportunity) and democracy provide the environment within which the individual's "energy of faculty" is finally liberated. From the very outset, however, Yen Fu escapes some of the more rigid dogmatic antitheses of nineteenth-century European liberalism. Precisely because his gaze is ultimately focused not on the individual per se but on the presumed results of individualism, the sharp antitheses between the individual and society, individual initiative and social organization, and so on, do not penetrate to the heart of his perception.[55]

It is worth noting here that the idea of democracy became the dominant political aspiration of the late Ching intellectuals, and the Confucian concept of *minben* (people-as-the-basis) was integrated into the Western concept of *minchu* (democracy).[56] To be sure, it was Dr. Sun Yat-sen who started the first "democratic revolution" in Chinese history. Significantly, though Sun's idea of democracy came from the West, he never failed to remind the Chinese people that there were many seeds of democracy in ancient China.[57] In the New Cultural Movement of 1919, "democracy" as an emancipatory institution was presented—together with "Science"—as one of the two fundamental "symbolic resources" in constructing a new Chinese culture. In contemporary China, most, if not all, intellectuals would probably agree that democracy is a necessary part of modern political life. What is significant is that even the most representative New-Confucian scholars have reached the point of contending that the development of democracy should not be thought of as something externally imposed upon China, but rather as the intrinsic necessity of Chinese cultural development.[58] They believe that if China is to carry forward her cherished tradition of developing a moral society, the promotion of democracy is both urgent and essential to the task.[59]

We can see, then, that there are elements in Confucianism that are compatible with democracy, and Confucianism has not constituted a real obstacle to the acceptance of democracy in China. However, the relationship between Confucianism and liberalism is quite a different matter. The gap between them is more difficult to bridge. In the view of Tu Wei-ming, the Confucian ethic,

> unlike the puritanic ethic which stresses a consciousness of one's rights, entails duty-consciousness. It stresses the importance of social solidarity and finding one's niche in a particular group. This means understanding one's role in society with reference to a whole body of social conventions and practices. It is more of a harmonizing than a competitive model. It assigns great importance to the personal cultivation and discipline (especially the spiritual and psychological discipline) of the self. It stresses consensus formation, not through the

imposition of a particular will upon the society at large but through the participation of a large segment of the group in a gradual process of mutual consultation. . . . It seeks to create a kind of fiduciary commitment to a larger and
more lasting goal.[60]

The basic difference between Confucianism and liberalism lies in their respective views on the relationship between the individual and society. Although both liberalism and Confucianism cherish the worth of the individual,
Confucianism does not see the individual and society in polar terms. As Fingarette asserts, "we would do better to think of Confucius as concerned with
the nature of 'humanity' rather than with the polar terms 'individual' and 'society'. The formulation in terms of individual and society reflects western preoccupations and categories."[61]

As mentioned above, liberalism and individualism have a special relationship, and Western modernity is linked to individualism.[62] But the East Asian
experience demonstrates that democracy and modernity are not necessarily
inseparable from individualism. Peter Berger holds that "the development of
modernity in the West suggests a reciprocal relationship with individualism"
and this has made various theorists of modernization assume that individualism is inevitably and intrinsically linked to modernity. But, he argues,

> The East Asian experience, at the very least, make this assumption less self-
> evident. . . . [I]t can be plausibly argued that East Asia, even in its most mod-
> ernized sectors, continues to adhere to values of collective solidarity and disci-
> pline that strike the Western observer as very different indeed from his
> accustomed values and patterns of conduct. The recent discussion about Japan-
> ese styles of business and industrial management has brought this feature into
> sharp relief. Could it be that East Asia has successfully generated a non-indi-
> vidualistic version of capitalist modernity? If so, the linkage between moder-
> nity, capitalism and individualism has not been inevitable or intrinsic; rather it
> would have to be reinterpreted as the outcome of contingent historical cir-
> cumstances.[63]

Though the Confucian value orientation cannot be neatly characterized as
collectivist, it is certainly not individualist.[64] Berger's observation that East
Asia has generated a "non-individualistic version of capitalist modernity"
should be of considerable interest to students of modernization. In the same
vein, it may be argued that the distinctive feature of Asian democracy is its
"non-individualistic" character.

Given the above analysis, it is plausible to suggest that "non-individualistic" Confucianism could be made a partner of democracy. If we consider an
Asian political system, it probably would not and should not be a "Confucian
democracy," in the sense that Confucianism would be the dominant partner
vis-à-vis democracy, but it might be and should be "democratically Confu-

cian," in the sense that democracy would be the dominant partner and Confucianism would operate within the limits set by it. A "democratically Confucian" political system, not unlike liberal democracy, would cherish and respect individuals, and their rights, but would define them and their rights in "communal" and "social" terms.[65]

Asian democracy, by which I mean a "democratically Confucian" political system, is still in the early stages of developing and unfolding. I am aware that there might be as "troubled" a relationship between democracy and Confucianism as there is between liberalism and democracy. (Indeed, the "trouble" might be even greater.) However, I see no intrinsic reason why Confucianism, and especially its reconstructed version,[66] cannot become a genuine partner of democracy. It may not be wide of the mark to say that if East Asia is going to become politically modern, this will most plausibly be as a "democratically Confucian" society. And, if there is to be a viable alternative to liberal democracy provided by the East, it will be this form of "Asian democracy."

NOTES

1. Marc F. Plattner, "The Democratic Moment," *Journal of Democracy* (Fall 1991), p. 40.

2. Samuel Huntington, "Democracy's Third Wave," *Journal of Democracy* (Spring 1991), p. 12.

3. Francis Fukuyama, "The End of History?" *The National Interest* (Summer 1989), pp. 3–18.

4. Francis Fukuyama, *The End of History and the Last Man* (New York: Free Press, 1992), p. 45.

5. Raymond D. Gastil, "What Kind of Democracy," *Dialogue* (no. 1, 1991), p. 10.

6. Leszek Kolakowski, "Uncertainties of a Democratic Age" in *The Global Resurgence of Democracy,* Larry Diamond and Marc F. Platter, eds. (Baltimore: Johns Hopkins University Press, 1993), pp. 321–24.

7. Charles S. Maier, "Democracy and Its Discontents," *Foreign Affairs* (July 1984), p. 54.

8. Louis Hartz, "Democracy: Image and Reality" in *Democracy Today,* N. N. Chambers and R. H. Salisbury, eds. (New York: Collins Books, 1962), p. 42.

9. Ken Jowitt, "The New World Disorder," *Journal of Democracy* (July 1992), pp. 16–17.

10. John Dun, *Western Political Theory in the Face of the Future* (Cambridge: Cambridge University Press, 1979), p. 11.

11. E. Gellner, "Democracy and Industrialization" in *Readings in Social Evolution and Future,* S. N. Eisenstadt, ed. (Cambridge: Cambridge University Press, 1979), p. 2.

12. David Held, ed., *Prospects for Democracy: North, South, East, West* (Cambridge: Polity Press, 1993), p. 14.

13. David Beetham, "Liberal Democracy and the Limits of Democratization" in *Prospects for Democracy: North, South, East, West,* David Held, ed. (Cambridge: Polity Press, 1993), p. 60.

14. See Roland Robertson, "After Nostalgia: Willful Nostalgia and the Phases of Globalization" in *Theories of Modernity and Post-Modernity,* B. S. Turner, ed. (London: Sage Publications, 1990), pp. 45–61.

15. *Asian Wall Street Journal* (June 1), 1994.

16. B. I. Schwartz, "Culture, Modernity, and Nationalism—Further Reflections," *Daedalus* (Summer 1993), p. 207.

17. Charles Taylor, "Inwardness and the Culture of Modernity" in *Philosophical Interventions in the Unfinished Project of Enlightenment,* Alex Honneth, Thomas MaCarthy, Claus Offe, and Albrecht Wellmer, eds., trans. William Rehg (Cambridge: MIT Press, 1992), pp. 88–110.

18. Consult C. P. Macpherson, *The Life and Times of Liberal Democracy* (Oxford: Oxford University Press, 1977).

19. Raymond Gastil, "What Kind of Democracy," *Dialogue* (January 1991), pp. 10–13.

20. Consult Reinhard Bendix, *Kings or People* (Berkeley: University of California Press, 1978). Karl Popper saw Athenian democracy as the classical form of democracy, in which one encounters the rule of the people as such, though he by no means endorsed it. See "Popper on Democracy: The Open Society and its Enemies Revisited," *The Economist* (April 23, 1988), pp. 23–26.

21. Gastil, op. cit., pp. 11–12.

22. Bhikhu Parekh, "Cultural Particularity of Liberal Democracy" in *Prospects for Democracy: North, South, East, West,* David Held ed. (Cambridge: Polity Press, 1993), p. 157.

23. Schwartz, "Culture, Modernity, and Nationalism," *Daedalus* (Summer 1993), p. 215.

24. S. N. Eisenstadt, "Cultural Tradition, Historical Experience, and Social Change: The Limits of Convergence" in *The Tanner Lectures on Human Values,* vol. XI. (Salt Lake City: University of Utah Press, 1990), p. 503.

25. B. Parekh, "Cultural Particularity of Liberal Democracy," p. 172.

26. J. Dun, *Western Political Theory in the Face of the Future,* p. 33.

27. David Riesman, "Egocentrism: Is the American Character Changing?" *Encounter* (August 1980), p. 21.

28. "A Whole Greater than Its Parts?" in *Time* (February 25, 1991).

29. See Stanley Vittoz, "The Unresolved Partnership of Liberalism and Democracy in the Americal Political Tradition" in *10 IOTOPIA,* Department of History, The Chinese University of Hong Kong, ed. (Hong Kong: 1993), pp. 282, 299.

30. Peter Berger, "An East Asian Development Model" in *In Search of An East Asian Development Model,* Peter L. Berger and Hsin-Huang Michael Hsiao, eds. (New Brunswick: Transaction Books, 1988), p. 4.

31. Max Weber, *The Religion of China: Confucianism and Taoism,* trans. H. H. Gerth (New York: Free Press, 1951).

32. A pertinent critique of Weber's work on Confucianism can be found in Thomas Metzger, *Escape from Predicament* (New York: Columbia University Press, 1977), p. 235ff.

33. I have argued elsewhere that Confucianism in traditional China should be conceptualized as "Institutional Confucianism" in that Confucianism provided the ideological and institutional infrastructure of the imperial system. See Ambrose Y. C. King, *Zhong Guo She Hui Yu Wen Hua* (Oxford: Oxford University Press, 1992), p. 110ff.

34. Roy Hofheinz, Jr. and Kent E. Calder, *The Eastasia Edge* (New York: Basic Books, 1982).

35. Peter Berger, "An East Asian Development Model," p. 5.

36. S. P. Huntington, "What price Freedom?" *Harvard International Review* (Winter 1992–93).

37. Seymour M. Lipset, "Some Social Requisites of Democracy: Economic Development and Political Legitimacy," *American Political Science Review* (vol. 53, March 1959), p. 80.

38. I have explored and analyzed elsewhere the plausible causes of democratization in Taiwan in a paper entitled "A Non-Paradigmatic Search for Democracy in a Post-Confucian Culture: The Case of Taiwan, R.O.C." in *Political Culture and Democracy in Developing Countries*, Larry Diamond, ed. (Boulder: Lynne Rienner, 1993).

39. Milton Friedman writes, "History suggests only that capitalism is a necessary condition for political freedom," and he adds, "clearly it is not a sufficient condition." Milton Friedman, *Capitalism and Democracy* (Chicago: University of Chicago Press, 1962), p. 10.

40. F. Fukuyama, *The End of History and the Last Man*, p. 238.

41. *Time* (June 14, 1993), p. 17.

42. Gilbert Rozman, "The East Asian Region in Comparative Perspective" in *The East Asian Region: Confucian Heritage and Its Modern Adaptation*, G. Rozman, ed. (Princeton: Princeton University Press, 1991), p. 12.

43. S. P. Huntington, "Democracy's Third Wave," *Journal of Democracy* (Spring 1991), p. 18.

44. Ibid., pp. 15, 21.

45. Ralph Milband, "The Socialist Alternative," *Journal of Democracy* (July 1992), p. 119. For C. P. Macpherson, liberal democracy has two meanings: first, "the democracy of a capitalist market society," and second, "a society striving to ensure that all its members are equally free to realize their capabilities." However, Macpherson was of the view that up until the 1970s "the market view has prevailed: 'liberal' has consciously or unconsciously been assumed to mean 'capitalist'." C. P. Macpherson, *The Life and Times of Liberal Democracy* (Oxford: Oxford University Press, 1977), pp. 1–2.

46. Seymour Martin Lipset, "The Centrality of Political Culture" in *The Global Resurgence of Democracy*, Larry Diamond and Marc F. Platter, eds. (Baltimore: Johns Hopkins University Press, 1993), p. 137.

47. Consult Gilbert Rozman, ed., *The East Asian Region: Confucian Heritage and Its Modern Adaption* (Princeton: Princeton University Press, 1991), p. 6.

48. Mou Zong San, *Sheng Dao Yu Zhi Dao* (Taipei: Guang Wen Shu Ju, 1974).

49. Richard Solomon, *Mao's Revolution and the Chinese Political Culture* (Berkeley: University of California Press, 1971), pp. 78–81.

50. Wm. Theodore de Bary, *The Liberal Tradition in China* (Hong Kong: The Chinese University Press, 1983).

51. Ambrose Y. C. King, *Shong Guo Min Ben Si Xiang Shi* (Taipei: Commercial Press Ltd, 1993). A somewhat negative version on *minben* can also be found in Andrew J. Nathan, *Chinese Democracy* (New York: Alfred A. Knopf, 1985), p. 127ff.

52. "A Roundtable Discussion of *The Trouble with Confucianism* by Wm. Theodore de Bary," *China Review International* (Spring 1994), pp. 36–52.

53. Chang Hao, "Intellectual Crisis of Contemporary China in Historical Perspective" in *The Triadic Chord: Confucian Ethics, Industrial East Asia and Max Weber,* Tu Wei-ming, ed. (Singapore: The Institute of East Asian Philosophies, 1991), pp. 325–50.

54. A brilliant and representative case study has been done by Benjamin Schwartz, *In Search of Wealth and Power: Yen Fu and the West* (New York: Harper Torchbooks, 1964).

55. Ibid., pp. 239–40.

56. Wang Er Min, *Wan Qing Sheng Zhi Si Xiang Shi Lun* (Taipei: Hua Shi Chu Ban She, 1969), pp. 220–76.

57. Ambrose Y. C. King, *Zhong Guo Min Ben Si Xiang Shi* (Taipei: Commercial Press, 1993).

58. Mou Zong San, Xu Fu Guan, Zhang Jun Li, Tang Jun Yi, *Zhong Guo Wen Hua Yu Shi Jie: Wo Men Dui Zhong Guo Xue Shu Yan Jiu Ji Zhong Guo Wen Hua Yu Shi Jie Wen Hua Qian Tu Zhing Gong Tong Ren Shi,* 1958.

59. Chang Hao, "Intellectual crisis of contemporary China in Historical perspective," p. 338.

60. Tu Wei-ming, *Confucian Ethics Today: The Singapore Challenge* (Singapore: Curriculum Development Institute of Singapore, 1984), pp. 110–11.

61. Herbert Fingarette, *Confucius: The Secular as Sacred* (New York: Harper Torchbooks, 1972), pp. 72–73.

62. Talcott Parsons defined modernity in terms of three inseparable dimensions: the market economy, democratic polity, and individualism. See Parsons, *The System of Modern Societies* (Englewood Cliffs: Prentice Hall, 1971), p. 14ff.

63. P. L. Berger, "An East Asian Development Model?" p. 6.

64. I have argued elsewhere that neither individualism nor collectivism can characterize the Confucian relationship between the individual and the group. I have instead advanced a view that the Confucian social theory adopts neither an individualistic nor a collectivistic but a "relational" perspective. I wrote, "For good or bad, the Confucian relational perspective did provide the Chinese with a way of creating a long-standing social system in which the individual who is a relational being endowed with a self-centered autonomy, finds himself in a complicated and humanly rich relational web he could hardly afford to escape." See Ambrose Y. C. King, "The Individual and Group in Confucianism: A Relational Perspective," in *Individualism and Holism: Studies in Confucian and Taoist Values,* Donald J. Munro, ed. (Ann Arbor: University of Michigan Press, 1985), pp. 65–66.

65. I am inspired here by the writings of Bhikhu Parekh, who argues for a political system which is "democratically liberal" rather than a liberal democracy. (See his article cited above.)

66. Tu Wei-ming points out that the new Confucian ethic "does not oppose western ideas of rights, individual dignity, autonomy, or competitiveness in the healthy and

dynamic sense." See Tu Wei-ming, op. cit., p. 111. One important task of the neo-Confucians' project is to assimilate the Confucian concept of self as having a Heaven-endowed inner nature to the German concept of freedom as focused on the idea of the moral development of the self and also to the Kantian idea of treating every individual person as an end. It is argued that "implied in these ideas of freedom are not so much the May Fourth's notion of democracy as an emancipatory institution as the conception of democracy as a participatory community of morally autonomous individuals." See Chang Hao, op. cit., p. 339.

Chung-Ying Cheng

CAN WE DO JUSTICE TO ALL THEORIES OF JUSTICE?

TOWARD INTEGRATING CLASSICAL AND MODERN PARADIGMS OF JUSTICE

I. METHODOLOGICAL OBSERVATIONS

Despite the many discussions on the subject, the problem of justice has always retained a freshness and incisiveness that challenges our understanding. This is because, in our search for a theoretical explanation of a theory of justice and a rational account of its applicability, we always start from an immediate and concrete sense of justice or injustice. Thus consider the recent problem of socialized medicine and healthcare in America: Which theoretical approach among the proprietarians, communitarians, utilitarians, and contractarians[1] will most fully satisfy our demand for (which is to say, our concrete sense of) justice? Or consider the rival claims being advanced in developing countries for economic development and political stability on the one hand and for human rights and democratization on the other: Which set of claims is to be granted priority here on the basis of our sense of justice? Even on a purely theoretical level, we might ask, must a man of virtue and a sense of duty be considered more just than a rational hedonist? It would seem that we could argue for many different theories of justice on the basis of our immediate and concrete sense of justice, and yet our concrete sense of justice is not likely to be entirely satisfied by any single theory of justice.

Our concrete sense of justice is embedded in a rich ambiguity of contexts and traditions, and consequently appeals to different theories for its explication and justification at different times and on different levels. Our theories of justice themselves, moreover, are all subject to certain intrinsic constraints and even contradictions and thus cannot be extended to cover all significant cases. MacIntyre, in confronting the existence of "rival justices" and "competing rationalities," has already asked: "whose justice" shall we adopt? and "which rationality" shall we recognize? I wish to explore somewhat further this issue of the existence of many justices, and to raise the question of whether and how we might be able to combine them. I feel that it is only fair and appropriate to at least attempt to do justice to rival justices by providing an account of their differences and considering the possibility of harmonizing them. As a small gesture toward tackling this larger project, then, in this paper I want to consider the possibility of integrating *some* theories of justice on two separate levels—the personal and the state level.

I will begin by examining two classical models of justice—the Platonic and the Confucian—which are very different in content and yet which share the aim of establishing an ideal state of justice for all humanity. These classical models of justice will then be compared with some modern theories of justice, which are grounded in our recently developed awareness of collective humanity, and which are intended to be realized in various kinds of social organization (i.e., the community or the nation-state). We shall see specifically how Rawls' theory of justice as fairness has been developed as a creative integration of two earlier positions—namely, natural rights theory and utilitarianism—and how, given its scope and the level of social organization to which it applies, it may have difficulties in assuring justice on a personal level, and thus may itself require integration and incorporation into a larger understanding of moral practice. In this light, we should come to see not only certain possibilities of synthesis with respect to the problem of justice, but also how Confucianism could be given a new direction that would have important implications for the development of political and social justice and democracy in contemporary China and the rest of the world.

II. TWO MODELS OF THE VIRTUE THEORY OF JUSTICE

In the *Republic,* Plato conceives of justice as a harmony of the soul—a harmony that is grounded upon knowledge of what we want and of what we can do, on a clear and objective understanding of what people's interests, rights, and obligations are. This understanding, moreover, must not be overwhelmed by our own private desires and passions. To be able to control those desires and passions is to exercise our rationality or reason for the purpose of leading a good and harmonious life, which is intrinsically valuable. The rational control of our desires and passions will not only enable us to see things in a true light; it will enable us to govern our actions with a sense of right measure and due proportion. The exercise of rational control over our desires and passions thus brings about a unity among the various parts of the individual human being.

We must note that the Greek term for justice (*dikaiosyne*) connotes a concrete sense of justice (*dike*: right, law, ethos, lawfulness) which applies to the individual person (*dikaios*) and his action in relation to other people. As rational control, justice is realized as the exhibition of different kinds of virtue in different relationships. For this reason, justice is not merely the sum of all virtues, but the source of all virtues. This means that justice enables a virtue to be a virtue and distributes the various virtues into an internally ordered pattern. Rationality, as the sense of proportion and ratio of the individual person, is thus the bringing together of different things in such a way that each thing will function well in the company of the others.

To the extent that an individual person has ordered his soul in justice and harmony, he can be said to have reached the implicit goal (*telos*) of self-realization. Like Confucius, Plato considered this implicit goal in relation to the function of human nature. He saw it as a capacity for "excellence" (*areté*) in the functioning of man and defined justice as the ideal state of virtue that brings out this excellence. There is, however, no speculation on the question of where this capacity for excellence comes from, even though Plato implied (via his Myth of Er in Book X of the *Republic*) that the human soul, having been exposed to the rational forms in its preincarnate state, must retain in its earthly incarnation a strong inclination to recover its sense of the whole of reality. This inclination thus stands as the ultimate source of justice and virtue.

The holistic nature of justice in Plato depends, of course, on a specific ontology of the human individual. According to Plato, the human soul has three parts—namely, reason, spirit, and desire—each of which has a virtue pertaining to it. These are wisdom for reason, courage or honor for spirit, and temperance for desire. As Plato sees it, the concrete and actual self is a product of the union of body and soul, the interaction of which gives rise to these three parts of the human individual, among which reason alone is immortal and separable from the body.[2]

Although Plato does not focus on knowledge of one's self and of other people as a basis for righteous action, it is clear that if justice is a goal to be reached, it requires this sort of practical knowledge (*phronesis*). Moreover, given Plato's understanding of justice as intrinsic to proper human functioning, it follows that justice, as excellence in the exercise of human faculties, is precisely that wherein the individual's well-being or happiness consists. In fact, all actions that contribute to the individual's well-being will have originated in the state of his soul that Plato calls justice. This means, of course, that we do not justify justice by an appeal to any external standard or goal. Justice is rather the goal that is reached if certain conditions are met that contribute to our living well or to the attainment of happiness.[3]

The question confronting us now is how is this view of justice to be applied to human society and the state. To some limited extent, of course, interpersonal justice can be brought about by the just person. But could the just individual achieve justice for a whole society or state on the basis of his own personal virtue? Hardly. In pursuing this question of the organization of a just society or state, Plato applied the logic of analogy—likening society as a whole to the individual human being and projecting social justice as a harmony between three social classes corresponding to the three parts of the soul. The question, however, is who in the state is to assume the ruling role of reason and who is to assume the supportive roles of spirit and appetite. Plato's answer, naturally, is that those individuals who excel in their cultivation of the virtues of reason and who thus possess wisdom should constitute the ruling class, whereas those individuals who excel in activities associated with spirit and desire should constitute the subordinate classes. Plato felt that there should be an internal harmony achieved among the three classes of individuals, each of which has a particular function to perform in the ongoing life of the state. This conclusion is difficult to accept, however, for a couple of reasons.

In the first place, if every individual is to achieve justice as an internal state, there seems to be no reason why one class of persons should be privileged with a ruling status. If everyone, as Plato's theory seems to imply, possesses the capacity to attain the state of personal justice, then each person deserves the same treatment as his neighbors, for they are equal and equivalent with regard to their proper functioning as human individuals. (The rational justification of class distinction and structures of command is not convincingly provided by either Plato or Aristotle. Perhaps it is not until modern times that theories concerning the origins of the state are proposed. But in contemporary—which is to say, twentieth-century—philosophy it is not until Rawls that the specific question of political institutional justice is seriously examined.)

In the second place, because Plato sees the state as an organism like the individual human being, he has argued for a very organic but closed system of government in which the three classes of citizens—philosopher-kings, warriors, and workers—are fixed in their vocations and in the relations in which they stand to each other. For the purpose of maintaining the orderly function of the state, individual freedom and mobility are to all effect abolished. In this sense, then, the rationally planned state deprives its individual citizens of their individuality. And thus, from the point of view of the attainment of personal justice as well as from the point of view of equality, Plato's Republic constitutes a closed society and a fundamentally unjust society.[4]

Plato's theory of justice, then, is a theory of justice as virtue based on the primacy of the paradigm of the individual soul, and he has failed to recognize the essential structural difference between the individual and a collection of individuals as a society. His application of the paradigm of the soul to the state thus constitutes a kind of category mistake and, conseqently, we need to move beyond this conception of social justice.

Where Plato based his idea of political justice on a model of the human soul, Confucius and his followers based their idea of social justice on the model of the human family. This new view of political justice, however, is also premised on the conception of justice as virtue, albeit a virtue conceived in the light of a different understanding of human nature. Confucius proposed an ideal norm according to which not only is the individual intended to attain the perfection of his life as a person, but society and the state are also intended to attain a desirable order and well-being, which are consistent with the internal ordering and individual well-being of the person.[5] For Confucius, the key to both is the notion and philosophy of *ren* (cohumanity).[6]

I shall argue that justice for Confucius and his followers (such as Mencius) consists in the cultivation of *ren* in the individual person and the obtaining of the *renzheng* (government by benevolence) in a state. In fact, we can see that in Confucianism justice is a rich and open concept that has undergone a process of development in terms of the notion of *ren* as a virtue and as a principle just as Plato's notion of justice was developed out of his understanding of rationality and of harmony based on rationality. Both *ren* and justice are complete or whole virtues under which other virtues can be subsumed. Although we can contrast *ren* as cohumanity with *dikaiosyne* as rationality and contrast justice based on *ren* with justice based on lawfulness, there is nevertheless a large measure of overlap in Confucian and Platonic efforts to define the just person as the whole person and justice as the whole of virtue. Nonetheless, with respect to their conceptions of political justice, the differences between Plato and Confucius are as significant as their similarities.

In spite of *ren*'s being conceived as the whole of virtue and as an ideal norm of human development, we may still ask whether there is a specific element of justice in *ren*. My answer to this is "yes." Among the many meanings of *ren* to be found in the *Analects,* the idea of negative reciprocity, as expressed in the Confucian statement, "One does not do to another what one does not desire others to do to you,"[7] and the idea of positive reciprocity, as expressed in that other Confucian statement, "In wishing to establish oneself, attempt to establish others; in wishing to reach for perfection, attempt to help others to do the same,"[8] offer two important principles and criteria for defining justice as an interpersonal relation. Both reciprocities capture the spirit of equity in our common sense of justice, for there cannot be justice if there is no reciprocity, either negative or positive.[9]

The substance of *ren* consists in loving people (*airen*), which means giving people consideration regarding their spiritual and material needs. This consideration is expressed in controlling one's own desires (*keji*) and behaving according to the rules of propriety (*fuli*). Confucius recognizes that, in cultivating his capacity for virtue, the individual human being must take particular care that his private desires and passions do not prevent or obstruct such development. Although Confucius does not speculate on how the individual can come to possess *ren*, his declaration that "If I wish to have *ren, ren* is right here"[10] leaves no doubt that he believes that there is something in the human constitution that naturally gives rise to the virtues. He does not elaborate on human nature (*xing*) as Mencius does later, yet he clearly has the strong belief that dispositions to virtues are indigenous in the human person and that one should pay attention to one's dispositions in order to realize virtues. He also believes, however, that there is a dark side to the human mind, which gives rise to prejudice (*yi*), dogmatism (*pi*), stubbornness (*gu*), and selfishness (*wo*).[11] To cultivate oneself is to avoid these undesirable qualities of mind and to concentrate on one's natural tendencies to do the right things. Once a person cultivates himself in this sense, he will not be motivated to harm other people. In fact, he will treat others as he wishes to be treated himself, and achieve justice as a whole virtue.

Li is to be understood as those conventions that regulate our relationships in such a way as to produce social and political harmony. Hence to achieve justice is not just a matter of controlling one's desires, but also a matter of articulating one's actions and attitudes in forms of *li*. As *ren* is the whole of virtue that each individual is to cultivate and pursue, we may see justice as embodied or subsumed in *ren* as the development of cohumanity in an individual and society. When Confucius urges his disciples to understand *ren* or explains to them how to understand *ren*, he implicitly answers the question of the nature of justice.

Given our explication of *ren* in terms of reciprocity, self-control, and the recognition of proprieties, it is clear that we could regard *ren* as a general principle of justice that would entail the performance of just actions by a just person. But if we wish to speak of specific acts of justice, we have to understand the specific principle of justice that is referred to in the Confucian discourse as *yi* (which is conventionally translated into English as "righteousness"). *Yi*, as it appears in the classical Confucian texts, is the general principle in accordance with which in each specific situation we reach a value judgement concerning the rightness or wrongness of a specific act.[12] In other words, in arriving at an assessment of the rightness or wrongness of a given case, one must look into specific circumstances, so that one's value judgment will conform to a proper understanding of the case. *Yi* directs one's attention to the specific meaning of a specific thing and as a principle will inform one's evaluation of the case in question. It is not accidental that the idea of *yi* as righteousness is derived from and closely related to the idea of *yi* as meaning or significance; both notions are derived from the idea of a good omen (the sheep) in ancient sacrificial ceremony.[13]

The meaning of a situation, unlike the meaning of a word, is what inspires and motivates people in their understanding of the situation and their consequent action toward the situation. It is also what gives meaning to a word if a word is used to refer to that situation. Thus *yi* can be understood as that which fits a situation and thus characterizes the situation. To act correctly and justly in a situation is, first of all, to realize the *yi* as the meaning of the situation, and then to see the relevant values and "oughtness" and thus the *yi* as righteousness with respect to the situation, and finally, to act appropriately in the situation. Hence *yi* provides an understanding of the meaning of a situation and suggests a norm for action in light of such an understanding.[14]

In this connection, we can sympathize with Gaozi in regarding *yi* as external to one's mind while regarding *ren* as internal.[15] Although Mencius has argued that, like *ren*, *yi* is a matter of judgment and feeling, we may nonetheless make a distinction between two levels of *yi*—meaning and norm—and thus reconcile the insights of Gaozi and Menzi. I call Gaozi's view an insight, because he has seen that the specificity of doing the right thing depends on the recognition of a specific state of affairs, and thus on the comprehension of the meaning of the situation. One can do justice to a thing only if one has identified the thing in question as that to which one is to do justice.[16]

Mencius, as a close follower of Confucius, made an important move toward consolidating the Confucian philosophy of justice as virtue, by focusing on human nature as an inexhaustible source of all virtues, including the specific virtue referred to as *yi*. He held that the feeling (or heart) of shamefulness (*xiuwuzhixin*) is the beginning of *yi* and that this feeling is rooted in human nature (*xing*) and amounts to a natural human propensity. This suggestion provides a way of integrating all of the virtues not only in terms of their singular origin but in terms of their mutual interdependence and ideal unity as the ultimate goal of human self-cultivation. Mencius' insight into the origin of *yi* as shamefulness focused on the inherent dignity of a person among his peers and in social relationships. To be able to foster *yi* in this sense is to be able to preserve the intrinsic dignity and social respectability of a person. Justice is thus essentially a matter of the preservation of human dignity— in both an individual and a social sense.

So far I have presented Plato's theory of justice and Confucius's theory of justice in order to show how these two theories, while different in many respects, could still have many things in common. One major characteristic that they share is that each conceives of justice on the basis of a holistic understanding of human purpose and human nature. Even though Plato appears to speak only of the human *telos,* he could easily (which is to say, quite compatibly with his other beliefs) have developed a theory of human nature that resembled the Confucian-Mencian philosophy of human nature. Both Plato and Confucius incline us to believe, then, that we will not be able to understand justice without an understanding of human purpose and human nature. Furthermore, it is important to note that the understanding of justice thus arrived at should be considered a realistic conception, rather than a conventional, or speculative, or aprioristic conception, being based as it is on deep reflection concerning human feelings and aspirations in the light of the rich historical experiences of man.

III. EMERGENCE OF MODERN THEORIES OF JUSTICE

The classical ideals of justice as *dikaiosyne* and as *ren/yi* were not successfully applied or incorporated on social and national levels even though their application and incorporation were attempted. Consequently, we must see them as an awakening of humanistic consciousness and a representation of humanistic ideals that were made possible by the troubled conditions of the societies in which they arose. The brutal facts of gross injustice aroused a strong reaction: stimulating profound reflection on human nature, out of which arose a sense of justice which in turn became a force for social and political reform. But we must admit that when these noble ideals were applied to actual political and social situations, they failed. Could we organize our society and state according to the Platonic metaphor of the tripartite soul or the Confucian metaphor of the family? Even though the Confucian social structure in the East lasted much longer than did the political experiments with Platonism in the West, it crumpled nevertheless in the modern period. But still there is no reason to doubt that the classical models of justice do give us an insight into how humanity aspired to justice and how a just personhood could be ideally cultivated to full fruition under ideal conditions. We must see them as belonging to a basic conception of justice in so far as interpersonal and intersubjective transactions between or among people are concerned.

The transition from the classical period to the modern period in human history is much too complicated a story to be rehearsed here. But it is important to notice that it is in the modern period that man comes to develop a radically new consciousness of the basic conditions for human society—one which is marked by a sense of the importance of the liberation of the human individual from traditional forms of domination, whether these be social, religious, or political. Given this new consciousness of individual freedom, the existence of society and the state require a new understanding and new explanation. For this reason, we may regard the combination of an individualistic consciousness with a contractarian explanation of the origin of the state and society as the overarching hallmark of modernity. We may cite the works of John Locke (1632–1704), Jean-Jacques Rousseau (1712–1778), and Immanuel Kant (1724–1804) as providing the first signs of modern political consciousness in the West. Even though Rousseau may not live up to our present standards of democracy,[17] he provided the possibility for the democratization of a state as well as the possibility for totalitarianism in a state—both, ironically, through his notion of the "general will." This makes him especially relevant for modernity, for in the modern period there appear both totalitarian and democratic state systems, both of which claim the right to rule based on an appeal to the will of the people. The most important elements of modernity, however, are still the recognition of the relative independence of an individual from society and the state as well as the recognition of the theoretical possibility that individuals are free to choose and rationally construct a society of their collective choice.

Although the liberation of the individual from political domination may have been achieved in the actual history of the West (insofar as it has been) through painstakingly slow and devious processes, it seems nonetheless that the goal has been (largely) attained primarily because of the revolutionary change in modern man's consciousness of the freedom of the human individual *vis-à-vis* society and the state. So long as this consciousness prevails, of course, the democratic ideal—understood as the general consent of the people to the decisions of those who rule, and their active participation in the decision-making process, by means of elections and the mechanisms of representative government—will remain central to the modern notion of social and political justice.

We must also recognize, however, that modern science and technology and international trade have been instrumental in shaping the structure of modern nation-states. The guiding spirit of their organization (and reorganization) has been economic development under the spur of advances in science and technology. The rise of the concept of the free market in the eighteenth century was not accidental and was contingent on the assertion of the individual's rights to use his own talents in the pursuit of his own profits.[18] Granted, this new economic freedom has abetted modern man's appetites and his greed, leading to the unrestrained pursuit of wealth and power, sometimes even under the pretext of glorifying God.[19] Still we need not to confuse the need for a free market with the craze for possessive exploitation of the market to the exclusion of humanistic considerations of equality and liberty. Clearly, though, the radical development of capitalism has resulted in evils which must be corrected.

Historically, the antidote that we have been offered to the evils of capitalism has been the communist movement, which, in the name of economic equality, asks us to forfeit the free market and with it the freedom of man. What I want to stress here is simply this: a large segment of humankind has experienced the radical oscillation from one politico-economic extreme to the other and has suffered under both forms of extremism—that of the right and that of the left—and this should give us ample reason to think carefully and to seek a system of justice that would avoid the errors of these two extremist positions. Modern man, in other words, should take into consideration both the positive and negative lessons to be gleaned from ancient and recent human history in forming his concrete sense of justice and meeting the challenges of the modern world.

It is noteworthy that radical capitalism thrives on the basis of unrestricted freedom and that the result of such licentiousness is not only the wide gap between the rich and the poor but the destruction of the equality of social and political liberty that was initially assumed. On the other hand, in radical socialism (i.e., communism) the original striving for equality under a proletarian dictatorship not only destroys both economic liberty and political liberty but eventually destroys the intended equality by introducing a permanent privileged class of the party elite. History has demonstrated the former irony in the nineteenth century and the latter irony in the twentieth century. What we have learned from these ironies is not simply that economic equality and political liberty may not be mutually compatible, but also that economic power may subsume political power just as political power may subsume economic power.

On the basis of these lessons, we recognize that we need a system of justice in which both economic freedom and economic equality are protected, and in which political freedom leads to economic equality rather than to economic inequality. Considerations of precisely this sort have led to the development of John Rawls' theory of justice as fairness. The spirit of contractarianism in Rawls is meant to resist the deleterious effects of excessive freedom on equality and simultaneously to resist the deleterious effects of excessive equality on liberty. Rawls wants both liberty and equality in his theory, but in formulating his two principles of justice, he nonetheless gives us the impression that his theory is biased toward political liberty at the expense of economic equality. His theory is bound to conflict with the socialist doctrine of justice that we can expect will emerge from this postcapitalist postcommunist era, and in which economic and social equality will be guaranteed on an equal basis with political liberty.

At present, I do not intend to critically evaluate Rawls' theory as a representation of our modern sense of justice, since many authors have already done this.[20] Nevertheless, it is interesting to note that Rawls rules out or simply ignores the possibility that his two principles of justice could be prioritized differently—namely, in such a way as first to guarantee basic equalities, especially economic, but noneconomic as well (which would thus include basic political liberties), and then to introduce social and structural constraints for the purpose of redistributing wealth, power, and status. His two principles of political justice are:

1. Each person is to have an equal right to the most extensive basic liberty compatible with a similar liberty for others.
2. Social and economic inequalities are to be arranged so that they are both (a) to the greatest benefit of the least advantaged and (b) attached to offices and positions open to all under conditions of fair equality of opportunity.[21]

But clearly, without basic economic equality an individual's possession of liberty is very much restricted. To speak of the individual's possession of basic liberties without guaranteeing his economic security is to address an ideal without giving any thought to the means of its implementation, which in turn is mere empty sloganizing.

Rawls, in other words, does not adequately consider how his second principle would impact upon his first principle. As it stands, one might argue that the first principle always acts as a constraint on the second principle, so that one would not allow the application of the second principle to affect the efficiency of the first principle. In actuality, however, whether the second principle will affect the efficiency of the first principle is not determined by either principle, but rather by the nature of the world and the opportunities it provides. Thus even though the acceptance of social and economic inequalities might bring immediate (economic) advantages to everyone, there is no guarantee that a gap would not eventually develop between the rich and the poor—a gap so wide that the rich would be in a position to seize all real power and in effect deprive the poor of their basic rights and liberties. (Many would claim, of course, that this has already happened in America.) Thus unless our basic rights and liberties include a guarantee of some measure of economic equality, the net result of the implementation of Rawls' two principles could well be a steady weakening of the first principle and eventually a distribution of power that would not square with our concrete sense of justice as fairness.[22]

Perhaps to profit from the lessons of the nineteenth century a theory of justice as fairness needs to include considerations of economic fairness and political fairness on an equal basis and to find a link between them, so that they may constrain each other on the one hand and promote each other on the other.

Still, Rawls' theory of justice as fairness better captures the significance of these lessons than does any other major theory. I have in mind here especially the two primary alternatives to his position, namely, proprietarianism and utilitarianism. Utilitarianism, of course, arose in a social context in which heavy industrialization and *laissez-faire* economic policy produced a huge gap between rich and poor, and utilitarianism was formulated with the intent of redressing these social and economic inequalities of the nineteenth century. Robert Nozick's proprietarianism, on the other hand, although it represents a reaction against the contractarianism of Rawls, and perhaps equally against utilitarianism as well, has its roots in the liberal tradition of John Locke, who stressed the inherent natural powers and rights of action of the individual. In this sense proprietarianism in fact antedates the liberal contractarianism of Rawls and can be said to provide the essential content for any notion of basic liberties.

Rawls' theory can be seen as a creative synthesis and modification of both proprietarianism and utilitarianism, but the question is how successful he has been in incorporating his predecessors' insights while avoiding their weaknesses. Of course, Rawls' theory of justice as fairness has to face the challenge of the future as well as the challenge of the classical past. In the final section of this paper, I shall explore how a general theory of justice must account for both justice on the social and political level and justice on the personal level, as these are formulated in Plato and Confucius, in order to meet the challenges and demands of our evolving concrete sense of justice.

IV. DOES THE JUSTICE OF A STATE ENTAIL THE JUSTICE OF ITS CITIZENS?

Even if a society is just, according to the criteria set out in Rawls' theory of justice as fairness, there is no clear mechanism that would transfer the quality of fairness from the social system to a person within the system, so that the individual himself can be said to be fair or just. This, of course, is because there are two levels of reference in play here—that of the individual and that of the state. How justice might be related *between* these two levels, however, is a crucial issue, and one upon which some light might be cast through a consideration of the classical conceptions of justice that we have been discussing.

Consider, for example, the case of a cold-blooded, calculating individual who has no concern for his community and no feelings of charity toward his neighbors, but who nonetheless meticulously obeys the laws of the land even while he manipulates the system to advance his personal interests at every opportunity. Obviously, this person could get along perfectly well in a Rawlsian just state, but he would be the sort of person whom neither Confucius nor Plato would consider just. On the other hand, a benevolent and righteous (i.e., dutiful) person, from a Confucian perspective, might have no sense of the rule of law as this is practiced in modern Western democracies and might thus be insensitive to human rights issues as we understand these today. It is quite conceivable, in other words, that one could have justice on the personal level without this entailing the recognition of justice as this pertains to the state.

In fact, this represents the permanent predicament of Confucian idealism in political philosophy: How does one realize outer kingliness on the basis of inner sageliness (*neisheng-waiwang*)?[23] Very often, however, history conspires to leave the Confucian only the hope of transforming the existing political authority into a moral power—which is to say, with the hope of realizing inner sageliness on the foundation of outer kingliness. But even this is not realistic. Not only need the ideal Confucian state not be just in the modern sense, but even where there is some beneficial influence of sagely wisdom on the ruler, it can be very limited and there is no guarantee that it will continue. Thus from a Confucian perspective one can only hope for justice on the personal level, without making it a demand at the level of the state. By contrast, in the modern state, founded on the principles of political liberalism, we may have the "outer kingliness" of law and order, but there is no guarantee that the "inner sageliness of humanity and virtue" will be realized. The question, again, is how social justice can be made to guarantee the existence of personal justice as the proper end of social communion.

The logic of virtue and the logic of political power or the pursuit of social interest are simply different logics, just as the state and the person are different entities. Each must have its range of application and each is important to the satisfaction and full realization of human potential. We should harbor no unrealistic hope of substituting one level for the other any more than we can insist on the self-sufficiency of either level for the well-being of humanity. Since both levels are levels of human behavior, it is desirable that they should become mutually supportive. But this mutual support must be premised on a recognition of the distinction between the logics of personal justice and of state justice.

I do not wish to contend that we might find a common denominator between personal justice and the justice of the state. What is important is our recognition that we have a genuine need for both given the very nature of our existence. Here we find that we have a common ground and a common measure on the basis of which we might achieve a synthesis of those values (the humanity of the individual and the rationality of the system) that we find embodied in the classical and modern traditions.

My concern here, then, is twofold: on the one hand, to harmonize the Platonic virtue of rationality with the Confucian virtue of co-humanity (*ren*); and on the other, to harmonize the virtue of rationality, as this is achieved at the level of the state, with the virtue of co-humanity, as this is achieved on the personal level. I am concerned, then, to work out the possibilities of mutual complementation. Co-humanity is needed to complement rationality at the level of state justice just as rationality is needed to complement co-humanity at the level of personal justice. Since, as MacIntyre explains, justices and rationalities can be contested, they can also be synthesized, providing we respect the various contexts in which they arose and the disparate functions they were intended to serve.

Given that the justice of individuals does not guarantee justice in the society or state, and vice versa, we might ask whether we could combine the Confucian conception of justice as the virtue of individual persons with the Rawlsian conception of justice as social fairness. There seems to be no intrinsic incompatibility between Confucianism and modern political liberalism. But, of course, if we are to effect a synthesis of the two conceptions of justice, we must ask the individual to simultaneously play two different roles: as a law-abiding citizen of the just state, on the one hand, and as a humane co-person in the network of interpersonal and social relationships, on the other. The individual must be prepared to resolve conflicts of interests and values through obedience to the laws, and yet he must be a morally cultivated individual in himself as well so that he may use his wisdom and understanding to resolve social and moral problems with or without the benefit of law.

With regard to the need to achieve a balance between laws and virtues in promoting benevolent government (*renzheng*), Mencius says something very instructive: "By mere virtues one cannot conduct government; by mere laws the government will not move by itself."[24] Mencius argues that a ruler may have the heart of *ren,* but if he does not use proven laws and norms from the past, he cannot make a good ruler. Notice that Mencius requires the ruler to be a good person first and then urges him to use good methods of rule. Thus although in practice Mencius sees an order of priority with respect to the two levels of justice—with individual justice coming before the justice of the state—he stresses the interdependence and mutual indispensability of state justice in the form of *fa* (laws and norms) and the individual justice of virtues.

Confucius too recognizes the need to distinguish between two levels of justice and speaks of the primordial importance and indispensability of *ren* at the level of the individual as the sustaining basis or foundation of state justice. Confucius also distinguishes between *ren,* as the whole of virtue, and *zhi* or knowledge. Although knowledge can also be regarded as a virtue, the special value of knowledge for Confucius is that it enables the individual to establish himself in society and to relate to other people. In a broader sense, it can also be said to imply the understanding of the nature of government.[25] Confucius argues, however, that even if one has the best form of knowledge, it will be lost if one does not preserve it with a human heart and carry out its dictates with propriety.[26] Confucius' message is clear: if we interpret *ren* as pertaining to justice on the personal level and *zhi* as pertaining to justice on the state level, justice on the personal level is not only the starting point for justice on the state level, it is the constant guard and moving (not merely motivating) force for state justice. Hence a just society cannot be just without just persons who will not even for a single moment abandon justice.

The distinction between the laws (*fa*) and the virtues (*shan*) in Mencius and the distinction between knowledge (*zhi*) and co-humanity (*ren*) in Confucius provide us with a clue on how to perceive the relationship between the two levels of the justice. For the Confucian, personal justice is absolutely fundamental. But even so the classical Confucian always recognizes the necessity of state justice, which can be achieved through the application of knowledge and which is to be expressed in norms and laws. There is therefore no reason why a Confucian theory of justice as virtue at the personal level cannot be integrated with a liberal and democratic theory of justice as fairness at the state level. The development of a framework for harmonizing the two levels of justice may take some time, but its importance in bringing about intertraditional recognition of justice as an all-encompassing system of human cooperation, mutual learning, and mutual support cannot be doubted. Rawls has made an important and successful step toward integrating the European traditions of natural rights theory and utilitarianism in a contractarian unity—all in the best Greek spirit of *logos.* Perhaps the next significant step would be an attempt to unify the modern liberal political tradition of human rights and democracy with the humanistic traditions of *renyi* and *dikaiosyne* from classical China and Greece. What I have attempted to do in this paper is to give some sense of what such a synthesis might involve.

NOTES

1. This terminology is borrowed from Philip Pettit, *Judging Justice: An Introduction to Contemporary Political Philosophy* (London: Routledge and Kegan Paul, 1980). See the introduction.

2. Unlike the Neo-Confucianists, Plato has not speculated on the metaphysical nature of mind and body (or *li* and *qi*—see below) and thus he leaves the nature of the spirit of man in large measure unexplained. But it is clear that it is in the union of soul and body that earthly life comes into being, which in turn makes the struggle of reason and desire a reality.

3. This point, of course, is developed at much greater length by Aristotle. There is an intrinsic teleology of the human soul in Plato which only becomes explicit in Aristotle. What interests us is the shift in the definition of justice as it moves from a reference to external behavior to motivational analysis and understanding. It can be summarized as follows: "Just actions depend on just persons."

4. See Karl Popper, *The Open Society and Its Enemies*, vol. 1 (London: Routledge & Kegan Paul, 1945). The following questions, then, need to be addressed: Must political justice sacrifice individual justice? What then would be the goal of political justice? And more explicitly, can there be political justice without a recognition of those rights that would guarantee the individual's free pursuit of his moral self-development? Plato has provided adequate answers to none of these questions.

5. One may call the ideal norm of human personal development "the way of acting as a person" (*weirenzhidao*) and the ideal norm of political well-being "the way of conducting political rule" (*weizhengzhidao*). One may call the *weirenzhidao*, *renxing* (the conduct of *ren*) and the *weizhengzhidao*, *renzheng* (rule by *ren* or rule by virtue—*dezheng*) which Mencius calls the way of the king (*wangdao*) as opposed to the way of hegemon (*padao*).

6. I shall translate *ren* as "co-humanity," although I take note of the earliest English translation of *ren* as benevolence in Legge's translation of the Four Books, and other English translations of *ren* as love, humanity, and goodness or good-heartedness.

7. See the *Analects,* 12–2 and 15–24.

8. Ibid., 6–30.

9. In explaining *ren* as reciprocity, Confucius refers both to what people would commonly avoid and to what people would commonly desire. To impose on others those things that people commonly avoid and to withhold from them those things that people commonly desire would constitute the grossest injustice. A person of *ren*, it follows, avoids harming others and endeavors instead to benefit them, at the same time as he endeavors to benefit and attempts to avoid harming himself. It is not simply that withholding harm and creating benefits constitute justice; it is the reciprocal considerations that make the relationship a just one. As for how we should define

these values and determine the modes of reciprocal relationship, these are questions related to how *ren* constitutes the whole of virtue.

10. *Analects,* 7–30 and 20–2.

11. Ibid., 9–4.

12. See my article "On *Yi* as a Principle of Specific Application," *Philosophy East and West* (July 1972), pp. 269–80.

13. In the first Chinese dictionary, written by Xu Shen in the Han period, Xu relates sheep to the idea of a good omen, which forms the referential basis for words like *shan* (goodness) and *mei* (beauty).

14. It is also clear that virtues governing the different human relationships and the virtuous actions which flow from these are also acts of *yi* or justice and must be recognized as such. There is a tendency to make this system of *yi* more explicit and even formal and lawful. In the first place, there comes into being the doctrine of five relations (*wulun*) as articulated in Mencius, and then comes the theory of three canons (*sangang*) in Dong Zhongshu, which changes the reciprocal relationships of the *wulun* into nonreciprocal and nonequal relationships. Finally, there comes the Confucianization of the legal codes in terms of the *sangang,* which lasts to the end of the imperial dynasty in China. See Toby E. Huff, *The Rise of Early Modern Science* (New York: Cambridge University Press, 1993), and in particular the section on Chinese law in chapter 7. One may say that the Confucian virtues of justice are eventually adopted or incorporated into the Chinese system of law. Thus we can regard traditional Chinese legal justice as a mirror of the Confucian virtue theory of *yi.*

15. See the Mencius, 6A-4 or the chapter Gaozi, I-4.

16. With this said, we can explain the content of justice in light of our understanding of the use of the term *yi* as specific justice in Confucius. Confucius has related *yi* to both integrity (*xing*) and candor (*zhi*). The reason for this is that with integrity and candor one is readier to respond to what one has perceived as righteousness in a situation. Where *ren* is the overall and basic propensity or response of an individual to human relationships, *yi* is a special call for action in a relationship that demands a recognition of specific circumstances. Hence *yi* is incorporated within *ren* and yet exceeds *ren* in terms of knowledge and practical wisdom. Thus Confucius's contrast between *ren* and *zhi* is instructive: *ren* is likened to mountain and *zhi* is likened to water; the person of *ren* lives long and the person of *zhi* enjoys himself. (See the *Analects,* 11–23.) Just action has to conform to specific circumstances and a just person should take pleasure in doing the just thing.

17. Locke published his *Second Treatise of Government* in 1689, Rousseau his *Social Contract* in 1762, and Kant his *Foundations of the Metaphysics of Morals* in 1785. Although Hobbes (1588–1679) may have published his political treatise on the origin of the state, *Leviathan,* as early as 1651, he retained the medieval theory of the divine origin of rulership, which rules him out from the consciousness of modernity as it is here defined.

18. Adam Smith (1723–1790) published his highly influential *The Wealth of Nations* in 1776, the same year that the United States declared its independence and affirmed the rights of all individuals to liberty, equality, and the pursuit of happiness. With Smith's idea of the free market, the basic ingredients for a modern theory of justice are complete. That man can manufacture higher quality goods in massive quantity through the use of machines and organized labor demonstrates how man is

capable of changing his own fate and controlling his own destiny (without necessarily having to give up faith in God).

19. Max Weber has in some sense legitimated the capitalist pursuit of wealth in terms of Protestant Ethics. But the relation between a genuine wish to honor God and material possessiveness remains obscure. There remains a question, then, as to whether God uses man or man uses God in the epoch-making rise of capitalism.

20. The most recent such discussion is to be found in Jürgen Habermas' article, "Reconciliation through the Public Use of Reason: Remarks on John Rawls' Political Liberalism," *Journal of Philosophy* (March 1995), pp. 109–31.

21. See John Rawls, *A Theory of Justice* (Cambridge: Belknap Press, 1971), pp. 60, 83.

22. One has to see this issue from the perspective of those who are born into disadvantaged circumstances, and who consequently suffer from a lack of opportunities to advance their life prospects, not for any lack of merit or effort on their own part. Consider, for example, the financial burdens involved in getting a decent education, or quality healthcare and medical treatment, or legal protection, in present-day America. Is it fair for one person to enjoy all of these benefits and for another to be deprived of them simply because of an accident of birth rather than a difference in merit, desert, and effort?

23. The phrase is derived from *tianxiapian* of the Zhuangzi. One can see the chapter entitled *Daxue* in *Liji* as an illustration and presentation of the thesis of *neisheng-waiwang*, which also becomes one of the main theses of Neo-Confucianism in the Sung Period.

24. See the Mencius, 4A-1. Of course, the laws (*fa*) that Mencius has in mind here are not laws in the modern sense, but norms of government as practiced by the early sage-kings.

25. There is a rich repository of Confucius's statements on knowledge—practical, theoretical, and metaphysical—in the *Analects*. I have discussed these in a number of articles. Cf. "Theory and Practice in Confucianism," *Journal of Chinese Philosophy* (vol. I, no. 2, 1974), pp. 179–98; "Lun Gongzi zhi zhi yu Zhuzi zhi li" [On Knowledge in Confucius and Principle in Zhuxi], in my book *Zhishi Yu Jiazhi* [Knowledge and Value] (Taipei: Linking Press, 1986), pp. 141–72.

26. Confucius says, "If one has knowledge, but cannot preserve it with benevolence, even if one has acquired the knowledge, one must lose it. If one has knowledge, and can preserve it with benevolence, but does not approach it with solemnity, then people will not show respect. If one has knowledge and can preserve it with benevolence and further [one] is able to approach it in solemnity, and yet act without following the propriety (*li*), this cannot be said to be good." See the *Analects*, 15–33.

Yü Ying-shih

THE IDEA OF DEMOCRACY AND THE TWILIGHT OF THE ELITE CULTURE IN MODERN CHINA

In his famous *Democracy in America*, Alexis de Tocqueville made the following most illuminating observation:

> If ever a democratic republic similar to that of the United States came to be established in a country in which earlier a single man's power had introduced administrative centralization and had made it something accepted by custom and by law, I have no hesitation in saying that in such a republic despotism would become more intolerable than in any of the absolute monarchies of Europe. One would have to go over into Asia to find anything with which to compare it.[1]

Needless to say, Tocqueville had France in mind when he spoke these words, which, however, have turned out to be startlingly prophetic about twentieth-century China. As we all know, China was the first country in Asia to abolish a highly centralized imperial system—one fully two millennia old—and establish in its place a republican form of government. On the other hand, exactly as Tocqueville had predicted, Chinese despotism in the twentieth century has indeed grown ever more intolerable on the waves of one revolution after another.

In this paper, however, I propose to discuss, not the reality of Chinese despotism, but the idea of democracy. The very fact that China, in 1912, was able to cast off its imperial past and adopt a republican system based primarily on the American model testifies unmistakably to the power of democracy as the political faith of the Chinese revolutionary elite. This simple but fascinating fact may serve well as the starting point of our inquiry into the vicissitudes of the idea of democracy in the political and intellectual history of twentieth-century China. The fact is fascinating because it raises a number of thought-provoking questions deserving further exploration. To mention just

199

a few: Why did so many Chinese intellectuals at the turn of the century, whose national history knew no other political model than hereditary monarchy after China's first unification in 221 B.C., become so readily attracted to the idea of democracy? Since the May Fourth period, Confucianism has been viewed as a major intellectual obstacle to China's democratization. As Ch'en Tu-hsiu (1879–1942) stated explicitly in 1919, "In order to advocate democracy, we are obliged to oppose Confucianism."² However, it is also an irrefutable fact that most, if not all, of the leading Chinese advocates of democracy at the turn of the century were, each in his own way, committed Confucians, notably Yen Fu (1853–1921), K'ang Yu-wei (1858–1927), Liang Ch'i-ch'ao (1873–1929), Chang Ping-lin (1868–1936) and Liu Shih-p'ei (1884–1919). Such being the case, how are we to account for their great enthusiasm for the creation of a democratic order in China? With the founding of the Republic of China in 1912, the idea of democracy enjoyed, indeed, a strong and auspicious beginning to its career in China. But, ironically, its subsequent career in China has turned out to be marked by frustrations and failures—at times, even of tragic proportions. Then a further question inevitably arises: Why was the idea of democracy able to help induce a fundamental change in political structure under the monarchical rule of China's last dynasty, while it has ceased to function in any meaningful way since the founding of the Republic? The rest of the paper will address itself to these intriguing questions. Due to limitations of time and space, however, no attempt will be made to deal with them in a general and comprehensive manner. Instead, I shall discuss them by specifically relating the idea of democracy to the elite culture in modern China.

I

There can be no question that the idea of democracy is of Western origin, traceable to ancient Greece. Even if we grant the possibility of some remote Phoenician influences on the beginning of Greek political wisdom, the historical fact nevertheless remains unaltered that it was in the Athenian *polis* that the idea of democracy was most fully institutionalized for the first time in the ancient world.³ When the idea was imported to China in the late nineteenth century, Chinese scholars showed no intellectual curiosity about its history. Rather, they were enormously interested in its modern institutional expressions as they found them in Britain, France, and the United States. They gave the idea several Chinese names—including *min-chu* ("people's rule"), *min-ch'uan* ("people's power"), and *min-chih* ("government by the people"), all of which have survived to this day. However, the first one, *min-chu*, is now generally accepted as the standard Chinese translation of the Western term "democracy."

It is significant that in the late nineteenth century open-minded Confucian scholars who visited the West for the first time almost invariably returned to China deeply impressed by the ideals and institutions of Western constitutional democracy. A few examples will suffice to illustrate this point. After a two-year trip to the British Isles and Europe in the late 1860s, Wang T'ao (1828–1897), the Chinese assistant to James Legge in the English translation of the Confucian classics, gave the following characterization of the British government and people:

> The real strength of England, however, lies in the fact that there is a sympathetic understanding between the governing and governed, a close relationship between the ruler and the people. . . . My observation is that the daily domestic political life of England actually embodies the traditional ideals of our ancient Golden Age. In official appointments the method of recommendation and election is practiced, but the candidates must be well known, of good character and achievements before they can be promoted to a position over the people. . . . And moreover the principle of majority rule is adhered to in order to show impartiality. . . . The English people are likewise public-spirited and law-abiding: the laws and regulations are hung up high (for everyone to see), and no one dares violate them.[4]

Later, in 1877, when Yen Fu and Kuo Sung-t'ao (1818–1891), China's first ambassador to England, were both in London, they often spent days and nights together discussing differences and similarities in Chinese and Western thought and political institutions. Interestingly, both men arrived at essentially the same conclusions as Wang T'ao's, apparently without being aware of the latter's writings. In the end, Kuo heartily agreed with Yen Fu's observation that "the reason why England and other countries of Europe are wealthy and strong is that impartial justice (kung-li) is daily extended. Here is the ultimate source."[5]

My last example is Hsueh Fu-ch'eng (1863–1894), who was concurrently China's minister to England, France, Italy, and Belgium from 1890 to 1894. In the May 1, 1890 entry of his diary, he wrote,

> Formerly Kuo Sung-t'ao frequently praised the merits of the governmental administration and popular customs of the West, which caused him to suffer criticism and ostracism from scholars who like to criticize others. I was also slightly surprised at the exaggeration of his words, which I checked with Ch'en Lan-pin [China's envoy to the United States in 1870s] . . . who said that his statement was correct. This time when I came to Europe and traveled from Paris to London I began to believe that the statements of Kuo Sung-t'ao could be verified in the parliaments, schools, prisons, hospitals, and streets.

Later in the same entry he also praised the United States highly, saying that "America is like the time of the Golden Age of Ancient China."[6]

I take the above examples as illustrative of the initial response of the Confucian elite to the idea of democracy. For all of them were deeply committed to Confucian values and therefore expressed their appreciative understanding of Western democratic ideals and institutions from a distinctly Confucian point of view. It is particularly revealing that Wang T'ao and Hsueh Fu-ch'eng praised, respectively, but independently of each other, England and America in terms of the Golden Age in China's high antiquity. It would seem to suggest that they saw the democratic West as the Second Coming of the Confucian Golden Age. This is indeed the highest tribute the traditional Confucian elite could have possibly paid to the idea of democracy. It is true that in their own times they constituted only a small minority and therefore can by no means be taken as representative of the Confucian elite as a whole. However, with the advantage of hindsight we also happen to know that they were a "creative minority" charting the future of China.

The equation of the Confucian idea of a Golden Age with that of Western democracy was soon to undergo a dexterous twist in the hands of Confucian reformers. When K'ang Yu-wei became acquainted with the ideas and institutions of Western democracy by reading journalism in the 1880s, he began to develop a theory which may be called the indigenous genesis of democracy in ancient China. He distinguished three types of government in Chinese history: namely, "the people's rule" (*min-chu*), "joint rule of monarch and people" (*chun-min kung-chih*) and "autocracy" (*chuan-chih*). The first type, *min-chu,* was actualized in the time of the legendary sage-emperors Yao and Shun. It was the highest and most perfect form of democracy. The second type, *chun-min kung-chih,* he attributed to the reign of King Wen of the Chou dynasty. It was a sort of constitutional monarchy. The last type *chuan-chih,* the lowest and worst possible form of government, was what China had practiced since its unification under the First Emperor of the Ch'in dynasty in 221 B.C. By way of extensive exegesis of certain Confucian texts, K'ang came to the conclusion that Confucius was a most enthusiastic advocate of democracy.[7] It may be noted in this connection that it was Wang T'ao who first identified these three forms of state in Europe, which he called, respectively, *min-chu kuo* or democracy, *chun-chu kuo* or monarchy, and *chun-min kung-chu kuo* or constitutional monarchy.[8] Quite possibly, K'ang may have been initially inspired by Wang's writing and built his theory on its basis. Thus K'ang introduced a completely new paradigm in Chinese intellectual history which dominated Confucian classical scholarship until the May Fourth period. The paradigm was not only taken over but also greatly extended by his political rivals—Confucian advocates of a republican revolution. Liu Shih-p'ei, for example, wrote a book entitled *Essentials of the Chinese Theory of Social Contract (Chung-kuo min-yueh ching-i)* in the early years of the twentieth century, which purports to trace the origins and evolution of democratic ideas in China—including democracy, equality, freedom, rights, etc.—from the ancient classics all the way to the philosophical writings of the eighteenth and nineteenth centuries.[9]

During the first decade of this century, the influential *Journal of National Essence (Kuo-tsui hsueh-pao)*, with which Liu Shih-pei and Chang Ping-lin were closely associated, carried numerous learned articles elaborating on this theme. As a result, there gradually formed a climate of opinion among the Confucian elite that democratic ideas had long ago been developed in ancient China by Confucius, Mencius, and other sages independently of the West and that it is the duty of modern Confucians to rediscover and repossess them from the Confucian texts. The following statement of Dr. Sun Yat-sen, Founder of the Republic, is worth quoting:

> In ancient China there were the abdications of Yao and Shun as well as the changes of the Mandate of Heaven (*ke-ming*, "revolution") of King T'ang (of the Shang dynasty) and King Wu (of the Chou dynasty). As for theories, there were such statements [as] "Heaven sees with the eyes of its people. Heaven hears with the ears of its people," "I have indeed heard of the punishment of the outcast named Chou [i.e., the "bad last ruler" of the Shang dynasty], but I have not heard of any regicide," and "the people are of supreme importance: the sovereign comes last," etc. So we cannot say that democratic ideas have been lacking in China. However, what we have are ideas but not institutions.[10]

Sun was not a Confucian scholar. But as Martin Wilbur rightly observes, "Sun's reformist prescriptions seem at all stages of their development to reflect the ideas currently fashionable among the then-radical Chinese intellectuals."[11] Therefore, this statement may be justifiably taken as representative of the view of the Chinese elite in the late nineteenth and early twentieth centuries. The idea of democracy proved to be so attractive to the Chinese elite that they not only adopted it, but went to great lengths to completely naturalize it.

II

With the beginning of the May Fourth era, the historical findings of the preceding generation with regard to the indigenous origin of democracy in ancient China was rapidly discredited. After 1919, few scholars, if any, would seriously believe that ideas like "democracy," "liberty," "rights," and "social contract," when truthfully interpreted in their original context, can be found in the Confucian tradition. Instead of viewing the Confucian classic as a repository of "democratic ideas," Confucianism was now repudiated as the very ideological cornerstone on which Chinese monarchy had stood from beginning to end. This anti-Confucian sentiment was so powerfully as well as multifariously expressed that it would still find a sympathetic echo in many minds today. Thus we find in modern Chinese intellectual history two major interpretations regarding the nature of Confucianism which are diametrically opposed to each other. Which one, then, should we follow? A detailed account of this controversy lies beyond the scope of the present paper.[12] Suffice it to say that Confucianism is such a complex system of values, beliefs, and ideas and has, moreover, undergone so many historical transformations that it does not easily yield itself to any one-sided characterization no matter how well grounded. Indeed, Confucianism can mean different things not only to different people but also to the same people in different contexts. Ch'en Tu-hsiu, for example, made the following remark to a friend in his prison cell in the early 1930s:

> Every feudal dynasty worshipped Confucius as a sage. The act of worship was inauthentic. Its true purpose was to strengthen dynastic rule. . . . This is the reason that during the May Fourth movement we came up with the slogan "Down with Confucius and Sons." However, intellectually speaking, the sayings of Confucius and Mencius are worth studying. Statements like "The people are of supreme importance; the sovereign comes last" (Mencius) and "In teaching there should be no distinction of classes" (Confucius) all deserve to be further explored.[13]

Clearly, at the time of this conversation, when his radicalism had subsided, he also distinguished Confucianism as state ideology from the true teachings of Confucius, Mencius, and other Confucians, thereby retreating from his earlier position that "Confucianism and monarchy were indissolubly bound."[14]

Hu Shih (1891–1962), another intellectual leader of the May Fourth movement, provides us with a slightly different example. He was responsible, more than anyone else, for making the anti-Confucianist battle cry—"Down with Confucius and Sons"—a household phrase in China. However, as a moderate liberal, he seemed to recognize from the beginning that Confucianism as state ideology must not be confused with those Confucian values that constituted the core of what he called "the humanistic and rationalistic China."[15] It is particularly interesting that in many of his English writings he often emphasized the compatibility of Confucianism with Western liberalism. He was, of course, intellectually sophisticated enough not to make any claim for China's independent discovery of the idea of democracy in ancient times. Nevertheless, he was bold enough to suggest that certain Confucian ideas and institutions may prove to be capable of furnishing China with a solid foundation on which constitutional democracy can be successfully established.[16] In "The Natural Law in the Chinese Tradition" (1953), he further proposed that both the Confucian Canon (Classics) and the Neo-Confucian idea of *li* or principle are more or less comparable to the Natural Law in the West, which "ha[s] always played the historical role of a fighting weapon in mankind's struggle against the injustice and the tyranny of unlimited human authority."[17] By contrast, he rarely favored Confucianism with such high credit in his Chinese writings, at least not so explicitly and focusedly, presumably for fear of making his compatriots too self-complacent to struggle for China's modernization.

The cases of Ch'en Tu-hsiu and Hu Shih seem to suggest that, in spite of their belligerent anti-Confucianist stance on the surface, at a deeper level of consciousness their early Confucian breeding, I suspect, may well have in some way helped to predispose them more readily to the idea of democracy. Ch'en was a most enthusiastic advocate of democracy during this period, and it was he who personified the idea, calling it "Mr. Democracy."

In the winter of 1919, John Dewey delivered a lecture on democracy in Peking. He analyzed the idea into four categories:

1. political democracy, including principally constitution and legislative representation;
2. people's rights, including freedom of speech, press, belief, residence, etc.;
3. social democracy, namely, the abolition of social inequalities; and
4. economic democracy in terms of the equal distribution of wealth.

Ch'en agreed with Dewey's analysis completely and supported it with an article entitled "The Basis for the Realization of Democracy," which appeared in the December issue of the influential *New Youth* together with Dewey's lecture. He emphatically pointed out that China must follow the British and American models in political democracy and at the same time also pay attention to the problem of social and economic democracy which had yet to be achieved anywhere in the world.[18] It was probably his concern with social and economic democracy that led him to the socialist revolution in the decade that immediately followed. However, his faith in democracy was never completely shaken, though temporarily suspended during his revolutionary years. In 1940, he expressed his final views on democracy in a number of letters and essays. He now realized that the so-called "proletarian democracy" was only a euphemism for totalitarian dictatorship. After six to seven years of deep thinking, he became fully convinced that democracy in any society, capitalist or socialist, must of necessity consist of a parliamentary system, elections, the due process of law, and civil rights protecting the freedom of thought, speech, the press, association, etc. On the basis of his own political experience, he stressed that "most important of all is the freedom of the opposition parties."[19]

What Dewey said in 1919 about democracy probably stayed in the back of his mind throughout the last two decades of his life. There can be no doubt that Ch'en's political, social, and ethical ideas as shown in his published writings through several stages of intellectual development are all, essentially, of

Western origin. Unlike late Ch'ing Confucian reformists or revolutionaries such as K'ang Yu-wei and Chang Ping-lin, he does not seem to have ever, as far as I can judge, justified his views by reference to the authority of Chinese classics. Such being the case, then, on precisely what grounds are we justified in suggesting that his advocacy of democracy, and for that matter also of socialism ("economic democracy"), may have been helped by his background in the essentially Confucian culture of the Chinese elite? I would like to suggest two possible grounds, one specific and one general. The specific ground is the fact that in his early years Ch'en first followed K'ang Yu-wei and then shifted to the revolutionary camp of Chang Ping-lin and Liu Shih-p'ei. Therefore, he was quite familiar with the common discourse of the two Confucian groups discussed earlier. By the May Fourth period he must have already dismissed the theory of the Chinese origin of the idea of democracy as nonsense. But the possibility cannot be completely ruled out that his initial acceptance of democracy as a value may well have been facilitated through the mediation of the sayings of Confucius and Mencius, such as those quoted by him in the early 1930s.

The general ground is that, in traditional Chinese elite culture, Confucian education often inculcates into the minds of the young, along with other values, the sense of justice, social responsibility, human equality, the well-being of the people, etc., which may be regarded as some of the closest Confucian equivalents to Western "civic virtues." Many late Ch'ing reformers and revolutionaries coming from the Confucian elite background were individuals imbued with this kind of public-spiritedness. It was also these Confucian intellectuals who were often susceptible to Western democratic ideas and ideals. In the end they might reject every established Confucian doctrine, thereby assuming an anti-Confucianist role. Nevertheless, they would still retain the public-spiritedness of Confucian origin. Of course, here I am speaking of an ideal type. But I would not hesitate to take Chen Tu-hsiu as a concrete illustration.

In this sense, we may indeed speak justifiably, with Wm. Theodore de Bary, of a liberal tradition in China, if the term "liberalism" is interpreted liberally without tying it to the Western conception of freedom under law. Having reexamined certain "liberal tendencies" in Neo-Confucianism from Chu Hsi (1130–1200) to Huang Tsung-hsi (1610–1695), de Bary deplores that these tendencies had become obscured by the May Fourth period. As a result, Neo-Confucianism was viewed by many young Chinese of the May Fourth generation as "a repressive, reactionary system." The following comment of de Bary's is insightful:

> Proponents of the New Culture movement in the twenties, whose newly Westernized education had made a sharp break with classical Confucian learning, were often left ignorant of the thinkers and works cited above. Nevertheless

their own thought processes may well have remained unconsciously subject to lingering Neo-Confucian influences. As members of what was still a privileged intellectual elite, they easily identified Western-style liberalism with the autonomy of the self which had already been a value in the earlier literati culture.[20]

I heartily agree with this observation of his. It also lends considerable support to my contention that, with all its imperfections, Chinese elite culture has proved to be, paradoxically, more receptive than hostile to the idea of democracy.

III

With the founding of the Republic in 1912, Confucianism ceased to serve as the philosophical foundation of China's political system. Before the advent of totalitarian dictatorship on the Stalinist model in 1949, the Chinese intellectual elite generally regarded constitutional democracy as the only acceptable norm of politics. Even as late as 1957 when Chinese intellectuals were urged to voice criticisms by Mao, they still had the audacity to demand the reestablishment of parliamentary systems and multiparty politics, only to be brutally suppressed as "Rightists." This is clearly the legacy of the May Fourth movement as many of these "Rightists" were students of the May Fourth generation.

If Confucianism has become politically marginalized almost to the point of irrelevance in China since the May Fourth period, can we say the same about it culturally? Undeniably, the influence of Confucianism in cultural and social realms has also been receding in the twentieth century. However, Confucian values and ideas have permeated Chinese everyday life for so many centuries that it is inconceivable that they can be eradicated in a span of several decades, even by revolutionary violence. Though considerably modified, and perhaps also somewhat distorted, Confucianism as a whole must nevertheless be taken seriously as a major component of Chinese culture at both the elite and popular levels. As Chinese society (as opposed to the state) has been gradually but ever increasingly regaining its vitality in recent years, signs are not lacking that Confucian culture is beginning to reemerge in a modern dress.

In late Ming China, as despotism was growing increasingly intolerable, many members of the Confucian elite abandoned their hopes concerning the imperial state above and began to focus their attention on opening up and expanding cultural and social space below. Some founded private academies, others devoted their lives to the building of local communities in various forms (including the well-known *hsiang-yueh* or community compact), and still others threw themselves into the business world. As a result, a profound reorientation was also taking place in Confucian social and political philosophy. For example, between 1600 and 1800, a number of leading Confucian thinkers advocated the primacy of "the private" over "the public" in the sense that private individuals can take care of their own interests much more effectively than the emperor could on their behalf. There was also a growing emphasis on the idea that wealth must remain in the hands of those who created it, and not be entrusted to the state treasury.[21] Today we seem to be witnessing a recurrence of this late Ming historical process in China.

If both Confucianism in its modern form and democracy are to coexist in China in, hopefully, a not too distant future—as is already beginning to happen in Taiwan—how will the two relate to each other? In this connection I would like to borrow a new concept developed by John Rawls after the appearance of his 1971 classic, *A Theory of Justice*. I refer to the concept of a "comprehensive doctrine." In *Political Liberalism*, Rawls says,

> An essential feature of a well-ordered society associated with justice as fairness is that all its citizens endorse this conception on the basis of what I now call a comprehensive philosophical doctrine. . . . Now the serious problem is this: A modern democratic society is characterized not simply by a pluralism of comprehensive religious, philosophical, and moral doctrines, but by a pluralism of incompatible yet reasonable comprehensive doctrines. No one of these doctrines is affirmed by citizens generally. Nor should one expect that in the foreseeable future one of them or some other reasonable doctrine, will ever be affirmed by all, or nearly all, citizens. Political liberalism assumes that, for political purposes, a plurality of reasonable yet incompatible comprehensive doctrines is the normal result of the exercise of human reason within the framework of the free institutions of a constitutional democratic regime. Political liberalism also supposes that a reasonable comprehensive doctrine does not reject the essentials of a democratic regime.[22]

Confucianism in its modern form clearly qualifies as a "comprehensive doctrine" as here described. In traditional China, theoretically speaking, political life was guided by Confucian ethical principles. As Confucius said,

> Guide them by edicts, keep them in line with punishments, and the common people will stay out of trouble but will have no sense of shame. Guide them by virtue, keep them in line with the rites, and they will, besides having a sense of shame, reform themselves.[23]

"Edicts" and "punishments" refer to legal principles whereas "virtues" and "rites" refer to ethical ones. The sage preferred the latter. By contrast, the political tradition of the West from its inception in the Greek *polis* has followed legal principles.[24] Now by embracing the Western idea of constitutional democracy the Chinese intellectual elite actually abandoned the traditional "rule of virtue" for the "rule of law."[25] It led inevitably to the end of Confucianism as a dominating political force.

Dissociated from political power, Confucianism in its modern form no longer occupies any privileged position and therefore becomes one of the comprehensive doctrines. Rawls, however, further distinguishes "reasonable comprehensive doctrines" from "unreasonable" ones. Unreasonable doctrines could undermine the unity and justice of a constitutional democratic regime and therefore must be contained. He does not specify, but we can reasonably assume, that they refer to certain forms of religious fundamentalism and, perhaps, also to some of the modern totalitarian ideologies.[26] On the other hand, he deliberately defines the idea of a "reasonable comprehensive doctrine" in a loose way so that it could accommodate as many religious, philosophical, and moral doctrines as possible. His examples include utilitarianism, Kant's moral philosophy with its ideal of autonomy, as well as "all the main historical religions."[27] In this light, Confucianism is not only a "comprehensive doctrine" but also a "reasonable" one at that.

Furthermore, according to Rawls, a conception of political justice shared by everyone in a democratic regime can be obtained only through an "overlapping consensus" of most, if not all, reasonable comprehensive doctrines. Each reasonable doctrine endorses the conception, but from its own point of view.[28] This seems to suggest that reasonable comprehensive doctrines as cultural resources contribute positively to the building of a commonly accepted conception of justice in a democratic society. Perhaps this is why he also refers to them as "background culture."[29] But not all reasonable comprehensive doctrines in a society can contribute equally to the "overlapping consensus" necessary for the establishment of a democratic order. This is logically implied in the following statement: "there are many reasonable comprehensive doctrines that understand the wider realm of values to be congruent with, or supportive of, or else not in conflict with, political values as these are specified by a political conception of justice for a democratic regime."[30] If I understand Rawls correctly, then what he says about how reasonable comprehensive doctrines and a conception of justice for a democratic regime are related to each other generally can apply with equal validity to the question of how Confucianism will be related to democracy in China specifically. Of all the reasonable doctrines in the Chinese tradition, Confucianism is clearly the most comprehensive and therefore also has most to offer a Chinese conception of political justice.

I am fully aware that Confucianism and Western liberalism are two entirely different and incommensurable systems of thought, each being the product of its unique historical experience. They cannot be translated into each other's terms without serious distortions. However, shorn of its accidentally acquired and now outmoded features, on the one hand, and with necessary readjustments to the changed and ever-changing conditions, on the other, the central ideas and principles of Confucianism may be shown to be largely compatible with many of the reasonable comprehensive doctrines of the West, liberalism itself included. Many people have already done valuable work along this line. In concluding this section, however, let me add one more example. Recently American liberals have turned their attention to the vice of cruelty. Of all the ordinary vices, Judith N. Shklar has chosen to "put cruelty first." As she expressed so powerfully, "Indeed, hating cruelty, and putting it first, remain a powerful part of the liberal consciousness."[31] Following Shklar, Richard Rorty specifically calls our attention to the books of what he calls "liberal ironists" which help us become less cruel. He tells us that both Nabokov and Orwell, each in a way uniquely his own, "met Judith Shklar's criterion of a liberal: somebody who believes that cruelty is the worst thing we do."[32]

Hating cruelty, I must emphatically point out, has also been a powerful part of the Confucian consciousness from the very beginning. Confucius says, "How true is the saying that after a state has been ruled for a hundred years by good men it is possible to get the better of cruelty and to do away with killing."[33] This is how Confucius "put cruelty first." Mencius also characterized Confucius' and two earlier sages' profound abhorrence of cruelty in the following words: "Had it been necessary to perpetrate one wrongful deed or to kill one innocent man in order to gain the Empire, none of them would have consented to it."[34] Rorty writes of "participative emotion" in the case of Nabokov thus: "the ability to shudder with shame and indignation at the unnecessary death of a child—a child with whom we have no connection of family, tribe, or class—is the highest form of emotion that humanity has attained while evolving modern social and political institutions."[35] This remark reminds me immediately of a well-known passage of Mencius on human compassion, which may be reproduced, in part, as follows:

> No man is devoid of a heart sensitive to the suffering of others. . . . Suppose a man were, all of a sudden, to see a young child on the verge of falling into a well. He would certainly be moved to compassion, not because he wanted to get in the good graces of the parents, nor because he wished to win the praise of his fellow villagers or friends, nor yet because he disliked the cry of the child. From this it can be seen that whoever is devoid of the heart of compassion is not human, whoever is devoid of the heart of shame is not human, whoever is devoid of the heart of courtesy and modesty is not human, and whoever is devoid of the heart of right and wrong is not human.[36]

Here we encounter the earliest Confucian discovery of "the highest form of emotion that humanity has attained." Space does not allow me to mention numerous Confucian writers of later ages who each had something to say about cruelty and suffering. But I cannot pass this topic without quoting a few lines from Tu Fu (712–770), China's greatest poet: "Behind the red-lacquered gates, wine is left to sour, meat to rot. Outside these gates lie the bones of the frozen and starved. The flourishing and the withered are just a foot apart—

It rends my heart to ponder on it."[37] This great Confucian poet surely deserves to be called a "liberal ironist."

IV

As shown above, the idea of democracy found its most sympathetic audience in China among the intellectual elite. From the late nineteenth century to 1919, leading advocates of democracy came almost invariably from the intellectual elite with a strong background in Confucian culture. For example, reformers like K'ang Yu-wei and Liang Ch'i-ch'ao, revolutionaries like Chang Ping-lin and Liu Shih-p'ei, and May Fourth leaders like Hu Shih and Ch'en Tu-hsiu were also top-notch scholars and thinkers holding the highest academic positions in China at one time or another. With the exception of Ch'en Tu-hsiu, all of them have made monumental contributions to Confucian scholarship. Needless to say, this does not mean to suggest, even slightly, that members of the Confucian elite from the late Ch'ing to the early Republican years generally endorsed the idea of democracy. On the contrary, it is not difficult at all to cite numerous instances showing that conservative Confucians during the same period were strongly opposed to change in general and to democracy in particular. All it suggests is that if the idea of democracy wanted to find a hospitable social space in China, it could only look to the Confucian elite, because other social groups, including merchants and peasants, were generally unmotivated to be actively involved in national or local politics. This was true in the last years of the nineteenth century as well as in the middle of the twentieth century. A sociological survey conducted in the late 1940s shows that "much of the Chinese peasantry . . . remained indifferent to and ignorant of political affairs."[38] Even today, a survey by Andrew J. Nathan and Tianjian Shi suggests that the same patterns still persist: the educated elite are more likely to be aware of the influence of government whereas the rest of the population has a very low level of awareness. In the judgment of the authors, "The contrast between the two patterns suggests that if a political crisis between the regime and the intellectuals occurs again, the majority of the population may once again not offer much backing for the demands for democratic changes."[39]

Why for a whole century has China not made much headway toward democracy? This is an immensely complex question a truthful answer to which would involve God-knows-how-many historical factors. Here I would venture to suggest that the waning of elite culture in twentieth-century China may have been one of the factors. In hindsight, the New Culture movement of the May Fourth era proved to be the last efflorescence of Chinese elite culture. It was in this era that both Chinese scholarship and Western studies reached a new height. In the humanities, especially, many great names date from this era. It was indeed a generation of "clusterings of genius," to borrow A. L. Kroeber's apt phrase. The idea of democracy is, after all, a Western concept. To translate it into a Chinese reality, it needed in this early phase native defenders as well as opponents. Only through penetrating debates and discussions, not only on the idea itself but also on many other topics directly and indirectly relating to it, could a clearer understanding be reached. Only then could it hope to take root in and grow on China's soil. A high level of elite culture is therefore an essential precondition. As Rawls says, the search for a generally acceptable conception of political justice must begin in the "background culture" or "public culture" as "the shared fund of implicitly recognized basic ideas and principles." It is very unlikely that democracy can flourish in a culturally impoverished land. To give a most recent example, the democracy movement in Tienanmen Square in 1989 was clearly related to the revival of elite culture in post-Mao China. Michael Walzer is certainly right in suggesting that student elitism was rooted in "pre-Communist cultural traditions specific to China."[40]

Unfortunately, post-May Fourth China immediately entered into a period of national crisis, revolution, and war. At the same time, as I have pointed out elsewhere, Chinese intellectuals were also undergoing a historical process of social and political marginalization, thanks particularly to revolution.[41] As a result, elite culture in the 1940s declined markedly in a war-ridden China. Without a powerful intellectual elite to champion it, the idea of democracy soon began to go through several ideological twists until it was distorted beyond recognition.

In linking the idea of democracy to Chinese elite culture so closely, I am running the risk of being seen as an advocate of elitism. But I am not really proposing anything new. On the contrary, I am only rethinking the wisdom of K'ang Yu-wei, Sun Yat-sen, and a host of other early Chinese advocates of democracy who insisted that, in the case of China, it is a matter of historical necessity that democratization in its initial state must begin with an elite leadership.[42] Subsequent history seems to reveal that by reducing the intellectual elite to a nonentity, on the one hand, and relying on the so-called "masses," on the other, democracy in China only degenerated into demagoguery. There indeed exists a tension between democracy and elitism. However, since democracy cannot function by itself without some kind of leadership, I am afraid, the tension is going to remain. As Arthur M. Schlesinger, Jr. forcefully argues,

> Of all the cants canted in this canting world, the cant about elitism is the most futile. Government throughout human history has always been government by minorities—that is, by elites. This statement is as true for democratic and communist states today as it was for medieval monarchies and primitive tribes. Masses of people are structurally incapable of direct self-government. They

must delegate their power to agents. Who says organization says oligarchy. Historians hardly needed Pareto, Mosca and Michels to demonstrate this point. The serious question is not the existence of the ruling elites but their character.[43]

Few today have Schlesinger's courage to tell this simple historical truth. He is also right to say that it is the character of the elites that is really at issue. This emphasis on character leads me directly to Irving Babbitt, a great American humanist and admirer of Confucius. In his *Democracy and Leadership*, published seventy years ago, he made quite a point about the great value of Confucian ethics in the molding of the character of a democratic leader. His view has been well summarized by Thomas R. Nevin as follows:

> In Babbitt's conception, Confucian ethics were the oriented complement of the Aristotelian, but with the critical difference that in the former there was a stress upon humility as a check upon self-reliance and, in the aggregate, upon popular will. Like Aristotle, Confucius placed mediatory virtues in a social setting; his teaching concerned not merely the individual of breeding but such a person's power to influence and regulate the masses. Babbitt's claim that "not justice in the abstract but the just man" or "man of character" was the only security for society was inspired by the Confucian keynote of exemplification. As a check upon the democrat's belief in the divinity of numbers, Babbitt posed a basically Confucian model in finding "here and there a person who is worthy of respect and occasionally one who is worthy of reverence."[44]

So, after all, there is also the possibility that Confucianism may offer something to democracy in return. Let my paper rest on this Confucian note.

NOTES

1. Quoted in Stephen Holmes, "Tocqueville and Democracy" in *The Idea of Democracy*, David Copp, Jean Hampton, and John E. Roemer, eds. (Cambridge: Cambridge University Press, 1993), p. 51.

2. Chow Tse-tsung, *The May Fourth Movement: Intellectual Revolution in Modern China* (Cambridge: Harvard University Press, 1960), p. 59.

3. Simon Hornblower, "Creation and Development of Democratic Institutions in Ancient Greece" in *Democracy: The Unfinished Journey, 508 B.C. to A.D. 1993*, John Dunn, ed. (Oxford: Oxford University Press, 1993), p. 2.

4. Ssu-yu Teng and John K. Fairbank, *China's Response to the West: A Documentary Survey* (Cambridge: Harvard University Press, 1954), p. 140.

5. Benjamin Schwartz, *In Search of Wealth and Power: Yen Fu and the West* (Cambridge: The Belknap Press, 1964), p. 29.

6. *China's Response*, pp. 143–44.

7. Kung-chuan Hsiao, *A Modern China and a New World, K'ang Yu-wei, Reformer and Utopia, 1858–1927* (Seattle: University of Washington Press, 1975), pp. 197–200.

8. *China's Response*, pp. 136–37.

9. Liu Shih-p'ei, *Chung-kuo Min-yueh ching-i* in *Liu Shen-shu shiang-sheng i-shui* [Posthumous Writings of Liu Shih-p'ei], vol. I (Taipei: reprint, 1975), pp. 673–713.

10. Quoted in Ying-shih Yu, "Sun Yat-sen's Doctrine and Traditional Chinese Culture" in *Sun Yat-sen's Doctrine in the Modern World,* Chu-yuan Cheng, ed. (Boulder: Westview Press, 1989), p. 94.

11. C. Martin Wilbur, *Sun Yat-sen: Frustrated Patriot* (New York: Columbia University Press, 1976), p. 7.

12. For an overview, see Chow Tse-tsung, "The Anti-Confucian Movement in Early Republican China" in *The Confucian Persuasion,* Arthur F. Wright, ed. (Stanford: Stanford University Press, 1960), pp. 288–312.

13. Quoted in Cheng Hsueh-chia, *Ch'en Tu-hsiu chuan* [Biography of Ch'en Tu-hsiu], vol. 2 (Taipei: 1989), p. 960.

14. Chow Tse-tsung, op. cit., p. 302.

15. See Hu Shih, "The Chinese Tradition and Future," Sino-American Conference on Intellectual Cooperation, Reports and Proceedings (Seattle: 1960), pp. 13–22.

16. Hu Shih, "Historical Foundations for a Democratic China," *Edmund J. James Lectures on Government: Second Series* (Urbana: University of Illinois Press, 1941), pp. 1–12.

17. Hu Shih, "The Natural Law in the Chinese Tradition" in *Natural Law Institute Proceedings,* vol. 5 (Notre Dame: University of Notre Dame Press, 1953), pp. 119–53.

18. See Chow Tse-tsung, *The May Fourth Movement,* pp. 228–31.

19. Ch'en Tu-hsiu, *Ch'en Tu-hsiu ti tsui-hou chien-chieh* [Ch'en Tu-hsiu's Final Views] (Hong Kong: 1950), with a preface by Hu Shih.

20. Wm. Theodore de Bary, *The Liberal Tradition in China* (Hong Kong: Chinese University Press, 1983), p. 104.

21. I have traced this new development in Confucian social and political thinking in a long article and, moveover, linked it to the acceptance of Western ideas by the Chinese intellectual élite in the late Ch'ing. See my "Confucianism in the Modern World: A Retrospective and Prospective Study" (in Japanese translation) in *Chugoku—Shakai to Bunka* [China—Society and Culture] (no. 10, June 1995), pp. 135–79.

22. John Rawls, *Political Liberalism* (New York: Columbia University Press, 1993), p. xvi.

23. Confucius, *The Analects,* trans. D. C. Lau (Harmondsworth: Penguin Classics, 1979), Book II.3, p. 63.

24. As Frederick Watkins pointed out, "Unlike the Chinese and other highly civilized peoples, whose political thought always tended to be ethical rather than legal in character, the Greeks had from the beginning to devote most of their political energies to the creation and enforcement of law." *The Political Tradition of the West: A Study in the Development of Modern Liberalism* (Cambridge: Harvard University Press, 1948), p. 8.

25. It may be noted that Huang Tsung-hsi made an important move by reversing the traditional Confucian formula to say that "only if there is governance by law can there be governance by men." *Waiting for the Dawn, A Plan for the Prince,* Wm. Theodore de Bary, trans. (New York: Columbia University Press, 1993), p. 99. See also de Bary's "Introduction," pp. 21–24. As Huang's book was a chief source of inspiration for the late Ch'ing Confucians, his new emphasis on the primacy of law over man must have some influence on them.

26. Rawls, op.cit., pp. xvi–xvii, 64.

27. Ibid., pp. 58–60, 169–170.

28. Ibid., p. 134.

29. Ibid., p. 14. Rawls also says, "We start, then, by looking to the public culture itself as the shared fund of implicitly recognized basic ideas and principles. We hope to formulate these ideas and principles clearly enough to be combined into a political conception of justice congenial to our most firmly held convictions" (p. 8). It seems safe to assume that these "basic ideas and principles" are largely provided by reasonable comprehensive doctrines. I must make myself clear that here I am only borrowing Rawls' idea of "comprehensive doctrine" as "background culture" to illustrate my own point about the Chinese case. This does not, however, commit me to Rawls' political conception of justice as a whole, early or late.

30. Ibid., p. 169.

31. Judith N. Shklar, *Ordinary Vices* (Cambridge: The Belknap Press, 1984), p. 43.

32. Richard Rorty, *Contingency, Irony, and Solidarity* (Cambridge: Cambridge University Press, 1989), p. 146.

33. *The Analects,* Book XIII.1, p. 120.

34. *Mencius,* trans. D. C. Lau (Harmondsworth: Penguin Classics, 1970), Book II, part A.2, p. 79.

35. Rorty, op.cit., p. 147. Here I am only comparing Chinese Confucians and Western liberals with respect to their attitudes toward cruelty. I am not exactly following Rorty's definition of "liberal irony." Nor am I accepting his antifoundationalism. For a criticism of Rorty's views, see Richard Wolin, *The Terms of Cultural Criticism* (New York: Columbia University Press, 1992), chap. 7.

36. *Mencius,* Book II, part A.6, pp. 82–83.

37. William Hung, *Tu Fu: China's Greatest Poet* (Cambridge: Harvard University Press, 1952), p. 88.

38. Kung-chuan Hsiao, op. cit., p. 219 where C. K. Yang's *A Chinese Village in Early Communist Transition* (Cambridge: Harvard University Press, 1959) is cited and discussed.

39. Andrew J. Nathan and Tianjian Shi, "Cultural Requisites for Democracy in China: Findings from a Survey," *Daedalus* (Spring 1993), p. 116.

40. Michael Walzer, *Thick and Thin: Moral Argument at Home and Abroad* (Notre Dame: University of Notre Dame Press, 1994), pp. 59–60.

41. See Ying-shih Yu, "The Radicalization of China in the Twentieth Century," *Daedalus* (Spring 1993), pp. 142–46.

42. Hsiao, op.cit., pp. 228–30.

43. Arthur M. Schlesinger, Jr., *The Cycles of American History* (Boston: Houghton Mifflin Company, 1986), pp. 428–29.

44. Thomas R. Nevin, *Irving Babbitt: An Intellectual Study* (The University of North Carolina Press, 1984), p. 108.

Daya Krishna

DEMOCRACY AND JUSTICE: PRESUPPOSITIONS AND IMPLICATIONS

Some Philosophical Reflections from a Non-Western Perspective

The demand for "equality" may be said to lie at the very roots of both democracy and justice. The one pertains to the realm of the political, while the other belongs to the legal domain. Yet, as everybody knows, the realm of politics is the realm of power, which is essentially asymmetrical in nature, and the realm of law is only a realm which legitimates existing inequalities. But if, in principle, not everyone can be equal in the political realm, then what is involved in the pursuit of "democracy"—which is prescribed as the ideal political form of government by everyone these days?

Perhaps democracy has to be understood differently. It may be seen not primarily as the achievement of equality in the political realm, but rather as an attempt to create institutional and procedural bulwarks against the misuse of power or the exercise of tyranny—which has been one of the perennial concerns of those who have thought about politics since ancient times, both in the East and in the West. It should be interesting in this regard to find what strategies have been suggested or adopted in different cultures to ensure that power is not misused by those who wield it, particularly for their own ends. The exercise of public authority for private ends is the perennial perversion that people have tried to prevent at all times and have generally failed to prevent, at least for significantly long periods of time.

This, however, is only the negative aspect of democracy; the other is its positive aspect, which may be described as participation in the decision-making processes of the polity. In fact, if we generalize, we may be able to see that participation in the decision-making processes in any situation and the creation of procedures and institutions to prevent misuse of power are twin aspects that are analogous in other fields to what is known as democracy in the political realm. Yet in both of these aspects, the presupposition is that people participating in the decision-making processes and those trying to

217

ensure that power is used for public welfare rather than private gain are motivated by the achievement of the "public good." However, this very notion of the "public good," or that which is not the good of any particular individual, is difficult to articulate in any satisfactory manner. Nor is there any mechanism to ensure that this becomes the motivating force among those who exercise their right of participation in the decision-making process.

The distinction between the public and the private realm is crucial for such a way of thinking, and yet the concepts are not as clearly identifiable as one would like them to be. Business corporations, for example, are public bodies and those who manage them may be motivated by the "good" of the company they represent and yet may completely ignore or deliberately violate the good of the community to which they belong. The story of the large industrial and commercial companies is well known, but the problems they raise in the context of the conflict between the larger public good and the narrower good of their own institutions has seldom been the subject of sustained theoretical reflection. Today, when institutions have achieved a global, multinational level, the problem has assumed dimensions that are of a qualitatively different order than the ones faced earlier when these institutions were subject to the political control of some one nation or another.

The problem is analogous to that encountered, on the one hand, in the relations between nation-states and, on the other hand, in the relations between international bodies, such as the United Nations, and the different nation-states. Today, if we have multinational corporations, we also have such institutions as the United Nations, which increasingly claim supranational authority over all nations. Beyond this, there is the strange spectacle of some of the nation-states, for example, the United States, assuming a role that is analogous to that of multinational corporations on the one hand and the agencies of the United Nations on the other.

In a sense, the story that is being repeated at a global level in contemporary times has analogues in earlier times when, between the purely personal good and the public good at the largest level, intermediate levels were conceived where the individual identified himself with the good of his family, clan, tribe, or village. At each of these levels, the individual had to subordinate, and sometimes even sacrifice his private good for the good of the larger community of which he happened to be a member and with which he identified to a substantive extent. The modern technical terminology for this in sociology is the role-expectation of norms that an individual is expected to fulfill or observe because of her membership in the group or community in the context of which she is assigned the role and assumes it voluntarily or semivoluntarily. The older Indian name for this was *dharma,* and the *dharma samkata*—or the conflict between various *dharmas*—was as much a subject of traditional reflection as it was the stuff out of which tragedy of epic proportions was depicted in literary creations. Role conflict in modern times does not seem to have resulted either in any significant moral reflection or in any literary creation comparable to that found, say, in the *Ramayana* or the *Mahabharata*, or for that matter in *Antigone*. Yet the dilemma deserves serious reflection at three levels—if we conceive the individual as the real center of these multiple and conflicting identifications and as transcending all of them in some sense or other.

The first relates to the very idea of the notion of a "public good" which transcends the good of each concrete specific group of which an individual happens to be a member, including the polity to which she happens to belong. Rousseau argued for the notion of a "general will," which was not the will of any individual or even the summation of all the individual wills constituting the society or the polity. The idea seems to have disappeared from political thought, and no longer enters into the deliberations of actual politicians. Yet the notion of the "general will" is inevitably linked to the notion of the "general good," from which it cannot be detached without making the notion meaningless and infructuous. However, there seems to be some asymmetry between the notion of the "general will" and the "general good." For while the two notions are intimately related and cannot be understood in isolation, nonetheless, the "general good" cannot be defined or understood apart from the particular goods not only of each individual but also of each group or community constituting the whole. The "general will," on the other hand, arises only when each individual forgets his own individual interests or even his own particular good and tries to strive for that which he apprehends as the good of the other or even his "interest" at a more mundane level. In fact, between the "general will" and the "general good" one has to postulate a "general reason" in which one participates for the apprehension of what is true and what is good for the whole. Yet while the will, at least theoretically, has to be bereft of any concern for one's own individual interest, the "public good" cannot and ought not, in principle, to be seen apart from and in isolation from the private goods of other people.

Today, the problem has assumed another dimension which, though not completely absent from earlier thought on the matter, shows a radical difference because of the contemporary widening of the notion of the "other" to include the whole realm of ecology, including the world of plants and animals in general. It is, of course, true that the earlier notion also included all of these, but not in the instrumental manner in which modern thought has usually conceived them. In earlier thought, the whole world of inanimate and animate matter, with all of its levels and gradations, was not only a continuum but also a community that did not stop with human beings alone but extended right up to the gods and beyond them to that ultimate infinite one that alone sustained the whole.

The problem with the "general will," then, extends beyond its relationship with the "general good," on the one hand, and the "general reason," on the other. The question is: How general is the so-called "general" itself? The general is not the universal, as, at the human level, the identification is always with something less than the universal, and it is bound to be so, for man just does not know, and perhaps cannot know, what the real universal is. It has, of course, usually been thought that it is the "general reason" in man which makes him capable of apprehending the real universal, both in the realm of the true and in the realm of the good. Those who have thought that reason cannot apprehend the good have generally relied on some other faculty in man which apprehends what is good. But this seems to be as mistaken as the belief that human reason can determine unequivocally and unambiguously what is the real good. The historicity in which man is essentially grounded precludes the identity of the general and the universal, which all seeking for objectivity normally generates as a necessary illusion.

There is a deeper problem here which has seldom been recognized or squarely faced. One cannot but identify oneself with the limited, particular, specific groups into which one happens to have been born and wherein one has grown. These are one's primary identifications just as one is born with a body and is bound to identify oneself with it. It is what is constant with one and which one continuously perceives as an object of knowledge, both internally and externally, and which at the same time is the basic instrument through which one may effectuate what one wishes to do.

Language is the other close analogue to the problem we are hinting at. One is born to a language, grows in it, and acquires a facility in its use which one normally does not possess with regard to any other language, however well one may come to learn it. The primary linguistic identification is with the language one has been born into and which one hears all the time and which alone one can use with ease and facility just as one uses one's body. And yet, there are other languages and other bodies and other cultures and other groups which also exist and which are as real as those to which one belongs and which belong to one. But while one may extend one's identification with them imaginatively, it is difficult to do so beyond a certain point, and when the moment of crisis arrives, one withdraws to one's narrower identifications until ultimately—when one is ill or in pain—one just becomes one's body and all the rest becomes the "other."

The expanding concentric circles of identifications radiating outward from one's body-mind complex and successively embracing larger and larger units thus create a dual dilemma for one's functioning in a representative capacity which, in a democratic framework, is necessarily imposed as an obligation almost on everyone who is supposed to be involved in the functioning of any institution that is expected to run on democratic lines. The eternal temptation is to use the larger identification to subserve the interests and purposes of that with which one identifies at a narrower level. This will be true even in situations where it may not be as obvious as in those instances where one uses a public office for private gain (and, of course, the "private gain" at stake may not be that of the individual, strictly speaking, but rather that of the family or clan or tribe or region or corporation of which one happens to be a member).

The situation, for example, is no different if a member of the United Nations uses the authority and power of the institution in the interest of his own nation rather than that of the world community as a whole—whatever that may mean. And yet, there are many people who think it legitimate and justified if international bodies are used for the advancement of the interests of their own nation, just as others will think it proper if they use the institutional mechanisms of the nation-state for the advancement of the interests of their particular group or the region with which they identify. It may be said that there is a radical difference between the use of public office for private purposes, including those of one's family or even the particular tribe, caste, or group to which one belongs and advancement of the interest of the region or a state to which one may belong, for one represents the interests of that particular region in the councils of the nation. But it will be difficult to draw a line or evolve criteria to demarcate between the legitimate and the illegitimate in this context. It would be considered invidious, for example, if one were to foster the interests of some particular corporation or company or some business interests while occupying a position in which one was supposed to foster the interests of the whole rather than of some one part at the expense of the other. Much has been written on the justice or injustice of fostering the interest of one *person* at the expense of another's, but not much attention has been paid to the question of fostering the interests of one *group* at the expense of another's.

Perhaps a distinction may be made even in the context of the ideology of democracy between representation in terms of articulation and representation in terms of action, and it may be argued that, while it is legitimate to articulate the specific interests that one may be said to represent for any reason whatsoever, if one has the responsibility to act, one cannot legitimately have a partisan viewpoint, as that would vitiate one's truly representative capacity at its very foundation. Thus, for example, one may articulate the interests of one's own region or country in the National Assembly or the United Nations, as the case may be, but one may not or rather ought not to pursue them if one happens to be a member of the government or belongs to an executive body of the United Nations.

Between the "general will," the "general reason" and the "general good" there thus lie certain specific goods that will have to be taken into account if the idealistic fallacy that led to totalitarianism in the West is to be avoided. For example, once one begins to conceive of the general good as transcending all specific goods, and even negating them if necessary, one is led to the paradoxical conclusion that one may legitimately impose untold suffering on a mass of people for their own "real" good. The distinction between the apparent and the real, though legitimate in certain contexts, should not be absolutized as it would then make almost everything "apparent" and the real would be known to hardly anyone (except, of course, those favored by the grace of God with special insight—insight which it would be possible to question only at the cost of being declared a heretic and possibly crucified.)

Here again we find the asymmetry mentioned earlier between the "general will" and the "general good," insofar as the "general will," unlike the "general good," is not only the summation of specific wills but is also supposed to transcend them in some manner. There is, of course, an analogous problem with the notion of "general reason," though it occurs in a different form and arises from different considerations. The problem with respect to reason relates basically to the issue of whether reason is ultimately rooted in culture, history, and tradition to such an extent that it is meaningful to talk of "cultural reasons" or "rationalities" as essentially multiple in character. This, of course, does not imply that they are completely closed to a possible dialogue with, or influence from, other "cultural reasons" or "rationalities." Each one of them is open to such a dialogue or influence, but it enters into such a relationship on its own terms—that is, in terms of what it is in view of its own history and cultural identity. The issue in fact relates at a deeper level to the question whether there are any ultimate, self-evident axioms or principles that every human being has to accept when he or she enters into a debate or argument with anybody else on any matter whatsoever. The law of noncontradiction is supposed to be one such principle, but one can always develop strategies to avoid it through a reformulation of what one has said or the claim that there is no real contradiction in what one has said, or that contradiction articulates the intrinsically opposed nature of the reality one is talking about. The deeper question, ultimately, is about the nature of reason itself. If reason exhibits only an "if-then" character, then unless one accepts the premise, one cannot be forced to accept the conclusion. The premises, moreover, cannot only be as multifarious as one pleases, but their "acceptance" has an element of arbitrariness and contingency about it which ultimately is what the notion of "culture" in the phrase "cultural reason" implies.

The issues of democracy and justice are thus intimately related to the way in which one conceives of the "general will," the "general good" and the "general reason." The notion of the "general will," as embodied in the idea of action in a "representative" capacity, and the notions of "general reason" and "general good," which appear to be closely related to cultural traditions rooted in history, on the one hand, and to the transcultural general human nature, on the other, seem to provide the parameters within which the problems of democracy and justice need to be posed and discussed.

It is, of course, true that the "general" always claims to be universal or at least aspires to be so, if it is self-consciously aware of its parochial character, rooted as it is in a particular cultural tradition and its historical development over time. The claim, on the one hand, and the aspiration, on the other, provide the dilemma for all cultures and civilizations, which it is almost impossible to resolve, since, in the first case, all other apprehensions apart from that of one's own culture are naturally regarded as incomplete or mistaken, while, in the second case, even where the parochial character is recognized to at least some extent, the aspiration to universality is generally sought in terms of one's own "cultural reason" or "cultural good." Thus even when cultures become aware of their own parochiality in the face of what others have apprehended and achieved, the search for universality through assimilation of what has been apprehended or achieved by others takes place only through the assimilation of that which one has been capable of apprehending given one's acculturation and socialization in one's own culture. This generally implies a rejection of incompatible elements and a substantial modification of those elements that are accepted and whose value is openly acknowledged and recognized. Universality thus is always at odds with generality, and the dilemmas that this generates in the realms of "reason," "will," and "good" are the dilemmas of a narrower and a larger identification.

The postulate of equality on which both democracy and justice are based thus runs counter not only to existent inequalities of every sort, but the inevitable perversions to which they are always liable because of the fact that one's identification is always with less than the whole of humanity—not to mention the larger identification with all living beings, toward whom one also feels an obligation because one is self-consciously aware that they too are capable of feeling pleasure and pain and that one can affect their lives positively or negatively by one's behavior.

Thus the demand for equality even as an ideal is always circumscribed by questions such as "Equality between whom and with respect to what?"—questions that are not easy to answer. Yet unless they are answered, no serious thinking about either democracy or justice can make any headway, for democracy and justice arise on the basis of a demand for equality in the political and legal realms. Ultimately, the demand is for equality between all human beings *qua* human beings, and that too in all respects, rather than just the few that some may consider more important than others. There is thus a transcendental dimension involved in the demand for equality as it not only negates the notion of difference among human beings, which itself implies inequalities of some sort or other, but also any relevant differentiation among the various attributes and dimensions that human beings inevitably have. Ultimately, the demand is that no discrimination should be made on any account whatsoever. In other words, there are no relevant differences among human beings that need to be taken into account, as all such differences are, in the final analysis, only of secondary importance.

The history of the implementation of the ideas of democracy and justice has shown an incessant drive toward this ideal, and yet the drive has always come into conflict with the fact that not only are many of these differences of great importance for human beings, but all societies and cultures strive for qualitative excellence among their people, particularly insofar as they have to compete with other societies, cultures, and civilizations. If the demand for the absolutizing of democracy and justice has been an imperative in modern times, so also has been the pursuit of incessant competition in all fields, so that gradually sports have become the paradigmatic exemplars of all that is sought for in society. The transcendental search for equality in every realm thus comes directly into conflict with the empirical situation of man, in which differences are not only endemic, but also valued, preferred, and rewarded. Such a system of preferences, valuation, and reward inevitably leads to an emphasis on competition in which inequalities of every kind are made visible to the minutest degree.

A remedy for the inherent contradiction in the situation is sought by making the rules of the competitive game as fair as possible. As a consequence, the enhancement of inequalities through the actual process of competition is supposed to be just and acceptable. But this is merely an illusion, for however "just" the competition may seem to be, it nonetheless celebrates inequality. And, as everyone knows, there are always ways to circumvent the rules or break them to one's own advantage. In a game, there at least *are* umpires or referees, even though the players may have found ways and means of cheating—by tampering with the ball, as some of the greatest bowlers in the game of cricket are supposed to have done, or by taking drugs to get that extra energy that enables one to break the record. In the political and economic arena, on the other hand, those who cheat are seldom caught and there are no umpires or referees. And so it is the one who can successfully cheat and get away with it who wins. And even if people vaguely remember how he or she has done so, they soon forget it. The legal system is supposed to be the watchdog for ensuring that those who violate the rules shall be punished, but as everyone knows, the legal system itself is not immune to the pressures that affect the realms of polity and economy. In fact, the more political or economic power one has the less likely it is, in most societies, that one will be legally convicted if one has done some wrong.

Yet the imperatives for establishing a better society are always there and one continuously tries to formulate rules and build institutions that one hopes will give everyone an equal chance in the running of society and ensure that if the rules of the game are not observed or if one willfully cheats, one gets punished. But along with this imperative, there is also a counterimperative, which demands that societies move forward in the realization of values with respect to which the rules to ensure that justice is done are seen as being only instrumental in character. There is thus always a tension, and even a conflict, between the demand for the enforcement of the rules that are supposed to ensure that no particular individual has any advantage over others in the competitive game for the realization of excellence and the pursuit of excellence itself. This inherent contradiction takes a sharper edge when a society pursues power, whether in the political or the economic realm, as the values of power and wealth are not only intrinsically asymmetrical in character but also asymmetrical in the bad sense of the term. This becomes apparent in the realm of international relations, in which the pursuit of goals of power and wealth at the national level are often harmful to the interests of those who belong to other nations. Thus those contradictions that are suppressed or masked or underplayed at the national level become visible at the international level, as there seems to be no real transnational identification to minimize or mitigate the contradictions.

The problem of "identification" thus is crucial to both democracy and justice, though it has seldom been seen as such. The simple reason for this has been that thinking about democracy and justice has primarily been done in the context of the isolated individual shorn of all identities with other larger groups of which he is inevitably a member. The Marxists tried to get rid of this monadic individualism, permitting only one identification as "real" and treating all others as evidence of a "false consciousness." In doing so, of course, they forgot that the characterization of any consciousness as "false" can only occur from the standpoint of some observer, in terms of a value judgment, and that when the so-called "false consciousness" is shared by a very large number of people, it consists not just of beliefs, but also of actions, which in turn transform social reality in the light of this consciousness that is supposed to be "false." The distinction between falsity and truth in the realm of social reality does not operate in the same way as it usually does in the case of transsocial reality or nature. On the other hand, if the criterion of falsehood is considered to be the failure of the action to which it gives rise, then one will have to wait for the failure to occur to declare whether the consciousness was false or not. The deeper question in this context, however, is how to define failure of action, particularly when it emanates from the so-called "false identifications" held by a large number of people.

Forgetting the exclusivist notion of real identification defined in Marxist terms, in which class consciousness or rather the identification of the self with the "class" is supposed to be the only real identification, there can, in principle, be no "real" identification, except perhaps with some ideal value that one wants to actualize or realize through action in one's own life, or with the community or society of which one happens to be a member or which can be regarded as the realm falling within the range of the effectivity of one's action.

There are, of course, powerful traditions, particularly in the Indian civilizations, that have argued that all identifications are the result of false consciousness or a primordial ignorance or *avidyà*, as the self cannot be anything other than itself. But as such a position has generally entailed the doctrine of the illusoriness of all action flowing from such false identifications, it is irrelevant for any serious thinking regarding the problem of how to bring into being an ideal society or polity through individual or collective action. In fact, the notion of collectivity will perhaps be the prime instance of false consciousness in such a perspective. That is perhaps the reason why, according to this perspective, one is supposed to renounce both society and polity and take *sannyàsa* and retire to the forest. That, of course, was only an ideal, since what actually obtained, even in India, was the community of renouncers who had an active involvement with society and polity, as they depended on it for their sustenance and support.

The philosophical point, however, is that not only has one inevitably to identify oneself with something or other in order to act (or even to feel oneself as oneself), these identifications are multiple in nature, and this multiplicity is both horizontal and vertical in character. It can expand sometimes, at least in imaginative empathy, to include the whole world, and at other times, shrink to the narrowest point, such as one's own body with its insistent desires and pains and pleasures. Consciousness, however, always has the feeling, however illusory it may seem to outside observers, that it has the capacity and the freedom to enlarge its identifications or shift from one identification to another. This felt freedom with respect to all determinate identifications leads both theoretically and existentially to the apprehension of one's ultimate reality as something that transcends all identifications and which is thus, in the real sense, as Professor Gandhi has recently argued, no-thing at all.

But such a move, though always tempting to any mind steeped in the Indian traditions, forgets the "otherness" of the other in a fundamental sense and thus not only dissolves but disowns the burdensome demands made by the other in its otherness, which is to be treated as equal to oneself in its own right. This is a demand for coordinate equality that not only preserves differences, but also values them. The debate in the Indian tradition regarding the preservation of ultimate difference or its denial has focused primarily on the *ātman* and the *brahman* or the *ātman* and the *iśvara*—that is, on the self and whatever is regarded as ultimately real, but never has it focused on the relation between selves, even at the transcendental level. The Advaita Vedānta, of course, recognizes no such problem, since for it there cannot be other selves in principle. But the question is not even raised by all those other schools that believe in the plurality of selves at the transcendental level.

Even at the empirical level, however, the problem of equality and inequality is not only complex, but remains unresolved, as each individual is a "subject" with respect to which everything, including other selves, are "objects," and thus, in their relationship to each other, individuals are both simultaneously "subjects" and "objects," ensuring a parity and a complementarity that is the ultimate foundation of all human dignity, though it tends to be forgotten most of the time because of the fact that all the other "subjects" cannot but be seen as "objects" by one's own subjectivity, even if one forgets or ignores the inequities in the relationships emanating from other dimensions. Yet as Sartre reminded us, anyone can be reduced to an object by the mere fact of being "looked" at by another or, a point that he did not make, by the more significant act of being "turned away from" by the other, which we might think of as involving the withdrawal of one's affection, regard, or respect. For, as everybody knows, even a child may in one way reduce one to a nullity—by showing its rejection of one. In fact, the multiple ways in which one's being can be negated or the corresponding alternative ways in which one can be restored to one's basic dignity have hardly been the subject of serious philosophical reflection.

Yet the very fact that the self is at the mercy of the other, and that at almost all levels there is a quantitative and qualitative inequality between selves, poses a problem that has seldom been seen in all of its ramifications. It has been mistakenly believed that equality between human beings can only be ensured by reducing or minimizing inequalities of all sorts and at all levels. But such an attempt is doomed to failure not only because the principle of variety constitutes the very nature of reality as we know it, but also because any such attempt requires coercion of a very high order to ensure that no fresh inequalities may emerge. Yet such an attempt at coercion can hardly be conceived without an enormous inequality between those who coerce and those who are coerced. It is true, of course, that certain forms of inequality are undesirable and have to be minimized to some extent in order to make collective living meaningful and worthwhile. But even the achievement of such a reduction will leave the essential problem unresolved, as it requires the apprehension and valuation of the subjectivity of the other self which demands to be treated on a par with one's own subjectivity, and such a situation can only be brought about by continuously reminding oneself and emphasizing, in social discourse, the equisubjectivity of all human beings, and even perhaps of all beings.

These considerations may seem unrelated to the actual problems of democracy and justice in the ordinary business of society and the polity with which most thinkers are concerned. But unless the problem of inequality is faced at its foundation, much of the actual functioning of democracy and the demand for justice may lead us in directions that will not seem very desirable from most points of view. There is a built-in dynamic by which democracy and justice press for equality in all directions, as there seems to be no justification for any inequality between human beings whatsoever. It is inequality, then, that has to be justified, since equality seems to require no justification at all and appears to be self-justified.

The demand for equality has shifted to other fields than those of politics and economy, which used to be the center of the debate between socialism and democracy. Now we have the issue of equality between the sexes and between different ethnic groups. But this is only the beginning. It is bound to be extended to other fields, as is already evident in many non-Western societies, where cultural constraints on the functioning of democracy do not obtain to the same extent that they do in the West. To take but one example: what would democracy mean in the context of the educational system, where there is a built-in inequality between the teacher and the taught? "Knowledge," it should be remembered, is not the sort of thing that can be possessed equally, even in principle. Not every person, after all, has the capacity to acquire it, even if he or she so wishes, the acquisition of knowledge requiring as it does a lot of discipline, which most people are not prepared to undergo for any considerable length of time. The acceptance of "democracy" in an educational institution might lead to a situation in which the students would determine the qualifications of admission, the material that is to be taught, the level at which it is to be taught, and the procedures of evaluation and examination. In a democratic arrangement, all of these are bound to be diluted to the utmost extent by the very logic of the situation, since those who are least desirous of learning and least qualified to learn are in the majority, and hence will decide the issue in any "democratic" system. The same would also be true of the teachers, as, in a thoroughly "democratic" manner, they will demand that persons with the least aptitude and least qualification for teaching should be appointed to teach in these institutions. There would thus be a collusion between the "democracy" of the students and the "democracy" of the teachers, resulting in incalculable harm to the very cause of learning for which the institution was created.

This obviously will not be confined only to the area of education but will extend to almost all fields where countercultural constraints are not operative to any significant degree. Any attempt at rectification of the situation will meet the organized resistance of the unions which, in the name of "democracy," will not allow even the mildest punishment of any transgressors, even if they have violated the most fundamental norms of social functioning. Add to this the fact that many of the criminal elements in society try to achieve legitimacy by achieving political power through electoral means. And if they are successful, who can say that they are not the true "representatives" of the people? And if they belong to the ruling party, these democratically elected representatives of the people, who once were "criminals," are entitled to rule in the name of the people.

These may seem unwarranted overstatements, but in fact they are understatements that hardly portray the situation as it increasingly obtains in India, where democracy has been successfully practiced for almost half a century now. The state of justice in such a situation can readily be imagined. In fact, one can easily go to a court of law and get a writ against anything for temporary stay in the execution of a decision and, as everything is justiciable, and the "rights" of the individual are always in jeopardy, practically nothing can be done that harms any vested interest.

Instances can be multiplied indefinitely, but the basic philosophical issue concerns the preconditions that underlie the institutions of democracy and justice, and in the absence of which democracy and justice can hardly achieve the values which political theorists had in mind. At a deeper level still, the dilemma that faces one is how to ensure the realization of these values in a situation where those preconditions are increasingly absent. Many of the new countries experimenting with Western forms of democracy and institutions of justice are increasingly faced with these dilemmas and, unless serious thought is given to these issues, there may eventually be deeper disillusionment with democracy than one imagines. The complacency in the West after the collapse of the alternative political institutions that went under the name of Socialism may prove temporary, as the increasing failure of political and legal institutions developed in the Western world may reveal the hidden preconditions of the culture in which they originated and within which alone they may successfully function. Moveover, the logic of the institutions may ultimately erode the cultural preconditions themselves and even the Western world may come to face the same problems that many of the non-Western countries are facing today. The problem ultimately emanates from the ideal of equality that the notions of democracy and justice imply, and unless that ideal itself is seriously subjected to a new philosophical scrutiny, the direction taken may become irreversible and lead to an increasing anarchy from which people may choose to escape even at the cost of giving up their hard-earned liberties.

Thus the basic problem for political philosophy today is how to reconcile the desire for equality with not only the manifest inequality derived from both genetic and environmental factors but also those inequalities that men cherish and foster and many of which result from the differential pursuit of ideal values on the part of different individuals. Unless this basic dilemma is recognized, the new values that are vaguely conveyed by terms such as democracy and justice may themselves be lost or jeopardized to a greater extent than we can imagine today.

Ramjee Singh

GANDHI'S CONCEPTION OF DEMOCRACY[1]

AMBIGUITY AND MISUSE

An inventory of the use of the term "democracy" is apt to become a barren enterprise in semantics.[2] However, no word is in itself either ambiguous or unambiguous, but only as it is used on this or that occasion.[3] There can hardly be any doubt that the term "democracy" has not only been used *ambiguously* and *vaguely*, but also that it has been *misused*. For example, during the two World Wars, which were solemnly proclaimed to have been fought in defense, and for the victory, of *democracy*. For this reason, the use of the term "democracy," without any historical, social, or political qualification, is apt to be ambiguous. There is another problem involved in the relationship between "formal" democracy, as an exclusively political concept, and "real" democracy, as a broad socio-economic-political concept.

However, in spite of the term's basic ambiguity and susceptibility to misuse, practical politicians and political theorists agree in stressing the "democratic" element in the institutions they defend and the theories they advocate. This acceptance of democracy as the highest form of political or social organization is the sign of a basic agreement. The other point of agreement lies in the fact that even the most sharply contrasting forms of democracy share a common tradition of humanism.[4] For example, they claim to uphold justice, equality, liberty, civilization, and true participation in public functions. But these basic agreements are overlaid with a complex array of disagreements. Given the important role that the term "democracy" played in the conflict of convictions after the Second World War, UNESCO felt the need in the early 1950s to organize a debate between nations, and between ideological camps, to help clarify the ambiguities and resist the sloganeering usage of the term. If we continue this project and pursue a further clarification of the issues today, we might show that there can be ideological opposition without bad faith.

THE ROOTS OF GANDHIAN DEMOCRACY

Gandhi's interest in democracy was less intellectual than practical. He may be called a liberal in the Lockean-Benthamite tradition and a radical in the Rousseauist tradition. Moreover, we can also call him a "revivalist," as he doggedly advocated for *Ram Raj*—or the Kingdom of God, according to Hindu belief. However, academic formulations do not penetrate very deeply with regard to Gandhi. Thought was only an aid to his life. According to him, "life alone is" and "life is unity." Neither the human mind nor human society is divided into watertight compartments corresponding to the social, the political, and the religious. All of these act and react upon one another. So also there is no real divide between individual *liberty* and *equality*. Gandhi viewed democracy in the context of a crisis in modern civilization, which, according to him, was no longer "governed by moral principle, and whose marvelous genius of discovery and invention is monstrously distorted towards its own ruin."[5] Roman Rolland, therefore, regards Gandhi as a new incarnation of Rousseau and Tolstoy, denouncing the illusions and the crimes of civilization, and preaching to men the return to nature, to the simple life. Gandhi decried the liberal democratic concept that "the power of man is his ability to command the services of others," because this leads to the "enslavement of man by the temptations of money and of the luxuries that money can buy."[6] The power of man lies in his potential for development based on the essential identity of all. This is the core of "Gandhian democracy growing from within, and not an imposition from above."[7] Gandhi did not accept the liberal individualist equating of man's powers with the extractive powers or with his ability to procure satisfaction by whatever means. Nor did he accept the democratic humanist ideal of John Stuart Mill and his utilitarianism. Gandhi's conception of man's power was based on the Indian Vedantic idea of the basic identity of everything that is individuated. Therefore, he believed in the essential goodness and the egalitarian nature of man, which are corrupted because of an uncongenial environment. Gandhi's concern, then, was not with the "power of man" but the "power of soul." In order to realize this essence, however, one has to discipline oneself through "self-restraint" and "self-purification."[8]

THE RULE OF RIGHTEOUSNESS

This spiritual legacy of Gandhi inclined him to believe that "the spirit of democracy cannot be imposed from without. It has to come from within."[9]

The Gandhian ideal of *Ram Raj,* which he described as the "sovereignty of the people based on purely moral authority,"[10] represents a democratic polity in which there is neither obscurantism nor utopianism. It cannot be equated with a theocratic Hindu polity, nor with a monarchy, nor with an autocracy. Hence there is no scope for "iniquitous inequalities." Gandhi's *"Ram"* is the symbolic expression of self. Thus he reiterated that

> without rule of self there can be no *Swaraj* or *Ramrajya.* Rule of all without the rule of oneself would prove to be a deceptive toy-mango, charming to look at outwardly, but hollow and empty within. Thus the problem of democracy is basically a problem of value. Unless the moral and spiritual qualities of the people are appropriate, the best of political systems and constitutions will not work.[11]

In a similar vein, Pitrim Sorokin observed, "if we banish moral considerations in politics, it will be a quagmire of opportunism and exigencies bound to create a morbid love of power and endless conflict."[12] Hence democracy presupposes "political ethics." This is "higher politics" or, as Karl Jaspers put it, the "religious politics of the 'self-revealing' man."[13] Aristotle long ago warned that a *polis* will cease to be a *polis* unless we bring ethical value to regulate the field of political activity. Gandhi, therefore, warned that "there is no politics devoid of religion"[14] and that "politics without religion is a death trap."[15] But his politics presupposed political ethics, and by religion he meant "ethical religion." For him, "to bring God into politics is to bring Truth and Love."[16] For "democracy is not a mere means to the attainment of other ends, but an independent value and an end in itself."[17]

DEMOCRACY AS A VALUE OF LIFE AND SOCIETY

Respect for the individual is the moral basis of democracy. "The individual is the one supreme consideration,"[18] said Gandhi. So, according to him, man is above institutions. "To slight a single human being is to slight [the] divine powers, and thus to harm not only that being but with him the whole world."[19] Democracy is the defender of individuality, a preserver of the spirit in man. Gandhi therefore said, "I am a lover of my own liberty and so I would do nothing to restrict yours."[20] This, of course, is also exactly what Lincoln proclaimed: "I would not like to be master even as I would not like to be a slave." No society can possibly be built on a denial of individual freedom. However, as a protagonist of self-discipline, Gandhi could not approve of unrestricted or "unbridled individualism [which] is the law of the beast of the jungle," but advocated instead "willing submission to social restraint for the sake of the well-being of the whole society of which one is a member."[21] Hence the individual, as Gandhi conceived of him, was not an isolated individual. The individual had no rights, but merely duties. As he put it, "The true source of rights is duty. If we all discharge our duties, rights will not be far to seek. If leaving duties unperformed, we run after rights, they will escape us like a will-o-the-wisp."[22] Nonetheless, he regarded the individual as an end in himself. Sovereignty is located in the individual conscience. The state exists for the sake of individual liberty, and hence obedience to the state is neither final nor absolute. Thus Gandhi "looked upon the increase in the power of the state with the greatest fear, because although while doing good by minimizing exploitation, it does the greatest harm to mankind by destroying individuality which lies at the root of all progress."[23]

The rule of majority, then, has a narrow application. That is to say, one should yield to the majority on matters of detail, but it is slavery to be amenable to the majority, no matter what its decisions are. Under democracy individual liberty of opinion and action is jealously guarded. The minority therefore has a perfect right to act differently from the majority. Gandhi was emphatic that "in matters of conscience the law of majority has no place."[24] Thus he was totally opposed to any armed coercion, either by a majority to bend the will of a minority or vice versa, because violence is the negation of democracy.

This is why Gandhi questioned the basis of the majoritarian principle underlying parliamentary democracy. In his philosophy of *Sarvodaya* or the welfare of *all*, Gandhi rejected the utilitarian principle of the greatest good for the greatest number, which is central to majoritarian democracy, since it might be used to justify the elimination of minority rights for the sake of an abstractly conceived majority. Gandhi's basic focus in political ethics was on "equality rather than majority." A democratic government—that is, government by the majority—is open to grave abuse. Lord Acton, therefore, warned against arbitrary resolutions of opinion.

> It will be the duty of the majority to see to it that the minorities receive a proper hearing and are not otherwise exposed to insults. *Swaraj* will be an absurdity if individuals have to surrender their judgment to the majority.[25]

In matters of truth, majority has no particular authority. Consequently, Gandhi advised, "let us not push the mandate theory to ridiculous extremes and become slaves to [the] resolutions of majorities."

The principle of majority rule involves a delicate balance of the rights of minority and the rights of majority. The minority has a right to influence the process of arriving at a decision by the free expression of its opinions and the right to have its wishes and interests taken into consideration. The majority has the obligation to respect those rights and to exercise its powers with moderation. The minorities acquiesce in the decision of the majority not only because they know they will have their day, but because they feel that every effort has been made to understand and meet their point of view. In short, majority opinion in democracy must be such that "while the minority may not share it, they feel bound by conviction, not by fear, to accept it, though only as a second best, and if democracy is real, the submission of the minority must be given ungrudgingly remembering that majorities also have rights."[26] Speaking about the *Panchayat* tradition of unanimity, Gandhi's able disciple, Vinoba Bhave, pleads for the transformation of "quantitative democracy" into "qualitative democracy." He writes, "Today a resolution is 'passed' by fifty-one as against forty-nine. This kind of democracy means the rule of evil. I want to see the fifty-one and the forty-nine working in harmony as one united hundred."[27] This "God in the majority" business is very dangerous. (Quakers, recognizing this, follow the method of unanimity.) Society must form the habit of coming to decisions either through unanimity or through broad consensus to avoid endless confrontation.

DEMOCRACY AND DECENTRALIZATION

The question of the relationship between democracy and nonviolence no longer remains merely an academic exercise; it has acquired practical relevance in the context of growing violence and terrorism in some democratic countries, striking at the very foundations of their democratic structure and values. "The state itself represents violence in a concentrated and organized form."[28] Thus increasing the power of the state is the most out-of-date idea today, because if the state uses more and more violence, "it will be caught in the coils of violence itself and fail to develop non-violence at any time." In fact, the modern state faces the paradox that it has more to do with power than with either individual freedom or democracy. The socialist state especially tends to be more than a Leviathan. The idea of a transitional dictatorship, of course, is a myth. While a people may choose a dictator, they cannot order him to abdicate. The welfare state, with ever-increasing responsibilities, has terribly strengthened its grip over individuals; and in the marriage between capitalism and democracy, capitalism becomes more important than democracy. Everywhere there is a moral and material fight between the omnipotence of the state and individual freedom. What is needed, then, is the decentralization of power that can be achieved through a "Great Society of Small Communities."

No doubt there is a lust for power, and the state represents the supreme power. There is presupposed, then, a clash for the seizure of power, which, once started, never seems to end. The state becomes enmeshed in the coils of counterviolence. Violence may destroy one or more bad rulers, but like Ravan's heads, others will take their places. Instead of futile attempts at the suppression of violence through violence (sponsored by capitalism or communism), the practical solution is decentralization, since "centralization cannot be sustained and defended without adequate force."[29] The dilemma of politics, then, persists: either it must evolve a nonviolent decentralized polity or remain in the clutches of violence. Hence Gandhi advocated the theory of "the least government," following Thoreau's dictum: "That government is the best which governs the least." Gandhi knew that "nowhere in the world does a State without Government exist."[30] The ideal of statelessness is thus a direction rather than a destination, the process rather than a consummation. And so Gandhi emphasized grass-roots democracy. When power belongs to the people at the grass-roots level, there is direct participation of the people in development and administration. The base will be widened and strengthened, while the apex bodies will not be burdened with such multifarious powers as they have today. Society as a whole will function like a well-coordinated machine, receiving explicit direction from the bottom, with the result that lust for power is reduced.

Centralization cannot be defended without adequate force. Therefore, Gandhi suggested for India a decentralized political structure based upon self-sufficient and self-governing village communities. "Every village has to be self-sustained and capable of managing its affairs even to the extent of defending itself against the world." The fundamental principle of political organization was that life should not be a pyramid with the apex sustained by the bottom. Instead, "it would be an *Oceanic Circle of Villages* till at last the whole becomes one life composed of individuals. The outermost circumference will not wield power to crush the inner circle but will give strength to all within and derive its own strength from it."[31] Today the state has become a Leviathan. If it wants, it can starve the whole nation. But a unit self-sufficient with respect to basic needs can offer nonviolent resistance to the power of the state. What Gandhi had in mind, however, was not "complete self-sufficiency" but rather "maximum self-sufficiency in basic needs." The structuring of power in this case is stratified, with only residual power passing upward from one stratum to the next. As a result of this stratification, with the passing on of only residual power, the greater portion of political power remains at the grass-roots level.

GANDHIAN CRITIQUE OF REPRESENTATIVE DEMOCRACY

The concentration of authority in the hands of central government has been criticized by many scholars. In Great Britain and America, complaints have been raised against "dictatorship of the cabinet" and "executive aggrandizement." But the challenge of politics is that, in order to preserve their liberties, citizens must delegate power to their governments in order that they may guard against those who would transgress against the moral law. Thus liberty and authority are held in a state of creative tension. As Locke argued, liberty in a social context cannot be absolute; it must be restricted within the framework of a civil society, of which government forms a necessary part.

Liberty by itself is not an absolute value, however; it needs to be complemented by equality. But equality, in order to be meaningful, must encompass not only political, but also social and economic equality. (This, of course, is where Western democracy has faltered and fallen short of its ideals.) Equality and liberty, however, are not entirely compatible goals. The more one achieves equality, the more thoroughly one has to limit individual freedoms in the name of conformity. Thus the more equality, the less liberty, and vice versa.

Aside from this formal contradiction, there are also some serious difficulties of a practical nature to be considered. The first has to do with the party system in representative/parliamentary democracies. The debate continues whether elected representatives are spokesmen for particular interests or for the national interest. In terms of political reality, however, they clearly represent the programs of party first, with the result that often the national interest is subjugated to that of the party. The second problem stems from the fact that the executive or cabinet has *de facto* control over the legislature, since, at least in a parliamentary system, the executive is formed by whichever party enjoys a majority. In fact, then, in the name of *democracy*, or "government by the people," there is actually rule by party, and within the party, by the party bosses. In truth, then, we have only veiled autocracy. As Gandhi painfully observed, "Western democracy is only so-called. It is diluted Fascism and Nazism."

Gandhi pointed out many defects in parliamentary democracy, which he dubbed a "costly toy of the nation." He observed, for example, that the "Prime Minister [is] more concerned about power than about the welfare of parliament," is "open to subtler influences," and is prone to "bribing people with honours." Parliamentary democracy has "neither real honesty nor a living conscience," and benefits from the "bewilderment of voters through dishonest press." There is a "lack of interest [on the part] of the members of the parliament in the actual business of the House," and the people at large, in their role as voters, are reduced to a mere "rubber stamp." As a consequence, Gandhi compared democracy to a sterile woman.[32] (Many Western thinkers will no doubt agree with the spirit of this Gandhian criticism.) He wanted not a representative but a participatory democracy, a people's democracy. (It is interesting to note that Gandhi prepared a constitution for the princely state of Aundh when the ruler decided to give self-government to his people in 1938. He called it participatory democracy at the grass-roots level.[33])

CONCLUSION

The ideals of democracy remain unachieved more so because of the prevailing belief in the efficiency of violence and lies than because of mere institutional inadequacies. No doubt, democracy is a form of government, or mode of society, but in reality it is an ideal and life-value. Respect for the individual is the moral basis of democracy. Still, democracy is also an institution, and therefore is liable to be abused. But there is no alternative to democracy. If there were to be an alternative, that could only be a better form of democracy. In that sense, democracy would be not only a governmental or political concept, but a holistic concept. It would touch all aspects of our life—political, economic, social, and spiritual. Although democracy seeks out the opinion of the majority, there must be no tyrannizing of the minority but rather magnanimity on the part of the majority, in which respect is freely granted to the opposition. Above all, democracy is essentially a way of life, in which we adhere to such ideals as the freedom and dignity of the individual, rule of law, social justice, individual freedom, equal economic opportunities for all, the desire for peace, the love of truth, and nonviolence.

Democracy is wholly inconsistent with the use of force. It cannot be cultivated through any method involving force. The democratic state will thus govern the least and use the least amount of force possible. It will involve primarily self-government, which means a continuous effort to be independent of government control as far as possible. The test of the strength of a democracy lies in the importance it accords to duties as opposed to rights, since every right is the right to do one's duty. As Gandhi observed, "the true source of right is duty. People who obtain rights as a result of performance of duty, exercise them only for the service of society, never for themselves."[34]

Democracy, as it is practiced today, seems to have been betrayed. It has ceased to be an inspiring ideal, having become autocratic and even highly ethnocentric, nationalistic and force-minded. Talking about the United States, the late Justice Robert Jackson declared, "No nation is more force-minded than our own." As he saw it, the special function of democratic law is to put "rational restraints upon the use of coercive power by those in authority" to prevent it from lapsing into communism in practice, which insists upon expressing the will of the dominant class—"the compulsive will of the state." It is impossible for the force-minded to either preserve or defend democracy. Aggressive democracy, which lives by tyranny and exploitation, is blasphemy against our democratic heritage. For a long time, Great Britain was a democracy fighting for her empire, and today we experience "the invisible empire of the United States." But as Nehru observed, "empire and democracy are two incompatibles; one must swallow the other." Democratic revolution cannot be limited to one nation. It must be a global phenomenon. Thus democracy cannot coexist with colonialism, exploitation, or racial suprematism. It can only be rooted in liberty, equality, and nonviolence.

NOTES

1. **Editors' Note:** The reader will remark that this paper is rather different in style and substance from the rest of the essays contained in this anthology. The editors have

chosen to include it because it is indicative of how the subject of democracy is commonly approached in many non-Western societies.

2. M. M. Bober, in *Democracy in a World of Tensions: A Symposium Prepared by UNESCO*, Richard McKeon, ed. (Chicago: University of Chicago Press, 1951), p. 18.

3. C. J. Ducasse, Ibid., p. 69.

4. Appendix II, ibid., pp. 522–24.

5. Roman Rolland, "Homage from a Man of the West to Gandhi" in *Mahatma Gandhi*, S. Radhakrishnan, ed. (Bombay: Jaico Publishing House, 1956), p. 197.

6. M. K. Gandhi, *Hind Swaraj* (Ahmedabad: Navajivan Publishing House, 1938), p. 35.

7. I. Rothermund, "Hind Swaraj and the Idea of Democracy," *Hind Swaraj: A Fresh Look*, N. Prasad, ed. (Delhi: Gandhi Peace Foundation, 1985), p. 130.

8. Gopi Nath Dhawan, *Political Philosophy of Mahatma Gandhi* (Ahmedabad: Navajivan Publishing House, 1946), p. 331.

9. M. K. Gandhi, *Young India*, 28.5.1931.

10. M. K. Gandhi, Address at Faizpur Session of the Indian National Congress, 1936.

11. J. P. Narayan, *A Plea for the Reconstruction of Indian Polity* (Bombay: Bhartiya Vidya Bhawan, 1960), p. 3.

12. Pitrim Sorokin, *Reconstruction of Humanity* (Bombay: Bhartiya Vidya Bhawan, 1960), p. 171.

13. Karl Jaspers, "Gandhi on his 100th Birthday," *Mahatma Gandhi—One Hundred Years* (Delhi: Gandhi Peace Foundation, 1968), p. 170.

14. B. K. Malik, *Gandhi—A Prophecy* (Bombay: Hind Kitabs, 1948), p. 90.

15. S. Radhakrishnan, Introduction to *Mahatma Gandhi: Essays and Reflections*, S. Radhakrishnan, ed. (London: Allen & Unwin, 1949), p. 14.

16. S. Painter-Briak, *Gandhi against Machiavellism* (Bombay: Asia Publishing House, 1960), p. 13.

17. Daya Krishna, "What Is Democracy?" in *Democracy in the New States* (New Delhi: Congress of Cultural Freedom, 1959), pp. 65–66.

18. M. K. Gandhi, *Young India*, 13.11.1924.

19. M. K. Gandhi, *An Autobiography* (Ahmedabad: Navajivan Publishing House, 1944), p. 337.

20. N. B. Sen, ed., *Wit and Wisdom of Mahatma Gandhi* (New Delhi: New Book Society of India, 1960), p. 131.

21. M. K. Gandhi, *Harijan*, 27.5.1939.

22. M. K. Gandhi, *Young India*, 8.1.1925.

23. M. K. Gandhi, *Modern Review* (Calcutta: October 1935), p. 413.

24. M. K. Gandhi, *Young India*, 4.8.1920.

25. R. K. Prabhu and U. R. Rao, eds., *The Mind of Mahatma* (London: Oxford University Press, 1946), p. 162.

26. A. Appadorai, Statement in *Democracy and Non-Violence*, Krishna Kumar, ed. (New Delhi: Gandhi Peace Foundation, 1968), p. 80.

27. Vinoba Bhave, *Democratic Values* (Kashi: Sarva Seva Sangh Prakashan, 1962), p. 112.

28. M. K. Gandhi, *Modern Review* (1935), p. 142.

29. M. K. Gandhi, *Harijan*, 30.12.1939.

30. M. K. Gandhi, *Harijan,* 15.9.1946.

31. M. K. Gandhi, *Harijan,* 15.9.1946.

32. M. K. Gandhi, *Hind Swaraj,* chap. V.

33. Indira Rothermund, *The Aundh Experiment: A Gandhian Grass-Roots Democracy* (Bombay: Somaiya Publishers, 1984).

34. M. K. Gandhi, *Harijan,* 25.3.1939.

Javid Iqbal

DEMOCRACY AND JUSTICE: ISLAM'S POLITICAL MESSAGE RESTATED

The political message of Islam is reflected in the Quran and the "Practice (*sunnah*) of the Prophet of Islam." The Prophet migrated from his ancestral home, Mecca, because the Meccans were not willing to accept the new faith. Arriving at Medina, and with the support of the citizenry, he founded a state there. Thus the state is an integral part of Islam from its inception.

As the head of this new state, the Prophet regulated political and military affairs, and as the Messenger of God, he was not obliged to consult others. But he consulted his companions in all matters other than those concerning revelation, in accordance with the command addressed to him in the Quran to the effect that he should consult them in affairs and when he had taken a decision, he should put his trust in God (sura 3:159). The command to the Prophet in this regard was for no other purpose than to emphasize the importance of "consultation" (*shura*) to the Muslims in the managing of affairs of state. In his personal capacity, the Prophet usually accepted the advice of others and did not impose his own decision.

In sura 42:38, it is specifically laid down that the Muslims are those who conduct their affairs by mutual consultation. Thus the Muslim community is expected to conduct all of its worldly affairs (*muamalaat*) by mutual consultation. The Prophet is reported to have said, "Difference of opinion in my community is [the manifestation of Divine] Mercy," and "My community would never agree on an error."[1]

In interpreting the verses pertaining to consultation, a very important question arises—to wit, whether the body to be created for this purpose is a consultative body or an advisory body. The Prophet always consulted a body of eminent members of the community in the conduct of the affairs of state. This was an advisory body, and the practice was subsequently followed by his four successors, the Rightly Guided Caliphs (from 632 A.D. to 661 A.D.).

241

However, the *Khawaraj* jurists disagree with this practice. According to them, under the relevant Quranic injunction a consultative body rather than a single head of state assisted by an advisory body (whose advice he could ignore) was required to conduct the affairs of the Muslim community. They maintain that after the death of the Prophet there was no obligation to render obedience to a caliph or imam as the head of state, because the Muslim community could govern itself by constituting a consultative assembly from among themselves, and if need arose, the assembly could nominate a head of state for its own convenience. Be that as it may, the principle that those who command authority ought in all matters of importance to consult the Muslims is undisputed.

The Prophet promulgated *Mithaq-al-Medina,* the first written constitution of the world, in the city state of Medina. This ancient document contains forty-seven articles. The first twenty-three deal with the mutual relations, rights, and duties of Muslims. It is under these articles that the "emigrants" from Mecca (*muhajirin*) were united with the "helpers" from Medina (*ansar*) in the fraternal bond of a community of faith, thus laying down the principle that, according to Islam, nationhood (*milla* or *ummah*) is to be founded on a common spiritual aspiration, rather than on common race, language, and territory. The remaining twenty-four articles are concerned with the relations between Muslims and the non-Muslim inhabitants of Medina or the valley of Yathrib, confirming the latter in their faiths as well as possessions and enumerating their rights and duties. The central concept of this part of the document is that non-Muslims are included "in" the Muslim *ummah,* which implies that, if the nationhood of Muslims is founded on a common spiritual aspiration, their unity with non-Muslim minorities in the state is based on patriotic considerations or the defense of a common territory.

The Muslims and non-Muslims, described as a "single community" (*ummah-tul-wahida*), are to help one another against whoever wars against the people of Yathrib, for as stated in the document: "Among them there exists sincere friendship, honorable dealing and no treachery." They are also expected to contribute or bear expenses equally as long as the war continues, and they are to collectively defend the valley of Yathrib, which is described as "sacred for the people of this document."[2]

The Prophet founded a confederal state, as the non-Muslim tribes governed themselves in accordance with their own laws and were fully autonomous in their own regions. It was only in accordance with the terms of *Mithaq-al-Medina* that they were united with the Muslim community.

The document also proclaims that "God is the most scrupulous and truest fulfiller of what is contained in this document." The proclamation is based on the concept that all authority in the universe is vested in God, who is the omnipotent and omnipresent creator of the universe and whose sovereignty is therefore absolute. But the sovereignty of God does not curtail the sovereignty of the state. The conduct of the Prophet while concluding the Treaty of Al-Hudaybiya indicates that an act performed in the interest of the state or the community by the head of state is sovereign and that the overall sovereignty of God does not impose any restrictions on the sovereignty of the state or the head of state as legislator so long as the action taken, functions performed, or laws interpreted are in the interest of the state or the community.[3]

In sura 38:27 of the Quran, while appointing David as Vicegerent in the land, God commanded unto him, "Verily We have made thee Vicegerent in the land; then judge between men with truth, and follow not thy desires lest they cause thee to err from the Path of God." It is evident that God lays emphasis on the adoption of a course of justice, honesty, and truthfulness on the part of the head of state, for this leads to the path of God, and he is not to allow his personal interest to influence his official conduct or decisions.

The traditional Islamic jurisprudence likewise acknowledges the powers of the head of state as legislator to suspend (*ta'wiq*) a Quranic rule of law, or to restrict (*tahdid*) or expand (*tausih*) its application if the conditions so demand or the interests of the state or the community so require. In the light of this reasoning, the overall sovereignty of God or the supremacy of His law do not interfere with or impose any limitations on the sovereignty of the state or the powers of the legislator (*mujtahid*) to implement that interpretation of the Quranic rule of law which suits the requirements of the state or the community. If the sovereignty of God is to be considered like the rays of the sun, the sovereignty of the state in Islam is like the flame of a candle. The light of the sun may overwhelm the fragile flame of the candle, but it does not obliterate it. Hence it is not correct to assert that the state is not fully sovereign or that the legislator can only exercise his powers in a restricted manner.

The Prophet, as the head of state, was concerned with the formation and unity of the Muslim community, and with its governance in accordance with Islamic law (*shariah*). In the Quran, only broad principles of law have been laid down, and the Prophet, as the chief executive authority, interpreted and implemented them. Thus the principle was laid down that, in the sphere of legislation, the head of state has to be a *mujtahid* (one who himself interprets) and not a *muqallid* (one who follows the interpretation of others). The basis of this principle is the Quranic verse: "And to those who exert We show our path" (sura 29:69).

The principle is further illustrated in the light of a tradition (*hadith*) of the Prophet. On the appointment of Muadh as the governor of Yemen, the Prophet is reported to have asked him how he would decide matters coming up before him. Muadh replied, "I will judge matters according to the Book of God." The Prophet continued, "But if the Book of God does not contain anything to guide you?" And Muadh replied, "Then I will act in accordance with the precedents of the Prophet of God." Again the Prophet pressed him: "But if the precedents also fail?" "Then I will exert to form my own opinion," replied Muadh.

The inference to be drawn from this principle is that worldly affairs (*mua-malaat*), as distinguished from religious obligations (*ibadaat*), being subject to the law of change, are bound to be such on occasion that the Quran and the "Practice of the Prophet" may not provide sufficient guidance. Muslims would then be expected to exert themselves in advancing their own solutions in interpreting Islamic law and implementing it in accordance with the needs and requirements of their respective times. In other words, a mechanism (*ijtehad*) is provided within the polity in order to make Islamic law flexible and dynamic rather than static.

Theoretically the supremacy of God's law is acknowledged by the state, but as for its interpretation and implementation, the legislator's supremacy cannot be doubted when he exercises his power to suspend, restrict, or expand the application of a Quranic rule of law (pertaining to matters other than *ibadaat*) in specific circumstances or uses his discretion by accepting or advancing a specific interpretation with due regard to the interests of the state and the community. Besides that, he is entirely free in the matter of "man-made" laws and their implementation in accordance with the requirements of the state or in order to benefit the community, so long as these laws are not repugnant to the injunctions of Islam.

Further, one cannot ignore the Sermons on Mount Arafat delivered by the Prophet during the Pilgrimage of Farewell, as these amounted to a partial exposition of human rights as enumerated in the Quran and fully implemented by the Rightly Guided Caliphs between 632 A.D. and 661 A.D.

Finally the judiciary (*qada*) is separated from the executive. According to the Quranic injunction laid down in sura 4:59, if any dispute arises between the citizens or between citizens and the state, the matter is to be referred to the judiciary for adjudication in accordance with the Book of God and Precedents of the Prophet, and the decision of the court is binding on the disputing parties.

To sum up, the directing principles derived from the "Practice of the Prophet" on which the Islamic Republican Order is founded are:

1. Ultimate sovereignty is vested in God. But the vesting of overall sovereignty in God or the supremacy of His law does not restrict the sovereignty of the state in conducting worldly affairs when the action taken is in the interest of the community or the state.
2. Since the state is an integral part of Islam, Muslims must aspire to establish a state of their own wherever it is possible to create a viable one.
3. The nationhood of Muslims is to be founded on a common spiritual aspiration, and commonness of race, language, and territory are secondary considerations.

4. The non-Muslim citizens of the state are to be confirmed in their faiths and possessions. They are to be governed by their own laws. Their national unity with Muslims is to be based on patriotic considerations and the defense of common territory.

5. Muslims and non-Muslims are collectively expected to defend the territories of the state and to bear its expenses.

6. The importance of consultation (*shura*) in conducting the worldly affairs of the state is emphasized.

7. The chief executive authority in the state is expected to interpret, implement, enforce and execute God-made laws as a *mujtahid* rather than a *muqallid*, as *ijtehad* by the lawmaker is a continuous and unending process.

8. The human rights enumerated in the Quran should be guaranteed and enforced in the state.

9. Taxes imposed for welfare purposes must be meticulously collected by state officials and disbursed among needy citizens or spent on the maintenance of the state.

10. The judiciary is separate from the executive so that it can decide matters before it independently.

11. Under sura 4:59, Muslims must, after God and the Prophet, render obedience to those who command authority among them so that order can be maintained in the state.

The Prophet died in 632 A.D. without nominating any successor. It is interesting to note that, in sura 4:58, Muslims are commanded by God to hand over their trusts to competent persons. However, the Quran itself does not lay down any method for the appointment of the head of state, because the Quran is mainly concerned with matters relating to right and wrong or good and evil, and is not concerned with matters relating to planning (*tadbir*). That the best person or persons are to be appointed is a matter relating to right and wrong. But the mode or process employed for determining the best person involves planning and is a matter relating to efficiency and wisdom in the light of prevailing conditions. Similarly, no procedure has been prescribed in the Quran for the removal of the head of state. The silence of the Prophet on matters of the nomination or appointment of any successor to him, or the laying down of any rule for the deposing of a successor, was deliberate, because such structures are to be evolved in the light of the good sense of the community from one occasion to the next. However, it is evident from the relevant Quranic injunctions and the "Practice of the Prophet" that the political message of Islam is to establish a republican order for the Muslim community.

During the period of the four Rightly Guided Caliphs (632–661 A.D..), different modes were adopted for the appointment of the head of state and in all cases the appointment was confirmed by the Muslim community—its consent having been formally obtained by means of *baiyat*. While the methods adopted during this period varied somewhat, they nonetheless shared a number of common features: the selection of the best man through initial election, nomination by the preceding caliph, or election through an electoral college, followed by a private baiyat, and subsequently the confirmation of the appointment through a public *baiyat* (or referendum). The course adopted in all cases was democratic, and the majority principle, although not specifically disapproved, was not followed, as the need did not arise.

Ibn Ishaq, in his biography of the Prophet, provides an account of how the first successor of the Prophet, Abu Bakr, was elected. Three distinct political groups were formed in Medina: *Muhajirin* (immigrants), *Ansar* (helpers), and *Banu Hashim* (the supporters of the family of the Prophet). The Muhajirin were led by Abu Bakr and Umar; the Ansar supported Sa'ad bin Ubaida; and the Banu Hashim were solidly behind Ali. The Ansar and Muhajirin assembled in the Hall of Banu Sa'ada. The Banu Hashim boycotted the session. The claim of the Ansar for power was advanced on the ground that they constituted the bulk of the armed forces of Islam, and they even suggested division of the government as the alternative. The Muhajirin stood for unity of the government and advanced their claim on the ground that the Arabs as a whole would only accept the leadership of those who were from the tribe of Quraysh. A political debate took place between the assembled groups. Eventually, Umar proposed the name of Abu Bakr as the head of state. Abu Bakr accepted the nomination by extending his hand upon request. Following the lead of Umar, the Muhajirin and most of the Ansar who were present then swore allegiance to Abu Bakr by way of *baiyat*. Subsequently, this private *baiyat* was confirmed by public *baiyat*.[4] Sa'ad bin Ubaida did not swear allegiance to him, however, and Ali as well as other members of the Banu Hashim swore allegiance to Caliph Abu Bakr only six months after his public *baiyat*.[5]

Caliph Abu Bakr's speech, after the multitude had sworn allegiance to him, is significant. He proclaimed,

> I am not the best among you; I need all your advice and all your help. If I do well, support me; if I [make a] mistake, counsel me. To tell [the] truth to a person commissioned to rule is faithful allegiance; to conceal it is treason. In my sight the powerful and the weak are alike; and to both I wish to render justice. As I obey God and His Prophet, obey me; if I neglect the laws of God and the Prophet, I have no more right to your obedience.[6]

The second caliph, Umar, was nominated by Caliph Abu Bakr. But since nomination had no legal precedent, it was merely a recommendation. However, the community reposed confidence in Caliph Abu Bakr, and therefore his recommendation of Umar was confirmed by a general *baiyat*.

Caliph Umar was murdered in the mosque at the morning prayers time. But before he died, he constituted an electoral council of the probable candidates in order that they might select one from among themselves to be put up as the sole candidate for succession. A council of six was formed, consisting of Ali, Uthman, Abdur Rahman, Sa'ad, Zubair, and Talha. Caliph Umar also appointed his own son, Abdullah, to cast a vote in the case of a tie, but Abdullah was specifically excluded from standing as a candidate for succession. The council, through a process of elimination, deputed Abdur Rahman to recommend whether Ali or Uthman should be the sole candidate. Abdur Rahman is said to have consulted as many people as he could in Medina, including women as well as students and those who had come from outside or happened to be present in Medina as wayfayers, and the majority of them expressed a preference for Uthman. Then Abdur Rahman questioned Ali and Uthman about the manner in which they would conduct themselves if one of them was selected as the successor. Eventually, Abdur Rahman supported Uthman and he was selected as the sole candidate. Later, the rest of the community swore allegiance to him in the form of a public *baiyat*.[7]

On the assassination of Caliph Uthman, some eminent members of the community gathered in front of Ali's house and asked him to agree to become the caliph. The uncle of the Prophet, Abbas, supported him as the sole candidate. But Ali refused to accept a private *baiyat* and insisted that if the community wanted to swear allegiance to him as the head of state, it should be openly done in the Mosque of the Prophet. This was accordingly done.[8]

It is evident from this brief survey that during the period of the Rightly Guided Caliphs, the head of state could only be appointed with the approval of the Muslims. Muslim women were not excluded from registering their consent. Furthermore, during this period hereditary rule, although known to the Arabs, was specifically excluded in the case of succession. The adoption of different modes for the appointment of the first four caliphs establishes the fact that, as long as the mode adopted was democratic, how the appointment was made was a matter relating to efficiency and wisdom in the light of prevailing conditions, and that therefore the restriction of these modes to some specific form of election or nomination would be contrary to the spirit of prophetic as well as Quranic teachings on this point. Evidently, the state in Islam is not a theocracy in the strict sense of the term, but nor does Islam desire the establishment of a political order strictly in conformity with the Republican Caliphate of the Rightly Guided Caliphs. Whatever the form of the Republican Caliphate, it was founded on the principles of democracy and justice and, accordingly, the Muslims are expected to reconstruct their polity on these principles.

During the course of history, a number of Islamic constitutional theories have been advanced by jurists, political moralists, and philosophers. The Khawaraj represent the extreme left wing of Muslim political opinion and, in modern terminology, may be considered strict social democrats. They require only moral qualifications in a caliph and restrict his authority by retaining the right to depose him if he is found unfit to hold office. They maintain that the caliph should be appointed by the approval of the entire Muslim community. They insist on a free election and hold that even a non-Arab or a slave is eligible for the office, provided he is a Muslim of upright character and takes the responsibility of performing the duties assigned to the office. Some of them maintain that even a woman can be appointed caliph; others reject the need of appointing a caliph and argue that, since it is not obligatory to do so, the Muslims can rule themselves by constituting a legitimate consultative assembly (*shura*). Nevertheless if the conditions so demand, a head of state can be elected.[9]

It is interesting to note that in the seventh century republican Islamic state three different categories of rights were evolved and enforced. These were: the rights of God (*haquq-al-allah*), the rights of human beings (*haquq-al-abaad*), and the rights that were common to both God and human beings (*haquq ban-al-allah wal-abaad*). Broadly speaking, the rights of God are the holding of congregational prayers, the observance of fasts in the month of *ramadan,* the payment of *zakat,* etc. The rights of human beings are numerous and include the prohibition of unlawful transactions, usury, false and defective scales, weights and measures, nonpayment of debt, etc. The rights that are common to both God and human beings are violated when, for instance, a divorced woman or a widow remarries without observing *iddat* (a period of time in which to ascertain whether she is pregnant), or when the leader of public worship (mosque *imam*) lengthens prayers unnecessarily so that the weak and old cannot stand it or people are hindered or delayed from performing other jobs, or when a *qadi* (judge) makes the petitioners wait before holding his court, etc. There existed a special department called *hisba* which enforced these rights and punished violations through *mohtasib* (ombudsman/moral censor).

Besides *haquq-al-abaad,* as briefly defined above, the citizens were familiar with "human rights" as laid down in the Quran as well as derived from the "Practice (*sunnah*) of the Prophet" (and as we understand them today). These were meticulously enforced.

The following are some examples taken from the Quran and the "Practice of the Prophet":

1. Equality of all citizens before law as well as equality of status and opportunity "O mankind! Be careful of your duty to your Lord who created you from a single soul and from it created its mate and spread from these too many men and women" (sura 4:1).
2. Freedom of Religion
   "There is no compulsion in the matter of religion" (sura 2:256).
   "For each of you We have appointed a law and a way. And if God had willed, He would have made you one (religious) community. But (He

hath willed it otherwise) that He may put you to the test in what He has given you. So compete with one another in good works. Unto God will ye be brought back, and He will inform you about that wherein ye differed" (sura 5:48).

3. Right to life
"And slay not the life which God hath forbidden save for justice" (sura 17:33).

4. Right to property
"And eat not up your property among yourselves in vanity, nor seek by it to gain the hearing of the judges that ye may knowingly devour a portion of the property of others wrongfully" (sura 2:188).

5. No one is to suffer from the wrongs of another
"That no laden one shall bear the burden of another" (sura 53:38).

6. Freedom of person
This is inferred from the "Practice of the Prophet" by Imam Khattabi and Imam Abu Yusuf. A tradition is reported by Abu Daud to the effect that some persons were arrested on suspicion in Medina during the times of the Prophet. A companion inquired as to the grounds on which these persons had been arrested. The Prophet maintained silence while the question was repeated twice, thus giving an opportunity to the prosecutor, who was present, to explain the position. When the question was put for a third time and it again failed to elicit a reply from the prosecutor, the Prophet ordered that the persons arrested should be released. On the basis of this tradition, Imam Khattabi argues in his *M'alim-al-Sunnan* that Islam recognizes only two kinds of detention: (a) under the orders of the court, and (b) for the purposes of investigation. There is no other ground on which a person could be deprived of his freedom. Imam Abu Yusuf maintains in his *Kitab-al-Kharaj*, on the authority of the same tradition, that no one can be imprisoned on false or unproved charges. Caliph Umar is quoted in Imam Malik's *Muwatta* as having said that in Islam no one can be imprisoned without due course of justice.

7. Freedom of opinion
"God loveth not the utterance of harsh speech save by one who hath been wronged" (sura 4:148).

8. Freedom of movement
"It is He who has made the earth manageable for you, so travel ye through its tracts and enjoy of the sustenance which He furnishes; but unto Him is the Resurrection" (sura 67:15).

9. Freedom of association
"And let there be formed of you a community inviting to good, urging what is reputable and restraining from what is disreputable" (sura 3:104).

10. Right of privacy

"It is not proper that ye enter houses through the backs thereof . . . so enter houses by the doors thereof" (sura 2:189).

"O ye who believe! Enter not houses other than your own without first announcing your presence and invoking peace (*salaam*) upon the folk thereof. . . . And if you find no one therein, still enter not until permission hath been given. And if it be said unto you: Go away again, then go away" (sura 24:27–28).

"And spy not, neither backbite one another. Would one of you love to eat the flesh of his dead brother? Ye abhor that so abhor the other" (sura 49:12).

11. Right to secure the basic necessities of life

"And in the wealth of the haves there is due share of the have-nots" (sura 51:19).

12. Right of reputation

"Neither defame one another, nor insult one another by nicknames. Bad is the name of lewdness after faith. O ye who believe! Shun much suspicion; for lo! Some suspicion is a crime" (sura 49:11–12).

"And those who malign believing men and believing women undeservedly, they bear the guilt of slander and manifest sin" (sura 33:58).

13. Right to a hearing

This is inferred from the "Practice of the Prophet" who, while sending Ali to Yemen, gave him the following directions: "You are not to take decision unless you have heard the second party in the same way as you have heard the first."

14. Right to decision in accordance with proper judicial procedure

"O ye who believe! If an evil-liver bring you news, verify it, lest you smite some folk in ignorance and afterward repent of what ye did" (sura 49:6).

The fact that citizens were highly aware of the human rights laid down in the Quran can be demonstrated by numerous examples. One night, for example, Caliph Umar, while crossing a street in Medina, heard the debauched sounds of a drunkard coming from inside a house. Losing his temper, he attempted to enter the house. But no one answered his knock or opened the door. He climbed on the roof and shouted down to the owner in his courtyard thus: "Why are you breaking the law by permitting such an abusive drunkard in your house?" The owner replied: "No Muslim has the right to speak like that to another Muslim. Maybe I have committed one violation, but see how many you have committed. 1) Spying, despite God's command, 'Thou shalt not spy' (sura 49:12). 2) Breaking and entering. You came in over the roof, despite God's order, 'Enter houses by the door' (sura 2:189). 3)

Entering without the owner's permission, in defiance of God's command, 'Enter no house without the owner's permission' (sura 24:28). 4) Omitting to invoke peace, though God orders, 'Enter not houses without first announcing your presence and invoking peace (*salaam*) on those within' (sura 24:27)." Feeling embarrassed, Caliph Umar replied, "All right, I forgive you your sin of permitting debauchery." The owner of the house retorted, "That is your fifth violation. You claim to be the executor of Islam's commandments. Then how can you say that you forgive what God has condemned as a crime?"[10]

Everyone was free to express his own opinion concerning the enforcement of Islamic injunctions about human rights and even the head of state was accountable for his conduct and actions. Sometimes the attitude of the citizens toward the caliph was improper and insulting; nevertheless, it was tolerated. On numerous occasions, Caliph Umar had to face such situations and to provide explanations. On one occasion, Caliph Ali was delivering a sermon (*khutba*) in the mosque of Kufa when some Kharijites interrupted him with insulting language. The companions of Caliph Ali urged him to punish them or at least to expel them from the mosque, but Caliph Ali declined to take such action on the ground that the Muslims' right to freedom of speech must not be imperilled.[11]

An eminent Muslim political thinker, al-Farabi (868–950 A.D.), who had been influenced by the ideas of Plato and Aristotle, and who had also made improvements on their thought, believed that the ideal state was that which implemented for its citizens the twofold concept of "happiness" as envisaged by Islam—i.e., well-being in this world and preparation for achieving "bliss" in the hereafter. According to him, the ideal state was that which was ruled by the prophet-imam (instead of the philosopher-king of Plato). Thus in the history of Islam, the perfect state was the city state of Medina governed by the Prophet himself as the head of state, as he was in direct communion with God whose law was revealed to him. He further believed that the citizens of that state attained real happiness and realized their true destiny.

Since it was impossible to realize the ideal or perfect state in the absence of the prophet-lawgiver-leader (*imam*), al-Farabi enumerated different varieties of imperfect states wherein the citizens could never achieve authentic happiness. This was because all imperfect states emerged from a false perception of religion and were due to corrupt convictions. However, he regarded democracy as closest to his concept of the ideal or perfect state. Probably he had in mind the republican era of the Rightly Guided Caliphs which immediately followed the ideal leadership of the prophet-imam. But when he maintained further that it was from democracy that most of the imperfect states emerged, one cannot help deducing that at the back of his mind was the transformation of the Muslim republican order to an absolute monarchy of different forms. Obviously, al-Farabi had a very deep perception of Islamic history, and in the course of the evolution of his political ideas, he kept an eye on the historical experience of the Muslim community.[12]

The four Rightly Guided Caliphs who laid the foundations of republican Islam in the light of the Quranic teachings and the "Practice of the Prophet" were certainly the greatest men Islam had produced after the Prophet. But their efforts for the permanent democratization of Islam failed, not because of any lapse on their part, but owing to the failure of the early Muslim peoples, emerging as they were out of the spiritual slavery of the pre-Islamic times, to realize that democracy had a discipline of its own. If they had understood the political message of Islam, revealed through the Prophet and very ably projected by the Rightly Guided Caliphs, the *shura* could have developed into a representative institution and the process of *ijtehad* might have been initiated in the form of lawmaking through *ijma* (consensus of the community). Instead, they divided themselves into numerous intolerant political groups and actually fought against one another. Thus the political message of Islam was subverted. The historian Ameer Ali rightly observes that with Caliph Ali the republic of Islam ended, and he closes the chapter of his famous book with a quotation of Oelsner to the following effect: "Thus vanished the popular regime, which had for its basis a patriarchal simplicity, never again to appear among any Mussulman nation."[13]

In the West, the emergence and development of democracy was the result of certain forces of a secular, rational, and materialistic nature. For instance, the Reformation, which was an outright revolt against the dominant church, separated religion from the state. The Renaissance, on the other hand, liberated man's mind from religious superstitions. As a result, in his quest for knowledge man learned to depend on reason, sense perception, and scientific thinking. The Industrial Revolution started changing the face of Europe, and with the French Revolution came the concepts of liberty, equality, and fraternity. It was in fact this awakening that led to the rise and growth of materialism in Europe. Cheap energy and labor were used for running factories and mills. Manufactured goods required markets for their sale. Through the emphasis on freedom of trade, the autocratic powers of monarchs were curtailed, and capitalist democracies were established on the basis of territorial nationalism. The search for markets and more raw material led to colonialism and imperialism.

The economic penetration and political expansion of Europe into the Muslim world disseminated ideas of individual freedom, territorial nationalism, patriotism, secularism, constitutionalism, radicalism, and so on. But as has been demonstrated above, it was not from the West that the Muslims learned about democracy and human rights. It can be said, however, that these new ideas did stimulate the desire of modern Muslims to rediscover and reinterpret the dynamic, progressive, and forward-looking spirit of Islam.

The main difference between Western and Islamic conceptions of democ-racy and human rights is that the former have been founded on secularism or materialism as well as certain compulsions of European history, whereas the latter claim to have religion or spiritualism as their original source.

Modern Western civilization, in the light of its historical experience, con-siders religion as a problem in matters of the state, and in order to deal with it, the development of two varieties of secularism has been encouraged. One type of secularism is based on the principle of "indifference toward reli-gion," and this norm has been adopted in the capitalist democracies of West-ern Europe, Great Britain, and the United States. The other type is based on the "suppression of religion" as state policy, and for a number of years this method was employed in the socialist countries, including the former Soviet Union. However, experience tells us that indifference toward religion not only engenders hypocrisy and double standards, but also leads to the de-mand for that variety of "freedom" which the French philosopher Albert Camus calls "tyranny," treading on the rights of others as well as moral way-wardness. Furthermore, the recent developments in the former Soviet Union and the countries of Eastern Europe indicate that atheism cannot be imposed on a people from outside through state terror. Whenever such an attempt is made, it is bound to fail. Thus the existing types of secularism have proven futile.

It is against this background that some Muslim thinkers reject contempo-rary methodologies of secularism, territorial or ethnic nationalism, capitalism, and atheistic socialism, as well as religious conservatism as drawing upon the psychological forces of hate, suspicion, and resentment, which tend to im-poverish the soul of man. They advance instead the view that the solution lies in the adoption of the policy, not of indifference toward religion or the sup-pression of religion, but of "respecting and liberating all religions, faiths, and creeds."

An eminent modern Muslim thinker of the Indo-Pakistan subcontinent, Muhammad Iqbal (1877–1938), welcomes the formation of popularly elected legislative assemblies in Muslim countries as a return to the original purity of Islam. He boldly asserts,

> I consider it a great loss that the progress of Islam as a conquering faith stulti-fied the growth of those germs of an economic and democratic organization of society which I find scattered up and down the pages of the Quran and the "Tra-ditions of the Prophet." No doubt the Muslims succeeded in building a great empire, but thereby they largely repaganized their political ideals, and lost sight of some of the most important potentialities of their faith.[14]

In his view, the pivotal article of Islamic faith—i.e., *tauhid* (unity of God)—as a working idea stands for human equality, solidarity, and freedom. There-fore, the state, from the Islamic standpoint, is essentially an effort to transform these ideal principles into space-time forces and an endeavor to realize them in a definite human organization.[15]

Further, in the light of the discoveries of modern physics respecting the essence of matter, Iqbal is of the opinion that materialists among political philosophers should reconsider their approach to materialism as well as secularism. He states,

> The ultimate reality, according to the Quran, is spiritual, and its life consists in its temporal activity. The spirit finds its opportunities in the natural, the material, the secular. All that is secular is therefore sacred in the roots of its being. The greatest service that modern thought has rendered to Islam, and as a matter of fact to all religions, consists in its criticism of what we call material or natural—a criticism which discloses that the merely material has no substance until we discover it rooted in the spiritual. There is no such thing as a profane world. All this immensity of matter constitutes a scope for the self-realization of spirit. All is holy ground.[16]

Iqbal's argument is that, since the Muslims believe that there can be no future revelation binding on man, they ought to be spiritually the most emancipated peoples on earth. He is convinced that the peoples of Southwest Asia, who accepted Islam at an early stage, could not understand the true significance of this basic idea, because they had just emerged from the spiritual slavery of pre-Islamic times and had no concept of spiritual freedom. But he thinks that modern Muslims are perfectly capable of appreciating their position. Therefore, he expects them to reconstruct their social life in the light of ultimate principles and "evolve, out of the hitherto partially revealed purpose of Islam, that spiritual democracy which is the ultimate aim of Islam."[17]

In modern philosophical and political literature of the Indo-Pakistan subcontinent, Iqbal is probably the only thinker who has used the expression "spiritual democracy" in order to define an Islamic state. The expression obviously means "a democratic state which is based on the principle of respect and freedom of all religions." It may be of interest to note that this humanistic approach of Iqbal in presenting his concept of the Islamic state as a spiritual democracy appears to be founded on sura 5:48 of the Quran in which God, addressing man, proclaims,

> For each of you We have appointed a law and a way. And if God had willed He would have made you one (religious) community. But (He hath willed it otherwise) that He may put you to the test in what He has given you. So compete with one another in good works. Unto God will ye be brought back, and He will inform you about that wherein ye differed.

If the state is an integral part of Islam (and according to Iqbal, the real aim of Islam, as a mode of life, is to establish a spiritual democracy in any multicultural society where Muslims dominate numerically), then Iqbal's conception of Islam, at least in the political sense, is a departure from the generally accepted position. But it must be realized that the conventional literature on Islamic political order was compiled during the times when the world of Islam had been afflicted with an absolute or rather a perverse kind of monarchy and when, in Iqbal's terms, the political ideals of Islam had been "repaganized."

NOTES

1. Such utterances of the Prophet are recorded in numerous collections of Traditions. For ready reference in English, see T. W. Arnold, *Caliphate* (New York: Barnes & Noble, 1966), p. 184.

2. For a complete English translation of the "Constitution of Medina," see Montgomery Watt, *Muhammad at Medina* (Oxford: Clarendon Press, 1956), pp. 221–25.

3. At the insistence of the representative of the pagans of Mecca, Suhail ibn Amr, that they did not regard him as the Prophet of God, the Prophet directed the scribe, in spite of the protests of his followers, to open the Treaty not as "between Muhammad the Prophet of God and etc." but as "between Muhammad son of Abdullah and Suhail ibn Amr." Ibn Ishaq, *Life of Muhammad*, trans. A. Guillaume, 9th Pakistan edition (1990), pp. 504–507; and *Tarikh-i-Tabari* vol. I (Sirat al-Nabi) Urdu trans. (Karachi: Nafis Academy, 1967), pp. 335–39.

4. Ibn Ishaq, ibid., pp. 683–87; and *Tarikh-i-Tabari*, vol. I, pp. 529–35.

5. *Tarikh-i-Tabari*, vol. I, p. 536.

6. Ameer Ali, *A Short History of the Saracens* (London: Macmillan, 1924), pp. 21–22; *Tarikh-i-Tabari*, vol. I, p. 539; and Ibn Ishaq, op. cit., p. 687.

7. *Tarikh-i-Tabari*, vols. I & II, pp. 300–439.

8. Ibid., vol. III, p. 27.

9. al-Mubarrad, *Kitab-al-Kamil*, W. Wright, ed., pp. 527–600; and Ibn Khaldun, *Muqqaddama*, pp. 196–202.

10. Sultanhussain Tabandeh, *A Muslim Commentary on the Universal Declaration of Human Rights*, trans. F. J. Goulding, pp. 31–32.

11. Ibid., p. 32.

12. Three works of al-Farabi can be examined: *al-Medina-al-Fadila, Kitab Siyasa Madaniya*, and *Kitab Tahsil al-Saada*.

13. *A Short History of the Saracens*, p. 54.

14. Syed Abdul Vahid, ed. *Thoughts and reflections of Iqbal* (Lahore: Sh. Muhammad Ashraf, 1964), p. 100.

15. Muhammad Iqbal, *The Reconstruction of Religious Thought in Islam* (London: Oxford University Press, 1934), pp. 122–23.

16. Ibid., p. 123.

17. Ibid., p. 142.

Majid Fakhry

WESTERN AND ISLAMIC VIEWS OF DEMOCRACY AND JUSTICE: A COMPARATIVE AND INTERPRETATIVE STUDY

THE BIRTH OF DEMOCRACY IN ANCIENT GREECE

Political theory, as the "disciplined investigation of political problems," writes George Sabine, was invented by the Greeks in the fifth century B.C."[1] But Greece, as he adds by way of highlighting the cosmopolitan character of political theory, "is the place where Europeans contacted the civilization of the ancient Middle East and it was there that man crossed the threshold of science, philosophy, and political theory."[2]

We will have occasion later on in this study to refer to the cultural interactions of Greece with the Middle East, of which the Islamic world was, and continues to be, an integral part. In fact, we proceed from the premise that, philosophically and culturally, the Islamic world is affiliated to the great Hellenic and Mediterranean cultural tradition of which Athens and Alexandria were the principal outposts in the ancient world.[3] As the heiress of Athens, Alexandria became, in the third century B.C., the custodian of Greek philosophy and science, the scene of the cultural encounter of East and West, and the battleground of intellectual and religious controversy well into the first three centuries of the Christian era. The names of Philo of Alexandria (20 B.C.–A.D. 40), Plotinus (205–270 A.D.), Origen (185–254 A.D.), Clement (150–217 A.D.), and Porphyry (ca. 232–303) are enough to demonstrate the continuity of Greek thought in the ancient and pre-medieval worlds and its interaction with Jewish, Egyptian, Phoenician, and Christian thought.

To go back to the birth of political theory in ancient Greece, it would be enough to mention the names of the first three great writers on political theory: Thucydides (460–400 B.C.), Plato (427–347 B.C.) and Aristotle (384–322 B.C.). Of those three, Aristotle is preeminent in the systematism and comprehensiveness of his analysis of political concepts, and his thought constitutes in many ways the consummation or synthesis of Greek thought, whether in the physical, metaphysical, or political fields. Emerging around the Aegean Sea as early as the eighth century B.C., Greek thought first took a mythological direction at the hands of Homer, Hesiod, and the other poets, then a cosmological form at the hands of the Ionian philosophers of the sixth century, with Thales of Miletus (fl. 585 B.C.), a Phoenician, at their head, and finally a metaphysical and ethical form at the hands of the fifth- and fourth-century humanists and system-builders, from Protagoras (d. ca. 411 B.C.) to Aristotle and Zeno of Citium (d. ca. 265 B.C.). Historians of Greek philosophy are no longer in doubt regarding the active cultural interactions of the Mediterranean and Middle Eastern peoples as early as the eight century B.C., and it is common knowledge today that the ancient Greeks learned a great deal from the neighboring nations, such as the Babylonians, the Phoenicians, the Egyptians and, to a lesser extent, the Persians and the Indians, in the fields of astronomy, geometry, cosmology, and mythology.[4]

With respect to the birth of democracy, the ancient Greeks invented, not only political theory but democracy as well. As Cynthia Farrar has recently argued, "Democracy was cobbled together, thousands of years ago, by the Athenians. . . . The citizens of fifth-century B.C. Athens lived democracy for the first time in the history of the world."[5] She credits Protagoras, Thucydides, and Democritus (460–360 B.C.) with espousing the ideas that gave birth to democracy. Thucydides, according to Farrar, injected a historical element into the study of human nature and underlined the role of "experience in the understanding of particular situations,"[6] which the philosophers tended to express in abstract terms. We owe it to Thucydides, at any rate, to have preserved the eloquent characterization of Athenian democracy by Pericles (d. 439 B.C.). "Our constitution is called a democracy," he is reported to have declared in the Funeral Oration, "because power is not in the hands of a minority, but of the whole people,"[7] and it is a constitution which is not modeled on those of others, but is rather "a model to others."

The other features of democracy that Pericles extols in the Funeral Oration are respect for the law, loyalty to the state, love of freedom, love of beauty, kindness to others, free public deliberation on matters of public concern, and the willingness to take an active part in politics. "We do not say that a man who takes no interest in politics is a man who minds his own business," says Pericles. "We say that he has no business here at all."[8]

If we cast a backward glance at those nations who preceded the Greeks in Asia and the Middle East, we may well agree with these sentiments of Pericles or with Aristotle's boast that: "Barbarians being more servile in character than Hellenes, and Asiatics than Europeans, do not rebel against despotic governments,"[9] and simply submit to tyranny.

In his analysis of democracy, which we might take, together with Pericles' eloquent exposition in the Funeral Oration, as the most forceful and comprehensive account, Aristotle isolates three essential ingredients of democracy: liberty, equality, and popular sovereignty. "One principle of liberty," he writes in *Politics* VI, "is for all to rule and be ruled in turn, and indeed democratic justice is the application of numerical, not proportionate equality; whence it follows that the majority must be supreme, and that whatever the majority approves must be the end and the just."[10]

Expressed in modern terms, those three ingredients, when predicated of the individual, are designated as civil or political rights, and today the test of democracy is the degree to which any state or nation is willing to guarantee these rights or respect them.

HUMANISM, A CORNERSTONE OF DEMOCRACY

From a philosophical and historical viewpoint, the gradual triumph of democracy over despotism was linked to the triumph of humanism over theocratic concepts of government in which God or his representatives on earth wielded political authority. Protagoras of Abdera (d. ca. 411 B.C.), who visited Athens many times and met with Socrates, should be regarded as the first exponent of an unqualified humanism. He is reported by the most ancient and reliable authorities, including Plato, to have enunciated two revolutionary maxims: "Man is the measure of all things," and "of the Gods we know nothing, whether they exist or whether they do not exist," his subtle reason being the difficulty of the problem and the brevity of human life.[11]

In modern times, the humanist or anthropocentric outlook has replaced the theocentric outlook (as Jacques Maritain has called these two contrasting positions) and become one of the foundation-stones of democracy. The example of John Locke (1632–1704), the champion of the Glorious Revolution of 1688 in England and of parliamentary government, may suffice. John Locke argues against such monarchists as Thomas Hobbes and Robert Filmer[12] that the state exists exclusively for the purpose of protecting the natural rights of the individual against royal usurpation, and although not explicitly enough, Locke mentions the rights of "life, liberty, and estate," as well as the rights of redress and retaliation.

> Man being born, as has been proved, with a title to perfect freedom and an uncontrolled enjoyment of all the rights and privileges of the law of nature, equally with any other man or number of men in the world, hath by nature a power, not only to preserve his property, that is his life, liberty and estate, against the injuries and attempts of other men; but to judge of, and punish the breaches of that law in others.[13]

Both Protagoras and Locke illustrate very well the Western view of man and his inalienable right to enjoy the boons of liberty, life, and just redress.

What, we might ask, are the Islamic parallels of these two Western views? and how does Islam describe man's relation to God and the bearers of authority among his fellowmen? The Quran in a number of verses stresses the duty of believers to "obey God and the bearers of authority among you" (Quran 4, 62).[14] The earliest successors of Muhammad met, on the whole, with little resistance, until the reign of the third caliph, 'Uthmān (644–656), who fell victim to insurrection and conspiratorial intrigues in Medina. His kinsman, Mu'āwiyah, founded the Umayyad dynasty in 661, with Damascus as its capital. Most Arab historians, including the famous Ibn Khaldūn of Tunis (d. 1406), accuse the Umayyads of the first serious divergence from the "orthodox" or "righteous" path of their predecessors and of a certain worldliness against which those predecessors had inveighed in theory and practice. Notwithstanding, the early Umayyad caliphs appear to have enjoyed the general support (or at least reticence) of the general run of (Sunni) Muslims. Those "loyalists," as one might call them, appear to have acquiesced in the Umayyads' view that the actions of the caliph or his agents, however cruel, are unimpeachable, because they are part of the divine decree. Committed to a rigid predestinarianism (*jabriyyah*), those loyalists and their masters sought in the Quran textual support for their views. However, their position was soon challenged by the first libertarians of Islam, known as the Qadaris, who laid down the foundations of a new humanism unknown hitherto in the world of Islam. In the process, those libertarians questioned the claim of the caliph to act arbitrarily and to justify his most repressive policies on the dubious ground that his actions, like the actions of his subjects, were foreordained or predetermined by God. Two of the early Qadari scholars are known to have paid dearly for their defiance: Ma'bad al-Juhani, who was killed by order of the Umayyad Caliph 'Abd al-Malik (685–705), and Ghaylān al-Dimashqi, killed by order of his son and successor, Hishām (724–743). A measure of the topicality of this issue in the seventh century may be gauged from a report of a meeting of Ma'bad with the great theologian and ascetic divine, al-Ḥasan al-Basri (d. 728). Ma'bad, we are told, addressed al-Basri as follows: "O Abu Sa'id, those kings (meaning the Umayyad caliphs) spill the blood of Muslims, seize their possessions, do this and that and say: 'Our actions occur according to god's decree (*qaḍā*')'." To which al-Basri, we are told, responded, "The enemies of God are lying."[15]

The Mu'tazilite school of theology, which continued the Qadari line of political and theological enquiry and flourished during the eighth and ninth centuries, pushed the libertarianism of its predecessors one step further and unleashed a distinctly humanist current, with far-reaching political and moral consequences. In the first place, the Mu'tazilite doctors defended the right of reason to probe the most abstruse moral and theological concepts and argued that the nature of right and wrong can be determined rationally "prior to the advent of revelation," as they put it; divine revelation (*sam'*) being, according to them, a divine "grace" whereby God merely tests or proves mankind. The goodness or badness of actions, however, is known to us intuitively and even the wisdom and truthfulness of God are rationally known, or else we would be involved in a *petitio principii*.[16]

Second, the Mu'tazilite theologians asserted, against traditionalist theologians, such as Aḥmad Ibn Ḥanbal (d. 855) and his school, that the human agent who is conscious of his actions is free, both in the domain of willing and that of doing. Accordingly, they developed elaborate theories of natural causation, known as generation (*tawallud*), to explain the manner in which the will can impinge effectively on the external world. Their rivals had favored an "occasionalist" metaphysics in which God is the supreme and unique Agent, who does not determine the sequence of events in the outside world only but the very direction of willing or choice.[17]

And third, they asserted the maxim of God's justice, as a necessary corollary of His goodness and wisdom, and rejected the view of their opponents that God can will evil and bring it about, on the ground that such a view would make a mockery of His wisdom and goodness. Wisdom, their opponents had argued, was synonymous with the divine decree itself; whereas goodness is simply the way in which God chooses to act. Therefore, neither wisdom nor goodness is an intrinsic attribute of God, as the Mu'tazilites maintained on rational grounds; they are simply the manner in which God has described Himself in the Quran, or chooses to act in the world.

The political and moral implications of the Mu'tazilite view of right and wrong can easily be discerned. Man, thanks to the God-given light of reason, is the arbiter of right and wrong, and the caliph or ruler is not at liberty to act in total disregard for the rights of his subjects or in violation of the universal precepts of justice. In fact, God Himself cannot act arbitrarily or fortuitously, but must also act in a manner that profits His creation or else His actions would be futile or senseless (*'abath*).

DEMOCRACY AND THE ELECTIVE PRINCIPLE

Regardless of how radical their moral and theological views and the degree to which they vindicated the right of the subjects to question the policies of their rulers, neither those early Muslim rationalists nor their rivals dealt adequately with the other major component of democracy: I mean the elective principle. From the earliest times, the election of the caliph was enshrined in political theory and practice, but such election was never identified with universal suffrage, but rather with the principle of allegiance or homage (*bay'ah*). This principle stipulated that it devolves upon the leading dignitaries, military commanders, tribal chieftains, and provincial governors, who formed the electoral college, so to speak, and whom Ibn Khaldūn calls collectively "the people who tie and untie," to elect the caliph, after adequate deliberation or consultation (*shūra*). It was left to the jurists to define specifically the conditions that both the electors and the candidates to the caliphal office should satisfy. The former, according to al-Māwardi (d. 1085), author of the classic *Principles of Government,* should satisfy three conditions: justice, knowledge, and sound judgment or wisdom; the latter, on the other hand, should satisfy seven conditions: justice, knowledge, soundness of senses, freedom from bodily infirmities, sound judgment, courage in the conduct of holy war (*jihād*), and membership of the tribe of Quraysh, Muhammad's own tribe.[18]

This theory of election can best be described as aristocratic or oligarchic, rather than democratic, but it is significant that it defined the constitutional framework for electing the legitimate successor to the highest executive office in the state in explicit terms. In practice, it was flouted in a variety of ways, but continued to be accepted as a constitutional fiction, at least in Sunni circles, until the official abolition of the caliphate by the Grand Turkish assembly in 1924. The Muslim world, ever since, without surrendering this fiction altogether, has been reconciling itself to the political realities of twentieth century life in a variety of ways. Some theologians, like M. Rashīd Riḍa (d. 1935), disciple of the famous Egyptian "reformer," Muḥammad 'Abduh (d. 1905) has identified the "electoral college" referred to above with representative bodies or parliaments and the *shūra* principle with that of democratic government.[19]

THE SOVEREIGNTY OF THE NATION (*AL-UMMAH*)

Perhaps the most distinguishing mark of democracy is the sovereignty of the people and the locus of this sovereignty within the state. In monarchy, sovereignty lies in the king, in oligarchy in the few, in military dictatorship in the army and, finally, in democracy in the people at large. What this last proposition signifies is that the people or their representatives have the ultimate authority to enact laws, elect the officials of the state, including the chief executive, superintend the application of the laws, impeach or bring to account those officials whenever they violate the laws of the state, and ensure the transfer of authority peacefully and constitutionally.

The principle of popular sovereignty, alluded to by Aristotle, was embodied explicitly for the first time in the French Declaration of the Rights of Man and the Citizen, issued in 1789, as a preamble to the draft constitution of the First French Republic. This declaration states in article 3 that "the source of all sovereignty is essentially in the nation; nobody, no individual can exercise authority that does not proceed from it in plain terms." And harking back to

Jean-Jacques Rousseau in Article 6, it defines law as "the expression of the general will" and adds that "all citizens have the right to take part personally or by their representatives in its formation."[20]

It would be instructive to search for parallels in Islam for the two Western principles of the sovereignty of the nation and the right of all citizens of the state to express the general will, and the way in which they are regarded as inseparable from democratic rule.

In the Quran the ultimate source of sovereignty is God, who bestows upon the rulers and their subjects alike the blessings of life and prosperity, but favors the rulers with the privilege of legitimate authority to which their subjects ought to submit.[21] The chief limitations upon this authority are the stipulations of the Holy law or *Sharī'ah* embodied in the Quran, the Traditions of Muhammad, and the interpretations of the jurists, who belonged originally to the four accredited legal schools, the Māliki, the Ḥanbali, the Shāfi'i, and the Ḥanafi (to which the Shi'ite Ja'fari school should be added). Because the so-called door of discretionary judgment (*ijtihād*) was closed, following the death of the last of the founders of these schools, Aḥmad Ibn Ḥanbal in 855, Islamic law has undergone very little change ever since, although constant attempts are made today at reinterpretation or adaptation in many Muslim countries, such as Tunisia and Egypt.

The bearing of this rigid attitude to law on political or constitutional developments is obvious; political leaders and legislative assemblies or parliaments in the Muslim world, with the exception of Turkey, are unable to introduce any legislation that appears to be in conflict with the sacred law or *Sharī'ah*, regarded as the fount of all legislation.

A parallel legal barrier against constitutional development or change is that of *ijmā'* (the consensus of the community), which, according to a prophetic *Hadith,* is infallible. The concept of *ijmā',* which is characteristically Islamic, is ambiguous, but linked to the concept of the Muslim *Umma* or nation it has been a potent force in shaping public opinion or determining policy. As one modern writer has put it, "The basis of political authority was the *Umma,* the 'Community,' an assemblage of individuals bound to one another by ties of religion. Within the *Umma* all were on an equal footing. There were no distinctions of rank, only of function. God alone was the head of the community and his rule was direct and immediate."[22]

However, it is significant that *ijmā',* which has tended to foster conformism and conservatism, has been challenged by almost all the radical or schismatic groups in Islam, including the Shī'a, the Kharijites, the Qarmatians, and others. Confronted with the challenge of Western ideas, starting in the nineteenth century, Muslim intellectuals and politicians have been able to moderate the pressure of religious conformism in a variety of ways. Perhaps the most significant change has been the wide acceptance of the principle of representative government, a cornerstone of democracy, for which legal scholars and theologians have found a basis in the Quranic concept of *shūra*[23] already referred to.

We cannot close this section without some reference to the most explicit discussion of democracy by the classical Islamic philosophers.

Al-Fārābi (d. 950), the founder of political philosophy in Islam, distinguishes in his utopia, modeled perhaps on Plato's *Republic,* four major corrupt or "opposite" forms of the perfect state: the necessary, the ignominious, the timocratic, the tyrannical, and the democratic (*al-madīnah al-jamā'iyah*).[24]

This last state (or city) is described by al-Fārābi as one whose inhabitants are entirely free and equal and are unwilling to recognize the right of any leader to rule over them without the "consent of the governed." Their favorite ruler is one who safeguards their freedom, protects them against aggression, both internal and external, and secures for them the means of attaining the necessities of life. Due to the variety of its constituent parts and the diversity of the pursuits of its inhabitants, the democratic state, argues al-Fārābi, is the most likely to become the "poaching ground" (or "emporium of constitutions," as Plato has put it) from which the perfect state could develop, and is therefore the best of the corrupt forms of government, being the nearest to the possibility of perfection.[25]

Ibn Rushd (Averroes, d. 1198), the great Aristotelian commentator, continued in his *Commentary on Plato's Republic* the same line of political speculation. Due to the selfishness and avarice of its rulers, the oligarchic state, according to him, soon degenerates into a democracy, in which the masses suddenly become conscious of their numerical strength and proceed to rob the rich of their wealth and their lordship. In this new regime, the love of freedom replaces the love of money, and equality becomes its political and social hallmark. Despite its weakness, this regime is superior to all the other corrupt forms of government, and it is not precluded, therefore, that "out of this city (or state) will come forth the virtuous city and the other kinds of these cities, because they exist in it potentially."[26] Averroes appears to regard the democratic state for this reason as the primordial form of government and attributes to Plato the view that "the wise ought to attend to such cities as these [i.e., the democratic ones] and choose from among them the good kinds that accord with the virtuous association (or ideal state)."[27]

JUSTICE, HUMAN AND DIVINE

The correlation between democracy and justice is paramount. For, the ultimate goal of democracy being to safeguard the right of every citizen to pursue his happiness or well-being in security and freedom, society has an obligation to create and guarantee the conditions necessary for such pursuit in an orderly and predictable manner. The greatest bane of social existence is chaos or tyranny: in the first case, because the individual is completely frustrated in his activities or designs; in the second, because he has no control over his actions or decisions and is completely subservient to a higher will. To remedy the two ills of chaos and tyranny, a principle of order is needed to regulate man's actions, in relation both to himself and to others. Such a principle is what we call justice.

It was Plato who first broached the problem of justice in its entire acuteness, both as a principle of moral probity at the individual level, and as a principle of political equilibrium at the collective level. An individual is just, as he has argued in the *Republic,* to the extent that the three parts of his soul—the rational, the spirited, and the appetitive—are kept in "their natural relations of control and subordination";[28] whereas the state is just to the extent that its three corresponding classes—the guardians, the auxiliaries, and the tradesmen—do not encroach upon each other's domain, but "each order, tradesmen, auxiliary, guardian, keeps to its own proper business in the commonwealth and does its own work."[29]

On the surface, Plato's "organic" concept of the just state would appear to be favorable to the concept of a democratic state or constitution, since it is of the essence of democracy to take full cognizance of the totality of classes or functions within the state, to regulate their relations, and to safeguard their interests. However, Plato was by temperament and breeding an antidemocrat, and the execution of his master and idol, Socrates in 399 B.C., by action of the Athenian Assembly, was a decisive factor in his revulsion at Athenian democracy, in particular, and democratic constitutions in general.[30] At any rate, he undoubtedly imparted to his disciple, Aristotle, this profound obsession with justice, which became one of the key factors in the latter's ethics and politics and which had a far-reaching influence on political and ethical writers of every stripe, including Muslim writers. First, we owe it to Aristotle to have distinguished between natural and legal (or conventional) justice. The former he defines as "that which has the same force and does not exist by people thinking this or that,"[31] as against the latter, which is a matter of convention or positive legislation, and accordingly changes from time to time and from place to place.

Natural justice, as St. Thomas Aquinas (1225–1274), the great Aristotelian and Scholastic theologian, was to maintain centuries after, is a corollary of natural law, which is an instance of the eternal law by which God governs the world and is closely linked to man's rational nature.[32] To the extent that positive legislation conforms to the dictates of this natural law, its justice is confirmed and the rights of the individual are safeguarded.

In Islamic ethical and political theory, justice has been an equally central concept. As already mentioned, it was the Qadari scholars of the seventh century who raised, for the first time in Muslim history, the question of political responsibility, as indeed of individual responsibility and its corollary justice, and challenged the claims of the caliphs to be unanswerable for their actions—which, according to them, were part of the divine decree. Their successors, the Mu'tazilite theologians of the eighth and ninth centuries, fully developed the ethical and political implications of this position and concentrated so thoroughly on the concept of justice, human or divine, that they became known as the People of Justice (al-Mu'addilah), chiefly by their opponents, who disapproved of such concentration.

The Muslim ethical philosophers were equally obsessed with the problem of justice and their discussions, on the whole, were closely linked to the views of Plato or Aristotle. To begin, almost all of them accepted the tripartite doctrine of the soul, which formed the groundwork of Plato's ethical and political theories, as we have seen. But in their elaborate analysis of justice and its subdivisions, they were primarily influenced by Aristotle's *Nicomachean Ethics*, as well as later Hellenistic writings on ethics.

Miskawayh (d. 1030) and al-Ghazāli (d. 1111) are the two most important writers on ethics in Islam and, despite their vast divergences, they appear to conceive of justice in analogous terms. In a short treatise entitled the *Essence of Justice*, Miskawayh speaks of conventional and human justice in terms that correspond to Aristotle's distinction of political and natural justice. Conventional justice is then divided by Miskawayh into the general and the particular and is said to be the attribute of those modes of legislation that are either generally approved by the whole of mankind or by particular states, nations, or households. As for human justice, it consists of a certain equilibrium or proportion of the three faculties of the soul, which Miskawayh interprets in numerical or Pythagorean terms.[33] It is manifested in three ways, corresponding to the three spheres of human activity: (a) that of the distribution of goods and honors; (b) that of the voluntary, including commercial transactions; and (c) that of the involuntary or violent transactions involving violence or repression.[34]

As a theologian and a mystic, al-Ghazāli identifies, in his ethical writings, two paths leading to happiness, the ultimate goal of human endeavor: the Sufi and the philosophical. And those two paths are, according to him, perfectly compatible. However, he believes that the philosophical or discursive path serves as a prelude to the Sufi or mystical. It consists in distinguishing the three powers of the soul and subordinating the irascible and the concupiscent to the rational. When this has been achieved, justice arises. This, as he puts it, is the foundation or mainstay of the heavens and the earth and is the pathway to religious piety and moral rectitude. Its divisions are three: (a) political justice, which is concerned with the orderly relation of the parts of the state to each other; (b) moral justice, which is concerned with the orderly relation of the parts of the soul to each other; and (c) economic justice, which is concerned with equitable business transactions.[35]

The climactic point of al-Ghazāli's ethics, however, is the mystical quest for God. Moral rectitude, together with compliance with the precepts of the Holy Law, are the first two steps leading to proximity to God. Those two steps should be supplemented by the renunciation of the world and a constant searching for God, accompanied by intense concern and solicitude.

> The basis of concern and solicitude is the apprehension of the beauty of the object sought, generating thereby yearning and love necessarily, whereas the basis of apprehending the beauty of that object is contemplation, or focusing the faculty of vision upon it to the exclusion of every other object. . . . In addition [your] love will increase by reason of constant fellowship, especially if in the process beautiful ethical traits, originally concealed, are now disclosed, so that love might be intensified.[36]

From this brief account, it appears how the love of God became, for this theologian and mystic, the capstone of moral and religious progress, the two pivotal points of which are justice and the fulfillment of the religious law.

MODERNISM, SECULARISM, AND FUNDAMENTALISM

We have, in the previous sections, isolated the essential ingredients of democracy and tried to identify areas of analogy or parallelism between the Greek-Western and the Islamic views of democracy. Complete identity, however, could not be demonstrated, because of the cultural distance that separates the Western and Islamic worldviews. We have been able, notwithstanding, to pinpoint important areas of agreement or correspondence. Thus for the sovereignty of the nation, defined in essentially populist and secular terms in the Western tradition, Islam substitutes the concept of the "general will" of the infallible community (*Umma*) as a cohesive religious and social unity which does not allow or tolerate radical divergence or dissent, the most serious instance of such divergence being apostasy, which is punishable by death.[37]

Second, humanism, which from the time of Protagoras we have identified as another ingredient of democracy, took in Islam a religious twist, because of the close correlation in Islam between the religious and the temporal. On the one hand, it marked, for the first time in Islamic history, the revolt against the arbitrary authority of the caliphs, who claimed that their actions, however unjust, were in total accord with the divine decree. On the other hand, it marked the vindication of the right of human reason, quite independently of revelation, to probe the most complex problems of responsibility, free will, and justice—both human and divine. This peculiar brand of humanism tempered and moderated in the process the unbounded enthusiasm of traditionalist jurists and scholars for the "revealed Word of God" (or the Quran), which so transcended human categories and norms, according to them, as to become well-nigh unintelligible.

Third, for the elective principle, as we have seen, Islam substituted the institution of homage or allegiance (*bay'ah*) paid to the caliph by the leaders or decision-makers of the community. However, the authority of the caliph was not regarded as absolute, but like every Muslim, the caliph's actions or decisions were subject to the precepts of the Holy Law (*Sharī'ah*). Should he violate these precepts, he would be disqualified or deposed.[38] Some extreme sects went so far as to advocate the assassination of the caliph who commits a grave sin (*kabīrah*) and flouts thereby the *Sharī'ah*.[39]

Fourth, it was perhaps in the domain of justice and equality that Islamic philosophical and theological theory fully accords with the Western tradition, stemming ultimately from the Greeks. The Hadith or Muhammadan Traditions express it in these terms: "An Arab has no superiority over a non-Arab, except by piety," and the Quran (49, 12) states: "O mankind, We have created you males and females and made you into peoples and tribes that you might know one another. Indeed, the noblest among you in God's sight is the most pious."

In practice, from the time of the earliest caliphs, the solidarity of the Muslim community was unbroken and even non-Muslims, such as Christians and Jews, referred to as the People of the Book (or *Dhimmis*) were regarded as part of a global domain or commonwealth known as the "World of Peace" (*Dār al-Silm*), which excluded pagans or infidels forming the "World of War" (*Dār al-Harb*). The People of the Book were tolerated and protected by Islam, provided they paid a polltax, but not the pagans, who were presented during the period of conquest with one of two choices, conversion to Islam or fighting to the death (Quran 9, 5 and 4, 47).

However, the rights of Muslims and non-Muslims (*Dhimmis*) were guaranteed by the *Sharī'ah* to which, as we have just seen, every Muslim— including the caliph—was subject. The two chief attributes of the caliph, again, were justice and knowledge, and it was his responsibility to ensure the universal application of the *Sharī'ah* and to administer justice effectively and indiscriminately.

In the last hundred years or so, Muslim intellectuals, theologians, and political activists have been grappling with the problem of the "viability" of Islam or its ability to cope with the political, social, and economic problems of the modern age. First came those theologians and activists known as reformists or modernists, such as Muhammad 'Abduh (d. 1905) and his disciple, M. Rashīd Riḍa (d. 1935), who took the position that the truth of Islam is timeless and incorrigible, and that the decadence of Muslims in this age should be imputed to the Muslims themselves rather than to their religion. In the political and social spheres, those reformists were willing to make certain concessions to the changing conditions of the times, but remained committed to the belief that Islam is the chief vehicle of salvation for the whole of mankind and not just for Muslims.

Over the last five decades, this position has hardened somewhat and has been succeeded by the "fundamentalist" position, which calls for a return to the ways of the pious ancestors (al-salaf al-ṣāliḥ) or first generation of Muslims as the only course open to Muslims today, if they are to overcome their decadence and deliver mankind from the evils of modern civilization. The fundamentalists, such as Abu'l-A'la Mawdūdi (d. 1979) in Pakistan, Sayyid Qutb (d. 1966) in Egypt, and Āyatollah al-Khomeini (d. 1989) in Iran, have been far more vehement than their predecessors, the "reformists," in their attack on the West—which they hold to be responsible for the decadence and misery of the Muslim peoples, on the one hand, and the spread of moral corruption that has plagued the world at large, on the other. As one would expect, the political regime of their choice is a theocracy that would restore the caliphate, or alternatively, an Islamic republic in which political authority would be vested in the learned religious scholars (ulema or mullas), who alone are qualified to implement or superintend the application of the Holy Law or Sharī'ah.

The fundamentalists have earned a great deal of notoriety in recent years, chiefly by reason of their radicalism and their open espousal of violence. However, there are in the Muslim and Arab worlds today large groups of Western-trained intellectuals, professionals, and academics who, although less vocal than their radical counterparts, are committed to the ideal of democratic or representative government and believe in the need to promote forcefully the cause of progress and political change, and especially the improvement of the lot of the masses—economically, educationally, and socially. They are hampered, however, by the strong hold that traditionalism and religious fanaticism continue to have upon the minds and souls of the masses.

The representatives of what I will simply refer to as the Westernized group in the Muslim and Arab Worlds include an assortment of strange bedfellows: secularists, Marxists, and plain liberal democrats.

The most important exponent of Islamic secularism continues to be the Azharite theologian and scholar, 'Ali 'Abd al-Rāziq (d. 1966), who published in 1925 a revolutionary treatise entitled "Islam and the Principles of Government," in which he attempted to disprove the thesis of the indissoluble bond between the temporal and the spiritual in Islam and to show that Islam allows for the possibility of social and political change through the processes of enlightened reason and sound deliberation. Islam, according to 'Abd al-Rāziq, is essentially a "spiritual call" addressed to the whole of mankind, rather than a political movement concerned with man's material needs or worldly affairs.[40]

The secularist thesis was pushed one step further in 1950 by another Azharite scholar, Khālid Muhammad Khālid, who was even more vehement in his advocacy of the separation of the political and the temporal in Islam and his onslaught on the Muslim clergy, whom he accuses of corrupting religion and using it for their own self-serving purposes.[41]

Other Western-leaning intellectuals and philosophers may be mentioned. Tāha Ḥusayn (d. 1975) and René Habachi, among others, have defended the thesis of a universal, Mediterranean culture—of which Arab-Muslim culture has formed an integral part, following Islam's encounter with Greek culture in the ninth century and even earlier. More radical in their advocacy have been a group of "positivist" philosophers, such as Zaki Nagib Mahmūd and Fu'ād Zakariya, who reject the authoritarianism, traditionalism, and verbalism of Arabic culture, and who call for the wholesale adoption of Western science and technology: first, as the only means of liberating the Arab mind from the shackles of authority and the "cult of language" and, second, as the highway of social and political progress.[42]

A similar line of thought has been advocated in recent years by a number of Arab Marxists, including Ṣādiq al-'Azm in Syria, 'Abdulla Laroui in Morocco, Ḥusayn Muruwwah in Lebanon, and many others. Although proponents of a class theory of the state, in which the bourgeoisie is pitted against the proletariat in a deadly struggle, Arab Marxists are fully committed to the democratic ideal and the just redistribution of wealth. Those two ideals are expressed in revolutionary terms, but moderate Arab socialists have acquiesced in the compatibility of Islam with European socialism and have subscribed to the democratic ideal of parliamentary government, while rejecting the revolutionary tactics of the Marxists in favor of peaceful methods of social and political change, including the just redistribution of wealth and the establishment of a constitutional system of government in which the rule of law and the rights of individuals are safeguarded.

NOTES

1. George Sabine, *A History of Political Theory,* 4th edition (Hinsdale, IL: Dryden Press, 1973), p. 3.

2. Ibid., p. 7.

3. See my *History of Islamic Philosophy* (New York: Columbia University Press, 1983), pp. 1–31.

4. See, for instance, F.M. Cornford, *Principium Sapientiae: The Origins of Greek Philosophical Thought* (Cambridge: Cambridge University Press, 1971); and W. K. C. Guthrie, *The Greeks and their Gods* (Boston: Beacon Press, 1951). Also, the *Theogony* of Hesiod reflects the influence of the Babylonian Epics, including the *Enuma Elish* and the *Epic of Gilgamesh*.

5. Cynthia Farrar, *The Origins of Democratic Thinking* (Cambridge: Cambridge University Press, 1988), p. 1.

6. Ibid., p. 131.

7. Thucydides, *History of the Peloponnesian War,* trans. M. I. Finley (London: Penguin Books, 1972), p. 145.

8. Ibid., p. 147.

9. Aristotle, *Politics* III, 14, 1285a20.

10. *Politics* VI, 2, 1317b2f. Cf. also *Politics* III, 11, 1281a40f; IV, 4, 1290a30 and 1291b30f.

11. Diogenes Laertius, *Lives* IX, 54. The first maxim is given and refuted in Plato's *Theaetetus* 152A, in the *Protagoras,* and elsewhere.

12. Locke's first Treatise of Civil Government was a direct attack on Robert Filmer's theory of absolute power and aimed only indirectly at Hobbes.

13. John Locke, *Second Treatise of Civil Government,* 2nd edition, Peter Laslett, ed. (Cambridge: Cambridge University Press, 1967), p. 341f.

14. Cf. Quran, 5,52.

15. Ibn Qutaybah, *Kitāb al-Maʿārif* (Cairo, 1969), p. 441.

16. Abduʾl Jabbār, *Kitāb al-Mughni,* vol. 6 (Cairo, 1962), pp. 18, 7, 43. Cf. M. Fakhry, *Ethical Theories in Islam* (Leiden: E. J. Brill, 1991), p. 33.

17. See M. Fakhry, *Islamic Occasionalism* (London: Allen & Unwin, 1958).

18. See *al-Aḥakām al-Sulṭāniyah* [Principles of Government] (Beirut, 1985), p. 6.

19. See M. Rashīd Riḍa, *al-Khilāfah aw al-Imāmah al-ʿUzma* (al-Manar, 1922–1923), French translation by H. Laoust (Beyrouth, 1938).

20. Quoted in Diane Ravitch and Abigail Thernstrom, eds., *The Democracy Reader* (New York: Harper Perennial, 1992), p. 54f.

21. Quran, 4,62. Cf. 5,52; 165; 7,13; 12,40.

22. A. K. S. Lambton, "Islamic Political Thought" in *Legacy of Islam,* Joseph Schacht and C. E. Bosworth, eds. (Oxford: Clarendon Press, 1979), p. 405.

23. Quran 42,36.

24. See al-Fārābi, *al-Madīnah al-Fādilah* [The Virtuous City], Albert Nader, ed. (Beirut, 1959), p. 110; and al-Fārābi, *al-Siyāsah al-Madaniyah* [The Political Regime], Fauzi Najjar, ed. (Beirut, 1964).

25. See al-Fārābi, *al-Siyāsah al-Madaniyah* [The Political Regime], p. 99f; Franz Rosenthal, *The Muslim Concept of Freedom Prior to the Nineteenth Century* (Leiden: E. J. Brill, 1960), p. 98f; and *Republic* VIII, 557c.

26. *Averroes on Plato's "Republic",* trans. by Ralph Lerner (Ithaca and London: Cornell University Press, 1974), p. 127.

27. Ibid., p. 128.

28. *Republic* IV, 444a (Cornford translation).

29. Ibid., IV, 434b. Cf. 432b.

30. I think Karl Popper made a good case for the antidemocratic character of Plato's Utopian project in the *Republic,* although he concedes Plato's profound aversion to tyranny. However, I think the problem is more complex than it appears from Popper's analysis, as his own portrayal of Socrates as a "democratic" critic of Athenian democracy clearly reveals. See *The Open Society and its Enemies,* vol. I (London: Routledge, 1962), pp. 158ff and 194ff.

31. *Politics* V, 1134b 19.

32. See *Summa Theologica* II, Q. 91, art. 2, where St.Thomas contends that the rational creature "has a share in eternal reason, whereby it has a natural inclination to its proper act and end; and this participation in the eternal law of the rational creature is called natural law." Cf. Ibid. art.1.

33. M. S. Khan, ed., *An Unpublished Treatise of Miskawaih on Justice* (Leiden: E. J. Brill, 1964), p. 17. Cf. *Tahdhib al-Akhlaq* [The Refinement of Character], C. K. Zurayk, ed. (Beirut, 1966), p. 112. In *Vita Pythag.* 130,1, Iamblichus reports that Pythagoras identified justice with proportion or equilibrium. Cf. M. Fakhry, *Ethical Theories in Islam*, p. 113f.

34. Cf. *Tahdhib,* p. 114. Cf. *Nicomachean Ethics* V, 1130b29f.

35. Cf. al-Ghazāli, *Mizān al-'Amal* [The Criterion of Action] (Cairo, 1342 A.H.), p. 196ff. Cf. M. Fakhry, *Ethical Theories in Islam*, pp. 197, 201.

36. *Mizān al-'Amal* [The Criterion of Action], p. 156f. Cf. M. Fakhry, *Ethical Theories*, p. 221f.

37. Cf. al-Māwardi, *al-Aḥakām al-Sulṭāniyah*, p. 69f.

38. Cf. al-Māwardi, op. cit., p. 19.

39. The sect in question was the Kharijites who revolted against Ali, the fourth caliph, and assassinated him in Damascus in 661 on the ground that he had committed a grave political sin by consenting to arbitration in the struggle against his Umayyad rival, Mu'āwiyah. Cf. al-Shahrastāni, *al-Milal wal-Nihal* [Religious Sects and Creeds] (Cairo, 1968), p. 116. Cf. M. Fakhry, *History of Islamic Philosophy*, p. 38.

40. Cf. 'Ali 'Abd al-Rāziq, *al-Islām wa Uṣūl al-Ḥukm* [Islam and the Principles of Government] (Beirut, 1966), p. 141.

41. Cf. Khālid Muhammad Khālid, *Min Hunā Nabda'* [From Here we Start] (Cairo, 1950), p. 47f.

42. Cf. Zaki Nagib Mahmud, *Tajdīd al-Fikr al-'Arabi* [Renewal of Arabic Thought] (Beirut, 1971), p. 253.

Part 4. Comparative Perspectives

David L. Hall and Roger T. Ames

DEWEY, CHINA, AND THE DEMOCRACY OF THE DEAD

On May 1, 1919, John Dewey arrived in China to begin his twenty-six month lecture tour. Three days later, the May Fourth uprising occurred in Beijing, initiating one of the most crucial periods in the history of modern China. In the beginning, the New Culture movement was particularly open to novel ideas and programs urging social reform, and given that the central subject of Dewey's numerous and wide-ranging lectures was to be that of "democracy," circumstances appeared auspicious for the positive reception of Western democratic ideas. Indeed, Dewey's influence was significant. Among other things, soon after his arrival, efforts were begun to transform the Chinese educational system along American lines.

But the circumstances that seemed so favorable in the beginning soon began to sour. Though initially the New Culture movement was anti-Confucian, hardly eight years later Sun Yat-sen and the Guomindang had nationalized China, employing a program which constituted a return to many of the traditional Chinese values. The later disputes between the Guomindang and the Communists aside, both groups were adamantly opposed to Dewey's ideas—the former in the name of a rehabilitated Confucius, the latter on behalf of Marxist-Leninist thinking. Under the pressure of these two opposing groups, Dewey's ideas would not survive. Shortly after the establishment of the People's Republic, a purge of Deweyan pragmatism was begun, and was completed by the mid-1950s.[1]

Now, given Dewey's insistence that democracy is expressed in attitudes rather than institutions, and that the sort of democratic attitudes entailed by his vision of democracy are both gradually formed by and reinforced through education, it would appear foolish to suggest that present-day hawkers of so-called democratic ideals will have any real influence in these decidedly less auspicious circumstances. Potential exporters of Western democracy to

275

China seem satisfied that internal changes among certain groups of Chinese, principally the student population, or the pressure of other so-called democratic nations, or the demands of the world market, abetted by a creative employment of the media, will work in a manner that Dewey's intelligent, patient, and altogether sensitive efforts did not.[2]

In our following remarks, we shall celebrate some of the central ideas of John Dewey's reconstructed understanding of democracy and note, despite many serious and significant differences, its surprising affinity with the traditional Chinese understanding of social organization. Then we shall suggest that, judged in terms of its resonance with many of the most pervasive Chinese beliefs and values, the Deweyan vision of democracy should be such as to engage the interest of a modernizing China.

We certainly realize that, even were a proposed dialogue between communitarian pragmatism and some form of left-wing Confucianism to come about, it would likely be drowned out by the voices of those engaged in other sorts of conversation. At the relatively innocent level of intellectual culture, self-proclaimed "postmodernists" from the West, celebrating Zhuangzi as the first true deconstructionist, are engaged by Chinese thinkers who argue for the relevance of Kant and Western modernism to the reconstruction of China. In this conversation, a modernizing China engages a postmodernizing West—and nobody wins.

Of course, the main conversation will likely proceed at the far darker level of practical politics and economics, where deals are made. In this dark place, where "democracy" is synonymous with a jerry-rigged form of market capitalism and nineteenth century party politics, a seedy capitalism faces an effete Marxism—and everybody loses.

In spite of the apparent practical futility of the exercise, we shall proceed with the effort to demonstrate the similarities between elements of Dewey's conception of democracy and Chinese understandings of community. Such a comparison may at the very least succeed in provoking some, on both the Chinese and Western sides, to introduce Dewey's ideas into future conversations concerning "China and Democracy."

1. A DEWEYAN VISION OF DEMOCRACY

1.1 Democracy and Contingency

The first thing to be said about Dewey's understanding of democracy is that it is decidedly historicist. Though the ideal of democracy is as old as civilized discourse, modern experiments with the implementation of democratic ideals were made possible by the confluence of a series of historical circumstances which included the spread of Enlightenment ideas, the effects of the French Revolution, the translation of dissenting sects to a distant geographical site in which unwanted constraints could be effectively abandoned, and the ascent of industry that not only undermined the institution of slavery but offered the possibility of a shift from a mentality shaped by the threat of scarcity to one stimulated by the possibility of abundance.

Of course, popular understandings of democracy tend to be naturalistic and essentialist. Roberto Unger has outlined the three central elements of these popular conceptions, which remain surprisingly effective even to the present day. They are:

> the idea of a science of human nature or of morals that would lay bare the basic laws of mind or of behavior . . . , the idea of a set of constraints rooted in practical social needs to produce, organize, and to exchange, . . . [and] the idea that these transformative constraints had a certain cumulative direction of their own.[3]

Classical political economy resulted from the combination of the first two of these elements; the belief in a manifest destiny for ideological movements such as Marxism and capitalism resulted from a combination of the second and third. These three assumptions have often been operative in tight conjunction with the ideal of democracy.

Dewey clearly held that democracy is not tied to any essentialist view of human nature, certainly not one that construes the human being as an acquisitive atom or a desiring machine. Whatever one may say about the original or biological nature of human beings, it is the cultural elements of a given society—its science and technology, industry and commerce, law and politics, arts of expression and communication, its most prized values, its general modes of individual and corporate self-understanding— that shape the meaning of the human being. And at the level at which it truly counts, the differences among cultures are of much greater importance than are the similarities.

Dewey also strongly affirmed that no set of economic constraints can define an economic order peculiar to normative socialization. There are simply too many ways of organizing for the same practical ends. Thus there can be no intrinsic connection between capitalism and democracy. Indeed, from Dewey's communitarian perspective, capitalism generally impedes and undermines the formation of democratic communities.

Finally, the idea that the advance of democracy or capitalism, or Marxism, will be inexorable is fundamentally at odds with pragmatism's historicist conception of the development of attitudes and institutions. A recognition of the sort of historical contingencies that allowed for the implementation of democratic institutions argues against wholesale attempts to export democracy. Indeed, the victories of democracy in the nineteenth century which were won in an accidental manner can now only be maintained through "deliberate and intelligent endeavor"[4] that meets the various problems that arise in a given society one at a time.

Our first summary proposition characterizing Dewey's understanding of democracy is this: *There is nothing inevitable about either the existence, the form, or the fate of democratic societies.*

1.2 Democracy and Aesthetic Activity

It should be recalled that for Dewey, "regarded as an idea, democracy is not an alternative to other principles of associated life. It is the idea of community life itself."[5] Further, the realization of the idea of democracy in some form, not as a set of political institutions, but as the expression of communal association, is the precondition for the development of true communication. Such communication, expressed in the form of free and open enquiry, grounds the employment of that intelligence which alone can move toward the achievement of the chosen ends of associated living.

If we conceive reason in objectivist and essentialist terms, Dewey's democratic ideal is precisely *not* a rational one. Democracy is, rather, the end for which "intelligence" serves as the means. Further, in its fullest sense, intelligence, as the perception of relationships between what is done and what is undergone,[6] comes at the end, not at the beginning of the process of social development. Thus democracy is more dependent upon imagination, emotion, and habits of thought and of action, than of anything which might be called reason.[7] For Dewey, "democracy" names a context in which human beings function principally in the support of things-in-common. It is these things that motivate the creation of groups—families, governments, churches, scientific associations, etc. The process infusing all these forms of association is that of communication, which Dewey calls "the miracle of shared life and shared experience."[8]

It is important to stress that this idea of democracy is not *political*. Government is only one of the groupings, and generally not the most efficacious one, promoting the aims of association and communication. The modes of association and the organizations that sustain them have as their implicit aim the protection and refinement of aesthetic activity. Contrary to those who would relegate Dewey's concern for art to his notion of "consummatory experiences," art and aesthetic activity, in their most fundamental forms, underlie a democratic community. In Dewey's words, "The expressions that constitute art are communication in its pure and undefiled form."[9] Further, "the language of art is not affected by the accidents of history that mark off different modes of human speech. . . . The difference between English, French, and German speech create barriers that are submerged when art speaks."[10]

This leads us to our second Deweyan proposition: *The sine qua non of a democratic community is the presence of widespread and effective communi-*

cation. Such communication can exist only within a community pervasively informed by aesthetic activity.

1.3 Democracy, Capitalism, and Technology

As Dewey well recognized, the assumption that democracy is intrinsically tied to the capitalist economic system is historically connected with the confluence of the industrial revolution and the articulation of modern democratic institutions. Specifically, this assumption derives from confusing the active force of industrial and technological development with the adjunctive or parasitical activity born from an economic system that combines a certain set of property rights with the motivation to acquire individual profit.

Scientific and technological advances which promise possible freedom from scarcity are only loosely connected with a capitalist system motivated by the need to concentrate the benefits of such advances in the hands of a few. The dynamism of science, and partly of technology as well, is cooperative effort leading to the most efficient and effective instrumentation of a set of ideas. The dynamism of capitalism, still motivated by the eighteenth and nineteenth century notions of individualism, is that of pecuniary profit. Technology, unsullied by entrepreneurial demands, is shaped by the aim of efficiency in the longest term permitted by the volatility of its augmentation. Capitalism is grounded upon desire for short-term profit, measured by brief segments of the productive life of individual entrepreneurs. It is only by tacitly including science and technology within one's definition of "capitalism" that one can argue for an intrinsic connection between capitalism and democracy.[11]

Dewey believed that strictly technological developments could promote freedom of access to the products of a community for all individuals. The final end of such a process would be that one day, when the shuttles weave without economic incentives determining what they weave and how much and to whom their products are affordable, then democracy in some finer form would be possible. Our third Deweyan proposition: *The view that not only democratic community but the scientific and technological activities supporting that community have conditioning features that, in principle, can swing free of capitalist motivations is at the heart of Dewey's conception of democracy.*

1.4 A New Individualism

Dewey claims that "assured and integrated individuality is . . . the product of definite social relationships and publicly acknowledged functions."[12] The loss of a sense of identity associated with such relationships and functions leads to a situation in which there is a confusion of roles and their attendant motivations. Dewey felt this to be one of the consequences of a capitalist economic system: "The business mind . . . is divided within itself . . . [since] the results of industry as the determining force in life are corporate and collective while its animating motives and compensations are so unmitigatingly private."[13]

If such divisions are to be healed, it can only be through a recognition of the corporateness of social life. In a democracy in which individuals recognize the intrinsic corporateness of life, there would be the recognition that the coherence of the individual is a function of the coherence of the community of shared experiences, and that the fullness of the individual's experience is guaranteed by that community. A consequence of this recognition would be that the achievement of an individual's principal rewards would be realized through her roles and the functions she performs, rather than through private pecuniary gain.

A fourth element of Dewey's vision of democracy is this: *A democratic community is comprised of individuals constituted by distinctive social relationships and publicly recognized roles. Such individuals realize their greatest satisfactions through these roles and relationships.*

We pause here to recognize that such individualism seems at present beyond the reach of at least North American democracy. Dewey's comment that "democracy begins at home, and home is a neighborly community"[14] has lost all but its nostalgic force. In the absence of "neighborly communities," which serve as the touchstone of democratic action, the best we seem able to do is to shift back and forth between the abstract and impotent extremes of individual absoluteness and individual relativity. Witness the liberal/conservative see-saw of the last several elections in the United States, the most recent phase of which has turned Washington D.C. into the Jurassic Park of democratic nations.

1.5 Democracy and Tradition

Our depiction of Dewey's understanding of democracy will conclude with some comments on the relation between democracy and tradition. As radical as were Dewey's reformist ideas, he well recognized the determinative power of customs and habits, particularly when they functioned in support of circumstances that allow for the most relevant employment of intelligence in the furtherance of community.[15] Ultimately, in fact, Dewey claimed that there is no moving beyond tradition. He said,

> The essential continuity of history is doubly guaranteed. Not only are personal desire and belief functions of habit and custom, but the objective conditions which provide the sources and tools of action . . . are precipitates of the past, perpetuating, willy-nilly, its hold and power.[16]

According to Dewey, "the underlying persistent attitudes of human beings were formed by traditions, customs, institutions, which existed when there was no democracy."[17] This raises one of the central issues involved in understanding the actual circumstances in the modern world that condition the implementation of democratic ideals. The barriers to the implementation of a democratic community are principally at the level of ingrained traditions that perpetuate attitudes, habits, and institutions incongruent with democratic ideals.[18]

Changes in social circumstances may be more rapid at some times than at others. In the Western world in the past three centuries, for example, the translation of a pioneering people to a novel geographical location, the American and French Revolutions, and the rise of industry and technology, all worked together to produce a situation which—though by all means cumulative and evolutionary—nonetheless gave the appearance of sudden and rapid transformation. This transformation led, moreover, among some, to the disintegration of old beliefs, and among others, to the perpetuation of beliefs broadly irrelevant to the changes taking place.[19]

With respect to the development of those attitudes conducive to democracy, much work is to be done in moving beyond the inertia of old habits and institutions. But this moving beyond must be one that employs the very traditions to be overcome as a means to that overcoming. Granted that "habits, customs, and systems can remain viable only when they are the objects of intelligent thinking,"[20] it is also true that, as Dewey says, "thinking is secreted in the interstices of habit."[21]

Our final characterization of Dewey's ideal democracy is this: *In a democratic community, habits, customs, and traditions are the grounds for the use of intelligence. Intelligent changes in tradition are evolutionary rather than revolutionary.*

2. THE DEMOCRACY OF THE DEAD

More often than not, Westerners who pride themselves on their democratic institutions see China, at worst, as a straightforward example of a totalitarian state. A somewhat more sympathetic, if equally condescending, view is that the Chinese are a people who have been "brought up by long habit to hug their chains."[22] Moreover, most of those who approach China with the idea of promoting democracy—many with unimpeachably sincere motivations—begin by flogging Chinese governmental institutions and practices with rhetoric born either from interests distinctly more economic than democratic, or from the vaguely idealistic and wildly irrelevant ideologies of contemporary North American, or North Atlantic, democracies.[23]

Were we to shift our perspective slightly, by reckoning that our form of capitalism frustrates rather than promotes a viable democracy, that our nineteenth century brand of individualism is precisely not an ingredient in the recipe of a truly democratic community, that claims to human rights do not have to be written in the heavens in order to be a reality on earth, that democracy, as the ideal of community life, follows different rhythms and time schedules in different cultural environments, and if, above all, we were to reject the Fallacy of the Wholesale Judgment that would offer the Chinese a democratic baby only on the condition that they accept, as well, its befouled bath water—that is to say, were we to look at China with John Dewey's democracy in mind—our vision might be transformed.

G. K. Chesterton once wrote,

> Tradition means giving votes to the most obscure of all classes, our ancestors. It is the democracy of the dead. Tradition refuses to submit to the small and arrogant oligarchy of those that merely happen to be walking about. All democrats object to men being disqualified by accident of birth; tradition objects to their being disqualified by accident of death.[24]

It is our intention now to take a look at China's "democracy of the dead" through the eyes of John Dewey. What we shall see might be as surprising to some of our readers as it has been to us, for as the ironic genius of history would have it, China is in many ways closer to the Deweyan ideal of democracy than is his own native land. Moreover, if there is to be mutually efficacious engagement between China and the West on the issue of democracy, it may well be the influence of China that brings the United States and other North Atlantic democracies closer to the Deweyan democratic vision. We are quick to say our comparison will not be made by appeal to Chinese and Western *governments*. We certainly hold, as did John Dewey, that the chief barrier to the implementation of democracy lies in the confusion of the democratic ideal with some political institution hypocritically claiming to embody it. Though governments are always involved, they are by definition almost always the followers, often *most reluctant* followers, in the march toward democracy.[25]

2.1 The Aesthetic Organization of Community

We turn first to the aesthetic organization of Chinese communities. It is difficult for many in the West to appreciate the aesthetic dimension of Chinese society. After all, Dewey claimed that "the function of art has always been to break through the crust of conventionalized and routine consciousness."[26] And given the ritualized, tradition-bound character of Chinese society, what is to be found there but a society literally ecapsulated by the "crust of convention"?

It is essential, therefore, that we understand the role of *li* 禮, or ritual action, in the promotion and maintenance of a community of shared experience—a *democratic community*—among the Chinese. In this manner we can most readily discern the paradoxical vitality of a *democracy of the dead*.

The notion of *li* is very broad, embracing everything from manners to roles and relationships, communications media, and social and political institutions. It is the determinate fabric of Chinese culture, and further, defines sociopolitical order. It is the language through which the culture is expressed. Ritual practice is not, of course, a purely Chinese innovation, but its prominence as an apparatus for ordering society and its dominance over formal legal institutions gives the Chinese *li* a unique status. To perform rituals is, on the one hand, to be incorporated as integral to that society such ritual practices define, and hence to be shaped and socialized by it. On the other hand, it is to contribute oneself to the pattern of relationships that ritual entails, and thereby to have a determinative effect on society. Because of this participatory emphasis of ritual practice in the Chinese context, *li* cannot be construed as involving passive deference to external patterns or norms; it is, rather, an artistic creation and re-creation of society that requires the investment of oneself, one's judgment, and one's own sense of cultural importances.

Although ritual practices initially lure the performer into social relationships by virtue of the stability and acceptability of their authorized forms, they are not simply given standards of appropriateness sedimented within a cultural tradition that serve to shape its participants in predictable ways. Ritual practices also have a creative dimension. In this sense, they are more exhortative than prohibitive. Rituals inform the participant of what is proper only to the degree that they are performed by her. Beyond any formal social patterning is an open texture of ritual that is personalized and reformulated to accommodate the uniqueness and the quality of each participant. From this perspective, ritual is a pliant body of practices for registering, developing, and displaying one's own sense of cultural importances. It is a vehicle for reifying the insights of the cultivating person, enabling one to reform the community from one's own unique perspective and, ultimately, to leave one's own mark on the tradition.

Given this vision of a community defined by *li*, we can appreciate that Dewey's hope for the effective role of aesthetic activity in Western democracies is definitely one shared by the Chinese. Dewey says,

> When the liberating of human capacity operates as a socially creative force, art will not be a luxury, a stranger to the daily occupations of making a living. Making a living economically speaking, will be at one with making a life that is worth living.[27]

2.2 The Confucian Individual

This leads us to a brief discussion of the traditional Chinese understanding of the individual. There are variable degrees of personalization in ritual practices and, as a consequence, the roles they establish are hierarchical. These roles form a kind of social syntax that generates meaning through coordinating patterns of deference. And to the extent that worth is a function of interest and attention, the process of extending and deepening these roles brings with it a greater felt significance.

Because ritual action can only take account of a person to the extent that one is differentiated and distinguished, the indeterminate masses (*min* 民) necessarily have a more passive and deferential role.[28] This same demand of ritual action as personal signature, while promising to make the most of available diversity, means also that the achieved community will in some important respect always be "local." It will be Dewey's "neighborly community," conditioned by the expectations and the imagination of its specific cultural leaders and the circumstances of its time and place. It thus falls to those who are the fullest participants in ritual practice and thus the fullest members of community, through effecting relations of deference rather than power, to formulate and creatively shape a future for their particular community, both in terms of goals to be achieved and minimal qualifications for participation.

The Confucian conception of the individual is dynamic, entailing a complex of social roles. It is the quality of these roles that focuses one's identity and is constitutive of oneself as a self. Not just role playing but *appropriate* role playing creates a self. Given that *other* is an always necessary condition for *self*, the cultivation of autonomous individuality is anathema to self-realization.

The Chinese conception of person as a specific matrix of roles will not tolerate an assertion of natural equality. Although persons stand in irrevocably hierarchical relationships that reflect fundamental differences among them, ritual practice serves the notion of qualitative parity in several ways. First, the dynamic nature of roles means that privileges and duties within one's community tend to even up across a lifetime. One's duties as a child are balanced by one's privileges as a parent. One's field of relationships over time produce a degree of parity in what is perceived as the most vital source of humanity— one's human relations.

Any discomfort we in the West might feel with respect to such an indifference to natural equality would be equally occasioned by Dewey's understanding:

> Equality [says Dewey] does not signify that kind of mathematical or physical equivalence in virtue of which any one element may be substituted for another. It denotes effective regard for whatever is unique and distinctive in each. . . . [Equality] is not a natural possession, but is the fruit of the community when its action is directed by its character as a community.[29]

2.3 Community and Tradition

Finally, we turn to the issue of the importance of tradition in the Chinese understanding of community. The Chinese are "the people of the Han." This act of self-designation roots the vast majority of Chinese people[30] in the traditions associated with the Han cultural synthesis culminating in the victory of Confucianism at the beginning of the first century of the Common Era. It is this that constitutes China as a "democracy of the dead".

It is commonly noticed that in China, from ancient times to the present, conflicts have almost invariably been settled through informal mechanisms for mediation and conciliation as close to the dispute as possible.[31] Society has been largely self-regulating, and thus has required a minimum of government. It is this same communal harmony that defines and dispenses order at the most immediate level that is also relied upon to define and express authoritative consensus without more obvious formal provisions for effecting popular sovereignty.[32]

The popular Western view is that the conformity associated with the conscious maintenance of a continuity with traditions of the past is undesirable, leading to unproductive inertia and stagnating inflexibility. By giving a pragmatist's endorsement to Søren Kierkegaard's aphorism, "We live forward, but we understand backward,"[33] William James emphasized that understanding in its most practical sense is always constituted by reflections upon the living past. The Chinese side with James and Dewey on this issue.

Further, Dewey claimed that "conformity is enduringly effective when it is a spontaneous and largely unconscious expression of agreements that spring from genuinely communal life."[34] The ideal of Chinese community is the maintenance of such spontaneity. Dewey claimed that "thinking goes on in the interstices of habit." In China, to be "reasonable" is to be in accord with *li* (*he li* 合理)). This entails an awareness of those constitutive relationships which condition each thing and which, through patterns of correlation, make its world meaningful and intelligible. All things evidence a degree of coherence as their claim to uniqueness and complexity, as well as their claim to continuity with the rest of their world.

Tradition is mediated through *li* 禮. *Li* establishes the ethos of given community. As such, *li* may never be considered as independent of context. There are no transcendent *li*. In the absence of teleological guidance, there is only an ongoing process of correlation and negotiation. One investigates *li* in order to uncover the patterns that relate things, and to discover resonances between things that make correlations and categorization possible. The nature of classification (*lei* 類) in this world is juxtaposition through some presumed similarity. Things are continuous with one another and thus are interdependent conditions for each other. In a tradition that begins from the assumption that existence is a dynamic process, the causes of things are resident in themselves and the project of giving reasons for things or events requires a tracing or mapping out of the conditions that sponsor them.

Li constitutes an aesthetic coherence in the sense that it begins from the uniqueness of any particular as a condition of individuation and is, at the same time, a basis for continuity through various forms of collaboration between the given particular and other particulars with which, by virtue of similarity or productivity or contiguity, it can be correlated. It is this collaboration that provides a ground for the various modes of analogical relationship that are the closest approximation to "reasoning" available in this tradition.[35]

In contrast to reasoning as the process of uncovering essences of which particulars are instances, *li* involves tracing out correlated details forming the pattern of relationships which obtain among things and events. Thus thinking has as its goal a comprehensive and unobstructed awareness of interdependent conditions and their latent, vague possibilities, where the meaning and value of each element is a function of the particular network of relationships that constitute it. Thinking, again to echo John Dewey, goes on in the interstices of the patterns of things and events.

2.4 Rights and Democracy

An important consequence of John Dewey's vision of democracy is his historicist understanding of human rights. Dewey believes it a fiction that "the individual is in possession of antecedent political rights."[36] Rather, he believes that "the concept of individual rights [must] be considered with reference to the society which grants them and the state which, through the agency of law, reenforces them."[37]

The Chinese have traditionally held, consistent with Dewey's view, that rights are granted by society, though in traditional China there is less of a tendency to stress the importance of the strictly legal enforcement of rights. On the relationship between human rights and law, R. Randle Edwards observes that "respect for individual rights is closely associated with formal legality. While laws can exist without respect for rights, rights cannot long exist without laws."[38] On the contrary, the Confucian alternative would suggest that almost all of the actual rights and duties recognized within a sociopolitical order are sustained by extralegal institutions and practices, and are enforced by social pressures rather than punishments. In fact, reliance upon the application of law, far from being a means of realizing human dignity, is fundamentally dehumanizing since it leads to the impoverishment of mutual accommodation, and compromises the *particular* responsibilities of the community to define what would be appropriate conduct.

The introduction of duties and obligations—the "power modes" of relatedness—has the effect of mediating and thus constricting the creative possibilities of the elements constituting a relationship. The emphasis on ritual, by contrast, is an attempt to optimize these possibilities. A careful and sympathetic look at the Chinese model might suggest alternative nonlegal mechanisms for resolving conflicts, and temper the readiness of the individual to pursue legal measures by providing reasonable alternatives. Movement away from formal procedures might also be a movement toward a greater sense of community.

3. CONCLUSION

Though we have dealt with our subject primarily at the speculative level, it has been no part of our purpose merely to advertise a set of ideas culled from the texts of two cultures, and to hold them high as occasions for inspiration and ennoblement. Exemplary principles, even when detached from particular circumstances, are truly abstract only if one treats them so. In the spirit of John Dewey, we have celebrated the ideas of democratic community expressed in Chinese and pragmatic understandings as a means of reminding ourselves that such ideas are deeply implicated in the most specific and local of the problems encountered by any engaged in the activities of living in and maintaining community life; that such ideas, in the form of relevant ideals, will always arise in the process of dealing with this problem and that, and that they then may serve as effective tools for intelligent action. Whether we actually employ these tools, or suppress their use by appeal to feigned necessities or covert interests will, of course, be largely a matter of choice.

NOTES

1. The reasons for Dewey's failure finally to influence China were largely associated with his refusal to take a wholesale approach to social problems. Always warning the Chinese against the uncritical importation of Western ideas (including, of course, his own), as well as the uncritical rejection of traditional Chinese values, Dewey, in spite of his radical reconstruction of the popular democratic ideal, was simply too moderate for a China in search of revolution.

Dewey's ideas for democratic reform were initially rejected by the Guomindang on the grounds that they were anti-Confucian, and by the Communist party because they supported "American monopolizing capitalists." An examination of the sense of Dewey's understanding of democracy, as it was promulgated both in China and in his native land, will show that, while Dewey's ideas are neither procapitalist nor anti-Confucian, the popular idea of democracy that Dewey was seeking to reconstruct entails both of these characteristics. Moreover, as Dewey and his ilk were hardly successful in reshaping the actual understanding of democracy and democratic institutions in the North Atlantic countries, it is the popular rather simple-minded idea of democracy that many are currently urging upon China, if only by default.

2. But much the same could be said of America. For Dewey's educational reforms in this country, misunderstood and only partially applied from the beginning, have

long since been effectively purged. And Dewey's understanding of democracy has never been the sense of the mainstream. In many ways, the opportunity to introduce a reconstructed idea of democracy seems to have been lost as surely in America as it was in China.

3. Roberto Mangabeira Unger, *Social Theory: Its Situation and Its Task*, vol. 1 of *Politics: A Work in Constructive Social Theory* (New York: Cambridge University Press, 1987), p. 85.

4. John Dewey, *Freedom and Culture* (New York: Capricorn Books, 1963), p. 173.

5. John Dewey, *The Public and Its Problems* (Athens, OH: The Ohio University Press, 1927), p. 148.

6. John Dewey, *Art as Experience* (New York: Capricorn Books, 1958), p. 45.

7. "Emotion and imagination are more important in shaping public sentiment and opinion than information and reason." *Freedom and Culture*, p. 10.

In the rhetoric of Western democracy, democratic institutions have been held to be among the highest attainments of reason. Partly this is so because of the (rather unrealistic) understanding of the rationality of classical Greek society, and the association of democratic institutions with the Enlightenment sensibility.

The fact is that one of the conditions sustaining democracy was grounded in the challenge to reason set out by Hume and the classical economic theory that found reason is always subject to the passions. The assault continued with Darwin, again a support to economic competition, and with Freud who provided a concept of civilized society as the sublimated product of libidinal impulses, further opening the door to the stimulation of desires by the production of objects satisfying those desires and of techniques of advertising and media stimulation that, when most efficacious, could actually create new desires where none were manifest before.

8. John Dewey, *Reconstruction in Philosophy* (Boston: Beacon Press, 1948), p. 211.

9. *Art as Experience*, p. 244.

10. *Art as Experience*, p. 335.

11. Dewey's point is that technological sophistication has led to a society that could potentially ground its aims and values in a sense of abundance rather than scarcity. Technology can, potentially at least, free individuals from attitudes long shaped by the need to wring from nature sufficient sustenance for the moment and to renew the struggle daily.

We are with Dewey in claiming that a worthwhile understanding of democracy requires that we conceive it in terms of a reversal of the dynamics that allow economic motivations to shape democratic institutions. We would conceive democracy in terms of the development of a community in which the goal of individual access to the ideals and goods of the community motivated the economic and technological matrix of the society. To say that one lives in a democracy until this is the dominant motive, or until the greater part of our energies are shaped by that desire, is to play with words in the most naive or cynical of manners.

12. John Dewey, *Individualism Old and New* (New York: Capricorn Books, 1962), p. 53.

13. Ibid., p. 57.

14. *The Public and Its Problems*, p. 210.

15. In *The Public and Its Problems*, pp. 159–60, Dewey quotes admiringly the oft-celebrated words of William James:

Habit is the enormous fly-wheel of society, its most precious conservative influence. It alone is what keeps us within the bounds of ordinance, and saves the children of fortune from the uprisings of the poor. It alone prevents the hardest and most repugnant walks of life from being deserted by those brought up to tread therein. It keeps the fisherman and the deck-hand at sea during the winter; it holds the miner in his darkness, and nails the countryman to his log-cabin and his lonely farm through all the months of snow. It protects us from invasion by the natives of the desert and the frozen zone. It dooms us all to fight out the battle of life upon the lines of our nurture or our early choice, and to make the best of a pursuit that disagrees, because there is no other for which we are fitted, and it is too late to begin again. [William James, *Principles of Psychology* (Cambridge: Harvard University Press, 1983), p. 125.]

16. *The Public and Its Problems,* pp. 161–62.

17. *Freedom and Culture,* p. 173.

18. Further, since "great changes in events and practical affairs [are] attended with marked cultural lags in verbal formulations" (*Freedom and Culture,* p. 48), we may not even have a proper language to characterize the ideals freed by the changes in social structure made possible by technological development.

Here we come face to face with the pragmatic interpretation of ideas and ideals. Unlike his contemporary, A. N. Whitehead, who accepts the efficacy, if not the primacy, of ideas and ideals in the "slow drift of mankind toward civilization," Dewey is less sanguine about the progressive interpretation of such a "drift" and finds that the drift is itself the context from out of which the articulated ideal (clothed now in appropriate beliefs, habits, and institutions) emerges. That is to say, Whitehead's accession to the positive influence of irrational forces illustrated by "steam and the barbarians" is met by Dewey's belief that it is "steam"—that is to say, technology—which is the primary causal agent in the development of mankind's potential. And it is the potential barbarous employment of technology, a consequence of habits and institutions we should long ago have outgrown, that presents the fundamental obstacle.

19. The role of education in democracy is to be recognized here. Dewey recognizes education as "truly conservative." Its function is "to conserve and transmit the best of our traditional cultural heritage [and at the same,] cultivate individuals who can cope with their environment." *Dewey—Lectures in China 1919–21* (Honolulu: University of Hawai'i Press, 1973), p. 188.

20. Ibid., p. 87.

21. *The Public and Its Problems,* p. 160.

22. *Freedom and Culture,* p. 10. Dewey is not referring to China here.

23. Typically there is an asymmetrical relationship set up in any comparison that bears the quality of critique. Social criticism is the most profound illustration of this claim, since the social critic attacks the practices of one social group while appealing to the ideals and theories meant to characterize her own, or compares the wrongful practices of her country, contextualized by mitigating circumstances, to the raw uninterpreted practices of her target. Responsible critique requires that we match ideals with ideals, and practices with practices, and then compare a selection of principles and practices that are plausibly deemed to be efficaciously related.

24. "The Ethics of Elfland" in *G. K. Chesterton: A Selection from his Non-fictional Prose,* W. H. Auden, ed. (London: Faber and Faber, 1970), p. 176.

25. We should, perhaps, offer reasons why our present effort is not totally irrelevant and utopian—why, that is to say, we have reason to believe that the international environment is volatile enough that we may reasonably expect relations among nations at the political, economic, and the broader cultural levels, to lead to real changes in the social structures of national communities.

Roberto Unger names three sources of dynamism in world politics: the rise of mass politics, the emergence of world history, and enlarged economic rationality (*Social Theory—Its Situation and Its Task*, pp. 52–60). With respect to mass politics, we may find that the very conception entails the view that it is the popular will, either through elected representatives or an oligarchic party system, that authorizes the power of the state. The shifts of power possible under such conditions are threatening to both current representatives and party members and policies. As for the dynamic of World History, Unger notes quite plausibly that "Every custom and dogma may be changed through deliberate policy, under the shadow of foreign threat, or by mass conversion, at the touch of foreign example" (*Social Theory*, p. 57). Certainly the presumed Marxian structure of China, stimulated by "the touch of foreign example" is an apt illustration of this dynamic. How deeply such changes go is a matter of dispute.

The third dynamic, enlarged economic rationality, expresses the flexibility of a society to "rearrange relationships, techniques, and organizations, according to productive opportunity or economic reward" (*Social Theory*, p. 59). The organization of China allows, at one level at least, for greater economic rationality than is to be found in most Western capitalist countries, since the aim of such rationality is that the place of an individual in the division of labor, or the control over capital, not be allowed to become vested rights. With respect to the division of labor at least, this is clearly less the case in China than it is, for example, in the United States.

It is plausible to assume, therefore, that present circumstances are not adverse to changes in social and economic organization within interacting nations. And though missionizing capitalists or liberal democratic reformers in Western nations may think that the changes ought to be from the side of China, there is no inherent reason why this must be so. Indeed, if we take as our standard the Deweyan ideal of democracy, we might say that an appeal to some Chinese models of human association might be the best means of realizing Dewey's dream.

26. *Reconstruction in Philosophy*, p. 211.

27. *The Public and Its Problems*, pp. 183–84.

28. See David L. Hall and Roger T. Ames, *Thinking Through Confucius* (Albany: State University of New York Press, 1987), chapter 3 passim, for this distinction between *ren* and *min* 民.

29. *The Public and Its Problems*, pp. 150–51.

30. The Han Chinese comprise, perhaps, 92 percent of the Chinese populace, the remaining 8 percent is comprised by at least 55 recognized minority groups representing a variety of ethnicities and linguistic families.

31. See Victor H. Li, *Law Without Lawyers* (Boulder: Westview Press, 1978), chap. 4 passim.

32. In China, political directives appear to take the form of broad and abstract slogans promulgated by the public institutions and the press. What is not apparent is the degree to which such directives require interpretation and application as they ramify back down through society. Communication and consensus is, in fact, arrived at by a

much less abstract mechanism than would be characteristic of a society comprised of strictly autonomous individuals. This is true in a large measure because the Chinese conception of humanness does not presuppose any notion of a moral order transcending the consensual order that could justify either demagogic appeals or appeals to individual conscience, and which might disrupt the consensus.

33. William James, *Pragmatism* (Cambridge: Harvard University Press, 1975), p. 107.

34. *Individualism Old and New*, p. 86.

35. See A. S. Cua, *Ethical Argumentation: A Study in Hsun Tzu's Moral Epistemology* (Honolulu: University of Hawai'i Press, 1985), for a discussion of the various modes of analogical thinking associated with *li*.

36. *The Public and Its Problems*, p. 102.

37. "There are no such things as individual rights until and unless they are supported and maintained by society through law" (*Lectures in China*, p. 151).

38. R. Randle Edwards, "Civil and Social Rights: Theory and Practice in Chinese Law Today," in *Human Rights in Contemporary China*, R. Randle Edwards, Louis Henkin, and Andrew J. Nathan, eds. (New York: Columbia University Press, 1986), p. 41.

Joseph Grange

THE DISAPPEARANCE OF THE PUBLIC GOOD: CONFUCIUS/DEWEY/RORTY

In this essay, I wish to describe the disappearance of the public good as a subject of philosophical discourse. The works of Confucius and of John Dewey contain robust concepts of the public good. But in the controversial work of Richard Rorty, the idea of the public good undergoes a radical transformation. I will examine *The Great Learning* of Confucius, John Dewey's *The Public and Its Problems* and Richard Rorty's *Contingency, Irony, and Solidarity.* What I hope will emerge from this cross-cultural study is a reconsideration of the relation between metaphysics and social philosophy.

I am aware that it is no longer fashionable to use the word "metaphysics," but such disdain is the result of an unreflective allegiance to postmodern modes of thinking. One outcome of this shift toward postmodernism is an inevitable confusion concerning the status of the public and the private realms. This essay is an attempt to clear up that confusion and at the same time justify the continued importance of metaphysics for the American pragmatic tradition.

I

The author of *The Great Learning* is at pains to demonstrate how a human being can become an adult and assume responsibility for her personal and communal life. In other words, *The Great Learning* is about the making of a good citizen. How does one grow in order to take up a valid position in the public realm? And how does one use one's personal life in order to participate in a fitting manner in social contexts?

The text offers us "three items" and "eight steps." But before taking these up in detail, it is important to note the kind of culture that *The Great*

293

Learning represents. As Hall and Ames argue, Chinese culture is through and through immanental.[1] There is no sense of any recourse to a transcendental source, power or being. Nor are the answers to human questions to be found in any fixed universal essences or scheme of things. Just as there is no higher court of appeal when it comes to assaying the human condition, so also there is no unshakable foundation to be sought for reasons of security, certainty, or assurance. Put as simply as possible, all the material for answering human questions and solving human problems are to be found on this earth and in this historical time. There are no other resources for confronting the great issues of human life. This is what is meant by dwelling in an immanental cosmos.

As Rorty might put it, this is a nonfoundational human world. Transcendental beings and principles are not to be discovered, and wrestling with the human condition must be done without the tricks of "backworldsmanship."[2] Given this insistence on immanence, the "three items" take on great significance for the theme of this volume, "Democracy and Justice." Each of the "three items" can be read as prescriptive advice for living justly in a democratic society. The text reads, "The Way of learning to be great (or adult education) consists in manifesting the clear character, loving the people and abiding in the highest good."[3] I propose that the act of *manifesting the clear character* refers to a way of living that puts the interests of the people on a level with one's own. The resultant clarity of character is the consequence of not mistaking one's selfish desires for the public good. *Loving the people* has to do with seeking in all circumstances to renew their hope for better outcomes and more civilized living conditions. *Abiding in the highest good* provides a perspective from which one can continually judge the worthiness of one's actions. The force of the term "abiding" is that of staying and dwelling. Those who would be good citizens must continually struggle to take up residence within the problem of the public good.

In an immanental social order, there is no fixed or ultimate solution to human problems. From the perspective of pragmatic philosophy, one can say that abiding in the highest good is the consequence of manifesting the clear character and loving the people. Without a sense of the public good, there is no possibility of ever renovating the lives of the people. And without the motivation provided by loving the people, there is no possibility of dwelling consistently in the highest good. There is a direct continuity established between the assumption of an attitude—the clear character—and its consequences, the recognition of the importance of the public good. Furthermore, there is a straight line to be drawn from the act of loving the people to acting consistently for the sake of the people. When this is carried out over a considerable period of time, a personal character is firmly established. It is this character that can be relied upon in judging what is the public good.

The "eight items" flow surely and steadily from this centering upon the public good. For our purposes, what is important is that each of the steps—

investigation of things, extension of knowledge, sincerity of will, rectification of the mind, cultivation of personal life, regulation of the family, national order and world peace—is a consequence of the "three items." In Confucian thought an absolute separation of the public and the private realms is a fallacy. Its falseness results from seeing the human person as somehow divided against itself and in need of separate spheres to sort out its priorities.[4]

On my reading of this text, what is required is not segregation but harmony.[5] Now harmony is not to be understood as some "nice" compromise between competing dimensions of the human condition. Neither is it a mere accommodation. Rather, harmony names something compellingly unique, a novel way of being that emerges from the conflicting claims of different human needs. A harmony is a special way of resolving the conflicting demands arising from the private and public levels of human life. This interpretation gains additional credibility when the means of working out this harmonic solution is grasped. The text states,

> Only after knowing what to abide in can one be calm. Only after having been calm can one be tranquil. Only after having achieved tranquility can one have peaceful repose. Only after having peaceful repose can one begin to deliberate. Only after deliberation can the end be attained. Things have their roots and branches. Affairs have their beginnings and ends. To know what is first and what is last will lead one near the Way.[6]

The key to creating a harmony between the private and the public is contained in these words. For what connects the public and the private is the sense of tranquility that results from abiding in the highest good. This repose is the result of knowing that not all private desires need to be satisfied. It is also the result of knowing that not all public goods require immediate instantiation. There is a time and a place for both the public and the private.

What The Great Learning requires of the adult person is the sense of assurance and poise that results from knowing each dimension will get its appropriate share. That, I believe, is the force behind the injunction to stay calm. Deliberation proceeds from maintaining a right relation to the good in its varying claims. The public and the private, the individual and the collective, the personal and the social require each other. Regardless of the shore from which one sets out, it is toward the other that one moves. This is the nature of human life at its richest and most profound. To tear one from the other is to deprive humanity of one of its most intense experiences—the unique tension felt by an individual as she takes her stand as a member of a community.

Finally, this interpretation of The Great Learning's understanding of the relation between the private and the public good is in accord with the central principle of Confucius' teachings. In the Analects, we are told of the thread that unifies the Master's teaching: "the Tao of the Master is Chung and Shu, nothing more."[7] I follow Hall and Ames in rendering these two key terms as follows: *Chung* means "doing one's best as one's authentic self"; and *shu* "is to be understood in terms of giving and receiving deference." Therefore the central act in forging a harmony between the public and the private is deploying the goodness of one's own personal self so as to light up the situation of others. To defer to the other is to be good enough to be yourself so that the other can also be good at the same time.

But surely this asks too much of the present times? How can our divided souls carry out so grand a project? A clue can be found in the relation spanning the Chinese organ of thought—the HeartMind—and the quintessential private and public act of living up to one's word. Within Chinese culture, one does not think solely with the mind. An equally important dimension of thinking is provided by the heart. To think is to carry out a harmonizing process that brings together thought and feeling, affect and insight. Furthermore, the register within which this deeply human activity is carried out is a verbal one, since the act of giving and receiving each other's word creates the bond that holds private and public orders together.

In summary, *The Great Learning* introduces many of the themes needed to work out a concrete philosophy of the public good. It insists on direct continuity between the public and private even as it recognizes the special character of each. Read in connection with the *Analects* and in the light of the most recent scholarship, this classic text shows that the public realm is dependent upon the construction of a common world of meaning. And equally important, it also demonstrates that such a common world of meaning can only be upheld through reliance upon the steady presence of private integrity. Acting by living up to one's word is the way in which the clear character is manifested. One loves and renews the people through the right deliberations of the heartmind. It is by reason of this same heartmind that human beings come to reside in the highest good. Abiding in this highest good involves envisioning the appropriate relation between the public and the private good—*a goodness that is different but not opposed.*

II

In 1927, John Dewey took up the issue of the public good in his classic study, *The Public and Its Problems.*[8] Even the title suggests Dewey's pragmatic approach. He is a functionalist who seeks the consequences of activities. Only then can genuine solutions be found. In bringing his pragmatic method to bear on issues of social and political concern, Dewey sought to reconstruct the relation between the private and public domains. His study rings a number of interesting changes on the themes so far discussed. He establishes, for the first time, a new category for political philosophy—the public and its concerns. Second, he elaborates on how the failure to recognize this category has brought about an absence of mediating social institutions. Without such instruments, the possibility of clearing up the confusions surrounding the connections between the public and the private realms remains decidedly dim. He also challenges political philosophy to accommodate new and profound changes in our thinking in order to bring about what he calls "the Great Community." This is obviously a *locus classicus* for American pragmatic philosophy.

For Dewey, the proper mode of doing philosophy is to attend to consequences, results, and outcomes. So when it is time to look at the various patterns human beings have employed to deal with each other, it is no surprise that Dewey will have no truck with *a priori* forms of social thinking. There is no usefulness in hypostatizing entities like "The State" or "The Government." The meaning of social issues lies in the results of our being with one another. Philosophers should not be talking about a national will as the cause of political institutions. All such causal thinking is anathema to the pragmatist. It is the results attendant upon a pattern of reasoning that reveal its truth. Behind all of Dewey's thinking lies this solid commitment to empiricism. The truth of any issue is determined by looking toward consequences and away from first principles.

Turning this instrumentalist attitude toward the social realm, Dewey finds that "the essence of the consequences that call a public into being is the fact that they expand beyond those directly engaged in producing them."[9] Therefore, a public arises each and every time one's actions spill over into the lives of others. This very strong reading of the public is an outgrowth of Dewey's relational metaphysics. For it is precisely the relational character of all reality that undergirds the pragmatic point of view. Since everything is connected with everything else, the important questions revolve around the precise manner and mode of those connections. For Dewey, the act of dividing the universe of relations is always a perilous one. The truth quality of any position is precisely the outcome of how one makes the appropriate cuts. Cut in the wrong place and the consequences could be disastrous. The world falls apart and hopes for justice and integrity vanish.

This insistence on the primacy of relations joined with the pragmatic stress on consequences brings about an important recasting of a series of related terms. First, there is no utility in keeping alive the distinction between the individual and the collective. It only prolongs useless ideological struggles concerning statism, liberalism, and collectivism. What counts are the consequences of using one or more of these forms of social organization. "The individual versus the collective" is but one more type of old thinking stifling our capacity to experiment with forms of governance. Similarly, disputes about the relative hierarchical status of private and public are misplaced. It is always a matter of the consequences that result from drawing particular lines of separation. Furthermore, it is individuals who act. The public does not act but rather reacts when consequences mount up. In fact, the basic problem faced by the public is finding its voice and gaining recognition.[10] This is not to say that a tyranny of the majority brought about by public opinion is an impossibility. It is to say that the problem is far too complex for the simple-minded solution of dividing off the public and the private as separate and inviolate spheres. Once again, it is the hard work of examining *empirically* the consequences of various patterns of relations that will deliver the truth.[11]

None of this should suggest that Dewey seeks to eliminate the place of the private, the personal, and the individual. In fact, Dewey accords it the highest possible place. It is within the sphere of the private that all genuine novelty and growth takes place. Left to its own devices, the public is an overwhelmingly conservative force. It seeks stability rather than creativity. Dewey recasts the category of the individual as that unique irreducible moment of fresh intelligence that turns the world of human experience in new and fruitful directions:

> Invention is a peculiarly personal act, even when a number of persons combine to make something new. A novel idea is the kind of thing that has to occur to somebody in the singular sense. A new project is something to be undertaken and set agoing by private initiative.[12]

Once again, in matters of definition, it is consequences that matter not putative transcendental features of human nature. For Dewey, the individual, the personal, and the private are defined by the degree of uniqueness exhibited in enacting behaviors and actions. It is a given that society needs to protect such spheres of creativity for its own self-interest.

What is at the heart of Dewey's reconstruction of the categories of the public and the private is his very common sense observation that there is no person, institution, entity, or thing that exists in isolation. A nonassociative way of being is ontologically impossible. Likewise, it is logically inconceivable to imagine a space wherein one remains unaffected by the deeds and acts of others. The "old individualism" proclaimed the existence of an atomic individual, inviolate in the possession of rights and isolated in terms of moral deliberation. Such a person never existed and such a theory is a myth built upon what Whitehead called "the fallacy of simple location." For Dewey there is no place to hide.

But some places are better than others. This conviction is behind the "Search for the Great Community."[13] In fact, the public good is the consequence of citizens participating in a community. It is most important to note that this participation is grounded in and through the act of communication. It is by sharing signs, symbols, and acts of togetherness that human beings both assert and achieve their humanity. In words that echo the major themes of *The Great Learning*, Dewey writes,

> To learn to be human is to develop through the give-and-take of communication an effective sense of being an individually distinctive member of a community; one who understands its beliefs, desires and methods, and who contributes to a further conversion of organic powers into human resources and values. . . . [T]he nature of the only possible solution [lies in] the perfecting of the means and ways of communication of meanings so that genuinely shared interests in the consequences of interdependent activities may inform desire and effort and thereby direct action.[14]

I conclude this analysis of *The Public and Its Problems* by noting, once again, the key to understanding Dewey's pragmatic method and its impact on his understanding of the conditions needed for the construction of the Great Community. First and foremost, there is the insistence upon looking at the consequences of given positions in order to determine their meaning. There are no final positions, no sacrosanct theories, and no distinctions that cannot be redrawn. In terms of communal life, experiments are the order of the day. In terms of the public good, democracy is the premier form of experimental social life. For it is only through democracy, understood as an experiment in self-government, that the public can find its voice and thereby gain recognition. This idea of active experimentation makes it necessary to lay down certain conditions for communal life:

> From the standpoint of the individual, it consists in having a responsible share according to capacity in forming and directing the activities of groups to which one belongs and in participating according to need in the values which the groups sustain. From the standpoint of the groups it demands liberation of the potentialities of members of a group in harmony with the interests and goods which are common.[15]

As with Confucius, what is always to be sought is a *harmony* of conflicting spheres of interests, which is always the outcome of very strenuous intellectual labor and debate. It is in finding the means whereby to communicate these harmonies that the tough and demanding experimental work underlying the Great Community consists. Dewey allows for no privileged hiding places in this search for the public good. The private and the public spheres constitute different dimensions of human experience but *they are not opposed*. In finding their harmonic relations we establish what is best and most unique about ourselves. Thereby we abide in the highest good.

III

David Hall has called Richard Rorty the "Poet and Prophet of the New Prag-matism."[16] In *Contingency, Irony and Solidarity,* we find many of the reasons for such a description. It contains a sustained treatment of the relation be-tween the public and the private realms as well as Rorty's summation of the place of philosophy at the end of the twentieth century. Four important com-mitments underlie Rorty's position on the public good. As an historicist, he locates his own thought in time through the invention of a narrative. As an heir to the tradition of Anglo-American analytic philosophy, he adopts a causal theory of language that makes linguistic activity the creative factor in the mak-ing of human experience. As a convinced postmodernist, he sees the self as a centerless web of appetites and beliefs. Finally, as a liberal he calls for a strict separation of the public and the private realms. This results in an attitude to-ward the public good that he calls "liberal ironism." A major result of this new way of thinking pragmatically is the permanent scuttling of any content-filled concept of the public good. Philosophically speaking, he is therefore influen-tial in what I have called the disappearance of the public good. An examina-tion of his central ideas suggests why such a judgment is a fair one.

In inventing a narrative of the history of philosophy, Rorty seeks to "hold his time in thought."[17] His narrative serves the function of any myth: the organization and celebration of a worldview. Rorty's myth is a nominalist, historicist reading of our efforts to understand the universe and our place in it. Viewing the failure of the human race to gain a permanent and lasting grasp on reality, Rorty concludes that it is now time to accept and proclaim contin-gency as the permanent character of the human condition:

> I have been arguing in this book that we try *not* to want something which stands behind history and institutions. The fundamental premise of the book is that be-lief can still regulate action, can still be thought worth dying for, among people who are quite aware that this belief is caused by nothing deeper than contingent historical circumstances. My picture of a liberal utopia . . . was a sketch of a so-ciety . . . in which the notion of "something that stands behind history" has be-come unintelligible, but in which a sense of human solidarity remains intact.[18]

In *The Linguistic Turn, Philosophy and the Mirror of Nature,* and *Conse-quences of Pragmatism,* Rorty worked out the epistemological details of this myth. The general plot is as follows. Philosophy has finally come to realize that its aim to provide a pure and exact rendering of external reality (read na-ture) is bankrupt. It is time to accept the pragmatic conclusion that there are no final answers, but only context driven situations that require solutions trimmed to the circumstances of the time. Second, the efforts of analytic phi-losophy to resolve the dilemmas surrounding the relation of language to thought and reality teach a parallel truth. We are forever locked into linguistic experience. This new *a priori* turns language into a causal agent that forever shapes reality and makes a pure access to reality impossible. There is simply no way out of this situation. Neither is there a privileged epistemological starting point guaranteeing certainty and truth. Searches for foundations are futile. The myth expresses the final acceptance of contingency through Rorty's celebratory formulas:

- *Philosophy is to be succeeded by literature.*
- *Democracy precedes philosophy.*
- *Freedom takes the place of truth.*

Having finally lost its capital "P," Philosophy is now philosophy. This is a good thing, for now we can get on with the business of humankind—which turns out to be a conversation about important matters. Philosophy can help make it "edifying."

Rorty is quite serious about this conversation, since it is the way in which our various "final vocabularies" get to rub against each other. In so engaging each other, what can be hoped for is expansion of understanding, tolerance, and the enlargement of meaning. Rorty shares with the Sophists a preference for persuasion through rhetoric. In place of propositional logic and scientific discourse, we are to substitute clusters of thoughts. It is for this reason that the metaphors become so very important. Through them the general ideas guiding social and personal thinking gain concrete purchase in our consciousness. They are the food by which our values are nourished. Or if that metaphor does not help, metaphors are the threads through which we weave the tapestry of our lives. The tenor and tone of a philosophic position is more important than its content. Thus metaphor pushes aside reason and figurative language replaces logical schemata. In fact, given the inevitability of interpretative linguistic experience, human reality can only be viewed as shifting sets of metaphors that either fall away or gain credence with the historical vagaries of contingency. Rorty is a nominalist who sees metaphors extending "all the way down." The Great Metaphor makes clear the next cultural need. We are to move from a scientized culture to a poeticized one.

Poets and novelists come to fill the place once occupied by philosophers. It is they who make possible imaginative identification with the suffering of others and thereby move the world in the direction of moral progress. Likewise, it is they who provide novel images for self-enlargement within the private sphere. In a world without foundations, talk about "essences" and "nature" and "reason" and "truth" is self-defeating nostalgia for a world that never was. It is to the literary genius that we must now look for the creation of new realms of meaning. And within these worlds—created, for example, by a Dickens, or a Kundera, or a Whitman, or a Baudelaire—we can take up our abode as public citizens and private persons. The decidedly aesthetic cast of this way of thinking has its own appeal. It sounds very much like dimensions of Confucius and Dewey discussed earlier. Indeed, even the musky scent of the existential hero clings to this narrative. It is the poet and the novelist who forge worlds of meaning in the face of lost certainties and cruel historical facts. If it is not by bread alone that men live, then metaphor and fiction are sources of nutritional supplement.

The need to check our impulse to establish transcendental categories of being is another reason for a strict segregation between the public and the private realms. In the absence of any shared "human nature," attempts to prescribe what should or ought to be thought only serve to prevent the search for new communicative powers. Our loneliness needs the solidarity fashioned from a well-spun story, narrative, or metaphor, not the solace of some transcendent ahistorical reality. We come to understand our solidarity with others when we can understand their stories, but all stories start in private. To invade that space would be to choke off the possibility of the shared understanding we so desperately need and desire. We must leave the individual alone so that the act of creation can take place.

But there is another, perhaps even stronger, reason for walling off the private from the public. It is what David Hall has called "the search for private perfection."[19] If what we do with our personal lives is our business, then whatever destinies await are also the business of the private self. This should be obvious to those who agree with Rorty's vision of the self as a centerless web of beliefs and desires. Battered by the contingencies of life, "we liberals," as Rorty would put it, still try to enlarge our selves, master our contradictions, and make coherent our place in the world. It is a brave and losing battle.

There is also the linguistic fact that private and public vocabularies are never the same thing:

> The language of the private sphere is the language of individual self-creation. The language of the public is the language of pain and humiliation—how to recognize them, who suffers them most, and how they might be alleviated. The historicist (read "poetic narrativist") turn releases us from the metaphysical desire for freedom from time and chance. The contingencies thus recognized are now divided among those associated with the search for self-perfection and those involving the desire for social good.[20]

The line drawn between the private and the public spheres is a defense against interference in the process of self-creation.

What, then, is left for the public to concern itself with? Rorty answers that this is the liberal hour, the time when the general usefulness of the liberal doctrine of tolerance shows itself. Being a liberal in the last years of the twentieth century demands joining irony to tolerance so that "we liberals" become "the people who think that cruelty is the worst thing we do."[21] Irony involves not taking our own final vocabularies as ultimate so that we can remain open to others. Cruelty is understood as both the infliction of pain upon others and the act of humiliating them by redescribing their experience so that it can be comfortably assimilated into our own worldview. Pain is chosen as a defining property because it is the empirical touchstone through which we acknowledge the existence of the other.

We see then the importance of the poet and the novelist for the public sphere. Through their art, they make available to us the pain of others. They thereby sensitize us to our liberal obligation to eliminate pain or at least reduce it. They bring about the act of imaginative identification around which the possibility of solidarity revolves. It is at this point that the disappearance of the public good begins to happen. For Rorty would have us believe that it is only through a text—such as a poem or a novel—that we recognize pain. The public good disappears between the pages of a book. What is equally telling is that this public good lacks all specificity. It has no content save that of remarking the cruelty being experienced by an other. Nor does this sense of the public good make evident any positive obligations we owe to others. These others, it should be recalled, like ourselves, can bear no rights, since they are themselves contingent, centerless webs of desires and beliefs. "We liberals" have long ago given up the possibility of founding human rights on metaphysical principles.

Rorty agrees that his position creates dilemmas with respect to the relation between the private and the public domains. "But they are never going to be resolved by appeal to some, further higher set of obligations which a philosophical tribunal might discover and apply."[22] In the private realm we experience autonomy, self-creation, and whatever enlargements of meaning that may come our way. In the public sphere, we encounter the question of justice, the reality of political discourse, and the sphere of *praxis*. It is time we gave up Plato's dream of uniting the private and the public realms through the experience of justice. Like everything else, the public good is a contingent notion dependent upon the forms of discourse and metaphoric vocabularies operating at particular times and places.

> Just as there is nothing which validates a person's or a culture's final vocabulary, there is nothing implicit in that vocabulary which dictates how to reweave it when it is put under strain. All we can do is work with the final vocabulary we have, while keeping our ears open for hints how it might be expanded or revised.[23]

This move away from principles and theories seems very much like Dewey's insistence upon the importance of fruits and consequences for defining the public good. There is an openness to experience that sounds very much like John Dewey's insistence on the concrete historical situation as the starting point for philosophic efforts. Indeed, Rorty's demand that ethnocentric beliefs be fully honored is in line with Dewey's recognition of the importance of local experience for building the Great Community.[24] Then there is the decidedly aesthetic cast of Rorty's thinking about matters of public concern, a theme that parallels Dewey's recognition of the importance of communication.

Is Rorty's vision of solidarity an updated version of Dewey's search for the Great Community? Has Rorty managed to find a way to translate the "three items" of *The Great Learning* into the vocabulary of late twentieth century political theory? Has the public good now reappeared in the pages of a novel or the stanzas of a poem?

IV

Rorty speaks often of a changed intellectual climate that requires new approaches and new analytic tools. And he cites John Dewey as one source of his new pragmatism. I conclude with some reflections on the legitimacy of such a move.

The ultimate pragmatic question is: Will Rorty's redefinition of the public good work? I think not. The injunction to eliminate cruelty as the new meaning of the public good is far too neutral and lacking in content. Nowhere in his work does Rorty define cruelty. He must think that we share an intuitive understanding of what constitutes the infliction of cruelty on another. Furthermore, there is a total absence of situatedness in this definition of the public good. It expresses exactly the kind of vacuousness that Dewey condemned in his social and political thought. For example, *Contingency, Irony and Solidarity* appeared at the end of the 1980s. During that decade, America witnessed an extraordinary shift of wealth to the upper class. At the very same time, our cities were overcome with crime, violence, poverty, and drug abuse. Now that is a fact which, if Dewey were alive, would interest him very much. Nor do I think that he would have to read *Oliver Twist* in order to be motivated to do something about it.

Rorty's invocation to read literature as a mode of access to the public good is exactly the participatory intermediate social structure one should expect from bourgeois intellectualism. But there is something quite desperate about this strategy. It is a perfect example of the "clean hands" liberalism Dewey condemned. The problem is that Rorty's liberal utopia lacks rootedness. It is not about anything historical or concrete. It is simply a set of rules for getting along with others. By making a virtue out of a negative definition of justice ("don't be cruel"), it violates the first commandment of pragmatism: to take up the facts as they are and deal with them. Dewey's pragmatism was built upon a very rich concept of experience. Because of his background in Anglo-American analytic philosophy, Rorty confines his thought to a very thin strip of experiential reality, the linguistic event. This impoverishment is compounded by his endorsement of postmodernism's love of "the text."

But we experience far more than the text. What about freedom marches, labor rallies, voter registration drives, acts of shared effort, acts of love and compassion, feelings of brotherhood and sisterhood? These are not textual experiences, but they are experiences nonetheless. By confining experience to the text, Rorty leaves out the greater part of humankind. In so doing, he makes the charge of cultural elitism inevitable. Dewey, I believe, wanted to return "Philosophy" to the people. Rorty's response would, I suppose, be that "Philosophy" no longer exists, and whatever versions of "It" are around are not worth giving to the people. Or given his nominalism, he might even deny the existence of the "People."

By making the literary image so central, Rorty for all his good intentions, risks driving the public good even further from our consciousness. Images, no matter how engaging, only deliver partial aspects of reality.[25] They are judged by their capacity to grab our attention. Their goodness resides precisely in their power to engage. Consideration of their truth or falsehood is secondary. Any reader of Plato's simile of the divided line knows this. There lurks in images as much danger as opportunity. Suppose the wrong image is used. But according to Rorty, we have no way of talking about such things as right or wrong, true or false.

We can, however, talk about cruelty. It is precisely at this point that a great confusion of realms takes over Rorty's thought. He confuses "the nice" with "the good." And this confusion comes through the banishment of what Rorty terms "all those things that Heidegger calls metaphysics." Bereft of anything but a nominalist, historicist linguistic world, anxious to promote the freedom and creativity of the individual, and unwilling and unable to bring the private and the public spheres together, Rorty settles on tolerance as the meaning of the public good. It is no accident that the act of tolerance is prepared for by the reading of literature. "We liberals" can do this at any time or any place. There is a general harmlessness in this act of reading. No one even knows that it is going on. Nevertheless, through it we can persuade ourselves that we do know something of the plight of others. This definition of the public good is especially appealing to a highly protected, bourgeois elite (of which I, like Rorty, am a member). It is the public good as envisioned by a well-insulated university professor.

An antidote to this cultural elitism lies in pragmatism's metaphysical side. Dewey fixed on the act of experience with full seriousness. He saw in it the generic traits of reality and used them to develop a deep understanding of the basic dimensions of the human condition. Thus all aspects of human life—the private as well as the public—exhibit an engaged, transactional quality. No ultimate distinction is to be made between them. Just as the public good influences the private sphere, so also private achievements have direct bearing on public life. Human activity—be it private or public—is always and everywhere norm-driven. The refusal to examine the worthiness of those norms is an act of intellectual irresponsibility. As a functionalist, Dewey regarded such a discussion as central to the philosophical project. As a nominalist, Rorty thinks it is impossible.

What then of Confucius/Dewey/Rorty and the disappearance of the public good? There are, I believe, in the "three items" of Confucius and Dewey's "Search for the Great Community" sufficient philosophic resources to renew debate on the public good. Its disappearance within the pages of great literature is not the last word. What is required is a synoptic vision that sees the lines of continuity that span the private and the public realms. Engendering such a vision has always been the traditional function of metaphysics. Just as we know that what happens between the pages of a novel is not always true, so we also know that words of dismissal do not make things go away. Recovery of a metaphysics of experience is what is needed to renew the promise of Dewey's pragmatism. One consequence would be the reappearance of the public good as a measure of our abiding in the highest good. Manifesting the clear character and loving the people would surely follow.

In the end, I suspect it is a matter of the relative ontological status one is willing to accord images. Solidarity, as defined by Rorty, is negotiated entirely in and through images. Community, as understood by Confucius and Dewey, is also anchored in a world of felt meanings. But the sweep of interests and concrete attention to detail that mark the public good to be found in the Chinese sage and the classic American pragmatist are of an entirely different order. Community entails solidarity, but solidarity does not imply community. That is a difference that makes a difference in the fostering of the public good.

NOTES

1. See David Hall and Roger Ames, *Thinking Through Confucius* (Albany: State University of New York Press, 1987), pp. 12–17.

2. The term is used by Nietzsche in *Thus Spoke Zarathustra.*

3. *The Great Learning* in *A Source Book in Chinese Philosophy,* Wing Tsit Chan, ed. (Princeton: Princeton University Press, 1963), p. 86.

4. See Tu Wei-Ming's *Confucian Thought: Selfhood as Creative Transformation* (Albany: State University of New York Press, 1985) for a sustained treatment of this attitude. Anthony Cua, *The Unity of Knowledge and Action* (Honolulu: University of Hawai'i Press, 1982), shows the development of this attitude in the Neo-Confucianism of Wang Yang-ming. A similar unification of the private and public spheres can be found in the other wing of Neo-Confucianism. See Wing-Tsit Chan, "Chu Hsi and World Philosophy" in *Interpreting Across Boundaries,* G. J. Larson and E. Deutsch, eds. (Princeton: Princeton University Press, 1988), pp. 280–93.

5. The doctrine of harmony as essential to metaphysical thinking and political life is explained and defended in Robert Neville, *The Cosmology of Freedom* (New

Haven: Yale University Press, 1974). The political consequences of adopting such a metaphysics can be found in William M. Sullivan, *Reconstructing Public Philosophy* (Berkeley: University of California Press, 1986). One is struck by the close affinity between Sullivan's theory of communitarian and early American civic republicanism and the Confucian ideal of the "authoritative person."

6. See *Analects*, 4/15 in Chan, op. cit.

7. See Hall and Ames, op. cit. pp. 287, 289. Angus Graham makes a similar point about *jen* and *The Great Learning*. See A. C. Graham, *Disputers of the Tao* (La Salle: Open Court, 1989), pp. 132–34.

8. John Dewey, *The Public and Its Problems* (Denver: Alan Swallow, 1927). Hereafter *PP.*

9. *PP,* p. 27.

10. *PP,* p. 77.

11. Dewey's full commitment to Democracy is wonderfully developed in Stephen Rockefeller's *John Dewey: Religious Faith and Democratic Humanism* (New York: Columbia University Press, 1991).

12. *PP,* p. 58.

13. See *PP,* chap. V, "The Search for the Great Community."

14. *PP,* pp. 154–55.

15. *PP,* p. 147.

16. Hall has written a brilliant critical analysis of Rorty's place in American culture. See David Hall, *Richard Rorty: Poet and Prophet of the New Pragmatism* (Albany: State University of New York Press, 1994). I am indebted to him for much of my understanding of Rorty. I do not, however, think he would agree with all that I have to say about Rorty.

17. Ibid., pp. 11–64. The phrase is Hegel's.

18. Richard Rorty, *Contingency, Irony and Solidarity* (Cambridge: Cambridge University Press, 1989), pp. 189–90. Author's italics and quotation marks. Hereafter, *CIS.*

19. Hall, op. cit. pp. 230–36.

20. Ibid., p. 135.

21. *CIS,* p. xv.

22. *CIS,* p. 197.

23. *CIS,* p. 197.

24. *PP,* pp. 210–13. See Hall, op. cit. pp. 174–82 for a discussion of Rorty's commitment to ethnocentrism. In fairness to Rorty, what is at stake in this discussion is not the sincerity of his commitment to the public good, but rather its ultimate effectiveness. See Rorty's eloquent defense of the radical legal theorist Roberto Mangabeira Unger in *Essays on Heidegger and Others* (Cambridge: Cambridge University Press, 1991), pp. 177–92.

25. Mark Poster has amply demonstrated the alienating power of imagistic thinking in his *The Mode of Information* (Chicago: University of Chicago Press, 1990). Of course, the first work to explode the innocent goodness of images in public life was Daniel J. Boorstin, *The Image: A Guide to Pseudo-Events in America* (New York: Harper, 1961). It remains required reading for all those interested in metaphors, cluster thinking, and images.

David Loy

FREEDOM: A BUDDHIST CRITIQUE

The growth of freedom has been the central theme of history, Lord Acton believed, because it represents God's plan for humanity. One does not need
such a Whiggish view of history to notice that the history of the West, at least,
has indeed been a story of the development of freedom (whether actualized
or idealized). We trace the origins of Western civilization back to the Greek
"emancipation" of reason from myth. Since the Renaissance, there has been
a progressive emphasis, first on religious freedom, then political freedom, followed by economic freedom, colonial and racial freedom, and most recently
sexual and psychological freedom. Today deconstruction and other postmodern intellectual developments free us from authorial intention and the stric-
tures of the text itself—what might be called "textual liberation."

So it is no surprise that freedom today is the paramount value of the Western world and, through the West's influence, it is becoming that of the rest of
the world as well. But is this value losing some of its luster? The history of
freedom itself contains enough contradictions to make us pause. As important as the Renaissance was for the development of personal freedom, we also
see in it the roots of the problems that haunt us today—in particular, the extreme individualism that liberated greed as the engine of economic development and that continues to rationalize the destruction of community bonds.
The French, Russian, and Chinese revolutions resulted in Napoleon, Stalin,
and Mao, respectively, vindicating Burke's warnings about the sudden disintegration of even oppressive political authority. And today our technological
freedom to transform the natural world is causing such despoliation that we
are in danger of destroying ourselves as well. If freedom is our supreme value,
then it is a problematic one. This paper will explore that problematic from a
perspective derived from Buddhism. I shall argue that making freedom
into our *paramount* value is dangerous, for freedom conceived in secular,

309

humanistic terms is fatally flawed, because it does not and cannot give us what we seek from it.

Part of our resistance to such a conclusion is due to the difficulty of considering freedom objectively. The ideal of freedom is so deeply involved in the way we understand ourselves that it is hard to look *at* it. Yet this value has a complicated genealogy that needs to be examined. We need to ask why the ideal of freedom arose in the West, when and where it did. And how does that value contrast with the primary values of non-Western cultures?

Another difficulty is that the very concept of freedom is extremely elusive. It is almost impossible to define in a satisfactory fashion, for the simple reason that the abstract concept loses meaning outside particular contexts of freedom *from*. . . .or freedom *to*. . . . In his recent study *Freedom in the Making of Western Culture,* Orlando Patterson distinguishes what he calls the "chord" of freedom into three notes: personal (being able to do as one pleases within the limits of others' desire to do the same), sovereignal (the power to act as one pleases, regardless of the wishes of others), and civic (the capacity of members of a community to participate in its life and governance).[1] Such a tripartite definition already suggests the tensions that have dogged the history of freedom from the very beginning. If freedom is a chord, it is evidently an unresolved one. The unfortunate fact is that throughout history it has been much easier to fight for freedom than to live freely, and it still is. Why is that so?

Most studies of freedom emphasize that the West has made the major contributions to the theory and practice of freedom. Patterson's also attempts to explain why freedom did not evolve in the non-Western world. His short, preliminary analysis discusses North and South American Indian tribes, African preliterate societies, a group of South Pacific tribes, ancient Mesopotamia, and dynastic Egypt, yet curiously it does not consider India and China, philosophically the most sophisticated non-Western cultures and therefore the ones we would expect to offer the most interesting alternative perspectives on the Western understanding of freedom. In India, for example, *mukti* has long been acknowledged by almost all schools of thought as the highest spiritual goal.

Patterson follows the received wisdom in concluding that the West's value complex of freedom is "superior to any other single complex of values conceived by mankind."[2] We may raise some questions about this by bringing to bear the Buddhist critique of the ego-self: the supposedly self-existing subject which, because it understands itself as separate from the world, is preoccupied with liberating itself from the bonds that tie it to the world.

Central to Buddhist teachings is a denial of the self (*an-ātman*). I think Buddhism anticipated the reluctant conclusions of psychoanalysis: that guilt and anxiety are not adventitious but intrinsic to the ego. This is because our dissatisfaction with life derives from a repression even more immediate than death-fear: the suspicion that *"I" am not real.* For Buddhism, the ego is not a self-existing consciousness but a mental construction, a fragile sense-of-self dreading its own no-thing-ness. Our problem arises because "my" conditioned consciousness wants to ground itself—i.e., to make itself *real.* If the sense-of-self is a construct, however, it can real-ize itself only by objectifying itself in the world. The ego-self is this never-ending project to objectify oneself in some way, something consciousness can no more do than a hand can grasp itself or an eye see itself.

The consequence of this perpetual failure is that the sense-of-self has, as its inescapable shadow, a sense-of-*lack,* which it always tries to escape. In deconstructive terms, the ineluctable trace of nothingness in our non-self-present being is a feeling of *lack.* What Freud called "the return of the repressed" in the distorted form of a symptom shows us how to link this basic yet hopeless project with the symbolic ways we try to make ourselves real in the world. We experience this deep sense-of-*lack* as the feeling that "there is something wrong with me," yet that feeling manifests itself, and we respond to it, in many different ways: I'm not rich enough, not published enough, not loved enough, etc. Such anxiety is eager to objectify into fear *of* something, because we have particular ways to defend ourselves against particular feared things. The problem with objectifications, however, is that no object can ever satisfy us if it is not really an object we want.

In this way, Buddhism shifts our focus from sexual desire and the terror of future annihilation to the anguish of a groundlessness experienced here and now. The Buddhist solution to the sense-of-self's sense-of-*lack* is simple although not easy. If it is no-thing-ness I am afraid of (i.e., the repressed suspicion that, rather than being autonomous and self-existent, the "I" is a construct), the best way to resolve that fear is to confront what has been denied—i.e., to accept my no-thing-ness by becoming no-thing. Meditation involves learning how to become nothing by learning to forget one's self, which happens when I become absorbed into my meditation exercise. Consciousness *un*learns trying to grasp itself, objectify itself, real-ize itself. For Buddhism, then, the only genuine solution is a "spiritual" one—that is, one that addresses the root problem by my "letting go" of myself in order to realize my interconnectedness with all things.[3]

If this Buddhist perspective is valid, it has two very important implications for the way we view freedom. First, any culture that emphasizes the individuality of the self will inevitably come to place paramount value on the *freedom* of that self. Freedom is usually defined as *self*-determination, and etymology (*de + terminus,* to limit, to set boundaries) reveals its connotations of separation, of establishing boundaries between the self and the not-self. Hence it is not surprising that, from its very beginning, the Western history of freedom has been strongly associated with the development of the self or, to put it another way, with subject-object dualism. Insofar as freedom is understood as freedom from *external* control, a discrimination is implied between internal (that which wants to be free) and external (that which one is freed from). This is important because what Patterson calls the "stillbirth" of freedom outside the West is connected with the fact that non-Western societies have had different conceptions of the self and its relationship with the other.

The second implication, and my main working hypothesis, is that if the self-existence and autonomy of that sense-of-self is an illusion, as Buddhism claims, then such a self will never be able to experience itself as enough of a self; in particular, it will never feel free *enough*. It will try to resolve its *lack* by expanding the sphere of its freedom, which can never become wide enough to be comfortable. This leads to a special way of experiencing time. Unlike traditional societies which emphasize natural cycles and patterns established in the past, a culture of such individuals will be aware of transcending its past and will feel a need to transcend the present, making it *future-directed.* This dynamic helped to generate what we know as the history of the West: a never-ending quest for genuine, i.e., *complete,* personal freedom. But can there be such a thing, if there is no genuine self to have it? We shall see that this relationship between the self and its freedom explains much about the curious development of Western freedom and perhaps a great deal about our predicament today.

I

To understand the West, we must begin with what existed before the West. Recent historical studies have emphasized that the value placed on freedom was generated out of its opposite, the "social death" of slavery. Since slavery was so common, however, this by itself does not go very far to explain why social freedom developed only in the West.[4] The basic problem is that among nonslaves the existence of slavery reinforced the sense of group solidarity and participation, and what the slave desired was never freedom in our evolved Western sense (which would have been fatal, since there was no place for a "free" person in such societies) but reduced marginality and partial resocialization into the master's community.

This already shows something important about the relationship between the individual self and its valuation of freedom: there is no social context for esteeming freedom until there is a social role in which the individual can function *as* an individual. Dynastic Egypt provides a good example of this. As Max Weber noticed, the "prevailing rule would be 'no man without a master,' for the man without a protector was helpless. Hence the entire population of Egypt was organized in a hierarchy of clientages." For Weber this reveals "the essential characteristic of a liturgy-state: every individual is bound to the function assigned to him within the social system, and therefore every individual is in principle unfree."[5]

Just as important is the implication for what Patterson calls sovereignal freedom, the power to do utterly as one pleased with another person. In spite of the authoritarian nature of most human societies, such sovereignal freedom did not normally exist, because all social relationship existed within a network of countervailing powers (including divine powers that limited human *hubris*). This points to one of the tragic paradoxes that have dogged the history of the West: personal freedom and totalitarianism are not opposites but brothers, for the historical conditions that made democracy possible also made totalitarianism possible. The self-directed individual could evolve only through the destruction or weakening of the "hierarchy of clientages" or (in more tribal societies, including pre-Cleisthenes Athens) of kin-based lineages; yet the authority-vacuum that that creates can readily be manipulated by those in a position to seize absolute political power once they are no longer limited by countervailing social forces.

This point may be made another way: the breakdown of hierarchies and lineages allows for the development of more autonomous, self-directed individuals, but it also allows for the creation of the *masses*. That brings out another disturbing aspect of this paradox: the eagerness with which plebs repeatedly embrace their autocratic rulers. Dostoyevsky's Grand Inquisitor emphasizes that man has "no more pressing need than the one to find somebody to whom he can surrender, as quickly as possible, that gift of freedom which he, unfortunate creature, was born with." We are not born free—what freedom we have is the result of complex historical conditions—but Dostoyevsky's arrow is otherwise right on target: if freedom makes us anxious, the more free we are, the more anxious we will be, and the greater our need to resolve that anxiety—usually by surrendering it to some authority figure or father protector.

The psychoanalyst Otto Rank divided our anxiety into two complementary fears. Life fear is the anxiety we feel when we stand out too much, thereby losing our connection with the whole; death fear is the anxiety of losing one's personhood and dissolving back into the whole. "Whereas the life fear is anxiety at going forward, becoming an individual, the death fear is anxiety at going backward, losing individuality. Between these two fear possibilities the individual is thrown back and forth all his life."[6] This can just as well be expressed in terms of freedom: we feel the need to be free, but becoming more free makes us more anxious and therefore more inclined to sacrifice that freedom to someone who promises us security (absolution for our sense-of-*lack*). In sum, human beings have two great needs—freedom and security—and unfortunately they conflict. This explains the temptations of totalitarianism:

Totalitarianism is a cultural neurotic symptom of the need for community—a symptom in the respect that it is grasped as a means of allaying anxiety resulting from the feelings of powerlessness and helplessness of the isolated, alienated individuals produced in a society in which complete individualism has been the dominant goal. Totalitarianism is the substitution of collectivism for community.[7]

Yet there is another "solution" to this dialectic, or an opposite temptation: the members of a society may decide instead that they are not yet free enough, that they must struggle further to become *truly* free. Unfortunately, this approach threatens to become viciously circular because it denies us any solace in community bonds, insofar as we never can feel free enough. To express it in terms of our sense-of-*lack,* today one of our main ways to objectify our *lack* is by feeling that we are not yet as free as we deserve to be. This is not to deny that there are always many human wrongs that need to be human-righted, but this does give us some insight into, for example, the popularity of *victimhood* in the United States. Victimhood is learning how to address the problem of one's life by discovering how one is being exploited or has been abused, so that one's anger and self-pity become justified and socially acceptable. From a Buddhist point of view, however, this is dangerous, since rather than indicating how to overcome one's sense-of-*lack,* it reinforces one's delusive sense-of-self—as that which has been abused.

II

The Greeks developed the higher religion of the self—i.e., humanism—and they also discovered that religion does not work. The Greco-Roman experiment with secular humanism failed, not for extraneous historical reasons (e.g., the barbarian conquest of Rome) but because it self-destructed. Its distinctive contribution to the development of freedom (and the individual self) survived only as sublated in the Augustinian synthesis of Neoplatonic thought with Christian theology, which could cope with the greater anxiety of greater inwardness only by postulating the existence of original sin (stemming from Adam's misuse of freedom) that would be resolved only in the afterlife.

In "discovering" the eternal *psyche* that persists unchanged, early Greek thought also discovered the idea of eternal substance. That which was believed to persist unchanged (the *psyche*) sought that which was believed to persist unchanged (Being). Beginning with Parmenides, the idea arises that only that which is permanent can be grasped by genuine knowledge, for comprehending transient things provides only a semblance of knowledge. From a Buddhist point of view, however, the knowledge that the Greeks sought was from the beginning a delusion, the glorious but vain quest of a constructed individual to ground itself by discovering the Ground of all things.

In setting up reason as the method whereby this *psyche* and this Being may be discovered, the Greek thinkers opened the door to what proved to be a blind alley. Despite its other fruits, rationality does not provide a handle to grasp and resolve the sense-of-self's sense-of-*lack*. The new religions of the self that tried to do so, such as Epicureanism and Stoicism, eventually reached a dead end in the speculations of Epictetus and Marcus Aurelius. Yet Neoplatonic emphasis on subjective inwardness survived in the Augustinian emphasis on the self's essential sinfulness. Sin required constant watchfulness and introspection, thus deepening the self's introversion, and it provided that self with a way to understand and cope with the deeper sense-of-*lack* shadowing it. Faith that this *lack* will be overcome (initially, in the return of Christ and the coming of heaven that his return would inaugurate) generated a future-orientation which would continue long after that faith had yielded to more secular hopes and preoccupations.

We have seen that in traditional societies *lack* was usually dissolved by integrating the individual into the social structure. In such cases, the issue of freedom does not arise because the individual does not exist. Questions about the meaning of one's life also do not arise because human society is likewise integrated into the cosmos, often through the vital role played by a priest-king in helping to maintain the cosmos. In such societies, there is no clear distinction between sacred and secular, which tends to preempt social revolution.

Insofar as this pattern was widespread, it is rather our distinction between sacred and secular that seems curious. What needs explaining is not the integration of secular with sacred but the split between them—i.e., the belief in a *transcendence* as that which is distinct from and superior to the natural world. Elsewhere I have argued that the category of transcendence is important for explaining the differences between South Asia (India) and East Asia (China and Japan).[8] In order to see this, however, transcendence must be understood to have at least three related but different meanings: as another "higher" reality, such as God or Brahman; as ethical universal or absolute, such as the Mosaic Decalogue (usually derived from a higher reality); and (remembering its etymology: *trans* + *scendere*, to climb over, to rise above) as that perspective by which we "rise above" the given in order to observe it critically and gain the leverage to change it. Although these three types tend to reinforce each other, Indian transcendence emphasizes the first, Hebrew transcendence the second, and Greek transcendence the third.

Why did explicitly transcendental perspectives arise in these places and not, for example, in Egypt or Mesopotamia or Japan?

"Transcendence," whether it takes the form of divine revelation or of theoretical cosmology, implies a search for authority outside the institutionalized offices and structures of the seeker's society. Even its most concrete form, the law code, implies a transfer of authority from the holders of office to the written rule. Transcendental impulses therefore constitute, by definition, an implicit challenge to traditional authority and indicate some dissatisfaction with it. . . . [N]ew transcendental visions are . . . likely to be presented by persons in a precariously independent, interstitial—or at least exposed and somewhat solitary—position in society. . . . [9]

In India a two-stage process created these conditions: first the Vedic development of complicated rituals led to the differentiation of priest from king, and then a new social role appeared—the renouncer who, being outside of traditional society, invented or discovered a "discipline of salvation,"[10] e.g., Sakyamuni, the founder of Buddhism, and Mahavira, the founder of Jainism. In Israel the "interstitial" Hebrew prophets, especially Amos, Isaiah, and Jeremiah, developed the ethical monotheism in the Mosaic covenant by fulminating against the impious people and their rulers.

While it is futile to seek the necessary and sufficient historical causes for Greek self-consciousness, we can observe how a number of factors reinforced each other to promote their particular type of transcendence. Generally, the Greek distinction between sacred and secular may be traced back to the "emanicipation" of reason from myth and the correlative distinction between *nomos* (convention) and *physis* (nature). Humphreys finds the necessary precondition for such a transcendental perspective on society in the privileged and relatively independent position of axial-age intellectuals, such as the sophists, whose special linguistic skills provided "the ability to recreate social relationships and manipulate them in thought."[11] Thales, Pythagoras, Herodotus, Democritus, Plato, and other pioneer thinkers traveled to other cultural centers such as Egypt and Babylon (and India?) to add to their learning. Exposure to different influences and contradictory customs encouraged skepticism toward their own myths. Thales founded natural philosophy when he did not use gods to explain the world. Unlike Moses, Solon, in giving Athens new laws, did not receive them from the gods. And in his funeral oration, a profoundly religious occasion, Pericles did not even mention the gods but celebrated the virtues of Athenian democracy.

One does not escape the gods so easily, however. Psychologically they serve a crucial function. We ground ourselves in a mythological worldview because it organizes the cosmos for us: it explains who we are, why we are here, and what we should be doing with our lives. In the process, our mythology usually explains what our *lack* is and how it can be resolved. If its vision becomes too fanciful or constrictive, its disappearance is likely to be worse, because that not only liberates the self, it also liberates our *lack*. And that points to the problem with Greek humanism and rationalism as an alternative: it did not and could not work insofar as it did not show the sense-of-self how to resolve its sense-of-*lack*; instead, the increased individuality of the Greeks aggravated their *lack*.

This accounts for what we now know about the "harmonious Greeks." Since Burckhardt and Nietzsche, it has become undeniable that the Greeks were not Apollonian but profoundly anxious and troubled, "an unusually energetic, restless, turbulent people, given to excess," who idealized harmony and balance because it was a virtue they rarely achieved. As Thucydides noticed, they "were born into the world to take no rest themselves, and to give none to others."[12] Greek competitiveness exceeded even our own. Despite their lack of lawyers, the Athenians were perhaps the most litigious people that ever lived, once they discovered that in this way one could conquer one's opponents without resorting to violence. In the fourth century B.C., only three Athenian generals were killed in battle, while at least six (perhaps eight) were sentenced to death in the Athenian courts, not for treason but for losing a battle.

The cultured flowering that continues to awe us is easier to appreciate in retrospect. Because it so fundamentally challenged the old ways of doing things, the explosion of creativity was profoundly disturbing to many people at the time. Most progressive thinkers were tried for heresy: Anaxagoras, Diagoras, Socrates, probably Protagoras and Euripides; later Plato and Aristotle wisely absented themselves. No one suggested liberating the slaves or emancipating women. When Athens became democratic, it became not less but more imperialistic and genocidal, as the Peloponnesian War demonstrates—which is to say that collectively the Athenians' impulses toward greed and domination may actually have been increased by the fact that they had evolved a new mode of self-governance.[13]

Such criticisms tend to be anachronistic. We should not criticize the Athenians for not living up to democratic principles that they were just beginning to develop. It is not surprising that there was no check on mob-rule, for the problem with mob-rule needed to be experienced for checks to be perceived as necessary. The concept of human rights requires a more evolved sense of autonomous personhood and the sanctity of the self, along with the development of empathy and altruism in place of the "stranger anxiety" predominant in classical Greece. Nevertheless, the problems mentioned above are precisely the sort to be expected if the increase in self-consciousness were shadowed by an equivalent increase in anxiety—i.e., *lack*. When this *lack*—the feeling that "something is wrong with me"—is not resolved in a sacred worldview that answers my doubts with a faith that grounds me in the cosmos, I try to ground myself in more individualistic, self-ish ways.

How did the more thoughtful members of Athenian society react to these developments? Aeschylus was proud of having fought in the Persian War that saved Athens from foreign domination, yet Euripides wrote his last unfinished play in exile, bemoaning that "we are slaves to the masses" and affirming popular kingship as an alternative. Most important for us, of course, were the responses of Plato and Aristotle. We do not know how much the former's political views were colored by his personal experience of Socrates' trial and execution, yet there is no doubt about his dislike of democracy, which he dismissed as "an agreeable, anarchic form of society, with plenty of variety, which treats all men as equal whether they are equal or not." The main concern of *The Republic* is the problem with city-state democracy; it addresses the root of the problem by analyzing the democratic personality, which lacks a coherent organizing principle and therefore follows the strongest pressures of the moment—a recipe for internal strife.[14] Aristotle is almost as critical of the democracies in which he lived, for "in these extreme democracies, each man lives as he likes—or, as Euripides says, 'For any end he chances to desire'."[15] He prefers a mixed constitution combining the best of oligarchy and democracy.

These elitist views were a response to changing social realities. If the fifth century was one of civic freedom, the fourth century (which began with Socrates' execution) increasingly became that of individual freedom and self-indulgence as the integrity of the *polis* declined in favor of the concern for personal advancement, which came to preoccupy those who controlled economic life and many of those who controlled political affairs. Demosthenes lamented that politics had become the path to riches, for individuals no longer placed the state before themselves but viewed the state as a way to promote their own personal wealth.

The consequences of this for Greek thought were profound. About the end of the fifth century—that is, at the same time as the development just mentioned—philosophical discourse on freedom took a radically new turn: a critical distinction was made between outer and inner freedom. Socrates' emphasis on knowledge—by means of which man can share in the universal and eternal—paved the way, by urging men to place their passions and impulses under the control of self-reflection. In the context of the philosophical inquiry that was primary for him and his successors—a search for the Truth about the human soul and human society—democracy had failed. But instead of freedom being renounced, it came to be redefined. *The Republic* makes a momentous analogy between harmony in the state and harmony in the soul. Internalizing the Greek sociological understanding of freedom and slavery as requiring each other, Plato came to conceive of reason as the master (hence the free party) with desire and emotion as its slaves. The virtue of freedom was retained by reconceptualizing it in terms of the self-mastery of self-consciousness. In contrast to the incoherent life of the democrat, who lived "for any end he chances to desire," the psychic tendencies of the spiritually developed individual harmonize with each other because they are governed by reason. Rather than solving the growing problem with civic freedom, however, this aggravated it. Like the merchants and politicians who retreated into the more private world of their own self-advancement, those who succeeded Plato retreated from commitment to the *polis* into the more private world of abstract thought, which for them became the only method by which *true* freedom may be gained. "Post-Aristotelian ethical philosophy was marked by a clean break between morality and society, by the location of virtue firmly within the individual soul."[16]

Restated in terms of *lack*, the democratic experiment in self-government had not worked to resolve the increased anxiety that the increased individualism of the "democratic personality" generated, for the self-governance of the *demos* clearly did not entail the self-governance of the *self*. Just as the sophists had realized that the state is a construction that can be reconstructed, so those after Socrates realized that the *psyche* is a construction that can be reconstructed, with reason as the master. And the aggravated sense-of-*lack* that shadowed increased individualism required such psychic reconstruction.

Needless to say, that reconstruction did not appeal to many. This meant that new gods besides reason would have to be found. In the early Hellenistic age, the cult of *Tyche* ("Luck" or "Fortune") became widely diffused. In the second century B.C., astrology suddenly became popular. In the first century B.C., people became increasingly preoccupied with techniques of individual salvation:

> There was a growing demand for occultism, which is essentially an attempt to capture the Kingdom of Heaven by material means—it has been well described as "the vulgar form of transcendentalism." And philosophy followed a parallel path on a higher level. Most of the schools had long since ceased to value the truth for its own sake, but in the Imperial Age they abandon[ed], with certain exceptions [notably Plotinus], any pretence of disinterested curiosity and presented[ed] themselves frankly as dealers in salvation.[17]

Dodds' conclusion is hard to dispute: "once before a civilized people rode to the jump—rode to it and refused it."[18] The great experiment of Greek rationalism, as a humanistic alternative to religion and superstition, had failed.

In retrospect, the fateful Platonic move was equating freedom with reason and understanding psychic reconstruction in terms of the domination of reason. The immediate philosophical heirs to this were Cynicism, Epicureanism and Stoicism, which developed into religions of the self, straddling between more conventional religions and philosophy as we know it today, the search for propositional truth. In place of salvation through ecstatic mysteries they offered a salvation to be gained from rational self-cultivation, but they are just as much religions insofar as they are designed to cope with the personal *lack* caused, as they now understood it, by the self's desires and passions. Their ultimate aim was *autarkeia,* inner freedom from negative emotions and their entanglements. For the Stoics the soul of the sage was in a permanent *apatheia,* absence of excessive emotions, and for the Epicureans the ideal psychic state was *ataraxia,* imperturbability of spirit. The aim of their theorizing was to contribute to the development of such states of tranquillity, which they equated with *autarkeia*. The metaphor of fortress became common. As the cynic Antisthenes put it, "Wisdom is the safest wall, and a fortress must be constructed of our own impregnable reason." But the sense-of-self's sense-of-*lack* remained a fifth column that no fortress could defend against.

The irony of their goal is that, insofar as they worked to develop and preserve the self's freedom from emotional bonds to the external world, they also contributed to the further bifurcation of self from other, of subject from object, that aggravated the sense-of-*lack*. The three stoas of Stoicism reflect this increasing introversion. The first stoa emphasized harmony between self and cosmos. The second stoa was more concerned about whether the *psyche* controls the body. And the third stoa became preoccupied with the personal freedom of the self-controlled individual, as described in the *Discourses* of Epictetus and the *Meditations* of Marcus Aurelius.

And just how *lack*-free was the self-controlled individual? Marcus Aurelius always held the deepest reverence for Epictetus, but when Epictetus, after one of his discourses on "the road which leads to freedom," was asked point-blank if he himself were truly free, he had to admit that while he wanted and prayed to be so, he was still "not able to look into the face of masters." Yet he could point to someone who is, or was: Diogenes the Cynic, who had died over four hundred years earlier! Evidently none of the Stoic masters had achieved it.[19]

Patterson explains the ultimate failure of Epictetus and Aurelius even by their own criteria.

> The uniqueness of Marcus and Epictetus was in searching not so much for freedom as for the source of the yearning for, and meaning of, freedom. Shifting the terrain from the outer to the inner world was the beginning, not the end, of the struggle.[20]

By both the philosophical and the conventional standards of his time, Marcus the Roman emperor should have been one of the freest men who ever lived; what his *Meditations* unwittingly reveal, then, is how little such freedom meant, both his sovereignal dominion and the reason-able freedom developed by his self-control. With him the Stoic tradition culminates in the realization that such freedoms do not bring personal fulfillment or peace of mind. In my Buddhist terms, they cannot resolve one's sense-of-*lack*.

The increased introversion entailed by psychic reconstruction enlarged the sphere of one's subjectivity, but identifying that freedom with reason provided no way to cope with the increased sense-of-*lack* shadowing it. Freedom understood in such secular terms proved to be unsuccessful. And so the stage was set for return to a more explicitly religious perspective: the

Augustinian discovery/construction of sin. If even the internal freedom of dominant reason does not satisfy, but freedom still remains one's ultimate value, then there must be yet another, even more internalized kind of freedom.

III

To understand the failure of classical humanism is to appreciate the importance of Augustine, who salvaged the inwardness of its enhanced subjectivity and bequeathed it to the Western tradition that developed after him and out of him. He was able to recuperate and revitalize this interiority of self-presence because he added a new element, or perspective: the awareness of sin, and particularly the incorrigibility of original sin. Sin provided precisely what the classical Greco-Roman tradition lacked, a way to understand and cope with the sense-of-*lack* that shadows the groundless sense-of-self. Human beings have been dislocated by an ancient Fall. Now I know what is wrong with me: I have sinned. And now I know what must be done: I must atone for my sins (including that of our father, Adam) and strive to sin no more in the future. The classical emphasis on reason is replaced by the primacy of will, a faculty unknown to the Greeks; the problem of reason, error, is superseded by the problem of will, which is sin. The rigorous self-examination and never-ending watchfulness that that required encouraged an ever-deepening inwardness exemplified in Augustine's own *Confessions*.

Yet there is an important difference between the Christian understanding of sin and my Buddhist understanding of *lack*. Belief in sin does not actually show the way to resolve *lack*; rather, one's anxiety is short-circuited by the belief that one's *lack* will (or can be) alleviated in the future. For the first Christians, this would happen at the Second Coming, which had been imminent but which by Augustine's time was becoming attenuated into a more generalized preoccupation with the future.

Augustine played a crucial role in this development. In his early years as a Manichaean and then a Neoplatonist, he shared the classical belief in the possibility of self-perfection. With his conversion to Christianity, he brought Neoplatonic free will with him: man is the author of his own degradation. Yet postulating an original sin made this degradation more foundational and difficult to cope with, as he himself soon discovered. The extraordinary book ten of the *Confessions* "is not the affirmation of a cured man; it is the self-portrait of a convalescent."[21] But the convalescent never fully recovered. What became distinctive in Augustine's religious attitude was "a sharp note of unrelieved anxiety about himself and a dependence upon his god." The later sermons and letters reflect his terrible realization

> that he is doomed to remain incomplete in his present existence, that what he wished for most ardently would never be more than a hope, postponed to the

final resolution of all tensions, far beyond this life. . . . All a man could do was
to "yearn" for this absent perfection, to feel its loss intensely, to pine for it.[22]

For Augustine, then, true freedom could only culminate a long process of
healing—a process so difficult that we cannot expect it to conclude during our
lifetime. But if perfection is not attainable in this life, it must be postulated as
attainable somewhere else: there must be a future state, after death, in which
our *lack* can be resolved. The stage was set for the medieval church. As God's
agent on earth, it gained a monopoly on the future dispensation of *lack*.

This was a complex, many sided legacy. Sin offered a way—indeed, developed a spiritual technology—to cope with *lack*, but the increasing subjectivity it promoted also deepened the sense-of-*lack* that needed to be coped with,
as the example of Augustine himself shows. According to how it was handled,
sin could liberate you from considerable anxiety or enmesh you more tightly
in labyrinths of self-doubt and self-hatred. Understood metaphorically, the
doctrine of original sin contained at its core an invaluable grain of liberating
truth: our sense-of-*lack* is the price of our individuality and freedom; my *lack*
teaches me that I am not self-present, but conditioned by something that it
is my spiritual responsibility to dis-cover. Understood more literally, original
sin enslaves my incipient freedom to those religious institutions that claim to
control its dispensation. Yet the radical inward turn Augustine encouraged,
by seeking God within, opened the door for the genuine spiritual freedom of
the great Christian mystics, such as St. Francis and Eckhart, who discovered
what according to Buddhism is the only true way to resolve our *lack*: liberation from self in nondual union with something greater than the self, a loss of
self-preoccupation that can lead to identifying oneself with all creation—not
only with the needy and sick, but with Brother Sun and Sister Moon.

IV

When we remember that the transcendental is, most fundamentally, that
which provides a perspective on the world and leverage for changing it, we
can see that transcendence has not disappeared from the modern West.
Rather, the transcendental dimension has been internalized in the supposedly autonomous, self-directed individual who began to develop again at the
end of the Middle Ages. The "rebirth" of Europe occurred when traditional
Christian answers to questions of ultimate meaning and *lack* no longer satisfied the cultural elites who went on to find or make their own solutions to the
problem of life. Luther encouraged this by sanctifying a more private relationship with God. Instead of believing in the corporate church as the means
to resolve *lack* and gain salvation, now everyone must work it out for oneself.
Personally having a direct line to Transcendence provides the leverage to

challenge all worldly authority, religious institutions as well as secular ones. Convinced he was following God's will, Luther refused to be silenced: "Here I stand; I can do no other." This sanctioned the principle that one's personal understanding and moral principles can provide an appropriate perspective from which to confront social structures. Thus Luther was more than a prophet: after him everyone had to become his or her own prophet.

Eventually God could abdicate, because by then his role had been largely assumed by the self-sufficient self-consciousness that Descartes described. The result was the Cartesian self: an increasingly anxious individual who relied on his or her own judgment, who measured the world according to his or her own standards, and who did not hesitate to use his or her own resources to challenge the present situation, the social environment as much as the physical one. A condition of this, of course, was personal freedom, which became and remains our paramount value.

But what does all this mean for *lack* today? For all the problems with sin, at least it taught a way to cope with the feeling that "something is wrong with me." Today, although our sense-of-self (and therefore our sense-of-*lack*) is stronger than ever, and although our subjective alienation from the objectified world is greater than ever, we no longer believe in sin. Therefore, we lack an effective, socially agreed upon way to understand and deal with our *lack*— which means that it tends to manifest in individualistic ways that further weaken community bonds and relationships. One of these, the need for greater freedom, has already been noticed: if freedom is our ultimate value, then when we feel that something is wrong with us, it must be that we are not yet free enough. This route is dangerous because it tends to become a vicious circle. It offers no resolution of *lack*, only its aggravation.

Suddenly, however, we find ourselves in a radically different situation which is beginning to transform our valuation of freedom. Like it or not, our paramount value must be reexamined from a new perspective. The ecological degradation of the earth, which is already damaging our own well-being and perhaps threatens our own survival, has superseded other problems. This situation cannot be understood in terms of, or be solved by, our need for greater freedom. On the contrary, freedom in this case is the problem, insofar as the human species has attempted to enlarge the sphere of its own "sovereignal" freedom by reshaping the whole earth into its own image.

I am amazed that, although the ecological crisis is already seriously degrading the natural cycles upon which we all depend, life otherwise goes on almost normally—it is, quite literally, business as usual. No doubt our habitual ways of thinking continue to be circumscribed by our consumerism, and our attention distracted by high-tech media addictions, but I think there is another problem: the environmental crisis is running up against the basic parameters of Western civilization, which has viewed progress in freedom as the solution to everything. As many have emphasized, what we need today is not a Declaration of Independence but a Declaration of Interdependence, which tempers our understanding of freedom by emphasizing that "complete" freedom is a delusion too dangerous to tolerate anymore.

To conclude in a slightly facetious way, what we need now is freedom from freedom—i.e., from our need for greater freedom. What we need, in other words, is responsibility. None of this denies the importance of freedom, any more than the Buddhist critique of self can be used to rationalize an Egyptian-like hierarchy of clientages. Yet it shows us that our understanding of freedom, like that of the self which values it, needs to be contextualized. The history of classical humanism and our present situation both show the problems that occur when the self and its freedom are understood solely in secular terms. Instead of being devalued, however, they can be redefined in "spiritual" terms, since that is what the *lack* of self requires. From a Buddhist perspective, our *lack* cannot be resolved in any other way, for the problem with the self that *lack* reveals also points to our need to discover what grounds the self if the self is not self-grounding. According to Buddhism, this quest can lead to the discovery of a different type of freedom, one that is necessary to empower our other freedoms: freedom from *lack*.

NOTES

1. Orlando Patterson, *Freedom in the Western World* (New York: Basic Books, 1991), p. 3.

2. Ibid., pp. 402–3.

3. For more on this, see David Loy, *Lack and Transcendence: Death and Life in Psychotherapy, Existentialism and Buddhism* (Atlantic Highlands: Humanities Press, 1995).

4. This does not mean that slavery was an integral part of many social economies. According to M. I. Finley, *Ancient Slavery and Modern Ideology* (New York: Viking Press, 1980), p. 9, there have been only two genuine slave societies outside of the Americas—classical Greece and classical Italy. If Finley is correct, it implies that the world's first democracy generated the world's first slave economy. The slave economy of Athens was a consequence of Solon's reforms, which gave political and economic rights to the *demos*. The loss of such a large source of involuntary labor was compensated by the decision to import large numbers of slaves from outside Athens, a solution welcomed by the *demos*. This explains the Greek understanding of freedom and slavery as opposites that require each other.

5. Quoted in *Freedom in the Western World,* pp. 36, 37.

6. Otto Rank, "Life Fear and Death Fear," quoted in Irvin Yalom, *Existential Psychotherapy* (New York: Basic Books, 1980), pp. 141–42.

7. Rollo May, *The Meaning of Anxiety* (New York: Norton, 1977), p. 212.

8. David Loy, "Transcendence East and West," *Man and World* (vol. 26, no. 4, December 1993), pp. 403–27.

9. S. C. Humphreys, "'Transcendence' and Intellectual Roles: The Ancient Greek Case," *Daedalus* (Spring 1975: a special issue on "Wisdom, Revelation, and Doubt: Perspectives on the First Millennium B.C."), pp. 92, 112.

10. Louis Dumont, "On the Comparative Understanding of Non-Modern Civilizations," *Daedalus* (Spring 1975), pp. 162–65.

11. "'Transcendence' and Intellectual Roles," p. 111.

12. Thucydides, *History of the Peloponnesian War,* I.10.

13. See Eli Sagan, *The Honey and the Hemlock: Democracy and Paranoia in Ancient Athens and Modern America* (New York: Basic Books, 1991), chap. 11 and passim.

14. Plato, *The Republic,* 565d, 561c–d.

15. Aristotle, *Politics,* trans. Ernest Barker (Oxford: Oxford University Press, 1958), 1310a.

16. *Ancient Slavery and Modern Ideology,* p. 120.

17. E. R. Dodds, *The Greeks and the Irrational* (Berkeley: University of California Press, 1951), pp. 242, 246, 248.

18. Ibid., p. 254.

19. Epictetus, *Discourses,* 4.1.

20. *Freedom in the Western World,* p. 278.

21. Peter Brown, *Augustine of Hippo* (Berkeley: University of California Press, 1969), p. 177.

22. Ibid., pp. 123, 156.

Michael Barnhart

BUDDHIST ETHICS AND SOCIAL JUSTICE[1]

It is hard to connect political theory or even ethics generally, in its Western philosophical guise, with Buddhism. And it is even harder to connect concepts of social justice with Buddhism. This is not to say that Buddhism lacks moral content. On the contrary, there are a wide range of Buddhist moral concerns, but they tend to bear on the process either attaining enlightenment for oneself or assisting others to do so, and rarely on the organization of society or the legal regulation of conduct within the society.

Recently, two attempts have been made to forge a connection, however. One comes from the perspective of a political theorist and the other from that of a Buddhist philosopher. The first is Fred Dallmayr's provocative suggestion that the Buddhist concept *śūnyatā* may have application in a nonessentialist "grounding" of democratic political structures and institutions.[2] The second is Abe Masao's extension of the Zen concept of self-awakening[3] to embrace a notion of global sovereignty.[4]

What is different and interesting in these two approaches is their insistence on focusing on the social-political aspects of Buddhist ethics. Dallmayr does so by articulating the political consequences of the concept of *śūnyatā* (emptiness), and Abe does so by addressing the question of the legitimate site of power or sovereignty covered by the Zen notion of "self-awakening." Both emptiness and self-awakening are part of the Mahāyāna Buddhist tradition specifically, and hence this discussion represents a departure from the more frequent treatment of these issues from the vantage point of Theravāda Buddhism.[5]

I

In "Hegemony and Democracy,"[6] Fred Dallmayr offers a sympathetic appraisal of *Hegemony and Socialist Strategy: Towards a Radical Democratic Politics* by Ernesto Laclau and Chantal Mouffe. According to Dallmayr, Laclau and Mouffe attempt to de-essentialize political categories or present a systematic rationale for doing so through an examination of the emergence of the concept of hegemony as an important feature of late Marxist or post-Marxist political theorizing. Thus they both justify and trace the progress of an emerging nonessentialism that challenges the once dominant economic determinism within Marxist thinking. The other target of such critique is the ontologizing of class identities, especially the favored working class. Basically, if the working class is both a real entity and the fountainhead of historical development, then there is no problem of hegemony in political life. Either the forces of history will work to elevate the working class to hegemonic status or, according to later Marxist critique, the ability of revolutionaries to articulate a working class identity and consciousness will create the necessary conditions for such hegemony. In any case, the problem of hegemony remains unformulated; it is a pseudo-problem at best.

By Laclau and Mouffe's account, hegemony cannot help but become a tremendous problem. Why? Well, for essentially postmodern reasons. As Dallmayr nicely puts it, "social formations are not causally fixed but the result of a symbolic fusion of plural meaning."[7] Social meanings are discursively adumbrated by what are called "articulatory practices," which means not merely intellectual but also behavioral activities in a social setting. Because the setting is social and beyond the scope of merely intellectual doings, as Dallmayr notes, such "articulatory enterprises . . . only selectively structure the social domain without reaching definitive closure."[8]

In other words, because the ontological categories and historical analysis of Marxist thinking are fundamentally discursive, they cannot but be part of the contestation that takes place on the social stage. They are true only to the extent that they can be made true through political as opposed to merely historical action. History, class, and so on are categories that require articulatory practices and as such have to compete for the social stage. Furthermore, they will be constitutively indebted to those forces involved in "the symbolic fusion of plural meanings." Additionally, such categories can only hope to "selectively structure the social as all meaning takes shape within a 'surplus' of plural meaning, polysemy." Hence, the degree to which Marxist categories are politically relevant is the degree to which political hegemony will always be a central rather than a marginal concern (as it has been in the past).

In terms of political staging, Dallmayr suggests that the account of Laclau and Mouffe commits them to a version of hyperliberalism and radical democracy, tendencies which are increasingly visible in contemporary thought. As Dallmayr notes,

> such struggles, they write, should locate themselves fully in the field of the democratic revolution and its expanding chains of equivalence; their task, in any case, cannot be to renounce liberal-democratic ideology, but on the contrary, to deepen and expand it in the direction of a radical and plural democracy.[9]

Further, they suggest that socialism has been ill-equipped to pursue this strategy and ambivalent about political engagement "due to its hankering for an 'essentialistic apriorism'."[10]

What seems to interest Dallmayr in all of this is the emergent view of the political as involving a concept of negativity or an interplay between positive and negative metaphysical principles. On the one hand, a "logic of difference" is deployed in the self-definitions that locate one on the political field. On the other hand, a logic of "equivalence" reduces all such distinctions to an equal ambiguity in the attempt to structure and fix the "social" by their means. Insofar as one succeeds in projecting constitutive categories onto the social, thus creating an identity, the forces of negativity (and differentiation) subvert the very meaning of these structuring categories. By negativity, Dallmayr means "the polysemy of meanings and the shifting parameters of social-political options and goals."[11] These are always irreducibly plural and ground any logic of difference that seeks to create an embracing vision of the social. Thus Dallmayr identifies this social logic of equivalence with a "nihilating force, which, on contesting positive integration, simultaneously nihilates or empties itself, thus cancelling its own predominance."[12]

From a Buddhist point of view, such a "logic" is extremely interesting, as Dallmayr observes, for it nicely encapsulates what is often termed the self-emptying of emptiness (*śūnyatā*). In short, it is a form of negativity that is quite congenial to the seemingly paradoxical concepts of *śūnyatā* and absolute nothingness. Emptiness (as well as absolute nothingness) has always been viewed as deeply problematic if understood as a purely negative formal principle. And whenever emptiness is talked about in Buddhist contexts, it is always in connection with positive principles such as form or suchness (*tathatā*). So, for example, the *Heart Sutra* claims that emptiness is not other than form and vice versa, and Nagarjuna proclaimed in his *Karikas of the Middle Way* that emptiness (*śūnyatā*) and the mutual dependence of all things (*pratītyasamutpāda*) were indeed nondifferent (which is not to say strictly identical). However expressed, the key view has routinely been that the universal emptiness of things does not mean their elimination or nihilation. *Śunyavada* is not nihilism. Rather, the emptiness of things (in general) means their essential codependence or mutual co-arising—and I would emphasize "essential." Or one could say that all relations are internal relations without constituting a closed system. What this means is not only that things lack their "own nature" or *svabhāva,* but that they also lack a fixed nature. Hence, the nature of things or reality is not amenable to analysis by means of fixed conceptual categories or designations. Consequently, any attempt to assert hegemony through meaning over a particular range of phenomena is by its very nature self-defeating, for what can escape the relational interdependence emptiness involves? Even the very concept of *śūnyatā,* if there is one, is subject to this dynamic of self-emptying. That is, should one try to fix the meaning of such dependence by reference to a particular set of relations or a formal account of relationality, the very meaning of emptiness and dependence is lost. In much the same way, on Laclau and Mouffe's account, the attempt to fixate the nature of the social or of a society will equally fail to capture or maintain hegemonic status. Hegemony, by its very nature, will shift in our attempt to assert it through the political process. (I suppose either by force or by persuasion.)

It is this similarity in pattern that captures Dallmayr's attention and leads him to talk suggestively of "the emptiness of the democratic public space." Interpreting emptiness in the Buddhist sense as the ultimate rejection of essentialism and adopting Claude Lefort's distinction between the political and the polity, Dallmayr notes,

> Seen as the empty place, democratic sovereignty cannot be manifestly actualized by any individual or group in society. What is manifest or visible in democracy are . . . the individuals or groups wielding political authority at a given time; but the constitutive matrix or space-time scheme of the polity remains hidden. In Lefort's words, democracy might even be described as the institutionalization of a "society without a body" or a society which "undermines the representation of an organic totality."[13]

In a similar vein, Abe Masao has attempted to explore the political implications of *śūnyatā,* especially in terms of a concept Dallmayr himself finds problematic—political sovereignty. In "Sovereignty Rests with Mankind," Abe attempts to adapt the well-known concept of self-awakening to the political arena in order to remedy what he sees as Zen's traditional abstinence from such important concerns. Generally, the lines of connection are similar to those laid down by one of Abe's close teachers, Hisamatsu Shin'ichi. After the Second World War, Hisamatsu was instrumental in founding the FAS society, the letters of which stand for Formless Self, All Mankind, Suprahistorical. What this is supposed to suggest is the self-awakening of all humankind without distinctions of race, ethnic background, creed, or gender, to the Formless Self that constitutes all of us in our very individuality. For Abe, such a transformation is involved in grasping all humanity as "a *single, living, self-*

aware entity." Only insofar as we see ourselves as the same self-aware entity are we then conscious of our intrinsic connectedness one to each other, or our essential equality with respect to each other. Once we succeed in experiencing such identity with each other, the distinction between saving myself and saving others drops away, thus fulfilling the *Bodhisattva* vow to enter enlightenment only when all are enlightened.[14] The process of self-awakening is the Zen answer to the Buddhist challenge to gain enlightenment and realize *nirvāṇa*. What Abe is adding in this essay is that such enlightening must proceed along a social, in fact global, dimension in order to qualify as bona fide.

The claim is that the very dynamic of self-awakening is social and must engage social concerns. This is quite startling. Traditionally, the process of self-awakening is represented in Zen as occurring on an individual level, often with the assistance of a teacher, but still mainly as the achievement of a particular pupil. However, as Abe points out,

> The ego is indeed nothing other than the basic source of all such distinctions and oppositions [between self and other, for example]. If we turn our backs on the world, there can be no investigation of the self. . . . The self-awakening which one awakens to by breaking through the ego transcends the ego and extends infinitely in every direction. There is nothing whatsoever which stands outside *this expanse of Self-awakening.*[15]

In effect, since in true self-awakening one sees the dissolution of all distinctions between self and other, self-awakening authenticates itself in our grasping ourselves as one body with others. The very dynamic of self-awakening itself mandates such identification with others. In fact, Abe explicitly extends this solidarity beyond the merely human realm, insisting that when fully self-awakened we are equally awakened to our solidarity with the nonhuman natural world as well.

In the Buddhist tradition and especially the *Soto* Zen tradition, the concept of self-awakening must be understood along the same conceptual lines as those in terms of which *śūnyatā* is understood. It is an all-pervasive negativity that negates or empties itself, philosophically speaking. Because its negativity, if petrified into a substance or thing, would contradict itself and lose all meaning, *śūnyatā* must be taken as functional negativity—as inherently depending on the relationality of things. Thus *śūnyatā* and *pratītyasamutpāda* or relational co-arising are routinely identified in the Buddhist tradition. Self-awakening, insofar as it expresses our awareness of our own emptiness, means an awareness of our deep-level dependence on all that we are not. There is a dynamic at the heart of our own individuality that drives the self-awakened to an instant identification with others along any number of relational dimensions.

Recognition of such identification with others is also not uncommon in other traditions of Buddhism. What is new in Abe's approach to this issue, however, is his emphasis on the political nature of sovereignty and its implications. By sovereignty, it seems pretty clear that Abe means something like the locus of political power or of legitimate political power. What worries Abe is the assumption of power by egocentric nation-states. As he puts it, "Moved by a blatant national egoism, the power of the state is now developing a demonic character as it destroys the balance of moral restraint and controlling power, which should be visible in the rationale of the state."[16] In short, under the banner of national sovereignty, the modern state has become the locus of political power itself. The danger is that the nation-state, because of its concrete role in human affairs and hence its relatively well-defined interests, is as vulnerable to egocentrism as is any individual. To act demonically in Buddhist terms is almost always to pursue narrow interests to the detriment of others—to be *only* self-interested. When a nation is purely driven by self-interest, it inevitably runs into conflict with others and experiences alienation from any form of larger community.

For Abe, it is not that the state has no role to play in human affairs. In fact, he treats the state in Hegelian fashion as a necessary stage in human moral evolution. "The ethical or moral force of the state is also often considered to be a higher form of human ethics *(Sittlichkeit),* transcending the birth and death of individual people and preserving the eternal continuation of races and peoples."[17] But one should not confuse such a stage with the absolute, and if we fail to evolve higher forms of social integration, we will inevitably suffer the consequences. That is, we will fragment into the warring camps that are all too familiar on the international scene.

In other words, sovereignty rests with the process of moral evolution and not with any particular stage. The way Abe chooses to describe the transforming process that is the only absolute, and hence the site of morally legitimate power in his view, is in terms of the dynamic of self-awakening. Self-awakening is, as I have argued, a deeply negative kind of process and Abe chooses the characterization "self-negation." To awaken to the true nature of the self is to acknowledge the nonreifiable transformative process that confers on us our place in the world and hence our very individuality. We are always in some sense beyond ourselves, or any concrete embodiment of ourselves. In terms of legitimacy and power, I take it that what this means is that we are only fully awakened as individuals when we acknowledge the full range of the community we inhabit. Such acknowledgement is, of course, only real in recognizing the full range of obligations one faces by virtue of such membership. The contrast is therefore with the egocentrism that characterizes the nation-state due to our failure to awaken to any higher form of solidarity that would mitigate our pursuit of national interest. However, such egocentrism is not only a problem for nation-states, but for any concrete embodiment of the various solidarities that define us.

I realize that there are many profound philosophical problems raised by this sort of treatment of sovereignty. But I do think that both Abe and Dallmayr stress the value of what is a neglected element in political theorizing—the negative. For Dallmayr, the negative is the functional negativity that empowers critique and reinforces the provisional nature of hegemony. The degree to which any political force succeeds in fixing the nature of the social and achieving "positive integration" is also the degree to which it will sow the seeds for contestation, given that the social can never be fixed. Sovereignty will always be an empty place of contestation where hegemony is forever an issue. Equally for Abe, the site of true power and legitimacy is always negative. Because it is in the self-negation of self-awakening that we connect with our true nature, the dynamic that makes us who we are in the sense of a full individual, our true political affiliations are really empty in a pregnant sense, not parochial (no matter how broadly we construe their limits). But since the political has to do with human relations and human community for Abe, the degree to which we are as one "self-aware entity" is the degree to which we have come to identify with each other in the strongest sense.

However, there is a built-in limitation to this manner of formulating the issues. From Dallmayr's point of view, the major issue neglected by a conception of democracy as an empty place is solidarity. If hegemony and hence sovereignty is always a point of contestation and debate, then the meaning of the social is never fixed. However, without a certain amount of social integration, there is the very real threat of social fragmentation and disintegration. Debate and contestation take place against a shared sense of political community involving commitment to institutions necessary to the staging of such political engagements. Thus, consensus in some sense is as vital as debate to the health of democracy. While not exactly criticizing Laclau and Mouffe's formulations, Dallmayr seeks to reorient their study toward a rethinking of "the Hegelian state"

> in such a manner that state no longer signifies a positive structure or totality, and certainly not simply an instrument of coercion, but rather the fragile ethical bond implicit in hegemonic political relations. Democracy under these auspices is still an arena of a struggle—but a struggle directed not simply toward domination but toward the establishment of a tensional balance between presence and absence, liberty and equality: that is, a struggle for mutual recognition (of differences).[18]

In short, how do we transform the *agon* of contestation and debate into a viable sense of solidarity and community? What exactly is the "fragile ethical bond" that serves this unifying role so necessary to maintaining a shared sense of community vital to any particular democratic society?

For Abe, there are certain insufficiencies implicit in a self-awakening based exclusively on the Zen experience. He writes,

> precisely because of its standpoint of Non-thinking, Zen has in fact not fully realized the positive and creative aspects of thinking and their significance which have been especially developed in the West. . . . [I]ts position of Non-thinking always harbors the danger of degenerating into mere not-thinking. . . . That Zen lacks the clue to cope with the problems of modern science, as well as individual social, and international ethical questions, etc., may be thought partly to be based on this.[19]

In other words, if sovereignty is to be based on individual self-awakening to our full solidarity with all of mankind and perhaps even all of nature, then self-awakening itself must in some manner incorporate this ethical and moral thinking, which has heretofore been at least inconspicuous in the nonthinking that underlies or is at the core of Zen self-awakening.

II

What both Dallmayr and Abe are arguing is very much that there is a regulative dimension to our conduct *vis-à-vis* others in both the political structure of participatory democracy and the subjective dynamics of self-awakening. The negativity inherent in each is also positive and reflective of equality and sameness (but not of a coercive sort) among peoples and persons. Abe goes on to suggest that this variety of sameness that Zen taps into is the source of the connection between wisdom (*prajña*) and compassion (*karuṇā*) within the Buddhist tradition. He never develops this connection in systematic detail to my knowledge, but it is this link that I think bears exploring in addressing the question of justice.

One can argue that, from its very inception, the Buddhist tradition has been informed by an ideal of compassion. To begin with, the target of Buddhist practice is suffering, and not just one's own personal suffering but the root cause of suffering for all sentient beings. Thus the very motivation of Buddhism is compassion—a sensitivity to suffering. Furthermore, one of the cardinal virtues that emerges in early Buddhist texts is freedom from hate. As is noted in the *Dhammapada*,[20] "Weeds harm the fields, hate harms human nature: offerings given to those free from hate bring a great reward." Many passages in both the *suttas* and the *Dhammapada* take hate to be an especially strong and damaging passion which condemns one to suffering.

The Mahāyanā tradition of Buddhism establishes this connection between compassion and self-overcoming even more strongly and obviously.

The distinctive contribution that Mahāyāna Buddhism makes is the *Bodhisattva* ideal as expressed, for example, through the figure of Avalokitesvara. Before entering Buddhahood, Avalokitesvara looks down and beholds the vast suffering of sentient beings and vows not to enter enlightenment or *nirvāṇa* until having made provision to bring all beings to enlightenment.

> He who is now so compassionate to the world,
> He will a Buddha be in future ages
> Humbly I bow to Avalokitesvara
> Who destroys all sorrow, fear and suffering.[21]

Another particularly provocative and interesting expression of this connection emerges in Shin Pure Land. As Shinran writes,

> When people attain this enlightenment, then with great love and great compassion immediately reaching their fullness in them, they return to the ocean of birth-and-death to save all sentient beings: this is known as attaining the virtue of Bodhisattva Samantbhadra. To attain this benefit is *come;* that is, "to return to the city of dharma-nature."[22]

It is not, however, until the efforts of contemporary Buddhist philosophers such as Nishida Kitaro that one finds an explicit attempt to connect compassion with ideas in Western moral philosophy. Nishida writes,

> Perfect sincerity is grounded in infinite compassion. It is this kind of perfect sincerity that I would place at the foundation of "practical reason" as well. Kant's ethics of practical reason was only a bourgeois ethics. A historically transformative ethics, I say, is one that is based on the vow of compassion.[23]

By sincerity, Nishida means "a form of selflessness, a pure response to the other,"[24] and he links such selflessness directly with Shinran's notion of "effortless acceptance of the grace of Amida." Indeed, in his discussion of the eighteenth vow of Amida Buddha, Shinran unpacks the phrase "sincere mind" as meaning "true and real" and connects it with Amida's vow as being true and real. In other words, "it does not arise from the hearts and minds of foolish beings of self-power."[25] To entrust oneself to Amida Buddha *sincerely* is to give oneself up fully to the Other-power which is Amida Buddha. Thus sincerity becomes fully selfless because it is full reliance on the other—Amida;. it is absolute self-surrender. Hence Nishida is clearly grounding ethics on a complete self-surrender to the absolute and, importantly, the compassion that flows from an absolute to a relative being.[26]

How can this be the ground of ethics? What does Nishida mean? In Nishida's view, a good example of the relation of relative to absolute being is that of the individual to God. Each individual is a limited and embodied being while God transcends such limitations or, at least, is not confined by such limitations. God is the true absolute. But a true absolute, Nishida argues, cannot merely oppose the relative—cannot remain ontologically distinct from the relative. If it did, it would no longer be absolute (because to be absolute is to be unlimited). Therefore, God must be immanent *and* transcendent. "The absolute must relate to itself as a form of self-contradiction. It must express itself by negating itself."[27] In short, as relative and contextual beings, we express the absolute's self-negation of itself at the same time as the absolute expresses us through our impermanence and limitation.

If this seems an impossible relationship, Nishida would argue that it seems so because of our commitment to only one form of thinking—one form of "logic." No one form of logic is adequate to thinking through the sorts of in-terexpressive relationships that he describes in the case of the absolute and the relative, God and man. In fact, to be religiously awakened, according to Nishida, is to be awakened to exactly this sort of dynamic interexpressiveness between God and man. Nishida entitles this the "identity of absolute contradiction" and sometimes the "absolutely contradictory identity of the many and the one." Furthermore, he does not restrict this relationship to God and man; it also pertains to what he calls the "dynamic world," which is social-historical in character. "The term 'world' does not signify for me that which stands over against the self, as it is commonly understood. It signifies the concrete world that has the logical form of a self-transforming matrix."[28] In other words, the world and God are interchangeable in that both play the same role with respect to the individual.

Admittedly, I am leaving out of account Nishida's analysis of the "world" into fully three transformative matrices: what he calls the physical, the biological, and the social/historical world. All of these categories of world express different relations between the many and the one, only the last of which is fully interexpressive. However, it is this last sense of world, where world and self are fully engaged, that is the most important. The individual both creates and is created by the social/historical world. This interexpressive relationship becomes the source of religious awakening on the part of the self. To the degree the self awakens to its engagement with the world, to that extent the self becomes "perfectly sincere." To be sincere is, of course, to be honest and open with respect to oneself—to hide nothing. Thus, to be fully honest with oneself or about oneself is to recognize the world as operative through oneself—oneself as the self-expression of the absolute—sincerely to trust in Amida, God, or the absolute. Recognizing one's complete reliance on, and identification with, God is to have surrendered, in a sense, all that one is. But equally, given God's own identification with the transformative character of the world, such sincerity is also compassionate engagement with the social and historical world. We give ourselves up fully to God—which is to engage the world, even to love the world, as Nishida explicitly contends. In short, because the relative and the absolute constitute an interexpressive identity, all relative beings are identical with each other in some sense. It is not a question of loving my neighbor; I am my neighbor in his or her individuality and difference.

I take it that Nishida sees this as the ground of ethics in that it forms the basis of a kind of binding obligation toward others. But it is a point of view that gives us no explicit guidelines in this respect. Given Nishida's interest in Kant and his emphasis on the dialectical power of that which is universal or aspires to be, one might see here a basis for an ethics of universal prescriptivism of some sort. I myself think that some form of situation ethics may be closer to Nishida's twin emphasis on compassion and the absolutely contextual aspects of human living.[29] But I do believe one can make a case for a conception of justice—justice as compassion.

III

In sketching out what I mean by justice as compassion and how I think it dovetails with the sort of negativity Dallmayr and Abe emphasize, I want to consider mainly two issues. First, what can be said generally about the nature of compassion in light of its development within the Buddhist tradition? Second, what do we expect of a conception of justice and how might compassion meet this expectation?

It is quite evident that compassion is as relevant to the process of self-awakening or enlightenment as is any other distinction or concept. In fact, compassion may have even more relevance to the phenomonology of enlightenment than a concept such as *śūnyatā*. After all, it is a distinctive emotion or affective demand on our attentions. But like *śūnyatā* or absolute nothingness, the concepts that impress Dallmayr, compassion is also part of a deeply transformative process of the self. Indeed, it is the culmination of such a process and the marker of authentic self-transformation. It is the sort of egoless openness to others that is *not* self-denial. This is why it also implicates a whole-hearted sincerity in that there is no ego left to hide. It is also profoundly nonjudgmental, because it involves an openness and acceptance of solidarity with all, no matter how evil any one person might be.

Thus compassion represents the complete emptying of the self in Buddhist terms. What this means phenomenologically, I believe, is that one gives up, or better, suspends all judgments of one's own. As Shinran would put it, we abandon all "calculation," and I think this would include moral calculation.[30] We judge not, to put it biblically. In so doing, we face the sense in which each of us is fully constituted by our relations with all others. Only in the space of such a nonjudgmental posture are we fully able to realize our complete interdependence with others. Compassion is the full measure of our acceptance that *nirvāṇa* really is *samsāra*—that enlightenment is simply acceptance of our samsaric relatedness to all being. It is the point at which we can maintain no privileged self-subsistent posture or place of judgment. In a sense, it is the "place" (in Nishida's sense) of no-judgment.

However, this does not mean that we do not make judgments at all. Rather, I think, it is a matter of the point from which judgments, especially moral ones, proceed. In a sense, we must be able to suspend judgments in order to truly make them or make them compassionately. I would like to think that judgment would be spontaneous and nonprejudiced if made from such a standpoint. From a Buddhist vantage point, we never escape *samsāra*, but we can be enlightened about *samsāra*—enlightened about delusion as Zen-master Dogen might have it. If so, then one might argue that we can never escape judgment and decision, samsaric features of our existence. But perhaps we can become enlightened in our judging, in our samsaric embeddedness.

We routinely expect justice to address two sorts of issues in public life. Ever since Aristotle, justice has been thought to embody those principles that regulate our behavior or conduct toward our neighbor. Thus justice prescribes remedies for harm that I do my neighbor and justice ensures fairness in the distribution of social goods and burdens. So justice covers those judgments we make regarding our appropriate interactions with others. From a Buddhist point of view, all theories of justice that purport to lay out the principles or standards in accordance with which such judgments must be made would be suspect. It is not that such principles are wrong. The libertarian emphasis on the rights of the individual as a source of value is not wrong, for example. Nor would the egalitarian emphasis on the desirability of maintaining real equality of opportunity be considered wrong. However, all such views would be regarded as partial. While they lay out important considerations regarding our interconnectedness with others, they lack a comprehensive approach to the problem of the standpoint from which we make judgments regarding the needs of people and the relative weights of such needs. Furthermore, such theories are, by their nature, insensitive to the situationatedness of all such judgments. Indeed, by their very abstractness such theories are designed to be noncontextual.

In many ways, Aristotle, in his emphasis on the virtues, and particularly in his insistence that justice itself is a virtue—that of fairness, most closely approaches the Buddhist emphasis on the factors that underlie principles of justice. In maintaining that justice is a virtue, what Aristotle might be seen as doing is suggesting that justice is a quality of judging well that cannot be reduced to explicit rules and guidelines. But in any case, I think compassion viewed as a nonjudgmental commitment to *samsāra* and an openness to others fully qualifies as an account of justice. In short, it says that justice is what flows out of the standpoint of compassion. In a sense, it is a view of what is constitutive of justice.

How does this remedy some of the concerns expressed earlier regarding Abe's and Dallmayr's views on democracy? In brief, the problem encountered in Dallmayr's conception of democracy as an empty place was that it left little room for a sense of solidarity either within or beyond the contestation and struggle for hegemony. In fact, the view of Laclau and Mouffe even seemed to suggest that democracy in some form was an inevitable product of struggle—at least of the struggle to persuade. All structuring of the social is inevitably partial and incomplete, open to revision. Could one participate in the process without any democratic commitment or commitment to democratic institutions?

The evident advantage of introducing the notion of compassionate justice into the picture is the solidarity to which it commits one. To enter the empty place of democratic staging, one must empty oneself. Democracy cannot be merely an empty process ruling impersonally over the *polis*. Democracy is also a commitment one makes to the institutions that provide the open forum which is the site of contestation and debate. I would think that, in order to enter such a forum, one would have to embrace its fundamental openness. Not only does the recognition of justice as compassion commit one to the requisite openness of the democratic forum, it also suggests the substance of public debate, or the guiding focus of public debate. We need not all be able to agree on what constitutes compassionate regard for others caught up in the intricacies of the social web, so long as we all agree that it is important to focus on what this might be. Furthermore, compassionate regard might be viewed as flexibly prescriptive in that it opens up a space within our moral and political judgments whereby we may equilibrate the inevitable divergence of viewpoints that Dallmayr's analysis suggests is endemic to the social. We are not the victims of our moral judgments; as long as we maintain compassionate regard for all others, we maintain a higher court of appeal for our moral judgments.

The problem that Abe raises with respect to Zen self-awakening—that it is too absorbed in the self-negating process of awakening and too little in the positive and ethical dimension of enlightenment—is also addressed by stressing the connection between justice, judgment, and compassion. In fact, Abe all but suggests such a strategy in the following remark:

> The crucial task for Buddhism is this: how can Buddhism . . . formulate a *positive direction* through which ethics and history can develop? . . . Here I must limit myself to suggesting that the Mahāyāna notion of 'compassion', which is inseparably connected with 'wisdom', and the idea of the 'Bodhisattva' which is

based on 'Emptiness' and 'suchness', can provide the foundation for such a Buddhist teleology.[31]

Without exactly touching on the point of teleology, one can argue that compassion in its connection to emptiness and emptying represents the inner core of judgments covering our social and political connectedness.

NOTES

1. I would like to thank the NEH for supporting research for this paper through a summer seminar in 1994 at Ohio State University led by Tom Kasulis.

2. Fred Dallmayr, "Śūnyatā East and West: Emptiness and Global Democracy," presented at the December, 1992 meeting of the Society for Asian and Comparative Philosophy in Washington, D.C.

3. This is Abe's preferred term for *satori*, presumably to avoid any associated "intuitionism" and to emphasize the self-transformative aspect of enlightenment.

4. "Sovereignty Rests with Mankind" in Masao Abe, *Zen and Western Thought* (Honolulu: University of Hawai'i Press, 1985), pp. 249–60.

5. See, for example, W. L. King, *In the Hope of Nibbana* (LaSalle: Open Court, 1964); or Damien Keown, *The Nature of Buddhist Ethics* (New York: St. Martins Press, 1992).

6. Fred Dallmayr, *Margins of Political Discourse* (Albany: State University of New York Press, 1989), pp. 116–36.

7. Ibid., p. 121.

8. Ibid., p. 122.

9. Ibid., p. 124.

10. Ibid., p. 124.

11. Dallmayr, "Śūnyatā East and West: Emptiness and Global Democracy," p. 29.

12. Ibid., p. 29.

13. Ibid., p. 33.

14. See Yoshifumi Ueda's discussion of *Mahāyāna* Buddhism and the Pure Land in *Shinran: An Introduction to His Thought* (Kyoto: Hongwanji International Center, 1989), chaps. 2, 3.

15. Abe, "Sovereignty Rests with Mankind," pp. 251–52.

16. Ibid., pp. 254–55.

17. Ibid., p. 254.

18. Dallmayr, "Hegemony amd Democracy," p. 136.

19. Masao Abe, *Zen and Western Thought,* pp. 119–20.

20. *The Dhammapada,* trans. Juan Mascaro (London: Penguin Books, 1973).

21. *Saddharmapundarika* 24, vol. 27, as collected in *Buddhist Texts Through the Ages,* Edward Conze, ed. (New York: Harper & Row, 1964), p. 196.

22. Shinran, "Going and Returning" in *Shinran: An Introduction to His Thought,* pp. 261–62.

23. Nishida Kitaro, *Last Writings: Nothingness and the Religious Worldview,* trans. David A. Dilworth (Honolulu: University of Hawai'i Press, 1987), p. 107.

24. Ibid., p. 107.

25. Shinran, "Primal Vow" in *Shinran: An Introduction to His Thought*.

26. Shinran argues that true compassion only proceeds from Amida Buddha and hence from an absolute to a relative being. So we discover the ground of compassion on embracing the Pure Land, but once there we must return, as the movement of compassion is always from Amida to sentient beings. This compassionate return, which is paradoxically part of entering the Pure Land, is called *genso*. See especially Ueda's discussion of this topic in chapter four of *Shinran*, pp. 179–82.

27. Nishida, *Last Writings*, p. 68.

28. Ibid., p. 73.

29. See Joseph Fletcher, *Situation Ethics: The New Morality* (Philadelphia: The Westminster Press, 1964).

30. Shinran's term is *hakarai,* and it involves the ultimate exercise of self-power, "a failure to recognize the self-attachment harbored in our perceptions and judgments, and . . . the imposition of those judgments on Amida's working" (*Shinran*, p. 222).

31. Abe, "Religion and Science in the Global Age—Their Essential Character and Mutual Relationship" in *Zen and Western Thought*, p. 248.

Part 5. Postmodern Perspectives

Rosi Braidotti

NOMADIC SUBJECTS: FEMINIST POSTMODERNISM AS ANTIRELATIVISM

> *Most people in the world*
> *are Yellow, Black, Brown, Poor, Female*
> *Non-Christian*
> *and do not speak English.*
> *By the year 2000*
> *the 20 largest cities in the world*
> *will have one thing in common*
> *none of them will be in Europe*
> *none in the United States.*
>
> *Audre Lorde[1]*

In this paper, I will defend a feminist poststructuralist position as a nonrelativist standpoint. This position rests on the assumption, which I shall outline presently, of the historical decline of the classical view of the human subject. By way of introduction, let me say that I see it as one of the historical tasks of feminism to elaborate an epistemological and ethical position that is suitable to postmodernity in a gendered perspective. I would also want to suggest that this position conveys a posthumanist vision of subjectivity as a de-essentialized and historicized entity—a multilayered (not a fixed) phenomenon, more akin to a process than a substantial unity, more like an event than an essence. This is what I have called, echoing Friedrich Nietzsche and Gilles Deleuze, nomadic subjectivity.

Before I get into the heart of the matter, however, let me confront the set of critiques coming from within feminism that tend to construe the poststructuralist critique of classical essentialistic notions of subjectivity as a relativist position. The charge of relativism has usually been made against

345

feminists by die-hard champions of European rationality, such as Ernst Gellner[2] and other militant masculinists. What is striking, however, is the extent to which this charge is now being made from within the feminist horizon. For instance, Sabine Lovibond[3] criticizes poststructuralist feminist theory because its radical reappraisal of epistemological and political values allegedly provokes a real "crisis" of rationality. Lovibond prefers the moderate readjustments proposed to the existing system of values by more "reformist-minded" feminists and concludes with a dismissal of poststructuralist feminist politics as both contradictory and pretentious in its relativistic understanding of human subjectivity[4].

For her part, Martha Nussbaum,[5] in keeping with the central premises of her work, claims an explicitly universalistic and neo-Aristotelian essentialist position. Nussbaum argues that this stance provides the only possible grounds from which to make judgments and defend fundamental moral values such as compassion and respect. Unwilling to take into serious consideration the more sophisticated case for difference, which has been made by poststructuralists and feminists,[6] Nussbaum shares Catharine MacKinnon's conviction that difference is a pernicious notion in that it carries pejorative connotations. Thus she chooses to concentrate instead on capabilities and functions that are central to all and common in human life.

In an important reversal of what had become the standard objection to postmodern feminism as "essentialistic,"[7] Nussbaum declares that all "difference-minded" feminists are antiessentialists. This strikes me as a major step forward toward a better understanding of the poststructuralist position after years of misunderstanding. The disadvantage of this reading, however, is that the antiessentialist feminists are represented as necessarily and inevitably relativistic in that they seek "norms defined relatively to a local context and locally held belief."[8] In other words, Nussbaum attempts to establish a context-independent sense of human nature and of human moral values, which leads her to formulate a sort of short list of essential points by which human subjectivity can be defined for all places and times.

In Nussbaum's rather simplistic reading, the deconstruction of essentialism, which is the cornerstone of poststructuralist philosophy, results in a collapse into subjectivism, which in turn is defined as a retreat into extreme relativism. This sequence of argumentative steps reveals beyond any possible doubt Nussbaum's attachment to liberal bourgeois notions of the individual and of the dualistic opposition self/other that it entails. In this view, the individual can only be conceived either as part of a global entity—family, state, nation, humanity, the cosmos—or, contrariwise, as splintered off and atomized. This simplistic reading positions language as an instrument of communication and banks on human affectivity—especially the qualities of identification and empathy—as the only possible moral bridges between the various atomized particles.

This philosophical tradition is obviously at the antipodes of poststructuralist philosophy: Nussbaum's liberal individualism has little in common with the materialist theories of subjectivity proposed by those philosophers whom she dismisses as relativists. For them, the critique of liberal individualism is yesterday's battle, and their main priority is to disentangle their own brand of materialism from the confining structure of Marxist theory. In this respect, the psychoanalytic theory of language plays a crucial role, in that it historicizes, and therefore politicizes, the process of subject-formation. According to poststructuralist psychoanalysis, language is what one is made of: it is an ontological site that defies rational, let alone individual, control. Thus to suggest that it is a "tool" is a humanist form of arrogance that does not help either the moral plan of bringing humanity together or the task of the social theorist who is supposed to account for processes of signification. Psychoanalysis also smashes any illusion of atomized individuality by embedding the subject in the thick materiality of a symbolic system of which language is the most available source. This allows for subtler analyses of the interaction between self and society and among different selves than does liberal ego-based psychology. Thus to say that Nussbaum utterly misconstrues the poststructuralist case would be an understatement.

I do not intend, however, to intervene at length in the debate on relativism, which has been so admirably dealt with by Barbara Herrnstein-Smith.[9] My aim in this paper is rather to try to decode the political and theoretical stakes of this debate within feminist theory today and to argue for poststructuralism as a nonrelativistic position. I want to stress that the reason why relativism is a problem for feminists is that it erodes the possibilities for political coalitions among women, thereby weakening feminist politics. I wish to suggest that a feminist postmodernist perspective manages to combine respect for differences with shifting yet productive foundations for political agency in a manner suitable to the complexity of our era.

In a paper that I consider to be of the greatest relevance, though it deals with cultural rather than cognitive or moral relativism, Clifford Geertz addresses this point.[10] He stresses the polemical and political use to which the "antirelativism" campaign is put (in this case, in the field of anthropology). In an argument that is analogous to the case feminists have made for strategic essentialism,[11] Geertz argues that a double negative does *not* amount to an affirmative. Thus to be opposed to antirelativism, does not make one a relativist. What this critical position makes possible is rather the possibility of deconstructing authoritarian modes of thinking that attempt to pass themselves off as universalistic. Geertz states that the fear of relativism is unfounded, because

the moral and intellectual consequences that are commonly supposed to flow from relativism—subjectivism, nihilism, incoherence, Machiavellianism, ethical idiocy, esthetic blindness, and so on—do not in fact do so and the promised rewards of escaping its clutches, mostly having to do with pasteurized knowledge, are illusory. Whatever cultural relativism may be or originally have been . . . it serves these days largely as a spectre to scare us away from certain ways of thinking and towards others. And, as the ways of thinking away from which we are being driven seem to me to be more cogent than those toward which we are being propelled . . . , I would like to do something about this.[12]

Accordingly, my reaction to the antirelativism charge is to go ahead and explore the ways of thinking from which the antirelativists are trying to scare us away. I will do so not in the spirit of polemic, but because I am convinced that these ways of thinking are far more cogent and useful than their critics suggest. Furthermore, and beyond the polemic, my position implies the historical need for the redefinition of our understanding of human subjectivity. It also assumes that feminist experiences have been elaborated in such a way as to be able to produce ideas that have a more general range of application than ever before. Contemporary feminist theory has a universalistic reach, if not a universalistic aspiration. As such it is not only a form of anti-antirelativism, but downright nonrelativistic.

FEMINISM AND POSTMODERNITY

Contrary to fashionable usages of the term, I take "postmodernism" to refer to a specific moment of the historical position of what can also be called late capitalism or postindustrialism. Not only is it the case that poststructuralist thought provides an adequate description of our historicity, but it also constitutes a constructive reaction to the sets of paradoxes that are engendered by this specific historical location. Thus postmodernity refers to an intellectual and ethical standpoint rather than a specific date—in that historians and philosophers alike do not seem to agree on its chronology. German critical theorists, especially Jürgen Habermas and Seyla Benhabib, argue against this notion, because they think that modernity is still to come, that it is a horizon toward which we are moving, like some kind of utopia. French critical philosophers, on the other hand, especially Michel Foucault, Gilles Deleuze, Jean-François Lyotard, and Luce Irigaray, argue that modernity is a philosophical and political project inspired by the Enlightenment, which has by now exhausted its historical function.

I find myself much closer to the French way of assessing the question of modernity. I believe that the central notions that animated the Enlightenment project, especially the belief in the fundamental reasonableness of the human being, the universal usefulness of reason, and the liberating powers of rationality and science—all these notions have been rudely shaken and contradicted by the events of modern history. More specifically, I am thinking of such phenomena as colonialism and European fascism, which are marked by episodes of genocide and industrial-scale exploitation and the elimination of people who were considered inferior and therefore disposable.

Moreover, my work on philosophical nomadism has made me aware of a sort of structural aporia in theoretical discourse and especially in philosophy. Discourse, understood in the poststructuralist sense as a process of the production of ideas, knowledge, texts, and representations, is an ongoing process upon which high theory rests, in order to capture and codify its diversity into an acceptable scientific norm. The normativity of high theory, however, also marks its limitation, because discourse, being a complex network of interrelated truth-effects, exceeds theory's power of codification. Thus philosophy has to "run after" all sorts of new discourses (those relating to, and produced by, for example, women, postcolonial subjects, youth, the audiovisual media, and other new technologies) in order to incorporate and codify them. As Donna Haraway[13] reminds us, high theory is a cannibalistic machine aiming at the assimilation of all new and even of alien and monstrous bodies. Fortunately, the conceptual nomads can run faster and endure longer trips than most.

Politically, the nomadic style expresses my doubts about the capacity of high theory to accommodate the very questions that I see as central: the critique of phallogocentrism and ethnocentrism and the affirmation of the positivity of difference. Philosophy, as a discipline of thought, is highly antinomadic. It holds a privileged bond to domination, power, and violence. It consequently requires mechanisms of exclusion as part of its standard practices. Philosophy creates itself through what it excludes as much as through what it asserts. High theory posits its values through the exclusion of many— nonmen, nonwhites, nonlearned, etc. The structural necessity of these pejorative figurations of otherness within a structure of thought that insists on claiming universal validity, makes me doubt the theoretical capacity, let alone the moral and political willingness, of theoretical discourse to act in a nonhegemonic, nonexclusionary and nonethnocentric manner.

Even closer to us, confronted by episodes of planned and thoroughly thought out violence, such as was displayed in Auschwitz, Hiroshima, the Gulag Archipelago, Vietnam, and by the Pol Pot regime, not to speak of the persistent pernicious effects of racism and xenophobia and the systematic destruction of the tropical rain forests and the events in Bosnia-Herzegovina—and this list is unfortunately open, of course—I think it would be irresponsible in the most sentimentally vacuous manner to go on believing in the reasonableness of the human being or in the coincidence of subjectivity with rational consciousness. Similarly, since the Manhattan project and the advent of the nuclear age, with its capacity to "overkill," science and technology—far from holding the key to our future progress and growth—have become the source of persistent anxieties about our present. As Fredric Jameson put it,

> The postmodern is an attempt to think the present historically in an age that has forgotten how to think historically in the first place. . . . Postmodernism may then amount to not much more than theorizing its own conditions of possibility, which consists primarily in the sheer enumeration of changes and modifications.[14]

This may well be the case, but given that cartographies are politically informed maps of the present, the sort of enumeration of changes that they are likely to offer tend to give rise to all sorts of contestations and dissonant readings. The first rule of the poststructuralist approach, therefore, is to compare notes on our respective cartographies, so as to engage in politicaly informed discussions on how to account for the present.

The enumeration of the changes and modifications engendered by the postmodern sociosymbolic space must begin with changes in the system of economic production, which are also altering traditional social and symbolic structures. In the West, the shift away from manufacturing toward a service and information-based economic structure entails a global redistribution of labor, with the rest of the world and especially the developing countries providing most of the offshore production through underpaid female and child labor.

The postmodern condition rests therefore on the paradox of the simultaneous occurrence of contradictory trends. On the one hand, we see the *globalization* of economic and cultural processes, which engenders increasing conformism in consumption and consumerism habits, and through them in general lifestyle. On the other hand, however, we also see the *fragmentation* of these processes: the resurgence of regional, local, ethnic, cultural and other differences not only between the geopolitical blocks, but also within them.

Following Stuart Hall, Paul Gilroy, and others, I believe that the single most important effect of this paradoxical historical situation is the ethnic mix that is coming upon the West through world migration. This is a huge movement of population from periphery to center, which has already affected and will continue to alter the alleged cultural homogeneity of European nation-states.[15] This new context demands that we shift the terms of the political debate from the issue of differences *between* cultures (East and West, Christian and Islamic, etc.) to differences *within* the same culture.

Gayatri Spivak puts it with customary wit: "The face of global feminism is turned outward and must be welcomed and respected as such, rather than fetishized as the figure of the Other."[16] The postmodern condition is about the becoming-Third-World of the First World, even as it continues the exploitation of developing countries. It is about the decline of "legal" economies and the rise of structural illegality as a factor in the world economy. It is about capital as cocaine. It is about the globalization of pornography and the prostitution of women and children; it is about the ruthless trade in human life. The postmodern predicament is about the feminization of poverty; it is also about the rising rates of female illiteracy and the structural unemployability of large sectors of the population, especially the youth.

It is also about the difficulties encountered by the law and traditional jurisprudence in trying to cope with such phenomena as the new reproductive rights, copyright laws as they relate to the use of photocopiers and videorecorders, the control of surrogate motherhood and artificial procreation, environmental control, and the problem of authorship on the Internet. These difficulties are what Foucault analyzed in terms of the decline of classical legal thinking and the rise of a system of diffuse and all-pervading surveillance and overregulation.

Postmodern culture is thus closely and powerfully linked to technology, which freezes time and displaces subjects, allowing for prosthetic extensions of our bodily functions and intellectual capacities: computers and answering machines augment our powers of memory, global telecommunications bring splinters of the globe into our living rooms, while electronic networks—telephones, faxes, and the Internet—make real-time communication a daily event.

Last but not least, the postmodern predicament is about the shift of geopolitical power away from the North Atlantic in favor of the Pacific and especially the South Pacific area. Cornel West put it succinctly, from a North American perspective: "Postmodernism . . . is a set of responses due to the decentering of Europe—of living in a world that no longer rests upon European hegemony and domination in the political, economic, military and cultural dimensions which began in 1492."[17] This shift in geopolitical power is both confirmed and theorized in poststructuralist philosophy in terms of the decline of European logocentrism. But philosophers such as Jacques Derrida and Massimo Cacciari[18] have pointed out an interesting fact about this shift in geopolitical power relations, which makes their discourse about the end of Western European hegemony radically different from the fascist and right-wing nostalgic discourse about the "decline of the West," which was popular at the end of the last century and which found expression in the work of, for example, Weininger and Spengler.

In a contemporary and more poststructuralist perspective, the more radical line of deconstruction of Eurocentrism runs as follows: what makes Western philosophical culture so perniciously effective is that it has been announcing its own death for over a hundred years. Since the apocalyptic trinity of modernity, Marx, Nietzsche, and Freud, the West has been thinking through the historical incvitability and the logical possibility of its own decline—so much so that the state of "crisis" has become the *modus vivendi* of Western philosophers. We thrive on it, we write endlessly about it; if the crisis did not exist, we would have to invent it, to justify our existence. Having written extensively about the metaphor of the crisis of philosophy in my first book,[19] let me just say here that I think nobody, let alone critical thinkers, should take the notion of the "crisis" of the West naïvely or at face value. White man always speaks with a forked tongue, and this state of prolonged and self-agonizing crisis may simply be the form that Western postmodernity has chosen in order to perpetuate itself. After all, Plato tells us that Socrates pointed out a long time ago that philosophy always loves a good crisis! Again, Gayatri Spivak makes the point:

> The agenda is to wrench these regulative political signifiers out of their represented field of reference. And the instrument of such a wrenching, such a re-constellating or dehegemonizing, cannot be ethnophilosophical or race-ideological pride. Given the international division of labor of the imperialist countries, it is quite appropriate that the best critique of the European ethico-politico-social universals, those regulative concepts, should come from the North Atlantic. But what is ironically appropriate in postcoloniality is that this critique finds its best staging outside of the North Atlantic in the undoing of imperialism.[20]

Spivak then goes on to argue that there are forces at work in the North Atlantic region that aim at rewriting universalism as "solidarity," thus reasserting the historical advantage of the center of the empire, in spite of evident signs of economic and cultural decline.[21] In Spivak's view, there is an implicit ethnocentric bias in this kind of universalism.

I think this insight highlights one of the central paradoxes of the postmodern historical condition, one that pitches center versus periphery in a manner so complex and so perverse as to require that we think the simultaneity of potentially contradictory social effects. This is the main consideration for rejecting antirelativism as an historically inadequate concept. The simultaneity of opposite factors, in fact, defies simplistic dual oppositions between wholeness and fragments and calls for subtler and more articulate modes of thought. As the artist Martha Rosler put it, "there cannot be fragments if there is no whole."[22]

Postcolonial thinkers have also emphasized the extent to which white mainstream philosophers resist this sort of displacement and dispossession, or tend to deny it, under the cover of neo-universalistic tendencies. Let me add to this another consideration: that in so far as poststructuralist philosophy makes manifest the crisis of Western modes of representation, it also evokes—especially in its opponents—the fear of loss of control and mastery.[23] In this regard, the appeal to neo-universalism on the part of Western philosophers fulfills a twofold function: it allows them to reject any suspicion of loss of conceptual mastery, and it helps them reassert that specifically ethnocentric Western concern that consists in passing itself off as the center of the universe. I want to argue that it is to the credit of poststructuralist thinkers like Foucault, Deleuze, Derrida, and others that, in their critique of a fixed subject position and the illusion of a coherent self coinciding with rational consciousness, they expose the web of violence and exclusion that lies at the heart of white heterosexual masculinist political economies. They also unveil the ethnocentric assumptions behind them.

The undeniable convergence between the discourse of the "crisis" of the West within poststructuralism and the postcolonial deconstruction of imperial whiteness is not a sufficient—though it is a necessary condition—for a political alliance between them. At the very least, however, it lays the grounds for the possibility of such an alliance. As Judith Butler and Joan Scott put it, the question then becomes:

> Where are the critical intersections between postcolonialism and post-structuralism that reveal the critique of Western logic as part of the critical decentering of colonial hegemony? What contradictions does Eurocentric theory face in trying to expose the constitutive logic of colonial oppression?[24]

I believe that facing up to these contradictions is our historical responsibility, because I am committed to thinking alongside my world and not to pretending that it does not exist or to hoping that maybe it will go away. As late-twentieth-century North Atlantic people, we are historically condemned to feeling responsible for our history, because we are the ones who come after the historical decline of the promises of the Enlightenment. Whether you choose to call our predicament "postmodern," "posthumanist" or "neohumanist" makes little difference. What does matter, however, is our shared awareness that living as thinking beings at the end of this millennium in the North Atlantic means that we must make ourselves *accountable* for the history of our culture without burying our head in the sand, but also without giving in to relativism or the decadent feeling that: "Alright then, if that's how things are, anything goes." It isn't true that anything goes.

In the specific case of the critique of European ethnocentrism, a poststructuralist perspective allows us to discuss quite seriously the grounds on which we postulate European identity. Identity is not understood by postmodernists as a foundational issue, based on fixed, God-given essences—of the biological, psychic, or historical kind. On the contrary, identity is taken as being constructed in the very gesture that posits it as the anchoring point for certain kinds of social and discursive practices. Consequently, the question is no longer the essentialist one, "What is national or ethnic identity?" but rather the critical and genealogical one, "How is it constructed? by whom? under which conditions? and for which aims?"

The bottom line is the need for a new nonessentialist politics; thus the relevant question is, as Stuart Hall put it,[25] who is entitled to claim an ethnic or national identity? Who has the right to claim that legacy, to speak on its behalf and turn it into a policy-making platform? These are questions about entitlement, agency, and subjectivity. In other words, to paraphrase Foucault, we need to address the paradox of exclusion and affirmation, of power and truth, which lies at the heart of the quest for, and the construction of, identity.

I do think that, on this point, a serious case of dissonance has emerged within the North Atlantic, namely, between Europe and the United States, on the issue of the political utility of French poststructuralism and especially of French feminist theories. As Cornel West points out, in American academic circles these theories have been given an apolitical and ahistorical reception, which does not do justice to either the spirit or the content of these theoretical movements. West suggests that French theories, including French feminist thought, are rendered in American academic debates in a neo-ethnocentric manner. This mistranslation fits within a broader scheme of commodification of European thought by the American academy.

> If one is talking about critiques of racism, critiques of patriarchy, critiques of homophobia, then simply call it that. Eurocentrism is not identical with racism. . . . Eurocentrism is not the same as male supremacists. . . . And the same is so with homophobia. *Demystify the categories in order to stay tuned to the complexity of the realities*[26] [my emphasis].

CRITICAL SPACES FOR FEMINIST RESISTANCE

One of the crucial points of intersection between poststructuralist philosophies and feminist theory is the desire to leave behind the linear mode of intellectual thinking, the teleologically ordained style of argumentation that most of us have been trained to respect and emulate. In my experience, the traditional mode results in encouraging repetition and dutifulness to a canonical tradition that enforces the sanctimonious sacredness of certain texts—*the* texts of the great Western philosophical humanistic tradition. I would like to oppose to them a passionate form of posthumanism, based on feminist nomadic epistemology. Nomadism is an invitation to dis-identify ourselves from the sedentary phallogocentric monologism of philosophical thinking and to start cultivating the art of disloyalty, or rather that form of healthy disrespect for both academic and intellectual conventions which in the West was inaugurated and propagated by the second feminist wave. The point for me is not loyalty to existing philosophies, but accountability for one's gender: a nomadic feminist is necessarily an undutiful daughter.

Let me therefore reiterate the main point: the shift of historical context entails in the West the decline of the traditional sociosymbolic system based on the state, the family, and masculine authority. As Inderpal Grewal and Caren Kaplan point out,[27] postmodernity corresponds to a reorganization of capital accumulation in a mobile and transnational manner. Given this new historical context of "trans"-national mobility, it is imperative for cultural critics to rethink their situation and their practices within this scheme, without romanticizing it, but also without nostalgia for an allegedly more wholesome past.

If you set these statements in the context of a postindustrial climate where the only constant is change, it becomes apparent that today the challenge for feminism and philosophy alike is how to think about and account adequately for changes and changing conditions. We do not need the comfort of static truths, but rather the stimulation of having to think through living processes of transformation.

As the feminist movement put it, well before Deleuze, we need to learn to think differently about our historical condition; we need to reinvent ourselves. This transformative project begins with the relinquishing of the historically established, phallocentric, eurocentric, hegemonic habits of thought which, until now, have provided the "standard" view of human subjectivity. We must relinquish all that in favor of a decentered and multilayered vision of the subject as a dynamic and changing entity, situated in a shifting context.

Nostalgia is one of the most pernicious traits of the reaction against the postmodern condition. As a feminist, I am firmly opposed to it. There is no need to mourn the decline of the West, the state, the nation, rationality, men, religion, and all the other pillars on which received ideas of "civilization" were built. Instead, we need to expose the deeply seated masculinism, misogyny, and racism of these ideals and, taking advantage of their historical decline, work toward replacing them with new and more adequate notions.

If we take, for instance, the idea of "national identity," a poststructuralist critical perspective, inspired by Homi Bhaba or Edward Said, can make us aware of the fact that common ideas of "the nation" are to a large extent narrative structures or imaginary tales, which project a reassuring but nonetheless illusory sense of unity over the disjointed, fragmented, and often incoherent range of internal regional and cultural differences that make up a nation-state. Moreover, any feminist knows to what extent the legitimating tales of nationhood in the West has been constructed over the body of women, as well as on the crucible of imperial and colonial masculinity.

The fact that these allegedly universal or all-encompassing ideas of "nation" or "national identity" are in fact flawed and internally incoherent does not make them any less effective, nor does it prevent them from exercising hegemonic power. But the awareness of the lack of coherence, consistency, and inner rationality of what Jean-François Lyotard named the "master-narratives" of the Western world, does open new spaces for critical opposition. As Jenny Lloyd pointed out in her critique of the role of rationality in the history of Western philosophy, it is not because masculinism, nationalism, and racism have superior inner rationality or logic that they have become hegemonic. Quite the contrary, it is because they were dominant that they have appropriated exclusive claims to rationality and logic.

Thus the postmodernist awareness of the profoundly unstable structure of the categories of political and philosophical analysis (the "metanarratives" mentioned above), far from giving way to a suspension of belief in the permanence of power—as the critics of postmodernism suggest—results in the acknowledgment of the historical decline of categories of political analysis both in the liberal and the Marxist tradition. This translates, however, into a renewed commitment to elaborating forms of political resistance that are adequate, that is to say, suited to the specific paradoxes of our historical condition. More specifically, a postmodernist political priority consists in dispelling the belief in the natural foundations and consequently the fixed nature of *any* system of values, meanings, or belief. In this respect, the deconstruction of essentialized identities of all kinds, including the political one, lies at the heart of this project.

The historical contradiction a feminist postmodernist is specifically caught in is that the very conditions that are perceived by dominant subjects as factors of a "crisis" of values are for women, as for other historically oppressed subjects, rather the opening up of new possibilities. The same historical conditions can be perceived as positive or negative, depending on one's historical and geopolitical location. Clearly, the postmodernist predicament cannot fail to affect our understanding of sexual difference, that is to say, the definition of woman as the "other" or the "second" sex, which is a typical feature of European cultures. In these cultures, masculinity has also become identified with the normal and is thus synonymous with subjectivity; hence the standard feminist joke at Descartes' expense: "I think, therefore *He* is!" Because "difference" has been predicated on relations of domination and exclusion, to be "different from" came to mean to be "less than," to be *worth* less than. In other words, in the West, difference has been colonized by power relations that reduce it to inferiority. Further, it has resulted in passing off differences as "natural," which transformed entire categories of beings into devalued "others" and therefore disposable others. To be disposable means that you are just as human, but slightly more mortal than the first-class subjects.

A feminist postmodernist therefore approaches the political analyses of difference in terms of power and discursive formations. Discourse is about the political currency that is attributed to certain meanings, or systems of meaning, in such a way as to invest them with scientific legitimacy. In the work of Michel Foucault, discourse analysis becomes a pragmatic form of materialism. Foucault's genealogical method consists in reading the scientific process in terms of mechanisms that discipline some truth-values and, consequently, also disqualify some others.

Let me provide an example. The belief in the inferiority of women—be it mental, intellectual, spiritual, or moral—has no serious scientific foundation; the same goes for racist beliefs. This does *not* prevent them from having great currency in political practice and the organization of society. The woman and the black as "others"—that is to say, as both empirical referents and symbolic signs of pejoration—function discursively as shapers of meanings, as organizers of differences in a hierarchical scale that divides man from woman, but also man from the animal, or nonhuman and the divine. The mark of differences fulfills the crucially important function of dividing the subjects along a set of axes of varying degrees of "difference." To divide, so as to conquer in a normative order the subversive or dangerous charge that is potentially contained in these "others"—this is how phallogocentric order is maintained.

As a corollary of the above, the pejorative use of the feminine, or of blackness, is structurally necessary to the phallogocentric system of meaning. By being structurally embedded, these differences of gender or race become paradoxically both abstract and invisible, except that the real-life, empirical subjects that are associated with them—women and blacks—experience in their embodied existence the effects of the disqualification (of the feminine and of blackness) that is effected at the symbolic level.

A poststructuralist approach to the analysis of power and discourse highlights the links that exist between scientific truth and discursive currency. Scientific discourse in particular is the master-narrative that has formalized the structural necessity for devalued difference in Western thought. Foucault's genealogical method emphasizes the need to historicize the analysis of the formation of scientific concepts *as* normative formations. Thus it allows us to take on the historicity of the very concepts that we are investigating. In a feminist poststructuralist frame, this emphasis on historicity means primarily two things. First, the rejection of dualistic schemes of thought. A discursive approach, for instance, makes us aware of the appalling simplicity of the dualism of Western science, but it also reveals the disconcerting fact that the banal simplicity of dualism is also the source of its success. Second, it implies that the scholar needs some humility before the eternal repetitions of history. We need to learn that there is no escape from the multilayered structure of language.

As a critical thinker, as an intellectual raised in the babyboom era of the new Europe, and as a feminist committed to enacting empowering alternatives, I choose to make myself accountable for this aspect of my culture and my history. Because of my own historicity and my specific location as a North Atlantic intellectual, I simply cannot leave the notion of "difference" alone, nor do I wish to delegate it to its traditionally hegemonic and pejorative meaning. I rather choose to, and desire to, *think through* difference, through the knots of power and violence that have accompanied its rise to supremacy in the European mind. This notion is far too important to be reduced to a problem of the relativity of values. What I will want to argue instead, is that difference can become the basis for the elaboration of *alternative* positive values in an historically embedded and politically accountable perspective.

IN PRAISE OF DIFFERENCES

Given my definitions of feminism and modernity, I see it as a priority to radicalize our understanding of human subjectivity, so as to achieve a double aim: on the one hand, to end the complicity between subjectivity and masculinity, and on the other hand, to incorporate difference as a positive value, instead of projecting it outward as a sign of inferiority. As end-of-millennium feminists, we need to radicalize the universal altogether, not merely get rid of it, or replace one dominant formation with yet another.

The postmodern feminist antirelativist question is indeed: *who* do we want to become? We need to hold onto identity (sexual, social, national) and onto the material foundations of identity in terms of graspable reference points that help us define it (this is what Stuart Hall has called, quoting Derrida, "a constitutive outside"), but we do not need beliefs in the natural, fixed, or universalistic structure of such identities. We need anchoring points, but we could certainly do without essences or universalistic principles, especially as we embark on the painful but historically necessary task of redefining human subjectivity in the light of respect for diversity.

Postmodernist antirelativist feminists who are committed to the project of redefining subjectivity raise the issue of sexual difference in the sense of analyzing the historicity and the power relations that are centered on the figuration of the feminine. Let me explain this, briefly, as follows: one of the more interesting consequences of the crisis of the Western subject is not only the crisis of masculinity that it inevitably entails. Of equal interest is the decline of classical femininity as a side effect of the postmodern predicament. This assumes that "woman as the other of man" had partaken in the historical construction of hegemonic and exclusionary practices of subjectivity. The "woman as other," the privileged "other" that Simone de Beauvoir analyzed brilliantly in terms of the "second" sex, is challenged, deconstructed, and thrown into question. This is only poetic and political justice: if white man is at a crisis point, so is white woman!

What I am saying is that the postmodern predicament, by opening up the conditions of possibility for the critical analysis of how certain forms of oppression have been structurally necessary (thus constituting "difference" necessarily as a mark of pejoration), also makes it urgent and necessary to deconstruct "woman." To deconstruct means that a notion is analyzed historically and politically, so as to make manifest the web of discursive and other power formations that constitute its identity and thus allow it to function as a signifier. This way of thinking calls for that flair for contradictions and paradoxes that I mentioned earlier—in this case, the paradox of woman as simultaneously powerless and powerful. The traditional Western notion of "woman" as "other" is certainly a pejorative, oppressed notion, but this does not mean that it is entirely powerless. On the contrary, that same notion is shot through with power relations—relations of class, race, ethnicity, etc.— that qualify and situate it historically and geopolitically and make it function in an internally contradictory manner.

To own up to the *complexity* and *multiplicity* of the power relations involved in the making of "woman" under patriarchy is not to deny her oppressed status. Quite the contrary, it is an attempt to radically redefine the political potential of a feminist position that is committed to accounting for and resisting the *simultaneity of potentially contradictory axes of oppression.* Postmodernist feminism is committed to thinking through this simultaneity, accounting for multiplicity and complexity only in order to find more adequate forms of resistance to them. What is at stake in this is the political but also the epistemological operation of moving "woman" out of the slot of devalued otherness to which she has historically been confined as the structurally necessary—and necessarily disqualified—"other." It is my way of reappropriating difference by tearing it apart from its hegemonic and exclusionary historical roots.

Quite clearly, this project raises issues that transcend the immediate perspective of "special interest groups." Some of these questions, as Butler and Scott suggest, are: How should we move politically in a world where the classical gender dichotomies no longer hold, because power is understood as the occurrence of simultaneous, complex, and multiple events? How should we act politically in a world where hybridization and cultural mix have come to occupy the place of the previous white male supremacist culture? What is the position of women in the new postcolonial world order and in non-Western patriarchal systems?

I have argued throughout this paper that a poststructuralist perspective is more relevant and constructive than its opponents claim, and that it offers more cogent ways of coming to terms with the challenges of today's world, than liberal or neo-universalistic approaches. I also think that the ways of thinking that poststructuralism offers are precisely what the "antirelativists" are trying to scare us away from. Thus while stressing as a conclusion the importance of maintaining an anti-antirelativist stance, I also want to emphasize simultaneously the theoretical irrelevance of this polemic. What is at stake in it is a set of deeper and more far-reaching concerns than the vicissitudes of the notion of relativism *per se*. To repeat the point made earlier by Cornel West, we are better off demystifying the categories in order to stay tuned to the complexity of the realities.

In response to these concerns, I maintain that we need to radicalize our vision of universal values, avoiding the double pitfall of relativism (i.e., dismissing the universal as redundant) and of essentialism (the nostalgic reassertion of essentialized identities). This is the challenge confronting the postmodernist antirelativist feminist and other critical intellectuals. I do believe that it will take more than the assault of nostalgia or the paranoia of those who fear "enemies within" to deter the feminists, the postcolonial and black subjects, the youth, and many others, from constructing viable alternatives to the decayed and nonetheless still operational ethno- and phallo-logocentric system, which, like an extinguished star, is still shining, though it is by now living on borrowed time.

NOTES

1. Unpublished poem, quoted in Audre Lorde's commencement address to Oberlin College, May 29, 1989. Cited in Chandra Mohanty, Ann Russo, and Lourdes Torres, eds., *Third World Women and the Politics of Feminism* (Bloomington: Indiana University Press, 1991), p. 1.

2. Ernest Gellner, *Postmodernism, Reason and Religion* (London: Routledge, 1992).

3. Sabine Lovibond in *New Left Review* (September/October 1994).

4. Contradictory because, in attempting to avoid relativism, poststructuralist feminists are drawn into complicity with the very rationalist tradition and the modernist kinds of value judgment that they criticize. Pretentious, because they do not live up to their own claims and fail to produce a radical alternative to dominant values.

5. Martha Nussbaum, "Women and Cultural Universals," paper delivered at the Seventh East-West Philosophers' Conference, Honolulu, Hawai'i, January 8–22, 1995. See also, "Human Functioning and Social Justice: In Defense of Aristotelian Essentialism," *Political Theory* (vol. 20, no. 2, May 92), pp. 202–46.

6. See, for instance, Carolyn Burke, Naomi Schor, and Margaret Whitford, eds., *Engaging with Irigaray* (New York: Columbia University Press, 1994); and Paul Gilroy, *The Black Atlantic* (Cambridge: Harvard University Press, 1993).

7. For an excellent survey of this polemic, see the special issue of the journal *Differences* (vol. 1, no. 2, 1989).

8. Paper delivered at the Seventh East-West Philosophers' Conference, Honolulu, Hawai'i, January 1995.

9. Barbara Herrnstein-Smith, *Contingencies of Value: Alternative Perspectives for Critical Theory* (Cambridge: Harvard University Press, 1988).

10. Clifford Geertz, "Anti Anti-Relativism," *American Anthropologist* (vol. 86, no. 2, June 1984), pp. 263–78.

11. For a study of this notion, see my *Nomadic Subjects* (New York: Columbia University Press, 1994).

12. Geertz, idem, p. 263.

13. Donna Haraway, "The Promises of Monsters: A Regenerative Politics for Inappropriate/d Others" in *Cultural Studies,* Lawrence Grossberg, Cary Nelson, and Paula Treichler, eds. (New York: Routledge, 1992).

14. Fredric Jameson, *Postmodernism or the Cultural Logic of Late Capitalism* (Durham: Duke University Press, 1991), p. ix.

15. In *What It Means To Be an American* (New York: Marsilio, 1992), Michael Walzer notes that European nation-states, being based on ancient and territorially based communities, find it harder to accommodate immigrant populations, especially from different religious backgrounds. Walzer opposes European intolerance to the greater flexibility of the United States, which is based on multiculturalism and pluralism. For a lucid comparison of the European and American brands of ethnocentrism, see Cornel West, *Prophetic Thought in Postmodern Times* (Monroe: Common Courage Press, 1994).

16. Gayatri Chakravorty Spivak, "French Feminism Revisited: Ethics and Politics" in *Feminists Theorize the Political,* Judith Butler and Joan Scott, eds. (New York: Routledge, 1992), p. 54.

17. Cornel West, *Prophetic Thought in Postmodern Times,* p. 125.

18. Massimo Cacciari, *Geo-filosofia dell'Europa* (Milano: Adelphi, 1994).

19. Rosi Braidotti, *Patterns of Dissonance: A Study of Women in Contemporary Philosophy* (New York: Routledge, 1991).

20. Idem, p. 57.

21. This remark is explicitly aimed at Richard Rorty's notion of "solidarity," with reference to his article "Solidarity or Objectivity?" in *Post-Analytic Philosophy,* John Rajchman and Cornel West, eds. (New York: Columbia University Press, 1985).

22. Martha Rosler, quoted at the "Decade Show" at the New Museum of Modern Art, New York City, 1990.

23. Poststructuralism is also known in Italian as *pensiero debole,* i.e., "weak thought."

24. Judith Butler and Joan Scott, eds., *Feminists Theorize the Political* (New York: Routledge, 1991), p. xi.

25. Stuart Hall, "'Race', Ethnicity, Nation: the Fateful/Fatal Triangle," W.E.B. du Bois Lectures, Harvard University, April 25–27, 1994.

26. Cornell West, idem, p. 20.

27. Inderpal Grewal and Caren Kaplan, eds., *Scattered Hegemonies: Postmodernity and Transnational Feminist Practices* (Minneapolis and London: University of Minnesota Press, 1994).

Ernesto Laclau

SUBJECT OF POLITICS, POLITICS OF THE SUBJECT

The question of the relationship (complementarity? tension? mutual exclusion?) between universalism and particularism occupies a central place in the current political and theoretical agenda. Universal values are seen either as dead or—at the very least—as threatened. What is more important, the positive character of those values is no longer taken for granted. On the one hand, under the banner of multiculturalism, the classical values of the Enlightenment are under fire and considered little more than the cultural preserve of Western imperialism. On the other hand, the whole debate concerning the end of modernity, the assault on foundationalism in its various expressions, has tended to establish an essential link between the obsolete notion of a ground of history and society, and the *actual contents* that, from the Enlightenment onward, have played that role of ground. It is important, however, to realize that these two debates have not advanced along symmetrical lines, that argumentative strategies have tended to move from one to the other in unexpected ways, and that many apparently paradoxical combinations have been shown to be possible. Thus, the so-called postmodern approaches can be seen as weakening the imperialist foundationalism of Western Enlightenment and opening the way to a more democratic cultural pluralism. But they can also be perceived as underpinning a notion of "weak" identity that is incompatible with the strong cultural attachments required by a "politics of authenticity." And universal values can be seen as a strong assertion of the "ethnia of the West" (as in the later Husserl), but also as a way of fostering—at least tendentially—an attitude of respect and tolerance *vis-à-vis* cultural diversity.

It would certainly be a mistake to think that concepts such as "universal" and "particular" have exactly the same meaning in both debates, but it would also be a mistake to assume that the continuous interaction of both has had

363

no effect on the central categories of each. This interaction has given way to ambiguities and displacements of meaning, which are, I think, the source of a certain political productivity. It is to these displacements and interactions that I want to refer in this essay. My question, put in its simplest terms is the following: What happens with the categories of "universal" and "particular" once they become tools in the language games that shape contemporary politics? What is performed through them? What displacements of meaning are at the root of their current political productivity?

MULTICULTURALISM

Let us take both debates successively and see the points in which each cuts across the central categories of the other. Multiculturalism first. The question can be formulated in these terms: Is a pure culture of difference possible, a pure particularism that does away entirely with any kind of universal principle? There are various reasons to doubt that this is possible. In the first place, to assert a purely separate and differential identity is to assert that this identity is constituted *through* cultural pluralism and difference. The reference to the other is very much present as constitutive of my own identity. There is no way that a particular group living in a wider community can live a monadic existence—on the contrary, part of the definition of its own identity is the construction of a complex and elaborated system of relations with other groups. And these relations will have to be regulated by norms and principles that transcend the particularism of *any* group. To assert, for instance, the right of all ethnic groups to cultural autonomy is to make an argumentative claim that can only be justified on universal grounds. The assertion of one's own particularity requires the appeal to something transcending it. The more particular a group is, the less it will be able to control the global communitarian terrain within which it operates, and the more universally grounded will have to be the justification of its claims.

But there is another reason why a politics of pure difference would be self-defeating. To assert one's own *differential* identity involves, as we have just argued, the inclusion in that identity of the other, as that from whom one delimits oneself. But it is easy to see that a fully achieved differential identity would involve the sanctioning of the existing status quo in the relation between groups. For an identity that is purely differential *vis-à-vis* other groups has to assert the identity of the other at the same time as its own and, as a result, cannot have identity claims in relation to those other groups. Let us suppose that a group *has* such claims—for instance, the demand for equal opportunities in employment and education, or even the right to have confessional schools. Insofar as these are claims presented as rights that I share as a member of the comunity with all other groups, they presuppose that I am not simply different from the others but, in some fundamental respects, equal to them. If it is asserted that all particular groups have the right to the respect of their own particularity, this means that they are equal to each other in some respects. Only in a situation in which all groups were different from each other and in which none of them wanted to be anything other than what they are, would the pure logic of difference exclusively govern the relations between groups. In all other scenarios the logic of difference will be interrupted by a logic of equivalence and equality. It is not for nothing that a pure logic of difference—the notion of separate developments—lies at the root of apartheid.

This is the reason why the struggle of *any* group that attempts to assert its own identity against a hostile environment is always confronted by two opposite but symmetrical dangers for which there is no logical solution, no square circle—only precarious and contingent attempts at mediation. If the group tries to assert its identity *as it is at that moment,* as its location within the community at large is defined by the system of exclusions dictated by the dominant groups, it condemns itself to a perpetually marginalized and ghettoized existence. Its cultural values can be easily retrieved as "folklore" by the establishment. If, on the other hand, it struggles to change its location within the community and to break with its situation of marginalization, it has to engage in a plurality of political initiatives that take it beyond the limits defining its present identity—for instance, struggles within the existing institutions. As these institutions are, however, ideologically and culturally moulded by the dominant groups, the danger is that the differential identity of the struggling group will be lost. Whether the new groups will manage to transform the institutions, or whether the logic of the institutions will manage to dilute—via co-optation—the identity of those groups is something that, of course, is not decided beforehand and depends on a hegemonic struggle. But what is certain is that there is no major historical change in which the identity of *all* intervening forces is not transformed. There is no possibility of victory in terms of an *already acquired* cultural authenticity. The increasing awareness of this fact explains the centrality of the concept of "hybridization" in contemporary debates.

If we look for an example of the early emergence of this alternative in European history, we can refer to the opposition between social democrats and revolutionary syndicalists in the decades preceding the First World War. The classical Marxist solution to the problem of the disadjustment between the particularism of the working class and the universality of the task of socialist transformation had been the assumption of an increasing simplification of the social structure under capitalism. As a result, the working class, as a homogeneous subject, would embrace the vast majority of the population and could take up the task of universal transformation. With this type of prognostic discredited at the turn of the century, two possible solutions remained open: either to accept a dispersion of democratic struggles only loosely unified by a semicorporative working class, or to foster a politics of pure identity by a working class unified through revolutionary violence. The first road led to what has been depicted as social-democratic integration: the working class was co-opted by a State in whose management it participated but whose mechanisms it could not master. The second road led to working class segregationism through violence and the rejection of all participation in democratic institutions. It is important to realize that the myth of the general strike in Sorel was not a device to keep a purely working class identity as a condition for a revolutionary victory. As the revolutionary strike was a regulatory idea rather than an actual possible event, it was not a real strategy for the seizure of power: its function was exhausted in being a mechanism endlessly recreating the workers' separate identity. In the option between a politics of identity and the transformation of the relations of force between groups, Sorelianism can be seen as an extreme form of unilateralization of the first alternative.

If we renounce, however, a unilateral solution, then the tension between these two contradictory extremes cannot be eradicated: it is there to stay, and the strategic calculation can only consist of the pragmatic negotiation between them. Hybridization is not a marginal phenomenon but the very terrain in which contemporary political identities are constructed. Let us consider a formula such as "strategic essentialism," which has been much used lately. For a variety of reasons, I am not entirely satisfied with it, but it has the advantage of bringing to the fore the antinomic alternatives to which we have been referring and the need for a politically negotiated equilibrium between them. "Essentialism" alludes to a strong identity politics, without which there can be no bases for political calculation and action. But that essentialism is only strategic—i.e., it points, at the very moment of its constitution, to its own contingency and its own limits.

This contingency is central to understanding what is perhaps the most prominent feature of contemporary politics: the full recognition of the limited and fragmented character of its historical agents. Modernity started with the aspiration to a limitless historical actor who would be able to ensure the fullness of a perfectly instituted social order. Whatever the road leading to that fullness—an "invisible hand" which holds together a multiplicity of diverse individual wills, or a universal class which would ensure a transparent and rational system of social relations—it always implied that the agents of that historical transformation would be able to overcome all particularism and all limitation and bring about a society reconciled with itself. This is what, for modernity, true universality meant. The starting point of contemporary social and political struggles is, on the contrary, the strong assertion of their particularity, the conviction that none of them is capable, on its own, of bringing about the fullness of the community. But precisely because of that, as we have seen, this particularity cannot be constructed through a pure "politics of difference" but has to appeal, as the very condition of its own assertion, to universal principles. The question that at this point arises is to what extent this universality is the same as the universality of modernity, to what extent the very idea of a fullness of society experiences, in this changed political and intellectual climate, a radical mutation that, while maintaining the double reference to the universal and the particular, entirely transforms the logic of their articulation. Before answering this question, however, we have to move to our second debate, that related to the critique of foundationalism.

CONTEXTS AND THE CRITIQUE OF FOUNDATIONALISM

Let us start our discussion with a very common proposition: that there is no truth or value independent of a context, that the validity of any statement is only contextually determined. In one sense, of course, this proposition is un-controversial and a necessary corollary of the critique of foundationalism. To pass from it to assert the incommensurability of context and to draw from there an argument in defense of cultural pluralism seems to be only a logical move, and I am certainly not prepared to argue otherwise. There is, however, one difficulty that this whole line of reasoning does not contemplate, and it is the following: how to determine the limits of a context? Let us accept that all identity is a differential identity. In that case two consequences follow: (1) that, as in a Saussurean system, each identity is what it is only through its differences from all the others; and (2) that the context has to be a closed one—if all identities depend on the differential *system*, unless the latter defines its own limits, no identity would be finally constituted. But nothing is more difficult, from a logical point of view, than defining those limits. If we had a foundational perspective, we could appeal to an ultimate ground that would be the source of all differences. But if we are dealing with a true pluralism of differences, if the differences are *constitutive*, we cannot go, in the search for the systematic limits that define a context, beyond the differences themselves. Now, the only way of defining a context is, as we said, through its limits, and the only way of defining those limits is to point out what is beyond them. But what is beyond the limits can only be other differences, and in that case, given the constitutive character of all differences, it is impossible to establish if these new differences are internal or external to the context. The very possibility of a limit and, *ergo*, a context, is thus jeopardized.

As I have argued elsewhere,[1] the only way out of this difficulty is to postulate a beyond, which is not one more difference, but something that poses a threat to (i.e., negates) all the differences within that context—or, better, that the context constitutes itself as such through the act of exclusion of

something alien, of a radical otherness. Now, this possibility has three consequences that are capital for our argument.

1. The first is that antagonism and exclusion are constitutive of all identity. Without limits through which a (nondialectical) negativity is constructed, we would have an indefinite dispersion of differences whose
   absence of systematic limits would make any differential identity impossible. But this very function of constituting differential identities
   through antagonistic limits is what, at the same time, destabilizes and
   subverts those differences. For if the limit poses an equal threat to all
   the differences, it makes them all equivalent to each other, interchangeable with each other as far as the limit is concerned. This already
   announces the possibility of a relative universalization through equivalential logics, which is not incompatible with a differential particularism, but is required by the very logic of the latter.
2. The system is what is required for the differential identities to be constituted, but the only thing—exclusion—that can constitute the system
   and thus make possible those identities, is also what subverts them. (In
   deconstructive terms, the conditions of possibility of the system are
   also its conditions of impossibility.) Contexts have to be internally subverted in order to become possible. The system (as in Lacan's object
   petit a) is that which the very logic of the context requires, but which
   is, however, impossible. It is present, if you want, through its absence.
   But this means two things. First, that all differential identity will be
   constitutively split; it will be the crossing point between the logic of difference and the logic of equivalence. This will introduce into it a radical undecidability. Second, that although the fullness and universality
   of society is unachievable, its need does not disappear: it will always
   show itself through the presence of its absence. Again, we see here announcing itself an intimate connection between the universal and the
   particular, which does not consist, however, in the subsumption of the
   latter in the former.
3. Finally, if that impossible object—the system—cannot be represented
   but needs, however, to show itself within the field of representation, the
   means of that representation will be constitutively inadequate. Only
   the particulars are such means. As a result, the systematicity of the system, the moment of its impossible totalization will be symbolized by
   particulars that contingently assume such a representative function.
   This means, first, that the particularity of the particular is subverted by
   this function of representing the universal but, second, that a certain
   particular, by making of its own particularity the signifying body of a
   universal representation, comes to occupy—within the system of differences as a whole—a hegemonic role. This anticipates our main con-

clusion: in a society (and this is finally the case of *any* society) in which its fullness—the moment of its universality—is unachievable, the relation between the universal and the particular is a hegemonic relation.

Let us see in more detail the logic of that relation. I will take as an example the "universalization" of the popular symbols of Peronism in the Argentina of the 1960s and 1970s. After the coup of 1955, which overthrew the Peronist regime, Argentina entered a long period of institutional instability which lasted for over twenty years. Peronism and other popular organizations were proscribed, and the succession of military governments and fraudulent civilian regimes that occupied the government were clearly incapable of meeting the popular demands of the masses through the existing institutional channels. So, there was a succession of regimes less and less representative and an accumulation of unfulfilled democratic demands. These demands were certainly particular ones and came from very different groups. The fact that all of them were rejected by the dominant regimes established an increasing relation of equivalence between them. This equivalence, it is important to realize, did not express any essential *a priori* unity. On the contrary, its only ground was the rejection of all those demands by successive regimes. In terms of our previous terminology, their unification within a context or system of differences was the pure result of all of them being antagonized by the dominant sectors.

Now, as we have seen, this contextual unification of a system of differences can only take place at the price of weakening the purely differential identities, through the operation of a logic of equivalence which introduces a dimension of relative universality. In our example, people felt that through the differential particularity of their demands—housing, union rights, level of wages, protection of national industry, etc.—something equally present in all of them was expressed, which was opposition to the regime. It is important to realize that this dimension of universality was not at odds with the particularism of the demands, or even of the groups entering into the equivalential relation, but grew out of it. A certain more universal perspective, which developed out of the inscription of particular demands in a wider popular language of resistance, was the result of the expansion of the equivalential logic. A pure particularism of the demands of the groups, which had entirely avoided the equivalential logic, would have only been possible if the regime had succeeded in dealing separately with the particular demands and had absorbed them in a "transformistic" way. But in any process of hegemonic decline, this transformistic absorption becomes impossible and the equivalential logics interrupt the pure particularism of the individual democratic demands.

As we can see, this dimension of universality reached through equivalence is very different from the universality that results from an underlying essence

or an unconditioned *a priori* principle. Neither is it a regulative idea—
empirically unreachable but with an unequivocal teleological content—
because it cannot exist apart from the system of equivalences from which it
proceeds. But this has important consequences for both the content and the
function of that universality. We have seen before that the moment of totalization or universalization of the community—the moment of its fullness—is
an impossible object that can only acquire a discursive presence through a
particular content that divests itself of its particularity in order to represent
that fullness. To return to our Argentinian example, this was precisely the role
that, in the 1960s and 1970s, was played by the popular symbols of Peronism.
As I said earlier, the country had entered into a rapid process of deinstitu-
tionalization, so the equivalential logics could operate freely. The Peronist
movement itself lacked a real organization and was rather a series of symbols
and a loose language unifying a variety of political initiatives. Finally, Peron
himself was in exile in Madrid, intervening only in a distant way in his movement's actions, being very careful not to take any definitive stand in the fac-
tional struggles within Peronism. In those circumstances, he was in the ideal
position to become the "empty signifier" incarnating the moment of universality in the chain of equivalences which unified the popular camp. And the
ulterior destiny of Peronism in the 1970s clearly illustrates the essential ambiguity inherent in any hegemonic process. On the one hand, the fact that the
symbols of a particular group assume at some point a function of universal
representation gives certainly a hegemonic power to that group, but, on the
other hand, the fact that that function of universal representation has been
acquired at the price of weakening the differential particularism of the original identity leads necessarily to the conclusion that this hegemony is going
to be precarious and threatened. The wild logic of emptying the signifiers of
universality through the expansion of the equivalential chains means that no
fixing and particular limitation of the sliding of the signified under the signifier is going to be permanently assured. This is what happened to Peronism
after the electoral victory of 1973 and Peron's return to Argentina. Peron was
no longer an empty signifier but the President of the country, who had to
carry out concrete politics. Yet the chains of equivalences constructed by the
different factions of his movements had gone beyond any possibility of
control—even by Peron himself. The result was the bloody process that led
to the military dictatorship in 1976.

THE DIALECTICS OF UNIVERSALITY

The previous developments lead us to the following conclusion. The dimension of universality—resulting from the incompletion of all differential identities—cannot be eliminated insofar as a community is not entirely

homogeneous (if it *were* homogeneous, what would disappear is not only universality but also the very distinction, universality/particularity). This dimension is, however, just an empty place unifying a set of equivalential demands. We have to determine the nature of this place both in terms of its contents and of its function. As far as the content is concerned, it does not have one of its own but just that which is given to it by a transient articulation of equivalential demands. There is a paradox implicit in the formulation of universal principles, which is that all of them have to present themselves as valid without exception, while, even in its own terms, this universality can be easily questioned and can never be actually maintained. Let us take a universal principle such as the right of nations to self-determination. As a universal right, it claims to be valid in any circumstance. Let us suppose now that within a nation genocidal practices are taking place. In that case, has the international community the duty to intervene or is the principle of self-determination unconditionally valid? The paradox is that the principle has to be formulated as universally valid but there will always be exceptions to that universal validity. But perhaps the paradox proceeds from believing that this universality has a content of its own, whose logical implications can be analytically deduced, without realizing that its only function—within a particular language game— is to make discursively possible a chain of equivalential effects, but without pretending that this universality can operate beyond the context of its emergence. There are innumerable contexts in which the principle of national self-determination is a perfectly valid way of totalizing and universalizing a historical experience.

But in that case, if we always know beforehand that no universalization will live up to its task, if it will always fail to deliver the goods, why does the equivalential aggregation have to express itself through the universal? The answer is to be found in what we said before about the formal structure on which the aggregation depends. The "something identical" shared by all the terms of the equivalential chain—that which makes the equivalence possible—cannot be something positive (i.e., one more difference that could be defined in its particularity), but proceeds from the unifying effects that the external threat puts to an otherwise perfectly heterogeneous set of differences (particularities). The "something identical" can only be the pure, abstract, absent fullness of the community, which lacks, as we have seen, any direct form of representation and expresses itself through the equivalence of the differential terms. But, in that case, it is essential that the chain of equivalences remains open. Otherwise its closure could only be the result of one more difference specifiable in its particularity, and we would not be confronted with the fullness of the community as an absence. The open character of the chain means that what is expressed through it has to be universal and not particular. Now, this universality needs—for its expression—to be incarnated in something essentially incommensurable with it: a particularity (as in our example of the right to national self-determination). This is the source of the tension and ambiguities surrounding all those so-called "universal" principles. All of them *have* to be formulated as limitless principles, expressing a universality transcending them, but they all, for essential reasons, sooner or later become entangled in their own contextual particularism and are incapable of fulfilling their universal function.

As far as the function (as opposed to the content) of the "universal" is concerned, we have said enough to make clear what it consists of. It is exhausted in introducing chains of equivalence in an otherwise purely differential world. This is the moment of hegemonic aggregation and articulation and can operate in two ways. The first is to inscribe particular identities and demands as links in a wider chain of equivalences, thereby giving each of them a "relative" universalization. If, for instance, feminist demands enter into chains of equivalence with those of black groups, ethnic minorities, civil rights activists, etc., they acquire a more global perspective than if they remain restricted to their own particularism. The second is to give a particular demand a function of universal representation—that is, to attribute to it the value of a horizon, giving coherence to the chain of equivalences and, at the same time, keeping it indefinitely open. To give just a few examples: The socialization of the means of production was not considered as a narrow demand concerning the economy but as the "name" for a wide variety of equivalential effects irradiating over the whole society. The introduction of a market economy played a similar role in Eastern Europe after 1989. The return of Peron, in our Argentinian example, was also conceived in the early 1970s as the prelude to a much wider historical transformation. Which particular demand, or sets of demands, are going to play this function of universal representation is something that cannot be determined by *a priori* reasons. (If we could do so, this would mean that there is something in the particularity of the demand that predetermined it to fulfill that role, and that would be in contradiction of our whole argument.)

We can now return to the two debates that were the starting point of our reflexion. As we can see, there are several points on which they interact and in which parallelism can be detected. We have said enough about multiculturalism for our argument concerning the limits of particularism to be clear. A *pure* particularistic stand is self-defeating, because it has to provide a ground for the constitution of the differences *as* differences, and such a ground can only be a new version of an essentialist universalism. (If we have a *system* of differences A/B/C, etc., we have to account for this systemic dimension and that leads us straight into the discourse of the ground. If we have a plurality of *separate* elements A, B, C, etc., which do not constitute a system, we still have to account for this separation—to be separated is also a form of relation between objects—and we are again entangled as Leibniz well knew, in the positing of a ground. The preestablished harmony of the monads is as essential a ground as the Spinozist totality.) So the only way out of this dilemma is to maintain the dimension of universality but to propose a different form of its articulation with the particular. This is what we have tried to provide in the preceding pages through the notion of the universal as an empty but ineradicable place.

It is important, however, to realize that this type of articulation would be theoretically unthinkable if we did not introduce into the picture some of the central tenets of the contemporary critique of foundationalism. (It would be unthinkable, for instance, in a Habermasian perspective.) If meaning is fixed beforehand, either in a strong sense, by a radical ground (a position that fewer and fewer people would sustain today), or in a weaker version, through the regulative principle of an undistorted communication, the very possibility of the ground as an empty place that is politically and contingently filled by a variety of social forces, disappears. Differences would not be constitutive, because something previous to their play *already* fixes the limit of their possible variation and establishes an external tribunal to *judge* them. Only the critique of a universality that is determined in all its essential dimensions by the metaphysics of presence, opens the way for a *theoretical* apprehension of the notion of "articulation" that we are trying to elaborate—as opposed to a purely impressionistic apprehension, in terms of a discourse structured through concepts that are perfectly incompatible with it. (We always have to remember Pascal's critique of those who think that they are already converted because they have just started thinking of getting converted.)

But if the debate concerning multiculturalism can draw clear advantages from the contemporary critique of foundationalism (broadly speaking, the whole range of intellectual developments embraced by labels such as "postmodernism" and "poststructuralism"), these advantages also work in the opposite direction. For the requirements of a politics based on a universality compatible with an increasing expansion of cultural differences are clearly incompatible with some versions of postmodernism, particularly those that conclude from the critique of foundationalism that there is an implosion of all meaning and the entry into a world of "simulation" (Baudrillard). I do not think that this is a conclusion that follows at all. As we have argued, the impossibility of a universal ground does not eliminate its need. It just transforms the ground into an empty place that can partially be filled in a variety of ways. (The strategies of this filling is what politics is about.)

Let us go back for a moment to the question of contextualization. If we could have a "saturated" context, we would indeed be confronted with a plurality of incommensurable spaces without any possible tribunal deciding between them. But, as we have seen, any such saturated context is impossible. Yet the conclusion that follows from this verification is not that there is a formless dispersion of meaning without any possible kind of even a relative articulation but, rather, that whatever plays such an articulating role is not predetermined to it by the form of the dispersion as such. This means first that all articulation is contingent and, second, that the articulating moment as such is always going to be an empty place—the various attempts at filling it being transient and submitted to contestation. As a result, at any historical moment, whatever dispersion of differences exists in society is going to be submitted to contradictory processes of contextualization and decontextualization. For instance, those discourses attempting to close a context around certain principles or values will be confronted and limited by discourses of *rights,* which try to limit the closure of any context. This is what makes so unconvincing the attempts by contemporary neo-Aristotelians such as MacIntyre to accept only the contextualizing dimension and close society around a substantive vision of the common good. Contemporary social and political struggles open, I think, the strategies at filling the empty place of the common good. The ontological implications of the thought accompanying these "filling" strategies clarifies, in turn, the horizon of possibilities opened by the antifoundationalist critique. It is to these strategic logics that I want to devote the rest of this essay.

RULING AND UNIVERSALITY: FOUR MOMENTS

We can start with some conclusions that could easily be derived from our previous analysis concerning the status of the universal. The first is that if the place of the universal is an empty one and there is no *a priori* reason for it not to be filled by *any* content, if the forces that fill that place are constitutively split between the concrete politics that they advocate and the ability of those politics to fill the empty place, the political language of any society whose degree of institutionalization has, to some extent, been shaken or undermined, will also be split. Let us take a term such as "order" (social order). What are the conditions of its universalization? Simply, that the experience of a radical disorder makes *any* order preferable to the continuity of disorder. The experience of a lack, of an absence of fullness in social relations, transforms "order" into the signifier of an absent fullness. This explains the split we were referring to. Any concrete politics, if it is capable of bringing about social order, will be judged not only according to its merits in the abstract, independently of any circumstance, but mainly in terms of that ability to bring about "order"—a name for the absent fullness of society. ("Change," "revolution," "unity of the people," etc. are other signifiers that have historically played the same role.) As for essential reasons, we have pointed out that fullness of society is unreachable, this split in the identity of political agents is an absolutely constitutive "ontological difference"—in a sense not entirely unrelated to Heidegger's use of this expression. The universal is certainly empty and can only be filled, in different contexts, by concrete particulars. But at the same time, it is absolutely essential for any kind of *political* interaction, for if the latter took place without universal reference, there would be no political interaction at all. We would only have either a complementarity of differences, which would be totally nonantagonistic, or a totally antagonistic one, one where differences entirely lack any commensurability and whose only possible resolution is the mutual destruction of the adversaries.

Now it is our contention that politico-philosophical reflexion since the ancient world has been largely conscious of this constitutive split, and has tried to provide various ways of dealing with it. These ways follow one or the other of the logical possibilities pointed out in the previous analysis. To suggest how this took place, we will briefly refer to four moments in the politico-philosophical tradition of the West in which images of the ruler have emerged that combine in different ways universality and particularity. We will successively refer to Plato's philosopher-king, to Hobbes's sovereign, to Hegel's hereditary monarch, and to Gramsci's hegemonic class.

In Plato the situation is unambiguous. There is no possible tension or antagonism between the universal and the particular. Far from being an empty place, the universal is the location of all possible meaning, and it absorbs within itself the particular. Now, there is for him, however, only *one* articulation of the particularities that actualize the essential form of the community. The universal is not "filled" from outside but is the fullness of its own origin and expresses itself in all aspects of social organization. There can be here no "ontological difference" between the fullness of the community and its actual political and social arrangements. Only one kind of social arrangement that extends itself to the most minute aspects of social life is compatible with what the community in its last instance is. Other forms of social organization can, of course, factually exist, but they do not have the status of alternative forms among which one has to choose according to the circumstances. They are just degenerate forms, pure corruptions of being, derived from the obfuscation of the mind. Insofar as there is true knowledge, only one particular form of social organization realizes the universal. And if ruling is a matter of knowledge and not of prudence, only the bearer of that knowledge, the philosopher, has the right to rule. *Ergo*: a philosopher-king.

In Hobbes, we are apparently in the antipodes of Plato. Far from being the sovereign who has the knowledge of what the community is, before any political decision, his decisions are the only source of the social order. Hobbes is well aware of what we have called the "ontological difference." Insofar as the anarchy of the state of nature threatens society with radical disorder, the unification of the will of the community in the will of the ruler (or rather, the will of the ruler as the only unified will that the community can have) will count so long as it imposes order, whatever the contents of the latter might be. Any order will be better than radical disorder. There is here something close to a complete indifference to the *content* of the social order imposed by the ruler and an exclusive concentration on the *function* of the latter: ensuring order as such. "Order" becomes certainly an empty place, but there is in Hobbes no hegemonic theory about the transient forms of its filling. The sovereign, the "mortall God," fills the empty place once and forever.

So Plato and Hobbes are apparently at the antipodes of the theoretical spectrum. For Plato, the universal is the *only* full place; for Hobbes, it is an absolutely empty place that has to be filled by the will of the sovereign. But if we look more closely at the matter, we will see that this difference between them is overshadowed by what they actually share, which is not to allow the particular any dynamics of its own *vis-à-vis* the full/empty place of the universal. In the first case, the particular has to actualize in its own body a universality transcending it; in the second case equally, although by artifical means, a particular has detached itself from the realm of particularities and has become the unchallengeable Law of the community.

For Hegel, the problem is posed in different terms. As for him the particularism of each stage of social organization is *aufgehoben* (sublimated) to a higher level, the problem of the incommensurability between particular content and universal function cannot actually arise. But the problem of the empty place emerges in relation to the moment in which the community has to *signify* itself as a totality—i.e., the moment of its *individuality*. This signification is obtained, as we know, through the constitutional monarch, whose physical body represents a rational totality absolutely dissimilar to that body. (This representation, in Hegel, of something that has no content of its own through something else that is its exact reverse has been very often stressed by Slavoj Zizek, who has contributed several other examples, such as the assertion, in the *Phenomenology of Spirit,* that "the Spirit is a bone.") But this relation by which a physical body, in its pure alienation of any spiritual content, can represent this last content, entirely depends on the community having reached, through successive sublation of its partial contents, the highest form of rationality achievable in its own sphere. For such a fully rational community, no *content* can be added, and there only remains, as a requirement for its completion, *the signification of the achievement of that functional rationality.* Because of that, the rational monarch cannot be an elected monarch; he has to be a hereditary one. If he were elected, *reasons* would have to be given for that election, and this process of argumentation would mean that the rationality of society would have not been achieved independently of the monarch, and that the latter would have to play a greater role than a pure function of ceremonial representation.

Finally, Gramsci. The hegemonic class can only become such by linking a particular content to a universality transcending it. If we say, as Gramsci did, that the task of the Italian working class is to fulfill the tasks of national unification that the Italian people had posed to itself since the time of

Machiavelli and, in this way, to complete the historical project of the *Risorg-imento,* we have a double order of reference. On the one hand, a concrete political program—that of the workers—as opposed to those of other politi-cal forces; but on the other hand, that program—i.e., that set of demands and political proposals—is presented as a historical vehicle for a task transcend-ing it: the unity of the Italian nation. Now if this "unity of the Italian nation" were a concrete content, specifiable in a particular context, it could not be something that extended over a period of centuries and that different histor-ical forces could bring about. If this, however, *can* happen, it is because "unity of the Italian nation" is just the name or the symbol of a lack. Precisely be-cause it is a *constitutive* lack, there is no content that is *a priori* destined to fill it, and it is open to the most diverse articulations. But this means that the "good" articulation, the one that would finally suture the link between uni-versal task and concrete historical forces, will never be found, and that all par-tial victory will always take place against the background of an ultimate and unsurpassable impossibility.

Viewed from this perspective, the Gramscian project can be seen as a dou-ble displacement, *vis-à-vis* Hegel and *vis-*à-*vis* Hobbes. In one sense, it is more Hobbesian than Hegelian, because, as society and State are less self-structured than in Hegel, they require a dimension of political constitution in which the representation of the unity of the community is not separated from its construction. There is a remainder of particularity that cannot be eliminated from the representation of that unity (unity equals individuality in the Hegelian sense). The presence of this remainder is what is specific to the hegemonic relation. The hegemonic class is somewhere in between the Hegelian monarch and the Leviathan. But it can equally be said that Gramsci is more Hegelian than Hobbesian, in the sense that the political moment in his analysis presupposes an image of social crises that is far less radical than in Hobbes. Gramsci's "organic crises" fall far short, in terms of their degrees of social structuration, of the Hobbesian state of nature. In some senses, the succession of hegemonic regimes can be seen as a series of "partial covenants"—partial because, as society is more structured than in Hobbes, people have more conditions to enter into the political covenant, but partial also because, as the result of that, they also have more reasons to substitute the sovereign.

These last points allow us to go back to our earlier discussion concerning contemporary particularistic struggles and to inscribe it within the politico-philosophical tradition. In the same way that we have presented Gramsci's problematic through the displacements that he introduces *vis-à-vis* the two approaches that we have symbolized in Hobbes and Hegel, we could present the political alternatives open to multicultural struggles through similar dis-placements *vis-à-vis* Gramsci's approach. The first and most obvious dis-placement is to conceive a society that is more particularistic and fragmented and less amenable than Gramsci's to enter into unified hegemonic articulations. The second, is that the loci from which the articulation takes place—for Gramsci they were locations such as the Party or the State (in an expanded sense)—are going to be also more plural and less likely to generate a chain of totalizing effects. What we have called the remainder of particularism inherent in any hegemonic centrality grows thicker but also more plural. Now, this has mixed effects from the viewpoint of a democratic politics. Let us imagine a Jacobine scenario. The public sphere is one, the place of power is one but empty, and a plurality of political forces can occupy the latter. In one sense, we can say that this is an ideal situation for democracy, because the place of power is empty and we can conceive the democratic process as a partial articulation of the empty universality of the community and the particularism of the transient political forces incarnating it. This is true, but precisely because the universal place is empty, it can be occupied by *any* force, not necessarily democratic. As is well-known, this is one of the roots of contemporary totalitarianism (Lefort).

If, on the contrary, the place of power is not unique, the remainder, as we said, will be weightier, and the possibility of constructing a common public sphere through a series of equivalential effects cutting across communities will be clearly less. This has ambiguous results. On the one hand, communities are certainly more protected in the sense that a Jacobine totalitarianism is less likely. But on the other hand, for reasons that have been pointed out earlier, this also favors the maintenance of the status quo. We can perfectly well imagine a modified Hobbesian scenario in which the Law respects communities—no longer individuals—in their private sphere, while the main decisions concerning the future of the community as a whole are the preserve of a neo-Leviathan—for instance, a quasi-omnipotent technocracy. To realize that this is not at all an unrealistic scenario, we only have to think of Samuel Huntington and, more generally, of contemporary corporatist approaches.

The other alternative is more complex, but it is the only one, I think, compatible with a true democratic politics. It wholly accepts the plural and fragmented nature of contemporary societies, but instead of remaining in this particularistic moment, it tries to inscribe this plurality in equivalential logics that make possible the construction of new public spheres. Difference and particularisms are the necessary starting point, but out of these it is possible to open the way to a relative universalization of values that can be the basis for a popular hegemony. This universalization and its open character certainly condemns all identity to an unavoidable hybridization, but hybridization does not necessarily mean decline through a loss of identity. It can also mean empowering existing identities through the opening of new possibilities. Only a conservative identity, closed on itself, could experience hybridization as a loss. But this democratico-hegemonic possibility has to recognize the constitutive contextualized/decontextualized terrain of its constitution and fully take advantage of the political possibilities that this undecidability opens.

All this finally amounts to saying is that the particular can only fully realize itself if it constantly keeps open and constantly redefines its relation to the universal.

NOTE

1. See Ernesto Laclau, "Why do Empty Signifiers Matter to Politics" in *The Lesser Evil and the Greater Good,* Jeffrey Weeks, ed. (London: Rivers Oram Press, 1994).

Chantal Mouffe

DEMOCRATIC IDENTITY AND
PLURALIST POLITICS

In this paper I want to take issue with those who assert that democracy needs rational foundations and that it is by providing such foundations that one will create allegiance to liberal democratic institutions. To criticize rationalism is, for them, to undermine the very basis of democratic citizenship. Hence their rejection of the so-called "postmodern" critique, which is presented as a threat to the democratic project.

I will argue, on the contrary, that it is only by drawing all of the implications of the critique of essentialism, which constitutes the point of convergence of the antirationalist approach, that it is possible to grasp the nature of the political and to acknowledge the challenge confronting the democratic project today. It is urgent that we realize that the universalist and rationalist framework in which that project was formulated during the Enlightenment has today become an obstacle to an adequate understanding of the present stage of democratic politics. Such a framework should be discarded, and this can be done without having to abandon the political aspect of the Enlightenment, which is represented by the democratic revolution.

I will follow the lead of Hans Blumenberg, who, in his book *The Legitimacy of the Modern Age*,[1] distinguishes two different logics in the Enlightenment—one of "self-assertion" (we could call it "political") and one of "self-grounding" (we could call it "epistemological"). According to him, these two logics have been articulated historically, but there is no necessary relation between them and they can be perfectly separated. It is therefore possible to discriminate between what is truly modern—the idea of "self-assertion"—and what is merely a "reoccupation" of a medieval position—i.e., an attempt to give a modern answer to a premodern question. In Blumenberg's view, rationalism is not something essential to the idea of self-assertion but a residue from the absolutist medieval problematic. This illusion of

381

providing itself with its own foundations which accompanied the labor of liberation from theology should now be abandoned and modern reason should acknowledge its limits. Indeed, it is only when it comes to terms with pluralism and accepts the impossibility of total control and final harmony that modern reason frees itself from its premodern heritage.

This approach reveals the inadequacy of the term "postmodernity" when it is used to refer to a completely different historical period that would signify a break with modernity. When we realize that rationalism and abstract universalism, far from being constitutive of modern reason, were in fact *re-occupations* of the premodern position, it becomes clear that to put them into question does not imply a rejection of modernity but a coming to terms with the potentialities that were inscribed in it since the beginning. It also help us to understand why the critique of the epistemological aspect of the Enlightenment does not put its political aspect of self-assertion into question but, on the contrary, can help to strengthen the democratic project.

THE CRITIQUE OF ESSENTIALISM

One of the fundamental advances of what I have called the critique of essentialism has been the break with the category of the subject as a rational transparent entity that could convey a homogeneous meaning to the total field of her conduct by being the source of her actions. Psychoanalysis has shown that, far from being organized around the transparency of an ego, personality is structured in a number of levels that lie outside the consciousness and rationality of the agents. It has therefore discredited the idea of the necessarily unified character of the subject. Freud's central claim is that the human mind is necessarily subject to division between two systems, one of which is not and cannot be conscious. The self-mastery of the subject, a central theme of modern philosophy, is precisely what he argues can never be achieved. Following Freud and expanding his insight, Lacan has shown the plurality of registers—the Symbolic, the Real, and the Imaginary—that penetrate any identity, and the place of the subject as the place of the lack, which, though represented within the structure, is the empty place that at the same time subverts and is the condition of the constitution of any identity. The history of the subject is the history of her identifications and there is no concealed identity to be rescued beyond the latter.

There is thus a double movement. On the one hand, a movement of decentering which prevents the fixation of a set of positions around a pre-constituted point. On the other hand, and as a result of this essential nonfixity, the opposite movement: the institution of nodal points, partial fixations that limit the flux of the signified under the signifier. But the dialectics of nonfixity/fixation is possible only because fixity is not pregiven, because no center of subjectivity precedes the subject's identifications.

It is important to stress that such a critique of essential identities is not limited to a certain current in French theory but is found in the most important philosophies of the twentieth century. For instance, in the philosophy of language of the later Wittgenstein, we also find a critique of the rationalist conception of the subject that indicates that the latter cannot be the source of linguistic meanings, since it is through participation in different language games that the world is disclosed to us. We encounter the same idea in Gadamer's philosophical hermeneutics in the thesis that there exists a fundamental unity between thought, language, and the world, and that it is within language that the horizon of our present is constituted. A similar critique of the centrality of the subject in modern metaphysics and of its unitary character can be found in different forms in several other authors, and this allows us to affirm that, far from being limited to poststructuralism or postmodernism, as some would have it, the critique of essentialism is present in the most important contemporary philosophical currents.

ANTIESSENTIALISM AND POLITICS

In *Hegemony and Socialist Strategy*,[2] we attempted to draw the consequences of this critique of essentialism for a radical conception of democracy, by articulating some of its insights with the Gramscian conception of hegemony. This led us to put the question of power and antagonism and their ineradicable character at the center of our approach. One of the main theses of the book is that social objectivity is constituted through acts of power. This means that any social objectivity is ultimately political and that it has to show the traces of exclusion that govern its constitution—what, following Derrida, we have called its "constitutive outside." But if an object has inscribed in its very being something other than itself, if, as a result, everything is constructed as *difference*, its being cannot be conceived as pure "presence" or "objectivity." This indicates that the logic of the constitution of the social is incompatible with the objectivism and essentialism dominant in social sciences and liberal thought.

The point of convergence—or rather mutual collapse—between objectivity and power is what we called "hegemony." This way of posing the problem indicates that power should not be conceived as an *external* relation taking place between two preconstituted identities, but rather as constituting the identities themselves. This is really decisive. Because if the "constitutive outside" is present within the inside as its always real possibility, the inside itself becomes a purely contingent and reversible arrangement (in other words, the hegemonic arrangement cannot claim any other source of validity than the power basis on which it is grounded). The structure of mere possibility of any objective order, which is revealed by its mere hegemonic nature, is shown in the forms assumed by the *subversion* of the sign (i.e., of the relation signifer/

signified). For instance, the signifier "democracy" is very different when fixed to a certain signified in a discourse that articulates it to anticommunism and when it is fixed to another signified in a discourse that makes it part of the total meaning of antifascism. As there is no common ground between those conflicting articulations, there is no way of subsuming them under a deeper objectivity which would reveal its true and deeper essence. This is why we assert that antagonism is *constitutive* and *irreducible*.

The consequences of this thesis for politics are far-reaching. For instance, according to this perspective, political practice in a democratic society does not consist in defending the rights of preconstituted identities, but rather in constituting those identities themselves in a precarious and always vulnerable terrain. Such an approach also involves a displacement of the traditional relations between democracy and power. For a traditional socialist conception, the more democratic a society is, the less power would be constitutive of social relations. But if we accept that relations of power are constitutive of the social, then the main question of democratic politics is not how to eliminate power, but how to constitute forms of power that are compatible with democratic values. To acknowledge the existence of relations of power and the need to transform them while renouncing the illusion that we could free ourselves completely from power, this is what is specific to the project of "radical and plural democracy" that we are advocating.

Another distinct characteristic of our approach concerns the question of the de-universalization of political subjects. We try to break with all forms of essentialism. Not only the essentialism that penetrates to a large extent the basic categories of modern sociology and liberal thought and according to which every social identity is perfectly defined in the historical process of the unfolding of being, but also with its diametrical opposite: a certain type of extreme postmodern fragmentation of the social that refuses to give the fragments any kind of relational identity. Such a view leaves us with a multiplicity of identities without any common denominator and makes it impossible to distinguish between differences that exist but should not exist and differences that do not exist but should exist. In other words, putting an exclusive emphasis on heterogeneity and incommensurability impedes our recognition of how certain differences are constructed as relations of subordination and should therefore be challenged by a radical democratic politics.

Democracy and Identity

Having given a brief outline of the main tenets of our antiessentialist approach and of its general implications for politics, I would now like to address some specific problems concerning the construction of democratic identities. I am going to examine how such a question can be formulated within the framework that breaks with the traditional rationalist liberal problematic and which incorporates some crucial insights of the critique of essentialism. One of the main problems with the liberal framework is that it reduces politics to the calculus of interests. Individuals are presented as rational actors moved by the search for the maximization of their self-interest. That is, they are seen as acting in the field of politics in a basically instrumentalist way. Politics is conceived through a model elaborated in the study of economics: as a market concerned with the allocation of resources, where compromises are reached among interests defined independently of their political articulation. Other liberals reject this view of democracy and propose a model of "deliberative democracy." Their aim is to create a link between politics and morality, and they think that it is possible to create a rational and universal consensus by means of free discussion. They believe that by relegating disruptive issues to the private sphere, a rational agreement on principles should be enough to administer the pluralism of modern societies. For both types of liberals, everything that has to do with passions, with antagonisms, everything that can lead to violence, is seen as archaic and irrational—as residues of a bygone age in which the "sweet commerce" had not yet established the pre-eminence of interests over passions.

But this attempt to annihilate the political is doomed to failure because it cannot be domesticated in this way. As was pointed out by Carl Schmitt, the political can derive its energy from the most diverse sources and emerge out of many different social relations: religious, moral, economic, ethnic, or other. The political has to do with the dimension of antagonism that is present in social relations, with the ever-present possibility of a we/them relation constructed in terms of friends/enemies. To deny this dimension of antagonism does not make it disappear; it only leads to impotence in recognizing its different manifestations and in dealing with them. This is why a democratic approach needs to come to terms with the ineradicable character of antagonism. One of its main tasks is to envisage how it is possible to defuse the tendencies of exclusion that are present in the construction of all collective identities.

To clarify the perspective that I am putting forward, I propose to distinguish between "the political" and "politics." By "the political," I refer to the dimension of antagonism that is inherent in all human society, antagonism that can take many different forms and can emerge in diverse social relations. "Politics," on the other hand, refers to the ensemble of practices, discourses, and institutions that seek to establish a certain order and to organize human coexistence in conditions that are always potentially conflictual because they are affected by the dimension of "the political." This view, which attempts to keep together the two meanings of *polemos* and *polis*, from which the idea of politics arises, allows us to grasp the real task confronting democracy.

In examining this question, the concept of the "constitutive outside" to which I have referred earlier is particularly helpful. As elaborated by Derrida, its aim is to highlight the fact that the creation of an identity implies the establishment of a difference, a difference that is often constructed on the basis of a hierarchy—for example, between form and matter, black and white, man and woman, etc. Once we have understood that every identity is relational and that the affirmation of a difference is a precondition for the existence of any identity—i.e., the perception of something "other" that will constitute its "exterior"—then we can begin to understand why such a relation may always become the breeding ground for antagonism. Indeed, when it comes to the creation of a collective identity—i.e, the creation of a "we" through the demarcation of a "them"—there is always the possibility of that we/them relationship becoming one of friend/enemy, i.e., becoming antagonistic. This happens when the "other," who so far had been considered simply as different, starts to be perceived as someone who puts in question our identity and threatens our existence. From that moment on, any form of we/them relationship—be it religious, ethnic, economic, or other—becomes political.

It is only when we acknowledge this dimension of "the political" and understand that "politics" consists in domesticating hostility and in trying to defuse the potential antagonism that exists in human relations, that we can pose the fundamental question for democratic politics. This question, pace the rationalists, is not how to arrive at a rational consensus reached without exclusion. Indeed, this would mean establishing a "we" that would not have a corresponding "them," which, as I have argued, is impossible. What is at stake is how to establish the we/them discrimination in a way that is compatible with pluralist democracy.

In the realm of politics, this presupposes that the "other" is no longer seen as an enemy to be destroyed but as an "adversary"—i.e., somebody with whose ideas we are going to struggle, but whose right to defend those ideas we will not put into question. We could say that the aim of democratic politics is to transform "antagonism" into "agonism." The prime task of democratic politics is not to eliminate passions, nor to relegate them to the private sphere in order to render rational consensus possible, but to mobilize those passions in order to promote democratic designs. Far from jeopardizing democracy, agonistic confrontation is in fact its very condition of existence.

Modern democracy's specificity lies in the recognition and legitimation of conflict and the refusal to suppress it by imposing an authoritarian order. Breaking with the symbolic representation of society as an organic body—which is characteristic of the holistic mode of social organization—a democratic society makes room for the expression of conflicting interests and values. For that reason, pluralist democracy demands not only consensus on a set of common political principles, but also the presence of dissent and institutions through which such divisions can be manifested. This is why its survival depends on collective identities forming around clearly differentiated positions, as well as on the possibility of choosing between real alternatives. The blurring of political frontiers between right and left, for instance, impedes the creation of democratic political identities and fuels disenchantment with political participation. This prepares the ground for various forms of populist politics articulated around nationalist, religious, or ethnic issues. When the agonistic dynamic of the pluralist system is hindered through a lack of democratic identities with which one can identify, there is a risk that this will multiply confrontations over essentialist identities and non-negotiable moral values.[3]

Once it is acknowledged that any identity is relational and defined in terms of difference, how can we defuse the possibility of exclusion that it entails? Here again the notion of the "constitutive outside" can help us. By stressing the fact that the outside is *constitutive*, it reveals the impossibility of drawing an absolute distinction between interior and exterior. The existence of the other becomes a condition of the possibility of my identity, since, without the other, I could not have an identity. Therefore, every identity is irremediably destabilized by its exterior and the interior appears as something always contingent. This questions every essentialist conception of identity and forecloses every attempt to conclusively define identity or objectivity. Inasmuch as objectivity always depends on an absent otherness, it is always necessarily echoed and contaminated by this otherness. Identity cannot, therefore, belong to one person alone, and no one belongs to a single identity. We may go further and argue that not only are there no "natural" and "original" identities, since every identity is the result of a constituting process, but that this process itself must be seen as one of permanent hybridization and nomadization. Identity is, in effect, the result of a multitude of interactions that take place inside a space the outlines of which are not clearly defined. Numerous feminist studies or researches inspired by the "postcolonial" perspective have shown that this process is always one of "overdetermination," which establishes highly intricate links between the many forms of identity and a complex network of differences. For an appropriate definition of identity, we need to take into account both the multiplicity of discourses and the power structure that affects it, as well as the complex dynamic of complicity and resistance that underlies the practices in which this identity is implicated. Instead of seeing the different forms of identity as allegiances to a place or as a property, we ought to realize that they are what is at stake in any power struggle.

What we commonly call "cultural identity" is both the scene and the object of political struggles. The social existence of a group needs such conflict. It is one of the principal areas in which hegemony is exercised, because the definition of the cultural identity of a group, by reference to a specific system of contingent and particular social relations, plays a major role in the creation of "hegemonic nodal points." These partially define the meaning of a signifying chain, allowing us to control the stream of signifiers and temporarily to fix the discursive field.

Concerning the question of "national" identities—so crucial again today—the perspective based on hegemony and articulation allows us to come to grips with the idea of the national, to grasp the importance of that type of identity, instead of rejecting it in the name of antiessentialism or as part of a defense of abstract universalism. It is very dangerous to ignore the strong libidinal investment that can be mobilized by the signifier "nation," and it is futile to hope that all national identities could be replaced by so-called "postconventional" identities. The struggle against the exclusive type of ethnic nationalism can only be carried out by articulating another type of nationalism, a "civic" nationalism expressing allegiance to the values specific to the democratic tradition and the forms of life that are constitutive of it.

By recognizing that identities comprise a multiplicity of elements, one could envisage an identity that accommodates otherness, acknowledges the porosity of its frontiers, and opens up toward that exterior which makes it possible. A democratic politics informed by an antiessentialist approach accepts that only hybridity creates us as separate entities; in that way it can defuse the potential for violence that exists in every construction of collective identities and create the conditions for a truly "agonistic pluralism." Such a pluralism is anchored in the recognition of the multiplicity within oneself and of the contradictory positions that this multiplicity entails. Its acceptance of the other does not merely consist in tolerating differences, but in positively celebrating them, because it acknowledges that, without alterity and otherness, no identity could ever assert itself. It is also a pluralism that valorizes diversity and dissensus, recognizing in them the very condition of the possibility of a striving democratic life.

POLITICAL LIBERALISM AND PLURALISM

The nature of the pluralism that I am advocating can be better understood by distinguishing it from the pluralism put forward by John Rawls. Indeed, in his recent work the question of pluralism has become central for Rawls, who now formulates the problem of political liberalism in the following way: "How is it possible that there may exist over time a stable and just society of free and equal citizens profoundly divided by reasonable religious, philosophical and moral doctrines?"[4]

The problem is, for him, one of political *justice* and it requires the establishment of fair terms of social cooperation between citizens envisaged as free and equal but also as divided by profound doctrinal conflict. Rawls' solution, as reformulated in his recent book *Political Liberalism,* puts a new emphasis on the notion of "reasonable pluralism." He now invites us to distinguish between what would be a mere empirical recognition of opposed conceptions of the good, the fact of "simple" pluralism, and what is the real problem facing liberals: how to deal with a plurality of incompatible yet *reasonable* doctrines. He sees such a plurality as the normal result of the exercise of human reason within the framework of a constitutional democratic regime. For that reason, a conception of justice must be able to gain the support of all "reasonable" citizens despite their deep doctrinal disagreements on other matters.

This distinction between "simple" and "reasonable" pluralism is in fact the denegation by the so-called "political liberalism" of its political stand. Indeed, it allows Rawls to present as a moral exigency what is in fact a political decision. Avowedly it is supposed to secure the moral character of the consensus on justice which precludes that a compromise should be made with "unreasonable" views—i.e., those which would oppose the basic principles of political morality. For Rawls, reasonable persons are persons "who have realized their two moral powers to a degree sufficient to be free and equal citizens in a constitutional regime, and who have an enduring desire to honor fair terms of cooperation and to be fully cooperating members of society."[5] This is obviously an indirect way of asserting that reasonable persons are those who accept the fundamentals of liberalism. In other words, the distinction between "reasonable" and "unreasonable" helps to draw a frontier between the doctrines that accept the liberal principles and the ones that oppose them. It means that its function is *political* and that it aims at discriminating between a permissible pluralism of religious, moral, or philosophical conceptions—as long as those views can be relegated to the sphere of the private and satisfy the liberal principles—and what would be an unacceptable pluralism, because it would jeopardize the dominance of liberal principles in the public sphere.

What Rawls is really indicating with such a distinction is that there cannot be pluralism as far as the principles of the political association are concerned and that conceptions that refuse the principles of liberalism cannot be accepted as legitimate in a liberal democracy. I have no quarrel with him on this issue, but this is the expression of an eminently *political* decision, not of a moral requirement. To call the antiliberals "unreasonable" is a rather disingenuous way of stating that such views cannot be accommodated within the framework of a liberal democratic regime. This is indeed the case, the reason for such an exclusion being that antagonistic principles of legitimacy cannot coexist within the same political association without putting in question the political reality of the state. However, to be properly formulated, such a thesis calls for a theoretical framework that asserts the primacy of the political association—which is precisely what liberalism denies. This is why Rawls has to pretend that it is a moral distinction. And he gets caught in a circular form of argumentation: political liberalism can provide a consensus among reasonable persons who *by definition* are persons who accept the principles of political liberalism.

Democracy and Consensus

Besides rendering him unable to adequately justify the limits of pluralism, Rawls' incapacity to recognize the primacy of the political also has serious consequences for his understanding of democracy. Let us examine from that angle his solution to the liberal problem: the creation of an "overlapping consensus" of reasonable comprehensive doctrines each of which endorses the political conception from its own point of view.

He declares that when the society is well-ordered, it is around the principles of his theory of justice as fairness that the overlapping consensus is established. Since they are chosen thanks to the device of the original position with its "veil of ignorance," those principles of the fair terms of cooperation satisfy the liberal principle of legitimacy that requires that they be endorsed by all citizens as free and equal—as well as reasonable and rational—and that they be addressed to their public reason. According to the standpoint of political liberalism, those principles are expressly designed to gain the reasoned support of citizens who affirm reasonable though conflicting comprehensive doctrines. Indeed, the very purpose of the veil of ignorance is to preclude the knowledge of citizens' comprehensive conceptions of the good and to force them to proceed from shared conceptions of society and personhood required in applying the ideals and principles of practical reason.[6]

In line with his project of establishing the specificity of "political liberalism" as a distinct liberal doctrine, Rawls is at pains to indicate that such an overlapping consensus must not be confused with a simple *modus vivendi*. He insists that it is not merely a consensus on a set of institutional arrangements based on self-interest, but the affirmation on moral grounds of principles of justice that have themselves a moral character. The overlapping consensus should also be distinguished from a constitutional consensus which, in his view, is not deep or wide enough to secure justice and stability. In a constitutional consensus, he states,

> while there is agreement on certain basic political rights and liberties—on the right to vote and freedom of political speech and association, and whatever else is required for the electoral and legislative procedures of democracy—there is disagreement among those holding liberal principles as to the more exact content and boundaries of these rights and liberties, as well as on what further rights and liberties are to be counted as basic and so merit legal if not constitutional protection.[7]

Rawls grants that a constitutional consensus is better than a *modus vivendi*, because there is a real allegiance to the principles of a liberal constitution that guarantees certain basic rights and liberties, and establishes democratic procedures for moderating political rivalry. Nevertheless, given that those principles are not grounded in accepted political conceptions of society and personhood, disagreements subsist concerning the status and content of those rights and liberties, and they create insecurity and hostility in public life. Hence the importance of fixing their content. This is provided by an overlapping consensus on a conception of justice as fairness, which establishes a much deeper consensus than one that would be restricted to constitutional essentials.[8]

Rawls acknowledges that those constitutional essentials (i.e., fundamental principles that specify the general structure of government and the political process as well as basic rights and liberties of citizenship) are more urgently in need of being settled, but he considers that they must be distinguished from the principles governing social and economic inequalities. The aim of justice as fairness is to establish a consensus of public reason whose content is given by a political conception of justice. "[T]his content has two parts: substantive principles of justice for the basic structure (the political values of justice); and guidelines of enquiry and conceptions of virtue that make public reason possible (the political values of public reason)."[9]

He seems to believe that, while rational agreement among comprehensive moral, religious, and philosophical doctrines is impossible, it can nevertheless be reached among political values. Once the controversial doctrines have been relegated to the sphere of the private, it should therefore be possible to establish in the public sphere a type of consensus grounded on Reason (with its two sides: the rational and the reasonable). This is a consensus that it would be illegitimate to put into question once it has been reached and the only possibility of destabilization would be an attack from the outside by the "unreasonable" forces. When a well-ordered society has been achieved, those who take part in the overlapping consensus should have no right to question the existing arrangements, since they embody the principles of justice. If somebody does not comply, it must be due to irrationality or unreasonableness.

At this point, the picture of the Rawlsian well-ordered society begins to emerge more clearly and it looks very much like a dangerous utopia of reconciliation. To be sure, Rawls recognizes that a full overlapping consensus might never be achieved, but at best only be approximated. It is more likely, he says, that the focus of an overlapping consensus will be a class of liberal conceptions acting as political rivals.[10]

Nevertheless, he urges us to strive for a well-ordered society in which, given that there is no further conflict between political and economic interests, such a rivalry would have been overcome. Such a society would see the realization of justice as fairness, which is the correct and definite interpretation of how the democratic principles of equality and liberty should be implemented in the basic institutions. It is independent of any interest and does not represent any form of compromise, but is truly the expression of free public democratic reason.

POLITICAL LIBERALISM AND THE END OF POLITICS

The conclusion that we can draw from our enquiry into the nature of the over-lapping consensus is that Rawls' ideal society is a society from which politics has been eliminated. A conception of justice is mutually recognized by rea-sonable and rational citizens who act according to its injunctions. They prob-ably have very different and even conflicting conceptions of the good, but those are strictly private matters and they do not interfere with their public life. Conflicts of interests about economic and social issues—if they still arise—are resolved smoothly through discussions within the framework of public reason, by invoking the principles of justice that everybody endorses. If an unreasonable or irrational person happens to disagree with that state of affairs and intends to disrupt that nice consensus, she must be forced, through coercion, to submit to the principles of justice.

How can a liberal defense of pluralism aim at the eradication of dissent from the public sphere? The explanation lies in Rawls' flawed conception of politics, in which it is reduced to a mere activity of allocating among competing interests susceptible to a rational solution. This is why he believes that political conflicts can be eliminated thanks to a conception of justice that appeals to individuals' ideas of rational advantage within the constraints established by the reasonable. According to his theory, citizens need, as free and equal persons, the same goods, because their conceptions of the good, however distinct their content, "require for their advancement roughly the same primary goods, that is, the same basic rights, liberties, and oppor-tunities, and the same all-purpose means such as income and wealth, with all of these supported by the same social bases of self-respect."[11] Therefore, once the just answer to the problem of the distribution of those primary goods has been found, the rivalry that previously existed in the political domain disappears.

Besides postulating the possibility of an agreement on justice, such a sce-nario presupposes that political actors are only driven by what they see as their rational self-advantage. Passions are erased from the realm of politics, which is reduced to a neutral field of competing interests. Completely miss-ing from such an approach is "the political" in its various dimensions of an-tagonism, undecidability, and coercion. This is precisely what "political liberalism" is at pains to eliminate. It offers us a picture of the well-ordered society as one from which antagonism, violence, power, and repression have disappeared. But it is only because they have been made invisible through a clever stratagem: the distinction between "simple" and "reasonable plural-ism." Exclusions are justified by declaring that they are the product of the "free exercise of practical reason" that establishes the limits of possible con-sensus. When a point of view is excluded it is because this is required by the exercise of reason.

This type of liberalism is clearly unable to provide an adequate framework to envisage the conditions of implementation of a pluralist democracy. While a pluralist democracy certainly requires a certain amount of consensus on the political principles that need to be shared by all its members, it also requires dissensus on the interpretation of those principles. It is precisely the tension between the consensus on the principles and the dissensus on their interpretation that constitutes the agonistic dynamics of the pluralist democracy. By eliminating the place of the *adversary,* Rawls' well-ordered society does not create the conditions for a more democratic society; what it does is negate the very conditions for pluralism. In a modern democracy, pluralism cannot be relegated to the sphere of the private; it must have its place in the public sphere, and that precludes that there could ever be a rational consensus on the principles of justice. Indeed, in such a society, justice should always remain an open question.

The superiority of the antirationalist approach lies in its emphasis on the irreducible alterity that represents both a condition of the possibility and a condition of the impossibility of every identity. The notion of the "constitutive outside" forces us to come to terms with the idea that pluralism implies the permanence of antagonism. It helps us to understand that conflict and division are not to be seen as either disturbances that, unfortunately, cannot be completely eliminated, or as empirical impediments that render impossible the full realization of a good constituted by a harmony that we cannot reach, because we will never be completely able to coincide with our rational universal self. By revealing that a nonexclusive public sphere of deliberation in which a rational consensus could be attained is a *conceptual* impossibility, such an approach protects pluralist democracy against any attempt at closure and provides a guarantee that the dynamics of the democratic process will be kept alive.

NOTES

1. Hans Blumenberg, *The Legitimacy of the Modern Age* (Cambridge: MIT Press, 1983).

2. Ernesto Laclau and Chantal Mouffe, *Hegemony and Socialist Strategy: Towards a Radical Democratic Politics* (London: Verso, 1985).

3. See Chantal Mouffe, *The Return of the Political* (London: Verso, 1994), for a further development of this thesis.

4. John Rawls, *Political Liberalism* (New York: Columbia University Press, 1993), p. xviii.

5. Ibid., p. 55.

6. Ibid., p. 141.

7. Ibid., p. 159.

8. Ibid., p. 227.
9. Ibid., p. 253.
10. Ibid., p. 164.
11. Ibid., p. 180.

Hans-Georg Möller

THE PHILOSOPHY OF SIGNS AND DEMOCRATIC DISCOURSE: COINCIDENCES BETWEEN CHINESE PRE- AND WESTERN POSTMODERNITY

INTRODUCTION

In this paper I will try to analyze social phenomena from a semiological perspective. Semiotic structures, constructed on the basis of certain explicit or implicit theories of (linguistic) signs, will be discussed in connection with political theories.

My methodological approach is structuralistic. I will talk about premetaphysical, metaphysical, and postmetaphysical structures and, analogously, about corresponding premodern, modern, and postmodern structures. These stages should not be understood as primarily chronological but rather as logical (or as semio-logical). Therefore, the description is general and based on ideal types.

In this way, I will first try to show the structural relationship between a certain linguistic theory in ancient China and a certain theory of authority. In contrast to this "premetaphysical" or "premodern" theory of language, which can be called "behavioral nominalism" and is connected with an autocratic and totalitarian concept of rulership, the semiotic structure of metaphysics can be connected with the political theory of modern democracy.

The semiotic structure of metaphysics involves an inner contradiction leading to another semiotical change. A third structure appears, which is called "postmetaphysical" or "postmodern." Today this process of change can be described in terms of language as well as social philosophy. Jürgen Habermas, for example, has already succesfully combined these different philosophical disciplines. I will try to make use of such postmetaphysical theories in order to reveal some characteristics of the postmodern democratic discourse that cause it to resemble a new kind of "behavioral nominalism" and which might even entail some rather "totalitarian" aspects.[1]

395

AUTOCRACY AND BEHAVIORAL NOMINALISM IN
PREMODERN CHINA

The term "behavioral nominalism," denoting the leading language theory in ancient China, is borrowed from Chad Hansen.[2] The features of the ancient Chinese language theory are quite different from modern language theories. I think that these features can be reduced to two specific structural distinctions. The first distinction is between signifier (or "designation") and signified (or "designated"), and the second distinction is between the named and the nameless. To understand how these two distinctions are interconnected is to understand the structure that underlies the ancient Chinese language theory.

The distinction between the signified and the signifier in early Chinese philosophy is somewhat "strange," because of the semiological status of the signifier.[3] The signifier—and this seems odd to a postmodern philosopher—is believed to be as "present" as the signified. Wang Bi stated that "Names and titles grow out of forms and shapes,"[4] a principle already current in his time, especially in Daoist "Huang-Lao philosophy." This principle is to be interpreted as meaning that the signifier comes into existence immediately along with that which it signifies. It appears to be a "natural phenomenon" and belongs to the world of the "ten-thousand things" (*wan wu*), to the realm of everything which "is there" or "present" (*you*). A "name" (*ming*) stems neither from conventions nor even thoughts. It appears along with the "form" (*xing*) or the "reality" (*shih*) of a thing and is likewise "essential." "There is a name, there is a 'reality': this is wherein a thing dwells," says the *Zhuangzi*.[5] Linguistic entities, namely names, are "objectively" present. They do not belong to thoughts or to "communication," but are "present" and proper indications of forms. The signified and the signifier belong to one semiological dimension; they likewise belong to the "realm of presence."

The distinction between the signifier and the signified is subordinated to the distinction between that which has names and that which does not. Things are things just because they have forms and names. Everything that has a form also has a name and is determined by its place in the world of phenomena, its function, its time, and its position. In their "objective presence" both the signifier and the signified constitute the things. And the whole of things in their togetherness and sequential order constitute the functioning of the world. The functioning of "present" and named things is dominated by that which is nameless.[6] In the *Book of Changes* (*Yijing*), there is an explicit distinction between the realm of things "within form" (*xing er xia*) and the realm "beyond form" (*xing er shang*).[7] This distinction is structurally equivalent to the distinction between the named and the nameless. That which is "beyond form" and that "which has no name" is called "*dao*."[8]

The nameless itself is separate from the distinction between the signified and the signifier. It "dominates" this distinction and is the basis of the realm of the named. The world of the present and named things is dominated and balanced by the nameless, which creates and maintains the steady process of the functioning from out of the motionless center. The hidden origin of the world belongs immanently to this realm and likewise encircles it completely. The origin of everything present is never absent: it is the nonpresence (*wu*) that gives rise to and includes all presence.

In this way, the semiotic structure is transformed into a structure of ruler-ship, authority, and order. This structure has been understood politically, namely, within Huang-Lao philosophy, which used this pattern of order to construct a theory of autocracy.[9] Therefore, political theory has to be under-stood in connection with a language theory, or rather, with a particular semi-otic structure which may be called "behavioral nominalism."

The sage (*sheng ren*) takes the place of *dao* and dominates the function-ing out of the center; he abides beyond names, overviews, and controls them.[10] His subjects, having names, are consequently subject to social oblig-ations. Having names, the ruled people have "mandates";[11] they have their specific functions, and their "performances" constitute the social world. The realm of the ruled is founded upon the specific semiotic distinction between "form and name." "Names" correspond to the "mandates"—i.e., to the spe-cific function of the specific position of every subject. And "forms" corre-spond to the actual "performance" that is expected and carried out.[12] In this way, names—and not universals—draw the distinctions (*fen*) in the world. They function in a "nominalistic" way. On the other hand, this nominalism can be called "behavioral" because of its social applicability. "Forms" in the political realm are performances. And in this respect, names guide action. The sum of all "actions" (*wei*)—corresponding to all of the names—consti-tutes the functioning of the world. And the sage, who namelessly practices "nonaction," rules over all societal operations.

The early Chinese conception of autocracy is structurally analogous to a semiotic pattern. The rule of the nameless goes along with the concept of *dao* or "the one" (*yi*).[13]

In the political world, the ruler who rules in accord with *dao* has to be alone. The "monarch" is the "one-man" (*yiren*)[14] and, while he is "alone," the world is "all-one."[15] Even though there are different kinds of autocratic concepts in Confucianism, Legalism, and Daoism, the structure remains the same. The variety of the named performances and the multiplicity of the subjects with their names or titles can only operate as an effective organism as long as the *single* and nameless sage-ruler guarantees the *oneness* of the world.

The "son of heaven has no companion."[16] In the same way as the unnamed *dao* rules as the one above the differentiated, the ruler rules as the one above the many; the semiotical monism is thereby carried over into a political structure.

DEMOCRACY AS OPPOSED TO BEHAVIORAL NOMINALISM

Owing to its two inherent semiotic structures, behavioral nominalism is es-sentially opposed to notions of democracy. To prove this assumption, I will attempt to show how some prime characteristics of "democracy" run counter to the two mentioned structures.

Democracy can be conceived of as the conception of the peaceful competition of political forces. The "electoral contest" is decided through the free and equal votes of all of the legitimate members of the political community. The peaceful competition between political forces in democratic societies is based on the competition of political interest groups, programs, and ideologies. Parties represent the political forces and claim to be aligned to a political belief. Traditionally, parties could be described as political "worldview societies."

Parties make use of signs. For example, they give themselves names, their members write texts, and hold speeches, all of which are supposed to "have meaning." What these signs mean, what they refer to, is a political program, a political "truth," or an ideology. The signs are arbitrary and of only secondary importance. What counts is the "meaning" or the "content" lying behind the signs. The democratic political arena involves a contest of signs, which represent "essential" ideas. This contest is based, therefore, on a certain conception and a certain use of "signs" and "meanings"—i.e., of "signifiers" and "signified." This semiotic conception can be called "metaphysical," because it is presupposed that there is a world of signs apart from the world of meanings (things and ideas)—i.e., a world of representation apart from a world of presence.[17]

Signs are "inessential" and representative; their meanings are "essentially" present. Thus a dualistic structure, dividing the realms of presence and representation, emerges. In the monistic view of behavioral nominalism, both the signifiers and the signified are "present."[18]

Semiologically speaking, the conception of democratic competition between political forces is based on the dualistic structure of metaphysics. Signs can be applied for debating about reality because they themselves do not belong to the essential reality. If signs and meanings were not metaphysically independent, but belonged both to one level of presence, then an *ideological* contest would be impossible.

In democratic theory, signs (like "votes") are vehicles of power and intellectual freedom, whereas under the rule of behavioral nominalism signifiers indicate the "form's" subservience. The semiotic structure of the theory of behavioral nominalism attributes everything that is articulated to the realm of the ruled, whereas the semiotic structure of metaphysics attributes the notion of freedom to the notion of "signs."

In "metaphysical" democracy, language becomes "autonomous": Every citizen can speak freely—that is, he utilizes the medium of signs to express his "thoughts." When signifiers are no longer present and constitute a level of "inessential" reality (i.e., the world of signs, *representing* "something else"), then the realm of presence is also qualitatively changed. What is "present" is still essentially real, but it is only accessible through the mediation of another world of signs. The gap between the signifier and the signified changes the semiotic monism into a semiotic dualism.

Politically, this means that ideologies are "transcendent" entities. Beyond signs, there are meanings that are essential and untouchable. They can only be expressed or represented. In this way, signs become dubitable in the long run. One cannot entirely trust language anymore, since it is at man's free disposal. It cannot be determined if people use the "right" signs to express a "meaning." Nonetheless, the democratic political discourse, conceived of as a contest of opinions, appears possible only with a semiotic structure that is based upon a hiatus between signifier and signified.

POSTMODERNITY AND DEMOCRACY

The semiotic structure of metaphysics is based on the hiatus between signifier and signified. A world of signs and one of "presence" coexist. Accordingly, a democratic system of power could develop, which is based on the conception that people use signs—i.e., "votes"—corresponding to what they "mean," in order to exercise power.

But today the semiotic structure of metaphysics is no longer universally regarded as valid, and democracy itself has had to change. It is developing into a new form of "behavioral nominalism," to which it was "originally" opposed. The "realm of presence," which is the realm of meanings, has never been directly accessible in metaphysics and has thus lost its credibility. Meanings are never actually at hand, other than through the mediation of signs. Consequently, postmodern philosophy has rightly stressed that the realm of "presence" has no primary status. "Difference"—i.e., the difference between the signifiers and the signified—makes the notion of presence possible.[19] What has been thought to be "present" is only mediated. The belief in a level of "pure presence" has become suspicious.

According to the semiotic structure of postmodern or postmetaphysical philosophy, the signified—i.e., the former "meaning"—also belongs to the level of signs, where no reduction to pure meaning is possible. Once there are signs, there is no way back to immediate or indifferent meanings.

The loss of the belief in pure meaning, the loss of the world of presence, has not occurred unnoticed by society. The meaning of democracy in the postmodern era is no longer modern. Postmodern democracy becomes less and less "democratic" in a metaphysical sense. And in the postmodern democratic discourse, the reference to ideology becomes more and more obsolete. Parties do not refer to ideologies anymore, but ply their political customers with "speech-act-offers," which may or may not be "accepted" by the political customers.[20] Signs are given in the hope that there will be a response of the voters when the democratic procedures of distributing power—i.e., the elections—are being held. The citizens then answer and approve these signs with further signs. "Communicative action"[21] via mass media constitutes a political discourse, hostile toward ideologies. "Tradiionally," ideologies had been the basis for the signs, constituting the political discourse of democracy, but in postmodernity, the reference to ideology seems "undemocratic." Those who argue ideologically, claiming their signs to be "true," are labeled "fundamentalists." In other words, this antimetaphysical label marks those sign-usages that deviate from the rules of the postmodern discourse.

Signs can only be discharged with signs. A political opinion should not entail a "fundamental" obligation. Whoever appeals to something that is more fundamental than signs threatens the "ethics" of the postmetaphysical democratic discourse. His or her success in the power struggle would precipitate a return to the old semiotic structure and involve the danger of "totalitarianism."

Apologists of postmetaphysical thought praise a sociopolitical discourse based on "communicative rationality" (*Verständigungsrationalität*),[22] which aims at intersubjective understanding, or on "liberality."[23] This kind of democratic discourse is regarded as progressive and conducive to a free, equal, and cooperative society. In this way, the semiotic structure of the postmodern democratic system is construed as a kind of "negative ideology." This theory claims negatively what it pretends to have abolished positively: it claims to know how to define the conditions of the "validity" of signs.[24] A totalitarian antitotalitarianism or ideology-free ideology comes to the fore.

BEHAVIORAL NOMINALISM AND POSTMODERN POLITICAL DISCOURSE

Along with the change of the metaphysical semiotic structure, the demise of the metaphysical theory of "meaning" can be observed politically. Metaphysics involved a contradiction: what it believed to be truly "present" had never been immediately at hand but was only accessible through signs. Thus the realm of presence could be discredited. In the postdemocratic discourse, a frankly "fundamentalist" or "metaphysical" argumentation is not welcomed. Accordingly, postmetaphysical democracy becomes structurally more and more similar to its monistic counterpart, behavioral nominalism.

The semiotic structure of postmetaphysics closes the semiological gap between the signifier and the signified. Both now belong to the realm of signs or representation, because what had formerly been the present "meaning" is now seen as dissolved into the discourse. The mediation has become total. The structural relationship of postmetaphysics to the semiotic structure of behavioral nominalism becomes evident. Both in postmetaphysics and in premetaphysics, the signifiers and the signified belong to "one world." In premetaphysics this world is that of presence; in postmetaphysics it is that of representation.[25]

In society, political authority is distributed within a certain discourse, within a system of communication, where names once again assume a nominalistic quality. The distinctions between names, not between ideologies, mark the political landscape—just as they mark the ballot. The names of the parties no longer relate to anything "present." Instead, it is the difference between the names that makes the political "language game" possible. The "Democrats" are no more "democratic" than the "Republicans," and there is no notion of "republic" that the "Republicans" could claim to be their specific and everlasting reference. Politics is discourse and only discourse.

The effective power of names in the postmodern discourse is related to the power of names in the premodern discourse. In premodern times the "name" fixed the "form." The names (and not universals) marked the distinctions in the social world. In the postmodern discourse, it is again names that mark distinctions. The division of the political world by means of party names on ballots reveals some kind of nominalistic language theory. During a political campaign, the names of the parties or candidates are linked to certain "images, "just as the names of consumer goods are tied to certain images through advertising campaigns. These "images" do not imply any fundamental meaning.

This kind of nominalism is also ostensively "behavioral." Using signs in the political arena is the way to "behave" politically. In modern democracy, someone could be a deeply convinced "democrat," but remain silent in the political debate. His intentions (meanings) are more important than his vote (sign). In the postmodern political discourse, abstention from the giving of signs is tantamount to refraining from political activity. Communication is, as many postmetaphysical philosophers have stressed, action.[26]

That is to say, political action is only possible through the use of signs. It is the articulated opinion that is of interest, not the man behind it. Communication in postmodern "democracy" requires signs, not minds. Thus the postmodern discourse seems to reveal some features of a new behavioral nominalism. The total discourse might replace the autocratic ruler.

NOTES

1. This table depicts the semiological scheme followed in this paper:

	Realm of presence	Realm of representation
Premetaphysics	Signified-signifier	
Metaphysics	Signified	Signifier
Postmetaphysics		Signified-signifier

2. Chad Hansen himself borrows the expression "behavioral nominalism" from Wilfrid Sellars, *Science, Perception, and Reality* (London: Routledge & Kegan Paul, 1963). Cf. Chad Hansen, *Language and Logic in Ancient China* (Ann Arbor: University of Michigan Press, 1983), pp. 31–32.

3. The most important sources of ancient Chinese language theory are connected with the so-called "theory of forms and names" (*xingming zhi xue*), which was developed within Huang-Lao-Daoism. Huang-Lao-Daoism and the theory of forms and names flourished in the third and second century B.C. and are mentioned frequently in the *Shiji*. This philosophy combines the thought of the pre-Han philosophers, especially in the field of the philosophy of language. The *Huanglao boshu* is the most important text in this respect. The main ideas of the theory of forms and names can be found in nearly all of the main philosophical works of this era, like the *Daodejing*, the *Hanfeizi*, the *Guanzi*, the *Zhuangzi*, the *Xunzi*, and the *Yinwenzi*. Cf. my book *Die Bedeutung der Sprache in der frühen chinesischen Philosophie* (Aachen: Shaker, 1994). Some important studies on ancient Chinese language theory, besides the works of Chad Hansen, are Bao Zhiming's "Language and Worldview in Ancient China," *Philosophy East and West* (vol. 40, no. 2, April 1990), pp. 195–219; and John Makeham's "Names, Actualities and the Emergence of Essentialist Theories of Naming in Classical Chinese Thought," *Philosophy East and West* (vol. 41, no. 3, July 1991), pp. 341–63.

4. Cf. Wang Bi, *Laozi zhilüe* in *Wang Bi ji jiaoshi* (Peking: Zhonghua, 1980), p. 199. Cf. the translation by R. G. Wagner for the sentence "*ming hao sheng hu xing zhuang*" or "Names and marks are born from the features and appearances," taken from "Wang Bi: 'The Structure of the Laozi's Pointers' (*Laozi weizhi lilüe*). A Philological Study and Translation." *T'oung Pao*, LXXII (1986), pp. 92–129.

5. *A Concordance to Chuang Tzu* (Taipei: Harvard-Yenching Institute Sinological Index Series, supplement no. 20, 1966), pp. 72–73.

6. Cf. chapter 32 of the *Daodejing*.

7. These expressions appear in the *Book of Changes*. Cf. *A Concordance to Yi Ching* (Taipei: Harvard-Yenching Institute Sinological Index Series, supplement no. 10, 1966), p. 44, chap. *Xici shang*, 12.

8. Cf. chapter 25 of the *Daodejing*.

9. The *Huanglao boshu*, but also chap. 22 (*zheng ming*) of the *Xunzi*, combine the "philosophy of names" with a theory of authority. Sinological interpretations that characterize the *Xunzi* as "conventionalistic" and thus as opposed to Huang-Lao philosophy—cf. John Makeham, *Name and Actuality in Early Chinese Thought*

(Albany: State University of New York Press, 1994)—are, in my opinion, misguided. The *Xunzi* as well as the *Huanglao boshu* ascribe the control over the names to the autocratic rule of a sage monarch who manifests *dao*.

10. Cf. chap. *jingfa* of the *Huanglao boshu* (part *lunyue*) or chap. 22 of the *Xunzi*.

11. In the texts named in notes 8 and 9, a connection between the "names" (*ming*) and the "mandates" (*ming*) issued by the ruler is evident.

12. Cf. John Makeham, "The Legalist Concept of Hsing-ming: An Example of the Contribution of Archaeological Evidence to the Re-interpretation of Transmitted Texts," *Monumenta Serica* (no. 39, 1990–1991), pp. 87–114. H.G. Creel translated *"xingming"* as "performance and title." Cf. the chapter "The Meaning of *Hsing-ming*" in his *What is Taoism?* (Chicago: University of Chicago Press, 1970), pp. 79–91.

13. This "metaphor" is used frequently in the *Daodejing* and in the *Huanglao boshu*.

14. This (self-)appellation of the ruler is mentioned already in the *Shujing*. Cf. Gu Jiegang, ed., *Shangshu tongjian* (San Francisco: Chinese Materials Center, 1978), chap. 10, character 0114f.

15. Cf. my *Laotse. Tao Te King. Nach den Seidentexten von Mawangdui* (Frankfurt: Fischer, 1994), pp. 20–21.

16. *A Concordance to Hsun Tzu* (Taipei: Harvard-Yenching Institute Sinological Index Series, supplement no. 22, 1966), p. 91.

17. In defining the word "metaphysical," I refer to postmetaphysical philosophers like Ludwig Wittgenstein, Jacques Derrida and Josef Simon.

18. This terminology, especially the term "presence" is borrowed from Jacques Derrida. In his "La Différance," he writes, "Le signe, dit-on couramment, se met à la place de la chose même, de la chose présente, 'chose' valant ici aussi bien pour le sens que pour le référent. Le signe représente le présent en son absence. Il en tient lieu. Quand nous ne pouvons prendre ou montrer la chose, disons le présent, l'étant-présent, quand le présent ne se présente pas, nous signifions, nous passons par le détour du signe. Nous prenons ou donnons un signe. Nous faisons signe. Le signe serait donc la présence différée. Qu'il s'agisse de signe verbal ou écrit, de signe monétaire, de délégation électorale et de représentation politique, la circulation des signes diffère le moment où nous porrions rencrontrer la chose même, nous en emparer, la consommer ou la dépenser, la toucher, la voir, en avoir l'intuition présente. Ce que je décris ici pour définir, en la banalité de ses traits, la signification comme différance de temporisation, c'est la structure classiquement déterminée du signe: elle présuppose que le signe, différant la présence, n'est pensable qu'a *partir* de la présence qu'il diffère et *en vue* de la présence différée qu'on vise à se réapproprier. Suivant cette sémiologie classique, la substitution du signe à la chose même est la fois *seconde* et *provisoire*: seconde depuis une présence originelle et perdue dont le signe viendrait à deriver; provisoire au regard de cette présence finale et manquante en vue de laquelle le signe serait en mouvement de médiation." *Marges de la Philosophie*, (Paris: Editions de Minuit, 1972), pp. 9–10.

19. Cf. Jacques Derrida's "La Différance" (see note 18).

20. These terms (in German: *Sprechaktangebot* and *Akzeptanz*) are used by Jürgen Habermas. See, for a quick reference, his essay "Handlungen, Sprechakte, sprachlich vermittelte Interaktion und Lebenswelt" in *Nachmetaphysisches Denken* (Frankfurt am Main: Suhrkamp, 1992), pp. 70–71.

21. Cf. Jürgen Habermas, *Theorie des kommunikativen Handelns* (Frankfurt am Main: Suhrkamp, 1981). See also his essay mentioned in note 20.

22. Cf. Jürgen Habermas, "Handlungen, Sprechakte, sprachlich vermittelte Interaktion und Lebenswelt" in *Nachmetaphysisches Denken* (Frankfurt am Main: Suhrkamp, 1992), p. 67ff.

23. Cf. Richard Rorty, *Contingency, Irony, and Solidarity* (Cambridge: Cambridge University Press, 1989).

24. Jürgen Habermas has proposed a *formalpragmatische Bedeutungstheorie* ("formal-pragmatical theory of meaning"), which replaces the metaphysical theory of meaning. Cf. his "Handlungen, Sprechakte . . . " pp. 75–81.

25. See table in note 1.

26. Two of the most reputed of these philosophers are Jürgen Habermas and John L. Austin.

James Buchanan

BEYOND EAST AND WEST: POSTMODERN DEMOCRACY IN A MODE OF INFORMATION

There is an unspoken but nevertheless widely held belief that the West holds the franchise and distribution rights on liberal democracy. It is *our* discourse and true democracy must proceed according to *our* forms. This attitude presents problems from at least two perspectives. First, there is the issue of whether or not there are forms of democracy which have developed in other cultures and which, while they may not look like Western forms, need to be included in a general discussion of what we might call "appropriate democracies." As interesting and important as this is, here I want to focus upon a second issue. This concerns the present state of the Western discourse on democracy. This discourse is in a state of great confusion, not only because of the disagreements between theorists but also because all of the theories to one degree or another neglect certain dimensions of "modern" Western culture, which, if included, would change the nature and possibly the direction of these discussions. These missing dimensions concern the fact that Western culture and increasingly the emerging world culture are technological.

I want to move the discussion beyond Western or Eastern models of democracy and claim that technology is increasingly the transversal vector and commonality of all social systems into which democratic forms are appropriated in the contemporary situation. Acknowledging this commonality does not imply that all forms of democracy will finally be reduced to some standardized form of technological democracy, though this is certainly a concern. The focus is upon new sites and new problematics that democracies face in the contemporary situation and which I want to claim increasingly transverse cultural specificities. I am concerned with those problematics and questions that arise from the fact of technological culture or the technologization of culture, particularly those related to what we might refer to as the "information age" or, using Mark Poster's terminology, "the mode of information."[1]

405

If we in the West are the master distributors of democracy, fundamental to the democracy we export is the technological wrapping in which it comes.

In particular, I want to focus on two characteristics that I consider to be fundamental to any form of democracy. These are *participation* and *diversity*. Both are critical to democracy, and both are sites of critical problematics in the current technological situation.

THE SITUATION: TECHNOLOGY AND DEMOCRACY

The liberal theorists, with the exception of Habermas (and him I except with reservations), either ignore technology or find in it an ally. The liberal vision avoids having to deal with the fact of technology by postulating an autonomous rational subject that remains essentially detached from any considerations of context. Democracy and justice as principles of rationality are intended to transcend not only difference in talents and positions in society but factors of society that enhance or diminish these differences. The autonomy of the will means that technology is seen as a set of tools or social structures that can be determined by a freely choosing agent just as that freely choosing agent makes any decision. Thus technology does not present itself as a particular problem for the formation of the will. In fact, historically, the growth of the liberal position has a close relationship to the technologization of culture. Philosophically there is an instrumentalism that underlies both the cultural transformation and the liberal approach to democracy. This parallel development has also led to that liberal side becoming increasingly instrumental in its approaches to social ills. William Sullivan agrees with this conclusion, saying, "The moral and political outlook of liberalism is instrumental in its view of politics and social life. . . . The logical goal of liberal rationality is a scientific social engineering that will be able to bring about a perfect adjustment of needs and wants."[2]

It is the growth of both the liberal tradition and America as a technological culture that leads us to conclude that, contrary to what writers such as Mill and MacIntyre say about the lack of an underlying notion of a good society in the liberal vision of democracy, there is a vision of the technological society as good. Boorstein and Borgman contend that, whatever else we might have to say about the problem of the good society, "Liberal democracy is enacted as technology."[3] In the contemporary situation, discussion of autonomous individualism needs to be associated with the possessive individualism that is tied to the types of consumer societies that fuel and are fueled by technological culture.

The communitarian theorists, with the exception of Borgman, seem to ignore the fact that technology is a factor at all. They counsel a neo-Aristoteleanism which emphasizes a return to participatory democratic communities like the *polis* without taking sufficient note of the difficulties of such a return in a technological situation. It is odd that, while one of their main points of contest with the liberals is over the notion of the subject as situated rather than autonomous, they make little of the fact that technology is a major factor in the contemporary situations that are constitutive of the self. If both the number and types of relationships we have as well as the types of social spaces within which these take place are not things we *have* but *what we are*, then technology becomes ontologically significant as constitutive of the democratic subject. A strong contextualist approach must take account of the reality of the transformation of the contexts themselves. In their own way, the communitarians are as "idealist" as the liberals, the difference being that instead of the subject itself being ideal it is the context that is idealized.

Technology becomes important on the global scene as well. As a practical matter, the United States is seen as the paradigm of democracy for the world. But this image is obscured by the fact that the United States is also seen as the paradigm of capitalism and of technological culture. The internal tensions between democracy and justice on the one hand and capitalism on the other were already an issue with Jefferson and certainly with de Tocqueville. Nor are they lost on modern theorists, be they liberal or communitarian. In fact, many of the internal debates within these camps are over issues of distribution of goods and services, issues of desert, etc., all of which assume capitalism as the economic form of democracy. But what also needs to be recognized is that capitalism is the economic system that grew up with and is best suited to the advancement of a technological culture. The result is that "democracy" is often reduced to little more than a rhetorical cover for both capitalism and technology. Capitalism is about consumption, which is the engine that feeds technological "progress."[4] The equation between market economics, technology transfer, and democracy is made far too easily today. The fact is that as other cultures look to America for models of their own future social forms, they may well describe what they want as democracy, even though when unpacked it becomes clear that what they want are the rights and abilities to consume at the levels we do. And because consumption and technologies go hand-in-hand, this amounts to the right to have technologies at the level that we enjoy.[5] The metanarrative for emerging global culture is closely akin to the technological imperative but it is a metanarrative with a difference. Instead of providing a coherent narrative of the past that grounds meaning and value, it is a narrative of the future, a narrative of the promise of progress that not only transverses cultural and geographical boundaries but overwhelms tradition in such a way as to disperse and fragment meaning and value. It is this odd combination of *de jure* totalization and *de facto* postfoundationalism that demands that we rethink democracy in the light of technology as postmodern.

DEMOCRACY AND THE MODE OF INFORMATION

Technology restructures the fields of symbolic exchange and practical inter-relationship. It does so in ways that neither liberal nor communitarian thinkers have taken into account. It is this that renders their theories suspect in terms of their resonance with contemporary experience and with contemporary problematics. It is the radical thinkers who seem to articulate best what Heidegger called the mood or tone *(Stimmung)* of life in a technological world. This is not to say that their answers (to the degree that they offer any) are adequate, but that their expression of the problem is the most adequate to the radicality of the problem.

Fredric Jameson notes that "no society has ever been quite so mystified in quite so many ways as our own, saturated as it is with messages and information. . . . "[6] The proliferation of information and messages for Jameson leads to an inability to discern meaning. Likewise Richard Terdiman claims that "In a world saturated by discourse, language itself becomes contested terrain."[7] It is this proliferation of information and of the reduction of the world to modes of information that most characterizes the contemporary situation. Mark Poster has argued that

> Electronic systems of communication are changing the fabric of advanced societies. A great historical upheaval is taking place, which promises to transfigure the structure of human interactions. What is going on today is comparable in significance to the industrial revolution of the nineteenth and early twentieth centuries.[8]

He goes on to suggest that, as we move from an industrial to a postindustrial society, our entire frame of reference shifts and so must our mode of analysis. This new form and context for analysis he calls the "mode of information." The mode of information "designates social relations mediated by electronic communications systems."[9] In the final section, we will extend the mode of information to include biotechnology.

The new communications technologies radically alter the time and space relations of the communicators; they transform the codes of language, radically altering not only the nature of communication but the nature of language as well. Poster bases much of his analysis upon Foucault's analysis of discourse/practice and knowledge/power. If discourse is a social practice and technology brings about a radical shift in the nature of discourse, then there is a corresponding shift in the nature of social relations and the subject constituted by them. What Charles Taylor calls "webs of interlocution" (which he claims are constitutive of the subject) are radically altered and the subject alters with them. As Poster puts it,

> [L]iberal . . . visions are badly suited to the present conjuncture with its mode of information because they presuppose the autonomous . . . rational subject as the basis of popular sovereignty. The world of electronically mediated communication disrupts the interpretive basis of this position. To the extent that the mode of information constitutes a variety of multiple, dispersed, decentered, unstable subjects which contest the culture of identity, a new political terrain may be mapped. . . . [10]

This new political terrain is characterized by the demise of anything like a metanarrative, which would provide a grid against which we ultimately gain meaning. Both Jean-François Lyotard and Jean Baudrillard speak of the end of the social and of history or traditions. For them, this is the end of a culture in which subjects gain their orientation in relation to some "rational" metanarrative (liberal or communitarian). In a highly mediated world, language tends to turn back on itself. It is less and less the case that signifiers refer or even give the illusion of representing the "real" world. Instead, the subject tends to relate to the flow of signifiers itself. This is what Eco and Baudrillard call hyperreality. It is a world in which it becomes increasingly difficult for the subject to separate the "real" world from that constant flow of signifiers. The social world that was presented as a stable grouping of material objects represented and ordered by the rationality of a masternarrative in the figure of "realism" now slips into a selfreferential flow of signifiers. What Henri Lefebvre and Baudrillard refer to as the "decline of the referentials" is characteristic of the mode of information. This linguistic instability entails a demise of the social as a unifying masternarrative within a culture of identity legitimated as fixed, natural, inevitable.

The radical thinkers provide us with the best philosophical description of the democratic problematic in a mode of information. For thinkers such as Lyotard, Laclau, and Mouffe, this demise of the social and of the unifying principles and traditions might be viewed as positive for democracy. Their vision of democracy seeks radical pluralism. One in which each member of the plurality is able to constitute his or her own validity. Democracy opposes any attempt to control or regulate discourse, allowing it a kind of free play. Democracy is not judged from the center outward; it is not about the goods and services provided to those already included. Rather, democracy can only be judged from the margins, in relation to those who are left out, marginalized, silenced. Laclau, using a term drawn from Derrida, speaks of the "constitutive outside" as the key to democracy. What distinguishes democracy from other social forms is that it is the outside that constitutes the inside. Democracy is to be judged and motivated by all of those "others" who are not yet included. Democracy should never be seen as stable since all

> principles of social organization, no matter how seemingly egalitarian and just, are constituted as such—are endowed with a determinate identity—through contrast with unstable constellations of "others," of what differs from themselves. This introduces an irremediable element of arbitrariness in all social orders, no matter how large the aspirations toward and the achievement of justice.[11]

To allow one or another version of the social to be constitutive of the other is totalitarian. "Democracy [is] the affirmation of the 'constitutive outside'."[12]

The mode of information may well be a case of what Lyotard calls self-legitimating narratives not subject to the "tribunal" of universalized reason or masternarratives. We are almost accosted by the small, local narratives that let the subject speak. This, for him, is the essence of democratic pluralism. Lyotard defines the postmodern as "an incredulity toward metanarratives."[13] He says that, without the grid or overarching principles of justification we find in metanarratives, we are left with a situation characterized by the "differend," which he defines as "a case of conflict, between at least two parties, that cannot be equitably resolved for lack of a rule of judgment applicable to both arguments. One side's legitimacy does not imply the other's lack of legitimacy."[14] Perhaps we can see the differend at work on television news shows such as *Nightline*, which proclaim themselves a discussion but are actually sheer presentation without even the pretense of conversation. Maybe for Lyotard this is not a bad thing, but there is something disturbing about the fact that the "participants" feel no need even to try to engage in conversation with their opponents. And perhaps the mark of a free society is found in its ability to allow for such irresolvable conflicts to remain so. Lyotard says that dissensus must be tolerated instead of forcing consensus that would wrong one or both of the parties. Politics for him is "the threat of the differend. It is not a genre but the multiplicity of genres, the diversity of ends."[15] The conflict between narrative traditions "has no tribunal before which it can be presented, argued and decided. For this tribunal would already have to be 'universal', human, have an (international) law at its disposal, etc."[16] This is precisely the problem we face with our notions of international justice or international rights. How do we adjudicate between competing claims without making harsh decisions that impact diversity? As disturbing as the seemingly arbitrary and relativistic implications of this postmodern vision of democracy may be for those of us who desire some type of foundation (and both liberals and communitarians fall into this category), their description of the play of signifiers, of the lack of overarching criteria, of a pluralism run wild is the best description of our experience in a technological situation. Mark Poster agrees, "The value of poststructuralist theory is its suitability for the analysis of a culture saturated by the peculiar linguisticality of electronic media."[17]

While the postmoderns raise troubling questions concerning consensus and the coherence of a democratic society, they also open us to a new engagement with what might be called the "democratic imagination." Democracy is not confined to the realm of rationality but is above all viewed as an act of the imagination. This shift from rationality to imagination understands democracy as inherently unstable, as process, even as a fiction caught in the play of signifiers. Botwinick calls this "continual waves of equalization,"[18] which never achieve equalization. Lyotard, Laclau, and Rorty all believe that politics must be constantly "experimental" if it is to be responsive to the other. The direction of this experimentation must always be toward the margins, and democracy can only be judged from the perspective of those "others" who are marginalized. Democracy rejects the relationship of reason to otherness as being one of the "strategies of containment." It sees in rationality's search for the meaning and means to include or find consensus with the "other" a drama enacting power relationships. It is only through the imagination that we are able to allow for the potential incommensurabilities presented by that Otherness. It is the democratic imagination that allows us to respect diversity in all of its radicality as part of and crucial to democracy. It is only through the engagement of this democratic imagination and through experimentation that we will find the new opportunities for democratic practice in a mode of information. Any theory of democracy that fails to take into account the fact of this shift into a mode of information risks being irrelevant to the actual practice of democracy.

PARTICIPATION AND THE NEW SOCIAL SPACES IN AN INFORMATION AGE

Democracy must also be participatory and ought to maximize opportunities for participation. This, it seems to me, is the single most important insight of the communitarians. The idea that those networks of relationships are not things we have but what we *are* means that the "good of community [is] seen to penetrate the person . . . so as to prescribe not just his feeling but a mode of self-understanding partly constitutive of his identity."[19] Their criticism of the liberal position is that its claim to autonomy abstracts from the sense of participation in community, which is always already the case. While I agree with the communitarians on the constitution of the self, they miss the point that communities and the modes and opportunities for participation in community are by no means static over time, as they seem to assume, but change, at times dramatically. In a technological society, characterized by the mode of information, this is certainly the case.

The importance of participation is indicated by the belief that in a democracy all citizens should be guaranteed equal access to participation in the governing process and the economic life of the society. But there is also the relationship between participation and self-development. John Stuart Mill held that participation is essential to the democratic goal of fostering self-development. Democracy promises the individual the possibility of both fulfilment and empowerment in society and participation is the route he or she must take to achieve this. Aryeh Botwinick says, "The underlying premise of participatory democracy—in contrast to liberal representative democracy—is that participatory democratic politics encompasses self-exploration and self-development by the citizenry."[20] The point is nurturance. I am nurtured by a context (a family, a community, etc.) only to the degree to which I am authentically a participant in it. Participation becomes a particularly crucial issue in an age of possessive individualism dominated by the valuing of abstract reason. The personal and social force of individualism is one that can result in a generalized mood of adversarial relationship and one that retards the sense of sacrifice for others which is crucial to democracy. If I do not feel authentically participatory in a situation, I am less likely to feel fulfilled by it or to commit myself to it fully. Participation is also important for aiding excluded groups to discover their self-interests. Herbert Gintis says, "Liberalism claims that the marketplace and the ballot box allow people to get what they want. But liberalism is silent on how people might get to be what they want to be, and how they might get to want what they want to want."[21]

Participation is also linked to the problem of responsibility. Without a genuine sense of connection and deep relationship to others, a sense that is developed most directly through participatory experience, there is little sense of responsibility.[22] Contemporary society in the United States is a testament to the variety of modes of irresponsibility and the refusal to take responsibility that develop when sectors of the society are cut off from participation in the political and economic system and, more importantly, are cut off from participation with each other in forms of community. Participation is the heart of community. Participation charges the will such that it is compelled to make the moral wager, even when that wager is into an abyss. Even a rationalist such as Habermas admits that it is the experience of solidarity shared by being consociates that is fundamental to the choice to be responsible. Clearly a sense of responsibility is more than a matter of rational argumentation and must include some reference to the sentiments and a self-awareness that is intimately bound up with the type of other-awareness that is only possible through mutual participation.

The question, then, is what happens to participation in an age of technology and particularly one characterized by the mode of information. One of the new sites of contestation for democracy will be the new cyberspaces that characterize the information superhighway. If one is a self among other selves, then how one is among those selves makes a profound difference. As Poster puts it,

> What the mode of information puts into question is . . . the very shape of subjectivity; its relations to the world of objects, its perspectives on that world, its location in that world. . . . In a mode of information the subject is no longer located in a point in absolute time/space, enjoying a physical, fixed vantage point from which rationally to calculate its options.[23]

Location is just the point. When we *are* in cyberspace, what and where *are* we? We are simultaneously everywhere and nowhere. One's physical location becomes little more than a transmission point connected to other transmission points.

> The "self" that emerges in an information age does not look at all like the self constituted in traditional communities such as the Aristotelian *polis*, which has now become an electronic *polis* with radically different modes and opportunities for participation.[24]

Nor is it just a matter of our being on the telephone or the "Net", or engaged by mass media, or in one of the many versions of cyberspace now available, but rather the way in which the increasing ubiquity of such new social spaces are constitutive of the subjects we *are* in spaces that are not (at least obviously) so mediated. It is also the way in which these highly mediated spaces now pass for the public sphere and the way in which these new information technologies restructure and reinscribe ordinary lived reality. One networks instead of connects. Technology becomes the "skin" through which we experience the world. The kinds of communities that will emerge out of this are imaginary communities or virtual communities bound together not by forms of communion (sacred or secular) but by webs of mass communication. Not only does responsibility become an entirely new type of problem within these spaces, but the question of the will to be responsible is also thrown open, because responsibility entails both the ability to respond and the will to do so. The issue is one of the modes of relationship in these new spaces. As we move into a world that is characterized by hyperrealities and virtual realities, do we become "virtual selves" within those spaces? It seems clear that these cyberpolitical spaces are sites of contest that cannot be overlooked or assumed to be neutral. The crucial point is that the modes and opportunities for participation have been radically altered, and we are left to ask what the implications for participatory democracy might be.

DIVERSITY AND MONOCULTURE IN A MODE OF INFORMATION

It might seem odd to raise diversity as an issue in an age in which what appears to be almost infinite option is spread out before us through the mass media. Indeed, technology has contributed to diversity at one level, namely, within technological culture. We have more technological options now than ever before. In fact, some say that we have entered a period in which too many options are presented to us. From the hyperrealities presented by movies and advertising to the daily overdose of news, we often seem left with a psychic callousness and nothing other than fashion or momentary emotion to act as judgement. Many critics of technology point out that the one option that goes missing in such a period is the nontechnological option. There is operative a "technological imperative" that demands that our response to the high-tech problems we create be always that of a higher-tech solution.

Generally speaking, diversity is problematic in our situation, because all options are increasingly technological. Technology or *technē* becomes a structure of thinking such that the nontechnological option can cease even to come up as an option. Again, my point is that there is here an assumed picture of a good society as a technological society. In the technological imperative is the threat of monoculture. We can already see this happening through the mechanism of mass media and globally systemic technologies. Increasingly we all watch the same movies (Hollywood dominates the global market); increasingly we all wear the same clothes; our children grow up playing with the same toys and games; we tend to know those figures who can gain access to mass media, etc. Granted there is diversity within these new technological structures and technologies are appropriated within cultures in different ways, but there is also a disturbing level of standardization worldwide. It is the overwhelming presence of global technology in its effects upon local knowledges and indigenous practices whether these be medical practices, agricultural processes, or other general cultural practices that is at issue. Eventually all will fall to the power of modern Western technology with the legitimation of "efficiency." But even this is problematic.[25] Again, there are many advantages to such global standardization, but if democracy is fundamentally about the preservation of and stimulation of diversity, then we must be careful that diversity is not limited to only technological diversity.

One of the important new sites of the contest of technological democracy in which diversity and monoculture are at issue are the broad global agreements such as the General Agreement on Trades and Tariffs (GATT) and the United Nations Conference on Environment and Development (UNCED). It is interesting to compare these two in terms of their visions of the future with respect to the sources of diversity. These are the two largest agreements signed in this generation. As such, not only do they provide a good signpost as to where we are, but they present the confusion of where we are in their very different visions of the future. While UNCED values diversity—cultural and biological—as its core value, GATT reduces everything to market value. GATT is a new form of political document written in the rhetoric of the "free market," which advances standardization and the monocultural world of transnational market economies. In these documents there are raised important issues of national sovereignties, the criteria of an international "level playing field," and the universalization of rules and standards, such as those connected with intellectual property rights, access to and protection of new technologies, etc. The enforceability of GATT and the nonenforceability of UNCED would lead to the conclusion that the global inertia is in the direction of monoculture. For good or ill, these will be among the new sites of contest of global democracy.

The UNCED agreements brings me to two further points concerning diversity. The first of these is the need to expand our notions of diversity to include "nature" or the nonhuman world within the democratic social, and the second is the need to expand our notion of the information age to include biotechnology.

Much of what radical thinkers refer to as other is "nondiscursive" in that it is otherness that for social reasons has not been allowed a voice. For Foucault, a postmodern politics is always transgressive in that it shifts the perspective from the center to the nondiscursive margins of the social, thus revealing the play of power where previously it operated unrecognized. It is a politics that attempts to establish a space for discourse based upon those types of "local knowledges" that do not meet the standards of legitimation and are thus suppressed. One of the thorniest problems facing democracy in a radically pluralistic situation is how far we should extend our offer of inclusion in a democratic society. This is precisely what worries not only the foundationalists but any of us who recognize that there are limits to those whom we are willing to admit into "the conversation." On the one hand, Foucault has taught us that the category of "all rational actors" is often one of the most dangerous power/knowledge constructs. On the other hand, it is a disturbing thought that the price of radical democracy might be the inclusion of a range of voices that might be better left in silence.

I want to claim a place within the democratic social for another more radical "nondiscursive other," another "nonrational actor." A postmodern, post-Rio democracy needs to expand its notions of diversity beyond cultural diversity to include biodiversity as well. Donna Haraway speaks of a "reinvention" of nature such that it is not outside of culture or society but included within it. This may be one of the most difficult leaps of the democratic imagination—an act of political experimentation that seeks to include what Haraway calls "monsters." Monsters are those odd "boundary creatures . . . which have had a destabilizing place in the great Western evolutionary, technological, and biological narratives."[26] "Nature" as an invention of modernity is an object to be classified and dominated. A postmodern approach would overthrow this colonization of the nonhuman world by instrumental rationality. Reinventing nature as part of a democratic society opens up nature as a new candidate for the nondiscursive, raising issues of responsibility, respect, and rights in new ways. In addition, I want to suggest that there is something important about healing this rift between nature and culture that is fundamental to learning participation and manifesting diversity in a democratic society. For any form of postmodern democracy to work, we must reinvent nature so that the "natural" monsters are admitted into a newly reformulated democratic social, a social that respects not just other persons but the diversity of being that is best captured by the term "nature."

Nature also comes under the control of a mode of information. First, nature is reduced to a category of information via mass media. Nature may be the best case in point that technology becomes the "skin" through which we experience the world. We now commonly mediate our encounters with nature through mass media. Nature is simulated by various media. The media that have done a wonderful job publicizing the plight of endangered species and nature worldwide also foster the illusion that once we have them on film we have preserved them in some fashion. Since it is only via media and zoos (which are simulations of another type) that most people will ever experience these creatures anyway, preservation as information in films and books is unconsciously accepted as adequate. The second way that nature enters the information age is within the new biological reinvention of nature in terms of the information coded in genetic structures. In fact, we do not speak of "natural resources" as much as "genetic resources" these days. This reclassification can be dramatically seen in the fact that one of the new modes of the preservation of species is now in gene banks. It is no longer necessary to consider a species that set of complex interrelationships that connects it to an ecosystem. Rather, we can view it as the information within the DNA that can be frozen and thus "preserved."[27]

There is in biotechnology a convergence of the cyberpolitical and the biopolitical spaces. Democracy will be contested at biotechnical sites not only for nature but for humans as well. Not only does biotechnology threaten diversity at the level of the genetic redesign of nature and humanity in accordance with instrumental purposes and current fashion but the new modes of ownership of life forms being contested as intellectual property rights is among the most problematic for democracy. The complexity of these issues is signaled by such recent cases as that of the oncomouse, in which a new genetically produced species has been patented. Given that the oncomouse is genetically engineered to develop cancerous tumors, questions are raised about intentionally creating a species designed to suffer. It also raises the question of where we draw the line on the patenting of life forms and what constitutes reasonable ownership. This issue is pushed further by the case involving John Moore, in which a cell-line developed from his spleen was patented. When Moore sought compensation, it was determined that he (and thus "we") did not have any ownership rights over his own genetic structure. The issue is raised as well by the genome project, which has filed for over three thousand patents on the human DNA structure (sequences),[28] and the patent recently filed by the Secretary of Commerce on aspects of the genetic structure of the Guyami Indians of Panama, which opens the door to the patenting of the genetic structure of indigenous peoples worldwide. I am not sure what the answers are to the questions raised by these events, but I am sure that these new biopolitical sites will challenge us with a range of disturbing new problems for democracy and justice.

These information age technologies, such as biotechnology, threaten to colonize nature and the body in dramatic new ways. Biotechnology reinvents nature from the inside out and, under the direction of the capitalistic marketplace, will orient design according to criteria of efficiency and productivity. As "big science" initiatives, such as the Human Genome Project, move beyond the mapping stage and into the development of genetic therapies, new and complex questions are raised concerning the value of diversity and the social constitution of categories such as "disease." Such categories will determine to what positive and negative limits we will allow the new forms of eugenics to develop. Will we eliminate not only Hodgkins disease and diabetes but obesity, baldness, etc.? As the marketplace takes control of these "therapies" will we move into an age of "designer babies"? And what of the loss of diversity in those areas we call "disease"? What is the cultural cost of such a leveling out of existence? We might ask, for example, about the relationship between the terrible physical disabilities of someone like Stephen Hawking and the abilities of his mind. This is not an argument for the maintenance of disease, but it does suggest that there will be new and interesting questions for democracy with respect to our "freedom" to choose such genetic options and our overall commitment to diversity. There is a question as to how "free" such choices would be in the first place. As we designate more and more human conditions as "disease" and thus legitimate their elimination, we come under greater threat of monoculture.

Again, I do not pretend to have the answers to the types of questions I have raised here. But what seems clear to me is that the contests for democracy and justice increasingly will be waged on these new technological and informational sites. They represent dramatic power shifts and new and complicated issues for the constitution of identity as moral or democratic. The more disturbing thought is that there are no longer any neat solutions, be they principles, sentiments, or any of the other candidates that are supposed to cut through the confusion. In a mode of information, the ambiguity is here to stay. It is vital that we search out the new sites of contestation and engage in the types of political imagination and experimentation whose orientation is always toward maximizing diversity and participation.

NOTES

1. Mark Poster, *The Mode of Information* (Chicago: University of Chicago Press, 1990).

2. William Sullivan, *Reconstructing Public Philosophy* (Berkeley: University of California Press, 1982), p. 26.

3. See Albert Borgman, *Technology and the Character of Contemporary Life* (Chicago: University of Chicago Press, 1984), particularly chapters 13–19.

4. For a good analysis of this, see *Technology and the Character of Contemporary Life*.

5. Again, see *Technology and the Character of Contemporary Life*.

6. Fredric Jameson, *The Political Unconscious* (Ithaca: Cornell University Press, 1981), pp. 60–61.

7. Richard Terdiman, *Discourse/Counter Discourse: The Theory and Practice of Symbolic Resistance in Nineteenth-Century France* (Ithaca: Cornell University Press, 1985), p. 43.

8. M. Poster, *The Mode of Information*, p. 125.

9. Ibid., p. 126.

10. Ibid., pp. 132–33.

11. Aryeh Botwinick, *Postmodernism and Democratic Theory* (Philadelphia: Temple University Press, 1993), p. 13.

12. Ibid.

13. Jean-François Lyotard, *The Postmodern Condition: a Report on Knowledge* (Minneapolis: University of Minnesota Press, 1984), p. xxiv.

14. J.-F. Lyotard, *The Differend* (Manchester: University of Manchester Press, 1988), p. xi.

15. Ibid., p. 167.

16. Ibid., p. 157.

17. M. Poster, *The Mode of Information: Poststructuralism and Social Context*, 417p. 82.

18. A. Botwinick, *Postmodernism and Democratic Theory*, p. 13.

19. Sandel, *Liberalism and the Limits of Justice* (Cambridge: Cambridge University Press, 1982), p. 161.

20. A. Botwinick and P. Bachrach, *Power and Empowerment: A Radical Theory of Participatory Democracy* (Philadelphia: Temple University Press, 1992), p. 10.

21. Samuel Bowles and Herbert Gintis, *Democracy and Capitalism: Property, Community, and the Contradictions of Social Thought* (New York, 1986), p. 125, quoted from A. Botwinick and P. Bachrach, *Power and Empowerment*, p. 11.

22. This is being developed in a forthcoming book entitled, *Wagers into the Abyss: Self, Responsibility and Participation in a Postmodern/Technological Situation*.

23. M. Poster, idem, p. 15.

24. James Buchanan, "In Search of the Modern Moral Identity: A Transversal Reading of Charles Taylor and the Communitarians," *Soundings* (vol. 78, no. 1, Spring 1995), p. 415.

25. If, for example, one determines efficiency in terms of per capita energy usage, it is clear that we are not more but less efficient in technological situations. Developed countries require between thirty and fifty times more energy per person than developing ones. It has also been suggested that many of the indigenous farming practices are more sustainable than the current agri-industry approach.

26. Donna Haraway, *Simians, Cyborgs, and Women: The Reinvention of Nature* (New York: Routledge, 1991), p. 2.

27. See my "The Information Age and Its new Lexicons: Biotechnology as a Case in Point," *Technology in Society* (Spring/Summer 1994).

28. The literature on these cases is extensive. For a good summary, see Andy Kimbrell, *The Human Body Shop: The Engineering and Marketing of Life* (New York: Harper Collins, 1993).

Part 6. Principles of Cultural Dialogue

Marietta Stepaniants

THE IDEAL OF JUSTICE IN THE CONTEXT OF CULTURAL DIALOGUE

While democracy was anticipated, it was said that it would come
for sure, but now that it has come, it is said that it can disappear.
                                                    Peotr Novgorotsev

The great integrative processes characterizing the twentieth century lead some people to forecast radical quantitative changes in the life of the world community, up to and including the emergence of a single planetary civilization with a new system of human values. Others, whose projections strike me as more probable, forecast the rise of a metacivilization that will become a kind of a cultural "common denominator," and which, instead of absorbing or pushing aside national, regional civilizations, will rather stand above all of them. Under any scenario of future developments, it is quite evident that the expansion of contacts and cultural dialogue—upon which depends, not only further progress, but the very survival of humanity—is vital.

For everyone who takes part in it, this dialogue has a different meaning. But the cultural dialogue is of particular significance for Russia, a country lying on the crossroads of the Eastern and Western "winds." Reflecting on the future of Russia, her enlightened minds long ago recognized the importance of its geographically central placement. As Peotr Chaadaev wrote in his first "philosophical" letter,

> While expanding between the two great divisions of the world, the East and the West, lying with one elbow on China and with the other on Germany, we should combine in ourselves the two great foundations of the spiritual nature—imagination and reason—in this way unifying in our enlightenment the historical fortunes of the whole planet.[1]

The dispute between "slavophiles" and *zapadniks* (Westernizers), which took place in the second half of the nineteenth and the beginning of the twentieth centuries, did not end in the discovery of a "golden middle way." Though Western-Oriental symbiosis occurred, it took the distorted form of the Russian brand of Marxism.

After seven decades, Russia once again faces the necessity of having to choose. It is true that slavophiles and *zapadniks* are not now what they were like in the past. Still, the core of the dispute between them remains the same. The stage through which Russia nowadays is passing is often called *perestroika,* which means "reconstruction." However, it seems it would be more precise to describe it as the condition of being "at the crossroads," since the Russian "architects" and "constructors" do not have a plan of action for the realization of any particular project. It is true that among them there are those who strongly believe that they need to build a "skyscraper," while others prefer to construct an *Izba* or "log cabin." As for the majority, they wish for themselves, and especially for their children and grandchildren, just to have a comfortable house where justice could reign.

A skyscraper and a log cabin are symbols of the two poles of the modern cultural dialogue, representing in their turn the traditional, and the posttraditional, liberal societies—in other words, what could be called "East" and "West." In spite of the plurality of problems being addressed in this dialogue, one can probably say that the central issue under discussion is how to establish the most humanitarian social system.

Many, especially in the West, have no doubt that the ideal political model for such a system is democracy. However, recently there have been many cases where democratic principles and institutions—viewed as alien "transplantations" forcibly imposed upon the local culture—have been rejected. (The anti-Shah revolution in Iran provides, perhaps, the best example of such an attitude.) There are a number of reasons for this. Perhaps the most important has to do with the different possible ways of understanding the meaning of *justice*—the very ideal that is supposed to be achieved through democracy.

Those who consider justice to belong to the set of so-called "universal human values" in fact tend to ignore existing differences in the interpretations of justice, and thus succumb to illusions about the essential sameness of all possible manners of its realization. The notion of justice, however, is always enclosed within the framework of a particular value system. And the traditional society typically differs in its approach toward the ideal of justice in at least four respects from the approach taken by the posttraditional society.

1) Before the emergence of Western liberal society, there were basically two types of moral prescriptions: the first, sanctioned by religion, and the second, by the local authority. Indian, Muslim, and Medieval Christian civilizations are characterized by the recognition of morality as a system of ethical norms prescribed by the corresponding religious belief. In the Islamic world,

for example, the source of any law, including the moral law, is Allah. Hence there is a rejection of any right to law-making by mere human beings and a demand that one strictly follow the law of Allah, *Shariah*. From this point of view, the statement the leader of Libyan Jamahiriya, Muammar Qaddafi, made in his *Green Book* is significant:

> The true law of any society could be either tradition, or religion. . . . [A] constitution is not the law of a society, because it is the product of human hands. . . . Non-religious, non-traditional laws are made by one man so [as] to use them against another, hence they are invalid being not founded on the basis of the natural source. . . . [2]

As for an authoritarian moral system, the most vivid example of it one can find is perhaps provided by the dominant Confucian tradition in traditional Chinese society.

2) The realization of justice in traditional societies usually refers not to the present but to the future, by which is meant the life after death, when we have passed from this mundane life. In Christianity and in Islam, justice will reign only at the Day of the Last Judgment, when God will treat each human in accordance with his or her sins and virtues. No human being or society, but God alone, is absolutely just:

> And I saw the dead, small and great, standing before God, and books were opened. And another book was opened, which is the Book of Life. And the dead were judged according to their works, by the things which were written in the books.[3]

Similarly, the Koran warns believers:

> For those who do good is the best (reward) and more (thereto). Neither dust nor ignominy cometh near their faces. Such are rightful owners of the Garden; they will abide therein. And those who earn ill-deeds, (for them) requital of each ill-deed by the like thereof; and ignominy overtaketh them—They have no protector from Allah—as if their faces had been covered with a cloak of darkest night. Such are rightful owners of the Fire; they will abide therein.[4]

According to the Indian tradition, after death, which is thought of as the death of the body, the soul transfers into another material form—that of a human being (either of a higher or of a lower status), an animal, an insect, a plant, etc. The transition is done in conformity with *karma* or deeds. It is in this way that justice is achieved.

3) Justice is related to a certain "collective" to which an individual belongs. That could be a caste, a community, a class or a social stratum, a religious confession, etc. For equal virtues or sins, different blessings or punishments could be expected. Thus, for example, when a *kshatria* (a mem-

ber of a caste of warriors) engages in violence or even kills on the battlefield, that is not only excused but considered a virtue. For those who belong to other castes, however, such behavior is considered to be criminal. In traditional society, where a "stratified labor division" (Max Weber's phrase) exists, an individual is expected to fulfill those functions that are prescribed as a result of his or her belonging to a particular social community. Here justice is measured on the basis of how successful an individual has been in following the prescribed behavior patterns of the social stratum to which he or she was assigned by birth. In this sense, it could be said that in the traditional society, justice has a tendency to be of an egalitarian nature.

The situation is quite different in the posttraditional society. Here the labor division is "functional," by which is meant that the place of an individual in the social stratification is determined by the function that he or she fulfills, and a change of that function can lead to a change in social status. Accordingly, here justice is measured strictly on the basis of the deeds of an individual; he or she carries personal responsibility for those deeds. It is not by chance that in English "justice" is defined as "reward or penalty as deserved." Similarly, in French "justice" means "acknowledgment and respect of the rights and dignity of everybody."

4) Justice is regarded only in terms of duty—which is to say, without any consideration of human "rights." It is significant that in Sanskrit there is no word that corresponds to "right." Similarly, the traditional Chinese ethical system presents a set of duties, rather than of rights.

The posttraditional or liberal society differs from the traditional one in all the above-mentioned respects. 1) The source of justice and the ultimate judge, ruling it, is the people itself, represented by the elected members of parliament and the courts. 2) Justice is thought of in terms of the categories of the present: it should be realized here and now, in this life. 3) Everyone should have an equal right to justice in full accordance with his or her own deeds. 4) Justice and the law are undivided.

The "middle" location of Russia has caused the dominance of a notion of justice that is stamped by the influence of both the traditional (Oriental) and liberal (Western) societies. The source of justice, for Russians, has both a sacred character (even Marxism has played the role of a kind of religious ideology) and an authoritarian nature. The absence of a civic society in contemporary Russia in fact precludes the legal mechanism for the realization of justice. At the same time, the general mood of the populace inclines them to demand equality for everyone, and during this life.

It is worth noting that, in the Russian language, the word for justice is the same as that for truth, namely, "*pravda*."[5] In Russian orthodoxy, justice is usually associated with the victory of the True-God, through the establishment of God's Kingdom, usually understood as "earthly paradise."

Having accepted the idea of the sacredness and divine mission of the state authority (an idea that first appeared in Byzantium), the Russian church, after the collapse of Constantinople in 1453, insisted on its own "blessed" status as the one chosen safeguard of Christ's truth in its purity, as well as on the status of the Russian monarchy in Moscow as the "third Rome." (Since the fourth Rome would never come, it followed that the Russian kingdom would survive until the end of the world.) The Russian tsar was regarded by the clergy as the agent of Divine Providence, who carried out justice in this world. Joseph Volokalamsky, a prominent clergyman of the late fifteenth and early sixteenth century, wrote, "The Tsar, by his nature, is similar to any human being, although by his position and power he is like God Almighty." Even more categorical is the statement made by the mitropolite Malaria, "You, ruler, have been chosen by God to replace Him on earth. He has raised you to the throne by passing you the blessing and life of the whole Christian Orthodoxy."[6]

The optimistic mood concerning the forthcoming earthly paradise as the blessed finale of human history, which had dominated Western thought from the end of the eighteenth century (in the writings of Rousseau, Kant, Hume, Spencer, Marx, etc.), once transplanted onto Russian soil, produced mutant fruits in full accordance with the logic of traditional society. It is not by chance that it was in Russia that the ideal of the Marxist utopia, based on the foundation of *absolute collectivism,* was first embraced. Russian Marxism, in spite of its materialist character, was in this sense fully in tune with the *soborny* spirit of the traditional society, which demands that the individual "merge with society," in this way rejecting, in fact, the value of the individual personality and the independent meaning of personal existence.

Equally in accordance with the traditional approach were the methods of realizing social justice, which excluded the mechanism of a legal system. The construction of communism in the Soviet Union as an "ideal society" with "universal justice" was brought about through the use of ideological propaganda and the tools of politico-economic enforcement, while genuine legal norms and institutions were ignored. The removal of Russians from real participation in the governing of the state and their legal ignorance can also be considered, indirectly at least, the fault of the ideologues of the traditional society—the slavophiles. These were, in general, the advocates of empire and the monarchy. For them the Tsar *was* the state, while the people—and the irony here is rich, since the slavophiles considered themselves to be the true Russian patriots—were the *object* of rule, rather than a self-governing force.

As P. Novgorotsev remarked, "among the slavophile's phantasies, maybe the most fantastic one was that according to which the Russian people do not consider political rights important and necessary for themselves. The West perhaps needs them, but that does not mean that we should follow its example."[7] The leading representative of that trend of Russian thought, K. Aksakov, claimed,

> The Russian people are no-state people: this means that they do not seek a state power, they do not wish for themselves political rights, and they do not possess even a bit of the lust for power. The Russian people, lacking the political element, have separated themselves from the state and do not want to rule. Not wanting to rule, the people pass to the government an unlimited state power. In return, the Russian people get for themselves moral freedom, freedom of life and of spirit.[8]

The faultiness of the slavophile's ideas and the possibility of their damaging consequences have been thoroughly demonstrated by the seventy years of Russian postrevolutionary history.

Not only today, at a time of *perestroika,* but much earlier, in the nineteenth century, questions such as, Who are we? Where are we going? In what direction should we move? became, what might be called, "Russian national questions." To these questions, some (and among them, the slavophiles) responded, "Seek for the internal spiritual, moral truth; love it with all the force of your soul, and thus you will get the ideal social life."[9] Others (the so-called Westernizers) opposed this attitude, contending instead that "Once the social life and social conditions have been improved to the state of perfection, individuals will naturally become oriented towards the good, towards moral development and perfection."[10]

The enlightened minds of Russia recognized the weak aspects of the above-mentioned polar trends of thought. The position of Vladimir Solovyov in this matter is quite significant. (See his "Opravdanie dobra" [Justification of the Good].) One is also reminded of the reasonable stand taken by P. Novgorotsev:

> Individual perfection is needed for social progress, but it is not enough, since there is also a need for certain social measures. The progress of social forms is needed for individual perfection, but it is not enough, since there is also a need of personal effort on the part of individuals. Thus the one-sidedness of polar moral objectivity and moral subjectivity is eliminated.[11]

The Russian revolution of 1917 involved an attempt to solve the old (as old as history itself) problem of the relation between the individual human being and society, between morality and politics. However, this was done without taking into consideration (and in fact, in opposition to) the necessity of eliminating the one-sidedness of, on the one hand, the claims of absolute collectivism and moral subjectivity and, on the other, the claims of absolute individualism and moral objectivity. Thus the experiment had been taken to synthesize noncombinable elements of two polar value systems, rather than trying to find a solution that would correspond to the logic of the internal evolution of Russian national culture.

The Russian synthesis of the influences of West and East, judging by the results of the past seven decades, has proven to be ineffective and lacking in perspective. However, it still could be useful as a lesson given to us, and to others who might emulate us, by history. By entering into the contemporary dialogue of cultures, we might perhaps be able to find the solutions to a number of unsolved problems, the answers to some as yet unanswered questions, such as the following: Is the principal difference in the notion of the ideal of justice (i.e., that between the traditional and the posttraditional viewpoints) an inevitable obstacle on the way to the introduction of democratic norms and institutions? Should we even consider democracy to be the imperative of the moment, the vital precondition of social progress? If so, then is there any possibility of the democratization of traditional societies without the radical reinterpretation of their cultural and religious traditions? Must that kind of reconstruction follow the model of the Reformation in Christianity? Is not the recent revival of religious fundamentalism evidence of the search for inner resources in the maintenance of cultural identity, *even as* the cultures in question pursue social progress? These and many other vital questions can be answered only in the process of a cultural dialogue. The success of this dialogue depends in large part on the recognition that the Western experience of democracy, though quite successful, still is one-dimensional, that democracy is *par excellence* a system of political relativity, for which "nothing absolute exists, which is always ready to permit anything—any political chance, any economic system that does not violate freedom," since democracy "is always a crossroad: no ways are closed, no directions are prohibited."[12]

NOTES

1. P. Ya. Chaadaev, "Filosoficheskie pisma. Pismo pervoe" in *Sochineniya* (Moscow, 1989), pp. 24–25. (The English translations of this and all other quotations taken from Russian language sources are those of the author.)

2. Muammar Qaddafi, *The Green Book,* vol. I (Tripoli), pp. 68–69, 76–77.

3. The Bible, Book of Revelation, chap. 20, verse 12.

4. Koran, Surah X, 26–27.

5. N. K. Mihailovsky, referring to the peculiarity of the Russian word "*pravda,*" wrote, "Every time that the word "*pravda*" comes to my mind, I cannot help but admire its striking internal beauty. . . . It seems that only in Russian are truth and justice called by the same word, thus becoming one great whole." See V.V. Zenkovsky, *Istoria russkoi filosofii,* vol. 1 (Paris, 1948), p. 19.

6. Cf. V.V. Zenkovsky, idem, p. 49.

7. See P.I. Novgorodtsev, *Ob obshchestvennom ideale* (Moscow, 1991), p. 530.

8. *Russ* (no. 26, May 9, 1881), p. 11.

9. Leo Tolstoy, adhering in fact to the slavophile's stand on subjective idealism, sincerely believed that "genuine social improvement could be reached only through the religious-moral perfection of individuals" and that "social perfection through the aid of external forms" is nothing but a crucial illusion that prevents "true progress." L.N. Tolstoy, "Ob abshchestvennom dvizhenii v Rossii," *Sochineniya grafa L.N. Tolstogo,* 12th edition (Moscow, 1911), pt. XIX, p. 313.

10. K.D. Kavelin. "Pismo F.M. Dostoevskomy," *K.D. Kavelin. Nash ymstvennyi stroi. Stati po filosofii russkoi istorii i kulturi* (Moscow, 1989), p. 448.

11. P.I. Novgorodtsev, idem, p. 202.

12. P.I. Novgorodtsev, *Demokratia na rasputie,* p. 553.

Yersu Kim

WORLD CHANGE AND THE CULTURAL SYNTHESIS OF THE WEST

As a century and, indeed, a millennium draw to a close, we stand today perhaps at the most open moment in the history of humankind. The cultural synthesis that it has taken the West well over four hundred years of the departing millennium to forge and which brought power and wealth to the West, but also a pervasive improvement in the material condition of humankind at large during the waning century is losing its once matter-of-fact validity and persuasiveness. The world a hundred years ago was in a very fundamental sense one. The world was ruled by the West—which is to say, by a few western and central European countries and the United States. Along the periphery of this world, a few non-Western, so-called "honorary" members of the West, such as Russia and Japan were mimicking the imperialist ways of their Western mentors. The rest of the world consisted of colonies and *de facto* colonies. Without exception, these were unanimous in seeing Westernization as the only means of ensuring themselves a viable future.

Today, instead of returning to its former condition of "oneness," as might have been expected given the end of the Cold War and the push for globalization brought about by revolutionary changes in communication technology and economic relations, the world is showing clear signs of cultural fragmentation. I am thinking here not only of the ethnic/religious fragmentation that has become the daily fare of international news. I am thinking primarily of the fact that the Western cultural synthesis, based on the ideas of individualism, rationalism, scientism, and belief in progress—a synthesis that had seemed self-evident and persuasive—no longer seems to offer a sure guide to human flourishing. And there seems to be no new synthesis persuasive enough to replace the old.

Many of the so-called "advanced" industrial countries seem to be going through a painful process of readjusting the cultural paradigm that brought

431

them democracy, freedom, and prosperity. In Europe, many countries are reducing welfare benefits and making significant revisions in their economic model. In the United States, there seems to be a not entirely articulated pendulum swing between liberalism and libertarianism (even perhaps libertinism)—a groping for some sort of balance.

Many of the nations in Asia have been able to break the vicious circle of poverty and underdevelopment and achieve a measure of peace, prosperity, and democracy. There is no question that this success was based to a great extent on the adoption and internalization of the Western cultural synthesis, but modified to fit the contingencies of economic, social, and political development. There is a growing sense in Asia today that even this modified cultural synthesis of the West is no longer adequate and there is now in progress a multitude of vigorous, if somewhat confused, attempts at forging a new cultural synthesis.

What is clear is that there is today no dominant and persuasive cultural model that compels full admiration and emulation in the way that the Western synthesis did in the past. The ideas and values that formed the backbone and the motor behind the rise and development of Western industrial civilization seem to be losing their once self-evident relevance and validity. It is becoming increasingly clear that those signs of stagnation and even of relative decline in the West are due not to an accidental configuration of factors, but rather to the tension and contradiction within the ideas or values that are at the core of the expansionist industrial civilization. It is becoming almost a commonplace to say that the expansionist dynamic inherent in the Western economic model may eventually come to destroy the very civilization built on that dynamic.

What I would like to do in the following pages is to put forward a rather simple thesis. It is that any large idea, including the idea of justice, is embedded in a larger historically conditioned context in which a set of ideas, values, and practices constitute a particular culture's conception of human flourishing. Without taking into account this embeddedness of the idea in a conception of human flourishing—to which I give the name "cultural synthesis"—the principles of justice or, for that matter, any idea that is of foundational importance in a society cannot be properly understood, let alone adequately justified.

In order to show that this is so, I will take Rawls' principles of justice— which are supposed to have been derived in such a way as to be radically ahistorical and acontextual, and thus universal—and try to show them to be firmly embedded in the historically conditioned context of the liberalism of individualistic provenience. Individualistic liberalism is understood as an essential ingredient in the cultural synthesis of the West that has provided a persuasive model of human flourishing for at least the last hundred years or so.

I hope to further strengthen the thesis of embeddedness by a brief excursus into the classical—that is, folk—Confucian conception of a good society, in which the Rawlsian concern for rights and liberties is of distinctly secondary importance, and this fact is traced to an embeddedness in a fundamentally different cultural synthesis. Then I will try to meet the charge of cultural relativism that could be leveled at the thesis of the embeddedness of the principles of justice in a particular cultural synthesis by proposing to regard the optimal cultural synthesis as a regulative principle in the Kantian sense.

PRIMACY OF JUSTICE: JOHN RAWLS

At the outset of his *A Theory of Justice,* Rawls makes a bold claim for the primacy of justice: "Justice is the first virtue of social institutions, as truth is of systems of thought."[1] Somewhat surprisingly, Rawls goes on to claim that just as an "untrue" theory, however elegant and economical, must be rejected, so "unfair" laws and institutions, however efficient and well-arranged, must be rejected. Justice then becomes the standard by which competing values and conceptions of the good are adjudicated.

Although Rawls describes the primacy of justice as "our intuitive conviction," its validity is intuitively far from obvious. Some societies may place (and, in fact, a number *have* placed) higher value on, for example, material well-being and solidarity than on rights grounded in a conception of justice. Justice does figure prominently in many of the classical ethical systems, but it was only as one virtue within a complex of many virtues. One finds no lexical equivalent of "justice" in some of the non-Western classical languages (Chinese, for instance), and modern words for "justice" in Korean and Chinese are of recent origin.

How, then, does Rawls argue for the primacy of justice? It is grounded, in part, in the privileged way in which the principles of justice are derived. The well-known Rawlsian principles of justice—the priority of liberty rule and the difference principle—are derived and justified without commitment to any substantive value or conception of the good, and thus they are presented as neutral principles. Rawls sees his conception of justice as fairness as exemplifying this very neutrality.

What are the conditions that must obtain in order to guarantee this neutrality? As is well-known, the centerpiece of the Rawlsian derivation of the principles of justice is his conception of the original position and the veil of ignorance. Each of the parties in the original position chooses principles of justice from behind a "veil of ignorance," depriving him of all information that could prejudice him in making his choice. He knows nothing of his place in society, of his class position or social status. He does not know what his abilities and assets are. Neither does he know his conception of the good or his plan of life. He has no knowledge of the particular circumstances of his own society. He does not even know to which generation he belongs.

Because of the veil of ignorance, the agent in the original position is an "essential" human devoid of all accidental particularities. He is assumed to be rational only in the sense that he is able to rank alternatives to advance his interests. A rational person is thought to have a coherent set of preferences for some of the options open to him, and he is capable of ranking these options according to how well they further his interests. But if the agents in the original position are deprived of all knowledge regarding their ends and interests, how can they decide which conception of justice is most to their advantage? In order to account for the parties' motivations in the original position, Rawls postulates certain "formal interests"—namely, the desire for primary goods, which include certain basic liberties, rights and opportunities, income and wealth, and the social bases of self-respect. It is assumed that the agent in the original position would prefer more "primary goods" rather than less. This so-called "thin theory" of the good is the "bare essential" necessary for derivation of the principles of justice, without jeopardizing the primacy of justice over the conception of the good. Through a series of complex and sophisticated deductive arguments, Rawls shows how the agent in the original position is bound to arrive at the lexical ordering of the principle of greatest equal liberty and the difference principle. The conditions and constraints that characterize the original position are intended to ensure justice as procedural fairness by removing human and historical contingencies. The principles agreed upon by the parties in a condition of procedural fairness cannot but be just. Rawls thus arrives at principles of justice that are radically ahistorical in their universality—valid for any social order, irrespective of particular motivations of human agents and contingencies of social and historical circumstances.

NEUTRALITY OF THE PRIMARY GOODS

Here we must raise the question: Is the thin theory of the good postulated in the original position neutral in the required sense—that is, does it avoid prejudicing the parties in the original position for or against a particular conception of the good? Rawls bases the thin theory of the good on what he calls "the facts of psychology" and "the general status of desires and ends."[2] Yet it seems clear that the primary goods stipulated in the thin theory are not equally valuable to all kinds of social and political orders found in history. The communitarian mode of life—as found in the feudal or the classical Confucian society—would need primary goods other than those of the thin theory. The socialist political order would require a communitarian value such as solidarity in its list of primary goods.

If the primary goods postulated in the thin theory are not equally valuable for all conceptions of the good, they must favor some conception of the good over others. If that is the case, the original position within which the thin list of primary goods operates cannot guarantee the kind of neutrality required for the justification of the principles of justice. Thomas Nagel, for one, argues that the list of primary goods as bare essentials changes according to different social and political orders, and Rawls' thin theory is especially congenial to the individualistic conception of the good. The original position, according to Nagel,

> contains a strong individualistic bias. . . . The original position seems to presuppose not just a neutral theory of the good but a liberal, individualistic conception according to which the best that can be wished for someone is the unimpeded pursuit of his own path, provided it does not interfere with the rights of others.[3]

THE CONCEPT OF PERSON

The basic individualism of the Rawlsian theory of justice can be seen clearly in the role the concept of person plays in it. The person in the original position is a rational being, a subject capable of choice, an autonomous will. The circumstances of justice require that there be conflicting claims, that there be a plurality of individuals with different sets of wants, desires, aims, and purposes. In the Rawlsian opus, the concept of person assumes an increasingly pivotal role. From the Dewey Lectures on, the conception of the moral person plays a fundamental role in the sense that it is the moral person who "both shapes the principles of justice and is shaped in their image through the medium of the original position."[4] The parties in the original position are moral agents endowed with two powers of moral personality: the capacity for a sense of right and justice, and the capacity for a conception of the good. In this way, the conception of an autonomous person becomes part of a conception of political and social justice from the very start.

It is not surprising that, in the Dewey Lectures, Rawls retreats from claiming neutrality for the original position and universality for his principles of justice. Here he disclaims attempts to find a conception of justice suitable for all societies, regardless of their particular social and historical circumstances. His claim now is only "to settle a fundamental disagreement over the just form of basic institutions within . . . a democratic society under modern conditions."[5] Rawls' theory of the good, then, is not based on a general form of social life, but on a special form of political structure in a democratic society. The liberal democratic ideal prefigures in Rawls' theory of the good.

CONTEXTUAL EMBEDDEDNESS

The larger political and social context in which Rawls' principles of justice are embedded involves the assumption that society consists of atomistic individuals competing with each other for scarce resources and goods. There is therefore a need for a set of principles and laws that will adjudicate between conflicting claims. This, in turn, requires a social contract, since these principles and laws must be agreed upon and respected by the individuals comprising that society. Since these principles and laws must be binding and enforceable, there is an obsession with the universalizability of these principles and laws at the conceptual level and an emphasis on the regime of law at the practical level. The regime of law is of course responsible for, on the one hand, prohibiting those actions inimical to the functioning of community and, on the other, protecting the basic rights of individuals. It is meant to guarantee the minimum conditions necessary to maintain a functioning society. As Rawls himself puts it, the principles of justice that the parties in the original position choose are ones that guarantee "a satisfactory minimum."[6]

A CONFUCIAN BENCHMARK

The essential embeddedness of the principle of justice in a larger set of ideas and values that together make up the notion of how a good society should be structured comes into sharper focus when we compare the assumptions of the Rawlsian conception with those of the Confucian notion of a good life. The liberal-democratic conception of justice began, as we saw, with the assumption that individuals in the circumstances of justice are autonomous subjects who are entitled to certain rights, simply by virtue of being born into a particular biological species. In the Confucian conception, a person becomes a human being only by virtue of participation in society. In Tu Weiming's felicitious words, a person "learns to become a human being."[7] Simply being born into a particular biological species is not enough to make one a human being. One becomes a human being as a consequence of personal cultivation and socialization. It is only through learning to participate in society and entering into harmonious relationships with others—the relationships between ruler and subject, father and son, husband and wife, between brothers, and between friends—that one can overcome the instincts and desires of animal nature, and develop cognitive, aesthetic, and spiritual capacities that make one distinctively human. Being a human being is not something that is given to people by right of birth; it is a condition that must be achieved.

As opposed to the Rawlsian assumption that a moral agent is an abstract rational being devoid of concrete social and political particularities, and thus presumably amenable to the universalization of first principles, the Confucian conception of the moral agent is predicated on the assumption that man is a social being in a particular social and historical context. We are part of a society and that society has a tradition. It sees persons in a network of deep historical roots and relationships based on the tradition of *li*. Sometimes translated as "rituals," "rites," or even "etiquette," *li* includes the full range of social customs and norms in the relationships and institutions of society. It is the repository of meanings and values handed down by tradition from the ideal past. It represents the wisdom of the ages, and Confucius claims himself to be a mere transmitter of this tradition.

The thrust of our moral life, therefore, cannot be the forging of universal laws and principles that would establish the minimum standards of basic rights for atomistic individuals bent on pursuing their self-interest. The essence of the Confucian synthesis is the hierarchical principle in social relations governed by the so-called "three bonds" and "five relations." In the Confucian system, morality and politics are inseparable because the self, the family, the society, and the state are linked together essentially by this principle. Confucianism as a political ideology therefore entails the ideas of self-cultivation, of family regulation, and of social harmony as different aspects of the same continuum that constitutes the Confucian conception of the good life. Our moral life should be directed toward the realization of a society based on the joint efforts of human beings cooperating and striving toward harmony in human relationships. Under this conception, a society that is compelled to secure a minimum level of basic rights devoid of any conception of the good must be deemed a failure.

CULTURAL SYNTHESIS

Our discussion of Rawls' attempt to derive principles of justice that are radically ahistorical in their universality has revealed the essential embeddedness of these principles in a larger historical context. The Rawlsian principles of justice are essentially part and parcel of the political ideology of individualistic liberalism, and cannot be properly understood, let alone justified, without recourse to the values and ideals of this ideology. Individualistic liberalism, in turn, is part and parcel of the Western cultural synthesis that has long provided the dominant and largely persuasive model of human flourishing. It is only within the context of this cultural synthesis that specific ideas and principles—such as those of justice—can be fully explicated and understood. By the same logic, a search for a new set of principles of justice adequate to the changed and changing circumstances of our world would have to be carried out as part of an attempt to forge a new cultural synthesis.

Each culture—of whatever time and place—strives to forge an optimal synthesis of ideas, values, and practices—a synthesis that would best enable it to meet the challenges of surviving and prospering within the constraints of its natural and historical circumstances. Each of the twenty-one civilizations identified by Arnold Toynbee was based on such a cultural synthesis. Such a synthesis must provide a clear conception, accepted by the majority of the members of the culture in question, of what constitutes the good life— the life that is worthy of human beings. When such a synthesis is successful, it will serve as the basis for a common perception of the world on the part of its adherents, it will set the goals and direct the activities of both individuals and societies, and it will provide the yardstick against which the worth of a society as a whole can be measured. Although each culture establishes its own criteria for determining what counts as an optimal solution to the problems of surviving and prospering, a particular synthesis, at some time and place, will be perceived both by those viewing it from inside and those viewing it from outside to have reached an optimal point—a point of reflective equilibrium in the interaction between ideas and values, on the one hand, and the recalcitrant and changing environment, on the other. Such a synthesis may thus become a model for emulation by other cultures, and even the yardstick against which the worth of other cultures' efforts at synthesis may be measured and evaluated.

Although the ambition of the cultural synthesis may be universalistic, its language and spirit must be fallibilistic. This must be so, because our knowledge of the world proceeds from a distinctively human and limited point of view, and is acquired by contingent, unprivileged, and biased means. If there is a valid insight in the philosophical arguments for cultural relativism, it is that man is finite. Our conception of reality as it presents itself to culture as a recalcitrant environment is never a fully accurate or unbiased picture of the world as it is. For this reason, the claim of the optimality of any given cultural synthesis holds only for a time.

But if our access to reality is thus contingent and biased, then cultures other than ours may have access to other aspects of reality and picture the world in terms of cognitive forms more suited to their interests and needs. So other cultures may process information regarding the world in such a way as to form a cultural synthesis that would in some sense be alternative to our own. Plurality and diversity of cultures are thus the consequences of human finitude. Since the worth of a cultural synthesis is a function of the extent to which it enables a culture to survive and prosper within a given environment, beyond a consideration of these factors it must not be judged absolutely, but rather always relative to its predecessors and rivals as being either more or less acceptable.

My proposal is to regard the possibility of an optimal cultural synthesis as a regulative ideal in the Kantian sense. It guides the efforts of different people at various times to forge a system of ideas, values, and practices that are perfectly adequate to the requirements of humans and the constraints of the environment. As our knowledge of the world increases and our horizons expand in the wake of ever greater contacts with other peoples and cultures, our notion of the optimal cultural synthesis is bound to undergo a similarly evolutionary process of revision and expansion.

We are encouraged in such a view by the fact that there are species-specific primitive experiences that are common to all humans, and by the fact that the basic constraints placed on the lives of humans by the recalcitrant world are essentially the same for all cultures and periods. Another contributing factor, of course, is the increasing homogeneity in the physical environment of different cultures. But these "universals" constitute only a minuscule part of what enters into the forging of an optimal cultural synthesis. The task of forging such a synthesis might be compared to that of the archaeologist who, on the basis of the most meager evidence, attempts to provide an overall picture of an ancient, little-known civilization. Just as the picture he offers must undergo changes, sometimes minor, sometimes radical, whenever some new evidence is discovered, and thus moves gradually closer to becoming the "true" picture of the civilization in question, so our knowledge of the world and our conception of how best to flourish in it undergo a continual process of disruption, correction, and expansion.

TASKS AHEAD

Whatever form and direction such a synthesis may finally come to have, there are a number of issues that must be dealt with in the process of conceptualizing anew a model of human flourishing. There is, first and foremost, the task of an appropriate revision of the aggressive individualistic ethics. Can it be tempered or even be replaced by a greater concern for the common good? Can we make the ethos and institutions of the traditional communalist societies relevant for the societies of tomorrow? Can familialism, which has often been pointed to as an essential element in traditional Confucian culture, be sublimated into a normative standard for a more inclusive and cooperative human relationship?

Another issue that requires reconceptualization is the attitude that sees human flourishing primarily in terms of the accumulation of material wealth. Such an attitude must be replaced by a more holistic perspective, which knows how to balance and coordinate satisfactions among many different dimensions of human existence. It would be an outlook that places "inner" satisfaction of the mind on the same or even on a higher level than material satisfactions. Art, music, poetry, and ritual would temper and enrich barren rationalism and materialism, thus regaining their commensurate places in the lives of humans. It would be a perspective in which reason and emotion, quality and quantity, future and past is each allotted its own appropriate and respected place.

Most controversial, no doubt, would be the problem of a fundamental readjustment of humanity's relationship to nature. In place of the current conception of the human as a being separate from nature, and obliged to conquer it, a less exploitative outlook must take root, one that sees humans as one species among others, embedded in the intricate web of natural processes that contain and sustain all forms of life. Such an outlook must be supported by the knowledge that there are limits to natural resources and that human intervention in the web of natural processes is bound to have far-reaching consequences, most of which are cumulative and some irreversible. It must be a relationship to nature that would enable us to manage our economy, including our technology, in such a way as to sustain the complexity and stability of nature. At the same time, it must enable us to manage the complexity and stability of nature so as to sustain our economy. The task ahead is not simply to control nature, but to control ourselves so that the economy can fit appropriately within the natural ecology. We would succeed better in this task through accommodating our interests and desires to the limits set by nature, rather than by trying to push at those limits in order to accommodate our insatiable desires.

Finally, intimately connected with the issue of individualism, the meaning of life, and our relationship to nature, the problem of justice—at both the national and international levels—is an integral component of any cultural synthesis. A search for a new set of principles of justice adequate to the changed and changing circumstances of our world must be carried out in creative interaction with each of these problems, as well as with the emerging cultural synthesis as a whole. These are only some of the issues that need to be worked through in the task of cultural synthesis that is ahead of us. We must carry out this task sometimes by harking back to the past, sometimes by bringing together the disparate ideas of the present into a coherent whole, but above all by articulating those thoughts that are not yet thought clearly.

NOTES

1. John Rawls, *A Theory of Justice* (Cambridge: Harvard University Press, 1971), p. 3.

2. John Rawls, "Fairness to Goodness," *The Philosophical Review* (1975), p. 538.

3. Thomas Nagel, "Rawls on Justice" in *Reading Rawls*, Norman Daniels, ed. (New York: Basic Books, 1975), pp. 9–10.

4. Michael Sandel, *Liberalism and Limits of Justice* (Cambridge: Cambridge University Press, 1982), p. 49.

5. John Rawls, "Rational and Full Autonomy," The Dewey Lectures, 1980, *The Journal of Philosophy* (September 1980), p. 518.

6. J. Rawls, *A Theory of Justice*, p. 156.

7. Tu Wei-ming, *Confucian Ethics Today: The Singapore Challenge* (Singapore: Curriculum Development Institute of Singapore: Federal Publications, 1984), p. 4.

Fred Dallmayr

JUSTICE AND GLOBAL DEMOCRACY

"Whose justice? Which rationality?"

Alasdair MacIntyre

Ours is a time of perplexing cross-currents. As we approach the end of the second millennium, we seem to enter the stage of a new *pax Romana*—but now on an unprecedented scale: a world order or world civilization, basically of Western design, encircling the globe with a network of universal/uniform ideas and practices. Among these ideas, easily the most prominent and influential is that of liberal democracy, a regime founded on popular self-determination and equal citizenship rights. Thus the near-providential advance of liberal democracy, apprehended dimly by Tocqueville over a century ago, seems to have reached in our time its destined goal and global fulfillment—an event celebrated by some observers as the completion and "end of history" construed as the dénouement of historical antagonisms and paradoxes.[1] Yet behind the din of global celebration, we cannot fail to perceive discordant sounds or noises disrupting the unison refrains—noises emanating chiefly from the upsurge of ethnic, national, and religious rivalries. The reasons for this upsurge are multiple—and not simply due to backward obstinacy. Even when transmitted through noncoercive or nonmilitary means, the blessings of *pax Americana* are bound to reach non-Western societies (and unassimilated groups in the West) as the offshoots of imperial hegemony—and thus are prone to be resented and resisted (precisely in the name of popular self-determination). On a more philosophical plane, global hegemonic rules—likes all rules—cannot possibly encompass or absorb the full range of otherness and historical contingency, an insight that inevitably disrupts or unsettles the complacent sway of liberal cosmopolitanism.[2]

443

As sketched, our global scenario may induce despair, or at least stark disillusionment. In contrast to the champions of historical fulfillment, some observers perceive our time only as the completion of *Realpolitik*, manifest in the relentless clash between center and periphery, between global domination and local particular resistance; in lieu of the triumph of universal rule-governance, world order in this view only signals global oppression or—in Max Weber's phrase—the advent of a "polar night of icy darkness." Although capturing elements of our situation, this outlook strikes me as too bleak and too closely akin to cynicism. Despite its hegemonic bent, *pax Americana* also buttresses the dissemination—sometimes through active intervention—of universal democratic principles, especially the principle of equal rights and liberties, around the world. To this extent, liberal democracy, raised to the level of global order, is not entirely divorced from considerations of public justice and equity, and thus not simply equivalent to *Realpolitik*. To be sure, care must be taken not to ignore the limits of these ethical concerns, that is, the complicity of liberal rule-governance in the process of global standardization at the expense of local and cultural differences. As it seems to me, public justice today requires a highly nuanced treatment, perhaps something like a double move (or double gesture) of affirmation and denial. Such a move was at least latently present in traditional conceptions, though rarely explicitly articulated. According to well-known classical formulas, justice means to "give to each his or her due" or else to "treat equal things equally and unequal things unequally." Buried in these formulas, of course, are complex questions of a judgmental sort: What precisely is everyone's "due," and what are the relevant respects in which things are either equal or unequal? For clearly, equality and inequality presuppose an act of comparison or, in Aristotle's phrase, an "intuitive grasp of the similarity in dissimilars" (and of dissimilarity in similars).[3]

In modern Western philosophy, this comparison has been weighted almost entirely in the direction of equality or the principle of equal rights—with the result that inequality or dissimilarity has tended to be marginalized if not obliterated. Differently phrased, equality of rights or "equal liberty" is assumed to be a natural fact (operative in a presocial "state of nature"), while inequality or difference is attributed to social convention. With regard to public justice, this means that the presumption is in favor of the equal treatment of all individuals alike, while unequal treatment requires justification in the light of circumstances. The proverbial "blindness" of justice has come to be viewed entirely in this light: the rule of justice (or "rule of law") is postulated to apply "blindly" or equally to all individuals irrespective of their color, creed, race, or gender. Undoubtedly, blindness of this kind is an enormous advance over arbitrary or willfully prejudicial modes of treatment (found in autocratic regimes). To this extent, "due process"—a process due to everyone—is surely an unrelinquishable part of modern democratic life. Yet approbation here cannot entirely escape critical scrutiny or the double gesture of dialectical inquiry—which gives rise to questions like these: Is the vaunted blindness of justice perhaps itself unjust? Construed in terms of radical indifference or neutrality, is the rule of law, with its accent on universal sameness of treatment, perhaps itself oppressive or repressive—namely, by suppressing or shunting aside important differences or distinctions that matter deeply to people in concrete situations? At this point, law as universal rule-governance seems to hover precariously at the border of justice and injustice—by not giving people their "due" (in not respecting the "dissimilarity in similars").

What is at stake at this juncture is not only the notion of justice as law but also, and more importantly, the question of the status and meaning of democracy, especially liberal democracy. In the following, it cannot be my aim to discuss—let alone resolve—all the facets of these complex issues. My more modest ambition is simply to bring into view the basic tension or ambivalence intrinsic to justice: its inevitable sliding or prevarication between neutral indifference and solicitous attention to difference. My approach will be in part phenomenological and in part dialectical (in Adorno's sense of "negative dialectics"); that is, I start from common sense assumptions regarding justice and then explore their tensional implications for ethical theory. In section I, I probe common sense beliefs undergirding modern Western conceptions of rule-governance, using as my reference point chiefly Jürgen Habermas' portrayal of the fabric of "moral consciousness." As I shall try to show, this portrayal leads Habermas to vindicate the prevalent (liberal) priorities of proceduralism over substantive ethics, of universal rule-governance over conceptions of the "common good," and generally (using summary labels) of "justice" over "solidarity." In section II, I turn to other common sense assumptions that, though usually sidestepped by liberal-individualist theories, have an equal *prima facie* appeal: assumptions that centerstage the role of particular traditions and cultural frameworks, thus affirming (or at least suggesting) the primacy of difference over sameness, of concrete context over rule-governance. Raised to the level of theoretical reflection, these beliefs support recent Western formulations of a "differential" justice, formulations attentive to group or community rights as well as the ethical relevance of gender and ethnicity. By way of conclusion, in section III, I extend the dispute over justice to the international scene, the arena of global (or globalizing) democracy. Here the basic question concerns the relation between Western-style equal rights and community bonds, and also between secular rationality and cultural-religious attachments. In light of the contest between global power and local resistance, the issue is ultimately "whose justice and which rationality" shall prevail.

I

Theories of justice sometimes start from abstract theoretical premises from which logical inferences are then drawn. Although fashionable among some professional philosophers, such theories seem to me to begin their construction with the roof. More plausible, in my view—and also sanctioned by a venerable Socratic tradition—are efforts that build from the ground up, namely, by exploring the common sense opinions of ordinary, nonacademic people, in order then to extract the "truth kernel" or theoretical yield of such opinions. As it happens, some prominent philosophical initiatives in recent times have basically followed this inductive-experiential approach. Thus, in *A Theory of Justice,* John Rawls took his point of departure essentially from common sense opinions or views widely held in Western liberal democracies, views that tend to accentuate the value of individual liberty and self-realization in a context of equal opportunities. Sifted through a theoretically imposed screen (called the "veil of ignorance")—a screen bracketing all nonrelevant differences or particularities—these opinions were then shown to yield a general conception of justice centered around the primary principle of equal liberty (of individuals).[4] In a somewhat modified form, a similar approach has also been adopted by Habermas in his elaboration of a communicative or "discourse ethics"—an elaboration that I take here as my guide because of its instructive insights. As Habermas observed in an important text, meant to lay the groundwork for his discursive framework, access to the moral domain can only be found from the vantage of ordinary experience and concrete life-world interactions; to this extent, ethical theory inevitably relies on a "phenomenology of morals." "As long as moral philosophy takes it as its task," he stated, "to clarify the everyday intuitions into which we are socialized, it must take its bearings (at least virtually) from the attitude of those participating in the communicative practice of everyday life."[5]

In delineating this grassroots approach to ethics, Habermas' text invoked the testimony of Peter Strawson who, in a number of writings, had articulated something like a "linguistic phenomenology of ethical consciousness." In Strawson's account, ethical theorizing had to be anchored in concrete moral sentiments or experiences—sentiments like the indignation or resentment arising from personal insults—with secondary attention being given to the articulation of such feelings in ordinary language or speech. Moral sentiments, for Strawson, were basically embedded in concrete life-world interactions and hence genuinely experienced only by participants, rather than mere onlookers, of such interactions. In terms of linguistic (or speech-act) theory, ethics happens in an illocutionary or performative, rather than merely denotative, mode. In Habermas' reading of these arguments, moral sentiments arise in everyday practices that are "accessible to us only in a performative attitude." This insertion in everyday practices lends to moral

feelings "a certain ineluctability": for we cannot "revoke at will our engagement in a life-world to which we belong"—for instance, by absconding into
a spectator's perspective. This insight has to guide or inform ethical theorizing intent on distilling the core of moral experiences. Thus naturalistic or
empiricist approaches that look at morals merely from the outside, that is,
the vantage of a detached observer, cannot possibly have an enlightening or
"clarifying effect" in this domain. In the end, Habermas shares Strawson's
conclusion that

> the personal reactions of an offended party—for instance, resentments—are
> possible only in the performative attitude of a participant in interactions. By
> contrast, the objectifying attitude of a detached observer cancels the commu-
> nicative roles of I and thou (first and second persons) and thus neutralizes the
> realm of moral phenomena as such. The third-person attitude causes this realm
> of phenomena to vanish.[6]

So far, Habermas' argument has remained close to the phenomenal domain of experience and thus seems largely unobjectionable. In pursuing further his theoretical objectives, however, his text makes a number of subtle
moves which, in light of the preceding, appear somewhat startling (though
not entirely surprising given the quasi-Kantian leanings characterizing his approach). One such move has to do with the proclivity to individualize moral
experience, that is, to examine ethical questions chiefly from the "first person" perspective of individual agents. Thus taking a leaf from Kantian teachings, Habermas formulates the root question of ethics as the quandary of
conscience: "What shall I do?" or "What ought I to do?" Although legitimate
in certain respects, this question immediately distances the individual agent
from the ordinary life context from which we began, that is, from "our engagement in a life-world to which we belong"; for all practical purposes, this
life context now appears as unreliable or unhelpful and perhaps as radically
defective in a moral or ethical sense. This distance or alienation is reinforced
in the text by a second, more crucial move: the ascent to the level of "discourse" or discursive argumentation where agents now encounter each other
as rational *cogitos* pressing against each other contested normative claims;
temporarily suspending ordinary interactions, discourse functions here as a
quasi-transcendental platform predicated on idealized conditions of speech
(guaranteeing the equal liberty of participants). With this ascent, the ban pronounced earlier against the detached onlooker seems to be nearly revoked.
In Habermas' account, moral experiences point to broader "normative expectations" beyond the level of ego-alter interactions, that is, to the realization that, in committing a moral offense, the perpetrator has "also violated
something impersonal or at least transpersonal, namely a generalized expectation that both parties hold." To this extent, feelings of guilt or obligation

"transcend the particular sphere of what concerns individuals in specific situations." As he adds,

> Emotional responses directed at individual persons in specific situations would be devoid of moral character were they not connected with an *impersonal* kind of indignation over some breach of a generalized norm or behavioral expectation. It is only their claim to *general* validity that lends to an interest, a volition, or a norm the dignity of moral authority.[7]

The accent on discourse or discursive validation is clearly the most distinctive and innovative feature of Habermas' theoretical approach. Since this feature is quite well-known, having been discussed widely in the literature, I shall refrain from recapitulating its details. For present purposes, the most noteworthy aspect of this approach is its centerstaging of the liberty and equality of participants, a centerstaging now accomplished through the medium of idealized speech (rather than a Rawlsian "veil of ignorance"). In terms of a theory of justice—which is here my main concern—this centering means a vindication of the moral weighting noted earlier in the case of Rawls: the assignment of priority to universal rules over particular contexts, to "equal liberty" over "difference" (where difference might arise from local contingencies or cultural-religious traditions). This weighting is clearly evident in Habermas' formulation of the "principle of universalization," seen as a "bridging principle" allowing moral consensus, and also of the more specific "principle of discourse ethics," construed as the avenue for the argumentative validation of moral claims. As his presentation makes clear, the first principle is simply a modified continuation of the Kantian categorical imperative, according to which only those norms can be accepted as valid that express a "general will" or that can be suitably elevated to the status of "universal laws." In the words of Habermas' text, universalization means or requires that "*all* affected persons can accept the consequences [of a norm] as well as the side effects that its *general* observance is likely to have for the satisfaction of the interests of *every* affected individual." For the sake of its procedure implementations, this principle of universalization is further coupled with the second principle (of discourse ethics) which stipulates that "only those norms can claim to be valid that meet (or could meet) with the approval of all potentially affected individuals in their capacity as *participants in a practical discourse.*"[8]

As can be gathered from these comments, justice in Habermas' account is basically equivalent to universal rule-governance—with rules being sanctioned through general (free and equal) argumentation; as in most liberal theories, justice here is assumed to be blind, that is, to turn a blind eye on differences of status, race, creed, or gender (as well as differences of intellect or moral striving). This procedural blindness or indifference is further accentuated and argumentatively fleshed out in the concluding part of Habermas' text. As he points out, discourse ethics is basically procedural and formal in that it revolves only around a method of argumentation or a means for validating contested norms; it provides "no substantive ethical guidelines" and no framework of "justified norms." Although not entirely devoid of content, discursive practices depend on contingent content being "brought into them" or being "fed into them from outside." The distinction between form and content also carries over into the division between procedural rule-governance and conceptions of the "common good" or of the "good life," conceptions that may pervade "the entirety of a particular life-form or of a particular life history." Here ethical formalism or proceduralism is said to be "incisive in a literal sense": for the universalization principle here "acts like a knife that makes razor-sharp cuts" between evaluative assessments of life-forms and strictly normative statements, that is, "between goodness and justice." This division or cutting deeply affects the status of cultural traditions and beliefs as well as the concrete meaning patterns of individual lives enmeshed in distinct cultural life-worlds. In Habermas' words, these patterns and beliefs are so inextricably intertwined with the whole fabric of particular life-forms that "they cannot by themselves claim normative validity in the strict sense"; they can at best function as *candidates* for an embodiment in norms that are designed to express a general interest" or general will.[9]

Habermas at this point considers the complex and tensional relation between substantive goodness (of life-forms) and procedural justice—generally concluding in favor of the primacy of the latter over the former. As he recognizes, individuals living in societies cannot entirely distance or extricate themselves from their cultural life-world or from the personal life history that has shaped their identity; yet they can extricate themselves, he insists, from contested norms or normative clusters, set off from the larger social fabric, and thus adopt "a hypothetical attitude toward them" by placing themselves on the quasi-transcendental level of discourses. Habermas also reviews certain hermeneutical qualms concerning procedural justice, qualms arising from the indisputable need to interpret procedural rules and their application in given circumstances. Discourse ethics, he acknowledges, cannot "resolve problems regarding its own application"; rather, rule application requires a "practical prudence" or judgment that seems to be already "presupposed" by the rationality of discursive argumentation. Despite this acknowledgment, however, Habermas is adamant in asserting the ultimate priority of rule-governance over interpretive judgment. Hermeneutical insights, he argues, cannot "undercut the claim of discourse ethics to transcend all local conventions or traditions"; in fact, no participant in argumentation can escape this claim "as long as he takes seriously the meaning of normative validity in a performative attitude." To illustrate this superior or "transcending" force, Habermas turns to the history of human rights in modern constitutional regimes, a history which is said not to vary contingently but to follow a "straight line" or teleology. What follows from this example is that rules take precedence over their application, which, in a given case, may "distort the meaning" of normative principles. Thus while rules are universal (and presumably univocal), "we can operate in a more or less biased way in the domain of prudent application."[10]

Behind the tension between substantive goodness and justice, Habermas argues further, there looms ultimately the deeper gulf between history or historical contingency, on the one hand, and reason or the "transcending claims and interests" of rationality, on the other. Using Hegelian terminology, the tension might also be rendered as the conflictual relation between "morality" and "ethical life" (*Sittlichkeit*), where morality retains a distinct Kantian flavor. Interpreting Hegel somewhat freely (perhaps misleadingly), Habermas views ethical life simply as a synonym for ordinary life practices and everyday beliefs—precisely those practices that are "distanced" and called into question on the level of discourses. As he notes, the ordinary life-world is an arena where "taken-for-granted cultural beliefs of a moral, cognitive or expressive sort are closely interwoven with each other"; in this sense, it functions as a "sphere of ethical life (*Sittlichkeit*)." In this sphere, questions of justice arise only "within the horizon of questions concerning the good life, where the latter are *always already settled*." Seen in their everyday context, questions of the good life are not "theoretical axioms incorporating an abstract 'ought'"; rather, they "shape the identities of groups and individuals in such a manner that they form an intrinsic part of the respective culture or personality." Discourse ethics, by contrast, operates on an entirely different level. From the vantage of participants in discourses "the relevance of life-world contexts pales" completely; the experiences of ordinary life appear now (one might say) from "an artificial, retrospective angle." Under auspices of procedural justice, the life-world nexus is unhinged. As Habermas states dramatically, "Under the stern moralizing gaze of the participant in discourses, this nexus has lost its taken-for-granted quality"; hence, "the normative potency of reality has vanished." In fact, due to this moralizing gaze, the entire "traditional storehouse of norms" has disintegrated and split into those norms that can be "justified in terms of principles" and those that "operate only *de facto*." As he adds, underscoring this disintegration,

> Thus the development of the moral viewpoint goes hand in hand with a differentiation in the practical realm between *moral* and *evaluative* questions. Moral questions can in principle be decided rationally, that is, in terms of justice or the generalizability of interests. Evaluative questions, by contrast, present themselves at the most general level as issues of the *good life* (or of self-realization);

they are accessible to rational discussion only *within* the unproblematic horizon of concrete historical life forms or the conduct of an individual life.[11]

As one should add, Habermas does not entirely ignore the need somehow to correlate goodness and justice, or lived experiences and procedural rationality. However, he finds the solution not in a genuine mediation or mutuality, but rather in the adaptation and transformation of everyday practices, that is, in their progressive "rationalization" in the direction of a greater conformity with discursive rules. Universalist modes of morality, he writes at the end of the cited text, have somehow to compensate or "make up" for the loss of concrete ethical substance, if they wish to retain their practical efficacy. To this extent, universalist moralities are dependent on life forms that are "sufficiently 'rationalized' to permit the prudent application of universal moral insights" and that thus move a good stretch of the way toward universalist principles. Here the weighting of priorities and presumptions surfaces again—now with clearly political implications (implications that sanction the hegemony of universal rule-governance). The same weighting also emerges in another essay, dating roughly from the same period, in which Habermas juxtaposed and rank-ordered the respective roles of "justice and solidarity." In its ordinary (or premoral) sense, solidarity signifies for Habermas simply the concrete context of everyday life, that is, the shared "engagement in a life-world to which we belong." At this point, solidarity is equivalent to conventional practices that need to be sifted through the filter of discursive argumentation and universal procedural rules. Once this happens, in tandem with a rationalization of life-world beliefs, a transformation occurs: solidarity—now construed as a "postconventional" category—becomes a corollary of justice by safeguarding the integrity of the context of moral discourses. In Habermas' words, justice concerns here the "equal freedom of unique and self-determining individuals," while solidarity protects the "welfare of consociates who are linked in an intersubjectively shared life form—and also the maintenance of the integrity of that life form itself."[12]

II

Moral proceduralism, as outlined above, is by no means the unique preserve of Habermasian discourse theory, though his formulation is surely distinguished by its verve and trenchant internal consistency. As indicated before, modern liberal democracy is to a large extent pervaded by a procedural conception of justice (with or without Kantian overtones), a conception privileging universal rule-governance anchored in the equal rights of all citizens. Despite its broad influence, and its salutary effect as an antidote to autocracy, this conception is not as incontestable or solidly grounded, however, as its proponents usually claim. With respect to discourse ethics, its limitations have been pointed out repeatedly, not only by overt opponents but by writers otherwise quite sympathetic to Habermas' perspective. What their criticisms have brought to light are certain deficits of proceduralism—especially in the areas of rule application and hermeneutical exegesis—deficits that are more serious than Habermas has been willing to admit. Thus, relying in part on Wittgensteinian teachings, Herbert Schnädelbach has drawn attention to the nexus of rule and rule application and the impossibility exhaustively to capture application in rules (which would involve an infinite regress of rule formulation). Proceeding from a slightly different angle, Albrecht Wellmer has shown the close interlacing of form and content, of procedural justice and qualitative "goodness"—a linkage illustrated by the fact that, to be meaningful, discursive exchanges already presuppose a sense of what "counts as" a good argument, and thus a shared framework of understanding (or preunderstanding).[13] Pressing this point further, one might question Habermas' "distancing" of normativity from life-world practices (or of "ought" from "is"). For if this distancing is radically performed—in other words, if lived experience is radically stripped of "normative potency"—then justice is literally stranded, suspended "lifelessly" in the void of abstract speculation.

Apart from theoretical quandaries or limitations, there are also political considerations affecting the role of proceduralism, considerations having to do with our contemporary global situation. In light of the asymmetry of center and periphery, of hegemonic power and nonhegemonic societies or groups, universal rule-governance can also mean the subjection of cultural particularities to hegemonic imperatives. In this situation, even the dissemination of equal human rights can entail a kind of disempowerment—namely, by disaggregating shared life forms, thus denuding them as reservoirs of resistance. An example here is the Spanish *conquista*. Propagating Western (Christian) standards, Spanish missionaries typically treated natives as individuals destined for personal salvation, thereby disrupting traditional cultural meaning patterns (as a corollary of conquest). Examples of this kind, illustrating "divide and conquer" policies, could readily be multiplied. What emerges here is a closer correlation, perhaps contamination, of justice and solidarity than Habermas allows—a correlation buttressed, I believe, by moral experience or the "phenomenology" of moral sentiments. As it seems to me, our sense of justice is violated not only when equal cases are treated unequally or prejudicially, but also when relevant differences (of cultures or persons) are ignored or repressed in favor of universal sameness. The plight of North American Indians can serve as a reminder of the deleterious effects of individualizing and homogenizing rule-governance. To mention just a few episodes: In 1868, a federal commission on Indian affairs recommended that "their barbarous dialect should be blotted out and the English language be substituted"—reasoning that "through sameness of language is produced sameness of sentiment and thought," such that "in the process of time, the differences producing trouble would have been gradually obliterated." And another government official is recorded as saying a decade earlier that "the great cause of civilization, . . . in the natural course of things, must exterminate Indians."[14]

In the meantime, sensitivity for such problems has greatly increased, even in the confines of Western liberal democracy. As a result, procedural blindness is no longer uniformly treated as the only yardstick of justice and/or ethical life. Attention to the relevance of difference (or nonsameness) can be found in prominent recent philosophical initiatives, both in North America and in Europe. In the North American context, the most eloquent treatment of the theme has been offered by Charles Taylor—though without any deprecation of equal rights. Elaborating on the Hegelian notion of mutual "recognition," Taylor, in an essay on "multiculturalism," has distilled two diverse meanings or implications of this term. On the one hand, he notes, recognition means "equal" recognition, that is, acceptance of a symmetrical relation. To this extent, the term endorses "a politics of universalism, emphasizing the equal dignity of all citizens," with an attendant commitment to the "equalization of rights and entitlements." Equality here militates against hierarchical social gradations and any kind of prejudicial discrimination; in this sense, sameness of treatment (of citizens) has become a cornerstone of modern liberal democracies everywhere. On the other hand, or by contrast, the second meaning of recognition gives rise to and supports a "politics of difference," that is, a politics nurturing and preserving precisely the distinctiveness or nonsameness of cultures or groups. Taylor notes a peculiar paradox operative in this latter sense, because recognition of difference is usually postulated as a general or universal rule. To this extent, we are asked to give general acknowledgment to something that is "peculiar to each"—thus in a way universalizing the particular. Basically, for Taylor, the two meanings are not just juxtaposed, but interpenetrate (and sometimes collide). In his words, under the rubric of equal citizenship,

what is established is meant to be universally the same, an identical basket of rights and immunities; with the politics of difference [by contrast], what we are asked to recognize is the unique identity of this individual or group, their distinctness from everyone else. The idea is that it is precisely this distinctness that has been ignored, glossed over, assimilated to a dominant or majority identity. . . . Where the politics of universal dignity fought for forms of non-discrimination that were "blind" to the ways in which citizens differ, the politics of difference often redefines non-discrimination as requiring that we make these distinctions the basis of differential treatment.[15]

In Taylor's presentation, the two strands or meanings of recognition are linked with prestigious philosophical or metaphysical traditions undergirding these diverse orientations. In the case of equal citizenship, he notes, the underlying idea is basically that all humans are "equally worthy of respect" due to a "universal human potential" that all humans share. The chief inspiration here comes from Enlightenment philosophy and especially from the writings of Kant and Rousseau (although the latter's impact is circumscribed by his demand for public unity). It was mainly Kant who centerstaged the notion of equal respect or dignity as something owed to humans as "rational agents" capable of directing their lives "through principles." The accent on difference or differential treatment, on the other hand, can be traced back to the teachings of Herder (and, in part, of Hegel), with the chief credit going to Herder's stress on distinct particularity—a particularity functioning, in fact, on two levels: not only "the individual person among other persons" but also "the culture-bearing people among other peoples." In modern democracies, the two strands or legacies inevitably have come into contact, leading to pragmatic sorts of accommodation. Yet on a theoretical level—and often also in practice—the two orientations clash and are difficult to reconcile. For the principle of equal liberty requires "that we treat people in a difference-blind fashion," while the other strand counsels us "to recognize and even foster particularity." This contrast fuels charges and countercharges. "The reproach the first makes to the second," Taylor observes, "is just that it violates the principles of nondiscrimination. The reproach the second makes to the first is that it negates identity by forcing people into a homogeneous mold that is untrue to them." The latter complaint is aggravated by the asymmetry or power differential between hegemonic and nonhegemonic cultures that presses minority life-forms into an alien mold. This, in turn, leads to the frequently voiced charge "that 'blind' liberalisms are themselves the reflection of particular cultures."[16]

Taylor's essay does not leave matters in this state of conflict or mutual recrimination. Faithful to the Platonic-Hegelian heritage of dialectical-dialogical reasoning, and also to the more recent work of Mikhail Bakhtin, Taylor explores the possibilities of a genuine reconciliation, which, without abandoning equal rights, would be properly responsive to the claims of otherness or human difference. In pursuing this goal, the essay distinguishes between two types of liberalism or liberal politics, of which only the second is found to be sufficiently nuanced or "differentiated." The first type is that of a narrowly procedural liberalism that emphatically privileges justice (as universal rule-governance) over goodness, and hence allows equal individual rights always to "trump" other considerations of ethical life. In Taylor's account, this type is mainly associated today with the names of John Rawls, Ronald Dworkin, and Bruce Ackerman, although he might well have included strands in Habermas' argument. In its distilled form, this approach sees liberal society as being devoid of any "particular substantive view about the ends of life," while being united only around "a strong procedural commitment to treat people with equal respect." As Taylor adds, this approach with its strong scheme of priorities has "become more and more widespread in the Anglo-American world," and derivatively in the rest of the Western world (as a hegemonic scheme). Taylor's own sympathies go toward another, more supple type of liberal democracy, one that tempers equal rule-governance with a greater Herderian (and Hegelian) appreciation of diversity, and hence makes room for a stronger recognition of distinct life forms. "A society with strong collective goals can be liberal, on this view," he asserts, "provided it is also capable of respecting diversity, especially when dealing with those who do not share its common goals; and provided it can offer adequate safeguards for fundamental rights." As illustrated by issues raised in French-speaking Quebec, such an approach might be willing "to weigh the importance of certain forms of uniform treatment against the importance of cultural survival, and opt sometimes in favor of the latter." In view of the increasingly multicultural character of many societies, the "rigidities" of procedural liberalism might turn out to be "impractical in tomorrow's world."[17]

In recent Western philosophy, attention to otherness or difference is nurtured not only by Herderian or Hegelian sources, but also by perspectives loosely gathered under the label of poststructuralism or "postmodernism." Although frequently accused of moral indifference, and even of harboring nihilism, these perspectives have by now generated their own ethical arguments—arguments which, though not entirely incompatible with earlier (Hegelian) teachings, are distinguished by their stress on "nonessentialism," that is, on the difference of everything from itself. What this stress entails or requires is an openness to the distinctness of fellow-beings, to their "alterity" above and beyond rule-governance (or in Heideggerian terms: to the excess of "being" over concepts). Among contemporary "postmodern" thinkers, crucial initiatives in this domain are due to Jacques Derrida. In an important essay entitled "Force of Law," Derrida—to the chagrin of his detractors—not only delineated a theoretical view of justice, but a view that in effect equates justice with "deconstruction." Deviating from procedural terminology (and perhaps from common sense usage), Derrida opposes "law" (*droit*) as universal rule-governance to "justice" seen as the disturbance or disruption of rules by the power of "unruly" particularities or contingencies. In his essay, the term "law" (*droit*) denotes basically, or at least in the first instance, equivalence or the "rule of law" conceived as a conceptually determinate and calculable principle. The term "justice," in its strong or primary sense, by contrast, refers to the domain of the unruly, incalculable, or (what he also calls) "undecidable." In large measure, the essay revolves around the correlation and conflict between these terms or, in Derrida's words, around the difficult and unstable distinction between justice and *droit,* between justice (infinite, incalculable, rebellious to rule and foreign to symmetry, heterogeneous and heterotropic), and the exercise of justice as law or right, legitimacy or legality, stabilizable and statutory, calculable, a system of regulated and coded prescriptions.

Invoking a notion with which his work has been prominently affiliated, he adds that it is precisely in the aporias of the ruled and the unruly, in the interstices between law and justice, that "deconstruction find its privileged site—or rather its privileged instability."[18]

The accent on justice as excess or radical heterogeneity, one should add, does not mean a simple dismissal of rule-governance or of the principle of equal rights. As Derrida emphatically states, the fact "that justice exceeds law and calculation, that the unrepresentable exceeds the determinable cannot and should not serve as an alibi for staying out of juridico-political battles, within an institution or a state or between institutions or states and others." What needs to be kept in mind is that the relation between law and justice is not one of thesis and antithesis or of affirmation and (logical) negation. Everything would be quite simple, he notes, if the relation were a "true distinction, an opposition whose functioning was logically regulated and permitted mastery." But as it happens and as it turns out, law (*droit*) "claims to exercise itself in the name of justice," while justice is "required to establish itself in the name of a law that must be 'enforced'." This ambivalence is clearly evident in the context of judicial interpretation where the court must "decide" or render a judgment about a particular case not foreseen by established rules. For a decision to be "just and responsible" in this situation, Derrida writes, it must be "both regulated and without regulation": it must "conserve the law and also destroy it or suspend it enough to reinvent it in each case"; since each case is different, each judgment is new and requires "an absolutely unique interpretation which no existing, coded rule can or ought to guarantee absolutely." On the other hand, if a decision were automatic, bypassing the "ordeal" of judgment, it would be only a "programmable application" or deduction: "it might be legal; it would not be just." These observations lead Derrida finally to comments about the "infinite idea of justice," comments that deserve to be pondered carefully (even by people not sympathetic to deconstruction). This idea is infinite, he states,

> because it is irreducible, irreducible because owed to the other, owed to the other before any contract, because it has come, the other's coming as the singularity that is always other. This "idea of justice" seems to be irreducible in its affirmative character, in its demand of gift without exchange, without circulation, without recognition or gratitude, without economic circularity, without calculation and without rules, without reason and without rationality. . . . And deconstruction is mad about this kind of justice. Mad about this desire for justice.[19]

In various modulations and combinations, arguments reminiscent of Taylor and/or Derrida have also infiltrated contemporary political and feminist theorizing. In the field of political theory, reference should briefly be made (among others) to the innovative study by Iris Young, entitled *Justice and the Politics of Difference*. In her book, Young critiques prevalent procedural conceptions as being wedded too closely to abstract standards of universality (or universalization), standards that tend to reduce equal liberty to equivalence and substitutability. This defect is manifest, in her view, in Rawls' model, especially in his bracketing of significant differences on the level of moral reflection (under the "veil of ignorance"). Although favoring some aspects of discourse ethics (especially the accent on public deliberation), Young also takes issue with Habermas' work, which she accuses of harboring a rationalist bias manifest in his privileging of general rights or interests over particular situations, and of reason over affectivity. Generally speaking, adepts of procedural justice claim to occupy a higher, decontextualized standpoint for the sake of fairness or "impartiality"—a claim Young takes to task for its neglect of the "heterogeneity" of life-forms and personal life histories and also for its tendency to homogenize individuals (at the expense of both social differences and their own differences with themselves). Drawing on a number of postmodern writers, including Derrida and Adorno, the book articulates a normative conception of the "politics of difference"—where the latter steers a course between the pitfalls of radical exclusivism (or essentialism) and harmonious convergence. This approach also involves a reformulation of the notion of "pluralism," which has long served as a staple in liberal political theorizing. Basically, in Young's account, the politics of difference underscores the genuine diversity of life forms in opposition to a mere juxtaposition of aggregate interests. In her words,

> The vision of liberation as the transcendence of group differences seeks to abolish the public and political significance of group difference, while retaining and promoting both individual and group diversity in private, or non-political, social contexts. . . . Radical democratic pluralism [by contrast] acknowledges and affirms the public and political significance of social group differences as a means of ensuring the participation and inclusion of everyone in social and political institutions.[20]

In the domain of feminist theory, the "politics of difference" has animated lively discussions in recent years, discussions that commonly (like Young's work) seek to bypass both essentialism and gender sameness. For present purposes, a brief glance at some of Luce Irigaray's writings must suffice. In Irigaray's view, prevalent Western conceptions of ethics and justice blend out or bracket gender differences, while celebrating universal rule-governance in the sense of procedural neutrality and impartiality; this celebration for her is part and parcel of traditional "patriarchy" with its entrenched male dominance masquerading under the veil of gender-blindness. Drawing on Derridean teaching and also, in part, on Lacanian terminology, Irigaray equates universal rule-governance with the "calculability" of law (*droit*) and with the "symbolic" structure of logical discourse (in opposition to the dimensions of the "imaginary" and the "real"). Being abstract and deductively linked, calculable rules inevitably have an exclusionary effect: by screening out and repressing concrete particularities, including above all the particularity of gender. Referring to the comprehensive system of rule-governance, as sanctioned by patriarchy, and its effect on women, she notes that the latter's "exclusion is internal to an order from which nothing escapes: the order of [man's] discourse." Given the concreteness of gender differentiation, the effect of the patriarchal order points up an issue that is prominent in postmodern thought (as noted before): the issue of the excess of being over categorical concepts or, in Lacanian terms, of the "real" over the "symbolic". This excess deeply pervades gender relations, in a manner that is bound to unsettle "equal liberty" or the simple postulate of the equalization of calculable rights. For Irigaray, genders are not substitutable. In her words, "one sex is not entirely consumable by the other. There is always a *remainder.*" The accent on gender difference, one should add, by no means implies here an endorsement of "essentialism" or of invariant (biological or cultural) essences—which would freeze both genders again in logical-symbolic categories. What the accent does encourage, however, and in a very emphatic way, is attention to the political and ethical significance of gender difference; for flexibly cultivated, such difference, she contends, might act "as a brake upon and a storehouse of resistance against a formalization that threatens life."21

III

Having outlined prevalent Western conceptions of justice, as well as their tensional or conflictual relation, I want now to turn to the implications of these conceptions for global politics and especially for the prospects of global democracy. As indicated before, our global scene is overshadowed today by a political asymmetry or conflict: that between the hegemonic center and the nonhegemonic periphery—an asymmetry that can be translated into the contrast between "universal" Western rule-governance and non-Western societies, cultures or traditions not yet fully submerged in this orbit. This contrast also raises profound issues of justice, primarily these: To what extent is the justice of (Western) rule-governance itself just? And what are appropriate, fair or "just" modes of response and resistance to this rule-governance? Thus the questions "Whose justice? Which rationality?" surface here again, and with full vigor. As it seems to me, our global scene today requires or entails a large-scale "politics of recognition," as this notion has been delineated by Taylor. Such a politics is bound to involve worldwide struggle and antagonism, but, hopefully, it can advance beyond the harsh "clash of civilizations"—to borrow Samuel Huntington's phrase—in the direction of a mutual learning process among cultures. To be sure, the obstacles to such learning are formidable on all sides—though they may not be equally distributed. If one takes one's cue from Hegel's portrayal of the "struggle for recognition," as manifest chiefly in the master-slave relationship, then the chances for learning (and a learning that liberates) are brighter on the side of peripheral or developing societies than on the side of the West in its role of hegemonic master. What obstructs (or may obstruct) learning on the part of Western culture is the arrogance of superiority, the complacent assumption of holding the key to justice and ethical truth. What, if not this presumption, would prompt Westerners to assert the completeness of the procedural yardstick, a completeness needing no attention to "alternative models" of ethical thought? As against this posture I find inspiring the idea of an "imparative" philosophy, as formulated by Panikkar, one in which commonalties are sought rather than presupposed. "Imparative" here is the very opposite of an "imperative" or commanding model which treats the West as "imperator" in a globally orchestrated *pax Americana*.[22]

What renders learning difficult, of course, are not only philosophical presumptions but real-life political and economic constellations, especially the noted asymmetry between center and periphery. Given the vast reach of Western media and market principles, the very encounter between West and non-West takes place no longer on any "impartial" ground, but under the auspices of Western civilization. This fact is illustrated (among other things) by the undisputed status of English as the worldwide *lingua franca*. Westerners, especially Americans, are notoriously loathe to acquire fluency in other languages, on the assumption or conviction that everything relevant is or can be made accessible in English—which means, that everything is universally translatable without loss. This conviction places a heavy onus on non-Western cultures—and even negates them completely, if credence is given to Heidegger's portrayal of language as the "house of being" (where the latter phrase means something like the home of indigenous experience and self-understanding). The problems arising from language barriers—and especially from the monolingual bias of most Americans—are ably pinpointed by Iris Young in her discussion of bilingual education. As she shows, the Bilingual Education Act of 1978 has remained largely a paper declaration. Half a decade later, three-fourths of Hispanic children in America still received no special bilingual instruction of any kind, while in Texas an even larger number of school districts were out of compliance with the legal mandate. In 1986 a referendum was even passed in California declaring English the official language of that state. In Young's words, the issue is not the requirement of a reasonable proficiency in English, but rather "whether linguistic minorities are recognized as full participants in their specificity, with social support for the maintenance of their language and culture."[23]

In seeking to promote "universal" standards, including the principle of universal rights, Western culture paradoxically tends to foster monolingual conformity, at variance with rights (or rightness). Precisely under democratic auspices, non-Western societies and people must be able to speak or "write back"—and they must be able to do so in their native tongue, which invariably is part and parcel of a cultural fabric or tradition. To this extent, it cannot be entirely correct to restrict the notion of rights to equal individual claims, as adepts of universal procedural justice are wont to do; at least in some contexts or under certain circumstances, claimants must also be entitled to speak on behalf of communal bonds, such as a shared language and distinctive conceptions articulated in that language. In his essay on multiculturalism, Taylor refers to the francophone community in Quebec, arguing—correctly, I believe—that the "survival and flourishing" of French language and culture in Quebec cannot be entirely a matter of individual choice (given the fact that there cannot be a completely individualized or "private" language game). As it happens, this flourishing is also mandated by the Canadian Charter of Rights and Freedoms, which proclaims as one of its objectives "the preservation and enhancement of the multicultural heritage of Canadians." Taylor also alludes briefly to the status of native Americans and "aboriginal peoples" in general—a point that is more fully developed by Iris Young. In Young's grim account—which no one can seriously dispute—American Indians (whether on or off the reservation) suffer "the most serious marginalization and deprivation of any social group"; by every conceivable measure, they are "the poorest Americans." At the same time, however, at least on an abstract legal level, Indians are not completely individualized but recognized as communities; in fact, they are "the only group granted formally special status and rights" by the American government. Thus in a manner confounding proceduralist axioms, the justice of recognizing collective group needs and rights has a "clear precedence" in American law. This precedent in the meantime has been extended to the global level, in the form of international charters of the rights of endangered communities (charters that match earlier declarations of the equal rights of individuals or citizens).[24]

To be sure, the notion of collective or cultural rights—like the principle of rights in general—must not be construed in a parochial or narrowly exclusivist fashion. In our steadily globalizing context, the "politics of recognition" necessarily has to be a two-way street, involving a process of mutual learning. On the part of non-Western societies or cultures, such learning is complicated by the legacy of colonialism with its tarnishing effects on Western liberal-democratic ideas—effects that still persist in our era of *pax Ameri-*

cana. Faced with the realities of global hegemony, non-Western cultures have to engage in a complex double move, or perform a double gesture: namely, to affirm or defend cultural traditions and identities, while simultaneously opening the latter up to critical scrutiny and revision (perhaps even of a radical kind). This double move, I believe, has been at the heart of the more inspiring national liberation movements in our century—movements that struggled valiantly against colonialism without retreating into a safely secluded or nostalgic counteridentity. Gandhi's entire lifework, it seems to me, can be understood along these lines. As will be recalled, Gandhi was a severe critic of Western modernity: particularly of its bent toward materialism, egocentrism, exploitation, and corruption; this criticism (articulated chiefly in *Hind Swaraj*), however, by no means implied a naive acceptance of traditional practices. Relying on indigenous sources (like the *Bhagavad Gita* and the poet-saints) and in part on Western teachings, Gandhi refashioned a vision of Hindu life as one devoted to tolerance, nonviolence, and respect for human rights (amplified by corresponding duties). A similar outlook pervaded liberation struggles in Africa—at least as seen from the angle of Amilcar Cabral and Frantz Fanon. As presented in Fanon's *Black Skin, White Masks,* Africans had to liberate themselves first of all from "Negrophobia" or an internalized self-hatred induced by the colonizers; this effort led naturally to the endorsement and counteraffirmation of blackness or *"négritude"*—but a *négritude* that is not simply a negation, but has to renegotiate its meaning constantly in a domain beyond fixed racial markers.[25]

This leads me, by way of conclusion, to a few further remarks on justice in the context of an emerging global democracy. As I have indicated, justice in the sense of universal rule-governance is today contested, or at least supplemented, in the West by alternative conceptions stressing individual and cultural differentiation. This contestation resonates well with many non-Western or nonhegemonic views of justice and ethical life. In the confines of Islam, rule-governance finds a loose equivalent in the *sharia* seen as a law governing equally all Muslims. Yet this rule-governance has always been tempered by the manifest need of interpretation (with different legal schools offering diverse interpretive schemes) and more thoroughly challenged by Sufism's emphasis on contingent and incalculable modes of experience. In the case of Hinduism, a distinction has traditionally been made between *samanya dharma* (meaning general rule) and *visesa dharma* (denoting a differentiated moral conduct), with the two terms seen not so much as polar opposites, but as closely interpenetrating perspectives. The closest interlacing of rule and nonrule can probably be found in the Asian notion of *dao,* usually rendered as "way" or way of life. Referring to the Western infatuation with universal calculable rules, D.T. Suzuki has pointed to the complicity of such rules with homogenizing forms of domination and control, forms that are at variance with the Buddhist attention to nonessential distinctiveness or "suchness" (*tathata*). The task facing most non-Western cultures, in our age of globalization, is how to preserve this attention to distinctness without lapsing into parochialism, or to put matters differently, how to democratize their life-forms without becoming a mere appendage of Western rule-governance. No doubt, a global politics of recognition is bound to put pressure on many time-honored formulas and traditional practices, but it is also going to put pressure on many Western ideas, including conceptions of human rights (to the extent that the latter are seen as private entitlements and as such linked with forms of economic privilege and exploitation). Fortunately, as Gandhi has shown, most cultures have resources that are empowering rather than disabling. In India, one may well want to remember the words of Akbar, the great Moghul ruler of the sixteenth century, who said,

> Now it has become clear to me that in our troubled world, so full of contradictions, it cannot be wisdom to assert the unique truth of one faith over another. The wise person makes justice his guide and learns from all. Perhaps in this way the door may be opened again whose key has been lost.[26]

NOTES

1. See especially Francis Fukuyama, *The End of History and the Last Man* (New York: Free Press, 1992); and for a recent critique Jacques Derrida, *Specters of Marx*, trans. Peggy Kamuf (New York: Routledge, 1994), pp. 56–68.

2. On the upsurge of particularisms see, e.g., Crawford Young, ed., *The Rising Tide of Cultural Pluralism: The Nation-State at Bay?* (Madison, WI: University of Wisconsin Press, 1993); and Mark Juergensmeyer, *The New Cold War? Religious Nationalism Confronts the Secular State* (Berkeley: University of California Press, 1993). In the above I do not mean to deny that certain rivalries are the result of "backward obstinacy" and hatefulness (witness the atrocities committed in Bosnia and in Rwanda).

3. Aristotle, *Poetics* 1459a3-8. For Weber's phrase, see his "Politics as a Vocation" in *From Max Weber: Essays in Sociology*, H.H. Gerth and C. Wright Mills, eds. (New York: Oxford University Press, 1958), p. 128.

4. See John Rawls, *A Theory of Justice* (Cambridge: Harvard University Press, 1970), pp. 3–22, 46–53, 60–65, 136–42. The study also clearly illustrates the weighting of presumptions mentioned before: in the sense that Rawls explicitly grants primacy to the "principle of equal liberty" over the "difference principle." More recently, Rawls has reformulated his approach (along more pragmatic lines), but without modifying this priority scheme. See Rawls, *Political Liberalism* (New York: Columbia University Press, 1993).

5. Jürgen Habermas, "Discourse Ethics: Notes on a Program of Philosophical Justification" in his *Moral Consciousness and Communicative Action*, trans. Christian Lenhardt and Shierry Weber Nicholson (Cambridge: MIT Press, 1990), p. 48. (In the above and subsequent citations I have slightly altered the translation for purposes of clarity.)

6. Ibid., pp. 45–48. Habermas refers mainly to Strawson's arguments in *Freedom and Resentment, and Other Essays* (London: Methuen, 1974).

7. Ibid., pp. 45, 48–49.

8. Ibid., pp. 63, 65–66. Habermas distinguishes basically between "theoretical discourses" concerned with the validation of empirical or logical "truth" claims and "practical discourses" concerned with the validation of normative claims.

9. Ibid., pp. 103–4.

10. Ibid., pp. 104–5.

11. Ibid., pp. 106–8. For a broader discussion of the relation between morality and ethical life (largely from a Habermasian prespective), see Wolfgang Kuhlmann, ed., *Moralität und Sittlichkeit: Das Problem Hegels und die Diskursethik* (Frankfurt: Suhrkamp, 1986). I have discussed this relation—and Habermas' vulnerability to Hegelian rejoinders—in my "Kant and Critical Theory" in *Between Freiburg and Frankfurt: Toward a Critical Ontology* (Amherst: University of Massachusetts Press, 1991), pp. 105–31.

12. See J. Habermas, "Discourse Ethics," p. 109; and also his "Justice and Solidarity: On the Discussion Concerning Kohlberg's Stage Six" in *The Moral Domain: Essays in the Ongoing Discussion between Philosophy and the Social Sciences*, Thomas E. Wren, ed. (Cambridge: MIT Press, 1990), p. 224. Compare in this context also Micha Brumlik and Hauke Brunkhorst, eds., *Gemeinschaft und Gerechtigkeit* (Frankfurt: Fischer, 1993).

13. See Herbert Schnädelbach, "Remarks about Rationality and Language," and Albrecht Wellmer, "Practical Philosophy and the Theory of Society: On the Problem of the Normative Foundations of a Critical Social Science" in *The Communicative Ethics Controversy*, Seyla Benhabib and Fred Dallmayr, eds. (Cambridge: MIT Press, 1990), pp. 270–92, 293–329. See also Wellmer, *Ethik und Dialog* (Frankfurt: Suhrkamp, 1986); and *The Persistence of Modernity: Essays on Aesthetics, Ethics and Postmodernism* (Cambridge: MIT Press, 1991). Compare on the same issues Georgia Warnke, *Justice and Interpretation* (Cambridge: MIT Press, 1993).

14. Quoted from *Washington Post,* March 14, 1993, and a bulletin of the American Indian Relief Council of August 1994. Regarding the Spanish *conquista,* compare especially Tzvetan Todorov, *The Conquest of America: The Question of the Other,* trans. Richard Howard (New York: Harper & Row, 1984).

15. Charles Taylor, "The Politics of Recognition" in *Multiculturalism: Examining the Politics of Recognition,* Amy Gutmann, ed. (Princeton: Princeton University Press, 1994), pp. 37–39.

16. Ibid., pp. 31, 41–44, 51. Taylor is at least in partial agreement with this charge. Pointing to the Salman Rushdie affair and the general linkage of politics and religion in Islamic societies, he states (p. 62) that "liberalism is not a possible meeting ground for all cultures, but is the political expression of one range of cultures, and quite incompatible with other ranges."

17. Ibid., pp. 52–54, 56, 59–61. Apart from Rawls' *A Theory of Justice,* Taylor refers chiefly to Ronald Dworkin, *Taking Rights Seriously* (Cambridge: Harvard University Press, 1977); and Bruce Ackerman, *Social Justice in the Liberal State* (New Haven: Yale University Press, 1980). The volume on multiculturalism also contains an essay by Habermas, designed, at least in part, as a response to Taylor. In this essay, Habermas seems willing to move some steps in the direction of Taylor's second type

of liberalism—but without renouncing his basic priority scheme (favoring universal rule-governance). With specific reference to the Canadian situation, Habermas asserts somewhat blandly that "when properly understood the theory of rights is by no means blind to cultural differences" and that, in fact, that theory is blind "neither to unequal social conditions nor to cultural differences." These statements, however, do not in any way abrogate the trump card held by equal individual rights, for liberal democracy demands "first and foremost, the right to equal individual freedom of choice and action, which in turn presupposes comprehensive legal protection of individuals." Hence, recognition of cultural distinctiveness "does not require an alternative model that would correct the individualistic design of the system of rights through other normative perspectives. All that is required is the consistent actualization of the system of rights." See "Struggles for Recognition in the Democratic Constitutional State," trans. Shierry Weber Nicholson, in *Multiculturalism,* pp. 112–13, 122.

18. Jacques Derrida, "Force of Law: The 'Mythical Foundation of Authority' " in *Deconstruction and the Possibility of Justice,* Drucilla Cornell et al., eds. (New York: Routledge, 1992), pp. 21–22. As Derrida notes, there are similarities as well as differences between his approach and that of Levinas—where the differences are also of a terminological sort (with Levinas approximating "justice" to rule-governance and ethics to the genuine excess of alterity). Compare Emmanuel Levinas, *Totality and Infinity,* trans. Alphonso Lingis (Pittsburgh: Duquesne University Press, n.d.), especially pp. 82–101.

19. J. Derrida, "Force of Law," pp. 22–25, 28. With regard to the status of human rights, Derrida adds without circumlocution (p. 28): "Nothing seems to me less outdated than the classical emancipatory ideal. We cannot attempt to disqualify it today, whether crudely or with sophistication, at least not without treating it too lightly and forming the worst complicities." While generally attracted to Derrida's account, I am somewhat troubled by his categorial juxtaposition of law and justice, rule and nonrule, reason and nonreason, and especially by his later association (in a second part devoted to an exegesis of Walter Benjamin) of justice with force or violence. On these points see my "Justice and Violence: A Response to Jacques Derrida," *Cardozo Law Review* (vol. 13, 1991), pp. 1237–43; and also my "Hermeneutics and the Rule of Law" in *Deconstruction and the Possibility of Justice,* pp. 283–304. In another context, I have discussed Heidegger's reflections on justice: see "Heidegger on Ethics and Justice" in *The Other Heidegger* (Ithaca: Cornell University Press, 1993), pp. 106–31.

20. Iris Marion Young, *Justice and the Politics of Difference* (Princeton: Princeton University Press, 1990), pp. 7, 100–7, 118, 166–68. Although emphasizing the public importance of difference, Young also seems willing to accept (p. 36) the priority of justice over the good life. In the domain of political theory, mention should also be made of William E. Connolly, *Identity/Difference* (Ithaca: Cornell University Press, 1991), especially the chapter on "Liberalism and Difference," pp. 64–94; Michael Walzer, *The Spheres of Justice* (New York: Basic Books, 1983); and Hannah Pitkin, *Wittgenstein and Justice* (Berkeley: University of California Press, 1972).

21. See Luce Irigaray, *Sexes and Genealogies,* trans. Gillian C. Gill (New York: Columbia University Press, 1993), p. 171; also her *This Sex Which Is Not One,* trans. Catherine Porter (Ithaca: Cornell University Press, 1985), p. 88; and *An Ethics of Sexual Difference,* trans. Carolyn Burke and Gillian C. Gill (Ithaca: Cornell University Press, 1993), p. 14. Compare as well Drucilla Cornell, *Beyond Accommodation: Eth-*

ical Feminism, Deconstruction, and the Law (New York: Routledge, 1991); and Deborah L. Rhode, *Justice and Gender* (Cambridge: Harvard University Press, 1989).

22. See Raimundo Panikkar, "What Is Comparative Philosophy Comparing?" in *Interpreting Across Boundaries*, Gerald J. Larson and Eliot Deutsch, eds. (Princeton: Princeton University Press, 1988), pp. 116–36, especially pp. 127–28; and also Samuel P. Huntington, "The Clash of Civilizations?" *Foreign Affairs* (vol. 72, 1993), pp. 22–49.

23. I.M. Young, *Justice and the Politics of Difference*, pp. 178–81.

24. Prominent among such charter declarations are the African Charter on Human and Peoples' Rights, adopted in Nairobi in June 1981, and the Declaration of Principles of Indigenous Rights, adopted at the World Conference of Indigenous Peoples in Panama in September 1984. For these and other documents, and their discussion, see James Crawford, ed., *The Rights of Peoples* (Oxford: Clarendon Press, 1992), pp. 179–212. Compare also C. Taylor, "The Politics of Recognition," pp. 52, 58; and I.M. Young, *Justice and the Politics of Difference*, pp. 181–83.

25. See Frantz Fanon, *Black Skin, White Masks*, trans. Charles Lam Markman (New York: Grove Weidenfeld, 1967), pp. 14, 134–35, 160. Regarding Gandhi, see, e.g., Bhikhu Parekh, *Gandhi's Political Philosophy* (Notre Dame: University of Notre Dame Press, 1989); and also my "Gandhi as Mediator between East and West" in *Margins of Political Discourse* (Albany: SUNY Press, 1989), pp. 22–38. The notions of a "critical traditionalism" and "critical modernism" are developed by Parekh in his *Colonialism, Tradition and Reform: An Analysis of Gandhi's Political Discourse* (New Delhi: Sage Publications, 1989), pp. 34–70.

26. Quoted from Michael Wood, *Legacy: Episode One* (Owing Mills, MD: Maryland Public Television and Central Independent Television, 1991), typescript, p. 31. See also K.J. Shah, "Of Artha and Arthasastra" in *Comparative Political Philosophy*, Anthony J. Parel and Ronald C. Keith, eds. (New Delhi: Sage Publications, 1992), pp. 141–62; Daisetz T. Suzuki, *An Introduction to Zen Buddhism* (New York: Grove Press, 1964); and Christopher Ives, *Zen Awakening and Society* (Honolulu: University of Hawai'i Press, 1992), especially pp. 114–44, chap. 6: "Zen Formulation of the Social Good."

CONTRIBUTORS

ROGER T. AMES holds a Ph.D. from the University of London. He is a professor in the Department of Philosophy at the University of Hawai'i at Mānoa, the editor of the international journal *Philosophy East & West*, and the director of the Center for Chinese Studies at the University of Hawai'i. Dr. Ames has been a visiting professor at the University of Cambridge, Peking University, the National Taiwan University, and the Chinese University of Hong Kong. His publications include *The Art of Rulership: A Study in Ancient Chinese Political Thought*, *Thinking Through Confucius* (co-authored), *Anticipating China: Thinking through the Narratives of Chinese and Western Cultures* (co-authored), *Nature in Asian Traditions of Thought: Essays in Environmental Philosophy* (co-edited), and *Sun-Tzu: The Art of Warfare*.

MICHAEL BARNHART received his Ph.D. from Temple University. He is currently teaching at Kingsborough Community College, CUNY. Dr. Barnhart has previously taught at Haverford College, Temple, and Drexel Universities. He has been a visiting scholar at the Hastings Center with a project entitled "Ideas of Nature in an Asian Context."

KENNETH BAYNES has been an associate professor of philosophy at the State University of New York at Stony Brook since 1987. Before receiving his Ph.D. from Boston University, he taught at the University of Massachusetts and Boston University. Dr. Baynes is currently the editor for the SUNY series in Political and Social Thought, as well as the book review editor for *Constellations: An International Journal on Democratic and Critical Theory*. His main publications are *The Normative Grounds of Social Criticism: Kant,*

Rawls, and Habermas and a translation of Axel Honneth's *The Critique of Power*.

RON BONTEKOE is an associate professor in the Philosophy Department at the University of Hawai'i at Mānoa. He received his Ph.D. from the University of Toronto. He is the author of *Dimensions of the Hermeneutic Circle* and co-editor, with Eliot Deutsch, of Blackwell's *A Companion to World Philosophies*.

ROSI BRAIDOTTI is a professor and chair of the Department of Women's Studies at the University of Utrecht in the Netherlands. She received her Ph.D. in philosophy from the University of Paris. Dr. Braidotti has been a visiting professor at the Institute for Advanced Studies, Princeton, at the Goethe University, Frankfurt, at the University of Rome, at the Universities of Jyvaskyla and Helsinki, Finland, and at Harvard University. Among her books are *Theories of Gender: Language is a Virus* and *Patterns of Dissonance: An Essay on Women in Contemporary French Philosophy*.

JAMES BUCHANAN received his Ph.D. from the University of Chicago, and is the Caroline Werner Gannett Professor at the Rochester Institute of Technology. He has also taught at the Hong Kong University of Science and Technology, the Chinese University of Hong Kong, the Chinese Academy of Social Sciences in Peking, the University of Chicago, Bucknell and Indiana University, and the University of Montana. He is the author of *The Myths of Understanding: Theory and Practice in Comparative Religions and Philosophy*.

CHUNG-YING CHENG is a professor of philosophy at the University of Hawai'i at Mānoa. He received his Ph.D. in philosophy from Harvard University. He has taught at Yale University, the City University of New York, National Taiwan University, Beijing University, and the International Christian University in Tokyo. His published works include *New Dimensions of Confucian and Neo-Confucian Philosophy* (in English) and *Knowledge and Value* and *Culture, Ethics and Management* (in Chinese).

FRANK CUNNINGHAM is a professor of philosophy at the University of Toronto and has held visiting positions in Japan, the Netherlands, and the People's Republic of China. He is a fellow of the Royal Society of Canada and current President of the Canadian Philosophical Association. His books include *Objectivity in Social Science, Democratic Theory and Socialism,* and *The Real World of Democracy Revisited and Other Essays on Socialism and Democracy*.

FRED DALLMAYR holds the Dee Chair of Political Theory in the Department of Government and International Studies at the University of Notre

Dame. He received his Ph.D. from Duke University and has taught there, as well as at Purdue University, the University of Georgia, and the University of Hamburg in Germany. He is the author of eleven books, including *Critical Encounters: Between Philosophy and Politics*, *Margins of Political Discourse*, and *G.W.F. Hegel: Modernity and Politics*.

MAJID FAKHRY is an emeritus professor of philosophy at the American University of Beirut, Lebanon, where he taught from 1954 through 1990. He received his Ph.D. from the University of Edinburgh, and has lectured widely: at Georgetown University, Princeton, the University of London, UCLA, the Lebanese National and Kuwait Universities. He is the author of fourteen books, including *Ethical Theories in Islam*, *Aspects of Philosophical Experience*, and *Arabic Ethical Thought*.

JOSEPH GRANGE received his Ph.D. from Fordham University and is a professor of philosophy at the University of Southern Maine in Portland. He is the author of *Nature: An Environmental Cosmology* and the editor of *City and Nature* and *The Pathway of Being and Being Human*.

DAVID L. HALL is a professor of philosophy at the University of Texas at El Paso. He received his Ph.D. in philosophy from Yale University. Dr. Hall is co-editor of the SUNY Press series in Chinese Philosophy and Culture and managing book review editor of *Philosophy East and West*. He is the author of seven books, including *Eros and Irony*, *The Uncertain Phoenix: Adventures Towards a Post-Cultural Sensibility*, *Richard Rorty: Prophet and Poet of the New Pragmatism*, *Thinking Through Confucius* (co-authored), and *Anticipating China* (co-authored).

TED HONDERICH is the Grote Professor of the Philosophy of Mind and Logic at University College London, where he was previously professor, reader, and lecturer. He received his Ph.D. from the University of London and has been a visiting professor at Yale and the Graduate Center of the City University of New York. His books include *A Theory of Determinism: The Mind, Neuroscience, and Life Hopes*, *How Free Are You?: The Determinism Problem*, and *Violence for Equality: Inquiries in Political Philosophy*. Dr. Honderich is also the editor of *The Oxford Companion to Philosophy*.

JAVID IQBAL is a member of the Senate of Pakistan and a former Chief Justice of Punjab. He received his Ph.D. from the University of Cambridge. The son of the most prominent Muslim philosopher and reformer of this century, Muhamed Iqbal, Dr. Iqbal is the author of a number of books on Muslim law, including *Pakistan and Islamic Liberal Movements*.

YERSU KIM has been, since 1977, a professor of philosophy at Seoul National University in Korea, and is a past President of the Korean Philosophical Association. At the present time he is on academic leave and is working with UNESCO in Paris. He received his degrees from Harvard College and the University of Bonn. His recent books include *Philosophy of Justice* and *Understanding Wittgenstein* (both in Korean).

AMBROSE Y. C. KING is the Pro-Vice-Chancellor and Chair Professor of Sociology at the Chinese University of Hong Kong. He received his Ph.D. from the University of Pittsburgh. He has been a visiting professor at the University of Wisconsin and the University of Heidelberg. Dr. King has held a number of advisory positions to the Hong Kong government. Among his published books are *From Tradition to Modernity: An Analysis of Chinese Society and Its Change, The Politics of Three Chinese Societies,* and *Salient Issues of Chinese Society and Culture.*

DAYA KRISHNA is a former professor of philosophy and ex-Pro-Vice-Chancellor at the University of Rajasthan, Jaipur, India. He has published nine books, including *The Art of the Conceptual, Indian Philosophy: A Counter-Perspective,* and *The Problematic and Structure of Classical Indian Thought about Man, Society and Polity.*

ERNESTO LACLAU received his Licenciado en Historia from the National University of Buenos Aires and his Ph.D. from the University of Essex, where he is currently a professor of politics. He has been a visiting professor at the Universities of Toronto and Chicago, at York and Cornell Universities, at the Nouvelle Sorbonne, and at the New School for Social Research. His books include *Politics and Ideology in Marxist Theory: Capitalism, Fascism, Populism, Hegemony and Socialist Strategy* (co-authored) and *New Reflections on the Revolution in Our Time.*

MARÍA PÍA LARA received her Ph.D. from the Universidad Autonoma de Barcelona. She is head of the Department of Philosophy at the Universidad Metropolitana, Iztapalapa, Mexico. Dr. Lara is the author of *Democracy as a Project of Ethical Identity.*

DAVID LOY is a professor in the Faculty of International Studies at Bunkyo University, Chigasaki, Japan. He is the author of *Nonduality: A Study in Comparative Philosophy* and *Lack and Transcendence: The Problem of Death and Life in Psychotherapy, Existentialism, and Buddhism.*

HANS-GEORG MÖLLER received his Ph.D. from Bonn University. He has published a translation of the Mawangdui manuscripts of the *Daodejing* and is currently working at the Institute of Sinology, Bonn University.

CHANTAL MOUFFE is Directrice de Programme at the College International de Paris. She received her M.A. in politics from the University of Essex, has taught at the University of London, and has been a visiting professor at the University of Toronto and the New School for Social Research, as well as a senior fellow, Society for the Humanities, Cornell University. Her recent books include *The Return of the Political* and *Hegemony and Socialist Strategy: Towards a Radical Democratic Politics* (co-authored).

RICHARD RORTY received his Ph.D. from Yale University. He is currently University Professor of Humanities at the University of Virginia, and taught previously at Wellesley College and Princeton University. His books (which have been translated into many languages) include *Philosophy and the Mirror of Nature, Consequences of Pragmatism,* and *Contingency, Irony and Solidarity.*

RAMJEE SINGH is the former Vice Chancellor, Jain Vishva Bharati Institute and is currently the director of the Gandhian Institute of Studies, Varanasi, India.

ERIKH SOLOVYOV received his Ph.D. from the Institute of Philosophy in Moscow, where he is presently main researcher. He is the author of four books, including *The Past Interprets Us* and *Kant: Complementariness of Morality and Law.*

MARIETTA STEPANIANTS, the director of the Seventh East-West Philosophers' Conference, at which the papers in this volume were originally delivered, is director of the Center for Studies in Oriental Philosophies at the Institute of Philosophy, Moscow. She received her Ph.D. in philosophy from the same institute and has been a professor at the Diplomatic Academy of Russia since 1980. She is the author of six books, including *Muslim Philosophy and Social Thought: 19th–20th Centuries* and *Sufi Wisdom.* She has also edited fifteen books, including *God, Man and Society in Traditional Oriental Cultures* and *Feminism: East, West and Russia.*

SVETOZAR STOJANOVIĆ received his Ph.D. from the University of Belgrade, where he is now a professor of philosophy and social theory. Dr. Stojanović has held a number of political positions in his native Yugoslavia. He was Chief Adviser to the President (1992–93) and a member of the National Political Council of the opposition Democratic Party. He is a member of the Institut International de Philosophie (Paris), and has been editor-in-chief of the journal *Praxis International* (Oxford) and the chairman of the International Humanist and Ethical Union (The Hague). He is the author of five books, including *Contemporary Meta-Ethics, Between Ideals and Reality, In Search of Democracy and Socialism,* and *From Marxism and Bolshevism to Gorbachev.*

CASS R. SUNSTEIN is the Karl Llewellyn Professor of Jurisprudence at the School of Law, University of Chicago, where he also teaches in the Department of Political Science. He received his Ph.D. from Harvard College and J.D. from Harvard Law School and went on to clerk at both the Supreme Court of Massachusetts and for the Honorable Thurgood Marshall, Supreme Court of the United States. He has advised on law reform and constitution-making efforts in various nations, including the Ukraine, Romania, Poland, South Africa, Israel and China. His published books include *The Partial Constitution*, *After the Rights Revolution*, and *Democracy and the Problem of Free Speech*.

J.E. TILES is a professor of philosophy at the University of Hawai'i at Mānoa. He holds a Master's degree in mathematical logic from the University of Bristol and a D.Phil. in philosophy from Oxford University. He is the editor of *John Dewey—Critical Assessments* (in four volumes) and the author of *Dewey, Things that Happen*, and *An Introduction to Historical Epistemology* (co-authored with Mary Tiles).

YÜ YING-SHIH is the Strater University Professor of East Asian Studies and professor of history at Princeton University. He received his Ph.D. from Harvard University and has taught there, and at the University of Michigan and the Chinese University of Hong Kong. Dr. Yü was elected to membership in Academia Sinica in 1974, and is the co-editor of *Asia Major* and the vice-chairman of the advisory board of *The Encyclopedia of Chinese History and Culture*. He is also the co-editor of *Power of Culture: Studies in Chinese Cultural History*.

INDEX